The 5 Knots

A guide to Being-Centred Therapy

How to undo the knots of your mind and rediscover Being

Claus Springborg, PhD

The 5 Knots

A guide to Being-Centred Therapy

How to undo the knots of your mind and rediscover Being

Sensing Mind Institute

Claus Springborg, PhD
Sensing Mind Institute
Copenhagen, Denmark

Sensing Mind Institute
Rosenvænget 8
3520 Farum, Denmark
info@sensingmind.com
www.sensingmind.com

Ordering Information:

Quantity sales. Special discounts are available on quantity purchases by corporations, associations and others. For details, contact the publisher at the address above.

Title The 5 Knots: A guide to Being-Centred Therapy

ISBN 978-87-971771-4-3 (printed book), 978-87-971771-5-0 (e-book)

Content

Content, detailed

List of Figures

List of Tables

1. Introduction

Mystical traditions teach us that the essence of our Being is an innate and boundless state of joy, peace, and fulfilment. Yet, when we observe the world around us, as well as our inner landscapes, we are confronted with suffering. This stark contrast raises a profound question: How can a reality of inherent bliss coexist with the suffering that permeates human experience?

To resolve this apparent contradiction, some dismiss the wisdom of the sages as comforting fairy tales divorced from reality, while others dismiss suffering as illusory and seek to transcend it by withdrawing into spiritual practices. Both perspectives, however, present significant issues. The first is problematic because it places unnecessary limits on the human potential for fulfilment. The second is problematic because it can lead to spiritual bypassing or escapism, preventing the individual from dealing with life.

The central thesis of this book is that human suffering, on the individual as well as societal level, is largely a consequence of people having lost awareness of Being and seeking to remedy the ensuing sense of loss through misguided strategies informed by widespread misconceptions about reality. This view is, thus, a middle way that acknowledges the reality of both Being and suffering. According to this view, the key to dissolving suffering is to understand the habits and patterns that cause us to lose awareness of Being, and through such understanding to regain this awareness. This approach forms the foundation of the Being-Centred Therapy outlined in this book.

The central thesis of this book is not new. It lies at the heart of many philosophical and spiritual traditions, from the non-duality teachings of Advaita Vedanta and the mindfulness practices of Buddhism, to the mystical insights found in Sufism and Christian contemplative practices. However, throughout history, it has been crucial to present knowledge of Being in a language that resonates with the people of the time.

In the 21st century, there are two major factors to consider when seeking to give the timeless teachings about Being a contemporary expression.

The first factor to be taken into account is that we are currently facing what can legitimately be called a mental health crisis. Statistics shows that at the start of the 2010s, rates of mental illness sharply increased, and this trend has continued since. Diagnosis of depression and anxiety among college students in the US doubled in the 2010s. Self-harm increased by 188% for teenage girls and 48% for teenage boys, and suicide increased by 167% for pre-teen girls and 91% for pre-teen boys. These numbers come from the US, but similar trends can be found in other Western countries, highlighting the urgent need for effective therapeutic interventions. In this context, I believe that it will be fruitful to integrate teaching about Being into therapeutic work, since cultivating awareness of Being can address not just the symptoms, but the root cause of psychological suffering. Furthermore, the prevalence of the mental health crisis can serve as motivation to engage with teachings specifically aimed at discovering inherent joy, peace and fulfilment. For this reason, I believe that therapeutic work is a particularly suitable vehicle for introducing these teachings, making a practical guide on incorporating awareness of Being in therapy both relevant and timely.

The second factor to take into account when adopting teachings of Being for the present-day context is the firm establishment of science.

Since the Enlightenment, the scientific method has become a fundamental tool for advancing human knowledge and prosperity. Science, both as a mode of inquiry and a body of knowledge, is deeply ingrained in modern society. It would be unwise and counterproductive to present teachings on Being in a way that requires people to reject science. Doing so would not only alienate many people but would also impoverish the teachings themselves by severing them from the vast repository of knowledge developed through scientific inquiry. Therefore, the Being-Centred Therapy presented in this book explicitly draws on scientific research and addresses common objections that may arise from a scientifically informed mindset, by highlighting how spiritual and scientific traditions when properly understood share much in terms of both knowledge and method.

In bringing this approach to light, my intention is not to dismiss traditional spiritual practices, but to integrate them into a contemporary framework that speaks to both our modern mental health challenges and our scientific sensibilities. By doing so, we can make the wisdom of Being accessible, practical, and effective for those navigating the complexities of 21st-century life.

Before diving into the principles and practices of Being-Centred Therapy, I will briefly introduce Being-Centred Therapy and the 5 Knots, define some key concepts and outline the structure of the book.

1.1. Being-Centred Therapy

In this section, I will describe, in more detail, Being-Centred Therapy's view on how suffering arises and what we can do about it.

The four key claims I will make in this section are:

- Being is all pervasive, and it is boundless joy, peace and fulfilment, but we do not notice this because we contain automatic processes which direct our attention away from Being towards behaviour aimed at dealing with our environment.
- The result is a sense of loss which we seek to remedy in ways that worsen it because *any* action we engage in takes our attention away from Being.
- When the sense of loss deepens, we tend to believe that we have not done enough – rather than recognising that it is precisely the acts we engage in to remedy the sense of loss that creates it.
- We can, therefore, dissolve suffering by becoming aware of both Being and the mechanisms that take our attention away from Being.

Being-Centred Therapy assumes that Being is, indeed, all pervasive and boundless joy, peace and fulfilment. Thus, Being is what anyone will experience if they focus their attention on the present moment rather than on various external or internal activities. In other words, boundless joy, peace and fulfilment are, in principle, available to anyone at any time.

However, we all contain a multitude of automatic and unconscious processes, which we, over time, have developed to deal with our environment, and many of these processes take our awareness away from Being in the present moment. Thus, if you are unable to disconnect your awareness from these processes, the joy, peace and fulfilment may be there, but you will not be able to notice it.

If you, for example, grew up in a family with parents who had severe mood swings, you would learn that it is important to constantly monitor your parents' mood and do certain things (or refrain from doing certain things) to keep them happy. To deal with this kind of family environment, you are likely to develop a tendency to continuously pay attention to your parents' moods and how their moods are affected by your behaviour.

Since how much you can be aware of at any given time is limited, the more awareness you spend on your parents' mood, the more you will lose awareness of Being. The result will be a deep sense of having lost something precious.

When you feel this loss, you will develop ideas about what caused it and how to remedy it. However, the ideas you develop are often wrong and will make you seek to remedy the loss in ways that worsen it.

For example, you may develop the idea that your sense of loss is caused by seeing your parents unhappy. According to this belief, the way to remedy your sense of loss would be to monitor their moods even more closely and modify your behaviour to keep them happy. However, it is precisely doing this that took your awareness away from Being in the first place. Thus, this strategy will not only fail to remedy your sense of loss – it is bound to deepen it.

To make matters worse, you are unlikely to discover that your explanation for why you feel a sense of loss is wrong, because your belief in this explanation creates the illusion that the explanation is correct.

If you believe your sense of loss stems from seeing your parents unhappy, you are likely to interpret the persistence of the feeling of loss as evidence that you have not done enough to make them happy – rather than as evidence that your beliefs about what causes and what would remedy your sense of loss are erroneous.

To understand how a belief in a particular explanation for a particular experience can make us unable to discover when our explanation is wrong, it can be useful to look at some everyday examples.

Imagine that you see yellow leaves on one of your houseplants (a particular experience). Imagine that the appearance of yellow leaves is just part of the plant's natural growth cycle (true cause), but that you assume it is due to lack of water (your explanation). Consequently, you will seek to remedy the situation by watering the plant. This may lead to overwatering and more yellow leaves. However, when you see more yellow leaves, you are likely to interpret this as evidence that the plant is still not getting enough water leading to even more overwatering, and so on.

Similarly, imagine that you run an online store and the sales begin to decline (a particular experience) due to a temporary market downturn (true cause), but that you assume the decline in sales is due to having an outdated webpage (your explanation). Consequently, you may try to remedy the situation by updating the webpage and adding fancy new features. This, in turn, may confuse and alienate your regular customers, causing further decline in sales. However, you may not see the further decline in sales as evidence that updating the webpage is a bad strategy but rather as evidence that you have not modernised the webpage enough, and so on.

These examples illustrate how a belief in a particular cause for something you experience can make it difficult to realise when your belief is wrong because the consequences of acting on your belief can be interpreted as evidence that you have not done enough – rather than evidence that you are doing the wrong thing.

Being-Centred Therapy seeks to cut through this kind of blindness and correct the mistaken beliefs that prevent clients from becoming aware of Being.

1.2. The 5 Knots

There are five different kinds of pattern that take our awareness away from Being and at the same time make us interpret the resulting sense of loss as evidence that we need to do something that further deepens our lack of awareness of Being. I call these five patterns The 5 Knots because their flawed circular logic is like a knot that must be untied.

Below is a brief introduction to each of the five knots, how each directs people's awareness away from Being, and how the knots relate to each other. The first four knots form a vicious circle, leading to an ever-deepening loss of awareness of Being. The fifth knot relates to the system of mental, emotional, and behavioural patterns produced by the first four knots (see Figure 1).

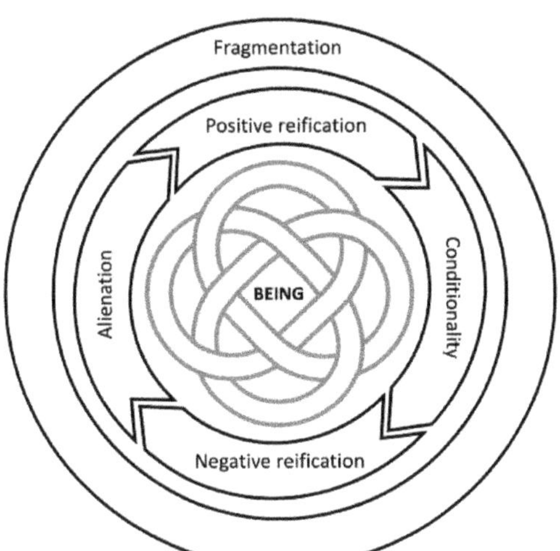

Figure 1: The 5 Knots model

- **The Knot of Positive Reification:** When people experience Being, they tend to perceive it as an experience of a (rare) positive thing, such as joy, connection, peace or love. Seeing Being as a positive thing will direct peoples' attention away from the experience itself and towards ideas about this thing.
- **The Knot of Conditionality:** Once people think about Being as a positive thing, they start developing strategies for how to create or acquire this thing. The implementation of these strategies monopolises peoples' awareness, making them less likely to become aware of Being.
- **The Knot of Negative Reification:** Seeking to create or acquire Being as if it were a positive thing leads to failure because Being is not a thing that can be created or acquired. Over time, the pain of such failures causes people to see experiences of Being as something negative they should avoid, making them actively turn their attention away from Being.
- **The Knot of Alienation:** Over time, the patterns that lead to the loss of awareness of Being become automatic and unconscious, leading to the sense that the absence of Being is the normal state, and the experience of Being is the exception. This creates a fertile ground for perceiving experiences of Being as the experience of (rare) positive things, i.e. the formation of the Knot of Positive Reification. This closes the vicious circle of the first four knots.
- **The Knot of Fragmentation:** The continuous development of the first four types of knots leads to a system of mental, emotional, and behavioural patterns that can be described as a system of entities pursuing Being through different and often mutually exclusive strategies. The result is a fragmented personality structure at war with itself. The inner conflicts monopolise the individual's awareness, leading to further loss of awareness of Being, which in turn intensifies the pursuit and, consequently, the level of conflict in the individual.

Since the five knots occupies our awareness, untying these knots frees up our awareness and enables us to become aware of Being, and because the true cause of so much suffering is the loss of awareness of Being, becoming aware of Being will dissolve a great portion of human suffering. In other words, becoming aware of Being is highly therapeutic.

Using awareness of Being in a therapeutic setting is common. Many approaches to therapy emphasise the importance of developing the capacity to be in the present moment and becoming aware of Being. These approaches promote many useful exercises that can help people do so. For example, in Mindfulness-Based Stress Reduction people are invited to do body scans, pay attention to their breathing and to chew a raisin while paying attention to all the different sensations involved in this action. In Gestalt Therapy people are invited to focus on current thoughts, feelings and emotions. In Ego State Therapy people are invited to visualise a safe place in ways that engage all their senses. In some Trauma therapies, therapists will invite clients to identify a certain number of things they can see, touch, hear, smell and taste. All these exercises aim to bring people's attention into the present moment and help them experience Being.

In many of these approaches to therapy, the patterns that prevent us from resting in the present moment and experiencing Being are called "ego" or "personality structure", and the techniques for turning one's awareness towards Being are often conceived as techniques for bypassing, overcoming or dismantling this ego or personality structure. In such cases, the details of the structure the therapy seeks to overcome are generally given limited attention.

Being-Centred Therapy, on the other hand, seeks to use a detailed understanding of the specific patterns that prevent a client from noticing Being as a means to point his/her attention towards Being. In other words, the very structures that take the client's awareness away from Being are used as signposts that point that awareness towards Being.

The reason this is possible is precisely that many of the patterns that take our awareness away from Being have been developed to remedy the sense of loss of Being. They are motivated by both a deep longing and a deep love for Being and they, therefore, contain intimate knowledge of Being.

Understanding The 5 Knots can greatly help therapists listen to their client's personality structure in such a way that this structure changes from being something merely preventing the client from becoming aware of Being to something guiding the client to develop this awareness.

In short, The 5 Knots model offers a way of listening to the ego that transforms it from an obstacle to a guide.

1.3. Definitions of key concepts used in this book

In this section, I define the following key concepts that I will use throughout the book.

- Being
- Aspects of Being (Essences)
- Personality Parts
- Personality Structure

These concepts have been employed in various ways by different authors. Thus, to avoid any confusion it is important to take some time to clarify, how I intend to use them.

Rather than following any particular therapeutic or philosophical tradition, I seek to define the above concepts in ways that are compatible with multiple traditions. I do this to allow therapists from as many different traditions as possible to benefit from and effectively experiment with the tools presented in this book without having to adopt any unnecessary metaphysical ideas.

The definitions provided in this section will be brief, offering an initial orientation. Each concept will be explored in greater depth in dedicated sections later in the book.

1.3.1. Being

One central concept that I use throughout the book is "Being". This concept has been discussed in philosophy for millennia. Consequently, there are many ways of understanding it. In this book, I will use the following definition:

> Being is the experience of unhooking one's attention from habitual thoughts and emotions.

It is worth noticing that the above definition says nothing about what the experience of Being is – only that it occurs when attention is unhooked from habitual thoughts and emotions, such as mind-wandering, rumination and habitual associations.

The advantage of defining Being in this way is that it is compatible with multiple metaphysical perspectives, and therapists are, therefore, not required to subscribe to any particular metaphysical ideas to adopt the Being-Centred approach to therapy presented in this book.

The metaphysical assumptions found among therapists can be grouped into three broad categories:

- **Optimistic reductionism:** Some therapists believe there is nothing beyond the physical. They will, therefore, believe the experience of Being can be explained fully by referring to physiological states in the brain and body.
- **Naturalistic dualism:** Other therapists believe that physical matter and consciousness are two separate and equally fundamental aspects of reality. They will, therefore, believe that the experience of Being should be understood as a state of consciousness – not a physical state.
- **Mysticism:** Yet other therapists believe in the existence of an all-pervasive divine or spiritual presence. They will tend to see the experience of Being as the direct experience of this presence.

Below, I describe these three perspectives in more detail and comment on how therapists operating from each may relate to the above definition of Being.

Optimistic reductionism

Some therapists believe that there is nothing other than physical states. From this point of view, any conscious experience including the experience of Being as defined above can, at least in principle, be fully explained through understanding the physical mechanisms of the brain (and potentially other physiological processes) that gives rise to this experience. This view is sometimes referred to as materialism or optimistic reductionism (Chalmers, 1995, 2010).

The main argument for optimistic reductionism is that because there is a tight correlation between certain physical brain-states and certain conscious experiences, then the brain-states must *cause* the experiences. If every single time an individual experiences a certain colour, there is the same activity in the same areas of this individual's brain, then (it is assumed) this activity in the brain must be what causes the experience of the colour.

For optimistic reductionists the definition of Being as what you experience when your attention is not occupied by thoughts and emotions, can be taken to mean that Being is the experience one will have when certain brain processes are inactive.

An optimistic reductionist may, for example, view thoughts and emotions as part of the body's regulatory system. Being can then be seen as the conscious experience that occurs when the organism is in homeostasis (a balanced state of internal physiological stability). In other words, the brain can be seen as a tool for self-regulation, and when there is no need for self-regulation because all regulated parameters are well within the acceptable boundaries, the brain can take a break, resulting in an experience of profound well-being – and that is Being.

Experiencing this state frequently may, furthermore, have profoundly transformative effects on the individual's experience of themselves and their environment.

Thus, optimistic reductionists can see therapy that focuses on becoming aware of Being as a therapy that focuses on learning how to think and feel in ways that enhance (rather than hinder) homeostasis.

Naturalistic dualism

Other therapists believe that consciousness is something fundamentally different from physical matter. This view is often referred to as naturalistic dualism (Chalmers, 1995) since it sees consciousness and physical matter as two equally fundamental types of phenomena in that neither can be reduced to an effect of the other.

From this point of view, the experience of Being is a state of consciousness, not a physical brain state. Thus, even though it is possible to observe certain brain states in experienced meditators when they have conscious experiences of Being, these brain states do not explain or cause the experience of Being.

The main argument for naturalistic dualism is that correlation is different from causation. Thus, observed correlations between brain states and conscious experience cannot be taken as evidence that the physical states cause the experience[1]. Furthermore, researchers have been unable to provide any explanation of how and why a physical state would bring about a conscious experience.

For naturalistic dualists, the definition of Being as that which you experience when your attention is not occupied with thoughts and emotions, can be taken to mean that Being is a particular state of consciousness.

A naturalistic dualist may, for example, differentiate between different states of consciousness, such as dreaming, rumination, flow and awareness of Being. Research has shown that the default state of consciousness while awake is

---

[1] Observing that A and B correlate does not tell us whether A causes B, B causes A or A and B are both caused by something else.

rumination[2] (Mason et al., 2007). In this state of consciousness, the individual's awareness is following strings of associated thoughts and emotions. Thus, naturalistic dualists can understand the above definition of Being as referring to the state of consciousness where the individual's awareness is still and not following these strings of thoughts and emotion.

Research has also shown that human beings are significantly more unhappy in rumination than in other states of consciousness. For example, people are happier when their attention is wholly absorbed in what they are currently doing (Csikszentmihalyi, 1990). Similarly, people are significantly happier when (for example during meditation) they are in the state of awareness of Being (Killingsworth & Gilbert, 2010). Furthermore, frequently experiencing awareness of Being has positive impacts, even when not meditating (Brewer et al., 2011). Such research supports the notion that helping clients enter into the state of consciousness called awareness of Being will have profound therapeutic effects.

Thus, naturalistic dualists can see therapy that focuses on becoming aware of Being as a therapy that focuses on learning how to shift one's state of consciousness from rumination to awareness of Being, which has profoundly positive effects on the individual's well-being[3].

It is worth noting that seeing consciousness as something different from physical matter does not automatically imply that there is anything supernatural about consciousness. Matter and consciousness are merely two fundamental properties of reality. To understand this, one can think about time and space, since these are also properties of reality that cannot be reduced to effects of physical matter[4].

---

[2] This state is also referred to as mind-wandering or the monkey mind.

[3] This would be analogous to learning to get better sleep since good sleep is another state of consciousness which has a profoundly positive impact on the individual's well-being – even when the individual is not asleep.

[4] There are physicists working with quantum field theory who challenge whether space is a fundamental property, by suggesting that it might be an effect of quantum entanglement – a property of matter. But for the purpose of illustrating how consciousness can be considered a fundamental property of reality the comparison with time and space suffices.

Mysticism

Some therapists are influenced by various mystical traditions[5]. While different mystical traditions differ in their beliefs, they often share certain core assumptions about the nature of reality, knowledge and what it means to live a good life.

- Mystics generally believe there is a divine or spiritual presence permeating and connecting all things and that this presence is what is real[6].
- Mystics generally believe that true knowledge or enlightenment comes through personal, direct experiences of this presence.
- Mystics generally believe that life's deeper purpose relates to spiritual growth through cultivating awareness of the divine presence, since this enables living life guided by true knowledge – rather than misconceptions.

For therapists who operate from these beliefs, the definition of Being as what you experience when your attention is not occupied by thoughts and emotions can be taken to mean that Being is the experience of the divine presence that permeates everything.

It is common to find definitions of the divine presence in mystical traditions that mirror the definition of Being used in this book. For example, in Advaita Vedanta (a mystical tradition within Hinduism) pure consciousness (a name for the divine presence) is defined as “not this”, meaning that anything that can be defined as an object is not pure consciousness. Thus, according to this definition pure consciousness is precisely that which is not only beyond physical objects, but also beyond thoughts and emotions. Pure consciousness is not an object but rather that to which all objects appear.

---

[5] Mystical traditions influencing various approaches to therapy include Sufism (Islamic mysticism), Kabbalah (Jewish mysticism), Christian mysticism, Hindu mysticism (Including Advaita Vedanta and Bhakti traditions), Buddhism, Taoism, various forms of Shamanism, Gnosticism (early Christian and pre-Christian mystical thought) and Theosophy to name a few.

[6] Different traditions have different names for this Divine presence, including Allah or the Divine Essence (Sufism), Ein Sof or the Infinite (Kabbalah), God, the Holy Spirit, the Divine Presence, The Christ Consciousness or the Divine Light (Christian Mysticism), Brahman or Atman (Hindu Mysticism), Dharmakaya or Buddha-nature (Buddhism), the Tao or the Way (Taoism), the One or the Divine Principle (Greek mysticism), the Great Spirit (some Shamanistic traditions), the Pleroma or the Fullness (Gnosticism), the Absolute or the Universal Soul (Theosophy), the Jiva or the Pure Soul (Jainism), Source, Universal Energy, or Divine Light (various New Age traditions).

Similarly, it is common to find approaches to therapy which directly state that the therapy brings about experiences corresponding to what mystics call the mystical experience. For example, Richard Schwartz, the founder of Internal Family Systems states that IFS is "a conceptual framework that seems to fit well with most of the world's spiritual traditions and it provides access, often much more rapidly than those traditions would believe [possible], to a kind of core essence in people that a lot of systems see as enlightenment" (Schwartz, 2018, Chapter 2). Similarly, Connirae Andreas, the founder of the Core Transformation Process, writes "One of the intriguing effects of the Core Transformation Process is that it taps directly into spiritual states" (Andreas & Andreas, 1994, p. 222).

To mystics, a therapy that focuses on becoming aware of Being is, thus, a therapy that focuses on creating circumstances under which clients may experience the divine presence directly and be transformed by this experience. Such transformation is therapeutic because it brings about knowledge that corrects the misconceptions about the world and the self that are the root cause of the client's suffering. This may include knowledge about the fundamental interconnectedness of all things which resolves psychological issues such as separateness, isolation and loneliness. It may include knowledge about the universality of unconditional love which resolves psychological issues such as low self-worth, self-hatred and feeling unloved. It may include knowledge about the impermanent nature of all phenomena, which resolves psychological issues such as greed, fear of loss, obsessive behaviour and anxiety about the future.

It is worth noting that to mystics the experience of Being is ineffable. Both the experience itself and the knowledge it brings is beyond ordinary language. For this reason, direct experience is necessary as the knowledge that comes with such experience cannot be fully communicated through language. The chemist and philosopher Michael Polanyi (Polanyi, 1969, 1974) writes that when seeking to communicate personal knowledge[7] through word, the words will only make sense to the people who already know.

Thus, therapists who are influenced by mystical traditions can see therapy that focuses on becoming aware of Being as a therapy that focuses on bringing about

[7] Polanyi wrote about personal knowledge arising from experience in general – not specifically about knowledge arising from the mystical experience. Nevertheless, his point is highly relevant in that context.

transformation of consciousness and attainment the knowledge that will resolve psychological issues and allow the individual to live a more fulfilling life.

Translating between perspectives

Throughout the book, I will use different concepts and phrases which at first glance may seem to be exclusive to the perspective of mysticism. I may, for example, write about "the divine", "the true nature of mind" or "the essence of the human being". Such phrases are, indeed, borrowed from mystical traditions. However, there is nothing preventing readers from translating such phrases into their preferred perspective.

For example, reductionists will generally reject accounts of encounters with the divine as superstition. However, it is possible to regard such accounts as poetic descriptions of the subjective experience of states of physiological homeostasis. Reductionists may even acknowledge that it can be necessary to resort to poetry to accurately capture certain subjective experiences. For example, for the purpose of communicating a subjective experience of watching a beautiful sunset, poetry may be far superior to a description of the physical processes involved, such as how photons with certain wavelengths affect the retinas and create electric impulses in certain regions of the brain. In the same way, the subjective experience of a state of homeostasis may be best described as "divinely pleasant" and the effects prolonged exposure to this state has on our subjective experience of ourselves and our environment may be best described as "divine blessings". Thus, therapists who prefer the reductionist perspective can read accounts of encounters with the divine as poetic descriptions of how certain physiological states *feel* to us in our subjective experience. Reductionists may regard such descriptions as valuable insofar as they, properly understood, can enable individuals to use their subjective experience to "monitor" their physiological states. Without the help of machines, it is difficult to point to a state of homeostasis. It is, however, possible to point to the subjective experiences that correlate with such a state. Thus, descriptions of the subjective experiences that correlate with homeostasis can establish a feedback mechanism that allows individuals to learn how to better self-regulate.

Similarly, naturalistic dualists will typically reject notions of divine love or an all-pervasive great spirit as supernatural. However, it is possible to understand such notions as referring to particular states of consciousness rather than to anything supernatural. Divine love can be understood as referring to a particular state of consciousness where the individual feels a profound sense of being both loved and loving. Similarly, the great spirit may refer to a state of consciousness where the individual acutely experiences the interconnectedness of all things. Having names for different states of consciousness that reflect the related subjective experience can be of great help when researching them.

Finally, mystics often reject the reductionist's focus on physiological states. However, it is possible to understand the reductionist's description of physiological states as descriptions of either the physiological effects of the mystical experience or the physiological prerequisites for attaining the mystical experience. Stanislav Groff, a prominent figure in transpersonal psychology, likens the brain to a radio receiver that enables humans to "tune in to" the divine presence. In short, much of what reductionists have to say about the correlations between subjective experiences and physiological states remains valid and valuable regardless of whether it is assumed that one causes the other or vice versa. Mystics also tend to reject the naturalistic dualist's notion of dualism, since many mystical traditions are monistic, meaning that they believe everything is made up of a single substance[8]. However, it is possible to engage with what naturalistic dualists claim about the antecedents and effects of experiencing different states of consciousness without agreeing on whether matter is created by consciousness or not.

[8] Pre-Socratic Greek philosophers believed that all was made of a single substance. Different philosophers proposed different substances, including water (Thales of Miletus), fire (Heraclitus), air (Anaximenes), the infinite (Anaximander) or atoms (Leucippus and Democritus). Others believe that all is made of consciousness. Theistic traditions can be seen as proponents of this view since they generally hold that the physical universe was created by God or the Gods. Yet others believe that both the physical and consciousness are empty in the sense that neither would exist without the other. This is the view held by scholars in the Madhyamika tradition (Tibetan Buddhism), such as Nagarjuna and Chandrakirti.

In short, it is not necessary to subscribe to a particular metaphysical perspective to benefit from the tools presented in this book. The only assumptions one would have to accept are:

- That when you unhook your attention from thoughts and emotions, you can have a particularly interesting type of experience.
- That the lack of this experience underpins much of the psychological suffering that makes clients seek therapy.
- That having this experience has profoundly positive effects on the individual beyond the duration of the experience itself.

It is my hope that the system presented in this book can provide a basis for respectful and mutually enriching dialogue between different perspectives on therapy. Far too often, such dialogue is prematurely terminated due to differences in assumptions – even when such assumptions are not strictly central to the topic of discussion.

Next, I will introduce the concept of Aspects of Being or Essences, which will help account for variation in individual experiences of Being.

1.3.2. Aspects of Being (Essences)

Another concept that I use throughout the book is the concept of Aspects of Being (or Essences), which I define in the following way:

> Aspects of Being are the qualitatively different ways in which individuals experience Being.

To understand why Being would be experienced in qualitatively different ways we can draw on a common metaphor for Being, namely space.

Drawing on this metaphor, we can see thoughts and emotions as analogous to physical objects and Being as analogous to the space that contains these objects. Switching one's attention from thoughts and emotions to Being is analogous to switching one's attention from physical objects to the space that contains them[9].

While space does not have any properties of its own, it can be experienced as having properties when compared to physical objects. For example, space is

---

[9] It is common to distinguish between "mind" and "consciousness" using this same metaphor, so that "mind" refers to the content of consciousness, including thoughts, emotions and sense impressions, and "consciousness" refers to the space in which this content appears – or as *that* to which this content appears. This distinction sees "consciousness" as synonymous with "Being".

lighter than any physical object, since space has no mass, whereas any physical object does. Space is also more stable than any physical object, since any physical object eventually deteriorates, whereas space does not.

In the same way, Being does not have any properties of its own, but it can be experienced as having properties when compared to different thoughts and emotions. For example, because judgements are thoughts and Being is defined as that which is beyond thoughts and emotions, Being is by definition non-judgemental. Similarly, because concerns and worries are thoughts, Being is by definition care-free. Because disturbances belong to the realm of thoughts and emotions, Being is peaceful.

Many approaches to therapies seek to harvest the therapeutic potential of what spiritual traditions refer to as "mystical experiences" and what here is referred to as the experience of Being. These approaches to therapy often contain classifications of the distinct characteristics of this experience.

For example, Core Transformation (Andreas & Andreas, 1994) operates with the qualities of wholeness, oneness, peace, love and OKness. Internal Family Systems (Schwartz, 1995) operates with the self-energies of compassion, curiosity, clarity, creativity, calm, confidence, courage and connectedness. The Diamond Approach (Almaas, 2002) and Diamond Logos operate with multiple Essences, such as freedom, grounding, vitality, peace, compassion, and joy. Such classifications are often inspired by a combination of client reports and classifications from spiritual traditions, such as the Latifa in Sufism, the chakras in Hinduism and the seven heavenly virtues in Christianity.

In this book, I will operate with a classification system consisting of ten aspects of Being. I will call these aspects of Being "Essences" and use colours to name each Essence[10]:

1. Unconditional Support, Grounding and Confidence (White Essence)
2. Unconditional Strength, Courage, Passion and Vitality (Red Essence)
3. Unconditional Peace, Power and Intimacy (Black Essence)
4. Unconditional Compassion and Loving-Kindness (Green Essence)
5. Unconditional Appreciation and Acceptance (Pink Essence)
6. Unconditional Joy, Happiness and Curiosity (Yellow Essence)
7. Unconditional Unity, Bonding and Surrender (Gold Essence)
8. Unconditional Nourishment, Satisfaction and Fulfilment (Cream Essence)
9. Unconditional Clarity, Intelligence and Guidance (Blue Essence)
10. Unconditional Freedom, Openness & Receptivity (Clear Essence)

This is not an exhaustive list of how people can experience Being. However, ten categories are enough for the purpose of this book. I will expand on these ten qualities of Being in Section 2.3 The 10 aspects of Being.

In the remainder of this section, I will explain why I use the qualifier "unconditional" in front of the words used to name each Essence.

The qualifiers "conditional" and "unconditional" can be used to distinguish clearly between situations where a word refers to a state of thought/emotion and situations where this same word refers to a quality of Being, which is beyond thought/emotion.

For example, "conditional peace" refers to a particular mental/emotional state that arises when an individual perceives their environment as not containing anything that would cause agitation. Conversely, "unconditional peace" refers to the fact that Being cannot contain agitation because agitation is a

---

[10] This classification system is an adaptation of the system used in the Diamond Approach/Diamond Logos tradition, which in turn is an adaptation and extension of the Sufi lataif system. Essence 1, 2, 3, 4, and 6 corresponds to the five lataif of God's Command and are labelled with the same colours used in the Punjab tradition within the Naqshbandi order: Qualb is yellow, Ruh is red, Sirr is white, Khafi is Black and Ikhfa is green (Almaas, 1986, pp. 142–143; Shah, 1971, pp. 145, 334, 340, 430). Essence 5 and 7, 8, 9 and 10 correspond to the essences used in Diamond Approach/Diamond Logos. However, Essences 8, 9 and 10 are labelled using colours different from those used in the Diamond Approach/Diamond Logos to keep a consistent practice of labelling.

mental/emotional state and Being is defined as that which is beyond thoughts and emotions.

Similarly, a person can be "conditionally non-judgemental" in the sense of actively suspending their judgements. Being "unconditionally non-judgemental" on the other hand refers to the fact that the experience of Being cannot contain any judgements because judgements are thoughts and emotions and Being is beyond thoughts and emotions.

I will expand on the distinction between conditional and unconditional phenomena in Section 3.2.

In this book, I will use "Essence", "aspect of Being", unconditional phenomena and the colour relating to each Essence interchangeably. Thus, I may refer to the first Essence in the above classification as "White Essence", "the White aspect of Being", "unconditional grounding" or simply "White".

1.3.3. Personality Parts

Several different approaches to therapy use the concept of "personality parts"[11].

Generally, the concept of personality parts is used to refer to distinct aspects or sub-personalities within an individual's overall personality, each with its own unique traits, behaviours and roles. These parts can influence thoughts, emotions, and actions, and can either be in conflict or work in harmony.

However, there are also differences between how the concept of personality parts is used in different approaches to therapy and by individual therapists. Some approaches operate with a fixed set of predefined personality parts, such as the super-ego, ego and id of the psychodynamic approaches. Other approaches to therapy operate with a potentially limitless number of personality parts which they classify according to their function, such as the managers (protective parts), firefighters (reactive parts) and exiles (parts carrying wounds) of Internal Family Systems or the parent, adult and child ego-states of Transactional Analysis. Yet other approaches to therapy, such as Gestalt Therapy, operate with an exploratory attitude towards both the number of parts and the function of these parts. Furthermore, some therapists will see the notion of personality parts as a

---

[11] For example, psychodynamic therapies, Transactional Therapy, Gestalt Therapy, Internal Family Systems Therapy and Relational Focusing.

metaphorical way of describing what is going on in the psyche, while others will consider personality parts to be actual entities operating within the individual.

In the interest of giving the tools in the present book the broadest possible appeal, I define a "personality part" as:

> A cluster of mutually supportive/reinforcing mental, emotional and behavioural patterns in the service of a single agenda.

Let's look at an example to illustrate how this definition works. Imagine an individual who has a mental habit of interpreting certain behaviour in other people, such as being late for meetings, as a sign that these people do not value him. This may give rise to feelings of insignificance or inadequacy. This emotional pattern may lead the individual to behave in ways that will give other people the impression that it is ok to be late for meetings with him. At the same time, if the individual feels insignificant and inadequate, he may be more likely to interpret other people's lateness as evidence that these people do not value him. These patterns may serve the purpose of avoiding abandonment by others by creating and maintaining a sense of low value which prevents the individual from asserting himself in ways that may lead to disruption of relationships with others. Such a cluster of mutually supportive and reinforcing mental, emotional and behavioural patterns in support of a particular agenda is what I refer to as a personality part. I will expand on this notion of personality parts in Section 6.1.

1.3.4. Personality Structure

A concept that is closely related to the concept of "personality parts" is "personality structure" or simply "personality". In this book, I define "personality structure" as:

> The total system of all of an individual's personality parts.

Below, I draw on the definition of personality parts to make two (relatively uncontroversial) claims about personality structure and propose that it follows from these claims that personality structure can be used as a guide to become aware of Being.

First claim: The personality structure is a layered structure

The purpose of any personality part is to reach a certain goal. Sometimes the way one personality part seeks to reach its goal will create problems, and another personality part develops around the goal of solving this problem. For example, an individual's personality structure may contain a personality part that seeks to produce the feeling of being connected with other people by going along with whatever other people want. However, a problematic side effect of following this strategy could be that the individual will disregard their own needs. Therefore, another personality part may develop which seeks to deal with this problem. This personality part may seek to create space for the fulfilment of the individual's own needs keeping other people at a distance. Following this strategy will, in turn, create other problems, and other personality parts may develop to deal with these problems. Consequently, the personality structure is a layered structure where many personality parts are reacting to problematic consequences of following the strategies of other personality parts. I will expand on the layered nature of the personality structure in Section 5.2.

Second claim: The goal of the personality structure is Being

Because the purpose of any personality part is to reach a certain goal, once the goal is reached the personality part becomes dormant, since it is only needed as long as the goal has not been reached. Consequently, one can say that all personality parts ultimately seek to make themselves redundant. Since personality parts consist of "pre-programmed" thoughts and emotions, one can further say that all personality parts ultimately seek the state beyond such thoughts and emotions. In other words, all personality parts, and by extension the entire personality structure, ultimately seek Being. I will expand on this idea in Section 2.5.1.

The personality structure can be used to become aware of Being

These two characteristics of the personality structure are important because they enable us to use the personality structure as a tool to become aware of Being.

Because all personality parts ultimately seek Being, it is possible to use a client's personality parts as tools to direct the client's awareness towards Being. We can do so by exploring what each part is ultimately reaching for since this will be Being. Because the personality structure is layered, we can also become aware of Being by repeatedly directing our awareness towards that which any personality part is reacting to. In other words, we can become aware of Being by exploring what is at the core of the layered personality structure. By exploring what precedes the activity of any personality part, we can discover what is beyond thoughts and emotions. In some approaches to therapy, this is captured in the metaphor of seeing therapy as the activity of peeling an onion.

In the above, I have briefly introduced and defined some key concepts used in this book, namely Being, Aspects of Being (Essences), Personality Parts and Personality Structure. I have sought to define these concepts in such a way that they are compatible with as many approaches to therapy as possible.

I will now briefly comment on what purpose I hope this book can fulfil.

1.4. The purpose of the book

As mentioned above, there are many approaches to therapy which directly or indirectly seek to harvest the therapeutic potential of what spiritual traditions call mystical experiences and what in this book is called experiences of Being.

However, the techniques employed by these approaches to bring about direct and personal experiences of Being may appear rather different. One of the reasons for this is that these different techniques focus on resolving different types of blocks that prevent clients from having experiences of Being. In the language of this book, different approaches focus on untying different knots.

The ambition of the present book is to compile and organise practices for bringing about experiences of Being in a comprehensive and detailed model.

Such a model can serve several purposes.

First, I see the potential for using the 5 Knots model to classify different approaches to therapy that work with experiences of Being according to which knot(s) they primarily work with. This can help illuminate advantages and limitations of different techniques for bringing about experiences of Being.

Second, the 5 Knots model can help therapists extend and develop their techniques by having a clear understanding of the knot the techniques are untying and comparing their own techniques with others that work with the same knot.

Third, the 5 Knots model can help therapists develop appreciation for techniques, which aim to untie knots that cannot be untied using the therapists' current techniques. In other words, the model can illuminate how different techniques for developing awareness of Being can be complementary.

Fourth, it is my hope that the 5 Knots model can support therapists and seekers from *any* tradition in harvesting the therapeutic potential the direct and personal experience of Being has to offer.

Fifth, it is also my hope that the 5 Knots model can offer a common language that can facilitate productive dialogue between not only practitioners in different therapeutic communities, but also between therapists, scientists, psychologists and mystics.

In the remainder of this introductory chapter, I give an overview of how the book is structured.

1.5. The structure of the book

The book is structured in seven chapters: One introductory chapter, five chapters outlining the 5 knots and how to untie them and a final chapter on how to integrate the experiences from Being-Centred Therapy in everyday life.

In Chapter 1, I have introduced the idea that lack of awareness of Being underpins many of the issues clients bring to therapy and that developing awareness of Being, therefore, can have great therapeutic effects. I have also outlined the purpose of the book as providing a model that can support therapists in harvesting the therapeutic potential of experiencing Being and facilitate dialogue between different approaches to therapy, and between therapists, scientists, psychologists and mystics. Finally, I have defined some key concepts I will use throughout the book.

In the following five chapters, I will describe five distinct mechanisms that prevent clients from developing awareness of Being and five therapeutic processes that can counter these mechanisms and help clients develop such awareness. Furthermore, I will describe the misconceptions underpinning the mechanisms and comment on how direct and personal experience of Being can replace these misconceptions with true knowledge.

In Chapter 2, I discuss how giving the experience of Being a positive name encourages individuals to perceive Being as an object and develop ideas about this object rather than letting their awareness dwell on the experience of Being. If this move of attention away from the direct experience towards ideas becomes automatic and pervasive, it will lead to loss of awareness of Being. Losing awareness of Being by conceptualising it as a positive thing is the Knot of Positive Reification. This knot lays the ground for all other knots. The Knot of Positive Reification is untied by encouraging the individual to move their awareness from the positive concept back to the underlying felt sense. This process is called Sensing Abundance.

In Chapter 3, I discuss how the things we seek in life are proxies for Being and how seeking these things will further take our awareness away from Being, thus exacerbating the sense of loss we seek to remedy through our actions. This is the Knot of Conditionality. This knot is untied by raising awareness of the felt sense the individual is ultimately seeking through their pursuits of various objects (external as well as internal). This process is called Sensing Completion.

In Chapter 4, I discuss two mechanisms through which the experience of Being can come to appear to us as something negative we must avoid. We can come to see Being as something negative when we, in our pursuit of one aspect of the experience of Being, dismiss another aspect of Being as irrelevant or as an obstacle. We can also come to see Being as something negative when we blame Being for the suffering created by the misconceived ways in which we seek it. Seeing Being as something negative will lead us to actively avoid it, thus exacerbating the sense of loss we feel when we lose awareness of Being. This is the Knot of Negative Reification. This knot is untied by exploring the felt sense of that which we avoid while setting aside our judgements. This process is called Sensing Taboos.

In Chapter 5, I discuss how the habitual and automatic nature of our acts of interpretation makes it difficult for us to recognise how these acts create the suffering we experience. Instead, we ascribe our suffering to external factors. However, seeking to deal with the external factors we believe are the cause of our suffering takes our attention away from Being, thus exacerbating the real issue. This is the Knot of Agency. To untie this knot, we must become aware of the acts of interpretation underlying our suffering. This process is called Sensing Agency.

In Chapter 6, I discuss how internal conflicts can be seen as the result of different personality parts seeking different aspects of Being in conflicting ways. Seeking to resolve such inner conflicts, whether by choosing one part over the other or by developing a compromise, will occupy our attention and draw it away from noticing Being. This will only deepen the sense of loss that each personality part seeks to remedy and, consequently, intensify the conflict. This is the Knot of Fragmentation This knot is untied by the simultaneous experience of the two aspects of Being our conflicting personality parts are seeking. This experience will reveal that while the strategies the personality parts employ may be in conflict, what they are seeking are not, since what they seek are two aspects of the same. This process is called Sensing Unity.

Chapters 2-6 each have five main sections.

The first section contains a general description of the knot and of any theoretical concepts needed to understand the knot.

The second section contains a description of the misconceptions that lead to the formation of the knots. For each misconception, I describe how it arises from other misconceptions, the implications understanding the misconception has for therapy and how these implications can be summarised in a corrective principle that can guide therapy.

The third section contains a process for untying the knot. Each process starts with techniques for recognising the knot followed by techniques for untying the knot by using the dynamics of the knot to make the client aware of Being. The section ends with follow-up processes that use the experience the client has gained from the main process to correct the misconceptions outlined in section two.

The fourth section provides examples of how to untie the knot in one-to-one sessions. It contains transcriptions of sessions that exemplify the process for untying the knot. Each session is written out with two columns. One column contains the dialogue between client and therapist and the other column contains commentary describing the observations and reasoning underpinning the therapist's questions and interventions.

The fifth section contains examples of how to untie the knot by using contemplation exercises, which students can engage with on their own or in couples. This is particularly useful when working with groups.

In Chapter 7, I focus on how to support clients in integrating and embodying the realisations gained by experiencing awareness of Being, so they can live their lives in accordance with these realisations. Many mystical and philosophical traditions refer to the process of becoming aware of Being as "realisation" and process of integrating and living from this awareness as "actualisation". In Chapter 7, I offer a fresh perspective on the process of actualisation. I propose that actualisation is the process of using conscious experiences of Being to alter the embodied grounding of one's conceptual systems in such a way that it becomes easier to sustain awareness of Being during interactions with the environment outside any therapeutic context and, thus, to live in accordance with such awareness and the knowledge it brings. This view on actualisation is derived from newer research relating to memory reconsolidation, Cognitive Metaphor Theory and Embodied Cognition.

And now, let's explore the first of the 5 Knots: The Knot of Positive Reification.

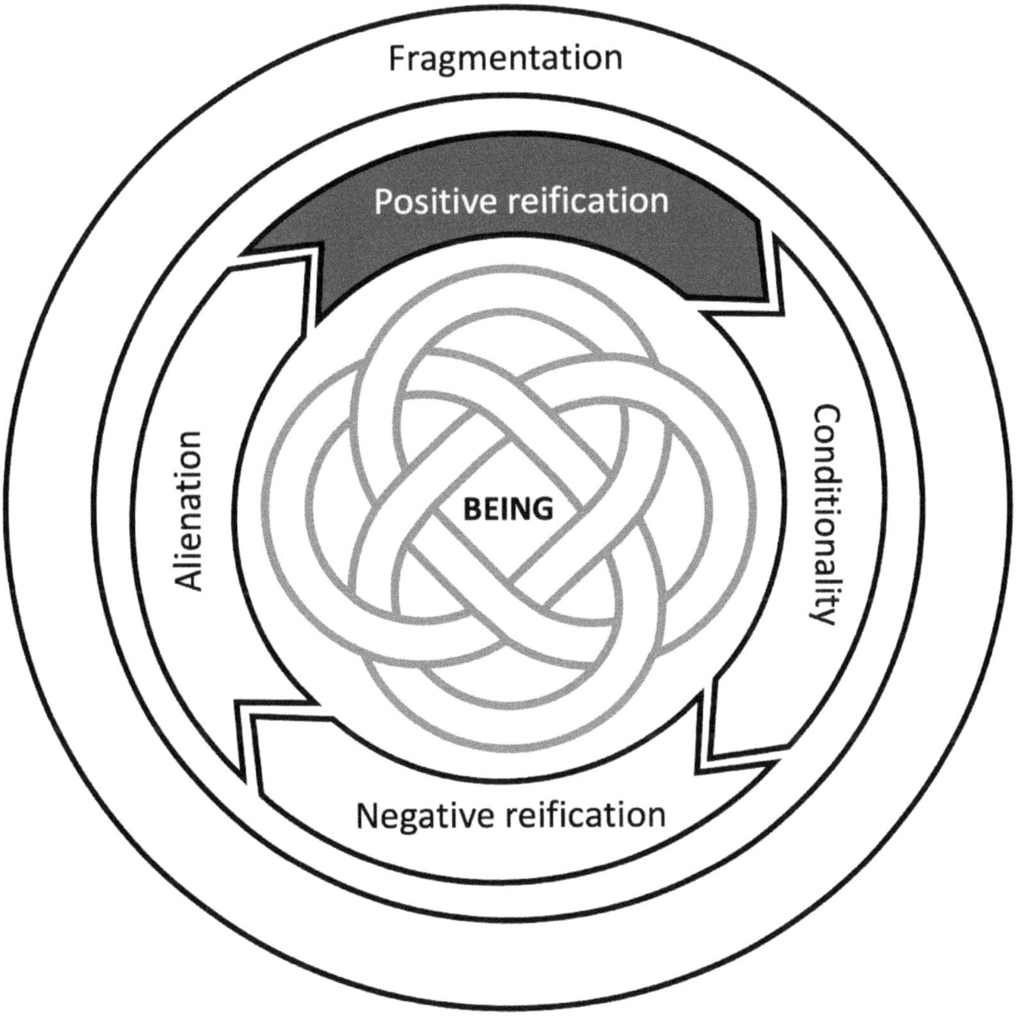

The Knot of Positive Reification

2. Knot 1: The Knot of Positive Reification

When we perceive Being, it is often a profoundly positive experience. We typically refer to experiences of Being as experiences of "love", "joy", "peace", "satisfaction", "confidence", "aliveness", "wholeness", etc.

Using such terms to refer to the experience of Being, does two things. It conceptualises Being as an experience of an *entity* (i.e., a thing), and it ascribes a *positive value* to this entity. This process of conceptualising Being as a positive entity is the process of "positive reification".

Reification is practical. The ability to refer to an experience using a single word is useful for communicating about the experience, reflecting on the experience, noticing more aspects of the experience, relating it to other experiences, etc.

However, positive reification of Being can also lead to three interrelated misconceptions, which have wide-ranging negative effects on our well-being.

First, when we refer to experiences of Being using many different words, we risk losing sight of the fundamental unity underpinning these experiences. Instead, we develop the misconception that these words refer to fundamentally different things. We come to believe that "love", "joy", "peace", "satisfaction", "confidence", "aliveness", "wholeness", etc., are fundamentally different phenomena – rather than different ways of experiencing Being. This, in turn, opens the possibility of developing false beliefs about how the pursuit of one of these phenomena can conflict with the pursuit of another. This lays the ground for a process of fragmentation of our personality structure where different parts of our personality structure will be in conflict with each other because they believe they pursue different and mutually exclusive phenomena[12]. Such inner fragmentation is detrimental to our well-being.

Second, when we conceptualise the experience of Being as a concrete entity, we use language in a manner that portrays this entity as something that is *separate* from ourselves. We talk about ourselves as a subject that can "find love", "lose joy", "attain peace", "run out of vitality", etc. Talking about Being in this way, we

---

[12] We will return to this in Chapter 6 Knot 5: The Knot of Fragmentation.

risk losing sight of our own fundamental unity with Being and instead perceiving ourselves as separate from it. This perception of ourselves as separate from Being, in turn, creates a deep sense of inner loss and a deficient sense of self that underlies a wide range of the psychological issues clients bring to therapy sessions. If we try to address these issues without addressing the underlying lack of awareness of Being, we are treating symptoms rather than the cause of the client's lack of well-being.

Third, using a single word to speak or think about an experience compels us to shift our awareness away from the experience itself and towards ideas connected with the experience. When we speak about "a flower", our awareness is directed towards that which we wish to say *about* the flower, diverting it from the immediate experience of the flower itself. In the same way, using a single word to refer to an experience of Being prompts us to say or think something *about* Being rather than letting our awareness dwell on the experience of Being itself. Over time the word replaces the experience, and we feel as though we have lost the experience because we have learned to consistently direct our awareness away from it. I will revisit this subject frequently throughout the book.

Thus, ironically enough, naming the experience of Being, compels us to divert our awareness away from Being and, over time, lose awareness of Being. This happens even if the name is associated with a positive value-judgement. This "paradox" is the Knot of Positive Reification.

The knot of Positive Reification is untied through the process of Sensing Abundance. The core of this process is to invite clients to regain awareness of the felt-sense experience that positive words for Being refer to. In other words, Sensing Abundance is a process of moving our awareness from the abstract word for Being back to the immediate experience of Being.

The process of Sensing Abundance provides experiences which dispel the mistaken beliefs connected with positive reification. If we have clear, frequent and sustained experiences of Being, we gain a clear and experientially grounded understanding of the difference between the word and the experience the word refers to; we learn that the experience of Being is an inherent aspect of existence and not a separate entity, and we learn that the many positive phenomena we seek in life are merely aspects of the same fundamental experience of Being.

Before expanding on the Knot of Positive Reification, a word on "reification" is in order as this term may be unfamiliar to some readers.

2.1. What is reification?

Reification is the process of perceiving something abstract and immaterial, such as “motivation”, “time”, “justice”, “will”, “nature”, “civilisation”, “the state”, etc., – as if it were a concrete and material thing. Reification is sometimes aptly referred to as *the fallacy of misplaced concreteness* because in essence it attributes concrete existence to something that has no concreteness in itself.

Reification is a useful tool in that it allows us to, among other things, imagine future scenarios, predict events, invent new things and processes, and combine things in new ways.

To understand this, we can look at the concept of “motivation”. When psychologists develop theories about “motivation”, they presume that humans possess something referred to as “motivation”, which drives them to act predictably under specific conditions. Once we have transformed “motivation” into a tangible concept, we can proceed to make claims about it.

Some claim that motivation propels humans to seek pleasure and avoid pain, suggesting that it is possible to influence people's behaviour by linking the performance of a particular behaviour with pleasure in the form of rewards and the non-performance of this behaviour with pain in the form of punishment or absence of rewards.

Others claim that motivation compels us act to fulfil needs, attain a sense of purpose, or acquire and display competency. From this perspective, we can predict that human beings will engage in behaviours which afford them the opportunity to fulfil needs, attain a sense of purpose or acquire and display competency.

Still others propose that motivation is derived more from *anticipated* outcomes rather than the actual results of our actions. This idea implies that promoting certain behaviours requires the manipulation of people's expectations about the outcomes of these behaviours. Ensuring that the behaviours in question genuinely lead to the expected outcomes is less important.

In short, envisioning a concrete entity called “motivation” that drives human behaviour allows us to construct theories that can help us predict human behaviour and better navigate our interactions with other people. This is invaluable to therapists, educators, managers, marketers – and many others.

Reification doesn't present a problem as long as we distinguish between the abstract and the concrete, even though we may discuss the abstract in terms that imply concreteness.

We can, for example, announce that we are "fighting for justice", and we understand that this is merely shorthand for "putting in an effort to ensure that certain social processes are conducted in a manner that most individuals perceive as fair". Likewise, we can assert that we are "wasting time", and we understand that this is a succinct way of expressing that "we are engaging in activities we believe are not worth doing, or that we are neglecting tasks we believe hold greater value than those we are currently engaged with".

However, reification *does* become a problem when we confuse the immaterial and abstract products of our thoughts with the tangible and concrete.

When we lose sight of the fact that a reified concept is our own creation and begin treating it as if it possesses an independent reality, then we may become entangled in our own creation – and even start fighting it[13].

For example, if we forget that "motivation" is an abstraction and not a tangible entity, we may start feeling that our motivation is deficient and that it does not supply us with the necessary energy to do the things we need to do, or that our motivation compels us to do things we don't want to do. We may begin to treat motivation as if it were an autonomous force within us that compels us to act against our own will (another reification). This, in turn, can lead us to fight with our motivation in an attempt to rectify or overwrite it. However, "motivation" is an abstract concept. It has no volition. It is not trying to impose anything on us. It is merely an idea we use to make sense of the world and our own behaviour. When we treat it as if it has a reality (and will) of its own, we can get into conflict with what is essentially a figment of our own imagination. We become like Don Quixote fighting imaginary giants and sorcerers.

The physicist and spiritual teacher, David Bohm, explains it in this way:

> "That's [a] mistake that thought makes. It produces a result, and then it says, I didn't do it; it's there by itself, and I must correct it. But if thought is constantly making this result and then saying, 'I've got to stop it', this is absurd. Because thought is caught up in this absurdity, it is producing all

---

[13] I will write more about this in Chapter 5 Knot 4: The Knot of Alienation.

> sorts of negative consequences, then treating them as independent and saying, I must stop them." (Bohm & Edwards, 1991, p. 14)

At this point, some readers might argue that surely "motivation" is a real and tangible force. They may contend that, one feels energy in the body when one is motivated, tasks are completed more swiftly when motivation is present, and it can be difficult to force oneself to act when motivation is lacking. If motivation produces all these effects, it must be a real force.

However, the energy, swift action, or inaction, are not "motivation" themselves. These are merely phenomena we presume to be related to "motivation"; we simply use the concept "motivation" to make sense of these phenomena. In fact, it is impossible to point to anything concrete and declare it to be "motivation". The word "motivation" does not correspond to any tangible phenomenon. This is how we know that "motivation" is the product of our thinking.

Similarly, you may feel that "justice" or "time" are real things beyond your mind because you are used to thinking about them as such. However, if you are in doubt about whether a word is a reification or not, you can test it by asking yourself the question: Can I point to the thing the word refers to? Upon asking this question, you will find that you can neither point to "justice" nor to "time" because both are abstract concepts.

If you take the time to examine a dictionary word for word, you will come to the disturbing realisation that most words are reifications. For example, in the previous sentence, the only word that refers to something you can point to is "words".

The reason we feel "motivation" is a real thing is because we are used to talking about it as if it were. In other words, we are committing the fallacy of misplaced concreteness – or reification. When we commit the fallacy of misplaced concreteness, we become trapped in a world of our own creation, which we have forgotten is our own creation.

The problem with reification, or the fallacy of misplaced concreteness, has been known for millennia. For example, stating that we can get trapped in a realm of reified concepts can be seen as a contemporary formulation of what Hindu and Greek philosophers (among others) referred to when they asserted that the common state of consciousness resembles being asleep while dreaming that one is awake or that we live in a state of ignorance, which includes the lack of awareness of this ignorance.

Similarly, the Judeo-Christian narrative of The Fall can be interpreted as a story about losing oneself in the creations of one's own mind. In this context, Adam and Eve eating the fruit from the Tree of Knowledge can be understood as the point where they develop the capacity for abstract thinking. Consequently, their expulsion from the Garden of Eden can be understood as the point where they become lost in their own abstractions and lose awareness of that which lies beyond their own mental constructs – that which has substance and reality – God[14].

In this book, I differentiate between positive and negative reification. Positive reification is the process of relating to Being as if it were a concrete and material thing that we place a *positive* value-judgement on. Negative reification is the process of relating to Being as if it were a concrete and material thing that we place a *negative* value-judgement on.

I differentiate between positive and negative reification and treat these in separate chapters because the conditions that lead to positive and negative reification, as well as the knots that can result from those reifications, differ in important ways[15].

Before we look in detail at the Knot of Positive Reification and the processes of Sensing Abundance through which we can untie this knot, it is instructive to comment on the conditions under which a reified concept gets to be seen as something positive.

2.2. Under which conditions do we perceive Being as positive?

Long-term meditators who are intimately familiar with the perception of Being often describe Being as neutral. They liken it to water or empty space. They describe it as simple, clear, open and neutral.

---

[14] Of course, religious traditions are notoriously famous for fostering multiple inspiring and profound interpretations. I will not pretend that the above interpretation is an exhaustive reading of any religious text. It is, however, an important interpretation in that it links modern science and ancient wisdom traditions and as such it can foster productive dialogue between modern and ancient traditions.

[15] If you wish to dive deeper into the concept of reification, you can, for example, read Wittgenstein's work on the topic or any of the introductions to his work.

This begs the question: Why do we so often experience Being as something distinctly positive? Or in other words: What are the conditions under which we judge the perception of Being to be the experience of something positive?

Understanding under which conditions individuals judge Being as something positive is useful when working with the Knot of Positive Reification because it can help us perceive Being more directly – as opposed to perceiving it through the filters that make it appear as a positive entity.

If you, as a therapist, are not clear on how positive reification is a product of perceiving Being under certain conditions, you are likely to fall into the trap of supporting the positive reification of your clients and joining them in turning attention towards narratives and ideas surrounding the reification and, consequently, overlooking Being itself.

If, on the other hand, you, as a therapist, clearly see positive reification as a result of perceiving Being under certain conditions, you are in a much better position to help the client side-step all the narratives and ideas surrounding the reification and instead turn their awareness towards the immediate experience of Being beyond its various appearances.

To understand how individuals evaluate the experience of Being as either positive or negative, it is essential to understand how humans evaluate phenomena in general. In particular, it is important to know that

1. humans rely on reference points when making evaluations
2. the reference points humans use when making evaluations are often arbitrary

I will now unpack these two assertions in detail.

Whether we judge something as good or bad largely depends on the reference points we use for comparison. For instance, you might feel that your salary is good when surrounded by peers who earn less but regard the same salary as inadequate when in a company of high-earning peers. Similarly, two lottery winners who both receive 500,000 USD may judge their winnings very differently if, due to a mistake, one was initially informed they had won 1,000,000 USD while the other was told they had won 250,000 USD. This effect has been demonstrated repeatedly in psychological research.

Furthermore, the reference points we use to make assessments are often not chosen deliberately and not even be relevant to the assessment. Instead, they are picked at random from among whatever happens to be present in our environment when we make the assessment. This was beautifully demonstrated in a piece of research by Tversky and Kahneman (Kahneman, 2011), who asked people to estimate the percentage of African countries in the United Nations but first had them spin a wheel with numbers from 0 to 100. The wheel was rigged to always land on either 10 or 65. The participants who saw the number 10 gave significantly lower estimates than those who saw the number 65. This, and similar research, shows that irrelevant reference points in our environment can impact our assessments and that we are unaware of what reference points we use in our evaluation processes.

We judge the experience of Being in the same way we judge anything else, namely, by relating the experience to arbitrary (and often irrelevant) reference points that occur in our environment. When it comes to Being, we tend to find such reference points among the mental, emotional and physical events we are aware of immediately before becoming aware of Being.

As mentioned at the start of this section, Being, in itself, is neutral and empty of mental, emotional and physical content. It is not inherently positive or negative as it is beyond concepts of positive and negative. This means that we will judge Being positively whenever we become aware of it immediately after being aware of mental, emotional and physical events we judged as negative.

To understand why we perceive a neutral experience as positive when it follows a negative one, consider the example of not having any particular sensations in your head. In itself, this is a neutral experience. However, you would be likely to judge it as profoundly positive if it comes after an intense headache. When you assess the absence of sensation using the reference point of a severe headache, you interpret the absence of sensation as a delightful relief.

Because most individuals live without an acute awareness of Being, their thoughts and emotions will be permeated by a pervasive sense of loss and separation. Even when we are optimistic and enthusiastic about something, it is often because we hope this something will deliver us from the pain of the loss and separation, and, as such, even our optimistic and enthusiastic thoughts and emotions are often marked by the sense of loss and separation. In short, when we are not aware of Being, our inner life is full of negative reference points.

Consequently, whenever we perceive Being, whether by chance or through deliberate practice, we are likely to evaluate this experience using a negative reference point. This is why we often perceive Being, which in itself is neither positive nor negative, as something distinctly positive.

The more our inner experience is marked by painful feelings of longing and separation and various (pessimistic or optimistic) derivatives of such feelings, the more likely we are to perceive Being as a positive relief from distressing feelings of desire and disconnection.

Thus, the conditions under which the perception of Being leads to positive reification are:

1. That we rarely experience Being or only experience it in certain (infrequent) situations.
2. That we experience Being after experiencing painful mental, emotional and physical content of our minds.

In other words, the rarer we have conscious and clear experiences of Being, the more likely it is that any experience of Being will lead to positive reification. At the same time, the more we believe in and pay attention to our positive reifications of Being, the more we lose awareness of Being itself. This cyclical process leads to deeper and deeper forgetting of Being. That is the Knot of Positive Reification.

In the next section, I present a classification of positive reifications of Being that I use in this book and in my education for therapists at the Sensing Mind Institute.

2.3. The 10 aspects of Being (Essences)

In the previous section, we saw that using *negative* reference points will make Being appear as a *positive* entity. Similarly, what *kind of thing* we perceive Being as depends on the *kind of thing* we use as a reference point. Thus, Being is not merely experienced as something positive but as a specific positive thing, such as peace, love, excitement, joy, connection, etc.

Using the comparison between Being and space can help us understand why Being has this chameleon-like nature in our minds.

If you see empty space in the middle of a wall, you perceive that space as “a hole” in the wall. If the empty space is square-shaped or circular, you may perceive it as “a window”. If the empty space goes all the way to the floor, you may perceive it as “a door”. If the space is surrounded by a prison wall, you may perceive it as “an escape route”. If you see empty space next to a cliff, you may call it “a precipice”. If you see empty space in a room that, last time you saw it, was full of clutter, you may call that empty space “tidyness”. If fact, when you see space (which happens a lot), you almost never perceive it as space. You almost always perceive it as something in relation to the objects in the space – even remembered objects as in the last example above. And because space is nothing, we tend to see it as the opposite of *whatever* reference point we use. In this way, space can appear as an endless number of phenomena.

Being is like space in that it is beyond all the inner objects. From the vantage point of the mind, Being is nothing. It is a gap in the stuff of the mind or the space in which this stuff exists. It is not a thought. It is not an emotion. It is not a sensation. It is not an energy. It is none of the things of the mind. It has no properties because properties belong to the mind.

Because Being is beyond the mind stuff, we tend to name the experience of Being by referring to what it is not. Thus, when we notice Being, our mind will give it a name, thus creating an object in the mind that we can use to refer to the experience of Being in that moment. This is reification.

As is the case with physical space, the type of object we perceive Being as, depends on what mental objects we use as reference points, and we do not choose these reference points consciously, we simply use whatever mental objects happen to be around. So, the mental objects (thoughts or emotions) that we are aware of, either while or immediately before we notice Being, determine what we see Being as, in that we will feel Being as the absence of those mental and emotional objects.

For example, when we perceive Being as the absence of the pushes and pulls of our thoughts and emotions (one possible reference point), Being may appear to us as "solid" and "grounded". When we perceive Being as the absence of the restrictions and deadness of our thoughts and emotions (another possible reference point), it can appear as "vibrant" or "alive". When we perceive Being as the absence of the noisiness of our thoughts and emotions, it appears as "stillness" or "peace". When we contrast Being with the tumultuous nature of our thoughts and emotions, Being may be perceived as "calmness". When our burdensome worries and concerns serve as a reference point, Being may be experienced as "joy" or "carefreeness". When we perceive Being as the absence of the fragmentation of our thoughts and emotions, it appears as "wholeness".

In this way, Being can be perceived in infinitely many ways because there are infinitely many mental objects that can serve as reference points. This is what gives Being its elusive and chameleon-like nature.

In this book, I will, for convenience's sake, use a classification that organises the thousands of positive reifications of Being into 10 broad categories. See Figure 2: The 10 aspects of Being (Essences) for an overview.

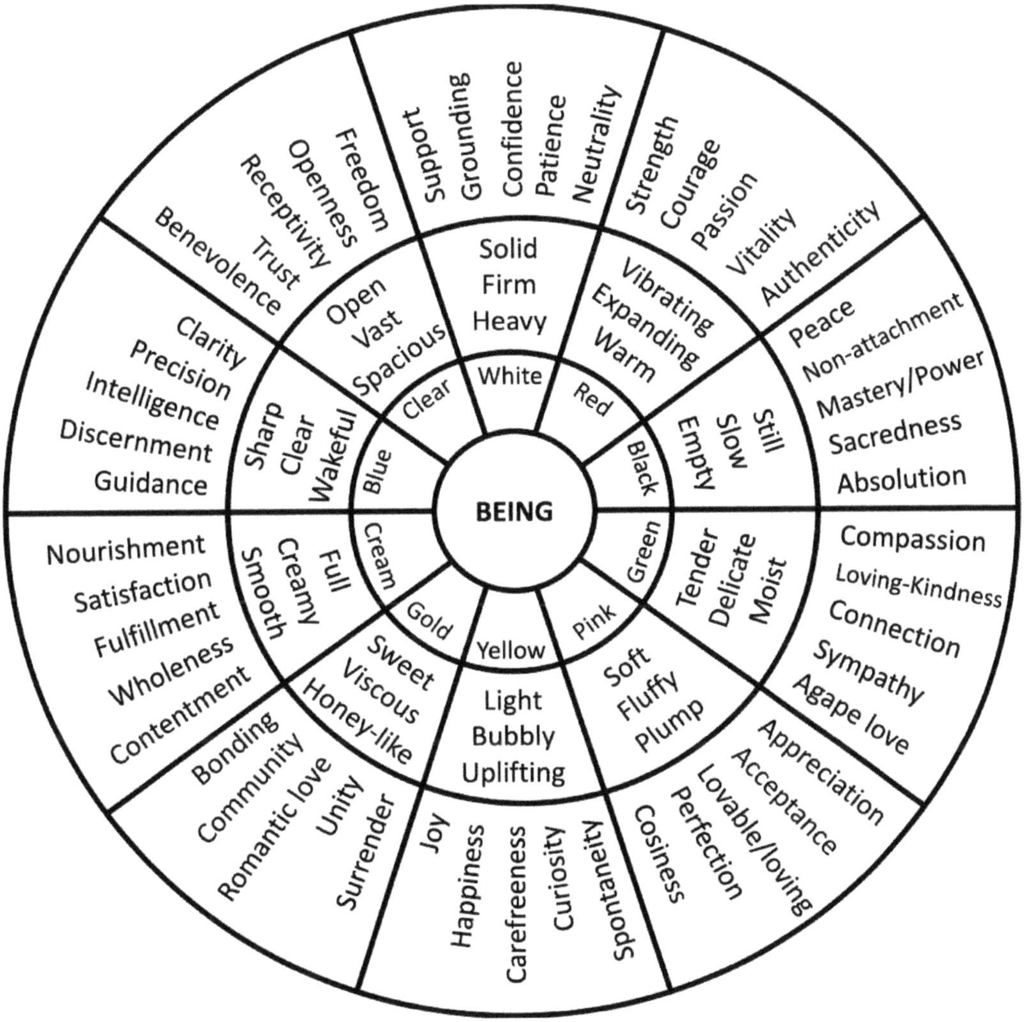

Figure 2: The 10 aspects of Being (Essences) and related positive reifications

In Figure 2, each slice of the pie represents one category of how Being can be perceived.

- The first circle contains the name/colour.
- The second circle contains the somatic reifications.
- The third circle contains the abstract reifications based on the somatic reifications.

If we, for example, look at the Red Essence, we can see that when our awareness is trapped in our thoughts and emotions, the flow of energy in our bodies are restricted by those thoughts and emotions. Therefore, when our attention shifts to Being, our energy starts flowing more freely. At a somatic level, this can feel like vibration, expansion and heat and these somatic states can, depending on the context, be interpreted as a range of positive abstract phenomena, such as "strength", "courage", "passion", "vitality" or "authenticity".

The clustering of concepts in Figure 2 should be considered as a typical way people reify Being. The connection between the somatic and more abstract reifications is not fixed. It is, for example, possible to find people who feel Being as "solidity" and interpret this solidity as "strength", while others would interpret such "solidity" as "grounding" and reserve the word "strength" for the felt sense of "free-flowing energy" mentioned above.

Nonetheless, Figure 2 illustrates the principle that becoming aware of Being gives rise to certain felt-sense experiences and that these are then interpreted as a range of positive concepts. It also illustrates how a vast range of abstract phenomena (The 50 mentioned in Figure 2 and beyond) are all different ways of experiencing Being.

I have organised the Essences in Figure 2 so that those placed opposite each other relate to reifications that can be perceived as opposite and mutually exclusive – both at the somatic and the abstract level. For example, "surrender" (Gold Essence) and "strength" (Red Essence) can be perceived as opposite and mutually exclusive abstract phenomena. Similarly, "full" (Cream Essence) and "empty" (Black Essence) can be perceived as opposite and mutually exclusive somatic phenomena. Understanding how such seemingly opposite and mutually exclusive phenomena are merely different ways of perceiving Being arising from interpreting Being in different contexts is key to resolving many internal conflicts. I will return to this in Chapter 6. The reason for calling the different aspects of Being "Essences" is precisely that this word emphasises that the essence of all the phenomena in the outermost circle is Being and that their differences derive from the context in which Being is experienced.

Table 1 illustrates how each of the 10 Essences can be understood as the experience of Being (that which is not mind) contrasted with particular properties of our thoughts and emotions (mind).

Table 1: Essences as the experience of Being contrasted with various properties of mind

Essence	Characteristics of mind
White	Because mind contains conflicting impulses and urges that push and pull us, what is not mind can feel stable and grounded.
Red	Because mind contains tensions that control and restrict our energy and impulses and because the objects of mind are dead in the sense that they are imprints of past experiences and, thus, have no life of their own, what is not mind can feel vibrantly alive.
Black	Because mind contains constant commentary on our immediate experience that is a form of inner noise and an intermediary layer between us and our experience, what is not mind can feel like peace and an increased intimacy with our experience.
Green	Because mind contains tensions that repress pain and hurt preventing healing, what is not mind can feel like tenderness, compassion and a healing inner touch.
Pink	Because mind contains judgements of aspects of oneself as unlovable or inappropriate, what is not mind can feel like appreciation and acceptance.
Yellow	Because mind contains burdensome worries and concerns, what is not mind can feel like joy, happiness and carefreeness.
Gold	Because mind contains borders around self and, consequently, a sense of separation, what is not mind can feel like bonding, unity and blissful surrender.
Cream	Because mind contains deprivation and dissatisfaction and because mental objects have no substance, what is not mind can feel like a nourishing inner fullness and satisfaction.
Blue	Because mind contains incoherence and amorphousness, what is not mind can feel like clarity and precision.
Clear	Because mind contains preferences and advocacy for particular perspectives that restrict the movement of our attention, what is not mind can feel like openness, receptivity and freedom.

A table with a fuller description of both felt sense and possible positive reifications for each aspect of Being can be found at www.the5knots.com/resources.

2.4. Absence vs. reduction of mental objects

Above, I have for the sake of clarity made a clear distinction between paying attention to mental objects and paying attention to Being.

However, we rarely, if ever, experience only mental objects or only Being.

Thus, in practice, the experience we reify is generally not the experience of pure Being, but rather the experience of a reduction in our occupation with mental objects.

To experience the solidity of Being, it is not necessary to experience a complete absence of any mental objects that push and pull our attention. Every time we experience a reduction in the mental objects that push and pull us, we can experience more Being and the change is experienced as an increase in stability.

For example, you may experience negative emotions towards your child and be concerned about whether this makes you a bad person. This concern is a mental object that pulls your attention. If during therapy, you learn to understand the source and intention behind the negative emotions and realise that having such emotions is normal and does not make you a bad person, the concern may cease. You may still have other mental objects that push and pull you but whenever a significant concern falls away, you will experience a reduction in the pushes and pulls of your mental objects. This makes it easier for you to become aware of Being and this change may appear as a sense of increased stability.

Thus, you do not need to experience the complete absence of mental objects to obtain a sense of Being. You only need to experience a lessening of your focus on the mental objects to gain a sense of their absence.

This is important, because it means that clients do not have to wait until the dissolution of all mental objects before they can experience Being. Instead, they can experience Being throughout the therapeutic work. It is the proposition of this book that such ongoing experiences of Being will not only greatly support the therapeutic process but will, in fact, be the main driver of the therapy.

In the next section, I will examine some of the main misconceptions related to the Knot of Positive Reification and the corrective principles that can be derived from these.

2.5. The Knot of Positive Reification and implications for therapy

The Knot of Positive Reification can be broken down into three interrelated misconceptions about the nature of the phenomena human beings seek in life. These misconceptions are all consequences of failing to understand the process of reification and believing that the positive phenomena we encounter in life have inherent existence.

Reification of experiences of Being as positive things creates the illusion that the things we seek in life, such as peace, joy, aliveness, connection, love, ease and freedom are essentially different things (1st misconception). Furthermore, it creates the illusion that we are separate from the things we seek (2nd misconception). Finally, reifying experiences of Being as positive things invites us to move our attention to ideas *about* these things instead of paying sustained attention to Being itself. In effect, reification makes us prioritise abstract ideas over direct concrete experience (3rd misconception).

To untie the Knot of Positive Reification, the therapist must shift each of these misconceptions by taking clients through lines of inquiry that will help them discover for themselves that all their desires are ultimately desires for Being (1st corrective principle); that because Being is inherent to all humans, clients are ultimately at one with what they seek (2nd corrective principle); and that when clients let their attention rest on Being, awareness of Being will, in turn, have profoundly positive effects on them that cannot they cannot get from grasping even the most insightful or subtle idea about Being (3rd corrective principle).

Correcting these three misconceptions is at the heart of the Being-Centred approach to therapy presented in this book. The root of many psychological issues is the lack of awareness of Being, even if they appear to be about other things. Thus, many psychological issues will dissolve when the client becomes aware of Being and, for this reason, helping clients to develop the capacity to pay sustained awareness of Being is a profound and powerful therapeutic intervention and the theme of the entire book.

2.5.1. Misconception 1: You seek many things

The first misconception related to the Knot of Positive Reification is that we seek many fundamentally different things in life, when, in fact, we only seek Being.

Because Being appears as many different phenomena, depending on which reference points we use in the process of reification, we develop the misconception that we are seeking many different things in life. We fail to see that all the things we seek are merely different appearances of that which transcends the realm of mental objects (i.e. thoughts and emotions), namely Being. In other words, we fail to see that the things we seek in life ultimately are one and the same.

The belief that we are seeking many different things pulls our awareness away from the Being by engaging us in speculations on which phenomena to pursue at the expense of other phenomena. This is particularly true if we perceive some of the phenomena we seek as mutually exclusive.

Thus, positive reification leads us to mistakenly believe that we seek many things in life and this, in turn, leads to the loss of awareness of Being which reinforces the process of positive reification.

Throughout the book, we shall see how this misconception grows with each knot we describe.

For example, in Chapter 3, Knot 2: The Knot of Conditionality, we shall see that the number of things we believe we seek is further multiplied when we start developing ideas about how to obtain the multitude of positive reifications of Being. If we desire “love” (a positive reification of Being), we also desire all the things we believe will bring us “love”, such as a loving partner, approval from others, physical attractiveness, social status, etc. Similarly, if we desire “peace” (another positive reification of Being), we inevitably start desiring anything we believe will bring “peace”, such as the elimination of conflicts, emotional control, a comfortable home, control over others, or massages and spa days. Thus, for each positive reification of Being we desire, not only the reification itself, but also all the things we believe will help us acquire or create this reification.

Similarly, in Chapter 4, Knot 3: The Knot of Negative Reification, we look at the negative reifications that are produced when comparing Being with mental objects we perceive as positive. Such negative reifications lead us to actively avoid Being and to desire anything we believe will help us in this endeavour.

However, in the rest of this present section, I will focus on the implications the misconception that we seek many things in life has for therapy. Furthermore, I will formulate a corrective principle that can guide therapists.

Implications for therapy

Understanding how the experience of Being can change radically depending on what arbitrary reference points the client uses in their reification process is crucial for therapists. It helps therapists learn to recognise the underlying unity of a seemingly diverse range of experiences, such as "love", "joy", "peace", "satisfaction", "confidence", "aliveness" and "wholeness". Recognising this underlying unity is particularly important to avoid becoming trapped in the client's (or the therapist's own) narratives about the mutual exclusivity of these phenomena.

For instance, a client may feel split between their desire for the aliveness they feel when they travel and the peace they feel at home. They want both, but they believe they cannot have both because they cannot travel and stay home at the same time.

If we (client as well as therapist) accept that "aliveness" and "peace" are two fundamentally different phenomena that can only be acquired by engaging in mutually exclusive actions, we may become trapped in reflections on how to strike a balance between the two or what we can do (instead of either travelling or staying at home) to satisfy both our desire for aliveness and for peace.

We can avoid this trap by realising that both "aliveness" and "peace" are aspects of the experience of Being, and that their perceived difference merely arises from the use of different reference points during the reification process. The reason the client feels "aliveness" when travelling and "peace" when at home is that they have different reference points available to them in these two situations.

When the client is at home in their familiar environment, they engage in automatic thinking and feeling, which is effective but also a bit lifeless. When the client is travelling, they are taken out of their automatic patterns because these do not provide good guidance in unfamiliar situations. Because the automatic thoughts and feelings feel lifeless, the absence of these appears to the client as "aliveness".

Similarly, the client may be prone to worry, but as long as they are at home in familiar environment, their patterns of worrying may be dormant. Because such patterns of worry contain a feeling of agitation, the absence of these patterns appears to the client as "peace".

From this perspective, both "aliveness" and "peace" are aspects of what the client experiences when their awareness is not occupied by mental and emotional patterns. The difference between "aliveness" and "peace" simply arises from which mental and emotional patterns the client experienced just before their awareness was unhooked from mental and emotional activity. In other words, both "aliveness" and "peace" are aspects of Being. Consequently, if the client's awareness is unhooked from both automatic thoughts and worries, they would feel "aliveness" and "peace" simultaneously.

Therefore, focusing therapy on achieving equilibrium between "aliveness" and "peace" is an erroneous strategy that can inadvertently reinforce the client's misconceptions about the nature of "aliveness" and "peace". This can result in inner conflict and turmoil, making it challenging for the client to allow their awareness to rest in the present moment.

Instead, therapy can focus on bringing awareness to the mental and emotional patterns that block the client's perception of the "aliveness" and "peace" of the present moment and, through this awareness, dispel the client's misconceptions about these phenomena – in particular, the misconceptions that "aliveness" and "peace" are different entities, that they are mutually exclusive and that they are created by certain external circumstances[16].

1st corrective principle: Ultimately, you seek Being

We are now ready to formulate the first corrective principle that can guide therapy.

> "Humans ultimately seek one thing, Being, which only appears as many different phenomena because it is interpreted in relation to many different reference points"

Thus, when a client feels they must choose between two positive states, it is because their ideas about these states are in conflict – not because the states themselves are mutually exclusive.

In other words, everything that is mutually exclusive between two desired states belongs to the *ideas* about these states; the states themselves can never be mutually exclusive since all positive states are reifications of one thing, Being.

---

[16] In Chapter 4, Knot 3: The Knot of Negative Reification, we will see that the range of experiences that arise when we use different reference points to reify our perception of Being also include negative experiences. These can be slightly more difficult to recognise as experiences of Being. However, having the ability to recognise these experiences as the product of a reification process using certain reference points can greatly enhance therapy. More on that in Chapter 4.

Links to other systems

This corrective principle can be found in many monistic spiritual traditions and in approaches to therapy inspired by the philosophy of monism.

Monism is a philosophical and metaphysical concept that posits the existence of a singular, unified reality or essence underlying all phenomena. It suggests that there is ultimately only one fundamental substance or principle from which everything in the universe emerges. Monistic traditions reject the notion of duality or multiplicity and emphasise the inherent unity and interconnectedness of all things.

Some famous examples of monistic traditions include:

- Advaita Vedanta is a Hindu philosophical tradition that emphasises the concept of non-duality. It posits that the ultimate reality, known as Brahman, is the fundamental indivisible essence from which all individual beings and objects arise.
- Taoism, an ancient Chinese philosophy and spiritual tradition, views the world as an expression of the Tao, which is the underlying and interconnected source of all things. Taoist philosophy emphasises the harmony and interconnectedness of the natural world, recognising the oneness and interdependence of all phenomena.
- Various mystical traditions across different religions, such as Sufism in Islam, Kabbalah in Judaism, and Christian mysticism, emphasise the unity of all existence.

All these traditions teach that there is a divine essence that permeates and encompasses everything in the world and that the goal of spiritual practice is to realise this essence and one's own unity with it.

It is possible to see the approach to therapy outlined in this book as a set of practical therapeutic tools to realise the goal of the monistic traditions.

Other therapeutic approaches that are inspired by the principle of the monistic spiritual traditions include:

- Mindfulness-Based Therapies, such as Mindfulness-Based Stress Reduction (MBSR) and Mindfulness-Based Cognitive Therapy (MBCT), draw on Buddhist and Zen principles and emphasise present-moment awareness, acceptance, and the interconnectedness of all phenomena as therapeutic tools.

- Transpersonal Psychology emphasises the unity of all existence and explores the therapeutic potential of developing awareness of transpersonal aspects of human experience and the interconnectedness between individuals, nature, and the cosmos.
- Holistic and integrative approaches to therapy emphasise the interconnectedness of mind, body, and spirit. Holistic and integrative approaches seek to facilitate the integration of various aspects of the self and the realisation of the individual as part of a larger whole.

These traditions remind us of the great therapeutic and transformative potential in recognising the fundamental unity of all things – not merely as idea but as lived experience.

2.5.2. Misconception 2: You are separate from what you seek

The second misconception related to the Knot of Positive Reification is that we are separate from that which we seek.

We seek Being and since Being permeates everything, we cannot be separate from it. However, when through positive reification, we depict Being as a desirable object, it is almost inevitable that we will start seeing ourselves as separate from what we seek.

If reification of Being leads you to believe that there exist concrete individual entities called "love", "joy", "grounding", "peace", etc. (the fallacy of misplaced concreteness), it is easy to start thinking of these "entities" as something that is separate from you, and as such, something that can be gained or lost, something that can be given to you or taken away from you, something you can have more or less of, etc.

In other words, by depicting Being as an entity, we can forget that Being is like space, all-pervasive and ever-present, and, as such, it can neither be lost nor gained.

To explain in more detail how the second misconception is developed and maintained, let's begin with an observation most people will recognise. The observation is that "love", "joy", "grounding", "peace", etc. seem to come and go.

Sometimes, you feel "love", and sometimes you do not. Sometimes, you feel "joy", and sometimes you do not. In certain situations you (more or less) consistently feel "peace" and in others not. There is nothing controversial in this. This is just a fact of life.

The second misconception is a misconception about *why* positive states seem to come and go. If you see words, such as "love", "joy", "grounding" and "peace", as referring to different entities which can be lost and gained, the explanation for why you sometimes feel them and sometimes do not is very straightforward. You feel "joy" when you have it, and when you do not feel "joy", it is because you have lost it.

This explanation implies that if you are not feeling "joy" and you wish to feel "joy", you will have to do something to get "joy". This line of reasoning will sound obvious and true to most readers. However, in the following, I will argue that it is, indeed, false.

If "love", "joy", "grounding", "peace", etc. are reifications of Being, then these words refer to something that is all-pervasive and ever-present – something that can neither be lost nor gained. If this is true, how come we sometimes feel these things and sometimes do not?

The answer to this question is that while Being is always present, we are not always aware of it. We feel "love", "joy", "grounding", "peace", etc. when we are aware of Being and we do not feel these things when we are not aware of Being. In other words, "joy" is part of the fundamental makeup of reality. We cannot lose it. But we *can* be unaware of it.

To understand this, consider your feet (or some body part that has been with you for your entire life). Before you read the previous sentence, you probably weren't aware of your feet. But now you are. Your feet can be out of your awareness and when that is the case, they are not part of your conscious experience. But that does not mean you have lost them. It simply means your attention is focused elsewhere – for example, on the words in this book.

In fact, most people will rarely pay attention to their feet. Unless there is something wrong with them or you are a dancer or have some other profession that requires you to pay frequent attention to your feet, they will probably not be part of your everyday experience.

The reason you do not fear that you have lost your feet every time you are unaware of them is that you can easily verify their existence whenever you wish. You can look at them, touch them, sense them, or pay attention to them in some other way. When you have verified the existence of your feet enough times, you develop the belief that they are always there – even when you are not aware of them.

Learning that your feet are always there, even when they are out of your awareness, happens at a very young age. There is a phase in early infancy, where babies become intensely fascinated by their own feet. This can be great fun to watch. Eventually, they lose interest and move on to other things. But the interest they take in their feet teaches them (among other things) that their feet are always around.

Learning that something is present even when you are not aware of it is what psychologists call developing object permanence. This happens at a very early age with the baby's own body parts. Later, babies develop object permanence in relation to external objects, such as toys. You can see that a baby has developed object permanence because they will start looking for toys you have hidden. This shows that even if the toy is not part of their current experience, the baby knows it wasn't erased from existence and that it is possible to find it if they look for it.

One way parents support their children in developing object permanence is through the popular game of Peek-A-Boo, where parents repeatedly hide and reveal their face (or body) to the delight of their baby. By seeing the parent disappear and reappear, the baby learns that the parents continue to exist even when they cannot see them.

Relating this developmental principle to Being, we can say that the reason Being can appear to us as if we can lose it and gain it despite it being ever-present is that we have not developed object permanence when it comes to Being.

We believe Being is gone when we are not aware of it. Just like the infant believes their feet are gone when they are not looking at them, or the toy is gone when it is hidden.

The reason we have not developed object permanence in relation to Being is that we have not gone through the phase of observing it disappear and reappear in our conscious experience until we understand that it is always there. In other words, we have not played enough Peek-A-Boo with Being to develop object permanence in relation to Being.

This is a radically different explanation for the fact that "love", "joy", "grounding", "peace", etc. seem to come and go. They are not entities that come and go. They are aspects of Being that we are sometimes aware of and sometimes not aware of. In other words, it is not "joy" that comes and goes, it is your awareness of "joy" that comes and goes. And because we have not developed object permanence in relation to Being, when we lose awareness of any aspect of Being, we think it is gone.

This explanation has very important implications for what to do when we do not feel "love", "joy", "grounding", "peace", etc. Rather than trying to get it, we should seek to become aware of it.

The reason we are not aware of it is, generally, that we spend our awareness on other things. Thus, to become aware of Being, it is a good idea to free up some of the awareness that is occupied by different tasks. We can do so through the practice of meditation. When we drop all the activities that occupy our awareness, we free up our awareness and then we may notice Being more easily.

From this perspective, trying to create the aspect of Being we believe we have lost is necessarily counterproductive. If the problem is that we are so busy with different projects that we have no awareness left to notice Being, then the last thing we should do is to add another project, such as trying to figure out what to do to acquire or create "love", "joy", "grounding", "peace", etc. If we do that, we make it less likely that we will notice Being.

This principle is sometimes summed up by saying that you do not notice Being because you are too busy looking for it.

One thing needs to be added to the argument. Some readers may think that there seem to be things one can do to produce "love", "joy", "grounding", "peace", etc. If, for example, every time you take a walk in the forest, you feel joy, it seems fair to say that walking in the forest produces joy. We all have many things that, more or less, consistently produce desirable states in us. If these states are truly aspects of something ever-present, why does it seem as if we can produce it through deliberate actions?

The reason is that we have mechanisms in our minds that keep our awareness busy in such a way that we rarely notice Being. Under certain circumstances, these mechanisms are paused, and when that happens, our awareness is freed up, and we may notice that which was there all along, namely, Being.

This is similar to the situation where you are absorbed in work, and when you finish work, you notice that you are very hungry. Presumably, the sensation of hunger has been there for a while, but it is only when you stop some activity that monopolised your attention that you notice it.

In the same way, when you take a walk in the forest, you stop certain inner processes that would otherwise occupy your awareness, and then you may notice Being and reify it as "joy", creating the illusion that the walk in the forest created this joy. The walk in the forest does not produce "joy" but it may reliably unhook your awareness from the patterns that prevent you from noticing it.

This shift of understanding has far-reaching implications for therapy.

Implications for therapy

Understanding that many of the "things" clients seek in life are aspects of Being is important in therapy because it means that the task of the therapist is not to help the client develop strategies for acquiring these things but rather to help them discover how they manage to stay unaware of these things, thus giving the client the option to cease distracting themselves from what they seek.

Let's look at an example, to see how this shift in understanding leads to radically different approaches to therapy.

You can imagine a client who tells you that they have problems with a lack of self-confidence.

If you operate from the assumption that the client is missing "confidence", you may try to help the client acquire or develop the missing confidence through different practices. These practices could include using positive affirmations, setting and accomplishing goals, doing things that are just beyond the client's comfort zone, making a list of past achievements the client is proud of, spending time acknowledging personal strengths and talents that the client may otherwise take for granted, etc.

Alternatively, if you operate from the assumption that "confidence" is an aspect of Being and, as such, the client is already inseparable from confidence, you may try to help the client in completely different ways. You can focus on helping the client discover what inner mechanisms take their awareness away from the confidence aspect of Being. You can pay attention to whether simply becoming aware of these mechanisms breaks the spell they hold over the client. And if this is not the case, you may help the client challenge the mechanisms and, in that way, disconnect from them[17].

---

[17] The practicalities of how to do this are described in the sections describing the five processes of Sensing Abundance, Sensing Completion, Sensing Taboos, Sensing Agency and Sensing Unity.

The more traditional practices used by therapists to *create* (rather than becoming aware of) confidence may still be useful, but you would use them for a different purpose. You would not use them to generate the missing confidence. Instead, you would use them to break the unconscious mechanisms that hold the client's awareness hostage.

For example, working with the client, you may discover that what takes their awareness is concerns about their competencies, which leads them to spend all their attention on learning new things, spotting mistakes in their work, and worrying about whether others think they are competent. If this is the case, you may select a practice that can help the client unhook their attention from this particular concern.

You can, for example, ask the client to describe what competencies they believe they need to feel confident and then ask them what they would feel if they had those competencies. Once they start describing the sense of confidence they believe would come with the competencies, you point out that they feel the confidence now – even if they have not developed any new competencies. In this way, you use the practice of developing competencies to teach the client to direct their awareness towards the aspect of Being they seek and in this way become aware of it. We will go much more in depth with this type of process in the next chapter as it is the core of the Sensing Completion process.

You may also pause the mechanisms that take the client's awareness away from Being in other ways by making these mechanisms strange. Often the mechanisms take our awareness because we never question the underlying assumptions of the mechanism. In the above example, you may ask the client why they need all that competency. This very question breaks the momentum of the client's mechanism because it questions the fundamental assumption that competency is something you can never get enough of. You may start exploring the downside of being competent, such as people starting to push tasks you don't want onto you because no one else can deal with them as well as you can.

Thus, the concrete interventions the therapist will use depends on whether the therapist believes the client is feeling a lack of something because they do not have it or because they are unaware of it.

Another important implication this shift in understanding proposed here has for therapy relates to when the client is expected to end therapeutic practices.

If the client engages in a practice because this practice generates what they seek, they will need to engage in this practice for ever. If your confidence is created by a particular practice, you must continue the practice for as long as you want confidence. This can be a problem if you want many things in life. Many people do indeed feel this issue. They have one practice to generate confidence, another to generate joy, another for love, and so on. But they only have a limited amount of time every day.

If, on the other hand, a practice is meant to dissolve the mechanisms that distract the client from noticing a particular aspect of Being, this practice is only necessary as long as the distracting mechanisms persist. If the mechanisms dissolve, there is no longer any need for the practice. If the function of a practice is to dissolve that which prevents a client to notice that they are already one with what they seek, the need for the practice ceases once the client reaches this realisation.

In summary, the perspective that what we seek is ever-present, but that we have difficulties in noticing it, shows that an important element of therapy is to practice recognition of Being. From this perspective, therapy becomes a place for developing object permanence in relation to Being.

Whereas the above argument may help open the client up to the possibility, an argument is rarely enough to shift such a fundamental aspect of how we perceive the world. What is needed is the experiential component of having frequent and clear experiences of Being across many different contexts in life. Such frequent and clear perceptions of Being will begin to challenge the misconception that we are separate from what we seek. If you can feel something whenever you turn your attention to it, regardless of the present context, you must be at one with it.

Thus, to dispel the second misconception related to the Knot of Positive Reification, therapists should aim to help clients develop the capacity to perceive Being directly, as opposed to only perceiving Being in certain circumstances. This game of spiritual Peak-A-Boo will, over time, correct the misconception that the client is separate from what they seek.

The process of Sensing Abundance described in Chapter 2.6 aims to do exactly that.

2nd corrective principle: You are already at one with what you seek

The above shift of perspective can be summed up in the second corrective principle that can guide therapy:

> "You are already at one with what you seek"

It only appears to you that you are missing something because you have lost awareness of Being and do not know how to become aware of Being again.

Links to other systems

This principle finds a forceful expression in the branch of Tibetan Buddhism known as Dzogchen. The central thesis of Dzogchen is the belief in the "innate perfection" and "intrinsic purity" of all beings and the possibility of recognising and abiding in this perfect state through direct experience, beyond conceptual understanding.

The Dzogchen teachings focus on the concept of "rigpa", the inherent nature of the mind, which is clear, open, and free from dualistic distinctions such as good and evil. Dzogchen teaches that this nature is present in all beings but is obscured by "karmic winds", or habitual patterns of thinking and behaving.

The goal of Dzogchen practice is to recognise and abide in the nature of the mind, the state of rigpa, without being distracted by thoughts or external stimuli. This recognition is not achieved by striving or effort but by relaxing and allowing the mind to settle into its natural state.

This state is sometimes described as "naked awareness", "non-conceptual wisdom", or "primordial purity". It's a direct, unmediated experience that transcends the ordinary mind and its conceptual frameworks.

What therapists can learn from the Dzogchen view is that there is a significant therapeutic potential in recognising any mental and emotional activity – including any self-development projects – as a form of distraction or agitation which, when relaxed, opens opportunities for the direct perception of Being as one's ultimate nature.

2.5.3. Misconception 3: Ideas are more important than direct experience

The third misconception related to the Knot of Positive Reification is that our ideas about Being are more important than our direct experience of Being.

People who are dedicated to spiritual practices may not consciously subscribe to this view. However, if we look at how people use their awareness in practice, it is evident that many of those who wouldn't subscribe to the above belief are, nonetheless, guided by it.

We will, for example, give a lot of attention to ideas about "joy", how to get it, what it is, what takes it away from us, and whether "joy" is more or less important than "kindness" or "hard work" or something else, etc. But we will give very little attention to the concrete experience of "joy", what it feels like, how it affects us, etc.

In fact, paying sustained attention to something like the experience of "joy" can seem pointless to some people. If you feel joy, all is well, and there is nothing for you to do. It is only when you are not feeling joy that you start paying attention to it, and your attention will be directed towards determining what has gone wrong and how to correct it – not towards the details of the direct experience of joy.

A part of this dynamic is what psychologists call "negativity bias" – the tendency to pay more attention to things that are problematic than to things that are not. The problem with negativity bias is that it skews our attention towards problems to such a degree that the positive things in life can become invisible to us.

However, negativity bias is only part of the story. The other part of the story is that once we place a label on something, we tend to begin paying attention to ideas about that on which we have placed a label. Once we have identified what something is, we tend to move our attention to questions of what we can do with that thing.

Using a single word to refer to a part of our experience is, as previously mentioned, beneficial as a shortcut in communication. It is much simpler to say: "can you bring me *the chair*" than to say: "can you bring me the dark brown wooden object with four legs standing next to the table". Naming things (as opposed to describing them) enables us to refer to them quickly and focus on the main point we wish to communicate. In the example above, the description of the chair is not important for the message. The speaker intends to express a desire for the chair to be brought to them. That is the essential aspect of the message.

However, this also means that naming things serves as a tool for shifting our attention away from the thing *itself* and towards some idea we wish to convey *about* the thing.

This property of language sheds light on how positive reification can lead to a loss of awareness of Being. Positive reification gives a name to Being, and in doing so, it compels us to move our attention from the *experience* of Being towards ideas *about* Being. The moment we assign a name to our experience of Being, this very act diverts our attention away from that experience itself and towards ideas about the experience. We might, for example, divert our attention to our appreciation of the experience, how this experience relates to other experiences, our desire to hold on to it, our worry about losing it, our beliefs about what caused it, and so on. Regardless of the nature of these ideas, they have one thing in common – they take our attention away from the experience itself.

In other words, our awareness tends to flow from immediate experiences to concepts that bundle and organise these experiences, to ideas about these concepts and how they relate. This process is illustrated in Figure 3. The first picture represents a rich, immediate experience. The second picture represents the process of using concepts to bundle parts of the immediate experience. For example, seeing a lot of sense impressions, such as a particular colour and material, a particular shape, and a particular position in relation to other shapes, as part of a single whole which we call a "chair". The third picture represents the process where the richness of the immediate experience has receded into the background, and we have moved our attention to examining the relationships between our concepts. The result is a model of the world that helps us navigate the world. Because such models are useful, once they are established, we tend to favour paying attention to these at the expense of our immediate sensory experience. We gain the ability to navigate the world but lose awareness of our immediate experience – including our experience of Being.

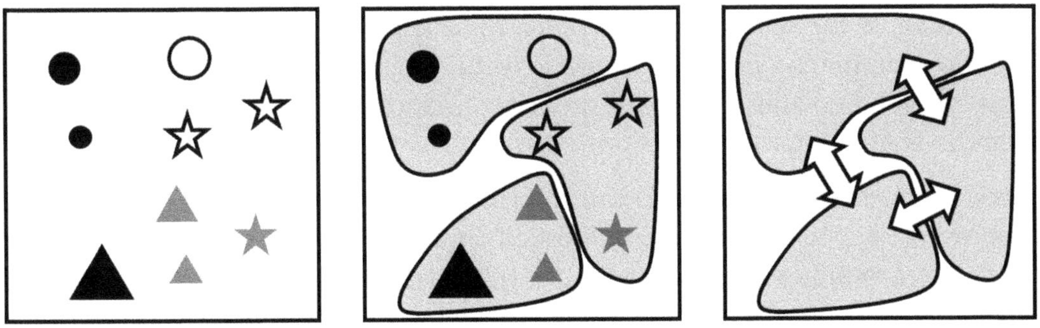

Figure 3: Loss of awareness of immediate experience through conceptualisation

The loss of awareness that results from prioritising ideas about our experience over the details of the experience itself can be observed in the common phenomenon that people may be aware of *the names* of their feelings – but are often not aware of the somatic states underpinning these feelings.

It is fascinating to observe how we, as human beings, can confidently pronounce that we feel "love", "joy", "peace", "satisfaction", "confidence", "aliveness", "wholeness", and many other inner states, yet struggle to describe the concrete felt-sense experience to which we ascribe these names.

You may, for example, ask a client what they feel, and the client may answer that they feel "peace". Let's, for argument's sake, assume that the client's statement is correct. The client feels peace, and they are aware that they feel peace.

However, if you ask the client what that state of peace feels like, they may not know. They may struggle to answer the question. Sometimes, clients will say that the peace feels "peaceful". But this is a non-answer. All they do is provide another form of the name for their inner state (the adjective corresponding to the noun).

Logically, there must be some sort of somatic state that the client recognises as a state of peace. And it should be possible to describe this in more detail. Individuals who have practised describing their inner states may describe the somatic state of peace by saying that it feels like "a light and spacious feeling in my head" or like "a soft and calm feeling in my belly".

As can be seen from the above descriptions, it does not take advanced vocabulary to describe the somatic states underpinning the names for states. Thus, it is not a lack of vocabulary that prevents people from describing the states but rather a lack of awareness.

This lack of awareness of the experience is a consequence of the continuous substitution of the felt-sense experience for a label for this experience. If every time you experience a particular somatic state, you say I'm feeling "X", this process of recognition becomes automatic and unconscious and leads you to stop paying attention to the details of the experience you have named.

To understand this process, you can think of a squirrel. You may be very good at recognising squirrels. But if you are asked to draw a squirrel, you may be hard-pressed to produce any degree of realistic details. Knowing enough to recognise the animal does not mean that you know much about what it looks like. I have a lot of squirrels in my garden and to recognise one, I just need to see something red and fluffy moving in a wavy fashion up a tree or across the lawn. But I have no idea what the shape of a squirrel's paws is or whether they have whiskers or not.

Like with the squirrel, once we recognise an inner state as fitting a particular category, we turn our attention towards ideas about this inner state, such as:

- What does it mean that we are feeling this state?
- Is it good or bad that we are feeling this state?
- How can we hold on to it if it is good?
- How can we change it if it is bad?

While our attention is occupied with such speculations, the experience itself slips out of our awareness. And, consequently, so does our possibility of becoming aware of Being as the essence of the inner state.

This is why giving names to Being, even if these are positive (positive reification), can lead to a loss of awareness of Being.

That we (in practice) tend to give more attention to our ideas about things than to the experience of these things has important consequences for therapy.

Implications for therapy

It is well known that human beings react to their model of the world rather than to the world itself. The reason we are offended by certain statements is that in our model of the world, these statements are offensive. Other people with different models of the world might find the same statements funny, enlightening or inconsequential. To quote The Bard: "There is nothing either good or bad but thinking makes it so".

A lot of traditional therapy, focuses on helping clients become aware of, evaluate and upgrade their models of the world. In doing so, the clients can develop models of the world which provide better guidance in life and thus helps them achieve their goals. This kind of therapy is illustrated in Figure 4. The first row shows one model of the world applied to a particular experience. The experience is organised into certain concepts, and these can be related in certain ways. The second row shows how a different model of the world might organise the same experience in a different way using different concept and, consequently, allowing the client to see different kinds of relationships. If therapy leads a client to change from the first to the second model, and this helps them thrive in life, that therapy has been successful.

Figure 4: Two different models of the world

However, as is evident from the illustrations above, any model of the world, regardless of how useful it is, takes awareness away from the immediate experience, and thus away from the experience of Being.

Therefore, another approach to therapy is to help the client move their awareness from *any* model of the world and towards their immediate experience. This can be understood as a form of relaxation or loss of interest in making sense of the world and instead simply experiencing it in its suchness.

A very effective way of doing so is to invite clients to describe their experience at the most concrete level available in language, namely, the level of felt sense. In practical terms, this means inviting clients to describe their experience using nothing but neutral sensory words, such as warm, cold, fast, slow, expanding, contracting, moving up, down, forward, backward, smooth, sharp, etc.

When clients direct their attention towards their felt sense, they are automatically directing their attention away from their models of the world, and they may, in this way, regain awareness of the fullness of their immediate experience. The process corresponds to reversing the normal movement from left to right in Figure 4 above and instead moving from right to left.

To illustrate the two approaches to therapy mentioned above, consider a client that comes to a session because they suffer from social anxiety at social gatherings. In particular, the client fears that other people think they are boring. At social gatherings, the client wants to say something interesting or entertaining. However, their fear that others will judge them as boring and reject them causes them to critically evaluate everything they might say and find it insufficiently interesting or entertaining. Thus, they stay silent. This silence compounds the issue since the longer the client stays silent, the more uninteresting and boring they feel and the more pressure they feel to say something brilliant to break the judgement they feel building up in the silence. The client may, furthermore, believe that the longer they stay silent, the more people will pay attention should they eventually decide to say something. In the end, the challenge of saying something interesting or entertaining may become insurmountable and the client ends up saying nothing for the entire duration of the social gathering while suffering from ever-increasing anxiety.

If we approach this issue in therapy in a traditional way, we may invite the client to examine the way they make sense of the world and challenge some of the taken-for-granted assumptions their model of the world is based on. This can lead the client to shift to a different model of the world that will enable them to enjoy social gatherings without anxiety. One could, for example, question the idea that other people pay close attention to what anyone is saying – usually, they do not. One could also turn the evaluation of who is boring on its head by saying that if you say something to someone at a party and they repeatedly refrain from engaging with you, that person is boring, and that it may be worth the client's while to talk to another person who is more up for social engagement. Such lines of inquiry can make the client question their taken-for-granted assumptions and create a new model of the world which offers better guidance. This would be a traditional form of therapy, and it can be very helpful when it comes to learning more effective ways to engage with the world.

However, changing your model of the world may not, in itself, help you become aware of Being[18]. Thus, the sense of dissatisfaction and separateness that plagues

---

[18] Of course, all the misconceptions discussed in this book are invitations to change one's model of the world. However, they are of a second order in that they are models of how models of the world work. This places the approach to therapy described in this book in the category that is sometimes called meta-cognitive therapy.

many people will not be touched by therapy that focuses on upgrading the client's model of the world.

It is, of course, possible that the client will become aware of Being if the new model of the world takes up less of their awareness. In the example above, by changing the model of the world, the client's awareness can be liberated from the concerns that consume them at social gatherings – and with their awareness freed up, they may spontaneously become aware of Being.

However, in traditional therapy, upgrading the client's model of the world is the primary concern and becoming aware of Being would be a fortunate by-product.

In Being-Centred Therapy, we change this priority around so that perceiving Being becomes the primary objective and upgrading the client's model of the world becomes a fortunate by-product.

This shift of priorities can lead to a different approach to therapy. In the above example, the therapist may, for example, encourage the client to examine what it is they are trying to attain by saying something interesting or entertaining. This can be done by asking the client to imagine that they, at a social gathering, effortlessly say things others find both interesting and entertaining, and then notice what is attractive about this scenario.

When the client imagines that others find everything they say interesting and entertaining and that being interesting and entertaining requires little or no effort on their part, the client may experience a visceral shift in their body and mind. They will *feel* what it is they are trying to achieve by being interesting and entertaining. Once this happens, the therapist can encourage the client to examine that experience. Since the experience is that of no longer having any concerns that occupy the client's awareness, it will be the experience of relaxing enough to become aware of Being.

Once the client experiences Being, their model of the world will automatically change, and the new model will be a better guide in life. This will happen because the new model of the world will no longer be built on the misconception that the client is separate from what they seek, and thus, it will be more in line with reality. And a model that is more in line with reality is a better guide.

Thus, this approach to therapy places primary importance on helping the client become aware of Being and relies on this as a means to change the client's model of the world to a new one that will better guide the client in life.

In other words, the implication for therapy is that rather than spending time on helping the client develop a new and better model of the world, the therapist can focus on helping the client become aware of Being – and let that experience do the work of upgrading the client's model of the world.

This approach has two significant advantages.

First, tuning in to Being and letting Being work on the client is less work for the therapist.

Second, tuning in to Being and letting new models of the world emerge from that experience mitigates the risk of the therapist pushing their own (possibly unhelpful) model of the world onto the client. No therapist can be certain that their own model of the world is superior to whatever would emerge in the client once they become aware of Being. Many times, I have observed understandings emerge in clients while they were aware of Being, which has taught me important lessons about how to engage with the world.

That being said, there are many situations where the traditional approach to therapy is useful. The important thing is to make sure it does not override the concern for cultivating awareness of Being.

3rd corrective principle: Pay attention to Being and let Being do the work

The third corrective principle that can guide therapy can be summed up as:

> "Awareness of Being is, in itself, therapeutic"

In other words, paying sustained attention to the experience of Being is more important than paying attention to the ideas we have about Being because simply letting awareness rest in Being can have profoundly positive effects on the individual. Thus, it is the role of the therapist to give space and time for the awareness of Being to emerge and work on the client.

In practice, this means that throughout the therapy session, the therapist must be on the lookout for opportunities to direct the client's awareness towards Being, and whenever the client becomes aware of Being, it is the job of the therapist to encourage the client to give time to this experience.

When a client becomes aware of Being and gives this experience time and space, the experience of Being becomes an important reference point for the development of the client's worldview. This will direct the development in such a way that many of the client's current issues dissolve because they are rooted in having a model of the world that does not recognise the existence of Being.

Clients will often mention the experience of Being in passing. Here the therapist will do well to pause the client and ask about the experience in more detail as a means to get the client to pay prolonged attention to the experience and develop their awareness of the experience.

In fact, the eagerness with which a client pursues an issue can be the root cause of this very issue. The pursuit of the issue can be the very thing that draws the client's awareness away from Being and the resulting sense of having lost something important can be the root of that issue.

Therefore, pausing the client in their pursuit and encouraging them to spend time noticing the particular aspect of Being that is present within their narrative can correct the client's perspective in such a way that they come to a resolution for the issue with minimum effort.

One way of expressing the first corrective principle is to say: "As long as you pay attention to Being, Being can heal you". Another way of saying this is: "When you pay attention to Being, this activates the self-healing property of your system". Yet another way is to say that: "Your responsibility is to pay attention to Being; everything else is the responsibility of Being". A fourth way of saying it is: "Let Being do you".

In the above statements, it should be understood that the word "heal" does not refer to changing anything about the client but rather to realising that nothing was wrong with the client in the first place. The healing is not related to the substance of the client – but rather to their false perception of being flawed.

Links to other systems

This principle is expressed to some extent in the branch of psychology known as Positive Psychology. The main thesis of positive psychology is that traditional psychology has primarily focused on diagnosing and treating mental illness, but it has largely ignored the positive aspects of mental health.

Positive psychology, therefore, seeks to focus on the positive aspects of life, including joy, happiness, and life satisfaction. It emphasises the development of human strengths such as resilience, courage, curiosity, integrity, self-knowledge, moderation, self-control, and wisdom. It also stresses the importance of positive relationships and positive institutions.

The field was popularised by Martin Seligman, who argues that psychology should not just be about moving people from a -5 to 0 (removing negatives), but from 0 to +5 (enhancing positives). This perspective shifts focus from pathology, victimology, and mental illness to positive emotion, virtue and strength, and positive institutions.

Whereas the motivation of positive psychology is (generally) not to increase awareness of Being, in effect the focus on positive emotions and well-being can greatly assist in overcoming the biases that prevent clients from noticing Being.

Another place where the third corrective principle is apparent is in the Dzogchen practice of pointing out the nature of mind.

"Pointing out the nature of mind" or "Pointing out instruction" is a key practice in some schools of Tibetan Buddhism and the philosophy of Dzogchen. This practice is a direct introduction to the nature of mind and reality as it is, generally done by an experienced teacher. The aim is to reveal the fundamental, clear and undistorted state of mind and awareness, often referred to as Rigpa, Buddha-nature, or simply "Being".

The teacher guides the student to recognise this natural state, which is free from conceptual elaborations, dualistic perceptions, and emotional disturbances. It's called "pointing out" because the teacher is essentially pointing directly to the nature of mind that is always present but usually overlooked due to habitual patterns of thought and perception.

This is not an intellectual understanding but rather a direct experiential recognition. Once recognised, the student then practises remaining in this state and integrating this realisation into all aspects of life, which can ultimately lead to the attainment of enlightenment.

The efficacy of pointing out instruction heavily depends on the student's readiness and capacity, the depth of the student's trust and devotion to the teacher, and the teacher's ability to effectively provide the instruction. It is considered an advanced practice and is typically given after the student has received preliminary teachings and has undertaken certain preliminary practices[19].

One of the principles often included in pointing out instructions is to rest in natural awareness. Once the student recognises the nature of their mind, the teacher often encourages them to rest in this natural state of awareness, without trying

---

[19] Concrete pointing out instructions vary depending on teacher, student and their relationship, and are primarily shared in oral traditions. However, the processes for untying the 5 Knots presented in this book can be understood as possible pointing out instructions.

to alter, modify or engage with the contents of the mind. This encouragement is beautifully expressed in the famous quote by Nyoshul Khenpo Jamyang Dorje:

"Rest in natural great peace
This exhausted mind
Beaten helplessly by karma and neurotic thought
Like the relentless fury of pounding waves
In the infinite ocean of samsara."

This encouragement corresponds to the third corrective principle described in this book of letting one's awareness rest in Being.

2.5.4. Summary

In the above, we have seen that the Knot of Positive Reification relates to three interconnected misconceptions. We have also seen how awareness of these misconceptions and their corresponding corrective principles can inform therapeutic interventions.

Table 2 summarises the misconceptions and corresponding corrective principles related to the Knot of Positive Reification.

Table 2: Misconceptions and corrective principles related to the Knot of Positive Reification

Misconceptions	Corrective Therapeutic Principles
You seek many things	You seek one thing, Being, which appears as different things when experienced in different contexts.
You are separate from what you seek	You are already one with what you seek.
Ideas are more important than direct experience	Awareness of Being is, in itself, therapeutic.

Table 3 summarises the differences between the questions that guide traditional and Being-Centred Therapy.

Table 3: How understanding the Knot of Positive Reification changes the questions guiding therapy

Traditional therapy questions	Being-Centred Therapy questions
How can clients find a balance between two desirable but mutually exclusive phenomena?	What are the ideas clients have about the two phenomena that makes them appear as mutually exclusive rather than as two aspects of Being?
What strategies can the client adopt to acquire the states they seek?	What mechanisms prevent the client from noticing that what they seek is already present? How can the client learn to become aware of what they seek and, over time, develop object permanence?
How can the client upgrade the model they use to make sense of the world in such a way that it offers better guidance in life?	How can the client learn to move awareness from their model of the world to Being? How does awareness of Being upgrade the client's model of the world?

So far, we have looked at the Knot of Positive Reification, three misconceptions related to this knot and three corresponding corrective principles that can guide therapy.

In the following section, I will describe in detail a therapeutic process aimed at untying the Knot of Positive Reification. This process is called Sensing Abundance because it aims at using the client's positive reifications of Being as a means to become aware of Being and recognise it as something that is abundant in the sense that it is always already present.

This perspective may be conceptually clear from reading the above (or similar texts). However, it is possible to understand the ever-present nature of Being conceptually, without this conceptual understanding changing anything about how we perceive Being, the world and ourselves. To engender such change, we need to go beyond conceptual understanding to direct experience, and let this experience update the beliefs that govern our behaviour. This is the goal of the process of Sensing Abundance.

2.6. Sensing Abundance – how to untie the Knot of Positive Reification

The Knot of Positive Reification consists of a system of interrelated misconceptions about the nature of Being, which encourages the individual to turn their awareness away from the felt sense of Being towards ideas about Being, leading to a loss of awareness of Being.

While under the influence of these misconceptions, the individual will not notice that the loss of awareness of Being is produced by the misconceptions. Instead, they will see the loss of awareness of Being as evidence in *support* of the misconceptions, thus giving rise to a stable system of ignorance.

The knot of Positive Reification is, in a sense, the easiest knot to untie as the client's attention is turned towards representations of Being, and the client is positively disposed towards these.

The knot merely consists of having replaced the felt-sense experience of Being with an abstraction in the form of a single word or phrase and, in the process, having lost awareness of the full richness of the concrete felt-sense experience the abstraction refers to.

The Knot of Positive Reification can, therefore, be untied through the four-step process of Sensing Abundance.

1. **Recognise the Knot of Positive Reification (positive entry points):**
   The first step is to notice the Knot of Positive Reification. This is done by noticing whenever the client uses abstract concepts to mention positive experiences they otherwise do not pay much attention to.
2. **Point to Being:**
   The second step is to use these abstract concepts as a means for moving the client's awareness to the concrete, felt-sense experiences the abstractions refer to.
3. **Sustain awareness of Being:**
   The third step is to use continuous description to help the client sustain awareness of this felt sense for as long as possible.
4. **Correct misconceptions related to the Knot of Positive Reification:**
   The fourth and final step is to use the experience of the previous steps as a means to correct the three misconceptions related to the Knot of Positive Reification.

Figure 5 provides an overview of the process. In the remainder of this chapter, I will describe how to guide the process of Sensing Abundance both in one-to-one sessions and in groups through a series of contemplation exercises.

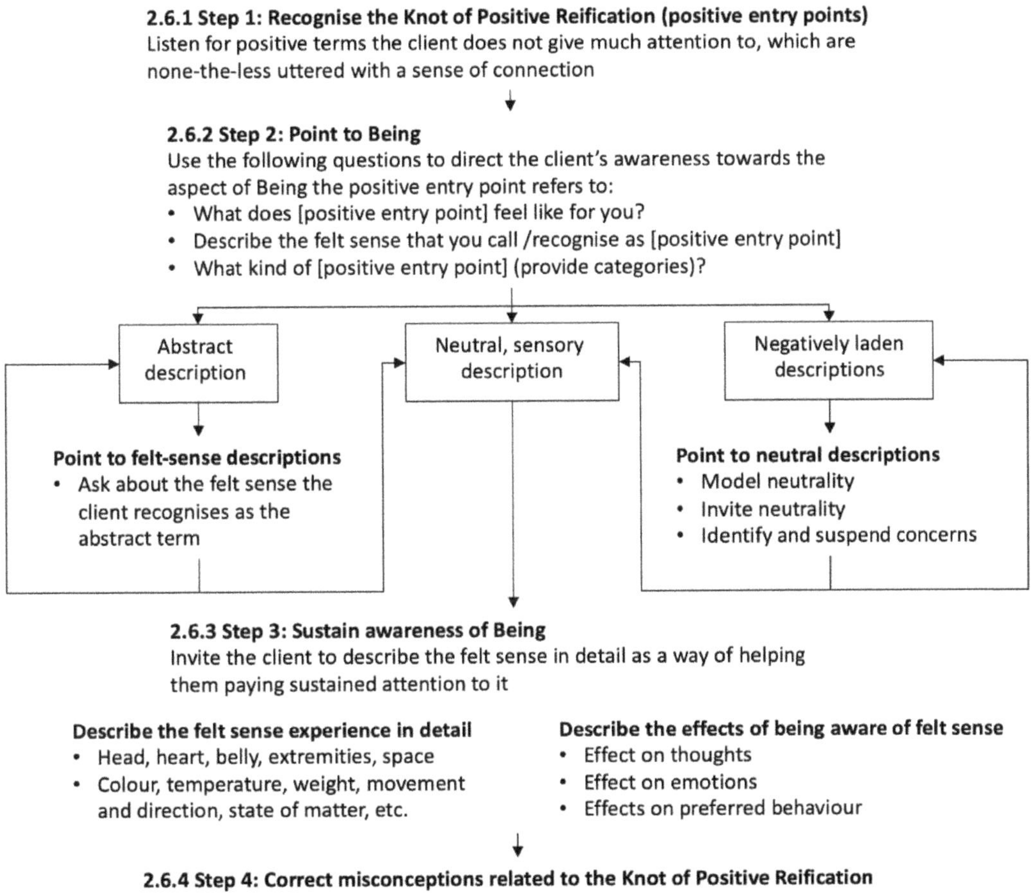

Figure 5: The Sensing Abundance process

2.6.1. Step 1: Recognise the Knot of Positive Reification - positive entry points

The first step in untying the Knot of Positive Reification is to detect it. You can do so by listening for words or phrases that refer to Being, which the client gives little attention to. I call such words or phrases "positive entry points".

The Knot of Positive Reification occurs when the client focuses their attention on an issue, neglecting Being, unaware that the issue they wish to address stems from the act of neglecting Being. That a client prioritises giving attention to an issue at the expense of attention to Being can be discerned in that they present elaborate descriptions of the issue while only referring to Being in a single word or phrase.

Therefore, therapists can detect the Knot of Positive Reification by listening closely for positively charged words or phrases related to experiences of Being, to which the client gives little attention in their eagerness to address a particular issue. Such words or phrases are "positive entry points" in that the therapist can invite the client to notice Being by asking them to focus their attention on these words or phrases.

Thus, to notice positive entry points, the therapist must, of course, *notice* when the client mentions positive experiences, such as experiences of feeling "loved", "loving", "peaceful", "relieved", "joyous", "open", "excited", "alive", "whole", "connected" or simply feeling "good".

However, not all words or phrases referring to positive states are positive entry points. That the client merely names a positive experience doesn't necessarily indicate a positive entry point. You know that a word or phrase is a positive entry point if the client "transmits" an aspect of Being when they utter the word or phrase. The client's expression must convey a visceral sense of the experience the expression refers to. When you encounter a positive entry point, you will experience that the client's words have power and that there is congruency between what is verbally expressed and the accompanying feeling. When a word or a phrase is a positive entry point, you can feel your own system responding or resonating with the client's words as if they were contagious. If the client speaks of "peace" while feeling tense, that is not a positive entry point. If, on the other hand, the client says the word "peace" and there is a bit of hush in the air, that is a positive entry point.

To understand this, you can think of a situation where a friend is talking about something they feel good about, and their emotions radiate through their words. As you listen to your friend, you start experiencing their positive inner states. If they are enthusiastic, you feel enthusiasm, even if the topic itself normally wouldn't excite you. If they express joy, you feel joyful, despite what your friend is talking about having no direct positive effect on you. If they are relieved, you sense relief, even if the issue they've resolved never concerned you.

Unlike the friend example, clients will generally not give much attention to their positive entry points. In fact, positive entry points are easily missed due to biases of both clients and therapists, which favour problems and problem-solving. Positive entry points refer to positive experience, and people typically do not seek therapy because they have positive experiences, nor do they focus on positive experiences when they do come to therapy. Thus, positive entry points will generally not play a prominent part in clients' stories. This makes them easy to miss. They are like brief flashes of light, perceptible only to the attentive therapist.

Familiarity with the different aspects of the experience of Being greatly enhances a therapist's ability to recognise positive entry points amid clients' narratives. For this reason, in the Sensing Mind Institute's educational programme, we give a lot of attention to familiarising students with different aspects of Being. This allows students to more easily recognise when words and phrases are connected to these aspects of Being – even when they are mentioned in passing.

The Knot of Positive Reification is untied by encouraging the client to give more attention to the experience of Being they down prioritise in favour of the issue they wish to discuss. Clients will often be surprised when you ask them to focus their attention on what they see as an unimportant side note in their narrative and, in doing so, neglect what they see as the main substance of the narrative. However, the effect of this shift of attention can be profound.

A client may, for example, tell you that they are having trouble with their meditation practice because while they feel a lot of tranquillity and peace in their chest, their head keeps feeling very tense, and they do not know how to release this tension in their head. It is clear that the client's focus is on the issue of tension in the head and that they are asking for your help or advice on how to release that tension. That is where their interest is. But in passing, they mention feeling a lot of tranquillity and peace in their chest. This is remarkable. But the client gives it little attention. In this case, you can say:

> "Before we look at the tension in the head, I'd like to hear a bit more about what you are feeling in the chest."

With these two sentences, you are doing two things.

The first sentence indicates that you intend to deal with the issue they want to deal with. As you will see, you may have no such intention, but by pretending that you do, you will put the client at ease and (hopefully) make it easier for them to follow what they are likely to perceive as a peculiar request.

The second sentence invites the client to refocus their attention from the issue to the positive entry point, namely, the sense of tranquillity and peace in the chest. As the client elaborates on this state, it is likely to start affecting them and calming them down, and importantly spread throughout their body – including the head.

After describing the state in detail, the tension in the client's head may be all but gone because the cause of the tension in the head was, fundamentally, a dissatisfaction with the limited experience of tranquillity and peace and the reason this experience was limited was that the client turned their attention away from it and towards the tension in the head. Thus, this was a classic case of not finding what you seek because you are too busy looking for it.

The reason the therapist may expect that they would not have to deal directly with the issue of the tension in the head is that they knew this tension was likely caused by the client turning attention away from the tranquillity and peace in the chest. However, it was necessary to pretend to intend to deal with the issue later to persuade the client to give their attention whole-heartedly to the positive state in their chest. It is, of course, also possible that the tension in the head has other causes and that it would, in fact, be necessary to return to it later.

In the above example, untying of the Knot of Positive Reification was very easy. The therapist simply asked the client to describe the experience of Being the positive entry point referred to.

In principle, this is how the Knot of Positive Reification is always untied. However, certain mental, emotional or behavioural patterns can distract clients from shifting their attention to Being.

In the following section, I will outline a detailed map of how to untie the Knot of Positive Reification. The map contains an overview of distractions clients might encounter when asked to shift their attention to the experience of Being indicated by a specific positive entry point. The map also contains strategies therapists can use to assist clients in maintaining their focus on Being, despite these distractions.

2.6.2. Step 2: Point to Being

The main tool for moving clients' awareness from an abstraction to the felt sense this abstraction refers to is to ask them to create rich and detailed descriptions of the felt sense using *neutral, sensory words*.

For example, during a session, a client may mention that in a particular situation, they felt love and then rush on to elaborate on their fear of losing this love. In this situation, it can be tempting for a therapist to take the same focus as the client and work with the fear of losing love. Depending on which therapeutic tradition you follow, you may engage the client in exploring the origin of the fear in their childhood family environment, exploring how their sense-making process creates the fear, challenging how realistic the fear is, exploring what can be done to mitigate any risks, using breathwork to relieve the fear, etc.

However, one important source of the client's fears of losing the love has to do with the knot of positive reification. They fear losing love because they experience this loss every time they, in their speech and thought, replace the rich, felt sense of love with the abstraction of the word "love". When they reduce the felt sense to the single word "love", the experience is impoverished, and the client experiences a loss which nurtures their belief that this love is easily lost.

If this issue is not addressed, working with the fear of losing love will not do much because the client is continually experiencing the loss due to their use of abstract language. Furthermore, every time the client turns their attention to the fear of losing love, it only exacerbates the issue because they, at that moment, turn their attention away from love and, in this way, lose it.

To solve the Knot of Positive Reification, the therapist can take time to ask the client what exactly they mean by the word "love" or, more precisely, what felt-sense experience they use the word "love" to refer to. This will direct the client's awareness to the felt-sense experience of love and undo the separation brought about by using the abstraction "love".

To help the client direct their attention to the felt sense underpinning any positive entry point (X), the therapist can ask questions, such as:

- What does X feel like for you?
- Describe the felt sense that you call X?
- Describe the felt sense in your body that you recognise as X?

Some clients will be able to answer such questions directly. They will give you rich and detailed descriptions of the love they feel – and their descriptions will have the mark of connection. Their description will be an outpouring of words and phrases that are imbued with the client's increasing awareness of the aspect of Being they identify as "love".

If this happens, step one of Sensing Abundance is complete, and you can move on to step two, where you help the client sustain their awareness of Being by expanding their description or simply spending time sensing what they have described.

However, some clients will need a bit more help. In the following three sections, we will look at the three main issues clients may encounter when asked to turn their awareness to the felt sense of a particular positive entry point. The three issues are:

- The client believes there is nothing much to say about their experience
- The client's description of the positive entry point is predominantly abstract
- The client's description of the positive entry point is negatively laden.

To direct the client's attention to the concrete, rich, felt-sense experience the positive entry point refers to, we have to deal with these three issues.

The client believes there is nothing much to say

Sometimes, the substitution of the felt-sense experience for the abstraction is so ingrained that the client feels there is nothing more to their experience than the abstraction they use to refer to it.

If a client mentions "love" and you ask them what this "love" feels like, they will be puzzled because they find this word to be a satisfying and complete description. They will say that love feels like love and that there isn't really anything more to say about it or that they don't know what else to say about it. In short, they will feel that their initial abstraction says it all.

In such cases, you can help the client by asking a more elaborate question in which you propose a few contrasting subcategories and some suggestions of felt sense words for each subcategory. In the case of "love", you could ask:

> "What kind of love are you talking about? Is it fiery, hot, passionate love? Is it tender, soft, caring love? Is it romantic love that feels like sweet honey in the heart? Or is it some other kind of love?"

This kind of question invites the client to sense into the concrete felt-sense experience they refer to when they use the word "love". This invitation works in two ways.

First, with this question, you invite the client to make more fine-grained distinctions in their experience of "love" by presenting the client with descriptions of a few contrasting experiences that could all be called "love".

By doing so, the client can realise that the term "love" is not well-defined and can refer to a range of qualitatively distinct experiences. This realisation can ignite the client's curiosity about the specific kind of "love" they're experiencing while simultaneously providing them with some examples with which they can compare and contrast their own experience of love.

You do not have to try to guess what the client's experience is like. It doesn't matter whether your suggestions match the client's experience or not.

If one of your suggestions *does* match the client's experience, they might respond: "Yes, that's precisely what I'm experiencing". This outcome is beneficial as your suggestion has aided the client articulate their concrete experience.

Inversely, if none of your suggestions match the client's experience, they will object and say, "No, that is not it; what I feel is...". This reaction is equally beneficial as your proposal has helped the client discover what their experience is not like, and in rectifying your suggestion, they find words that more accurately describe their concrete and tangible experience of love.

Indeed, I often deliberately propose ideas that I suspect won't align with the client's experience. This is because the impulse to rectify misconceptions about oneself is powerful for most individuals. When they respond to this urge, their corrections often emerge in a spontaneous, rapid fashion that circumvents intellectualisation, ensuring the client *feels* the answer rather than trying to think their way to it.

Second, with the above question, you invite the client to pay attention to the felt-sense experience by modelling the use of neutral sensory words as a means to describe their experience of love.

In the above example, I used "fiery and hot", "tender and soft", and "sweet honey in the heart" to describe the various felt-sense experiences the word "love" could refer to. In doing so, I modelled attention to felt sense.

I also mix in a few abstract words, such as "passionate", "caring" and "romantic". The purpose of this is to give the client something more familiar to relate to and ensure that the client understands that the groups of words refer to qualitatively different experiences – since the client is (most likely) used to thinking about these abstractions as qualitatively different.

However, the felt-sense words are important because whereas presenting the client with the above-mentioned subcategories of love *does* help the client make more nuanced descriptions of their experience, they may not help clients gain awareness of the felt-sense aspect of their experience – and the main purpose of Sensing Abundance is to help clients move their awareness to the concrete, felt-sense level of their experience.

Another way of helping the client put words to the felt sense is to pay attention to the client's body language. Many times, the client's hands will answer the question about how an abstract concept feels before the client is able to put the answer into words.

For example, a client may mention a sense up feeling "uplifted", and you may ask the client to describe the felt sense of this experience. While the client searches for words, they may move their hands upwards and outwards. This motion of the hands may precisely describe the motion of the felt sense the client calls "uplifted". Pointing out to the client that their hands are providing an answer, can help them either find the words or simply continue using their hands to answer the question. Non-verbal descriptions of felt sense will also help clients become more aware of this felt sense.

One can also look at respiration patterns, body posture, facial expressions, etc. for non-verbal descriptions of the felt sense.

The client's description is abstract

Sometimes, clients will answer the question of how a particular abstraction feels to them by providing more abstractions.

For example, when you ask a client what the love they experience feels like, they may say it feels like passion, intimacy, care, appreciation, trust, and so on. This is great because it shows that the clients are making the kind of distinctions that will deepen their experience of love.

However, it is still necessary to encourage the client to move their awareness through the abstractions to the felt sense underpinning these abstractions. You can do this by congratulating the client on their increased discernment and asking what the new abstraction feels like.

If, for example, the client says that the love they experience feels like passion, you can say:

> "Great, and what is the felt sense of passion?"

The client may answer such a question with a description of their felt sense. In the above example, the client may answer that the passion feels like intense vibration in their chest, belly and genitals.

Even if the ultimate goal is to help the client become aware of their felt sense, it is very important to welcome abstractions when clients use them to answer our initial questions. Becoming aware of the felt sense is a gradual process and using abstractions can be a helpful part of this process. In the above example "passion" was an important step on the way from the more general word "love" to the felt sense of intense vibration.

When clients use abstractions, some therapists will see it as a sign that the client is "in their heads", and they will tell clients to "get out of their heads and into their bodies". While the intention is good (seeking to help clients become aware of felt sense), setting up a dichotomy between being in the head and being in the body and seeing the former as bad and the latter as good can be unhelpful.

It is good to point the client's awareness in the direction of the felt sense if they get stuck in abstractions. However, outright dismissing of the abstractions as "unhelpful head stuff" can come across as an interruption to the flow of the client's exploration.

Therefore, it is better to ask the question about felt sense in a way that does not imply that there is something wrong with the abstractions. This is why I suggest signalling that the abstractions are great and then building on them rather than dismissing them by asking about the felt sense of the new emerging abstractions.

Sometimes, clients will answer the question of how a particular abstraction feels to them by providing felt-sense descriptions and then start speculating in abstract terms on these felt sense descriptions.

For example, when you ask a client what the love they experience feels like, they may say it feels like being bathed in a gentle light. This is a description of the felt sense. However, instead of deepening their description of the felt sense, the client may go on to say that this gentle light feels like connection with the Divine. In this second statement, the client starts to interpret the felt sense and moves into abstractions. To guide the client back to the felt sense, one can simply ask the same question as above:

> "Great, and what is the felt sense of divine connection?"

This question is likely to guide the client's awareness back to the felt sense. It is important to note that you as a therapist do not have to agree with the interpretation or even believe in the concepts the client uses. You may think that the gentle light they are talking about has nothing to do with anything divine. You may be an atheist and believe there is no such thing as "the Divine". None of this matters. If you begin to discuss such things with the client, you will take them away from their exploration of the felt sense. By accepting both interpretation and the conceptual framework of the client, you can keep your focus on what matters, namely helping the client become aware of the felt sense of the positive experience they are presently having.

It is also worth noting that not all abstractions are equal.

Some abstractions, such as "heartful", "uplifting", "fulfilling", etc., contain clues as to what the felt sense they refer to is. It can be good to use these clues.

For example, if the client says that the love they experience feels "heartful", the word indicates that they feel the love in the heart area and that it feels like a fullness. You can use this and ask:

> "Great, and what does the substance that fills your heart feel like?"

If needed, you can add a few categories to help the client along the way.

> "Does it feel like honey, water, or cream? Is it liquid or solid? Is it warm or cool? How can you describe that which fills you heart?"

Similarly, the word "uplifting" will likely refer to a felt sense of moving upwards or being carried upwards, and the word "fulfilling" will likely refer to a felt sense of being filled by some substance.

Other abstractions are very intellectualised and offer no clues as to what felt-sense experience they refer to. This is not to say that they do not have a clear and conscious connection to a felt-sense experience for your client. It is just worth being aware that they might not.

For example, if a client says that the love they experience is "passion" or "care", "trust" or "appreciation", you may, from experience, know what felt sense people, in general, are referring to when using such words, but it is good to keep your questions open. You may be surprised by what a specific client answers.

In other situations, the client may use highly intellectualised words, such as "eros", "agape", or "philia". In this case, you will have even less idea what the felt sense the client is referring to is. Furthermore, words like this are often indicators that your client has their awareness thoroughly place in the realm of ideas and will need extra coaxing to turn away from philosophical definitions and technicalities and towards their own immediate felt sense related to their experience.

In such cases, it can be good to build on the client's inquisitiveness and encourage them to be pioneers of discovery. If the client speculates that their experience of love is philia, you may, for example, ask:

> "Great, so you have a sense that the love you feel is more related to "philia", as opposed to "eros" or "agape". This is interesting. One way of knowing this is to note that your behaviours, attitudes and perspectives match those related to philia. But different forms of love must also feel different. Would you be able to describe how "philia" feels inside you right now?"

In this question, I start of by matching the client in their more intellectual approach to resolving the question of what kind of love they are feeling. I then move on to inviting them into an active (and pioneering?) exploration of the felt sense. Furthermore, I insinuate that this is a matter of capability. People who respond in a highly intellectualised manner will often have a sense of pride around their own capabilities. Thus, they are unlikely to back down from such a challenge.

If the client keeps answering the question of what the love they experience feels like with abstract descriptions, you can directly ask them to describe their experience using only neutral, sensory words. To ensure they understand what you mean by that, you can tell the client that neutral, sensory words are words you can use to describe physical substances, such as warm, cold, heavy, light, rough, textured, moving forward, upward, downward, outward, inward, etc. You can find a list of neutral, sensory words at www.sensingmind.com/5-knots-resources.

Finally, in some cases, clients are unable to find concrete words that describe their felt sense. The abstractions they use are really the best words they can find to express their felt sense. If you feel that an abstract word for a particular client clearly refers to a felt sense, it can be better to leave the description as it is. If you force the client to describe their felt sense using sensory words, the client may end up feeling that they cannot describe their experience in a way that satisfies the therapist. And that is not a productive dynamic. The point of the description is not to satisfy the therapist. The point of the description is to deepen the client's awareness of felt sense.

Continuously inviting clients to make descriptions of their experience less abstract and more concrete is important because the purpose of Sensing Abundance is to help clients move their awareness to the concrete, felt-sense level of their experience.

The client's description is negatively laden

It may be surprising that clients would use negative descriptions when asked to describe a positive entry point. However, this does happen. I will elaborate much more on how to deal with negatively laden descriptions when we get to the Knot of Negative Reification. However, because it can happen even when dealing with the Knot of Positive Reification, a few words on the matter are appropriate at this point.

I always encourage clients to describe their experiences using neutral, sensory words. The reason for using sensory words is that such words help the client move from abstractions to felt sense. The reason for using neutral words is that by using neutral words, we separate the description of our experience from value-judgements about this experience. This makes it easier to focus our attention on the felt sense and not be distracted by evaluations of this felt sense.

Both positive and negative evaluations of a given experience can divert the client's focus from the felt sense of this experience. Positive evaluations may cause the client to focus on how to preserve the experience, while negative evaluations may lead them to focus on how to avoid, eliminate or alter the experience. However, in practice, negatively laden language is more problematic than positively laden language. This is because, whereas the grasping that arises out of positive evaluations does not make the client averse to engaging with the felt sense of the experience, the aversion that arises out of negative evaluations does.

The way to deal with negatively charged descriptions is similar to the way we deal with abstract descriptions, in that the therapist should encourage the client to describe in neutral, sensory terms the felt sense underlying the negative description.

For example, when a client is asked to describe how "love" feels in a certain situation, the client might say that it feels like "infatuation". This is good insofar as it is more specific than the word "love", and as such, it *does* help qualify what kind of love the client is experiencing. However, there are two problems with the word "infatuation".

First, it is an abstract word and does not reveal anything about the felt sense it refers to. We have already covered how to deal with abstractions in the previous section.

Second, for many people, "infatuation" carries a negative connotation. If we describe love as "infatuation", we are invoking the idea of love as something fickle, fleeting, volatile and potentially regrettable. The client may feel that love comes quickly and can disappear equally quickly, and that love can take over and make one do things one might later regret. This can lead the client to speculate on whether what they feel truly is infatuation or something more palatable, whether it might be ok for them to feel infatuated under certain circumstances, and what those circumstances might be. In case the client believes that infatuation is decisively bad, they may furthermore start strategising on how to eliminate it. All these lines of thought divert the client's awareness away from the concrete, somatic experience of love and will, in this way, compound the client's fear of losing love because they lose awareness of the felt sense of love whenever their awareness is captured by any of these speculations.

As therapists, we can respond to such negatively laden descriptions of love by congratulating the client for taking this step towards a more detailed description of the love they feel and then prompt them to describe it in terms of felt sense. If this leads to a neutral sensory description, we can move on to the second phase of Sensing Abundance, where we focus on sustaining awareness of the felt sense.

However, the client may preserve the negative value-judgement as they move to the felt sense. They may, for example, say that the infatuation feels like being "overheated".

The word "overheated" is better than "infatuation" because it refers to a somatic experience. However, it still has the problem of containing a negative value-judgement. The prefix "over-" indicates that the heat is too much according to some standard of how much heat the client believes they are supposed to feel when in love. This value-judgement is likely to make the client engage in considerations that will take them away from the somatic experience, such as how much heat is too much heat, is it ok to feel this much heat, when is it ok to feel this much heat, what are the risks connected with feeling overheated, how can one mitigate these risks, and so on. Once again, if the client's awareness is captured by such speculations, they are likely to lose awareness of the felt sense of the love, and this will compound their fear of losing love and their belief that love is fickle and easy to lose.

Once again, as therapists, we can congratulate the client on finding a word that describes the felt sense in more detail and then prompt them to take the value-judgement out of the description. We can do this by modelling neutrality, inviting neutrality or suspending concerns.

Modelling neutrality: We prompt the client to suspend their value-judgement by modelling neutral language. We can, for example, ask:

> "Where do you feel the heat?"

In this question, we simply remove the part of the word carrying the value-judgement. In other cases, we might replace the word carrying negative connotations with a more neutral one. It is possible that the client objects to this, but in many cases, if the rapport between therapist and client is good, they will go along with the change and leave behind their value-judgement.

Inviting neutrality: We can also prompt the client to suspend their value-judgement by suggesting that they reverse it. We can, for example, ask:

> "How would you describe the sense of being overheated if it was a good thing?"

This invites the client to take the negative judgement out of the description and puts to rest their concerns. Often the client will be able to find a neutral word that describes the felt sense without any value-judgement.

Suspending concerns: Sometimes the client will insist that what they feel is negative. In those cases, it is good to ask what negative consequences they imagine will come from having the felt sense. The client may say that this overheated love will lead to burnout, manic action or something else. Once the client's concerns are clarified, you can ask them what the love would feel like if they knew that none of the negative consequences would occur. In essence, you ask them what the love feels like if you remove the standard according to which the heat is too much.

Finally, it is worth noting that sometimes clients will describe their experience using sensory words, which in themselves are neutral, but the client's tone of voice, facial expression or other physical aspects reveal that the client *perceives* the word as something negative. They may, for example, state that the love feels "sweet", and when they say the word "sweet", there is a contraction in their face or a twitch in their voice, which reveals disgust or dismay.

In this case, it is good to invite the client to neutralise the word using one of the three techniques described above:

- **Modelling neutrality:** Using the word in a neutral way yourself

- **Inviting neutrality:** Pointing out that it seems that the client doesn't like sweetness and, if this is confirmed, inviting them to consider what sweetness would feel like if it was a good thing.
- **Suspending concerns:** Mapping out what the client's concrete concerns about sweetness are and inviting them to notice what sweetness feels like if it is separated from their concerns.

If you manage to make the client curious about the details of their experience and you deal well with both abstract and negative descriptions, your client has moved through the positive entry point and into the felt-sense experience of an aspect of Being.

At this point, the task becomes to help the client sustain awareness of this felt sense. The longer the client retains awareness of Being, the more this experience will positively affect the client and dissolve their issues.

2.6.3. Step 3: Sustain awareness of Being

Once the client has moved their awareness from a positive reification to the underlying felt sense, you can help them sustain awareness of this felt sense by "interviewing" them about it in a manner that leaves ample time for sensing.

Interviewing your client about the felt sense will not only help them deepen their experience of the felt sense, but more importantly, it will help them sustain their awareness of it because as long as you ask your client questions about it, they will have to keep paying attention to it to answer your questions.

It is, therefore, good to have an arsenal of questions you can use in this phase of the Sensing Abundance process. In particular, you can ask about details and effects.

Details: You can ask the client to describe details about the felt sense itself:

- Where in the body do you feel it the most?
- How does it feel in the head/heart/belly/arms/legs/space around the body?
- Does it have a colour?
- What is its temperature?
- What is its weight?
- What state of matter does it resemble (air, liquid, solid, plasma)?
- Does it move or is it still?
- If it moves, how can you describe the movement? (clear direction, shifting directions, expanding, contracting, tempo)

Effects: You can also ask the client how it affects them to be aware of the felt sense:

- How does being aware of this felt sense affect your thoughts?
- How does being aware of this felt sense affect your emotional state?
- How does being aware of this felt sense affect what you would like to do?
- How does being aware of this felt sense affect your sense of self/the world/others, etc.?

If, for example, the client has found that the "love" they feel in a particular situation corresponds to a felt sense of warmth in the body, you can start asking questions, such as:

- Where in the body do you feel this warmth the most? Do you feel it in the head, heart, belly, the whole body, around the body or somewhere else?
- What is the temperature and state of matter of the warmth? Is the heat like a hot bath, a hot sauna space, lava, a warm stone, or something else?
- Is the warmth still, or does it move?
- If the warmth is moving, how does it move? Does it move up, down, or forward? Does it expand, vibrate, oscillate, or something else?
- Now that you are feeling this warmth, does it change what you want to do in the situation?

As a rule of thumb, the therapist should use such questions to help the client sustain awareness of the felt sense for as long as possible. Depending on the client, this can be a few seconds or the entire session.

The frequency of the questions should also strike a balance. If you ask too many questions too quickly, it can take the client out of sensing rather than support it. On the other hand, if you ask too few questions, the client's attention may drift, and it can be difficult to get back in touch with the felt sense. Thus, it is good to ask a single question and notice the effect. If the client shows signs of being in touch with the felt sense, you can just stay silent. Once the client shows signs of starting to drift away from the felt sense, you can ask another question to invite them to refocus on the felt sense.

It is important to be aware that the client may lose awareness of the felt sense before they stop answering the questions. When a client loses awareness of the felt sense, they may still try to guess the answers to your questions but their words will turn stale and the visceral sense of the client speaking from direct awareness of the felt sense will disappear. In other words, the magic is gone, and the description becomes boring to listen to. Then it is time to move on with the session.

The reason it is good to help the client sustain awareness of the felt sense is that the longer the client pays attention to the felt sense, the longer the experience of the felt sense will have to undo the Knot of Positive Reification and related issues.

In the next section, we look at how awareness of the felt sense can undo the Knot of Positive Reification by providing experiential counter-evidence to the misconceptions that are related to the Knot of Positive Reification.

2.6.4. Step 4: Correct misconceptions related to the Knot of Positive Reification

The process of Sensing Abundance unties the Knot of Positive Reification by providing the client with direct experience that contradicts the misconceptions that are created by and sustain the Knot of Positive Reification.

Misconception 1: You seek many things

When clients pay sustained awareness to Being, it is common that the experience transforms from one positive state to another. The client may start by experiencing the felt sense of joy as a fountain in the heart and after a while the fountain transforms into a quiet flow and then dissolves into deep peaceful darkness, like inner velvet, and then out of the darkness a sense of tenderness and softness emerges, and so on. It is also common that the felt-sense experience the client becomes aware of is a combination of sensations the client would normally see as mutually exclusive, such as a sense of fullness and emptiness, heavy grounding and lightness, vast openness and closeness, and so on.

Both kinds of experience reveal to the client that many of the things they thought were different kinds of things are not really different. There is a link between all things we seek in life. We do not seek many things, but one thing experienced in many ways.

Whenever a client has such experiences, it is beneficial for the therapist to highlight them and point out how these experiences point to the unity of things the client would normally see as different or even mutually exclusive. A client may, for example, see peace and vitality as two positive but mutually exclusive phenomena. If the client at some point experiences a felt sense they describe as still yet vibrantly alive, it is good to point out that this is an experience of feeling peace and aliveness at the same time and that this shows the two are not mutually exclusive after all.

Misconception 2: You are separate from what you seek

The longer the client lets their awareness rest on any aspect of Being, the clearer it becomes to them that they are not separate from Being and that they will experience it for as long as they direct their attention towards it.

For example, the longer a client pays attention to the felt sense of love, the longer they will feel this love, and this will quench their thirst for love. This experience reveals to them that they are not separate from the love they seek but that this love is always present and all they have to do to feel it is to pay attention to it.

If a client vividly experiences a positive state while describing it, this experience can be used to correct the misconception of separateness. As a therapist, you can simply propose that the client feels the state while describing it because describing it requires the client to pay attention to it, and if the client feels a state whenever they pay attention to it, it must be because this state is always available as an integral part of the client.

Misconception 3: Ideas are more important than direct experience

The longer the client pays attention to an aspect of Being, the more this experience will change them. Experiencing the healing, nourishing and transformative effects of the direct experience of Being, reveals to the client that sustained awareness of Being can be far more therapeutic than analysing ideas about Being (or about anything else, for that matter).

The time aspect is important. We are not trying to change the misconceptions that constitute the Knot of Positive Reification through logical arguments but rather by providing the client with an experience that contradicts these misconceptions, and the more we can prolong this experience, the more time it will have to shift the client's misconceptions.

In other words, the longer the client can sustain awareness of Being, the longer this experience will have to work on the client.

It is important for the therapist to understand the distribution of work between the therapist, client and Being. It is the role of the therapist to help the client direct their attention towards Being. Once this is done, the experience of Being will do the rest.

One mistake I see therapists make is that they keep trying to do something even after the client becomes aware of Being. But this is the time for the therapist to step back and only prompt the client to stay with the experience if the client's attention drifts towards something else.

Summary

To sum up, the process of Sensing Abundance is the process of going through a positive reification of Being to the underlying felt-sense experience and then pay sustained attention to this felt sense.

Clients can become aware of the felt sense underlying a positive reification of Being by describing positive states using neutral, sensory words.

Clients can sustain awareness of the felt sense by describing it in more detail and describing the effects being aware of the state has on them.

The more familiar you, as the therapist, are with the various experiences of Being, the easier it is for you to recognise when words refer to such experiences. It is as if the words lights up like small stars, or as if you get a small taste of Being when the client utters these words. That is how you know which words to pursue. I call these words "positive entry points", and I always listen for them, when clients are telling me their stories.

2.6.5. Dealing with distractions

At any point during the process of Sensing Abundance, the client may become distracted by some tangential line of thought.

Below are four conversations between a therapist and a client that illustrate four typical distractions.

When this happens, the first thing to try is to agree with the client's observation or statement (whatever it might be) and invite them to refocus their attention on the felt sense of Being. The first two examples illustrate this process.

Example 1: The accuracy of an example

In the following exchange, the therapist invites the client to describe the felt sense underpinning their experience of "love" by providing a few examples of possible descriptions.

Instead of engaging in the investigation of the felt sense, the client becomes distracted because one of the examples appear inaccurate or false to them.

In such cases, it can be tempting for the therapist to defend their example; however, engaging in a discussion of the accuracy or veracity of an example will only side-track the process.

It is, therefore, better to use the client's objection as an illustration of the point the list of examples were meant to make, namely, that a given word may refer to very different felt-sense experiences for different people, and then restate the invitation to describe the felt sense of the state the word refers to for the client

Therapist: What kind of love are you talking about? Is it fiery, hot, passionate love or tender, soft, caring love or romantic love that feels like sweet honey in the heart or some other love?

Client: I don't think romantic love feels like honey...

T: Romantic love will, of course, not necessarily feel like honey. Different people might feel it differently. This is why it is so interesting to examine how love feels to us. So, how does the love you experienced feel to you?

Example 2: The nature of the phenomenon

In the following exchange, the client responds to the therapist's list of examples by putting forward a philosophical claim about the nature of "love". Thus, the client does not object to any individual example but rather to the idea that there are different kinds of love.

Once again, engaging in a philosophical discussion about the nature of love will only side-track the investigation of the felt sense underpinning the client's experience of love. Therefore, the therapist simply acknowledges that the client's claim may well be true and then redirects the conversation back to the investigation of felt sense.

T: What kind of love are you talking about? Is it fiery, hot, passionate love or tender, soft, caring love or romantic love that feels like sweet honey in the heart or some other love?

C: I believe that all forms of love are fundamentally the same.

T: True. Different experiences of love may very well ultimately be different expressions of one single source. What I'm curious about is what the specific form of love you experienced in the situation you mentioned feels like.

Sometimes, the distractions have more momentum, and you find that it is not possible to refocus the client's attention on their felt-sense experience. This is often a sign that the client is caught in a different knot. Thus, you are no longer dealing with just the Knot of Positive Reification. If this happens, you must switch processes to deal with the new knot that has revealed itself. The following two examples are illustrations of this.

Example 3: Equation of phenomenon and circumstances

In the following exchange, the client gets distracted by the fact that they have felt the love they explore in a kind of situation that is no longer part of their life.

The therapist initially tries to agree with the client's observation that this particular situation is no longer available to them and then refocuses the client's awareness on the felt sense of love itself.

However, the distraction persists. This reveals that the client strongly believes that "love" is dependent on certain circumstances for its existence. Thus, the client equates the loss of the possibility to create these circumstances with the loss of the possibility to experience "love".

This is one of the misconceptions related to the Knot of Conditionality. Therefore, it can be beneficial at this point in the therapy session to shift to the process for untying this knot. This process is described in Chapter 3, Knot 2: The Knot of Conditionality.

T: What kind of love are you talking about? Is it fiery, hot, passionate love or tender, soft, caring love or romantic love that feels like sweet honey in the heart or some other love?

C: I remember this feeling so well from my youth. When I and my partner were on holiday and swam together in the ocean. I no longer have the strength to do this. That makes me sad.

T: Yes. Sometimes we recall situations in the past where we had the feeling, and we may feel sad when we think that we can no longer experience those particular situations. But we can still explore the felt sense. What does the love itself feel like now?

C: It feels like loss and sadness. What is the point in exploring the feeling of love when I can no longer have it?

Example 4: Internal conflict

In the following exchange, the client gets distracted by negative ideas about the felt sense of love. The therapist initially tries to agree with the client's observations and refocus them on the felt sense. The therapist employs two techniques to accomplish this.

Firstly, the therapist uses language that is slightly less intense than that of the client, such as "a bit much" and "we might find ourselves pondering".

Secondly, the therapist ascribes the uncomfortable part of the felt sense, the dizziness, to the thoughts the client harbours about love, thereby differentiating it from the felt sense of love itself.

Nevertheless, the client doesn't accept the invitation. Rather, they convey a distinct aversion to the felt sense they experience. The client's second statement exposes a voice of a personality part that is strongly opposed to embracing the felt sense of love. This reveals a conflict within the client between two internal parts: one that is seeking love, and another that opposes the felt sense of love. We will explore how to deal with such inner conflict in Chapter 6, Knot 5: The Knot of Fragmentation.

T: What kind of love are you talking about? Is it fiery, hot, passionate love or tender, soft, caring love or romantic love that feels like sweet honey in the heart or some other love?

C: It feels hot. Very hot. I get dizzy. I don't think this is healthy. It feels wrong.

T: True. Sometimes, love can be a bit much, and we might find ourselves pondering whether it is healthy or not or whether it is right or wrong. Such thoughts might make us dizzy. But what does heat feel like – apart from any such speculations?

C: I don't want to feel this. I don't know if it is love – or if it is then I don't know if I want to feel love.

In summary, when a client's exploration of the felt sense related to a particular aspect of Being is disrupted by a distraction, the therapist can initially attempt to agree with the distracting observation and then refocus the client's attention on the felt sense.

However, if the distraction persists, it may indicate the activation of significant patterns in the client. In such scenarios, it can be beneficial to acknowledge and explore these patterns before continuing the exploration of Being.

Determining whether to bypass or address a distraction is an important judgement call on the part of the therapist. On the one hand, if we engage too often with distractions, we may become entangled in the client's confusion. On the other hand, if we sidestep too many distractions, we risk engaging in what is known as "spiritual bypassing", which could exacerbate the client's sense of fragmentation. I will return to these themes in Chapter 6, Knot 5: The Knot of Fragmentation.

2.7. Examples of Sensing Abundance

In this section, you can read transcriptions of two therapy sessions applying the process of Sensing Abundance. The sessions, like all sessions in this book, are fictional but representative of sessions I have had with clients.

Furthermore, the sessions are abbreviated so they only include the key parts of the exchange. Real sessions often contain more exploration, longer narratives, tangents, pauses, etc. That being said, the Knot of Positive Reification, can in some cases, be untied in a matter of minutes. In such cases, the examples below would represent full transcriptions of the therapeutic exchange.

The examples are written in two columns. In the left column, you can read the client and therapist's conversation. In the right column, you can read the observations and considerations that guided the therapist during the exchange.

2.7.1. Session 1: The fountain in the heart

This session is a typical example of how a client experiences Being (in this case reified as a positive experience of "love") but does not ascribe this experience much value or give it much attention because their attention is drawn to a situation, the client (falsely) believes is the hindrance to their well-being.

However, when the client is encouraged to give more attention to Being by exploring the felt-sense experience of "love", the problem they wanted to talk about dissolves effortlessly because the real problem was always lack of awareness of Being and not the situation the client believed to be the problem.

In this case, the imagined problem dissolved almost entirely. Or more precisely, it shifted from being a problem that was severe enough to bring to a therapy session to a minor matter the client felt they could easily deal with in an undramatic fashion.

This scenario is very typical for any of the processes described in this book. The client believes their problem is a particular situation but because the real problem is lack of awareness of Being, the moment the client gains awareness of Being the problem they believed they had is reduced to a more or less banal situation they can easily deal with.

Process	Comments
Client: I have a problem with a friend of mine. He invited me and my partner for dinner, and it started off really well. We walked to the restaurant together and I felt deep love walking arm in arm with my friend and my partner. But at the restaurant my friend kept talking about these heavy issues, and I was really not in the mood. But when I told him so, he got offended and said that these topics were important, and that I should show more gratitude because he had invited the two of us to this nice restaurant. I didn't want to be ungrateful. But I also didn't want him to ruin the dinner with these heavy topics.	The client is focused on the problem of how to deal with her friend and her own conflicting emotions in relation to the situation. However, it is interesting to see how she skips past the words "deep love". When she uttered these words, she lit up, indicating that this could be a positive entry point. Therefore, I chose to develop the client's connection to the sense of deep love before anything else.
Therapist: You mentioned that you feel "deep love" on the way to the restaurant. I'm just curious. Could you tell me more about what that feels like?	I invite the client to explore the felt sense of love with an open question. I use the present tense (even if that is grammatically wrong) to invite the felt sense into the present moment.
C: It feels like a water hose. Like a fountain in the heart. Just bursting up and out. I feel soft in the whole body and uplifted. This is why I didn't want to talk about...	The client is good at describing the felt sense. She uses neutral, sensory words, and it is visible that she feels what she is describing. However, she is eager to move on to the problem.
T: Let me just pause you there. We will get to the difficulties with your friend, but I'm curious about the fountain. Do you feel it now that you are talking about it?	I interrupt the client to direct her awareness back to the felt sense of love to give it more time to work on her. I do so by first ensuring her that we will get to the issue and then asking a question about the sense of love.

Process	Comments
C: Yes, I do actually	She confirms and it is visible that she feels the sensation of love
T: And if you just take some time to enjoy this feeling, what can you notice about it? Is the fountain a water fountain or a honey fountain or something else? What does it do to your thoughts and emotions to hang out with the feeling of this fountain?	I suggest questions that expand her perception and enable her to sustain her awareness of the love. I ask some relating to the felt sense and some relating to the effect of being aware of the felt sense. This is a menu. The client can answer any of the questions.
C: I can feel my whole body relaxing... I think I really long for this feeling... It's like a fountain of love in the heart... It's sweet and light... It is not as fast as before... it is more mellow... I think I normally disconnect from this feeling and start finding faults with people. I can still see the faults – but somehow, they seem less important. They seem to mean something different...	I give the client ample time to sense. At this point the client may speak very slowly and take long pauses. This is fine. This is the part of the session where insights flow in and it is good to give space for this process. There is very little for the therapist to do. When the client has a felt sense awareness of Being, Being takes over the therapeutic work, so to speak.
T: How does feeling this state affect the way you feel about the heavy topics your friend brought up at the dinner.	I will often ask how awareness of the state affects the issue the client wanted to address to test whether this is still an issue or not. I sometimes ask what clients would like to do in the situation because this can help the client change behavioural patterns in such a way that it becomes easier for them to maintain awareness of Being.

Process	Comments
C: (laughs). That's just how he is. Melodramatic. Somehow, it doesn't affect me at all. It's almost cute. I don't even remember why it was such a big deal for me... that's strange... I think I'd just change the topic. No need to berate him for bringing the heavy stuff.	This is a typical change in terms of behaviour. A simple, uncomplicated option emerges. In this case it was: "Just change the topic". It is important to note that changing the topic from a state of love is a very different act than changing the topic from a place of judgement.
T: Enjoy the love fountain	I like to end sessions like this with an encouragement to go on enjoying the state and not leave it just because the session has come to an end.
C: Thanks. I will.	

2.7.2. Session 2: Finding wholeness

So far, we have primarily discussed positive entry points as words or phrases that refer to positive experiences the client gives little attention to because they focus on exploring a specific problem.

The Knot of Positive Reification can also reveal itself through the client's idealisations. The client may see another person, a place, an ideology or something else as perfect and extremely attractive. Such idealisations can also be used as positive entry points.

To use idealisations as positive entry points, it is key that the therapist refrains from reflecting on whether the client's idealisation is justified or healthy. Idealisations are generally a matter of the client projecting their sense of Being onto the object of their idealisation. What they see when they look at the idealised object is a reflection of their own light – their own experience of Being. Thus, in this context, idealisations are always justified – even when the idealisation of the particular object in question can lead to issues, such as unhealthy attachments or a disowning of one's power that leaves one open to abuse.

The therapist can use the client's idealisations as a tool to direct their awareness towards Being. If the client idealises a person, the therapist can encourage the client to imagine what it would be like to be or merge with that person. Similarly, if the client idealises a lifestyle, the therapist can engage the client in imagining what it feels like to already live this lifestyle.

In such explorations, the therapist must steer clear of pitfalls, such as working with the client's lamentations of not being the person or planning how the client may attain the idealised lifestyle. The goal of the exploration is to bring to awareness the felt sense the client is projecting onto the object, which is what gives the object its allure.

In the following therapy session, the idealised object is a potential romantic partner. At the outset of the session, the client experiences a mix of infatuation, excitement, trepidation and fear of loss when considering expressing their feelings to the potential romantic partner.

Instead of delving into these emotions, the therapist invites the client to explore the felt sense underpinning the attraction. In doing so, the client gains awareness of Being in the form of wholeness (and other aspects).

After this awareness is established, the problematic emotions are dissolved, and the client's view of the situation loses its gravity and gains a measure of playfulness and light-heartedness.

This session illustrates the advantages of cultivating awareness of Being during therapy. By doing so, all issues that are rooted in the lack of awareness of Being dissolve, and those that remain become more manageable and easier to work with.

Process	Comments
Client: I have met a man, Gregg, who is so perfect. He is funny, caring, wise, strong, in touch with his emotions... and so very good looking. He has been working with healing for over 10 years and teaches it. I met him on one of his courses, and we got talking and one thing led to another. I don't know if it is a thing. I'm afraid of telling him how I feel. I don't want to come across too strong. I really don't want to blow my chances with this one. I'm afraid I'll mess it up if I tell him all I feel.	The client is obviously infatuated with the man. The fact that he is taking an interest in a student indicates an ethically problematic behaviour which the client gives no attention to. Her focus in on the issue of managing her own "demons" so as not to "blow her chances". When people idealise another, it is often because they project Being onto them, thus turning their image of the person into a positive entry point.
Therapist: Wonderful. I'm curious about how the qualities you see in Gregg fit with your own ideals.	With the word "wonderful", I acknowledge the client's positive view of the situation to settle any trepidation she might feel about my reaction. Therapists are sometimes known to be buzzkills focusing on hidden motivations. I then ask about the fit with her own ideals to test my hypothesis that she sees a personal ideal in Gregg.
C: He is everything I wish to be.	This confirms my suspicion that she sees her own ideal in Gregg and this is part of the attraction.
T: What does looking at this perfection connect you with in yourself?	Here I start inviting the client into the felt sense underpinning the positive entry point.
C: I feel inferior.	Here emerges a distraction of a negative self-image. This is the reason she seeks the ideal externally.

Process	Comments
T: Yes, when we see perfection in others, we sometimes feel a bit inferior. But that is not why you like looking at him. What is it you like?	I choose to make a mental note of the sense of inferiority, and treat it as a distraction (for now). I then refocus the client on the felt sense of perfection.
C: My heart melts. I want to merge with him and melt with him.	Melting is often a sign that what keeps the client separate from Being is starting to dissolve.
T: Wonderful. What does that feel like?	Therefore, I encourage her to continue. I use present tense as an aid.
C: Warm, exciting, special, beauty, love, joy, esoteric, on a soul level, divine, infinite cosmic. I feel it in my entire body. In particular in the heart and belly. I feel whole.	The client speaks slowly and gradually deepens her awareness of this aspect of Being. I stay silent throughout the exploration and let the client's awareness of Being work its magic.
C: It is strange. I no longer feel deficient. I feel whole. I'm still excited about seeing Gregg but I want to see all of him. It's like I no longer need him to be perfect. Strange... I'm a bit worried about not seeing Gregg as perfect. What does that mean?	The root of the client's deficiency was lack of awareness of Being. Becoming aware of Being dispelled the deficiency and spontaneously changed the client's view of the situation. As Being is internalised Gregg loses some of this shine. This worries the client.
T: Just let it unfold. Feeling whole tends to make one feel a bit more grounded as well. It's all unfolding by the book.	Once again, I treat the worry as a distraction. I encourage the client to not give it much attention by describing it as a normal (and insignificant) aspect of the process.
C: (laughs) Now it doesn't feel like a big deal to tell him how I feel. It feels much lighter. It's just nice to feel like this.	The original problem of worrying about how to share her feelings has dissolved.
T: Enjoy!	Normally, I would say a bit more to round off a session. But the Sensing Abundance process is concluded here.

2.8. Untying the Knot of Positive Reification through contemplations

In Section 2.6, I have outlined how the Knot of Positive Reification can be untied in one-to-one sessions with clients.

In this section, I will present two contemplation exercises that are specifically designed to untie the Knot of Positive Reification. These exercises are well suited to group work. The instructions are sufficiently simple to be given to a group, and the exercises can, for example, be performed in pairs or as individual writing exercises.

These contemplation exercises can be deepened through one-to-one processing, as outlined in the previous section. When working with groups, I often begin by inviting the students to do the contemplation exercise in pairs or individually. Afterwards, I work one-to-one with a few students in plenum. This approach has the advantage that although I only work with a few students directly, the other students, having completed the contemplation exercise, can partake in the one-to-one processing vicariously.

2.8.1. What does meditation/relaxation feel like for you?

A good general way of gaining experience with untying the Knot of Positive Reification is an exercise I like to use when I introduce the work to new students.

The exercise consists of two parts. First, I guide a simple meditation or relaxation exercise to help people disengage their attention from thoughts and emotions, thereby increasing the potential for becoming aware of Being. The relaxation students generally experience during this part of the exercise can then be used as a positive entry point. Thus, after the meditation/relaxation exercise, I ask the students to describe in detail what the relaxation felt like for them at a felt-sense level.

The first part of the exercise can vary. Sometimes, I use a simple body scan, guiding people through sensing one body part at a time until they have gone through the entire body. Other times, I invite people to spend some time doing nothing – to abandon any projects, refrain from planning anything in the future or reflecting on the past, and even from trying to get something out of the exercise. The instructions may include:

- Sitting with closed eyes and letting time pass – or as I sometimes phrase it: "Deliberately wasting time".
- Letting any thoughts or emotions that might emerge be – without trying to repress, alter or engage with them.
- Regarding anything that occurs internally as irrelevant background noise.

For the second part of the exercise, I ask how people felt during the meditation/relaxation exercise. Initially, most people will agree that the experience was extremely relaxing and pleasant – including those who have never practised meditation before.

However, when I use this sense of relaxation as a positive entry point and ask people to describe the felt sense underpinning their individual experience of relaxation in more detail, it quickly becomes evident that the experience of relaxation can vary significantly among individuals.

Some people experience the relaxation as a peaceful dark night, others as a sense of lightness or of being uplifted, yet others feel the relaxation as if everything falls into place inside of them.

When people hear these qualitatively different experiences of relaxation, they usually relate to all or most of them. They recognise that each description is, in some measure, a valid way of describing the state that emerged in themselves. Thus, hearing other people's descriptions expands their own experience of Being.

This exercise creates an experience that reveals how we tend to reduce the profound experience of Being to a single word, such as "relaxation" and how we, in doing so, risk overlooking the richness of the experience. Thus, the exercise creates an experience that makes it possible for the participants to observe positive reification in action.

Furthermore, by recognising the descriptions from other people as revealing overlooked aspects of one's own experience, we gain the experience that the different words used by different people all relate to the same unified experience. In this way, the exercise provides experiential evidence that gently starts to correct the misconception that different words for positive inner states refer to wholly different phenomena (misconception 1).

Similarly, the exercise shows that it is possible to experience profound and valuable inner states by doing nothing. This experience can, when repeated, start correcting the mistaken belief that we are separate from these states and that we, therefore, must do something to acquire them (misconception 2).

Finally, when each individual in a group becomes aware of Being and describes this experience, the atmosphere in the room becomes very delicious and nourishing. As mentioned previously, when people feel Being and speak about their experience their words become contagious. Thus, through this exercise people are together building up a field of awareness that has a visceral and positive impact on everyone in the room. This provides experiential evidence that simply paying attention to Being has great therapeutic potential, thus correcting the misconception that paying attention to ideas is more important than paying attention to immediate experience (misconception 3).

When I work with experienced meditators, I can skip the first part (if needed due to time restraints) and simply ask the question: What does meditation feel like for you? If I ask this question in a group of 10 people or more, I'm likely to receive enough qualitatively different answers necessary for the exercise to work.

2.8.2. When have you had positive and uncomplicated experiences of X, and what did that feel like in the body?

Another contemplation exercise I frequently use to untie the Knot of Positive Reification involves examining the felt sense of positive phenomena, such as "confidence", "love", "appreciation", "peace", "joy", or "connection".

For this exploration, I typically ask two interconnected questions.

- When have you had positive and uncomplicated experiences of X (the positive phenomenon)?
- What did that feel like in the body?

Each of these questions serves a distinct purpose, which I will describe in the following two sections.

When have you had positive and uncomplicated experiences of X?

The purpose of the first question is to access memories of concrete situations in which the client has experienced the phenomenon they wish to explore. This is important because it enables a real investigation.

Recalling concrete situations in which the client has experienced the positive phenomenon is akin to a researcher collecting empirical data that will help them answer a research question.

Doing so allows the client to investigate and discover the answer to the second question about what the phenomenon feels like in the body by investigating their lived experience of the phenomenon.

Asking only the second question, "What does X feel like in the body?" might result in the client responding with a list of preconceived notions and beliefs about what the phenomenon feels like. However, such beliefs may be false or inaccurate. Recalling concrete situations in which the client has felt the phenomenon allows the client to *discover* the felt sense of this phenomenon rather than merely *recall* preconceived notions about it.

The question also contains the two qualifiers "positive" and "uncomplicated". The reason for this is that it is easier to discover what a certain phenomenon feels like if we explore situations that are not cluttered by other phenomena.

For example, you may wish to explore what "joy" feels like by considering a situation where you sat in the sun and felt "joy", and there were no complications. As you recall this situation, you may notice that you feel light and spacious, and you may conclude that this is what joy feels like.

If, on the other hand, you were to explore the felt sense of "joy" by recalling a situation where you experienced joy upon passing an important exam which your best friend failed, you may feel the same lightness and spaciousness as in the previous example but you may also feel a host of other feelings. You may feel sad on behalf of your friend, guilty for feeling joyful when your friend is not, concerned about making your friend's day worse because you passed the exam and they did not, resentment towards your friend for dampening your joy, ashamed for feeling such resentment, sad about not being able to share your joy with them, and so on. Each of these thoughts and emotions will influence your felt sense as you recollect the situation, and it is not always easy to separate what part of your felt sense pertains to "joy" and what part pertains to other phenomena present in the situation.

Thus, when exploring the felt sense of any positive phenomenon, it simplifies the process if you draw on memories of positive and uncomplicated experiences. In contrast, drawing on memories of experiences where the phenomenon you wish to explore was mixed with other phenomena can add unnecessary complexity and potentially hinder the exploration.

Exploring the felt sense of a positive phenomenon by recalling positive and uncomplicated experiences of this phenomenon is akin to exploring what a clarinet sounds like by listening to a clarinet playing solo. This is considerably easier than attempting to discern what a clarinet sounds like by listening to a full symphonic orchestra performance. While the clarinet is part of the overall sound, it is not always easy to distinguish the part of the sound that pertains to the clarinets from the sound that pertains to the oboes, flutes or other instruments.

Focusing one's attention on the felt sense of a single phenomenon among the plethora of associated concepts and ideas can be challenging without proper preparation. For example, consider the phenomenon of "confidence", which for many people is associated with "competency", "courage", "optimism", "self-esteem", "assertiveness" and more. Each of these concepts is, in turn, associated with both positive and negative ideas and emotions. "Competency" may be associated with pride and self-esteem, but also with incompetence, shame and lack of value. Similarly, "courage" might be associated with assertiveness and self-reliance, but also with danger, fear and cowardice. As a result, when we call to mind experiences of any phenomenon, we trigger a whole web of associated concepts and emotions, and clients may not always discern between the felt sense of the phenomenon they set out to explore and the felt sense of associated concepts and emotions. For example, if you ask a client what "confidence" feels like to them, without framing the question by first asking the client to identify positive and uncomplicated experiences of this phenomenon, they might respond that it feels like a "tight knot in the stomach". However, this tight knot is not the felt sense of "confidence" but rather the felt sense of an associated idea. Perhaps upon being asked about the phenomenon of "confidence" the client recalled a situation where they felt they needed to be confident because they doubted their capacity to handle the situation. Thus, the knot in the stomach may actually be the felt sense of this doubt.

In summary, when investigating the felt sense of a positive concept, it is beneficial to reference tangible, real-life examples instead of trying to answer the question abstractly. Furthermore, choosing examples that are "positive and uncomplicated" allows for a clearer and more direct exploration of the felt sense of the phenomenon, unobscured by the felt sense of associated ideas and emotions[20].

What did that feel like in the body?

The purpose of the second question is to invite the individual to turn their awareness from the abstract concept representing the phenomenon (and the

---

[20] In a sense, asking what a positive concept feels like "in itself" is a trick. When we ask this question, we decouple the concept from all associated ideas and emotions and in this way, we arrive at the felt sense of no ideas or emotions – which is Being.

network of associated ideas and emotions) towards the felt sense of the phenomenon itself. In other words, this question invites the client to use the concept as a positive entry point through which they may become aware of the felt-sense experience of Being. In so doing, the Knot of Positive Reification is untied.

If the ground has been prepared well by identifying examples of situations where the client had positive and uncomplicated experiences of the phenomenon in question, the exploration process will be fairly straightforward.

Even if the client cannot recall their exact felt sense in the identified situations, they can still observe the felt sense that emerges in them when they recall these situations. It is not crucial to provide an accurate account of what the client felt in the original situation. It is still possible to use the recollection of the situation as a means to point the client's awareness towards Being.

To facilitate this exploration, it can be useful to have a rough map of what felt sense typically underpins various phenomena. Table 4 (page 104) lists the felt sense and the positive phenomena typically associated with each of the ten Essences (aspects of Being) used in this book.

Some of the essences share similar felt sense features

In the table, both Red and Blue Essence is described as relating to the felt sense of being "energised" and Pink, Yellow and Gold are all related to "sweetness". Such overlaps occur for several reasons.

First, the overlap occurs due to the limitations of language. There is infinite variety in felt sense experience and for this reason each word must refer to a range of experiences. Thus, while it may be possible to *feel* the difference between the Red and Blue energy and the Pin, Yellow and Gold sweetness, it would be impractical to have different words for every possible nuance of felt sense. I have, however, introduced some distinction between the Gold sweetness which is often denser than the Yellow and Pink sweetness.

Second, the overlap in descriptions of the felt sense of the different Essences is due to the fact that Essences are categories describing different aspects of one single experience, namely, the felt sense of Being. As such, there is no clear boundary separating one Essence from another. People will frequently experience Being as a mix of multiple Essences, making it difficult to draw clear lines.

Table 4: Essences and related felt sense and concepts

Essence	Felt sense	Positive phenomena
White	Solid. Firm. Heavy. Downward movement. Relaxed immobile. Calm. Easeful.	Support. Grounding. Confidence. Patience. Neutrality. Perseverance. Discipline. Commitment
Red	Vibrating. Expanding. Warm. Energised. Free flow. Charged. Forward movement. Dynamic.	Strength. Courage. Passion. Vitality. Excitement. Authenticity. Truthfulness. Assertiveness. Liberation.
Black	Still. Slow. Sense of being erased. Empty. Inward movement. Absorption. Velvety soft. Dark.	Peace. Intimacy. Power. Mastery. Sacredness. Absolution. Intuition. Mystery. Magic. Non-attachment.
Green	Tender. Delicate. Moist Calm flow. Fresh or minty.	Compassion. Loving-Kindness. Human Connection. Sympathy. Agape Love. Understanding. Open hearted
Pink	Soft like cotton. Fluffy. Plump. Sweet (light). Warm. Calm.	Appreciation. Acceptance. Being Lovable. Being Loving. Perfection. Cosiness. Welcomed.
Yellow	Light. Bubbly. Uplifting. Upward movement. Sweet (light). Laughter.	Joy. Happiness. Carefreeness. Curiosity. Spontaneity. Optimism. Innocence. Light-heatedness. Unburdened. Simplicity. Desire.
Gold	Sweet (dense). Viscous. Honey-like. Soothing.	Bonding. Community. Romantic love. Unity. Surrender. Harmony. Value. Generosity.
Cream	Fullness. Creamy. Smooth.	Nourishment. Satisfaction. Fulfilment. Wholeness. Contentment. Fullness.
Blue	Sharp. Clear. Wakeful. Crisp. Fresh. Energised.	Clarity. Precision. Intelligence. Discernment. Guidance. Alertness. Inspiration.
Clear	Open. Vast. Spacious. Light.	Freedom. Openness. Receptivity. Trust. Benevolence. Loving holding.

To understand this, consider the experience of eating an apple. If the apple is good, sweetness, juiciness and crunchiness are three aspects of this experience. While we can talk about these aspects individually and choose to focus on one aspect at a time, they are ultimately part of the same experience and, as such, not altogether separate.

Some words can occur both in the concept column and in the felt sense column

In the table, I have chosen not to use the same words to describe felt sense and the positive phenomena. However, some words have dual meanings and could, therefore, be used both to describe the felt sense and a positive phenomenon based on that felt sense. For example, the word "tenderness" could appear both in the concept and felt sense columns for Green Essence, since "tenderness" can refer to an attitude (They treated the child with tenderness) as well as to a felt sense (The meat was very tender). Words that refer to both concepts and felt-sense experience reveal the strong link between phenomena and underlying felt-sense experience.

Some concepts may seem at odds with the corresponding felt sense

Some of the concepts in the table may seem to match well with their corresponding felt sense descriptions, while others may seem not to match. For example, looking at White Essence, you may find that "grounding" matches nicely with the felt sense of "heaviness" and "ease" but that "perseverance" does not. Instead, you may associate "perseverance" with a sense of energy, tension or the feeling of pushing through something.

Such seeming mismatch arises because the felt sense we experience when we contemplate a particular phenomenon is a fusion of the felt sense of the phenomenon itself and the felt sense of various associated phenomena. Thus, the sense of energy, tension or push you feel when you think about "perseverance" is the felt sense of "effort", a phenomenon that many people associate with "perseverance". However, if you focus your attention on the felt sense of "perseverance" isolated from the felt sense of "effort", you may begin to perceive it as a form of "heaviness" and "ease", as suggested in the table. Then perseverance is just the simple act of continuously putting one foot in front of the other. If there are no temptations or distractions, this act is effortless.

The more positive and uncomplicated the situations, the more likely it will be that the felt sense of the positive phenomenon we explore will match the felt sense in the table above.

That being said, as one explores the felt sense of any positive phenomenon, one will discover depth and richness that is beyond what can be captured in words. Sometimes, it can be good for clients to develop their own words and phrases that capture the experience for them. Thus, I have had clients describe the experience of Being as “inner sparkles”, “gold dust”, “inner hammock” and “dipping sauce”. If a client finds such personal names for the experience of Being, I will usually adopt these names – even if the experience the client describes fits perfectly with one of the categories I would normally name by the colour in the above table. This is because personal names often have more power for the client.

2.9. Summary

In this chapter, we have explored the Knot of Positive Reification. This knot occurs when we give an experience of Being a positive name and, in doing so, divert our attention away from Being and towards ideas related to that name.

The Knot of Positive Reification produces and is sustained by three misconceptions: that the many names we give to the experience of Being refer to wholly different entities, that these entities are separate from ourselves and that it is more important to pay attention to ideas about these entities than to simply sense them.

The way to untie the Knot of Positive Reification is through the process of Sensing Abundance, where we turn our attention back from ideas about the positive name we have given to the experience of Being and towards the felt sense that the positive name refers to.

We looked at how this process can be facilitated in one-to-one sessions and through two contemplation exercises.

Next, we look at the Knot of Conditionality in which we formulate strategies for attaining Being but in doing so only accomplish deepening our lack of awareness of Being.

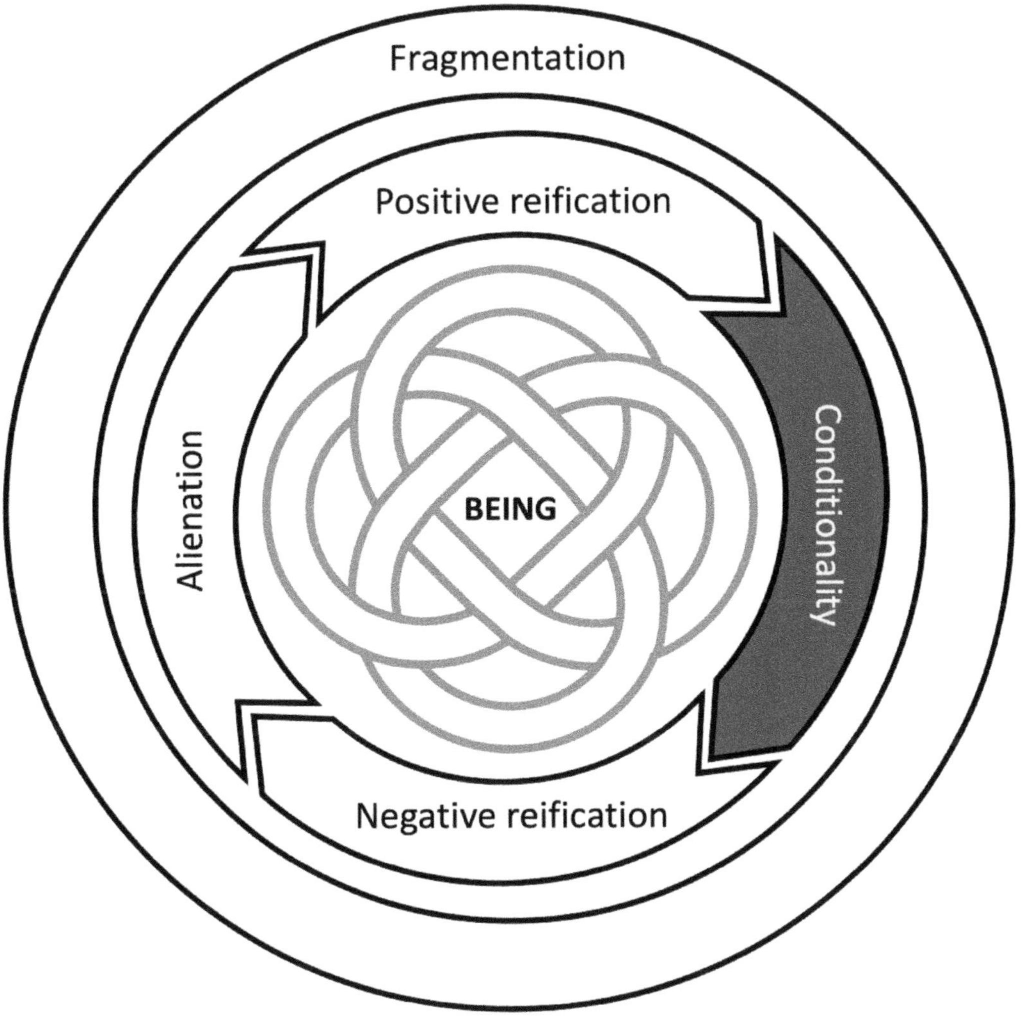

The Knot of Conditionality

3. Knot 2: The Knot of Conditionality

When we, through the process of Positive Reification, come to see Being as a positive object separate from ourselves, we are compelled to ask:

"Under what conditions can I acquire and hold on to this positive object?"

This question leads us to formulate ideas about what conditions we must fulfil to attain and hold on to Being in the form it appears to us through the process of Positive Reification.

If, for example, we experience Being as "peace", we may formulate ideas, such as, "to feel peace, I need to finish my to-do list", "to feel peace, I need to have resolved all conflicts", etc. If, on the other hand, we experience Being as "joy", "vitality", "connection", "confidence" or something else, we may formulate different ideas about how to attain and hold on to these reifications of Being.

The ability to formulate and test hypotheses about how to attain and hold on to various objects is a very useful ability. However, when applied to Being, which is not an object and does not need to be attained as it is permanently present, formulating such ideas will needlessly draw your attention away from Being. Thus, ironically enough, by trying to answer the question of how to attain Being, we can end up losing awareness of it. This is the Knot of Conditionality.

The Knot of Conditionality is untied through the process of Sensing Completion. Just like the core of the Sensing Abundance process is to use positive reifications to regain awareness of Being, the core of the Sensing Completion process is to use our desires, wishes, obsessions and compulsions to regain awareness of Being. In practice, this is done by exploring what we imagine we would feel like if we completely fulfilled the conditions we desire to fulfil. In doing so, we direct our awareness towards the ultimate goal of our desires, and this will always be the felt-sense experience of Being.

Many traditions present desires and compulsions as something which block awareness of Being and should be overcome. This is true insofar as they can be distracting. However, the Sensing Completion process provides a beautiful alternative perspective on desires and compulsions. It shows that desires and compulsions ultimately are grounded in deep love for Being and that they therefore, properly understood, can point our awareness straight to Being.

3.1. Typical conditions for reaching the 10 aspects of Being

In Section 2.3, I introduced the ten aspects of Being, which are ten distinct felt-sense states people commonly experience when they become aware of Being. For each of these aspects, I listed a range of positive phenomena, which are conceptual names people typically give to these different experiences of Being.

Table 5 expands this model by providing examples of the conditions clients typically believe they must fulfil to create or acquire the positive phenomena related to each of the ten aspects of Being[21].

Having a map like the one presented in Table 5 can greatly assist therapists in developing their ability to detect Knots of Conditionality in clients. Knowing which aspects of Being clients are typically seeking when they express a desire to fulfil certain conditions can help therapists understand clearly both what feeling the client hopes to attain by fulfilling their desired conditions and why fulfilling these conditions can never result in the creation of this feeling.

Looking at the third row in Table 5, we can, for example, say that some people seek to obtain a sense of confidence (a positive reification of the White aspect of Being) by working hard to acquire skills and achievements. They believe that acquiring more skills and achievements will give them a sense of confidence. However, working hard to acquire skills and achievements will take their awareness away from Being and, thus, from the felt sense they interpret as confidence. When this happens, the individual will interpret the absence of this feeling as lack of confidence and as evidence that they are not working hard enough. Consequently, there is no upper limit to how hard they will work.

Thus, the map sheds light on how workaholism can derive from a client's desire to feel the White aspect of Being combined with the positive reification of this aspect as "confidence" and the false idea that the confidence the client longs for is created by acquiring skills and achievements through hard work.

---

[21] The conditions mentioned in Table 5 are far from exhaustive. However, they do illustrate the principle of how the desires to fulfil certain conditions can be motivated by a wish to reach specific aspects of Being. More extensive lists will be made available in the book series dealing with the details of each aspect of Being.

Table 5: Conditions people fulfill to create or acquire positive reifications of the 10 aspects of Being

Essence / felt sense	Positive reification	Conditions
White	Support	Maintain stability in work and relationships
Solid	Grounding	Resist influence
Firm	Confidence	Acquire skills & achievements
Heavy	Patience	Repress frustration. Give up
	Neutrality	Be indifferent. Have no opinions
Red	Strength	Dominate others. Pick fights
Vibrating	Courage	Face fears. Leave comfort zone
Expanding	Passion	Suspend control & reason. Infatuation
Warm	Vitality	Thrill-seeking. Excessive risk-taking
	Authenticity	Challenging social norms
Black	Peace	Withdraw
Still	Non-attachment	Erase personal wishes & desires
Slow	Mastery/Power	Eliminate disturbances
Empty	Sacredness	Disinterest in the world
	Absolution	Renunciation
Green	Compassion	Reduce sadness & hurt
Tender	Loving-Kindness	Forgive transgressors
Delicate	Connection	Share hurt & vulnerability
Moist	Sympathy	Help vulnerable people
	Agape Love	Self-sacrifice
Pink	Appreciation	Give & receive gratitude
Soft	Acceptance	Gain fame & fans
Fluffy	Lovable/loving	Focus on the positive in self and others
Plump	Perfection	Living up to an ideal
	Cosiness	Create a comfortable environment
Yellow	Joy	Seek entertainment & novelty
Light	Happiness	Prioritising personal enjoyment
Bubbly	Carefreeness	Reject seriousness & difficulties
Uplifting	Curiosity	Perpetual exploration
	Spontaneity	Impulsive actions & decisions
Gold	Bonding	Relinquish boundaries
Sweet	Community	Give up individuality & autonomy
Viscous	Romantic love	Nurture emotional connection
Honey-like	Unity	Eliminate or downplay differences
	Surrender	Let go of control
Cream	Nourishment	Fulfilling needs
Full	Satisfaction	Seek instant gratification
Creamy	Fulfilment	Accomplish goals
Smooth	Wholeness	Avoid change to preserve coherence
	Contentment	Limiting or denying needs
Blue	Clarity	Brutal honesty
Sharp	Precision	Measure & quantify everything
Clear	Intelligence	Acquire & display knowledge
Wakeful	Discernment	Follow a doctrine unquestioningly
	Guidance	Critique others' ideas frequently
Clear	Freedom	Reject all constraints
Open	Openness	Accept all ideas and opinions equally
Vast	Receptivity	Reject discernment & filtering
Spacious	Trust	Excessive / insufficient scepticism
	Benevolence	Offer unsolicited advice or help

It is important to mention that clients are different and whereas the map can help in developing useful hypotheses about which aspect of Being a client is longing for, it is always necessary to test such hypotheses through the conversation with the client. The map should be used to enhance the therapist's live investigations – not to replace them.

It is also worth mentioning that different people may seek the same aspect of Being through opposite strategies.

For example, some people try to get a sense of "trust" (a positive phenomenon related to the Clear aspect of Being) by engaging in excessive scepticism and distrusting everything. Such people believe that they can only trust things and people after thorough testing.

Other people try to get a sense of "trust" by abandoning scepticism altogether. Such people believe that they can only feel trust by being trusting and that this means setting aside all scepticism.

Insofar as "trust" refers to an aspect of the felt sense we experience when we are aware of Being, both the above strategies are problematic because following them takes our awareness away from Being in the present moment.

For the first strategy, the activity that takes the individual's attention away from Being is testing trustworthiness; as long as their attention is monopolised by this activity, they will not *feel* trust even if they have every reason to trust. The individual will interpret this absence of the felt sense of trust as evidence that they have not tested enough. Consequently, they will never end their testing.

For the second strategy, the activity that takes the individual's attention away from Being is cultivating the naivety they call "being trusting", for example by inventing excuses for any indication of deception; again, as long as their attention is monopolised by this activity, they will not *feel* trust. The individual will interpret this absence of the felt sense of trust as evidence that they have not become trusting enough. Consequently, they will never cease in their attempts to eliminate even the most legitimate of concerns.

Thus, different people may seek a particular aspect of Being through opposite strategies. However, because aspects of Being are not created through any action, both strategies will result in the Knot of Conditionality.

A more extensive table with more positive reifications and conditions people seek to fulfil to create or acquire them can be found at www.the5knots.com/resources.

3.2. Conditional vs. unconditional phenomena

It can be useful to distinguish between conditional and unconditional phenomena. This distinction allows us to express the Knot of Conditionality as the fallacy of perceiving that which is unconditional as conditional.

To understand this, we can look at the popular concept of "unconditional love".

Unconditional love is a core concept in many spiritual traditions. Unconditional love is often depicted as an infinite, ever-present love that is inherent to the fabric of reality. It is not an emotional state but rather a pervasive truth about the intrinsic worth and connectedness of all beings. Unconditional love is often likened to the sun in that it shines equally on all, irrespective of their actions or the paths they choose in life. Thus, unconditional love is unconditional in the sense that no conditions needs to be fulfilled for it to be present.

Unconditional love is contrasted with conditional love. Conditional love is conditional in the sense that it is only present if certain conditions are fulfilled. It is contingent upon, for example conforming to certain norms, meeting certain criteria or fulfilling certain expectations. Sentences such as "I love you if...", "I love you when..." or "I love you because...", and "I feel loved when..." are expressions of conditional love.

When clients seek love, they seek unconditional love. But the way clients seek love is by trying to figure out what conditions they must fulfil to feel love, and what clients find in this way is conditional love.

Sometimes, "unconditional love" is, mistakenly, understood as the act of setting aside any reservation one has about loving. However, a love that can only be experienced if we fulfil the condition of having no reservations is a conditional love.

Of course, people may be more friendly disposed towards us when we meet their expectations and conform to certain norms. We can call this friendly disposition conditional love if we like. But it is important to recognise that it is a radically different phenomenon from unconditional love and that it gets its appeal, beyond the purely practical level, from being mistaken for unconditional love. Conditional love is like the moon that reflects the light of the sun but has no light of its own. We seek conditional love because in it we see the reflection of the unconditional love we truly long for.

In the same way that we can make the distinction between conditional and unconditional love, we can make the same distinction for all other positive phenomena. We can distinguish between conditional joy that can only be experienced when we fulfil certain conditions, such as succeeding with a project, and unconditional joy which is an inherent part of Being. We can distinguish between conditional peace that can only be experienced when we fulfil certain conditions, such as having no conflicts with other people, and unconditional peace which is an inherent part of Being.

When we work with the Knot of Conditionality, we examine conditioned phenomena and gradually separate them from all conditions we have associated with them. This work reveals that the essence of any conditioned phenomenon is an unconditioned phenomenon. By exploring the light of the moon, we discover the sun as the source of this light.

Next, we will look at how understanding the Knot of Conditionality sheds light on five misconceptions clients typically operate from that make unconditional phenomena appear conditional. We will also look at how this understanding changes what kind of questions guide therapy.

3.3. The Knot of Conditionality and implications for therapy

The Knot of Conditionality can be broken down into five interrelated misconceptions. The first of these is a consequence of the positive reification of Being discussed in the previous chapter. The subsequent four misconceptions are derivatives of the first, emerging in a causal chain. Consequently, these five misconceptions form a continuum of beliefs that progressively steer the client away from the awareness of Being.

Seeing Being as an entity that is separate from oneself leads to the belief that at different times it may be present or absent (4th misconception). This leads to the belief that to have what you seek you must create or acquire it (5th misconception), by actively doing something you are not currently doing (6th misconception). This leads to *specific* beliefs about what conditions you must fulfil through your actions to create or acquire what you seek (7th misconception). Because you see the fulfilment of certain conditions as what causes the positive phenomenon you seek, this activity will take on a certain level of importance and, over time, you may forget that fulfilling these conditions is a means to create or acquire Being and instead come to see the fulfilment of the conditions as a goal in itself (8th misconception).

For example, the moment you see "peace" as something separate from yourself, you will perceive it as something that is there sometimes and not at other times (4th misconception). You will believe that "peace" can be created or acquired (5th misconception) and that to create or acquire "peace", you must actively do something (6th misconception). You may develop specific ideas about what conditions will bring you "peace", such as finishing your to-do list or resolving all conflicts (7th misconception). Over time, you may start to perceive the fulfilment of these conditions (finishing your to-do list or resolving conflicts) as goals in themselves, forgetting that the reason you desire to do this is that you believe doing so is a way of creating or acquiring "peace" (8th misconception).

To untie the Knot of Conditionality, the therapist must shift each of these misconceptions by taking the client through lines of inquiry that will help them discover for themselves that what they seek is always already present (4th corrective principle); that rather than creating or acquiring what they seek, they must become aware of it (5th corrective principle); that to become aware of what they seek, they do not need to do something they are *not* currently doing but rather cease doing something they *are* currently doing which prevents them from noticing Being (6th corrective principle); that what they are doing to create or acquire what they seek is counterproductive because any form of searching will monopolise their attention in such a way that they become less likely to notice Being (7th corrective principle); and lastly, that their perceived goals are often merely the conditions they believe they must fulfil to reach their actual goal which is the reified felt sense of Being (8th corrective principle).

It is useful to notice clients' position within the continuum of misconceptions at the beginning of a therapy session as this can give clues as to what misconception to focus on in the therapeutic work. For this reason, I have included in the subsequent descriptions of the five misconceptions some observations on how clients typically present their problem at each stage of the continuum.

3.3.1. Misconception 4: What you seek may come and go

The first misconception underpinning the Knot of Conditionality is the belief that what we seek can come and go, that it is the kind of thing we can acquire and lose.

This misconception is a consequence of reification. The moment we view Being as a concrete thing, we will assume that it can be acquired and lost just like any other concrete thing, such as chairs, apples or houses.

It is due to this misconception that it feels normal to us to talk about “finding love” or “losing love”, “gathering up courage” or “losing one’s courage”, “seeking peace” or “finding no peace”, and so on. All such phrases are based on the perception of “love”, “courage”, “peace”, etc. being phenomena that can be acquired or lost.

However, insofar as love, courage and peace are aspects of Being, and Being is inevitably always present, these phenomena are not the kind of phenomena that *can* come and go.

The nature of these phenomena, like the nature of Being, is akin to physical space. Space is not like concrete things. There is never more or less of it. It can contain more things or fewer things, but the amount of space is always the same. We can be aware of it or not. But even if we are not aware of space, it is still there – unchanged.

Sometimes, people will, of course, think about space as if it were a concrete thing. One might talk about “taking space for oneself” or “having no space”. However, these expressions are not really about “space”. If, for example, we “take space” in a conversation, we mean that we are directing other people’s attention to what we have to say. Thus, in this context “taking space” isn’t about getting more space per se but rather about influencing what others pay attention to. Similarly, when we talk about having “no space”, it is often a description of our plan for what to do in the future. “I have no space in my calendar next week” means that we have made a lot of appointments and that it is unrealistic to try to do more things that particular week. Similarly, “I need to have more space for myself” generally means that we feel we are spending too much time on things relating to others and not enough on things we want to do ourselves. In none of these examples are we suggesting that there is more or less space. Instead, we use the word “space” metaphorically to talk about attention or how we have allocated time to different tasks in the future.

Thus, whenever a client says that they would like to have more “love”, “aliveness”, “peace”, “connection”, and so on, they are not being precise. They speak as if these phenomena are present in insufficient amounts or are altogether missing. But if these things are aspects of Being, they cannot be missing – just like space can never be missing. Thus, what the clients are really saying is that they do not *feel* these phenomena. Understanding this distinction is of vital importance in therapy because it leads to very different lines of inquiry.

Implications for therapy

At first glance, the distinction made above might seem trivial, but it is not. It carries profound implications for therapy.

For instance, if a client experiences a deficiency of "love," it is important to know whether it is because the client is lacking "love", or because the client is unable to perceive the "love" that is already there. It's not just a matter of semantics. It fundamentally changes the central question to be explored in the therapeutic process.

Traditional approaches to therapy may begin from the question:

- What is wrong with the client? or What is the client lacking?

Being-Centred Therapy, on the other hand, begins from the questions:

- What prevents the client from recognising that there is fundamentally nothing wrong with them?
- What prevents the client from perceiving that they are fundamentally whole and lack nothing?

If the client (and therapist) believes the client is truly missing love, the therapy will focus on answering the question of how to acquire love. However, trying to answer this question is exactly what creates the Knot of Conditionality. Imagining what conditions we need to fulfil to get what we mistakenly believe we are missing distracts us from noticing that we already have it.

If, on the other hand, the client merely cannot feel love, the question becomes why the client cannot feel something that is always present. Answering this question will reveal the blocks and open the possibility for circumventing them.

The answer to this question generally falls in one of two categories.

First, the client can have prejudices against love that makes them avoid noticing it, and this entire process is unconscious.

Second, the client can be so caught up in some project that they have no awareness left to notice love. Ironically enough, the project that blocks the client's awareness of love is often the project of trying to figure out how to obtain love. This is what is meant by not noticing it because you are too busy looking for it.

Thus, when a client says they lack love, peace, vitality, joy, connection, etc. the guiding question you should hold as a therapist is not "How might the client acquire what they lack?" but rather "How is it possible that the client fails to recognise that they are already full of what they are seeking?"

Of course, simply telling clients they already have what they seek will be of little use. They will most likely not believe you, and presenting a viewpoint that is so at odds with a client's perception of the situation could potentially harm the therapeutic relationship.

Thus, in practice, your task as a therapist is to provide your client with experiences that challenge and make them doubt their established narrative of deficiency.

One way of doing this is the process of Sensing Completion, which I will describe later in this chapter. This process focuses on encouraging the client to imagine that they have already fulfilled all the conditions they believe they need to fulfil to gain what they seek and then describe what that feels like. If, for example, the client believes they need to be more charming to attract love, you can first invite them to imagine that they are the most charming person on the planet and that they have attracted love. Next, you can ask them to describe this love. In doing so, you invite the client to move their attention from the project of fulfilling the conditions to the felt sense of that which they seek. And since what they seek is already here, the client will experience it when they direct their attention towards it. Once the client feels what they seek, you can simply point out that they now feel the love they seek, without having to become any more charming. This experience will sow the seed of doubt in the client; they will no longer be certain that they lack love and must increase their charm to acquire it.

4th corrective principle: What you seek is always already present

The 4th corrective principle is:

> "Clients always already have what they ultimately seek, because what they ultimately seek is always Being and Being is always present."

This principle helps us avoid being drawn into the clients' narratives of lack or deficiency. Holding this principle in mind helps us recognise our clients as inherently whole. Despite their personal interpretations of themselves and their environment, which might make it challenging for them to navigate the world, they fundamentally lack nothing.

This principle reminds us that the issues clients face is not that they are deficient but that they are unaware of their inherent wholeness. The issues are akin to a mechanic working on a functioning car with a faulty tool or a functional computer running software that contains bugs.

3.3.2. Misconception 5: What you seek is created or acquired

The second misconception related to the Knot of Conditionality is the belief that what you seek must be either created or acquired.

This misconception is a consequence of the previous one, that it is possible for you to not have what you seek. If what you seek can be absent, then there are only two ways of obtaining it. Either you can create it yourself, or you can go out and find it.

Clients may say that they want to "create more connection in their life", "create more confidence in themselves", "acquire peace within themselves", "get more joy into their daily routines", "cultivate love for themselves and others", "manifest joy in their lives", "create harmony in their relationships", "acquire serenity amidst life's challenges", "manifest strength in the face of adversity", etc.

All the above statements share a common structure. They describe a domain (life, themselves, their daily routines, their relationships, etc.) that is perceived to be lacking something, which, thus, needs to be created or acquired.

Consequently, these statements embody a distinct interpretation of the client's predicament. They see the situation they describe as akin to a situation where a container (their life, themselves, etc.) needs to be filled with a certain substance (connection, confidence, peace, etc.) which is currently absent or insufficient.

Insofar as that which the client is missing is an aspect of Being, any understanding taking the above form is at odds with reality and will, therefore, be a poor guide for the client.

Implications for therapy

When clients frame their issue as a matter of a certain place or container lacking something, which the therapist recognises as a reification of Being, the therapeutic process should aim at challenging this perspective rather than supporting the client in finding ways to fill the perceived void.

If the therapist accepts the client's perspective, the therapy will end up reinforcing the client's misconceived way of understanding the situation and, thus, making it even more difficult for the client to realise that they already have what they seek.

In practice, this often involves guiding the client through a series of questions that will lead them to become aware of Being in the present moment. Through this process, the client can discover for themselves that what they seek is not something that can be created or acquired but rather an ever-present reality they can become aware of. All the processes in this book aim to do just that.

5th corrective principle: You don't create what you seek; you become aware of it

The 5th corrective principle of Being-Centred Therapy is

> "Because what clients seek is already present, the remedy to their perceived lack lies not in creating or acquiring what they believe they lack, but in becoming aware of its presence."

Bearing this principle in mind helps you avoid becoming entangled in the client's metaphor of their issue being analogous to the challenge of filling an empty container with the right substance. It is worth reminding yourself that the client has most likely operated from this understanding for many years, yet despite years of striving, they have failed to create or acquire what they perceived to be lacking; that is, after all, the reason they have sought your help.

Whenever a particular understanding has persistently failed to yield results, it is crucial to question the understanding itself[22]. Clients often come to therapy with the preconceived notion that they need help finding a way to create or acquire what they feel they lack. As a therapist, it is your job to challenge the taken-for-granted assumption about deficiency that has been guiding the client's efforts so far. You must help the client discover that the reason they haven't been able to remedy their perceived lack is that there is no lack to remedy.

The way to do this is to help the client become aware of what they thought they were lacking in the present moment. This process can be likened to a client approaching you, distressed over how to rectify their perceived lack of a nose, and you, as the therapist, simply holding up a mirror so they can discover for themselves that they already have a nose. Engaging in dialogue about how to create or acquire a nose, when a nose is clearly present, is counterproductive. It doesn't address the actual misperception responsible for the client's distress.

---

[22] Gregory Bateson refers to this shift in the focus of one's inquiry as Deutero Learning, Learning 2 or second order learning (Bateson, 1972a, c). Argyris and Schön have popularised Bateson's concept in organisational studies as double-loop learning (Argyris, 1977; Schön, 1986). I will return to second order learning in Section 5.4.

3.3.3. Misconception 6: You get what you seek by doing something

The third misconception related to the Knot of Conditionality is the belief that you create or acquire what you seek by actively *doing* something.

This misconception is a consequence of the previous one. If you believe what you seek must be created or acquired this implies that you must play an active part – that you must *do* something – to get what you seek.

Thus, the client will say they have come to therapy to find out "*how* to create more space for myself", "*how* to find and hold on to love", "*how* to become more confident", "*how* to find meaning in my life", "*how* to be more resilient", etc.

Such problem formulations presuppose the two previous misconceptions: that the client is missing something and that what they are missing must be created or acquired. It is these two misconceptions that lead the client to ask: *How* can I create or acquire what I lack?

If you, as a therapist, uncritically engage with these types of questions, you inadvertently endorse the two embedded misconceptions, and the subsequent therapy will, thus, reinforce and solidify them. When the client's desired states are reifications of Being, such as space, love, confidence, meaning and resilience, it is the role of the therapist to push the pause button and invite the client to examine the assumptions embedded in their understanding of their situation before continuing their exploration. Exploration that is based on false assumptions will be likely to only lead the client astray. For exploration to lead to genuine insight and growth, it must be based on a sound foundation.

Implications for therapy

When an assumption we build our understanding of a situation on is reversed, it reverses how it makes sense for us to address the situation.

If we assume that we are lacking something, it follows that to experience what we miss, we need to do something.

If, on the other hand, we make the opposite assumption that we already have what we seek, it follows that we must be doing something to block our perception and, thus, to experience what we miss, we need to *stop* doing that something.

In practical terms, this means that the therapy aimed at bringing the client in touch with what they seek should not focus on identifying what actions the client should take to create or acquire what they seek but rather on identifying what the client is already doing that distracts them from noticing that they already have what they seek. Rather than encouraging the client to do more, we should encourage the client to do less.

In other words, if what you seek is already present, you must be doing something actively to prevent yourself from noticing this. Thus, the problem is not that there is something you are *not* doing that you should be doing. The problem is that there is something you *are* doing which, if you stopped doing it, would make it easier to perceive what you seek.

For example, a client may tell you that they find their life has no meaning and that they would like to work with you to find out how to make their life more meaningful. In other words, they perceive a lack of "meaning" and believe they have to do something to create or acquire meaning, but they are not sure what.

It might be tempting to accept the client's premise and assume that the client doesn't feel meaning because they fail to do things in life that are meaningful to them. From this perspective, the therapy might revolve around uncovering what the client finds meaningful and what limiting beliefs and/or circumstances in their life hold them back from doing that.

If you engage in this line of inquiry, you may, for example, find that the client has a deep passion for history, but they have chosen to work as a banker because they believe that one cannot make a living as a historian. In this case, the therapy may address this belief, see its origin and challenge its veracity. The outcome of the session may be that the client finds ways of engaging with their passion for history – professionally or in some other way. The hope is that this will bring a sense of meaning to the client's life.

Alternatively, you may find that the client may have a deep desire to start a family and raise children as they believe this would be profoundly meaningful for them. However, they may be with a partner who doesn't want to have children or doesn't feel ready to have children. In this case, the therapy may explore why the client stays in a relationship that prevents them from doing what they find meaningful, or, if the therapist works with the couple, they may explore whether the partner's reluctance to start a family arises from certain interpersonal dynamics in the relationship and what can be done to resolve these.

In both cases, the assumption guiding the therapy is that if the client finds ways of doing what is meaningful to them, they will acquire the sense of meaning in their life they currently feel they lack.

However, from the perspective of Being-Centred Therapy, "meaning" is an aspect of Being and thus the reason the client is not feeling meaning should be sought by asking what the client is currently doing that prevents them from being aware of the sense of meaning inherent in Being.

This perspective encourages the therapist to view the absence of meaning the client experiences as something peculiar in want of an explanation. They should ask themselves how the client manages to avoid noticing the meaning that is inherent in their very existence.

Listening from this perspective might reveal to you that the client who is passionate about history tends to be passionate about whatever they are not doing and grow easily bored with whatever they are doing. Thus, they have a pattern of perpetually seeking new thrills, and that pattern takes their awareness away from Being and the present moment. If they managed to turn history into their new profession, they would be excited for a while and then grow bored and long for the next thing they don't have. Thus, to become aware of Being, the client should not *do* something extra (turn history into their profession); rather, the client should *stop doing* something (engage in seeking thrills by trying new things).

Similarly, if you ask yourself how the client who wants to start a family manages to overlook the meaning that is inherent in their very existence, you may find that they are perpetually focused on lamenting what they do not have. They might have a pattern of glass-half-empty thinking. If you become curious about what motivates this thinking, you may find that the client uses stories of misfortune as a means to connect with and elicit support from other people. It is this constant concern with what they do not have (and others do have) that occupies their awareness in such a way that they do not let their awareness rest in Being. If the therapy helped them find a partner and start a family, it is likely that they would start lamenting things that were missing in their partner, their relationship, their children, etc. To become aware of Being, the client does not have to do something they are not already doing (start a family). Rather, they should *stop doing* something (use stories of what is missing in their life to try to create connection and support).

It is worth noticing that in both of the above cases, the client may indeed briefly experience meaning once they achieve what they wanted, i.e. once they turn history into their profession or start a family, respectively. However, this is not because these actions create meaning but because these actions momentarily pause the patterns that take the client's awareness away from Being. On the first day in the new job, the first client will not be concerned with finding a new thrill. In the first month(s) building a family the second client may forget to look for what is missing in their lives. Thus, in both cases the sense of meaning comes because the client's awareness is not monopolised by their patterns. However, it is easy to mistakenly see the sense of meaning the client experiences as caused by what they did – rather than by what they stopped doing. I will describe this in more detail in the section The mechanism of Sensing on page 142.

The purpose of Being-Centred Therapy is to help the client notice Being in general.

Doing something to remove a single distraction is nice but it is treatment of a symptom rather than the cause.

Identifying the patterns that block the client's perception of Being and inviting them to relinquish these patterns, on the other hand, will have a lasting effect since it works on the root cause of the client's suffering.

Finally, it is worth noting that in the above examples the patterns that prevent the clients from noticing Being are motivated by a wish to find Being. The first client is distracted by the pattern of looking for new thrills. This pattern is a search for "excitement", which is a reification of Being. The second client is distracted by the glass-half-empty pattern. This pattern is a search for "connection" and "support", both of which are reifications of Being.

Thus, if these clients become aware of Being, they will not only feel their life is inherently meaningful; they will also feel excitement, connection and support, and this will make the patterns that take their attention away from Being superfluous. Because our search for Being takes our awareness away from Being it is counterproductive. This is the topic for the next section. But first, let's summarise the above discussion with a corrective principle that can guide therapy.

6th corrective principle: You become aware of what you seek by stopping doing something.

The 6th corrective principle of Being-Centred Therapy is:

> "To become aware of Being, you should not ask what you need to do but rather what you need to stop doing."

Bearing this principle in mind helps us remember to look for what blocks the client's perception of what they seek rather than hypothesise about what might create it. It directs our attention towards the cause of the client's suffering rather than towards the symptoms.

Links to other systems

The principle that it can be more effective to do less rather than more is expressed by many thinkers in both psychological and spiritual traditions.

Philosophers from Epicurus to Henry David Thoreau have emphasised reduction of desires and striving in life as a path to tranquillity.

The principle is also found in the world of art in the minimalist notion: "less is more".

Some approaches to therapy, such as Mindfulness-based Stress Reduction (MBSR) and Acceptance and Commitment Therapy (ACT), focus on accepting one's inner experience as it is, rather than struggling with it or trying to control it. Other therapeutic approaches, such as Gestalt Therapy and Expressive Arts Therapy, emphasise the importance of spontaneous expressions, which are less effortful than more deliberate expressions.

Among spiritual traditions, the principle is reflected in the Buddhist encouragement to let go of desires and expectations, in the Sufi encouragement to surrender to the will of God, and in the Hindu encouragement to be detached from the fruits of one's labour.

However, the 6th corrective principle is probably most elegantly expressed in the Taoist notion of Wu Wei, which can be translated as "non-action" or "effortless action". Wu Wei suggests that one can achieve optimal results by aligning with the natural flow of things rather than exerting forceful or excessive effort. Wu Wei encourages acting spontaneously, intuitively, and in accordance with the natural course of events. This involves being in a state of harmony, allowing actions to arise naturally without resistance or interference. It is a practice of surrendering to the Tao, the ineffable principles that govern all things. When the practitioner of Tao allows actions to arise in this manner, they embody the principle of "doing without doing".

While this principle is popular and widespread as an idea, it is far from easy to put into practice. One of the main challenges is that non-doing or effortless doing can become the new agenda. If one struggles to implement the principle, one is not following it. I will expand on this in Chapter 7, where I explore different methods for embodying teachings, such as the Taoist teaching on Wu Wei.

3.3.4. Misconception 7: You get what you seek by fulfilling certain conditions

The fourth misconception related to the Knot of Conditionality is the belief that you need to fulfil certain conditions to create or acquire what you believe you lack.

This is a misconception for two reasons. First, insofar as what you seek is an aspect of Being, there are no conditions you need to fulfil to create or acquire it. Second, and more importantly, focusing your attention on the task of fulfilling any conditions can take your attention away from noticing Being. Thus, engaging in the very actions you believe will bring you what you seek is, in reality, preventing you from noticing that it is already here. Thus, trying to create aspects of Being is likely to be counterproductive.

This misconception is a consequence of the previous one. Formulating ideas regarding what specific conditions to fulfil to remedy perceived deficiencies is a response to the idea that you must do *something* to resolve such deficits. Clients with this type of misconception will enter therapy, not only with the belief that they must take action to create or acquire what they feel is lacking, but with specific notions about *what* they need to do. Hence, it's not uncommon for clients to arrive at therapy with a fully conceived plan they hope the therapist will assist them in executing.

Clients may say things such as "if only I could find the right partner, I'd feel happy", "I want to learn to find joy in the small things in life", "I want to be more grateful for what I have, so I can be at ease", "I need to build inner peace through mindfulness", "my life feels meaningless without a family of my own", "I want to find a job where I can feel valuable and feel I'm making a real difference", or "I want to establish a habit of exercising so I can get my vitality back".

The above statements all embody the previous three misconceptions and add a concrete idea about what specific conditions the client believes they need to fulfil to attain what they feel they lack. Thus, all the above examples explicitly state:

- A notion of what the client is seeking: Happiness, joy, ease, peace, meaning, value, and vitality.
- A strategy of how the client believes they can attain this: By finding the right partner, learning to appreciate the little things, being grateful for what they have, engaging in mindfulness practices, starting a family, finding the right job, and establishing a habit of exercising.

As a therapist, you may believe in some of these methods while being sceptical of others. Thus, it can be tempting to engage either in a discussion of how to implement the client's proposed method if you believe it is good, or in a discussion about finding alternatives to the proposed method if you believe it is problematic. Traditional therapy may, for example, evaluate clients' goals using the SMART framework which states that good goals should be specific, measurable, achievable, relevant and time-bound.

However, if you, as a therapist, engage the client in discussions about *any* method for creating or acquiring what they feel they lack, you have accepted the client's view of themselves as someone who is, indeed, lacking happiness, joy, ease, peace, meaning, value, vitality, or whatever the client seeks.

Since these phenomena are reifications of Being, the client is not lacking any of them. The reason they do not feel them is that they are too busy meddling with themselves and their habits to notice Being. Regardless of whether you are successful in finding a good plan and helping the client implement it, any session with such a focus will unintentionally reinforce the idea that the client is, at present, lacking what they seek – which from the perspective of Being-Centred Therapy is one of the misconceptions that are the root cause of the client's suffering. In other words, a session with a focus on methods is a session focusing on chasing mirages.

Thus, it is good to be sceptical about the plans clients bring to therapy – not only because these plans may be bad but, more importantly, because the whole idea of needing a plan presupposes a misconception around the true nature of what the client seeks.

Implications for therapy

When clients arrive at therapy with fully conceived plans for how to "fix" themselves, it is recommendable to play along to preserve the therapeutic relationship while (secretly) gathering what you need to reveal to the client the counterproductive nature of their project and point their awareness towards Being.

Even if it is a misconception, it is still useful to listen carefully to the client's ideas about what conditions they need to fulfil to create or acquire what they believe they lack. I frequently encourage clients to provide detailed accounts of their plans to remedy their deficiencies.

The reason for doing so is not to help the client implement their plan in real life; rather the reason is that the client's ideas about what conditions they believe they need to fulfil contain information you can use to construct scenarios or thought experiments that can point the client's awareness towards Being and help them discover that what they seek is already present and that trying to fulfil those conditions is exactly what has prevented them from noticing this earlier.

Before you can effectively challenge the client's current view of their situation, you need to understand intimately and in detail the mental, emotional and behavioural patterns they use to make sense of their situation.

A detailed understanding of the client's way of making sense of the situation will, at minimum, include answers to the following questions:

- What is the client seeking?
    - What aspect of Being is the client ultimately reaching for?
- What does the client believe they have to change about themselves to get what they seek?
    - Do they want to acquire new behaviour/habits?
    - Do they want to change certain beliefs or thoughts?
    - Do they want to feel differently about certain things/situations?
- What does the client believe they have to change about others, or the world, to get what they seek?
    - How does the client want others to see them?
    - How does the client want other people to feel?
    - How does the client want other people to behave?
- What does the client see as the main barriers to making the changes they believe they need to make to get what they seek?
    - Do they see their plan as unrealistic?
    - Do they see potential negative side effects of implementing their plan?
    - Do they know what they want to change but not how?

With this information, you can create a scenario in which the client has got exactly what they want. And if you ask the client what they feel when considering this scenario, they are likely to provide a description that contains positive entry points, which you can then use to direct their awareness towards Being.

To make these scenarios effective, you need concrete and specific information. If your understanding of the client's plan is too generic, you cannot trigger their experience of Being. It is not enough to know that the client wants to be a better person or wants a more loving partner. You need to know exactly what "better" or "loving" means to the client in concrete terms.

It is important to note that the plan the client presents doesn't have to be good for this to work. The plan can be fraught with negative consequences, unrealistic expectations and psychologically naïve assumptions. None of that matters. As long as the client is enthusiastic about their plan and believes it can bring them what they feel they lack, it can be used to create a scenario that points the client's awareness towards Being.

Using clients' own ideas about what conditions they need to fulfil in order to attain what they believe they lack, as a means to make clients aware that what they seek is already present, is the core of the process Sensing Completion which I will describe later in Section 3.4 Sensing Completion – how to untie the Knot of Conditionality .

Once a client has connected with the aspect of Being they seek in the therapy session, you are in a good position to challenge the misconception that they need to fulfil certain conditions to create or acquire what they seek. To do so, you need only ask them whether they feel what they seek, and if they say "Yes" (which they should do if you have used the positive entry point effectively), you can point out that, in this very moment, they are feeling what they were seeking even though they have not fulfilled the conditions they thought they needed to fulfil. Thus, they must have used a "shortcut".

If you really want to challenge the client's view of their situation, you can suggest that the reason they do not feel what they seek is not that it is lacking (after all they feel it currently) but rather that they are too busy trying to fulfil the conditions to notice it. Thus, the project of fulfilling the conditions they believe they need to fulfil to attain what they seek is not only inefficient – it is counterproductive.

Making these observations at the right time can be very powerful. I will describe this process in more detail in Section 3.4.4, Step 3: Correct misconceptions related to the Knot of Conditionality, in the sub-sections

- Access and the 4th and 5th corrective principles
- Non-doing and the 6th corrective principle
- Counterproductivity and the 7th corrective principle

7th corrective principle: Fulfilling conditions is counterproductive

When a client comes to a therapy session and asks you to help them learn to fulfil certain conditions, they believe they must fulfil to remedy a perceived lack in themselves, it is useful to remember the 7th corrective principle:

> "Fulfilling conditions is often counterproductive because it distracts you from noticing that what you seek is already present and, thus, reinforces the experience of and belief in the separation (2nd misconception)."

Remembering this principle can help you avoid the pitfall of engaging in discussions about what constitutes good or bad methods for acquiring love, peace, harmony, connection, vitality, joy, and other reifications of Being.

It helps you remember that the things the client seeks are inherently a part of their true nature, Being, and that the real questions to answer through the therapy are:

- What specific patterns in the client block the perception of their Being?
- How can you use information about these patterns to point the client's awareness towards Being?

3.3.5. Misconception 8: Fulfilling conditions is a goal in itself

The fifth misconception related to the Knot of Conditionality is mistaking the conditions one believes one must fulfil to achieve one's goal for the goal itself.

This misconception arises from the previous ones which lead you to believe that you are lacking something and that you need to fulfil certain conditions to create or acquire what you lack. Consequently, you find yourself working tirelessly to fulfil these conditions, oblivious to the fact that this pursuit is, in fact, counterproductive. The longer this state of affairs continues, the more likely it is for you to lose sight of why you embarked on fulfilling these conditions in the first place, with only the belief in their importance remaining. Eventually, you might mistakenly start viewing the fulfilment of these conditions as an end in itself, rather than the means to an end. This is the fifth misconception related to the Knot of Conditionality.

To understand this misconception and its resolution, it is instructive to look at a parallel situation that will be familiar to any therapist.

In therapy, it is common to see clients retaining, in adult life, behavioural patterns they initially evolved as coping strategies to handle challenges in their childhood family environment. These patterns, despite being potentially burdensome to uphold, may persist long after environmental shifts have rendered them unnecessary; this is because the clients may have lost sight of the patterns' original purpose and now view the maintenance of these behavioural patterns as an important goal in itself. In other words, they come to see the behaviour as intrinsically significant, forgetting that it was initially a means to an end.

In such cases, therapy can help the client realise the initial objectives of their behaviours and recognise that those same objectives can be met more effectively, and with less distress, in new ways because their current circumstances differ significantly from their childhood environment.

As an example of this, one can think of an individual who, as a child, was the peacemaker in a family where the family members frequently were in conflict with each other. This person may have developed the habit of always putting others' needs before their own, trying to defuse any hint of tension, even at the expense of their own needs and feelings. The goal of this behaviour is to ensure the individual's own safety and well-being by defusing conflict between the family members the child depends upon.

As an adult, this individual might continue this habit in their relationships, continually suppressing their own desires and emotions in order to maintain peace. This behaviour could lead to feelings of resentment and frustration over time, as they continually side-line their own needs – undermining the individual's relationships and well-being. Moreover, this habit may not even be necessary in their current relationships or environment, where open communication and mutual respect may be the norm. Thus, this once adaptive behaviour has turned into a burdensome and unnecessary habit in their adult life.

In such cases, therapy can help the individual realise that diffusing conflicts is not a goal in itself and that in their present environment, there are better ways of ensuring the original goal of safety and well-being, which do not involve setting aside one's own needs and feelings.

This example illustrates three points of importance to Being-Centred Therapy.

First, the above example illustrates how what we perceive as *goals* in our adult life can, in fact, be *methods* to achieve certain goals we had in our childhood family environment. Thus, what we see as goals today are, in fact, means to an end where we have forgotten about the end.

In the same way, much of what we perceive as goals in our lives are, in fact, methods for achieving the goal of experiencing Being, which have taken on an importance in themselves because we have forgotten that the real goal is Being.

Second, the above example also illustrates that the methods that worked in the context of our childhood family environment can become counterproductive in the context of our adult life.

In the same way, the methods we employ for experiencing reifications of Being are, more often than not, counterproductive because engaging with these methods takes our awareness away from perceiving Being in the present moment.

Finally, it is worth noticing that as long as the client in the above example perceives the act of defusing conflicts as a goal in itself, they may be motivated to improve their ability to function as a peacemaker. However, if a therapist helps them in this project, they are doing the client a disservice because they are helping the client deepen their fixation on an unhelpful coping mechanism.

Similarly, helping clients achieve the goals they wish to achieve can be a disservice insofar as doing so only deepens their lack of awareness of Being, thus sacrificing their ultimate goal in favour of a partial one.

Let us use this perspective to look at some of the issues clients typically bring to sessions.

When talking about their goals for therapy, clients may typically say they want things such as:

- More respect from family members, partners or work colleagues
- More self-confidence and less self-criticism
- Becoming better at managing their anger
- Becoming better at setting boundaries and not letting others walk all over them
- Becoming better public speakers and have less performance anxiety
- Establishing an intimate relationship and/or a family of their own

However, upon taking a closer look, it is easy to see that the above goals cannot be the client's end goal. Rather, they are something the client wishes to achieve because they believe that achieving them will enable them to achieve other, more important goals.

The client may want more respect from work colleagues because they believe this will enable them to shine in their position and increase their chances of being promoted. The client may want to have more self-confidence because they believe this will enable them to ask a potential partner out. Becoming better at managing anger or better at setting boundaries may both be attractive goals because they, in different ways, will improve the client's relationship.

Thus, the clients' goals usually are attractive to them, not in themselves, but rather because they hold the promise of achieving other, more important, goals. This begs the question of what the ultimate goal might be.

One way of answering this question is to repeatedly ask clients what achieving their goal would bring them that they regard as even more important to them. Every time the client answers, we can use their answer to restate the question until we reach something that truly is a goal in itself, rather than a means to an end.

If we pursue this line of inquiry, we discover that the client's ultimate goal, which makes all the partial goals attractive to the client, is always a feeling, such as happiness, peace, love, connection, aliveness, unity, value, etc.

For example, the client may want to become a better public speaker because they believe this would make people look up to them and they want people to look up to them because they believe this would make them feel "valuable". Thus, the feeling of being valuable, and not the ability of public speaking or even being looked up to, is the client's ultimate goal.

That this is true is evident in that the client would be disappointed if they managed to become an excellent public speaker but still didn't feel valuable. This type of scenario is very common. People will often achieve goals such as attracting a certain partner, reaching a certain level of wealth, acquiring a certain skill, and so on – only to be disappointed because achieving that goal doesn't make them feel what they believed it would make them feel. Such disappointment shows that a feeling – not the partner, wealth or skill – was always the client's actual goal.

So, the ultimate goal is always a feeling, and these feelings are, in turn, nothing other than positive reifications of Being. Thus, the ultimate goal that motivates the vast majority of people's actions is the wish to experience Being. As we shall see later, this changes when people gain a stable awareness of Being. But as long as people do not have a stable awareness of Being all their desires are masked desires for Being.

In summary, the goals clients bring to therapy are generally only the first step in the client's more or less conscious plan for reaching the experience of Being.

Implications for therapy

It is important for therapists to understand that the goals their clients present in therapy are frequently nothing more than the first step in the client's (ill-conceived) plan for reaching the experience of Being.

Consequently, it is generally wise to be sceptical of the client's own conception of the goals for the therapy and not accept those goals without thorough testing. The process of Sensing Completion presented later in this chapter can be understood as a way of illuminating what the client is truly seeking.

Let's unpack the implications for therapists a bit further.

When clients first come to therapy, they often have an idea about what is wrong in their life and what they need to do to fix it, but they have not been able to do it on their own. In other words, they have a plan, and they want the therapist's help to implement it.

However, from the perspective of Being-Centred Therapy, the plans people formulate all suffer from the same flaw, namely, that clients are unaware that the cause of their discomfort is that they don't pay attention to Being and that the harder they try to implement their plan, the more they distract themselves from Being – exacerbating the very discomfort they seek to remedy.

Therefore, the challenge for the therapist is to make the client aware of the fallacy of their plan – without breaking the client's trust in either the therapeutic process or the therapist. In other words, the therapist needs to pretend to help the client achieve their goal in ways that lead the client to realise the futility of their plan and give it up. Once the client does this, their awareness is freed so they can become aware of Being – thus dissolving the true source of the client's discomfort.

A good way of doing this is to invite the client to inquire into what they are ultimately reaching out for because once they become aware of what they are ultimately seeking, they will feel it and, thus, notice that they actually already have it.

Imagine that a client tells you they would like to have more respect from their partner – or, alternatively, that they would like to find a partner that showed them more respect than their previous partner(s). It is, of course, a good idea to have mutual respect in any partnership and pronounced disrespect should not be tolerated or (even worse) become the norm. Thus, on the surface the client's wish is sound. However, before rushing to the client's assistance, it is worth testing whether there is more to the situation than the client is aware of at present.

To test this, you can ask the client what their partner would say and do to show respect and what they believe obtaining this kind of respect from their partner would give the client. The reason for asking what respect would look like is to make the situation more concrete and easier to examine. Furthermore, it is a good idea to couch the question by saying that, obviously, respect is important but that you are curious about what the client finds most important about it. That way, you can invite the client into the inquiry without breaking the rapport between you and the client by saying something the client could construe as a challenge to the legitimacy of their wish to be respected.

The client may answer that if they received respect from their partner, they would feel seen by their partner. You may proceed by acknowledging the importance of being seen and asking what being seen would give them. The client may answer that being seen would make them feel safe. When asked about what feeling safe would give, the client may say that that would enable them to relax. At this point, you may recognise the word "relax" as a positive entry point and start asking what this particular relaxation feels like to the client (using the present tense to amplify the client's experience). The client may at this point breathe a sigh of relief and say that the relaxation feels solid, peaceful and grounded – as if something lands in their belly. You may recognise this as the White aspect of Being.

In this example, we see that receiving respect from the partner is not the true goal but merely the first step in a plan to be able to experience the White aspect of Being. Thus, the client's plan can be summed up as follows: Getting respect from their partner => feeling seen => feeling safe => relaxing => feeling solidity, peace and grounding (the White aspect of Being).

In this example, helping the client reflect on ways to gain more respect from their partner would have been a disservice to the client because it would have kept their awareness fixated on this issue, preventing them from becoming aware of Being, which is what they ultimately were longing for. The idea of gaining respect from their partner was merely a symbol for the White aspect of Being.

Once the client becomes aware of the White aspect of Being, it is highly likely that this awareness will make them more at ease and grounded in such a way that their partner will be more respectful – or that the client will develop self-respect that makes them uninterested in disrespectful partners.

On the other hand, if we had tried to help the client elicit more respect from their partner without first helping them become aware of the White aspect of Being, our efforts would most likely have failed for several reasons.

Firstly, if they try to elicit respect without feeling grounded in themselves, they are likely to end up pleading for it, and having to plead for respect only confirms its absence.

Secondly, because the client is ultimately seeking the White aspect of Being, they will only feel that they have received sufficient respect from their partner when they feel the White aspect of Being. But since no amount of respect can deliver the White aspect of Being, the client will never feel that they have quite succeeded – regardless of their partner's behaviour. Thus, trying to obtain respect without feeling the White aspect of Being they are truly seeking, leads to the development of an insatiable need (a neurotic need). It is exactly this state of affairs that got the client stuck in trying to achieve the first step of their plan, consequently losing awareness of their ultimate goal.

8th corrective principle: Fulfilling the conditions is a method – not a goal

The 8th corrective principle of Being-Centred Therapy is:

> "In therapy, the conditions clients wish to fulfil is never a *goal* in itself but rather a *method* for achieving the goal of experiencing Being."

Thus, when a client asks for your help in achieving a goal they have not been able to achieve themselves, the first thing to do is to explore what the client is ultimately reaching for through achieving this goal.

In other words, in Being-Centred Therapy, the client's goals are often regarded as symbols for aspects of Being and before engaging in reflections on how to achieve the goals themselves, it is important to use these symbols to help the client become aware of Being.

Such awareness will transform the client's relationship to the initial goals. Sometimes, the client will completely lose interest in their initial goal. At other times, the client will still want to achieve the goal but they will have much clearer ideas about how to go about it and the drama will be taken out of the project because achieving the goal is no longer conflated with the goal of reaching Being.

Links to other systems

The 8th corrective principle is the foundation for Connirae and Tamara Andreas' Core Transformation Process (Andreas & Andreas, 1994).

The Core Transformation process generally is framed as a process of exploring behaviour the client perceives as problematic. This starting point adds to the power of the process. Whereas it can be profound to discover that one's goals are motivated by a wish to experience the positive states that are aspects of Being, it is even more profound to discover that what one sees as problematic behaviour in oneself is driven by that same wish to reach Being, our true home. I will return to this point in Section 6.3.2 Misconception 17: Clients contain inner enemies and obstacles.

The Core Transformation Process is a ten-step process where the client is invited to explore the positive purpose behind what they see as problematic behaviour in themselves. Once they have formulated this positive purpose, the therapist asks a question, such as: "If you have fully achieved this purpose, what would that give you that is even more important?" This will reveal a deeper purpose, and the therapist can repeat the above question for that deeper purpose.

What Connirae and Tamara Andreas discovered was that clients going through this process would end up in what they call "core states". They distinguish between five such core states: "oneness", "beingness", "peace", "OKness" and "love". In the language of this book, these core states are positive reifications of Being.

Connirae and Tamara Andreas' book has a lot of interesting details on how to facilitate the process and is highly recommendable. It is beautiful and to the point – a pleasure to read.

I will return to the Core Transformation process in Chapter 3.4.3, Step 2: Point to the felt sense the client is ultimately reaching for, in the section on *The distraction of realism*.

3.3.6. Summary

In the above, we have seen that the Knot of Conditionality relates to five interconnected misconceptions. We have also seen how awareness of these misconceptions and their corresponding corrective principles can inform therapeutic interventions.

Table 6 summarises the misconceptions and corresponding corrective principles related to the Knot of Conditionality.

Table 6: Misconceptions and corrective principles related to the Knot of Conditionality

Misconceptions	Corrective Therapeutic Principles
What you seek can come and go	What you seek is always already present.
What you seek must be created or acquired	You don't create what you seek; you become aware of it.
You get what you seek by doing something	You become aware of what you seek by stopping doing what distracts you.
You create or attain what you seek by fulfilling conditions	Fulfilling conditions is counterproductive because it distracts you from noticing what you seek.
Fulfilling conditions is your goal	Fulfilling the conditions is a method – not a goal.

Table 7 summarises the differences between the questions that guide traditional and Being-Centred Therapy.

Table 7: How understanding the Knot of Conditionality changes the questions guiding therapy

Traditional therapy questions	Being-Centred Therapy questions
What is wrong with the client? What is the client lacking?	How is it possible that the client fails to recognise that they are already whole and full of what they are seeking?
What does the client need to do to create or acquire what they lack?	What is the client currently doing that blocks their awareness of Being and, thus, creates the illusion of lack?
Is the client's plan for reaching their goal realistic and effective?	How can you use information about the client's plan to point their awareness towards Being?
Does the client want things that are good for them?	What is the client ultimately reaching for? (The answer is always a felt-sense aspect of Being).

So far, we have looked at the Knot of Conditionality, five misconceptions related to this knot and five corresponding corrective principles that can guide therapy.

In the following section, I will describe in detail a therapeutic process aimed at untying the Knot of Conditionality. This process is called Sensing Completion because it uses the client's desires, obsessions, wishes and compulsions as a means to become aware of Being by noticing what the client is ultimately reaching out for. Because the client's desires are always ultimately a desire for Being, becoming aware of the completion of the client's desires is becoming aware of Being.

This perspective may be conceptually clear from reading the above (or similar texts). However, it is possible to have a conceptual understanding of how all our desires are ultimately derivatives of our desire for Being, without this conceptual understanding changing anything about how we perceive Being, life and ourselves. To engender such change, we need to go beyond conceptual understanding to direct experience, and let this experience update the beliefs that govern our behaviour. This is the goal of the Sensing Completion process.

3.4. Sensing Completion – how to untie the Knot of Conditionality

The Knot of Conditionality consists of five interlinked misconceptions about the nature of Being. These misconceptions direct the client's awareness away from the felt sense of Being and towards formulating hypotheses about what conditions must be fulfilled for Being to be present, planning how to fulfil these conditions or lamenting about not being able to fulfil them.

When the client directs their awareness towards concerns about what conditions to fulfil to create or acquire Being, they lose awareness of Being as it is in the present moment. However, while under the influence of the misconceptions, the client will interpret this loss of awareness of Being as an actual loss of Being itself, thus, reinforcing the perceived need to fulfil the conditions they believe would reverse the loss they have suffered – even though doing so only deepens the loss as it takes the client's awareness further away from Being. This gives rise to a stable system of ignorance.

The Knot of Conditionality, like the knot of Positive Reification, can be untied by utilising the client's desire. Clients are generally highly motivated to talk about the conditions they would like to fulfil and the great things that would result.

Since the ultimate result is experiencing Being, moving the client's attention from the plan to the end goal can be an effective way of making them aware of Being.

The Knot of Conditionality can be untied through the three-step process of Sensing Completion.

1. **<u>Recognise the Knot of Conditionality:</u>**
   The first step is to notice the Knot of Conditionality. This is done by noticing whenever the client expresses a strong desire to change something about themselves or their environment.
2. **<u>Point to the felt sense the client is ultimately reaching for:</u>**
   The second step is to use the client's desires for change as a means for moving the client's awareness to the concrete, felt-sense experiences they are ultimately hoping will result from making the desired change. The two main things to navigate in this step are 1) the client's desire to talk about *how* to fulfil the conditions if they believe they can do it and 2) the client's despair if they have lost faith in the possibility of fulfilling the conditions.
3. **<u>Correct misconceptions related to the Knot of Conditionality:</u>**
   The third step is to use the experience of the previous steps as a means to correct the five misconceptions related to the Knot of Conditionality. This can be done through four different processes designed to highlight four important observations:
   a. **Access:** What the client seeks is accessible in the present moment.
   b. **Non-Doing:** It is easier to feel what the client seeks when they do less.
   c. **Counterproductivity:** Trying to fulfil the conditions the client believes they need to fulfil to feel what they seek is often counterproductive as it makes it more difficult to notice that what they seek is already present.
   d. **Non-Urgency:** The sense of urgency the client feels around fulfilling the conditions disappears or is significantly reduced when they are aware of Being.

Noticing these things will help the client become aware of the fallacy of the misconceptions they operate from and correct them.

Below, I will describe how to guide the process of Sensing Completion in more detail. Figure 6 provides an overview of the process.

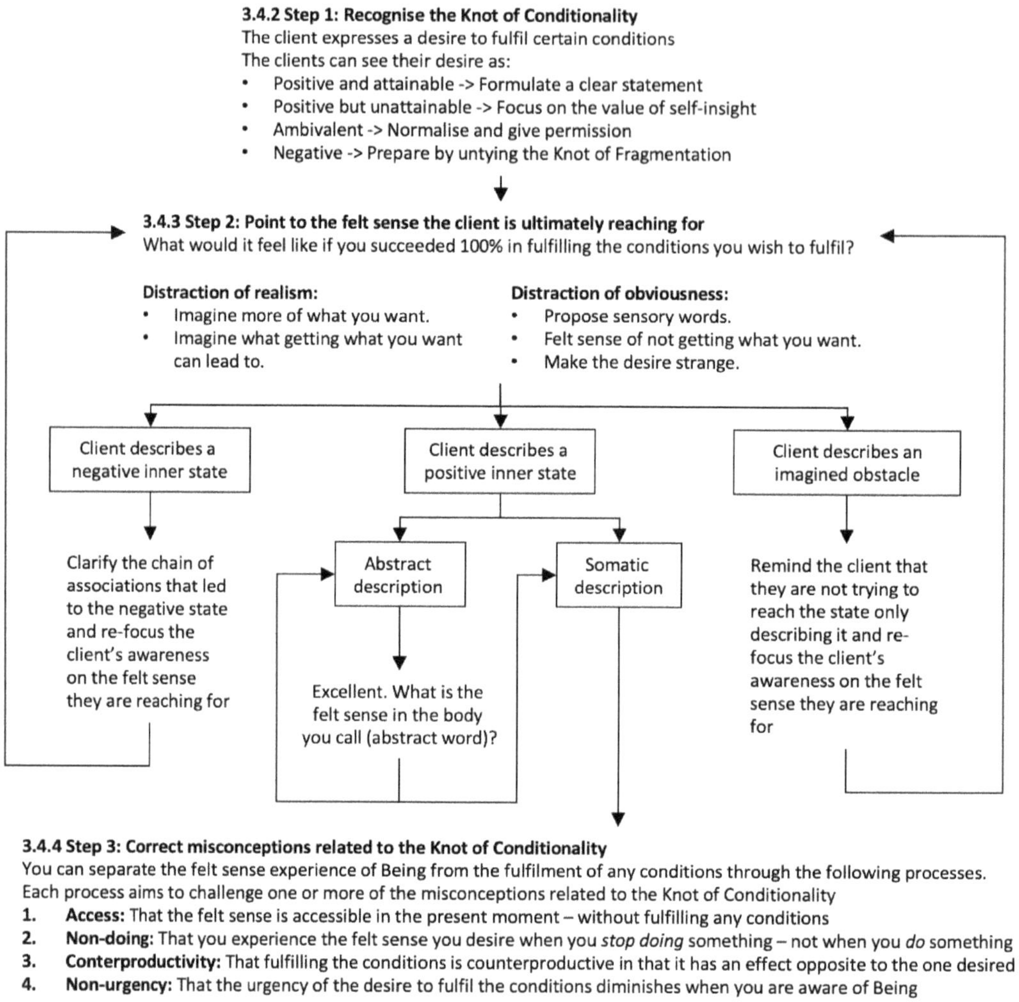

Figure 6: The Sensing Completion process

3.4.1. The mechanism of Sensing Completion

Before describing the individual steps in the Sensing Completion process, I will briefly elucidate the mechanism behind the somatic experience elicited by this process. Understanding this mechanism is crucial for successfully facilitating the process.

When we imagine fulfilling certain desirable conditions, it often triggers a positive visceral felt sense. For example, when imagining having a loving partner one might start feeling soft and energised. Similarly, when imagining being wealthy one might start feeling ease, settledness or value.

To effectively facilitate the Sensing Completion process, it's crucial to understand precisely why these feelings emerge, and to know that most people's default explanation for this phenomenon is misleading.

Because most people operate from the misconception that positive states are caused by actions on their part, the default explanation of why they feel good when *imagining* having fulfilled their desired conditions is that that the positive felt sense is a preview of the felt sense the *actual* fulfilment of the desired conditions would create in them (see Figure 7). For example, if you feel valued when you imagine receiving a compliment, you might assume that compliments *cause* you to feel valued. Similarly, if you feel joy when imagining being promoted, you may assume that promotions *cause* happiness in you. People tend to interpret the fact that they feel a positive state when they imagine the fulfilment of their desire as evidence that the actual fulfilment of their desire must produce in them an even stronger version of that state.

Figure 7: Fulfilment of desire causes positive felt sense

This belief, however, is incorrect, and it is important that you, as the therapist, do not buy into this explanation as it would render you unable to facilitate the Sensing Completion process.

The real reason imagining the fulfilment of desired conditions is followed by a positive felt sense is that, by imagining the fulfilment of the desire, you deactivate a range of thought patterns related to fulfilling the desire which, when active, monopolise your awareness in such a way that you lose awareness of Being. When these patterns are deactivated, you can become aware of Being, and you will experience this as a positive felt sense (see Figure 8). Therefore, merely imagining the fulfilment of the conditions is enough for you to obtain a visceral experience of the positive felt sense.

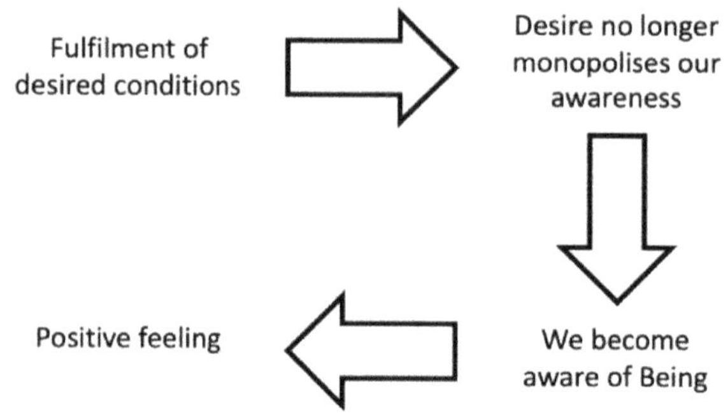

Figure 8: Link between fulfilment of desire and awareness of Being

First and foremost, imagining 100% success in fulfilling the desired conditions deactivates your struggle to succeed. When you imagine 100% success, you momentarily stop planning how to fulfil your desire, pushing yourselves to do what you believe you need to do to fulfil your desire, and worrying about failing.

If you desire respect and you imagine you have all the respect you could possibly want, you will momentarily stop planning how to get respect, pushing yourself to do what you believe you need to do to get respect, and worrying about not getting respect. With all of that out of the way, your mind become much less active, and, as a result, you are much more likely to notice Being.

Furthermore, you usually imagine that attaining a single desired object will solve a whole range of problems for you. For example, you might imagine that getting respect will make you feel more valuable, make you more attractive to certain partners, make it easier to earn more money, etc. Thus, imagining 100% success in getting one desired object will deactivate a whole range of thought patterns related to other desires that otherwise would be active and take your awareness away from Being. Once again, when these patterns are deactivated, you become much more likely to become aware of Being.

Thus, imagining fulfilling a desired condition will create a momentary gap in the activity of your mind, and in that gap, you are more likely to perceive Being.

It is important here to note that even if the client's belief about how to get what they seek is false, it is useful that they have this belief because it affords us an opportunity to help them learn how to direct their awareness towards Being. Thus, the therapist should not challenge the client's theory – no matter how bad it is – at least not at this point.

Thus, when facilitating Sensing Completion, you as therapists will pretend to be exploring the wonderful feeling created in the client when they attain their object of desire. However, in reality, you are laying the groundwork for undermining the client's belief in a causal relationship between their object of desire and the positive felt sense, and for showing the client how to access this felt sense directly by directing their awareness towards it.

We pretend to be exploring the felt sense the client will feel when they fulfil certain desired conditions. But we know that once the client becomes aware of the felt sense they are reaching for by fulfilling these conditions, they will either no longer care about fulfilling the desire or their motivation will profoundly change. As a result, they are freed from the compulsion because they now have what they were truly after.

Thus, the process is a trick. We get the client to engage with the process by pretending to be helping them attain their object of desire. But we know that by engaging with the process, the client will have to direct their awareness towards Being and, in doing so, discover for themselves that that is all they really need to do, and that fulfilment of the desired conditions is unnecessary. We have to facilitate the process as a trick because if we told the client that we wouldn't help them reach fulfil their desired conditions, they would not engage with the process and, consequently, not discover the secret of how their mind works[23].

If you, as a therapist, do not understand the above, you are likely to make one of two mistakes:

1. **Supporting the client's plan:** If you buy into the client's plan, you may start to help the client achieve the fulfilment of their desired conditions. This would only strengthen the misconception that what they seek is caused by fulfilling certain conditions.
2. **Challenging the client's plan:** If you challenge the client's plan, you may engage the client in reflections on whether there might be other conditions

---

[23] Some therapists may feel uncomfortable with the idea of tricking clients – even if the trick is in the client's own interest. However, accepting and going along with a client's perspective, allowing them to discover for themselves issues the therapist is already aware of, is a key therapeutic tool. This method is impactful because it allows clients to learn through their own realisations. Additionally, it can reveal insights the therapist may not have anticipated, making the process more valuable for both parties. At the same time, I like calling the technique a "trick", as this helps therapists to be mindful of and avoid potential misuse.

that are more desirable to fulfil. Again, this would also only strengthen the misconception that what they seek is caused by fulfilling certain conditions.

Below, I will comment on each of these typical mistakes.

Supporting the client's plan

Sometimes, a client's plan to get a particular feeling by fulfilling certain conditions may seem reasonable to you. You may even be trying to do something similar in your own life. For example, one client might express their desire to improve at establishing clear, healthy boundaries, believing that this would give them a sense of empowerment and ease in their life. Similarly, another client might express a desire to curb their habit of shouting at their children when they misbehave, believing this would improve their self-esteem and foster a better environment for their children.

In such cases, it can be tempting to dive directly into assisting the client in fulfilling their desired conditions, i.e. help them find ways of setting clear boundaries or managing their children without resorting to shouting.

There is, of course, nothing wrong with the kind of projects mentioned above. Learning such skills can be of great use in life. However, the belief that either being good at setting clear boundaries or raising children without raising your voice is a prerequisite for experiencing the kind of positive inner states that are facets of Being, is a problematic foundation for these projects and will most likely undermine the possibility of success.

The problem is that the arrow of causation has been turned around. It is not that once you set clear boundaries you will feel empowered and at ease; rather, when you feel empowered and at ease, setting clear boundaries becomes natural. It is not that learning to stop your children from misbehaving in a calm way will make you feel good about yourself; rather, when you feel good about yourself, it is much easier to teach your children how to behave in a calm and effective manner.

Therefore, before engaging in any discussion of how to learn the things the client wants to learn, it can be a good idea to use the process of Sensing Completion to check whether the conscious goal is conflated with an unconscious desire to feel Being. If that is the case, it is worth separating the two and to become aware of the felt sense of Being the client is reaching out for before dealing with the situation the client brought to the therapy session. When the client has become aware of Being, they will get much better ideas for how to do what they want to do. If the client does not include awareness of Being at the outset, their ideas for how to deal with the situation they wish to deal with are likely to make the situation worse because these ideas for action are conceived on a faulty foundation.

Challenging the client's plan

Sometimes, a client's plan to obtain a particular feeling by fulfilling certain conditions may sound quite unreasonable to you. For example, a client may tell you they want to be rich and famous because they believe this will make them happy. Or a client may tell you that they want to learn to ignore their sadness and vulnerability because they believe this will help them feel stronger and become more assertive in life[24].

In such situations, it can be tempting to challenge the client on their assumptions about what they would feel should they succeed in fulfilling their desired conditions.

You may have worked with wealthy and famous people and, from this work, learned that wealth and fame bring their own set of problems and that wealthy and famous people can be as miserable as everyone else. Similarly, you may know from your professional and/or personal experience that hardening yourself and repressing sadness and vulnerability leads to a whole host of psychological issues and only provides a brittle form of strength.

However, if you enter into a discussion with the client about whether the conditions they seek to fulfil will bring the inner states they assume, you lose the opportunity to use the client's beliefs to help them receive a deep and visceral experience of the felt sense they seek, and you rob them of the transformation that such an experience can bring.

Rather than relying on your own capacity to change the client's mind about their projects, you will do well to entrust that task to the experience of Being. Once the client has the deep visceral experience of happiness inherent in Being, their attitude towards wealth and fame may change. Once the client has a visceral experience of the strength of Being, they may no longer be disturbed by sadness or vulnerability because they will be strong enough to embrace the full range of their emotional states.

---

[24] I assume most therapists will consider these two strategies as unlikely to be successful – however if you believe one or both are good strategies, feel free to fill in your own examples of action plans that include doubtful predictions of future affective states.

In short, the client desires to fulfil certain conditions because they believe doing so will create certain positive feelings in them. Whether these beliefs are good or bad is irrelevant to the process of Sensing Completion, because the purpose of Sensing Completion is not to figure out what one needs to do to feel good but rather to question the premise that the felt-sense experiences we seek are the result of something we do.

The purpose of Sensing Completion is to use the client's theories of what they need to do to feel something they want to feel to help the client learn to let their awareness rest on that feeling. The purpose is not to develop a plan of action. The purpose is to help clients learn to unhook their awareness from the turbulence of thoughts and emotions.

Therefore, it doesn't matter whether the client's theory is sound or not. The client may not know what they will actually feel if they get what they desire. In fact, research has consistently shown that human beings are extremely bad at making accurate predictions about their own affective states in various future conditions[25]. Clients have some positive felt sense in mind that they project onto a particular scenario, causing them to desire this scenario. The purpose of Sensing Completion is to help the client focus their attention on that felt sense and experience it as vividly as possible. This is why whether the client's theory of what conditions would enable them to feel the felt sense they are after is a good or a bad theory is completely irrelevant.

In this way, Sensing Completion is a trick. We go along with the client's plan, not because we believe in it but because we know that doing so enables the client to deactivate a whole set of mental, emotional, and behavioural patterns, making it easier for them to become aware of Being. And this is something, we cannot ask the client to do directly.

For this trick to work, the client needs to obtain the visceral sense of what they are ultimately reaching for. However, when exploring the question of what 100% success in fulfilling a desire would feel like, the client can become preoccupied with many different distractions, preventing them from having a conscious experience of the felt sense they are ultimately reaching for. The Sensing

---

[25] If you are in doubt, you can ask yourself what you believe would make you happier – winning the lottery or becoming paraplegic. Data on these two groups show that after a year there is not much change to the baseline happiness felt by either group – but that is generally not what people predict (Brickman et al., 1978).

Completion process is designed to navigate these distractions and help clients become aware of what they ultimately seek in such a way that they experience it in the present moment. The first step in the process is to recognise the Knot of Conditionality

3.4.2. Step 1: Recognise the Knot of Conditionality – urgent desires

The first step in untying the Knot of Conditionality is to detect it. The way to do so is to listen for phrases or stories revealing a fixation on a particular objective combined with a sense of urgency in relation to reaching this objective.

The desired object can be virtually anything. It can be external objectives, such as a particular romantic partner, a promotion, monetary wealth, more leisure time, recognition from certain people, or material goods. It can also be internal objectives, such as more assertiveness, more compassion or love, increased composure, inner calm, or having fewer thoughts and being better at meditating.

To recognise when a client is fixated on a desired objective, it is important to know that such fixation can be expressed in many different ways. The way the fixation appears in the client's narratives is influenced by the degree of control they have over their desire, how they feel about having this desire, and how they evaluate their chances of attaining their desired object. Thus, the desire may manifest as obsession, compulsion, infatuation, preoccupation, drivenness, enthusiasm, craving, despair, dejection, desperation, wretchedness, disheartenment, and so on. All these states are ultimately expressions of passionate love shaped by different beliefs about the possibility and the ethical appropriateness of being united with one's beloved – i.e. with Being.

To facilitate the Sensing Completion process, it is important to remember that the client's desire ultimately is the desire to become aware of Being. The desire the client presents is, thus, a symbolic representation of their desire for Being. For this reason, it is unimportant whether it can be considered healthy or even ethical for the client to pursue their desired object. Because any desired object is a representation of Being, any desired object can be used as a means to regain awareness of Being. And once the client gains awareness of Being, their actions tend to gain a natural health and ethics as they are no longer influenced by the anguish of feeling separate from Being.

Understanding that the client's desire is ultimately a desire for Being can help the therapist engage in conversation about the desire without judgement. This can be particularly valuable if the client judges their own desire as unhealthy or unethical as it supports the client in exploring their desire with genuine curiosity – unburdened by guilt, shame, or fear.

Understanding that the client's desire is ultimately a desire for Being can also help the therapist avoid the trap of accepting the client's premise that their object of desire is their ultimate goal.

In the following, I will describe four variations on how a client's fixation on a desired object can appear in sessions: Positive desires clients see as attainable, positive desires clients see as unattainable, desires clients are ambivalent about and desires clients see as negative.

Positive: Desires clients admit to and see as good

Often, clients will directly tell you what they desire to attain. In fact, this can often be the reason they come to therapy. Clients may express desires such as:

- Earning more respect from partners, family, friends, bosses, co-workers, etc.
- Increasing their self-confidence
- Boosting their sex drive
- Earning more money
- Overcoming feelings of loneliness
- Learning to be kinder to themselves
- Finding a partner and starting a family
- Leaving an unsatisfying relationship

Each of these goals may represent a particular facet of a client's desire to experience Being more fully in their lives. In therapy, it is your role to help the client understand that these desires, while seemingly varied and specific, are all connected to a deeper yearning for wholeness and presence.

Of course, even if clients have full awareness of Being, they may still have goals in life. However, such goals feel very different from the goals most of us experience as long as our awareness of Being is somewhat limited. When an individual is aware of Being, they may, for example, still wish to find a life partner and start a family or earn money for some purpose but the individual's approach to such projects will be lighter and not marked by the same urgency and desperation that characterises the same projects when they are conflated with an unconscious desire for Being.

Spotting when conscious desires for specific goals are conflated with the unconscious desire for Being is key to recognising when a client is caught in the Knot of Conditionality.

Clients may talk about a goal they see as positive in very different ways depending on whether they believe their goal is attainable or not.

Attainable positive goal

When clients perceive their desired object as both positive and attainable, they will typically speak about it with enthusiasm and a sense of urgency, compulsion or obsession. You may experience that the client's desire has a non-negotiable edge to it, as if it were a matter of life and death.

To understand the intensity of these emotions, it is good to remember that ultimately the driving force behind the concrete desire the client speaks about is the desire to reconnect with Being. It is because awareness of Being is of such crucial importance to any individual that the concrete desired objects appear as a matter of life and death to the client.

When clients perceive their desired object as both positive and attainable, they will also, typically, be certain about the importance of attaining it and see it as *self-evidently desirable*.

Your client may, for example, desire to climb the organisational ladder and increase their salary even though their present job and salary are more than adequate for supporting their lifestyle. Your client may wish to overcome their procrastination and increase their productivity even though they have already achieved a significant level of success in their life. Your client may want to become a more helpful person even though they already spend a significant portion of their resources on helping others.

If you ask them why they want to increase their salary, be more productive or be more helpful, they may find your question strange because they see these objectives as self-evidently desirable and as something every reasonable person would want.

The presence of one or more of the following elements is a good indicator that the client is caught in the Knot of Conditionality and that they view the desired object as positive and achievable:

- Enthusiasm
- Sense of urgency
- Compulsion
- Obsession
- Non-negotiability
- Certainty
- Seeing the goal as self-evidently desirable

When clients view their goal as positive and attainable it is relatively easy to formulate what the client's goal is. It can be useful for the therapeutic process to agree on a succinct phrase that captures the client's goal as this will allow the therapist to refer back to the goal later in the process.

Unattainable positive goals

When clients perceive their desired object as positive but unattainable, they will typically speak about it with a sense of hopelessness, despair or desperation.

Sometimes this affective state is the result of having tried and failed to attain the desired conditions for a very long time and, thus, having become discouraged and pessimistic about the possibilities of success.

A client may, for example, believe that happiness comes from establishing a family, but as they have been unable to find a suitable partner, they now feel that happiness is not attainable for them.

At other times, this affective state is the result of having succeeded in attaining the desired conditions and being disappointed because this achievement didn't deliver on the client's expectations – even if these expectations are not always completely conscious.

For example, a client may have believed that happiness comes from establishing a family. However, after finding the perfect partner and having some great children, they still do not feel happy. Consequently, they may have lost belief in the possibility of happiness.

As with the enthusiastic clients, it is good to remember that the intensity of the affective states displayed by the pessimistic clients also derives from the conflation of their conscious desire for a particular object and their unconscious desire for Being. It is because the loss of the desired object is equated with the loss of Being that it results in strong emotions such as hopelessness and despair.

Thus, clients in pursuit of fulfilling certain desired conditions generally appear very optimistic, and clients who have failed to fulfil such conditions, or where the fulfilment of these conditions has failed to deliver what the client had imagined, generally appear very pessimistic. But despite this pronounced difference in the affective state, the underlying knot is, in both cases, the Knot of Conditionality. Whether the client is optimistic or pessimistic about their prospects, they are still caught in the idea that what they seek is created or acquired by fulfilling certain conditions.

Thus, hopelessness, desperation and despair can also be good indicators that the client is caught in the Knot of Conditionality.

When the client perceives their goal as positive and attainable, they are naturally interested in exploring it. When the client, on the other hand, perceives their goal as positive but unattainable, they may have little interest in exploring it. After all, why explore how wonderful something would be if it can never come true? In such cases, it can be useful to frame the therapeutic exploration as a way of gaining important self-insight that can be helpful even if the client never achieves their goal. Highlighting the value of self-insight can help motivate the client to explore their "impossible dream" when the hope of realising this dream cannot.

The client's attitude towards their own desire

Clients can hold (at least) three different views on their own desires.

- **Positive:** They fully own their desire and see it as a positive aspiration – regardless of whether they believe they can attain what they desire.
- **Ambivalent:** They are ambivalent about their desire and hesitant about admitting to it because they have negative judgements about the desire.
- **Negative:** They are disturbed by the desire and find it unacceptable.

Sensing Completion is easiest with the first type of desire, doable (and often very powerful) with the second but requires some extra preparation with the third.

Above, we have examined situations where the client regards their desire as positive. Below, we will explore how to recognise the Knot of Conditionality in situations where clients hold ambivalent or negative attitudes towards their own desires.

Ambivalent: Desires clients are hesitant about owning

When clients are ambivalent about having a particular desire, they will often talk about this desire in a veiled or indirect manner. They can appear shy about their desire and unwilling to admit to it. They feel shame and guilt about having the desire, and they will often engage in rationalisation or in "rewriting" the desire into something they perceive as more socially acceptable or more aligned with their self-image.

In these situations, it can be beneficial to assist the client in candidly acknowledging their true desires. This can be achieved by suggesting more straightforward expressions of their desire with a neutral and understanding attitude. Doing so helps normalise the client's desire, so they can feel more comfortable with it and let go of any associated guilt or shame.

If, for example, a client says they would like to "*deal with* their loneliness", you may understand that what they are really saying is that they want to "*get rid* of loneliness" but they know enough about therapy to know that "one does not get rid of emotions". In this scenario, you could ask: "So, if it were possible, would you like to just not feel lonely?" If the client hesitates and responds with something along the lines of "I don't believe that one can simply get rid of loneliness" or "it's not that I never want to feel lonely", you can say: "Of course, you know that emotions cannot simply be removed – but even though something cannot be done, we might still wish that we could do it. I think most people would like to not feel lonely". This way, you give the client permission to have and express their true desires by showing understanding and normalising it.

Similarly, if a client says that they wish their colleagues would take more responsibility and be more collaborative, you may understand that your client would like to throw their colleagues out of the window – but social convention prevents them from admitting to this desire. Once again, by saying: "It sounds to me as if you would kind of like to throw your colleagues out of the window, which, by the way, is very common. Is that it?" In this way, you give the client permission to have this desire and you normalise it. You may, of course, be wrong. But if you are, you have still proposed a rather radical desire and showed that you wouldn't judge it. So, whatever the client's desire is, they are likely to be more willing to own it and give it a more direct expression.

It is important to remember that the purpose of the therapy is not to help the client fulfil their desires but rather to help them become aware of what felt-sense state they believe would result from fulfilling the desire. Consequently, neither your client's nor your own personal beliefs about whether acting on the client's desire would be healthy or ethical are of any relevance. The primary objective is to clarify what the client finds attractive about their goal.

Furthermore, the fact is that when understood in terms of wishes to reach positive inner states, all human desires become very normal and understandable. Who wouldn't want to feel all the pleasures the world has to offer? Who wouldn't want the power to ensure others were always nice? Who wouldn't want people they dislike to magically disappear? It may be easy enough to see how such wishes are unrealistic or might lead to negative consequences, but it is also easy to see their immediate appeal. Human desires can be problematic when acted upon – but I've never encountered a human desire that wasn't understandable when framed as a wish to reach a positive inner state.

When clients feel they have permission to bluntly express desires they are otherwise a bit shy about, they usually light up and own their desires wholeheartedly. This combination of guilt, shame and shyness on the one hand and a real attraction on the other is a good indicator that the Knot of Conditionality is present in the client.

Negative: Desires clients find unacceptable

It can also happen that clients are mortified when they discover their desire because it is severely at odds with who they believe they are as a person.

For example, a client may believe they are a person who gives a lot of freedom to others and be mortified when they discover that they desire to have complete control over their partner. Similarly, a client may believe themselves to be a modest person and be mortified when they discover they desire to have other people worship them. A client may believe themselves to be a kind and loving person and be greatly disturbed when they discover a real desire to cause harm to someone they dislike.

These desires are an excellent starting point for the process of Sensing Completion. Understanding what these desires are ultimately about can be a great relief to the client because it absolves them from the judgement they hold over the desire.

However, it often requires a bit of preparation before the client is ready to explore desires they abhor in themselves. The strong reaction against the desire reveals that the client contains two conflicting desires – the uncovered desire and the desire to be a certain kind of person, which is at odds with the first desire. We will look more in depth at how to work with such inner conflicts in Chapter 6, Knot 5: The Knot of Fragmentation, but the essence is to acknowledge both desires as valid and work with them one by one.

Thus, mortification and shock can also be indications of the Knot of Conditionality.

Summary

The Knot of Conditionality can be detected by listening for phrases or stories revealing a fixation on a particular objective combined with a sense of urgency in relation to reaching this objective.

However, such fixation can be surrounded by various affective states depending on the client's view of their desire.

If the client perceives their desired object as both positive and attainable, they may display enthusiasm, urgency, compulsion, obsession, non-negotiability and certainty and they may see their desire as self-evident.

If the client perceives their desired object as positive but unattainable, they may display hopelessness, despair, desperation or despondency.

If the client is ambivalent about their desire, they may display shyness, guilt, shame and engage in rationalisation or substitution of their desire for something they perceive as more palatable.

If the client is negatively disposed towards their desire, they may display mortification, severe shame or denial.

It is important to be able to recognise the Knot of Conditionality in all of these affective climates.

3.4.3. Step 2: Point to the felt sense the client is ultimately reaching for

Once you have clarified and, if necessary, normalised the client's desire, you can guide them to imagine that they have already attained what they desire in a way that leaves nothing wanting and ask them to notice what this would feel like.

Often, the mere suggestion of imagining 100% success can prompt a visceral experience of the somatic state the client ultimately aims to achieve.

The client may, for example, experience profound feelings of relief, elation, joy, peace, connectedness, and so forth. If this is the case, you can transition to the process of Sensing Abundance, aiding the client in expanding and sustaining their awareness of the felt sense they have just tapped into. This is illustrated in Figure

6 (page 142) by placing a simplified version of the Sensing Abundance process under "client describes a positive state".

If, for example, the client says: "that would be such a relief", you can say: "wonderful, what does that relief feel like? Is it a spacious relief, a melting relief, a sense of a burden being lifted, or something else?"

It is important that the client discovers what 100% success would feel like by attending to their felt sense in the moment they imagine such success, rather than by deducing it from previously held beliefs.

Sometimes, clients will respond to the question about how it feels to achieve their goal too hastily and in a detached manner. This is typically an indication that they are sourcing their response purely from previously held beliefs. While this is acceptable if no other options are available, the Sensing Completion process is far more potent when the client retrieves the answer from their felt sense in the moment.

Sometimes, the felt sense that emerges in response to the question can surprise the client. For instance, they might be taken aback by the extent of relief they anticipate upon achieving their desire. Surprise is a good sign as it means the client is open to learning new things. Surprise is typically an indication that the client is sourcing their answers from felt sense in the moment as it shows what they discover runs counter to or modifies their predetermined expectations.

While it is possible for clients to become aware of the felt sense they are ultimately reaching for immediately after being invited to explore what it would feel like to fulfil their desired goal, it is common for them to be distracted by thoughts and emotions related to the desired goal.

In the remainder of this section, I will outline common distractions clients may encounter during the Sensing Completion process and offer strategies to work with these distractions in ways that help refocus clients' awareness on discovering the felt sense they ultimately seek.

Distractions

When we invite clients to focus their awareness on what they are ultimately seeking, one of two things may happen. Either they become aware of what they are ultimately seeking, or they are distracted by one of the patterns that keeps them from noticing what they are ultimately seeking. Both are great outcomes.

When the client becomes aware of what they are ultimately reaching for, they become aware of Being. This is great because it solves the problem of lack of awareness of Being. When this happens, you can continue with the process of Sensing Abundance, helping the client pay sustained attention to Being.

When the client becomes distracted, it affords them an opportunity to notice the patterns that prevent them from becoming aware of Being. This is also great because becoming aware of these patterns affords the client the opportunity to learn to disengage their awareness from them. When you can see the pattern that normally distracts you, the pattern no longer determines what you can see and will, therefore, no longer distract you.

Below we look at a range of common mechanisms of distraction and how we can help clients learn to disengage their awareness from these and refocus their awareness on the felt sense they are reaching for, i.e., on Being.

The distraction of realism

The first distraction is that of realism. When clients describe what they desire, they may experience a very limited somatic response because they scale down their desire to a level they consider realistic.

In this case, it can be good to give the client permission to imagine levels of desire that are a bit above what they give themselves permission to imagine. You may even directly encourage them to set aside any considerations of what is realistic and to acknowledge desires that are not realistic.

When the desire is increased, it is likely to trigger a stronger somatic reaction in the client and, thus, make it easier to become aware of what felt sense they are ultimately reaching for.

This can, however, be a bit of a balancing act. If you paint a picture that is too far beyond what the client can imagine, they may get hung up on the lack of realism or pull back because this picture seems exaggerated to them. If this happens, simply reduce the scenario a bit until the client finds it attractive again.

You can increase the attractiveness of the desired scenario in two ways:

1. By encouraging the client to imagine they get more of what they want
2. By encouraging the client to imagine they fulfil chains of desires, i.e. to notice what more they want once the initial desire is fulfilled.

Inviting clients to imagine getting more of what they want

One way in which clients try to scale their desire down in the interest of realism is to ask for less than what they truly want. A client may say they just want their partner to be nice to them, when, in fact, they want their partner's undivided love and adoration. A client may say they want their work colleagues to at least *consider* their proposals every now and then, when, in fact, they want their colleagues to do what they tell them to do without question or delay. A client may say they want a little time for themselves when, in fact, they want someone else to take over all their chores and have a few years off to do whatever pleases them – and possibly never return to their present duties.

If you give your client permission to admit to their true level of desire, without judging it for being unrealistic (or problematic in any other way), it can make the somatic response to the imagined scenario much stronger and clearer.

If your client hesitates in acknowledging the true level of their desire, you can simply remind them that you are not creating an action plan but simply exploring what felt sense they are reaching for through the desired scenario – and that realism is not important for this exploration.

Inviting clients to imagine fulfilling chains of desires

Another way in which clients scale down their desires in the interest of realism is by focusing exclusively on the first step in a chain of desires.

You can help clients acknowledge more of their desires by asking them what fulfilling the desire they are aware of would make possible and that is even more important to them.

If you ask this question repeatedly clients will, after a few steps, describe aspects of Being, such as oneness, love, peace, wholeness, etc. directly as this is ultimately what they are reaching for[26].

A client may, for example, say that they would like their partner to consult with them before making plans for their weekends. When asked what it would give them if their partner started doing this consistently, the client may say it would make them feel respected. When the question is repeated, the client may say that when they feel respected, they can relax, when they can relax, they feel alive and

---

[26] This question is the foundation of the Core Transformation process developed by Connirae Andreas, where it is used to integrate parts of the client's psyche that has been disowned or left behind in the client's development by revealing that these parts ultimately are reaching for very positive states. We return to this in the chapter on the Knot of Alienation.

playful, and when they feel alive and playful, they are at one with love. By the time the client gets to talk about being at one with love, they will most likely have a strong felt sense of this. Thus, the desire to get their partner to consult with them when planning their weekends is ultimately a desire to be at one with love.

Another client may say that they desire a promotion in their current organisation. When asked what this promotion would give them, they may say that it would give them financial stability. When the question is repeated, the client may say that when they have financial stability, they would feel relieved because they can provide for their family, when they can provide for their family, they feel worthy, and when they feel worthy, they feel whole. Thus, the desire for financial stability is ultimately a desire for feeling whole.

Of course, the initial desires often have value in themselves. It is practical to coordinate your time with your partner. It is also great to have financial stability for yourself and your family. However, part of the attraction felt by the clients in the above examples derives from the clients having projected aspects of Being onto coordination and financial stability.

Thus, uncovering the chain of desires does not neglect the validity of the first desire; it simply reveals that this desire has been conflated with a desire for Being and, in doing so, helps the client become aware of Being. And this is the purpose of Sensing Completion.

Limited expressions of the positive somatic state

It is worth mentioning that limited expressions of the positive somatic state do not necessarily mean that the client is scaling down their desires. Some clients are simply less expressive than others. Even if they feel a positive state clearly, they may not express it very forcefully. This is not a problem. As long as the client *feels* the positive state, we can proceed with the process of Sensing Completion.

Finally, the absence of a visceral response to the imagined scenario can also occur when the client isn't talking about something they actually desire. Sometimes, clients will, through the process of Sensing Completion, discover that they don't care about achieving what they thought they wanted. This is a very valid outcome of the process. If this happens, you may ask the client what it feels like to acknowledge that they do not really want what they thought they wanted. Discovering that they do not want what they thought they wanted can be a relief because it deactivates the struggles to achieve the objective and the conflict about this struggle that is inevitable when we push ourselves to achieve things we do not desire. If the client feels this relief, you can use it as a positive entry point and ask about the felt sense of the relief following the Sensing Abundance process.

The distraction of obviousness

Another common distraction is that of obviousness. When clients describe what they desire, they may not connect it to any felt sense because they think what they desire is obviously attractive in itself – and they do not need any further reason for why they find it desirable. In other words, the client's desired condition seems so obviously attractive that they are convinced it is the end goal and that there is nothing more to say about it (this is misconception number 8).

The client may, for example, say they want "respect", and they feel that this is a self-evidently desirable thing. If you ask them what it would give them to be respected, they will answer that it will give them respect.

You can deal with the distraction of obviousness by:

- proposing what fulfilling their desired conditions might feel like
- exploring what not fulfilling their desired condition feels like
- making the desire strange to spark curiosity.

Proposing what fulfilling the desired condition might feel like

One way of helping the client become aware of the feeling they believe fulfilling their desired conditions would give them is to simply offer them a menu of possible feelings to choose from. You don't have to worry about getting it right. If you guess correctly, the client will now have words to describe the felt sense they are reaching for. If you guess incorrectly, the client will usually correct you and, in doing so, will become aware of what felt sense they are reaching for.

If, for example, the client desires respect, you can present them with a range of possible felt-sense experiences that people typically connect with feeling respected. You can ask whether having respect would make them feel relieved, feel a sense of value, feel safer, or feel something else. The client may respond by choosing one of these words and saying, "Yes! That's it." Or the client may say: "No, it is none of that." If the latter is the case, you can then ask the client: "Ok, so if it is none of these feelings, which feeling is it?"

Once the client finds a word that describes the felt sense, be it relief, value, or safety, you proceed with the process of Sensing Abundance and explore what that feels like at a somatic level.

Exploring what not fulfilling the desired condition feels like

Another way of getting the client to connect with the positive felt sense they believe comes from fulfilling their desired conditions is to ask what it feels like when the condition is not fulfilled or what they would feel if the condition were never fulfilled. Usually, it is easy for clients to connect with the negative felt sense. And once they do, you can propose that fulfilling the condition must give the opposite feeling.

If, for example, a client desires to be respected by others, you can ask what it feels like not to be respected. The client may answer that they feel deflated or collapsed. Now you can suggest that if they get respect, they will not feel deflated and collapsed. Once they agree, you can then ask what they believe they would feel instead. It can be a good idea not to immediately suggest the opposite feelings to the client as it is not always obvious what the opposite feeling is. For some the opposite of "deflated" is "inflated", but that is generally not a positive word. The opposite could also be "valued", "safe", "shining", or something else. If the client cannot make the translation, you can suggest a range of possible feelings that could be seen as the opposite of what the client feels when their desired condition is not fulfilled.

Making the desire strange

Yet another approach to getting beyond the client's perception of the fulfilment of their desire as a goal in itself is to point out that one can imagine that some people would not care about this particular desire. In doing so, you make the desire strange which is a general technique to spark curiosity about things that seem obvious[27]. If what the client wanted was obviously desirable, everyone should desire it – but not all people do.

Some people may, for example, not care about whether other people respect them. So, if the client does desire respect, there must be something the client imagines respect will give them that makes respect desirable, which other people

---

[27] One source of inspiration for how to make the obvious seem strange is Bertolt Brecht's "Verfremdungseffekt" or "alienation effect". Brecht was a playwright who used techniques, such as direct address, breaking the fourth wall, using episodic or fragmented narratives, and emphasising the theatricality of the production, to prevent the audience in the theatre from becoming fully immersed in the narrative and to encourage critical reflection on the social and political themes presented on stage.

might not imagine they can get from respect. The question then becomes: What is it the client believes respect will give them that makes them desire respect?

In short, it can be good to present clients' desires as strange to spark their curiosity about why they desire what they desire. This helps engage them in the exploration of what they imagine fulfilling the desire would feel like.

The distractions of realism and obviousness prevent clients from recognising that when they seek to fulfil their immediate goal, they are reaching for a particular felt sense.

Once these distractions are dealt with, and the client is ready to explore what felt sense they are reaching for, the client's attention may then be caught in two ways:

- The emergence of negative inner states
- Concerns about how to deal with imagined obstacles.

In the remainder of this section, we look at how to deal with these two situations.

Negative inner states

Sometimes when you ask a client how it would feel to get exactly what they desire, the client will answer that it would feel bad.

Such an answer may be confusing because there appears to be a mismatch between the client stating that they desire something and stating that they would feel bad if they got it. So, why would a client desire the fulfilment of certain conditions if they believed doing so would produce negative inner states?

The reason for this kind of answer is generally that the client does not, in fact, answer the question. Instead, their mind has jumped a few steps down a chain of associations, and they are describing the felt sense of the place where their awareness has landed.

When a client mentions a *negative* felt sense as the result of fulfilling a desired condition, their awareness will typically have jumped to one of the following four places:

1. **Imagining lack of success:** The negative felt sense is a felt sense the client associates with *not* succeeding in getting what they desire.
2. **Imagining a negative consequence of success:** The negative felt sense is a felt sense of a negative consequence the client associates with succeeding in getting what they desire.

3. **Imagining struggling for success:** The negative felt sense is the felt sense of the client's struggle to fulfil the desired conditions and impatience in finishing this endeavour.
4. **Imagining a negative perception of the desire:** The negative felt sense is a felt sense associated with a negative prejudice against the desire and/or the struggle to fulfil the desire.

The way to deal with all these cases is to clarify how the felt sense the client is currently experiencing is created, by imagining something other than fulfilling the desired condition, and then refocusing the client's awareness on the felt sense the client imagines would result from fulfilling the desired conditions.

There are, however, some variations in how you might do this. So, let's look at each of the four scenarios in turn.

The negative state is caused by imagining lack of success

Sometimes, when you ask clients what they feel when they imagine 100% success, they will answer that they feel sad, empty, despondent, etc.

Though such answers are surprising, clients are answering truthfully in that they are reporting the felt sense emerges in their awareness when they imagine 100% success. What they are not aware of are the steps they go through to get from the imagined success to the negative felt sense they are experiencing.

Our awareness often leaps quickly from one association to another, and sometimes we are unaware of a few of these leaps. This can create the illusion that one experience is directly following another when, in fact, there are a few steps between the two.

When clients tell you that the feeling that emerges from imagining 100% success is one of sadness, emptiness, despondency, or something similar, it is often the result of a chain of associations, such as:

1. The client imagines success in fulfilling the desired conditions
2. They feel the attractive felt sense they associate with the fulfilment of these conditions
3. They think of how this felt sense is lacking in their life and how much they long for it
4. They feel sad, empty, or despondent.

The client's awareness simply jumps so fast from step one to step four that the client is not aware of the two intermediary steps.

To clarify the origin of the sadness, emptiness or despondency and refocus the client's awareness on the felt sense they associate with the fulfilment of the desired conditions, the therapist can say:

> "Yes, what you are describing is what you feel when you do *not* succeed. But what would you feel when you *do* succeed?"

In this statement, the therapist first points out a cause for the felt sense the client is aware off. The purpose of doing so is to help the client lose interest in the felt sense their awareness is currently occupied with and show them that this negative state is not directly related to the experience of fulfilling the desired condition. This creates a space for the therapist to then use a question to refocus the client's awareness towards exploring what felt sense they are reaching out for by trying to fulfil the desired conditions.

In other words, first the therapist points to the steps in the chain of associations the client has missed and then asks specifically for the content of the second step.

The negative state is caused by imagining a negative consequence of success

Of course, feelings, such as sadness, emptiness and despondency can be the result of different lines of association. Another common string of associations that can be triggered when imagining fulfilling a desired condition is:

1. The client imagines success in fulfilling the desired conditions
2. They feel the attractive felt sense they associate with the fulfilment of these conditions
3. The client feels there is no longer any need to strive
4. They interpret the absence of striving as a "loss of purpose"
5. The client feels sad, empty, or despondent.

In this example, imagining the complete fulfilment of the desired conditions does not trigger a sequence of associations that take the client's awareness to the felt sense related to failure. Rather, it triggers a sequence of associations that take the client's awareness to a felt sense related to some negative outcome the client associates with 100% fulfilment of the desired condition – in this case, the loss of purpose.

To clarify the origin of the negative inner state and refocus the client's awareness on the felt sense they associate with the fulfilment of the desired condition, the therapist can, in this example, say:

> "Of course, if you have been striving to reach something for a long time, you may feel a bit empty when you succeed. You may even feel a bit purposeless. However, that is not the reason you found the goal you were striving for attractive in the first place. What made you want to strive is that you imagined the goal you were striving for would feel good in some way. What kind of good feeling do you imagine succeeding will bring – apart from maybe purposelessness?"

In this statement, the therapist points out the sequence of associations that create the negative inner state and then uses a question to refocus the client's awareness on the felt sense they are reaching for by trying to fulfil the desired conditions.

It is worth pointing out three tricks employed in the above answer to the client.

Unconditional confirmation of the client's experience

First, the therapist starts with the words "of course" to indicate unconditional confirmation of the client's experience.

Downplaying the magnitude of the negative state

Second, the therapist downplays the magnitude of the negative state by saying "a bit empty" or "a bit purposeless". Doing so diminishes the grip this negative state has on the client. Often clients accept this suggestion and relax. Occasionally, a client may react to such downplaying of the negative state and exclaim that they feel *very* empty and purposeless. In such cases, the therapist can simply acknowledge that yes, one may indeed feel *very* empty and purposeless and proceed to ask about the positive felt sense that the client is reaching for.

Downplay the importance of the negative state

Third, the therapist ends by clarifying that they are looking for a part of the client's experience that is separate from the purposelessness, and they use the word "maybe" to further place the purposelessness in the category of something not particularly interesting, which helps to refocus the client's awareness on what is key, namely the positive felt sense that motivated them to try to fulfil their desired condition.

These tricks help the therapist turn the client's awareness from the negative state towards the felt sense the client associates with the fulfilment of their desired condition by framing the former as less interesting and the latter as more interesting.

The negative state is caused by imagining struggling for success

Other common negative inner states that can emerge when asking a client what fulfilling their desired conditions would feel like are states related to the effort and struggle the client believe is required.

There are two sides to the struggle: Spending one's energy and having spent one's energy.

If the client's awareness jumps to the felt sense of spending their energy, they may say that they feel forced, pushed, pulled, or even shackled. This can be the result of a chain of associations such as:

1. The client imagines success in fulfilling the desired conditions
2. They feel the attractive felt sense they associate with the fulfilment of these conditions
3. The client imagines that fulfilling the condition will be a Herculean task
4. The client feels that they have no choice but to complete this task because losing the felt sense is unacceptable to them. They feel obliged, compelled, or even enslaved by the task
5. The corresponding felt sense is a sense of being forced, pushed, pulled, or even shackled.

If the client's awareness jumps to the felt sense of having spent their energy, they may say they feel exhausted, drained, weak or depleted. The chain of associations that leads to such inner states may look like the following:

1. The client imagines success in fulfilling the desired conditions
2. They feel the attractive felt sense they associate with the fulfilment of these conditions
3. The client imagines that fulfilling the condition is a Herculean task
4. The client feels exhausted, drained, weak or depleted at the thought of the task.

These examples show how the words the client use to describe the negative felt sense can contain important clues as to what chain of associations precedes the negative felt sense.

A word like "shackled" implies being enslaved. As a therapist, you may ask yourself: How might the client construct their experience so that it leads to a sense of being enslaved? A reasonable answer would be that they feel they have no choice but to carry out a task they don't really want to engage with because doing so is the only way to acquire the positive feeling they *need*.

A word like "exhausted", on the other hand, implies spending great amounts of energy. As a therapist, you may ask yourself: What is the client spending so much energy on that they feel exhausted? In this case, it is highly likely that the client imagines that fulfilling the desired condition is an arduous task.

Using logic to deduce what the words clients use to describe negative inner states imply about how the client constructs their experience is a very useful therapeutic tool. It helps us deduce and point out the associations that cause the negative inner state before we refocus the client's awareness on the felt sense they are reaching for by trying to fulfil their desired condition.

The negative state is caused by a negative perception of success

Finally, a common response to the question of what fulfilling the desired condition would feel like is a sense of tension, as if one is pushing something away or moving away from something in a gesture of antipathy, disgust or animosity. This typically happens when the client contains two parts with opposing attitudes to fulfilling the desired conditions.

A client may, for example, have a wish to be more confident and at the same time see confident people as obnoxious. In this case, imagining success in becoming 100% confident may trigger a chain of associations like the following:

1. The client imagines success in fulfilling the desired conditions
2. They feel the attractive felt sense they associate with the fulfilment of these conditions
3. The client "remembers" their negative perception of people who fulfil these conditions
4. The client feels a sense of tension, as if they are pushing something away or moving away from something in a gesture of antipathy, disgust or animosity.

Depending on the strength of the negative opinion about the desired state, you, as the therapist, can try one of two things.

First, you may try to side-line the objection or negative perception. To do so, you will first have to understand what the negative perception is. Then you must create a clear distinction between the desirable and the undesirable aspects of the condition in question. This distinction will then allow you to invite the client to focus their attention exclusively on the desirable aspect.

In the example of a client with an ambivalent relationship to becoming confident, this process may look like this:

> Client: "I'd like to be more confident"
>
> Therapist: "What would it feel like to be 100% confident?"
>
> Client: "I hate it. It feels yucky"
>
> Therapist: "What do you hate about being confident?"
>
> Client: "I just hate confident people. They are so obnoxious. They never listen. They just bulldoze you"
>
> Therapist: "Ok. So, what do you think it would feel like to be confident if it had nothing to do with being obnoxious? What would it feel like to be confident in a way where you enjoy listening to others, and you are not bulldozing anyone?"
>
> Client: "That feels better. That just feels calm and settled"
>
> Therapist: "Say more about that felt sense of calmness and settledness..."

In this exchange, the therapist deduces from the client's experience of hate and yuckiness that the client must have a negative perception of confidence in addition to their desire for confidence. As it is not possible to know what the negative perception is, the therapist asks the client to clarify their negative perception. Once the client puts their negative perception into words, the therapist can establish a clear distinction between what the client finds desirable and repulsive about confidence and use a question to focus the client's awareness on the desirable inner state. Once the client describes this inner state with a few positively laden words, the therapist can continue with the process of Sensing Abundance and have the client elaborate on this state until they have a strong visceral experience of it.

Sometimes, however, the objection is so strong that it is not possible to side-line it in the above manner. The client may completely lose the wish to become confident. Once the negative perception is triggered, they may state that they actually do not want to be confident at all; that they thought they wanted to but now they realise they do not.

This means that the client is now so strongly identified with the part of their psyche that is formed around the negative perception of "confidence" that it is not possible to continue the process of Sensing Completion.

Instead, you may try to inquire into what the part of the client's psyche that objects to confidence desires. For example, this part may desire to be empathetic or understanding, or something else. Doing so will calm down the part as it will feel heard. You may then follow the Sensing Completion process with this part instead. If this part connects to the aspect of Being it seeks, it may cease to object to the exploration of confidence, and you can return to the process of Sensing Completion for the first part.

However, on occasions, when you shift to work with the second part, the first part of the client's psyche that is formed around the desire to be more confident may interfere. If you experience the client flip-flopping between opposing parts in this manner, you are experiencing the Knot of Fragmentation and must shift to the process of Sensing Unity. I will describe this process in Chapter 6, Knot 5: The Knot of Fragmentation.

Getting the chain of associations right

In the above sections, we have examined how to deal with various situations where negative inner states draw the client's awareness away from noticing the aspect of Being they are reaching for by fulfilling certain desired conditions.

The key is to notice and put words to the chain of associations along which the client's awareness moves and then redirect the client's awareness back towards Being.

For this to work, it is important that the therapist gets the chain of associations reasonably right. If the therapist, in collaboration with the client, can come to an understanding of how the negative inner state is constructed through a sequence of associations, the client is likely to feel that the emergence of the state is understood and that they do not have to explore it further.

If you, as the therapist, get the chain of associations wrong, the client may become caught up in discussing the origin of the negative inner state. They may, furthermore, get attached both to understanding it and trying to do something about it. This is irrelevant for the purpose of the process of Sensing Completion and will only trap the client's awareness and make it more unlikely that they will notice Being.

As mentioned above, clients will often say things from which the therapist can deduce the steps in the chain of associations that leads from imagining the fulfilment of the desired condition to feeling the negative inner state.

- If the client feels shackled, they must imagine that there is something binding them and preventing them from moving freely. That is what a shackle is.
- If the client feels empty, they must imagine a transition from being full of something to no longer being full of that something, and you can ask directly about this: What is it you are empty of?
- If the client feels exhausted, they must imagine that there is a strenuous task they have to complete, and you can ask directly about that: What is it you are trying to do?
- If the client feels lost, they must imagine that there is somewhere they need to get to, and you can ask directly about that: Where are you trying to get to?
- If the client feels frustrated, they are often imagining they need to do something, and you can ask: What are you trying to do right now?

However, sometimes you may not be sure about the chain of associations. In such cases, you can use a general formulation to redirect the client's attention back to the felt sense they hope to connect with by fulfilling their desired conditions. Such a general formulation could be:

> "Right now, you are aware of this negative inner state, and there might be many reasons why imagining [the fulfilment of your desired condition] triggers this feeling in you. However, this is not the feeling that made [the condition] look attractive to you. To be attracted to something, we must assume that it will bring a positive feeling. What is the feeling you hoped to get by [fulfilling the condition]?" (Substitute the parts of the formulation in brackets with the concrete desired condition the client is pursuing).

Here the therapist uses the logic that we cannot be attracted to something we perceive as negative in order to redirect the client's awareness towards the felt sense that initially motivated them to try to fulfil their desired condition.

You cannot always be sure *what* chain of associations leads a client's awareness from the imagination of fulfilment of a desired condition to a negative inner state. You can, however, be sure that there must be *some* chain of associations. If the client had a direct association from the fulfilment of a condition to a negative inner state, fulfilling that condition would not appeal to them – and the whole starting point for the process is the client's urgent desire to fulfil a condition.

Now that we know how to deal with situations where the client's awareness is caught up in negative inner states, we will turn to situations where the client's awareness is caught up in considering possible obstacles to fulfilling their desired condition.

Imagined obstacles

Sometimes, the client will answer the question of what 100% success in fulfilling their desired conditions feels like by telling you what prevents them from achieving success. Rather than answering the question, they get hung up on why they cannot fulfil their desire.

Just like with the negative inner states, the client's awareness arrives at the imagined obstacles through a chain of associations and gets stuck thinking about these obstacles. Rather than paying attention to what state they are reaching for by trying to fulfil their desired condition, their attention gravitates to the obstacles they face when trying to fulfil these conditions.

In other words, rather than noticing *why* they want to fulfil their desired conditions, they spend all their awareness on various complications related to *how* they can fulfil these conditions.

The client may, for example, become concerned with:

- necessary preconditions to fulfilling their desired condition
- negative consequences of fulfilling their desired condition
- the unpleasantness of their struggle to fulfil their desired condition
- their impatience if they feel fulfilling their desired condition takes too long
- their hopelessness if they feel that fulfilling their desired condition is impossible
- or the client may tell you that they don't know what fulfilling their desired condition feels like because they have never experienced it.

The general way of dealing with such distractions is by first acknowledging the client's concern and then refocusing the client's awareness on the felt sense they imagine fulfilling their desired conditions would bring. A good way of doing so is to invite the client to imagine what it would feel like if they already had what they are seeking.

Sometimes, the client's concern about obstacles to fulfilling their desired condition has too much momentum. Then we have to pause the Sensing Completion process and shift to another process but many times it is fine to simply side-track the chain of associations the client's awareness has been taken by and refocus the client on the felt sense they are reaching for.

Throughout the rest of this chapter, I will describe the particulars of how to deal with four different types of obstacles that clients' awareness frequently gets taken by. I will round off the chapter with some reflections on how to deal with hidden motivations clients may have for focusing on the obstacles rather than on the felt sense they wish to reach.

The obstacle of necessary prerequisites

One very common way in which clients become distracted from letting their awareness rest on the felt sense they imagine they will get when their desired condition is fulfilled is what could be called planning mode.

The chain of association would look something like:

1. The client imagines success in fulfilling the desired conditions
2. They feel the attractive felt sense they associate with the fulfilment of these conditions
3. The client starts mapping out what they believe they need to do to fulfil their desired condition, including how they may do it, what might get in the way of fulfilling their desire and how they can get around those potential obstacles.

In other words, instead of exploring the felt sense they wish to reach, the client is thinking about what they need to do to fulfil their desired conditions, how they can do it and when they can do it. They will almost pull out their calendar and start writing tasks in.

If, for example, the client wishes to obtain a promotion (their desired condition), they do not pause to consider what they believe getting the promotion would feel like because they are too busy considering who they need to build a relationship with, what projects to take on that will place them in a good position to be considered for the promotion, who their rivals for the promotion might be and how they can side-line these individuals. If the client believes that the path to gaining a promotion is simply through hard work, they might become stuck in thinking about how to deliver better projects and how to free up more time for work. Regardless of what the client's strategy for getting the promotion is, the execution of this strategy can easily take up all the client's awareness so that none is left to notice what felt sense state they are chasing through the promotion.

In such cases, the therapist can listen to the client and collect a list of what the client believes they have to do to fulfil their desired condition. Then the therapist can use this information to ask the client to imagine that they have done all that. Asking the client to imagine they have completed all the individual steps they believe they have to take is more powerful than asking the client to simply believe they have achieved their goal because it speaks to the way the individual client believes they would arrive at their goal.

For example, the client may desire to be promoted and believe that if they work really hard then their hard work will be noticed and rewarded with the desired promotion. In this case the therapist can say:

> "Good. So, imagine that in the next few months you really outdo yourself and top management notices all your outstanding work and gives you the promotion. What does that feel like?"

This is a much stronger statement than merely asking the client what they would feel like if they got the promotion because it includes the client's imagined storyline.

When you ask a client a question like the above, they may remain in planning mode and add more necessary preconditions. In the example above, the client may say that a few months wouldn't suffice since many of the projects they have at work will not show significant results before two or three years.

In that case, you simply modify your narrative to include the additional preconditions. Thus, you may say:

> "Very well. So, imagine that you have worked for three years on a project and done an outstanding job, and by the end you are promoted for your excellence. What do you feel when that happens?"

At some point, when you have included enough prerequisites, the client will draw a sigh of relief and light up. Then they are feeling it and you can ask:

> "That! What you are feeling now. What is that?"

At this point, you continue with the process of Sensing Abundance and support the client in unpacking the felt sense they were striving for as they feel it in the present moment.

It is worth pointing out three tricks employed in the above answer to the client.

Making it sound easy

Even though the client said they believed that "hard work" would get them the promotion, I changed this phrase into "outstanding work" in my response. The reason for this substitution is that the phrase "hard work" might lead the client on to the feeling of exhaustion or even hopelessness as discussed in the section "The negative state is caused by imagining struggling for success". Furthermore, it is clear that the client is talking about being noticed for outstanding work and not merely for putting in a lot of hours. Thus, using the phrase "outstanding work" is both more precise than the client's own phrase and has the advantage of not invoking the sense of struggle – at least not directly.

Making small substitutions that make the strategy sound lighter can support the client in imagining that they have already completed the strategy.

Using present tense

When asking what the imagined scenario would feel like, I deliberately use the present tense – even if it is grammatically incorrect. Thus, I ask: "What *does* that feel like?" instead of "What *would* that feel like?" The reason for this is that the present tense suggests to the client that they are feeling it now, whereas the use of the (grammatically correct) conditional tense subtly suggests a separation in time between the client and the felt sense. Furthermore, the present tense implies that we are talking about something that is reality whereas the conditional tense implies that we are talking about something hypothetical.

When the client exhibits physical signs showing that imagining the scenario has evoked a positive felt sense in them, I further reinforce the fact that the client is experiencing the felt sense in the present moment by saying it directly: "That! What you are feeling now. What is that?"

Do not discuss the client's strategy

Finally, it is important not to challenge the client's ideas about how to fulfil their desired condition – even if you are convinced that the strategy will not work. Many times, you will work with clients who have peculiar ideas about what they need to do to fulfil their desired conditions.

However, challenging the client's ideas will only side-track them. When facilitating the Sensing Completion process, it does not matter whether the client's idea about how to fulfil their desired condition is sound or not. Thus, discussing this is, at best, a waste of time. You can use whatever strategy the client believes in as a means to direct their awareness towards their ultimate goal – which you know is always Being. Even the most flawed strategy can be used for this purpose as long as the client believes in it.

The client may, for example, believe that they will get their promotion through hard work alone because that hard work will be seen and rewarded. If you have some experience as a business coach, you may be very sceptical of this strategy. You may believe that hard work is not enough and that the client would do well to learn a bit of networking and self-promotion skills – or whatever you believe would help them to obtain the promotion they desire. You may be right about this. However, it is important to remember that in Being-Centred Therapy in general and in the process of Sensing Completion in particular, the goal is not to help the client fulfil their desired condition. The goal is to help the client become aware of Being and let that awareness transform the client. Any other agenda will only get in the way by activating the client's mind and drawing their awareness away from Being.

The obstacles of struggle, impatience and impossibility

Another common way in which clients become distracted from letting their awareness rest on the felt sense they imagine they will get when their desired condition is fulfilled is negative opinions about what they believe they need to do to fulfil the condition.

The chain of association would look something like:

1. The client imagines success in fulfilling the desired conditions
2. They feel the attractive felt sense they associate with the fulfilment of these conditions
3. The client starts mapping out what they believe they need to do to fulfil their desired condition
4. The client objects to having to do what they imagine they have to do. They may think it is too much of a struggle, that it takes too long or simply that it is not possible.

In short, the client objects to their own ideas about what they have to do to fulfil their desired condition as if those ideas were the indisputable truth. This line of associations shows how clients can become trapped in their own imagined world by reacting to their own imagination as if it were merely observations of facts.

A client may, for example, wish to be more confident (their desired condition). When they consider how to become more confident, they may imagine that this requires them to learn to control their anxiety, repress their self-doubt, formulate and achieve certain goals, practice self-assured body language, use positive affirmations daily and change their circle of friends to surround themselves with supportive and confident people. After imagining that they must do all that, they may object and say, this feels like a struggle, this will take way too long, or even that it is just not possible.

It can be very tempting to engage in a reflection on whether they really need to do all they believe they need to do or whether it would really be as much of a struggle as they imagine. However, since the purpose of Sensing Completion is to direct the client's awareness towards the aspect of Being they are ultimately reaching for, doing so would be a mistake.

Instead, you can simply acknowledge the client's frustration with the process and invite them to imagine what they would feel like if they woke up one morning and all they believe they would have to do had already been done.

In relation to the above-mentioned example, you might say:

> "Yes. Engaging in positive affirmations, goal setting, emotional control, changing body language and social circles is a lot of effort. Fortunately, you do not have to do any of that to *imagine* what confidence feels like. Imagine you had already done all of the above and notice what the confidence you now feel is like. What *does* confidence feel like?"

In this response, I provide a succinct summary of the client's plan, distilling each part into a word or two. The purpose of this summary is to acknowledge the client's plan while at the same time giving it as little attention as possible. The summary effectively treats the entire plan as a single uninteresting unit. Afterwards, I propose that *noticing* what felt sense the client is reaching for does not require any specific action. It is fully possible to state the purpose of a plan without executing it. As in the previous section, I use the present tense to help the client feel what they are reaching for in the present moment.

If the client remains fixated on the topic of the struggle associated with fulfilling their desired condition, you can invoke "magic" or "parallel universes", to help detach the client's awareness from the topic of the struggle. You might say:

> "Imagine you woke up tomorrow and somehow you are confident. You don't know how it happened. But it is there now. What does that feel like?"

By suggesting a magical transformation, you turn the plan into a black box and remove the possibility of feeling that the transformation was a struggle.

Not all clients are willing to suspend disbelief and imagine this kind of scenario, but many are. So, it can be worth a try. You could also say:

> "Imagine a parallel universe where your positive affirmations are an integral and effortless part of your daily life, where you have already achieved a succession of significant goals, where emotional control and confident body language is second nature to you, where your social circle is full of supportive and confident people, and where you don't even know what it feels like not to be confident. What does it feel like to be you in this universe?"

In this statement, you spend more time on addressing each aspect of the client's plan, not as a struggle, but as something that is natural, effortless and already in place. Talking about the plan as something already achieved without effort, might unhook the client's awareness from the imagined struggle. Once again, not all clients will engage with this scenario, but many will. So, it can be worth a try.

One of the trickier ways clients can get hooked on the difficulties they imagine they will have to go through to fulfil their desired condition is when they say:

> "Why imagine having what you cannot have? That only enhances the pain."

In such cases, it is (as always) good to acknowledge the client's concern before redirecting their awareness towards the felt sense. Furthermore, it can be good to hint at the separation between the felt sense the client is reaching for and the ideas they have about how to get it.

You may, for example, say:

> "True. If you truly cannot have something there is no need to rub it in. That would just be self-torture. However, before you can determine whether you can have it or not, you need to know what it is you are ultimately reaching for. What you want is not the positive affirmations, goal setting, emotional control, new body language or new social circle. These are just a means to an end. What you want may not even be confidence. What you want is a particular feeling. If you were the most confident person on the planet but you didn't get the feeling you sought, confidence wouldn't

necessarily matter much to you. So, what is the feeling you think you would get if you were confident?"

This is a bit of a speech. For those who are schooled in forms of therapy or coaching that emphasise the need for the therapist/coach to speak less than the client, this might seem like a lot to say in one go. However, this little speech can be seen as a form of mental massage. It is designed to orient the client's mind in such a way that it becomes easier for them to perceive Being – despite their fear of pain and disappointment. Making persuasive arguments that turn the client's worldview on its head can be useful to soften up some of the client's fixated ideas.

The obstacle of lacking experience

Sometimes, clients will claim that they cannot describe what fulfilment of their desired condition would feel like because they have never experienced it.

Your client may, for example, say they wish to feel loved but that since no one has ever loved them, they don't know what that feels like. Or your client may wish to be wealthy, but that since they have always been poor, they have no idea what being wealthy feels like.

On the surface, this may appear to make sense. You cannot know what something feels like if you haven't experienced it. You cannot know what an apple tastes like if you have never eaten one. So, how can you know what parental love feels like if you grew up with parents who didn't love you? How do you know what affluence feels like if you have been struggling to make ends meet all your life?

However, the question is not what the fulfilment of the client's desire *actually* feels like but rather what the client *imagines* it would feel like. As a therapist, you can know with certainty that the client *imagines* that fulfilling their desired conditions will feel amazing in some way because if they didn't, there would be no desire.

You can use this distinction to refocus the client's attention on exploring the felt sense they are reaching for. First, you acknowledge the validity of the client's objection by saying that they cannot know for sure what fulfilling their desired condition will feel like, and then you ask about what they imagine it would feel like.

For example, if the client desires to be loved unconditionally but say they don't know what this feels like because they have never experienced it, you can say:

> "Of course, you cannot know what unconditional love feels like if you have not experienced it. However, the fact that you desire unconditional love shows that you must believe that it will feel good. If you didn't have *any* idea about what unconditional love feels like, you would not be attracted to it. So, what do you believe being loved unconditionally feels like?"

It is worth noting that I completely avoid taking a stance on whether the client claims that they have never experienced what they seek. It is reasonable to doubt what the client says. It is highly unlikely that anyone has lived a life with no love at all. It can be tempting to challenge this belief and help the client remember situations where they have indeed felt love.

However, while the intention of challenging a false belief underpinning the client's suffering is good, doing so directly would side-track the Sensing Completion process needlessly. The goal of this process is to bring awareness to the felt sense the client is longing for and give them a deep experience of the felt sense by helping them to have sustained awareness of the felt sense.

If the client's experience in the moment is that they have never felt loved, that is fine. If you challenge it, you only give the client an excuse to keep avoiding the felt sense of being loved by engaging in a discussion about the character and actions of their parents.

If, on the other hand, the client starts describing the felt sense of being loved and starts feeling it, that felt sense is likely to trigger the client's memory, and they might start to remember times in their childhood when they did feel loved.

This is a much more effective way of challenging the client's belief since it does not involve contradicting the client but allows the client to discover the fallacy of their beliefs for themselves.

Furthermore, if the client insists that they have never felt loved before but still get a sense of the feeling they are searching for, that is wonderful. Then the day of the session is the first time they feel it, and that can only make the experience more powerful and memorable. And who knows what positive changes in the way the client perceives their life and life story will emerge as they become more acquainted with the felt sense of love? Your job, as a therapist, is to bring the client's awareness to Being. It is Being's job to do the rest.

The obstacle of negative consequences

Finally, clients are often distracted from focusing on the felt sense they believe will come from fulfilling a desired condition by their objections to either having the desire itself or the actions they think are necessary to achieve it.

The chain of association would look something like:

1. The client imagines success in fulfilling the desired conditions
2. They feel the attractive felt sense they associate with the fulfilment of these conditions
3. The client "remembers" their negative perception of the fulfilled condition and objects.

This is the same chain of associations that we looked at in the section *The negative state is caused by a negative perception of success*. The only difference is that the client's awareness lands in the negative perception rather than in the negative inner state related to this perception.

The way to deal with this is to modify the desired scenario so it includes a sentence about the absence of the negative consequence.

A client may, for example, wish to be wealthy. However, when you ask what the client believes being wealthy would feel like, they will tell you that wealth corrupts and that they don't want to be corrupted. In this case, you may restate the question as follows:

> "Yes. One can certainly find many examples of how wealth corrupts. And being corrupted is obviously not what attracts you to the idea of being wealthy. So, what might it feel like to be wealthy if you knew for sure, that it wouldn't corrupt you in the slightest?"

In this response, the therapist starts by unquestioningly agreeing with the client. If you are aware of concrete examples of the corruptive power of wealth, you may want to include a brief mention of one or two of these examples. Strengthening the client's objection in this way is likely to make them feel understood and, consequently, open to listening to what comes next.

In the second part of the response, the therapist restates the question of what fulfilling the desired condition would feel like – but with a modification that excludes the negative consequence the client is concerned about.

Sometimes, the negative consequence is not related to the fulfilment of the desired condition but rather to having the desire in the first place.

A client may, for example, be disturbed by simply having the desire to be wealthy. They may believe that this is already a sign of corruption.

In this case, it can be good to normalise the desire and to point out that wealth is not the end goal but that the goal is a feeling they hope to attain through being wealthy. In other words, you can propose to the client that "wealth" is merely a symbol for that which they truly desire, namely the feeling, and that there is nothing corrupt about desiring the feeling.

You may, for example, say:

> "The desire to be wealthy is an extremely common desire that most people will recognise. Furthermore, it is often not the wealth itself people desire. It's not even the things wealth allows you to do. What people generally desire is the feeling they believe they will get if they are wealthy. It could be relaxation or enjoyment or peace or something else. And everyone desires these kinds of feelings. That is just human. And the world would probably be a better place if more people felt these things deeply. So, if you set aside for a moment any worries about what it means that you desire wealth, do you know what positive feeling you are hoping to get from being wealthy?"

In this response, the therapist first normalises the desire for wealth, then points to a deeper desire and normalises this desire by pointing out that it is a universal human desire which is harmless or even beneficial. This is all aimed at soothing the client's concern about their own desire so that they can focus their awareness on exploring what felt sense they are reaching for.

As mentioned in the section on *The negative state is caused by a negative perception of success,* sometimes, the negative perception is so strong that we will have to pause the process of Sensing Completion and shift to Sensing Unity described in Chapter 6, Knot 5: The Knot of Fragmentation.

Finally, it is worth mentioning that it is good for the therapist to resist the temptation to challenge the client's beliefs about negative consequences – even if they appear to be flawed.

You may, for example, believe that wealth does not necessarily corrupt. And you may think that if only you can make the client see this, they would be able to embrace their pursuit more wholeheartedly. There can, of course, be value in challenging the client's beliefs. However, given the purpose of the Sensing Completion process, engaging clients in such discussions is likely to simply derail the process and make it more difficult to become aware of the aspect of Being they are reaching for through fulfilling the desired conditions.

Sensing Completion is a process where we enter into the client's system of associated beliefs and emotions and search for the heart of this system – the aspect of Being the whole system revolves around. This is best done by accepting the system as it is and trusting that once the client becomes aware of Being this experience will transform their system of associated beliefs and emotions in ways that are far more intelligent than anything any therapist could do by challenging individual beliefs directly. The less we disturb the client's system, the faster we can penetrate to the heart of it and open the client's awareness up for Being.

Hidden motives behind imagined obstacles

Sometimes, the client will encounter many negative states and imagined obstacles when they are asked what they believe fulfilling their desired condition would feel like. Every time you deal with one negative state or imagined obstacle, another emerges.

In such cases, you may get the feeling that the client is invested in keeping their desire unfulfilled. In other words, the client may have a covert attachment to the longing and the separation.

In such cases, the client generally has an unconscious agenda. They are trying to achieve something positive through the behaviour that runs counter to their conscious agenda. We will deal with this in Chapter 5, Knot 4: The Knot of Alienation, but it is worth mentioning here.

This concludes the second part of the Sensing Completion process. By now the client has become aware of the felt sense they are ultimately reaching for, and "tasted" it in the present moment, so it is now time to look at how to separate this felt sense from the fulfilment of the desired condition.

The following section contains four processes which can make the client aware that the felt sense they seek is an ever-present aspect of Being and not the direct product of fulfilling the desired condition. Each process is related to one or several of the corrective principles described in Section 3.3.

3.4.4. Step 3: Correct misconceptions related to the Knot of Conditionality

In the first step of Sensing Completion described above, the therapist helps the client become aware of the felt sense they are reaching for by trying to fulfil certain conditions. Furthermore, the therapist helps the client steer clear of various chains of association that take the client's awareness away from this felt sense. If done correctly, the result is that the client has a vivid and visceral experience of the felt sense they desire – even though the client has not fulfilled any conditions.

This experience opens the possibility of powerfully suggesting the five corrective principles related to the Knot of Conditionality. The second phase of Sensing Completion consists of processes with this purpose.

In the sections that follow, I will outline four processes that aim at suggesting the five corrective principles related to the Knot of Conditionality.

- Access suggests the 4th and 5th corrective principles
- Non-Doing suggests the 6th corrective principle
- Counterproductivity suggests the 7th corrective principle
- Non-Urgency suggests the 8th corrective principle

During therapy sessions, I rarely use all four processes. I prefer to select one or two that seem to be most impactful for the specific client and the specific context.

The rationale behind this is that if a client gains a powerful insight, it is best to allow space and time for this insight to land. If you overload the client with additional insights, you risk confusing them and potentially diluting the power of the initial revelation.

Access and the 4th and 5th corrective principles

In the first part of Sensing Completion, the client becomes aware of the felt sense they are ultimately reaching for when they are trying to fulfil their desired conditions, and they pay attention to this felt sense long enough to feel it in their bodies.

This experience reveals to the client that they can access what they are reaching for simply by paying attention to it – and without fulfilling the conditions they believed were the cause of the felt sense. In other words, it shows that what they are reaching for is always available to them (4th corrective principle) and that, therefore, to feel it they simply have to pay attention to it, not create or acquire it (5th corrective principle).

The Access process helps the client draw these conclusions from their experience in the first part of the Sensing Completion process.

First, you need to obtain the client's explicit acknowledgement of the fact that they are currently feeling the state they were seeking. You can do so simply by asking:

> "Do you feel the state you are describing?"

Securing the client's explicit verbal confirmation of their felt-sense experience enables you to more effectively draw the client's attention to the conclusions that necessarily follow from this experience.

Clients tend to change their perception of events if these events challenge long-held beliefs[28]. Therefore, if you indicate that the client's experience in the first part of the Sensing Completion process shows that what they seek is always present and that their belief about what conditions cause the state is misguided, the client may start to doubt, forget or deny that they felt the state just by paying attention to it – even if they, minutes earlier, proclaimed to be feeling the state vividly.

When the client verbally confirms their experience, they are more likely to remember it, and if they forget, you can remind them more persuasively by referring to their own verbal confirmation. The client may be perplexed as to why they said that they felt the state, but it is harder to doubt or deny what they *said* than to doubt or deny what they *felt*. Thus, securing explicit verbal affirmation from the client aids you in compelling them to resolve the cognitive dissonance[29] created by the Sensing Completion process by re-evaluating their beliefs, rather than by altering their perception of the experience.

Timing is essential when asking a client if they are experiencing the state they are describing.

---

[28] The reason for this is that holding conflicting beliefs, values, or behaviours is uncomfortable. Leon Festinger (Festinger, 1957; Festinger & Carlsmith, 1959) called this kind of discomfort "Cognitive Dissonance". His research shows that people will often radically alter their perception of events rather than having to change established beliefs.

[29] Leon Festinger's (Festinger, 1957; Festinger & Carlsmith, 1959) research on cognitive dissonance also showed that when someone verbally states a belief or commitment, it creates a stronger sense of accountability, making them more likely to alter their beliefs to align with what they've expressed, to reduce the dissonance between their words and their internal state.

If you ask prematurely, the client may not have developed their awareness of the felt sense state sufficiently. Consequently, they are likely to answer that they do *not* feel the felt sense they are talking about. In that case, you should dedicate more to developing the client's awareness of the felt sense state through description.

If you ask too late, the felt sense may have faded and the client may no longer be aware of it. In that case, you can ask whether they felt the state as they spoke about it. If they confirm this, you can still proceed with the Access Process. However, if they do not, you have most likely missed your opportunity. You can attempt to return to the description phase, but often it will be better to allow the session to naturally flow onto the next topic.

The optimal time to ask the question is when you notice physical reactions in the client indicating that they are experiencing the state they are describing. For instance, if the client talks about relief, the time to ask the question is when you see them heave a sigh of relief, drop their shoulders or show other signs of relief. If the client talks about feeling energised, the time to ask the question is when they start speaking louder or faster, start gesticulating more, or show other signs of being energised or excited. If the client talks about feeling peace, the time to ask the question is when they cease talking, their face softens, or they show other signs of feeling peace and tranquillity. With experience, you will learn to recognise these physical indications. Additionally, if you are familiar with the various aspects of Being, you can also recognise when clients are experiencing the states they are talking about, by noticing when these states emerge in you as you are listening to the client.

Once the client has confirmed that they are, in this moment, feeling the state they were seeking, you can point out that they are feeling the state despite not having fulfilled any conditions. All they did was paying sustained attention to the state. You can do so by asking a question in which this assertion is embedded:

> "How is it to notice that you are now feeling the state you were seeking, even though you have not fulfilled the conditions you believed to be the cause of the state?"

Delivering this obvious fact at the right moment can be an immensely powerful way to introduce the 5th corrective principle: You don't create what you seek; you become aware of it.

If the client accepts this principle, you can further expand your suggestion to include the 4th corrective principle: What you seek is always already present. You do so by suggesting that the reason the client doesn't always experience the desired state is not because it is absent, but rather that they are not always aware of it – they become distracted, so to speak.

Most clients will be puzzled at this point. And it is essential to allow them sufficient time to absorb both the experience and the proposed interpretations.

Even if clients do not deny outright what they experienced in the first part of the Sensing Completion process, they may still resist adopting the suggested interpretations of these experiences. This is normal and healthy and should be welcomed. After all, if new perspectives cannot withstand challenges, they are not worth adopting. It is only by confronting and overcoming challenges that new perspectives mature into strong and valuable convictions.

In the following, I will comment on four of the most common objections clients have to interpreting their experience during the Sensing Completion process as evidence of the 4th and 5th corrective principles. These objections are:

- Yes, I feel the state, but it's not real, I just imagined it
- Yes, I feel the state, but I would feel it more if I fulfilled the condition
- Yes, I feel the state, but I cannot give up trying to fulfil the condition because I've spent so much time on this. It cannot all have been for nothing
- I feel the state because you (the therapist) are here.

It's not real, I just imagined it

Sometimes, clients may argue that what they feel isn't real but just a product of their imagination.

To deal with this objection, you can simply invert the argument. If mere imagination is sufficient to elicit the state, then why go through the arduous work of fulfilling the conditions the client thought were the cause of the state?

The client's objection is based on flawed logic. They claim that the desired state is caused by fulfilling certain conditions, and if the state emerges without the client fulfilling these conditions, it means the state is not real. However, the occurrence of the state without the conditions being fulfilled is clear evidence that the conditions cannot be the only thing that can cause the state – and if something else can cause the state, there is no guarantee that the emergence of the state is ever caused by fulfilling the conditions. The conditions and the state may simply have occurred simultaneously in the client's experience until now and correlation is not causation.

One way of showing the fallacy in the client's logic is to ask them in what sense a feeling they are experiencing in the present moment isn't real. After all, the reality of a feeling must depend upon whether the client is feeling it, not on whether the client has fulfilled the conditions they *believe* to be the cause of it.

Another way of showing the flaw in the client's argument is to create a parallel example in which the feeling is replaced by something more tangible. You can, for example, say that if you believe that wearing your lucky socks is what causes your favourite basketball team to win, and one day you forget to wear your socks, but the team still wins, you wouldn't say that this victory is not real.

I would feel it more if I fulfilled the condition

Sometimes, clients acknowledge that they are experiencing the state they desire, but they believe they would feel it with more intensity if they were to fulfil the conditions they believe to be the cause of the state.

The flaw in this argument lies in the client objecting to a claim about causality by making an irrelevant and unwarranted statement about intensity.

That the client feels the state they are seeking with any level of intensity and without fulfilling any conditions shows that fulfilling the conditions is not what causes the state to emerge.

Therefore, when a client suggests that fulfilling certain conditions would cause a stronger sense of the state, they are, essentially, claiming that doing more of something that does not cause the state would result in a more intense feeling of that state. Clearly, this cannot be true.

To point out the fallacy of the client's argument, you can respond:

> "The important thing in this exploration is not how strongly you feel the state but that you can feel it at all without fulfilling the condition. This is enough to show that the condition is not the cause of the state you long for. If you feel it now, it is possible to feel it without doing anything. What determines the intensity is a separate question that we have yet to answer – all we know is that it cannot be the fulfilment of the conditions."

Inviting the client to leave the question of intensity unanswered is a good way of inviting them to stay open to new insights.

It cannot all have been for nothing

Sometimes, clients object to the experience of directly becoming aware of the state they are seeking without doing anything to create or acquire it because they struggle to accept how much unnecessary pain they have caused themselves simply because they didn't know this was a possibility – they didn't know the true nature of what they were seeking.

Listening to this objection can be heart-breaking. The client may have spent a lot of time and effort on needlessly pursuing irrelevant goals. The client may have expended a significant amount of time and effort in the pursuit of what they now realise were inconsequential objectives. In this moment of the therapeutic process, they might feel as though a considerable portion of their life was wasted in this fruitless pursuit. They may feel like the punchline of a cruel cosmic joke.

To support the client in grappling with this challenging realisation, it's vital to provide them with all the time they need and simply be there with them as they process the pain of it. You can help the client coming to terms with the reality of their situation by encouraging them to focus on the future rather than the past:

> "I understand it can be hard to accept that your struggle may have been unnecessary. But better acknowledging it now than spending the rest of your life in the same unnecessary struggle."

This objection is, essentially, an example of what economist, Daniel Kahneman, calls the "sunk cost fallacy". Sunk costs are costs that have already been incurred and cannot be recovered. For decision making related to the future, sunk costs are irrelevant and should be disregarded. However, because people get emotionally invested in projects they have spent time and energy on, sunk costs can make people stick to projects even after it has become clear that these projects offer no benefits. The time and effort a client has spent on pursuing the fulfilment of irrelevant conditions, because they falsely believed it would bring them a positive inner state, is a sunk cost.

However, if a client reaches this stage, it is good to be aware that they may be grieving a loss they have only just begun to recognise. It is important to allow the grief to unfold naturally.

I feel the state because of the therapy

Sometimes, clients may accept that the conditions they once believed would create the state they seek cannot do so. However, rather than realising that no external conditions will produce the state they desire, they shift their focus to new conditions. A common example is clients believing they feel Being because of the presence of the therapist.

This belief is created the way Knots of Conditionality are typically formed. When clients experience a pleasant state of Being, they attribute it to some external factor that happens to be present in the environment. In therapy, clients often choose the therapist as the external factor they see as the source of the states they feel.

Refuting the belief that you, as the therapist, are the source of your clients' experiences of Being can be challenging, as your presence is indeed a constant factor in all your clients' experiences of Being during sessions.

However, it's crucial to address this misconception. If the client starts seeing the therapist as the source of their experiences of Being, it can lead to highly problematic relational dynamics with negative consequences for both client and therapist.

It hurts clients by reinforcing their sense of personal lack, deficiency, and separateness, while also creating an unhealthy dependency on you as their therapist. It also hurts the therapist as the reason you would accept clients seeing you as the source of their Being is generally a wish to mask your own sense of lack, deficiency and separateness and by masking it you reinforce it. If multiple clients (or disciples) see you as the source of their experiences of Being, it can inflate your self-image, making it harder for you to remain grounded in Being. When you allow clients to put you on a pedestal, you are setting yourself – and them – up for disappointment and disillusionment when your human imperfections inevitably are exposed.

A good way of showing clients that you, as the therapist, are not the source of the Being they experience in sessions is by employing the Non-Doing process described in the next section. In this process, you help the client identify the specific actions through which they disconnect themselves from the state they seek in their everyday life. Once they recognise how their own actions create this separation, you can explain that therapy helps them stop these activities, allowing them to sense Being more easily. The therapist, therefore, is not the source of Being but simply facilitates the client's ability to stop blocking it.

Other objections

Clients may present other objections to the adjustment of their misconceptions. In such cases, try to be creative. The client has already acknowledged that what they are pursuing is an inner felt-sense state, and that they are experiencing it simply by paying attention to it. The conclusion that the conditions are unnecessary is inescapable. If they resist this understanding, allow them to do so. The experience will eventually land. All you can do is sow the seed of insight and patiently wait for it to take root and grow within the client.

The Access Process is summarised in Figure 9: The Access Process.

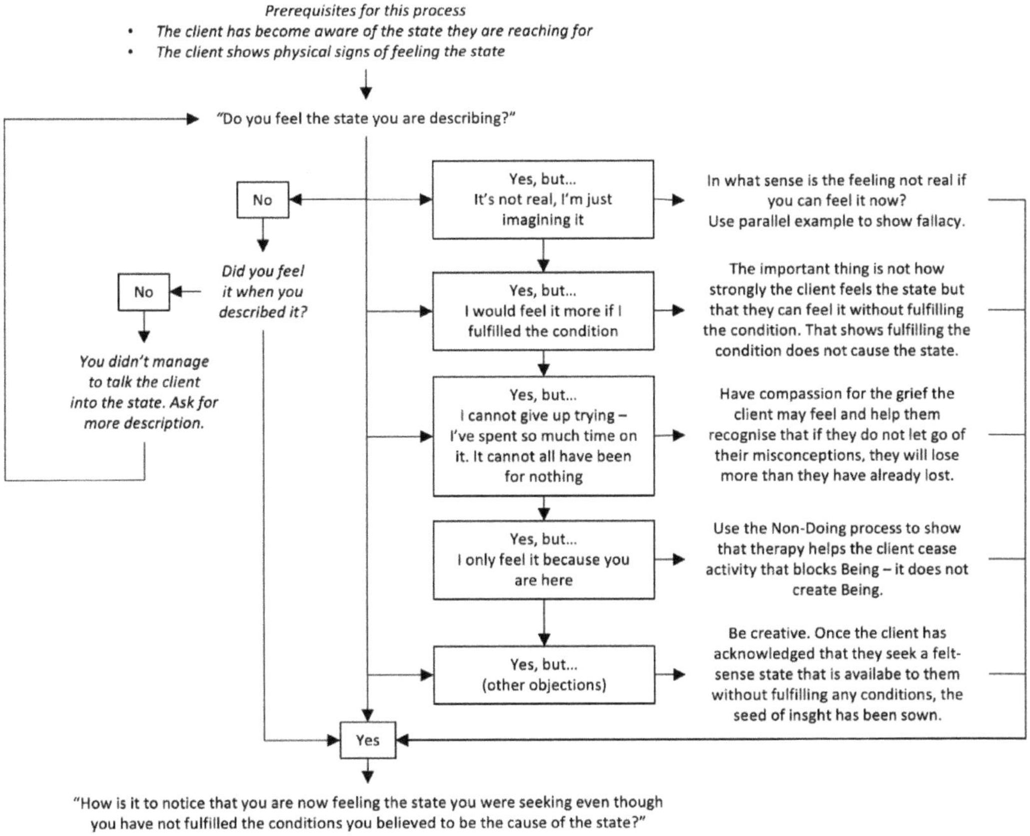

Figure 9: The Access Process

Non-doing and the 6th corrective principle

Once the client has experienced that they can feel the desired state simply by paying sustained attention to it, they are also receptive to the 6th corrective principle that you don't get to feel the state you seek by *doing* something to create or acquire it, but rather by *ceasing to do* something that currently takes your awareness away from it.

As discussed in Section 3.3.3, the question that should guide the therapy session is not: What can the client do to create or acquire the desired state?, but rather: What is the client currently doing that keeps them unaware of the state?

Thus, the therapy can be likened to checking the activity monitor on a slow-running computer to identify those programs that are draining the computer's processing power and then shutting them down.

In a client, the "programs" are mental, emotional and behavioural processes that occupy the client's attention, leaving insufficient attention capacity for awareness of Being. These processes are often automatic and unconscious. They are like programs that are running in the background on your computer – you don't see them but they still drain the computer's processing power.

With every program/process that is identified and shut down, the client will "free up" more awareness and the probability that the client will become aware of Being increases. Thus, non-doing is a process of noticing what activity occupies the client's attention and then inviting the client to cease that activity – if even just momentarily. The reason it is enough to stop the processes momentarily (not permanently) is that this is enough to notice Being, and once the client notices Being, this experience will grab their attention in such a way that they are much less interested in restarting the programs. In practice, the client will experience this as having a lot on their mind (worrying, planning, etc.) which seem very important to them, but once they notice Being these things seem much less important.

Thus, after the client, in the first phase of the Sensing Completion process, has experienced that they can feel the state they are seeking without fulfilling the conditions they thought were the cause of the state, you can invite the client to reflect on what prevented them from noticing this state earlier. You can formulate this invitation in the following way:

> "So, if it is possible for you to feel this state simply by paying attention to it, how then do you manage to not feel it all the time? What do you pay attention to instead of this state?"

If you, during the first part of the Sensing Completion process, have gained a sense of what mental, emotional and behavioural processes take the client's awareness away from Being, it can be powerful to point out that, instead of trying to create the state they seek, they can simply stop blocking it with those particular patterns. It is, however, recommendable to treat any hunch you may have about what processes block awareness of Being as a hypothesis and present it as inspiration for the client's own reflection – not as a statement of fact.

For example, a client may ask you to help them better control their frustration. You then engage in the Sensing Completion process and discover that the client wants to get better at controlling their frustration, so they can become better at mediating interpersonal conflicts they encounter at work as well as in their private life, and that by mediating such conflicts they are reaching for a state of harmony and tranquillity.

When considering what the client is doing that prevents them from noticing the harmonious and tranquil aspect of Being, you may have noticed that they create elaborate narratives about how interpersonal conflicts can spin out of control and lead to negative outcomes far beyond anything they have ever experienced.

Thus, to feel harmony and tranquillity, rather than trying to mediate every conflict the client comes across, the client could focus on ceasing to create such disaster narratives. Whereas this may not be easy for the client, it is the more promising of the two paths to harmony and tranquillity – and the one that would best guide the therapeutic process.

You can propose this view by saying:

> Therapist: "It seems that you often give a lot of consideration to quite severe potential outcomes of interpersonal conflicts – even when such outcomes are highly unlikely and beyond anything you have ever experienced. Would you agree?"
>
> Client: "Yes."
>
> Therapist: "You may not know how to do it, but what do you think it would feel like if, now, you *could* stop worrying about any negative outcomes you have never experienced?"
>
> Client: "I'd feel much more at ease..."

If you do not get the client's confirmation after the first question, it may be because your hypothesis is wrong. In that case, simply continue reflecting together with the client on what takes their awareness away from harmony and tranquillity.

There are, of course, many processes that can take the client's attention away from Being. It can be useful to think about three categories of such processes.

- **Obsessing:** The client is busy with something they see as more important than the state they seek
- **Worrying:** The client is busy navigating problems they associate with the state they seek
- **Searching:** The client is busy looking for the state they seek.

In the following, I will describe the two first types of process and how to help the client to stop them. The third type of process is the topic of the next section on the counterproductive nature of clients' strategies for creating or acquiring the states they seek.

Obsessing: The client is busy with something they see as more important

Sometimes, clients are very occupied with achieving something, and if feeling the state is not relevant to this mission, or if feeling it will get in the way of completing the mission, the client will ignore it.

To invite the client to stop obsessing, you can ask them to consider a scenario where this obsession is irrelevant.

Consider, for example, a client that is longing for "silence and peace", but who is obsessed with making a difference in the world. This client may feel that peace will have to wait until they have completed their mission in life. In practice, this means that they will never give attention to peace because there is always something more they can do to increase the positive impact they have on the world.

It is, of course, commendable to wish to make a positive impact on the world. However, if this wish then prevents the client from ever feeling at ease, it has turned into an obsession. And since making a difference in the world is a marathon, not a sprint, resting periods are of vital importance.

One way of inviting the client to pause their obsession is to invite them to consider a scenario where the obsession is no longer relevant.

In the above example, you can invite the client to:

- consider that during the session, they have no opportunity to work on their mission, and so, they can drop it
- let go of making any impact on the world for 30 seconds, since such a short time will make no difference to their goal
- consider how it would be if someone trustworthy and capable took over their mission for a day.

There is ample room for creativity when you formulate such scenarios. What scenarios you should propose will depend on both the nature of the obsession and the temperament of the client. Any scenario that will make the client pause their obsession, even briefly, will do.

If the client feels the state they long for when pausing their obsession, you can point out that the reason they do not always feel peace is that they are too concerned with making a difference in the world.

The process of non-doing brings clarity around how an obsession can cut the client off from resource states they long for. Even if the client still wants to make a difference in the world, having clarity around how this can lead them to ignore an important resource can help them reinvent how they go about making a difference.

The problem is not that the client wants to make a difference in the world but that they go about this in a way that takes their awareness away from Being. When the client understands this, they are more likely to become curious about what it might mean to make a difference in the world while remaining (continuously) aware of the peaceful aspect of Being.

If you succeed in constructing a scenario in which the client's obsession is irrelevant, this scenario can help the client experience how letting go of their obsession will free up their awareness and allow them to become aware of Being – including the silent and peaceful aspect.

Worrying: The client is busy with problems they associate with the state

Sometimes, the processes that occupy the client's attention are attempts at navigating problems the client associates with the state they seek. The client is attracted to the state, but the moment they start feeling it, it triggers concerns about what feeling the state means, and when these concerns start occupying the client's awareness, they lose awareness of the state again.

To invite the client to stop worrying, you can ask them to consider a scenario where this worry is irrelevant. In particular, you can separate the concerns from the state itself[30].

If a client is seeking the state of "lightness and joy", they might be distracted by worrying about whether it is permissible to feel lightness and joy if there are people in the world, particularly people close to them, who are suffering in one way or another. The client may believe that:

- It is offensive to feel joy when others are not feeling it
- If you feel joy, it will exacerbate others' suffering
- It is immoral to feel joy when others are suffering
- Setting aside your own joy helps people who suffer feel better.

However, *feeling* joy and lightness cannot be offensive, immoral or affect others' suffering one way or the other if the feeling is separated from *any* action. In principle, you could feel joy and lightness without anyone ever knowing.

You can use this perspective to invite the client to separate the state of joy and lightness from any worries they may have and, thus, help them stop those worries so they no longer take the client's awareness away from the state of joy and lightness. You can do so either by making the worry irrelevant in the present moment, by challenging the validity of the worry, or by turning the logic of the worry on its head. Here are some examples of how to do that:

- "Right now, during this session, it will not affect anyone if you feel lightness and joy"
- "If someone has plunged into a hole, jumping into the hole with them only prevents you from being of service to them"
- "Joy is a resource. If you set aside your resources, you will be less able to be something for someone else"
- "When you feel joy, you can inspire others to do the same"
- "Sure, singing and dancing with joy may be a bit inappropriate when someone has just told you about their pain. However, no one can see what you feel in the privacy of your own inner world. So, allowing lightness and joy internally can never harm anyone"

---

[30] I will explore this in much more detail in the next chapter in Section 4.4, Sensing Taboos – how to untie the Knot of Negative Reification.

The purpose of such sentences is not to convince the client of anything, but rather to turn off the concern that, at present, is drawing the client's awareness away from Being. They are sentences constructed to put the client's concern at ease and free up their awareness so they may notice Being.

Once the concern is turned off, the client's awareness will return to its default state of Being, as it exists before they engage in any activity, and this includes lightness and joyfulness.

If you succeed in separating the problem the client worries about from the felt sense they long for, this can help them experience how letting go of their worrying will free up their awareness and allow them to become aware of Being – including the light and joy.

Objections

Once the client starts understanding that everything, they seek can be found by doing less rather than doing more, two objections typically arise.

1. **But what I do, does work sometimes:** The client may point out that they do, in fact, sometimes feel the desired state when they fulfil certain conditions.
2. **But then I'd never do anything:** The client may worry that if they don't have to do anything to feel good they would become inactive in life and never do anything.

An important part of the non-doing process is to be able to deal with these two objections. Below, I will comment on each objection in turn.

But what I do, does work sometimes

It is true that clients may experience the desired state immediately after fulfilling the conditions, they believe are needed to create or acquire this state. It is precisely because clients have such experiences that they come to believe that fulfilling certain conditions is necessary to create or acquire the desired state.

However, this experience does not come about because fulfilling the conditions create the state but rather because the fulfilment of the conditions incidentally disrupts one of the automatic and unconscious processes that, under normal circumstances, block the client's awareness of the desired state.

A client may, for example, experience a sense of value whenever they receive a compliment from their partner, not because the compliment generates a feeling of value but because receiving it interrupts the client's automatic process of self-deprecation that, under normal circumstances, takes the client's awareness away from the valuable aspect of Being.

Having a clear understanding of why fulfilling the conditions occasionally seems to produce the desired state is important because it reveals that fulfilling the conditions is not an energy-efficient approach to connecting with the desired state. In doing so, you end up spending energy both on the automatic and unconscious process that obstructs your awareness of the state *and* the conscious effort to fulfil the conditions that interrupt this unconscious process. It will always be more energy-efficient to simply cease running the automatic and unconscious process and, thus, cease to block your awareness of the desired state.

You can understand this by thinking of a shopping cart with a skewed wheel that pulls the cart to the left. The first scenario is akin to making the shopping cart go straight by distorting another wheel so it pulls the cart equally to the right. It works, but now it takes a lot of energy to push the cart. The second scenario is akin to fixing the first wheel, so the cart naturally goes straight. This approach is far more energy-efficient[31].

When clients point out that fulfilling the conditions does create the state they seek, you can use the above explanation to counter their objection.

But then I'd never do anything

Clients will sometimes object to the 6th corrective principle that you get to feel the state you seek by doing less, not more, by saying that if they can experience all their desired states without doing anything, they no longer have any reason to do anything. And sitting on the couch all day, doing nothing, may not appeal to the client.

Beneath are two responses to this objection.

First, it is worth noting that the objection reveals that the client is still operating from the assumption that they need to do something to feel good. That they find complete passivity objectionable reveals that they believe activity is important for their well-being.

---

[31] This distinction is parallel to a distinction between learning to overcome the negative effects of a deeply held belief by installing a new competing belief vs. changing the problematic belief. I will return to this in Section 7.5 on memory reconsolidation.

However, if the client truly felt all aspects of Being, doing nothing would not diminish their well-being in any way, and they would be absolutely fine with sitting on the couch all day. In fact, experienced meditators, who practise paying sustained attention to Being, will frequently report experiencing that they in meditation feel they could sit for ever and be perfectly happy.

Thus, when the client objects to complete passivity, you can ask them:

> "What do you think you would miss out on by never doing anything?"

This will reveal what the client is reaching out for through activity. In other words, you can do a Sensing Completion process starting from the client's desire to be active.

Second, it is also worth noting that the client has posed an important question

> "If I can access all desirable states just by paying attention to them, why then would I ever do anything?"

The reason it feels as if we would not do anything if we develop the capacity to be continuously aware of Being is that, when we are not aware of Being, almost all our activity is motivated, at least in part, by our desire to feel Being. Thus, we have very little experience of actions that are not motivated by trying to remedy a perceived lack of Being.

However, this does not mean there is no other form of motivation – only that we may not have experienced it much.

In fact, motivation can be divided into two different kinds. There is "lack-motivation", where we are motivated to do something to remedy a lack (real or imagined). This is the motivation we are used to. But there is also "abundance-motivation", where our inner sense of abundance spills over into action.

If all we know is lack-motivation, it makes sense to assume that we would not do anything if we felt nothing is lacking. However, if you know abundance-motivation, you also know that you can be active when you do not feel any lack.

One way of getting a sense of abundance-motivation and how it differs from lack-motivation is to think of days you felt really good and felt that nothing seemed to be lacking in your life, you might remember that those days you also felt you had a lot of energy and that precisely because you felt good and energised, you felt like doing things. You didn't do things because you hoped doing these things would make you feel good; rather, feeling good made you want to do things. This is how it feels to operate from abundance-motivation.

Another way of getting a sense of abundance-motivation and how it differs from lack-motivation is to think of times you have done something out of pure curiosity. You were not trying to remedy any lack in yourself or gain anything from your actions – you were just curious. Maybe you tried a new recipe or visited a place you hadn't been before, or maybe you asked a friend a question that had sparked your curiosity. You were active but not motivated by a sense of lack.

If you cannot connect with abundance-motivation in yourself, you may be able to connect with it in other people.

Think about the activity level of small children when they are in a good mood. At the time of writing, my son is two years old. When he is running around on the playground, climbing things or "driving" around on a toy scooter he is not doing all of that to fix some perceived lack in himself. He just has a lot of energy to spare. His activity is pure joy in action. One way of connecting with abundance-motivation is to imagine what it feels like to be a happy child on a playground.

Similarly, you can think of Buddhist masters. They are supposedly in touch with Being and have no problem sitting and enjoying Being for hours on end. In other words, their actions are not motivated by a sense of lack. Yet, many of them travel extensively, open schools and write books at a pace few others could keep up with. If you are curious about what such masters feel, you might get a sense of abundance-motivation.

Thus, while awareness of Being does make it possible to do nothing, it doesn't preclude action. Rather, it changes the nature of one's motivation.

This concludes the description of the non-doing process, which can help solidify the 6th corrective principle in the client.

The process of non-doing is summarised in Figure 10: The Non-doing Process.

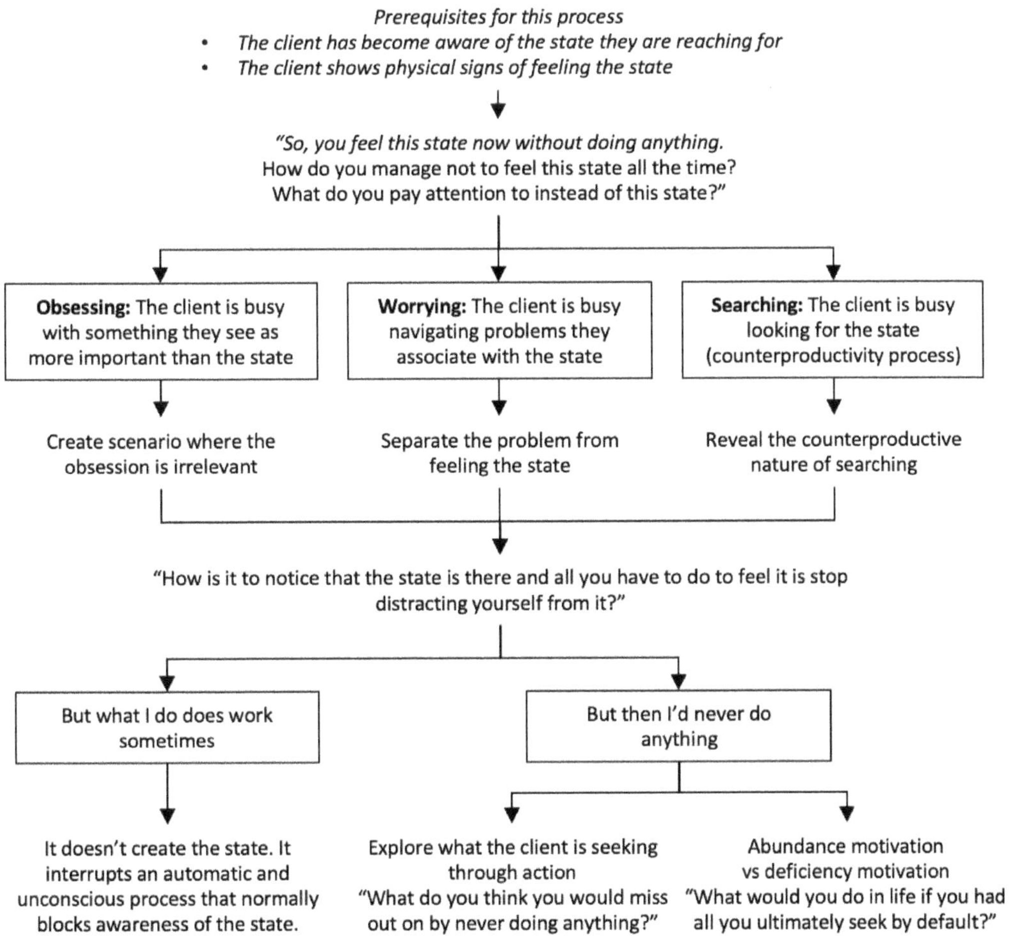

Figure 10: The Non-doing Process

Counterproductivity and the 7th corrective principle

The reason a client doesn't experience a desired state is not due to its absence but instead because their attention is preoccupied with a particular activity, preventing them from noticing the state. Ironically, the activity that occupies the client's attention is often the very activity they engage in for the purpose of creating or acquiring the state they desire. In other words, clients often do not feel their desired state because they are too busy searching for it.

Consequently, actions clients take to create or acquire a certain state are invariably counterproductive. This is the 7th corrective principle described in Section 3.3.4.

In therapy, it can be very powerful to highlight the counterproductive nature of the way the client tries to create or produce their desired state.

One way of doing this is to ask the client to compare the feeling they have *while* engaged in fulfilling the conditions with the feeling they believe fulfilling the conditions will bring them (which they uncovered in the first part of the Sensing Completion process). You can do this by asking two questions:

> "What do you feel *while* trying to fulfil the conditions?"
>
> "How does this feeling compare with the feeling you desire?"

Because any mental, emotional or behavioural process tends to take the client's awareness away from Being, the client will often notice that while they are occupied with fulfilling the conditions, they will feel the exact opposite of the state they are striving to create or acquire.

If this is the case, you can ask the client how long they believe they need to do something that produces one state in order to get to the opposite state. The absurdity in this statement captures the counterproductive nature of the client's project and will often be a powerful way of making the client lose their enthusiasm for this project and cease searching.

For example, a client may criticise their own work performance harshly. During the first phase of the Sensing Completion process, they may find that they do this to motivate themselves to get better at what they do, so they will deliver impressive results, so others will look up to them, which they believe will make them feel safe and ultimately able to relax. When you ask what the client feels while they are criticising themselves, they may say that they feel very tense. Now you can ask the client:

> "How much tension do you need to create in yourself to make yourself relax?"
>
> "How long do you need to feel tense before this makes you relax?"

Of course, no amount of tension will lead to relaxation. When the client understands what state they seek, and they see that the activity through which they seek this state creates the direct opposite state, they recognise the absurdity of the whole project and may drop it.

The reason clients do not recognise the absurdity of their own project is that every individual step in the chain of causal links seems to make sense. Criticising yourself *can* indeed make you work harder, putting in more hours *can* make you better at what you do, etc. It is only when you look at the full scope of all the assumed causal links that you recognise that the project cannot work.

In other words, this process tests the client's plan by taking the chain of causal links mapped out in the first phase of the Sensing Completion process and placing the initial action next to the final outcome the client is reaching for. This always results in an absurd proposition because the whole project is based on the false premise that the state the client is reaching for needs to be created or acquired when, in reality, it is already present.

In practical terms, it is beneficial to divide the process into two separate questions. First, you ask:

"What do you feel *while* trying to fulfil the conditions?"

You will expect the client to give a negative answer because the whole project springs from a desire to remedy a perceived lack in themself. However, sometimes the client will give positive answers. The client may feel hopeful, joyful, excited, confident, etc. Usually, these feeling derive from the client being optimistic about their prospects. If they feel they are about to fulfil the conditions and they are looking forward to their expected reward, they may feel relatively good about their situation and downplay the sense of lack that is driving the project.

To deal with such answers, you can acknowledge that the client feels good about their prospects and ask whether the process might also involve some strain or discomfort. Usually, clients will emphatically confirm this, as if that goes without saying. Many times, clients fail to mention the negative feelings because they are simply too obvious to them.

When clients acknowledge the negative states they feel while striving to fulfil the conditions they believe will lead to positive inner states, you get a clear picture of the counterproductive nature of the client's strategy.

Knowing some of the counterproductive strategies clients typically follow will help you facilitate the process of counterproductivity. Beneath is a selection of common counterproductive strategies[32].

---

[32] These are the counterproductive strategies at the heart of each of the nine Enneatypes in the Enneagram personality typology framework. These are not the only ones you will encounter but they are extremely common and worth familiarising yourself with.

- Clients force themselves to live up to impossibly high standards to avoid criticism and feel appreciated. However, appreciation cannot come from self-criticism.
- Clients reject parts of themselves others won't like, hoping this will make them feel accepted for who they are. However, acceptance cannot come from self-rejection.
- Clients engage in perpetual upgrading of themselves to feel inherently valuable. However, inherent value cannot come from focusing on flaws that must be upgraded.
- Clients are putting themselves down to avoid being abandoned and feel loved. However, love cannot come from self-deprecation.
- Clients are cutting themselves off from resources as a way of avoiding depleting interactions with others and ensuring they have what they need. However, needs cannot be fulfilled through isolation.
- Clients are constantly looking for dangers in the hopes that this will make them feel safe. However, safety cannot come from paranoia.
- Clients are constantly looking for or fantasising about the next pleasure. However, pleasure cannot come from constant anticipation of future events.
- Clients are denying their own vulnerability and doubt in order to feel strong. However, strength cannot come from self-denial.
- Clients are setting aside their own needs to preserve harmony in their relationships. However, harmonious relationships cannot come from eradicating one side of the relationship.

When you understand both what state the client is ultimately reaching for *and* what they feel while trying to create or acquire this state, you can construct very powerful questions that sum up and exhibit the counterproductive nature of the client's strategy. You can do this simply by placing the desired state next to what the client feels while attempting to create or acquire this state.

- "How much do you need to raise the bar to eliminate your worry about falling short?"
- "How long do you need to reject yourself before you will feel accepted?"
- "How many upgrades do you need before you can feel your inherent value?"
- "How much self-deprecation does it take to create a sense of feeling loved?"
- "How does cutting off the supply lines secure having enough?"
- "How many dangers do you need to scare yourself with before you feel safe?"

- "How many potential pleasures do you need to collect before you take time to enjoy any of them?"
- "How will running away from your own vulnerability ever make you feel strong?"
- "How much of yourself do you need to set aside to have a harmonious relationship?"

As is visible, one can work with the language in a way that highlights the way in which the client's action is at odds with their desired end state. For example, by referring to the repression of vulnerability as "running away from vulnerability", one can present this act as an act of weakness rather than strength. The client would probably refer to it as "controlling their vulnerability", which makes it sound like an act of strength. Thus, it can be good to practise and build up an arsenal of these powerful one-liners.

As a variation, you can also display the counterproductive nature of the client's strategy by suggesting that, to reach their goal, they should do the exact opposite of what they are doing. In doing so, you take the energy in the client's desire and set it against their strategy. This is a form of inner Aikido in that you use the momentum and energy of the client's own desire to dismantle the strategy they are following. By turning the client's logic against itself, you defeat it. By "short-circuiting" the client's logic, you free them from it. This can be a particularly fun and creative way of working. I think of it as "messing up" the client's logic, so it no longer has a hold on them.

Below are some examples of how to do this. Each sentence can be read as an alternative to one of the questions above.

- If you want to be perfect, you must discard all ideals since no ideal is perfect
- If you really want to feel accepted as you are, you should embrace all sides of yourself, in particular those others reject
- If you want to feel your value, you must see the value in how you are now – not in how you could be
- If you want to feel loved, you should talk yourself up – not down
- If you want to ensure you have enough, you must connect with others
- If you want to feel safe, you should focus on developing trust – not distrust
- If you want to experience pleasure, you need to reduce how many pleasurable things you do, so you have time to savour them
- If you want to be strong, you must have the strength to be vulnerable
- If you want harmony, don't do anything that you later will resent

It is important to note that sentences such as those above should not be taken as universal rules. Rather, they should be regarded as custom-made sentences designed to short-circuit specific patterns that take a specific client's awareness away from Being.

Thus, if two clients have opposing patterns that take their awareness away from Being, you would argue for one thing when working with one client and for the exact opposite when working with the other client.

Dealing with reactions to the counterproductivity process

When you highlight the counterproductive nature of the client's strategy, they may be relieved or disturbed.

Some clients feel relieved when they realise the counterproductive nature of the strategy they follow when searching for their desired state because it means they no longer have to follow this strategy. Often the relief they experience when they drop the search is the exact feeling they were looking for. If this is the case, you can point out that the client achieved the desired state the moment they stopped trying to create or acquire it.

Other clients feel deeply disturbed when they realise the counterproductive nature of their strategy. They may feel grief for having spent so much time and energy on a flawed strategy. As before, it is good to give them time and to remind them that it is better to drop the strategy now than later. They may also feel stupid. If this is the case, it can be good to remind them that we are all stupid. No one is born with in-depth knowledge of how this world functions – and many never achieve such knowledge. The important thing is to become a little bit less stupid every day.

The process of counterproductivity is summarised in Figure 11: The Counterproductivity Process.

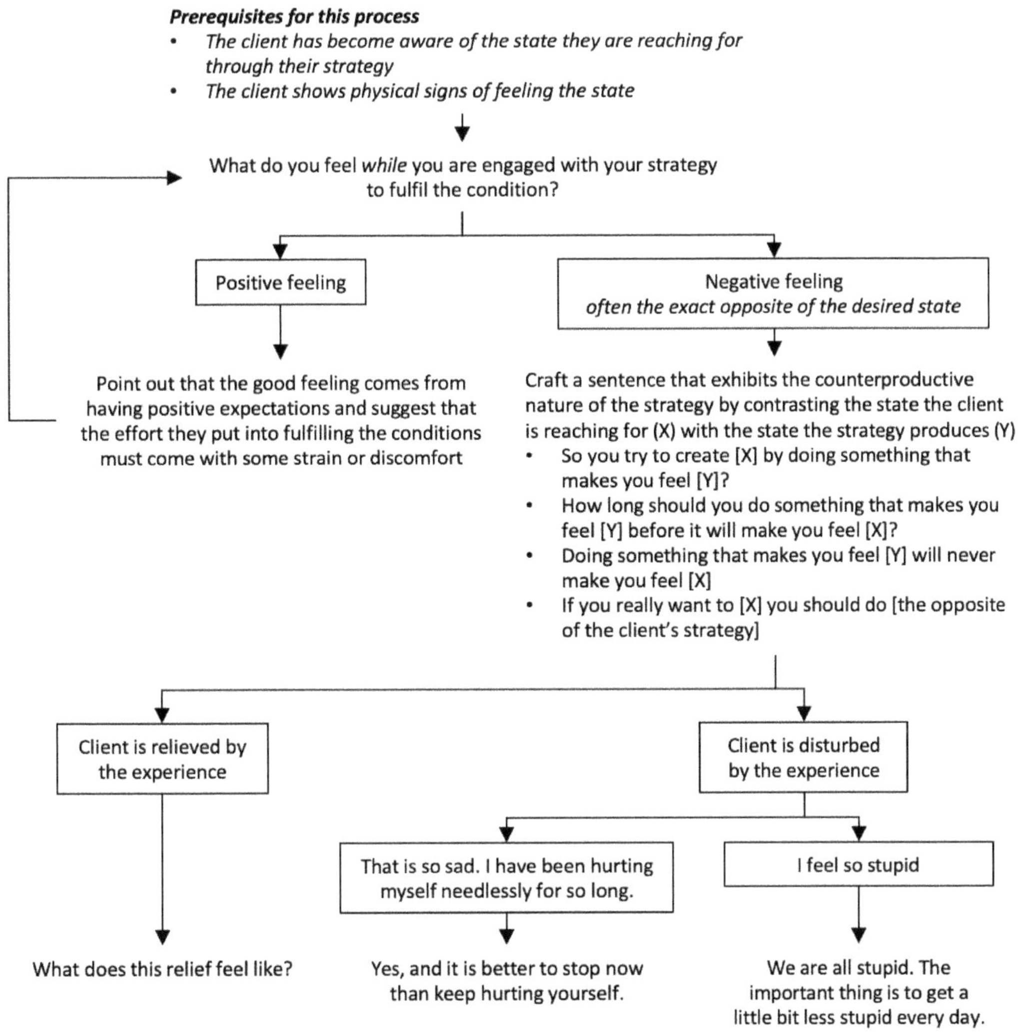

Figure 11: The Counterproductivity Process

Non-Urgency and the 8th corrective principle

The reason clients feel it is urgently important to fulfil certain conditions is that they believe it will bring them in touch with Being.

Therefore, it can be very powerful to invite clients to reflect on what they feel about fulfilling these conditions after they have become aware of Being.

Thus, when the client has completed the first part of the Sensing Completion process and they are feeling the state they were seeking, you can ask:

> "While you remain in touch with the state you are now feeling in your body, what do you feel about [the conditions the client wanted to fulfil]?"

Clients will typically experience one of three things:

- The client is no longer interested in fulfilling the conditions
- The client still feels it is urgently important to fulfil the conditions
- The client still wants to fulfil the conditions, but the drama has gone.

Below, I will describe each of these scenarios and how you, as a therapist, can respond to them.

The client is no longer interested in fulfilling the conditions

Often, once the client has become aware of Being, they no longer care about fulfilling the conditions. This shows that fulfilling the conditions was only attractive insofar as the client believed doing so would bring them a desired inner state. Fulfilling the conditions holds no appeal in and of itself.

For example, a client may feel it is urgently important to receive compliments from their partner and they, therefore, wish to become more attractive to their partner. During the first part of Sensing Completion, the client learns that the reason they seek compliments is because they believe this will bring a sense of worth. When the client describes the sense of worth they seek, and, through this process, starts feeling the state of worth and value, they may completely lose interest in eliciting compliments from their partner. Obtaining compliments may be nice but they hold no further appeal for the client. The drama around getting or not getting compliments is all but gone.

If this is the case, you can congratulate the client on having found what they were searching for and point out that fulfilling the conditions was always merely a method the client employed to reach their real goal, namely, an inner felt sense. This is the 8th corrective principle.

In the above example, receiving compliments was merely a method to get to a sense of worth. Once the client has reached their goal, the method becomes irrelevant.

The client still feels it is urgently necessary to fulfil the conditions

Sometimes, upon being reminded of the conditions they wished to fulfil they, once again, are gripped by a sense that this is of urgent importance. Usually, this is because they have only partially discovered what they were reaching for by fulfilling the conditions. Thus, in this scenario, you can go back to the first part of the Sensing Completion process and explore what more the client is reaching out for.

For example, while feeling a sense of value, the client in the example above may still feel it is urgently important to receive compliments from their partner. In this case, you can invite the client to, once again, imagine that they get an abundance of just the right kind of compliments and ask them to notice what this gives them, other than a sense of value. Then the client may discover that compliments also give them a sense of safety and ease. You can then ask the client to describe this sense of safety and once they feel it, check how they feel about getting the compliments when they have both a sense of worth *and* safety.

You can repeat the process either until the client no longer feels the urgent need to receive compliments or until the exploration grows stale. If you choose to round off the exploration before the client has found all they believe they can get from fulfilling the conditions, you can simply tell the client that there is more but that, for now, they can explore connecting directly with the state they have found through the exploration.

That it is possible to find multiple aspects of Being by exploring the same situation has an important implication. Often clients will experience issues in their life that are persistent. They come to therapy. They go through a process. They feel the issue has been resolved. But a few weeks (or hours) later, the issue returns. In such cases, the clients can feel discouraged because they evaluate the success of the therapy by whether the issues they work with disappear.

However, there is another way of evaluating the success of therapy. If every time you engage with a particular issue, you learn to become aware of another aspect of Being, then your issues become like a tool for treasure finding. If you can use a single issue to become aware of multiple aspects of Being, this issue is pure gold, and in a sense, it would be a loss if it disappeared.

Thus, if the client after going through the Sensing Completion process is still obsessed with fulfilling certain conditions, it may still have been a successful session if the client has also become aware of and deeply felt an aspect of Being.

The client still wants to fulfil the conditions, but the drama has gone

Finally, sometimes the client's desire to fulfil the conditions is motivated by two objectives simultaneously. They want to fulfil the conditions both because it will give them something practical *and* because they believe it will help them create or acquire a desired state.

For example, a client may wish to become a better communicator, both because it is practically useful for them in their line of work *and* because they hope this will make them feel more valuable. Another client may wish to resolve a long-standing conflict in their relationship, both due to pragmatic concerns about how this conflict is affecting the children *and* because they believe resolving the conflict will bring a sense of love they currently feel they are lacking.

The sense of urgency and drama is typically connected to the latter of these two objectives. Making sure work colleagues understand what you wish to communicate and making sure that your children grow up to be healthy and happy are both important tasks in their own right. But the sense of urgency and drama that one feels when engaging in these tasks often comes from the second objective, to remedy a perceived lack of value and love, respectively.

When a client is motivated simultaneously by a practical concern and a perceived lack of an aspect of Being, the client will still want to fulfil the conditions even after becoming aware of Being, but they will no longer feel the same level of urgency and drama in relation to fulfilling the conditions. Their project will feel much more matter-of-fact and concrete. It will be "reduced" to a mere practical matter.

When the task of fulfilling the conditions for practical reasons is separated from the task of noticing Being, the client tends to become much more able to fulfil the conditions. In general, the more we are aware of Being, the better ideas we get for dealing with our environment and the situations we face in our daily lives.

Thus, if the client says that they still want to fulfil the conditions but that they feel much less drama around this project, it is beneficial to invite the client to reflect on how they can imagine going about fulfilling the conditions, while noticing Being.

> "Good. So, now that we have separated the project of connecting with the inner state from the project of dealing with the situation, the situation is much more manageable.

What ideas for action do you get now that you no longer feel separate from the inner state you were seeking?"

Clients can answer this question in two ways. The client may suggest:

- Dealing with the situation in the same way as before but with less drama
- Dealing with the situation in a radically new way.

Below, I describe these answers and how to respond to them.

Dealing with the situation in the same way as before but with less drama

Sometimes, when clients become aware of Being, they still wish to fulfil the same conditions as before and to do it in the same way as before.

At first glance, it can appear as if nothing has changed. However, this situation merely indicates that while the strategy the client was following was not effective in remedying the perceived lack of Being, it may still be useful for dealing with practical matters.

For example, a client may seek a sense of value by getting a promotion and a pay rise. After connecting with the sense of value inherent in Being, the client may still want to pursue the promotion and pay rise, not out of a need for value, but because it is a practical step towards achieving financial stability. Thus, the strategy remains relevant, even though the deeper issue of self-worth has been resolved through awareness of Being.

In such cases, the client will often be able to carry out their strategy with more grounding and ease. They may do the same as before, but it will feel radically different.

Dealing with the situation in a radically new way

Sometimes, when clients become aware of Being, they will create completely new ideas for dealing with the practical problems in their lives. Such new perspectives emerge when the client has conflated the practical problems with problems of creating or acquiring Being in the form of positive inner states. Thus, awareness of Being removes this additional layer of complexity from the practical problems, opening up new possibilities.

For instance, when the problem of improving a client's financial situation is separated from the problem of finding an inner sense of worth, the client may start to consider options they have never previously considered. This happens because there are more feasible solutions to financial problems than there are to the financial and inner worth problems combined.

Similarly, if a client no longer conflates the problem of choosing a career path with the problem of finding meaning in life, choosing a career may seem much more straightforward. As a result, the client will be more able to be guided by curiosity and exploration.

In the same way, when the problem about solving a conflict the client is experiencing, is separated from the problem of finding love and acceptance, the risk of failing will be significantly reduced. Consequently, the client will have more freedom to experiment and learn through trial-and-error.

Sometimes, clients will say that they still want to fulfil the conditions they originally intended to fulfil because this is the best way they can conceive of solving a practical problem in their life. However, their attitude will have changed significantly. The drama and urgency are completely gone. Fulfilling the conditions becomes just something that needs to be done, much like taking out the rubbish or doing the dishes.

In these cases, it is beneficial to point out to the client that the changes in how they perceive the situation result from separating their practical problems from problems of becoming aware of Being. These two problems must be dealt with in completely different ways. Practical problems may require changing the environment, whereas the problem of Being can only be addressed by becoming aware of Being – not by changing anything external. Separating the two types of problems allows the client to deal with each in an effective manner.

The Non-Urgency Process is summarised in Figure 12.

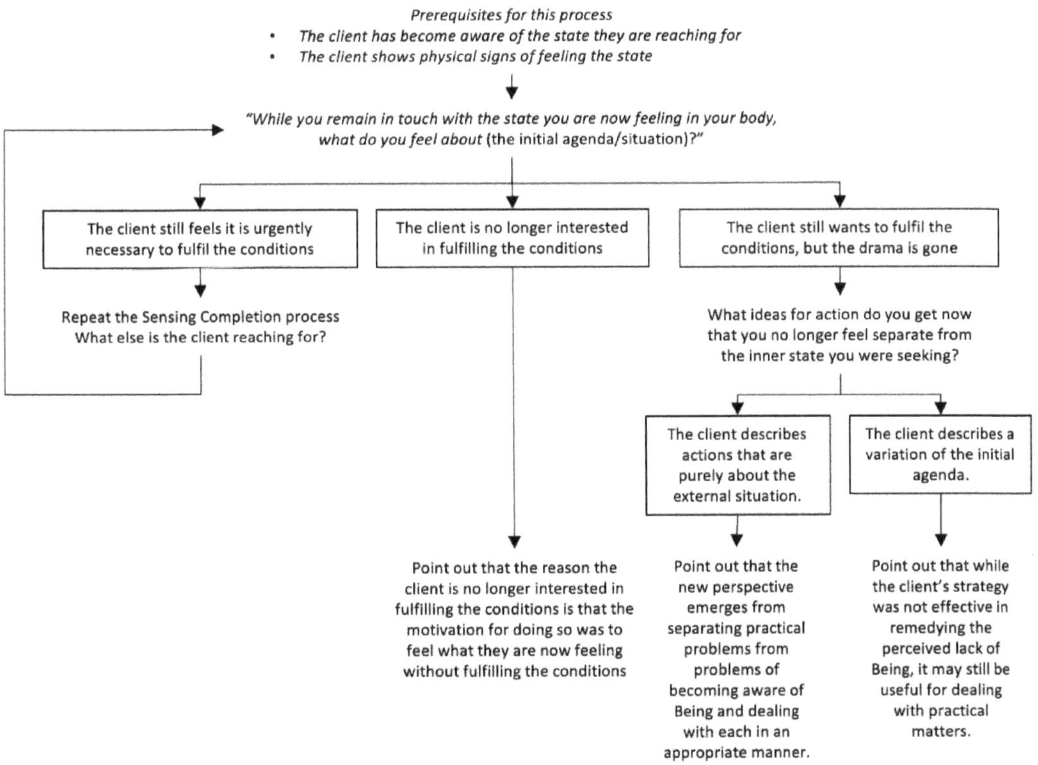

Figure 12: The Non-Urgency Process

3.5. Examples of Sensing Completion

In this section, you can read transcriptions of two therapy sessions applying the process of Sensing Completion. The sessions, like all sessions in this book, are fictional but representative of sessions I have had with clients.

Furthermore, the sessions are abbreviated so they only include the key parts of the exchange. Real sessions often contain more exploration, longer narratives, tangents, pauses, etc. That being said, the Knot of Conditionality can, in some cases, be untied in a matter of minutes. In such cases, the examples below would represent full transcriptions of the therapeutic exchange.

The examples are written in two columns. In the left column, you can read the client and therapist's conversation. In the right column, you can read the observations and considerations that guided the therapist during the exchange.

3.5.1. Session 3: Finding stability through a partner

The following session is a typical example of a session where the client from the start asks for assistance with a very particular project, namely finding a stable partner they are attracted to so they can start a family.

Rather than helping the client carry out this project, I engage the client in an exploration of what they are ultimately reaching for. As the client discovers what state they are ultimately seeking, they start feeling the state.

I then use elements of the Access process and the Counterproductivity process to interpret this experience for the client in a way that corrects the client's misconceptions that the state they seek is separate from them and that the source of the state is the fulfilment of the conditions of finding a partner and starting a family.

The Sensing Completion process is only one possible approach to working with this client's issue. Later, I will return to this case to show other possibilities.

Process	Comments
Client: The problem I have is that I pick the wrong partners. I always get involved with partners who are unstable, and I end up having to support them and help with all their problems. I'd like to have a stable partner. Someone who can help me out once in a while. But whenever I find someone who is stable, I feel no attraction. I'd like help figuring out how to be attracted to partners that are good for me.	Here the client presents a desire to fulfil a particular condition, namely having a stable relationship.
Therapist: Good. So, this might sound like a funny question, but what do you think you would feel, if you got a stable partner?	I ask what fulfilling this condition would give the client.

Process	Comments
C: Isn't it obvious? With all the drama in my current relationships, they never last. I'd like to eventually have a relationship that lasts. I want to start a family. This way, I will not get a family. The clock is ticking.	The client reveals the next step in their plan. The stable relationship will bring a family.
T: So, you want a stable relationship so you can have a family. Good. This is very understandable. Many people want this. But different people may have different beliefs about what would be good about it. So, I'm curious about what you believe having a family would feel like? Why is this attractive to you?	I ask what fulfilling this new condition will give the client. I start by demonstrating understanding for the wish and then propose that different people would have different reasons. I do so to make the exploration feel natural and to trigger a sense of curiosity.
C: I just want that sense of "home" and "love". I want to have a place where I belong.	The client reveals the state they seek by fulfilling the desired conditions.
T: Excellent. And what does having a place where you belong feel like?	I ask the client to translate the abstract word "belong" into a felt sense description.
C: (sighs with relief) I feel I can finally relax. Like something settling in my stomach. Like a big warm rock filling my belly. This feels wonderful.	The sigh reveals that the client is connecting with the felt sense state. And they describe the state nicely using neutral, sensory words.
T: Are you feeling this now?	I ask for the client's acknowledgement of the presence of the felt sense.
C: Yes. I am actually.	The client confirms that they feel it.
T: Good. And how does it affect you to feel this warm rock in the belly?	I ask for effects to give the client more time in the felt sense they sought.

Process	Comments
C: It is like my whole body relaxes. It feels like I've come home. I'm not so much out there – searching.	The client describes effects.
T: How does it affect your thoughts and emotions?	I ask for more effects.
C: I feel a sense of calmness and ease. My head feels much clearer. My heart feels warm.	The client describes more effects.
T: How is it to notice that you are feeling this now – even if nothing has changed regarding your relationship status?	I ask the client to notice that they are presently feeling the state without having fulfilled what they believed to be necessary conditions. This is the process of access.
C: Somehow, the relationship thing doesn't bother me. Strange.	The client notices that their interest in fulfilling the conditions has diminished.
T: Yes. This feeling is the home you were looking for. You were just too busy looking for a partner to notice it.	Here I hint at the counterproductive nature of the client's original plan for creating or acquiring the state.
C: What?	The client expresses surprise.
T: Right now, you are feeling the sense of home you thought would come from finding the right partner. But that you are feeling it now means you already have it – it does not come from a partner. How do you feel about stability in a partner now?	I reiterate the conclusion that if the client can feel the state without fulfilling the conditions, they must have direct access. I then ask a question to direct the client's attention and avoid that they question the proposed conclusion.
C: It's funny. Somehow it seems more attractive. I don't know why I was so attracted to unstable partners.	The client notices that their preference in relation to potential partners has shifted.

Process	Comments
T: Yes. When you are aware of the stability in yourself, you enjoy it in others as well. Enjoy.	I interpret this observation for the client in a way that supports the shift

3.5.2. Session 4: Breaking things and bossing people around

The following process is an example of using the Sensing Completion process to explore a desire the client feels a bit ambivalent about, namely their desire to "break things and boss people around".

On the one hand, the client is attracted to letting go of control and niceness. On the other hand, the client is worried about potential repercussions – in particular, about not fitting in and getting fired.

Thus, this process is an example of a Sensing Completion process in which the therapist must work around the obstacle that the client's attention is occupied with a potential negative consequence of fulfilling their desire.

In such cases, it is useful to remind the client that you are not suggesting that they do anything in particular – only that they imagine what it would feel like if they did do what they would like to. Furthermore, it can be useful to map out the consequences the client is worried about and create a "parallel universe" scenario in which the social rules are different in such a way that the client's concerns are no longer relevant. Such a scenario can greatly assist the client in imagining doing what they want without holding back and, thus, discovering what they are ultimately reaching out for by taking such actions.

Process	Comments
Client: I'm having a difficult time at work. Often, I sit in meetings and get annoyed at what other people discuss.	Annoyance is often an indication of wanting to do something but feeling ambivalent about doing it.
Therapist: What annoys you?	I ask for the client to be more specific

Process	Comments
C: They never want to take a stand. I know what they say to each other when talking one-on-one. But in meetings, they all pretend everything is fine. Sometimes, I just want to scream at them.	Here, the client reveals what they want to do. They want to scream at their colleagues.
T: What would you like to scream?	I ask for the client to be more specific.
C: I want to shout that they should stop being such cowards.	Here the client reveals their desire in more detail.
T: What do you think it would feel like to do this?	I ask what fulfilling their desire might feel like.
C: I can't go around shouting at people.	The client objects because they believe it isn't possible to do what they want to do.
T: What in particular do you think would be the problem with that?	I ask the client to specify what negative consequences they fear.
C: It doesn't really fit the culture. People might take offence. That might have negative repercussions for me.	The client seems to imply that the negative consequence of fulfilling their desire is to be fired.
T: So, you are afraid you might get fired?	I test this assumption.
C: Yes.	The client confirms.

Process	Comments
T: Of course, I'm not suggesting that you go back to work tomorrow and start shouting at people. That might, indeed, get you in trouble. However, it can still be interesting to notice what you find attractive about doing it. What if you had a contract that meant they couldn't fire you under any circumstances. Then what would it feel like to shout at people?	First, I acknowledge the validity of the client's concern and reassure them that I am not proposing that they simply follow their urge. Then I present a modified scenario in which the client's concerns are no longer relevant. It can be a bit of an art form to get these scenarios right. A good scenario makes the client willing to consider fulfilling their desire without reservations.
C: (laughs) I see myself as a diva walking around and breaking things and bossing people around.	The scenario works and the client connects with their desired state through an image.
T: What does that feel like?	I ask for the felt sense.
C: I feel I'm finally standing on my own. It is so liberating.	The client describes the felt sense.
T: Describe this feeling a bit more.	I ask the client to expand.
C: I feel I can breathe. I feel energised and warm. All this tension is lifted.	The client expands.
T: How is it to see that what you truly desire is to feel this sense of standing on your own and being liberated and that shouting at people merely is what you believe you have to do to get there?	Here I suggest the 8th corrective principle that the conscious desire is merely a method for reaching the true desire, which is a particular inner state. To bypass the client's evaluating mind, I embed the suggestion in a question.
T: It's a relief.	This statement shows that the client has accepted the embedded suggestion in my question.

Process	Comments
T: Can you feel it as you talk about it?	I ask the question that marks the transit to the second phase of the process.
C: Yes.	The client confirms.
T: Good. And you got there without screaming at anyone. Now, as you feel this energy and warmth, as you feel that you are liberated and can stand on your own, what do you think about the situation?	I suggest the 4th corrective principle, that the client has access to the desired inner state without doing anything to create it and immediately redirect the client's attention by asking them to elaborate on the consequences of feeling the state. I do this so the client does not have time to evaluate the suggestion. This way it can dodge conscious scrutiny and be accepted readily.
C: I still think it would be good if people were more honest. But I guess they are also worried about losing their jobs. That's fair enough. Maybe I can set up working groups where people can be free to speak their mind. It might help if they come together around their concerns and support each other. They can't fire all of us (laughs).	The client talks with much less agitation. This is because when they connect with the desired state, the situation is no longer about the client's sense of freedom and strength but "only" about a communication issue. As the issue of connecting to the energetic aspect of Being is taken out of the equation the client can consider the issue of communication in a more calm and deliberate manner.

Process	Comments
T: You seem to speak in a different way now. Do you notice a difference in how you feel about the situation?	I invite the client to notice the urgency is gone now that they feel the desired state. This is an indirect way of suggestion the 8th corrective principle that fulfilling the desired conditions (screaming at people) is a method and not a goal. The goal being the state they now feel.
C: It doesn't feel so charged. It's just another thing to do. I can try out some things. If they work, they work – if not, well, no harm, no foul.	The client recognises the urgency is gone as they say, "it doesn't feel so charged".
T: Excellent. Enjoy the liberation!	I invite the client to enjoy the state.

3.6. Untying the Knot of Conditionality through contemplations

In Section 3.4, I have outlined how the Knot of Conditionality can be untied in one-to-one sessions with clients.

In this section, I will present two contemplation exercises that are specifically designed to untie the Knot of Conditionality. These exercises are well suited to group work. The instructions are sufficiently simple to be given to a group, and the exercises can, for example, be performed in pairs or as individual writing exercises.

These contemplation exercises can be deepened through one-to-one processing, as outlined in the previous sections. When working with groups, I often begin by inviting the students to do the contemplation exercise in pairs or individually. Afterwards, I work one-to-one with a few students in plenum. This approach has the advantage that although I only work with a few students directly, the other students, having completed the contemplation exercise, can partake in the one-to-one processing vicariously.

3.6.1. What are your ideas about how to create or acquire X?

In this chapter, we have seen that one of the main reasons students do not notice a particular aspect of Being, such as "joy", "vitality" or "peace" is that they believe they need to do something to create or acquire it, and that they, therefore, are so busy searching for it that they overlook that what they seek is already present.

To help students unhook their attention from their search for a particular aspect of Being (X), it can be helpful to invite them to contemplate the following question:

> "What are your ideas about how to create or acquire X?"

Seeing the ideas that compel the students to engage in the search can help them unhook from this project, because when one pays attention to an idea, it diminishes this idea's power to control what one is paying attention to.

This contemplation exercise is effective in groups, because when each student shares their insights into what patterns distract them from a particular aspect of Being, it can help other students notice similar patterns in themselves, which they might otherwise overlook. Thus, working with this kind of contemplation exercise in a group can help raise awareness of each member.

If, for example, you ask a group to contemplate what ideas they have about how to create or acquire peace, you may get answers such as:

- To feel peace, I need to resolve all interpersonal conflicts
- To feel peace, I need to finish my to-do list
- To feel peace, I need to get better at meditating
- To feel peace, I need a clear conscience
- To feel peace, I need to control my emotions.

Each of these answers reveals a condition the individuals believe they need to fulfil to feel peace.

Sometimes, the answers will not state the condition explicitly, but it can be deduced. For example, someone may say: I cannot feel peace when the world is in such turmoil. This implies that the condition this person believes must be fulfilled for them to feel peace is complete harmony in the world's international affairs. The reason they do not state this in the form above is that they probably feel fulfilling this condition is beyond their capacity. But in principle, what they are saying (and feeling) is: To feel peace, I need to resolve all the world's conflicts.

How to introduce the exercise

When you introduce this contemplation exercise, it is good to frame it using the following six instructions:

- The purpose of the exercise is just to see (not to change or evaluate) the ideas
- Do not evaluate the ideas
- Let all parts of you speak

- Expect contradictory ideas
- List all ideas you have been exposed to (whether you believe them or not)
- Notice what happens as you list out the ideas

The purpose of the exercise is just to see the ideas

The purpose of the exercise is to see the ideas that distract you from noticing the peaceful aspect of Being. Nothing else.

We are usually not aware of these ideas. But they do influence what we pay attention to. And it is precisely because we are not aware of them that they can fulfil this function. Thus, when we focus our attention on these ideas, their capacity to control our attention is limited[33]. What you focus your awareness on cannot control what you are aware of.

Do not evaluate the ideas

Because the purpose is to become aware of the ideas that guide us and nothing else, it is important to encourage clients not to evaluate the ideas as they become aware of them. For the purpose of this exercise, it is not important whether the ideas are true or not. Engaging in such reflections would occupy your attention rather than freeing it. You would go from spending your attention on how to fulfil the condition to spending it on evaluating the proposition that fulfilling the condition creates the desired state. The purpose is to notice the proposition and leave it alone.

Let all parts of you speak

It is also important to encourage clients to let all parts of them speak. Different parts of our personality may hold very different ideas about how to create or acquire an aspect of Being and we want to map out all ideas – not just the ones we like or endorse. Often, we have one set of ideas that we espouse and another

---

[33] Michael Polanyi makes a useful distinction between subsidiary and focal awareness. What we have in our subsidiary awareness are tools for examining what is in our central awareness. For this reason, we are only aware of things in subsidiary awareness in terms of what they tell us about that which is in our focal awareness. Polanyi illustrates it using the example of hammering a nail into the wall. The nail is in focal awareness. The hammer and the hand and arm used to wield the hammer are in subsidiary awareness. We are using awareness of these to guide our interaction with the nail in our focal awareness. Polanyi writes: "When we bring down the hammer we do not feel that its handle has struck our palm but that its head has struck the nail" (Polanyi, 1974, p. 57).

set of ideas that guide our behaviour[34]. The same person may say that they seek peace by detaching themselves from concerns about what other people think, while at the same time they do everything in their power to resolve interpersonal conflicts and make sure that people see them in a positive light. Thus, this person is influenced by to ideas about how two create peace:

- To feel peace, I should not worry about other's opinions about me
- To feel peace, I must make sure no one is angry with me

In this exercise, the client should be encouraged to reveal both ideas.

Expect contradictory ideas

When introducing the exercise, it is useful to explicitly mention that it is common to contain contradictory ideas about how to create or acquire an aspect of Being. Containing contradictory ideas is often a major contributor to why our attention is so occupied. We are trying to fulfil two (or more) mutually exclusive conditions. Discovering this is part of the exercise.

List all ideas you have been exposed to

The ideas we have about how to create or acquire an aspect of Being come from people around us. Many of them are embedded in our society or the social environments we have been part of. We often internalise such ideas without consciously deciding to do so. Consequently, we are likely to be affected by ideas we have come across without knowing that we are. So, to ensure we list out all ideas that are affecting us, it is useful to list out all ideas we have been exposed to – not just the ones we *are aware of* having internalised.

Notice what happens as you list out the ideas

Finally, since the very act of seeing the ideas is what has an effect, the clients should pay attention to what happens within them as they list out the ideas. This is because, as they list out the ideas, their awareness is freed from them and they become more likely to notice Being.

---

[34] Chris Argyris and Donald Schön distinguish between espoused theories and theories-in-action.

Challenge ideas about how to create or acquire an aspect of Being

Sometimes, when clients list out their ideas there will be some of them that the clients will feel are just observations of how things are. They will feel it is strange to call these "ideas" as they perceive them as fact.

In the contemplation exercise described above, it is good *not* to evaluate the ideas about how to create or acquire an aspect of Being that one is listing out, as the point of the exercise is to see what happens when one sees these ideas.

However, as a follow-up exercise, it can be useful to take some of the ideas that seem like facts and challenge them using the two questions below:

- When have you experienced X without fulfilling the condition?
- When have you fulfilled the condition without experiencing X?

These two questions both challenge the causal relationship between fulfilment of the condition and the inner state X.

If you have experienced X without fulfilling the condition that means, at the very least, that X can be caused by something else and not only by fulfilling the condition. This, in turn, means that there might be a simpler way of creating or acquiring X that makes fulfilling the conditions superfluous. The central proposition in this chapter is, of course, that the experience of X is "caused" by paying attention to X – the simplest possible path.

If you experienced that fulfilling the conditions does not result in the feeling of X, that means either that fulfilling the conditions does not cause X or that there sometimes is something that cancels out the effect.

It is worth noting that both questions are formulated in such a way that they presuppose that the client has, in fact, experienced each of the two scenarios. It is important not to ask: "Have you ever experienced…" as this formulation would open the possibility for the client to simply answer "No" without any real investigation of their lived experience.

Finally, it is worth noting that the purpose of these explorations is not to come to any conclusions but merely to loosen the client's certainty about the causal relationship between fulfilling the conditions and the inner experience of X. Softening the client's sense of certainty about how things are paves the way for the realisation of the true nature of X as fundamentally uncaused.

3.6.2. What would it feel like if you were 100% successful?

The previous contemplation exercise can be followed up by a contemplation on the central question used for the Sensing Completion process, namely, what it would feel like to be completely successful in fulfilling the conditions the client believes will create or acquire a particular reification of Being.

When you invite a group of people to engage in this contemplation, you can ask them to pick one of the ideas they listed out in the previous exercise that seems particularly attractive to them.

If you are working with the reification "peace", a client may feel particularly attracted to the idea that they can create peace by having a clear conscience. In that case, the exercise would be to imagine what it would feel like to have a completely clear conscience.

Below are a few things to consider when using this contemplation exercise in groups.

Use scenarios

To explore what it feels like if certain conditions are fulfilled, it is good to imagine concrete scenarios in which the desired conditions are fulfilled. If one tries to imagine the fulfilment of the conditions in the abstract, the exercise tends to become too theoretical.

For example, directly asking what it would feel like to have a completely clear conscience is more likely to lead to an intellectual discussion than to bring forth a somatic response. Asking what a concrete scenario in which the conditions are fulfilled would feel like, is much more likely to bring forth that felt sense as a response to the scenario. Thus, to imagine having a completely clear conscience one might use one of the following scenarios:

- Imagining that one has lived a life without doing anything of a questionable ethical nature
- Imagining having made amends for any and all past moral transgressions
- Imagining having been completely forgiven by anyone one has wronged in any way
- Imagining that the son of God has taken on the burden of any past moral transgressions.

In most cases, there will be many possible scenarios in which the conditions the student believes are necessary to experience a particular reification of Being are fulfilled. A good scenario is one where, when the student hears it, they experience an immediate positive response. For example, if working with "peace", some of the above scenarios may appear too unrealistic or strange for the student to engage with or relate to, while others might cause the student to heave a deep sigh of relief and exclaim that that would be wonderful. When this happens, the exercise is simply to explore the feeling the student experiences in that moment.

When introducing this exercise, it is a good idea to illustrate how to craft concrete scenarios by working one-to-one with a few students to find scenarios they resonate with. If I work with smaller groups, I will often develop scenarios for each student as it can sometimes be a bit difficult to craft a good one and, ideally, the student should spend the contemplation time sensing what happens when they think about the scenario.

Imagine no negative side effects

One of the pitfalls of the Sensing Completion process is that students may become distracted by imagining negative side effects of fulfilling the conditions or of experiencing the state they seek. For example, if a student imagines the peace they would feel if they had a completely clear conscience, they might start worrying about how boring it would be to never make any moral transgressions or they might worry about other people feeling threatened by them or be unable to relate to them due to their moral superiority.

As you cannot directly intervene in each student's process when you work in a group, it is important to mitigate this risk through the way you frame the exercise.

You can do this simply by encouraging the students to imagine scenarios where there are no negative side effects of fulfilling the conditions or of experiencing the state they seek. Thus, in the above example, the student would imagine having a clear conscience in a way that neither entails boredom nor moral superiority.

Let your felt sense answer the question

The other main pitfall of the Sensing Completion process is that students may become distracted by abstractions and not notice the felt sense.

To mitigate this risk, it is good in your introduction to the contemplation exercise to emphasise that the answer to the contemplation question is going to come through the felt sense. It is how the student *feels* when they contemplate the scenario that is the answer to the question: How would it feel if....?

One-to-one work after the exercise

It can be beneficial to follow this exercise up with one-to-one work in plenum.

If the student did not get a sense of the state they were seeking, it is usually because they were distracted by concerns about negative side effects or they tried to answer the question in an abstract way. Then the one-to-one work can focus on modifying the scenario to exclude the possibility of negative side effects and drawing the student's attention to their felt sense.

If the student did get a sense of the state they were seeking, you can focus the one-to-one work on letting the client describe the state. When a student feels a reification of Being and describes it, it has a contagious effect, which will benefit everyone else in the group.

You can also use one of the four processes from the second part of the Sensing Completion process (Access, Non-Doing, Counterproductivity and Non-Urgency) to draw out the corrective principles from the students' experiences with the exercise.

3.7. Summary

In this chapter, we have explored the Sensing Completion process in detail. The heart of this process is to follow the client's desires, wishes, obsessions and compulsions to their natural conclusion as a way of pointing the client awareness to Being.

Taking any condition the client wishes to fulfil as starting point, we ask them to describe what they believe fulfilling these conditions would give them. As they become aware of what they are ultimately reaching for, they become aware of Being.

Connecting with Being in this way powerfully demonstrates to the client that Being is always present and that they experience it whenever they pay attention to it.

When the client becomes aware of Being they will either completely lose interest in fulfilling the conditions or they will still want to fulfil the conditions, but the sense of urgency and drama will be gone. The first scenario occurs when the only motivation for the client's desire to fulfil the conditions is to remedy a perceived lack of Being. The second occurs when the motivation is a combination of a practical concern and the concern for remedying a perceived lack of Being.

Thus, the Sensing Completion process is fundamentally about separating issues of awareness of Being from practical issues and, thus, simplifying those practical issues significantly. Once the two are separated, the client usually does not need therapy to deal with the practical issues and, therefore, your role as a therapist will have ended.

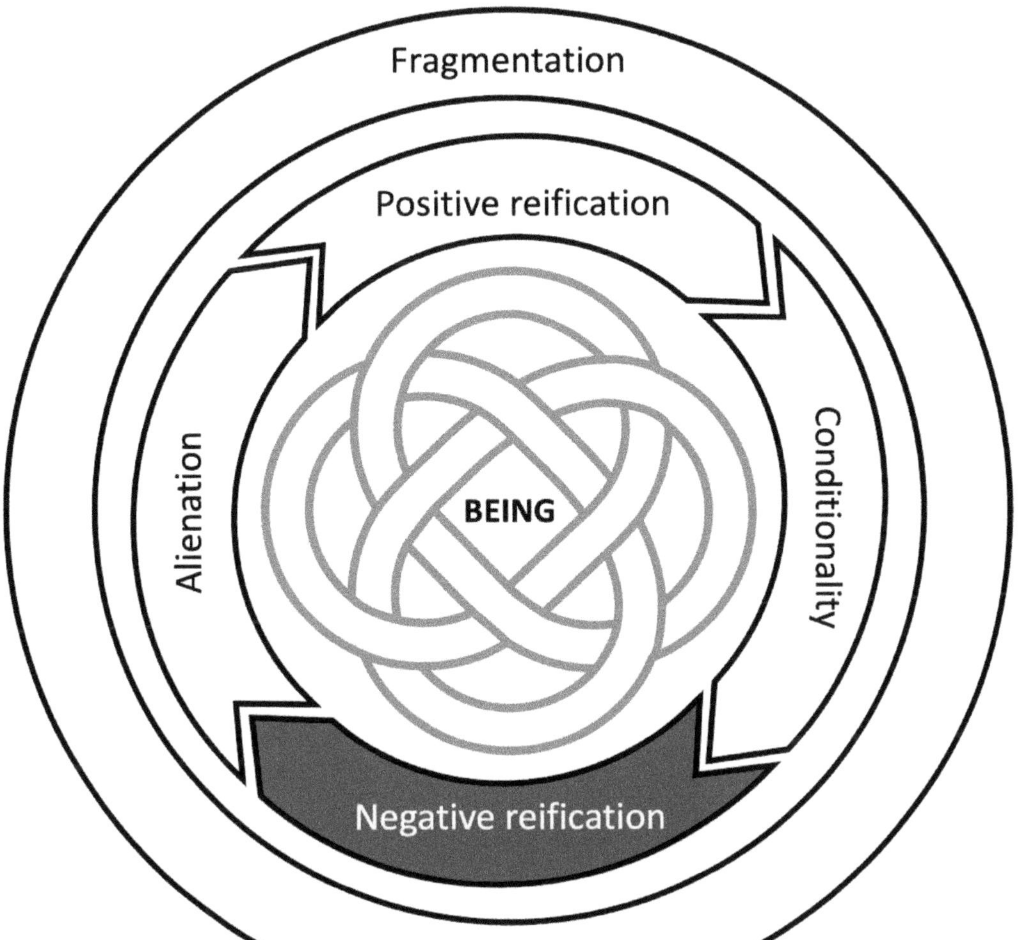

The Knot of Negative Reification

4. Knot 3: The Knot of Negative Reification

When we have adopted beliefs about what conditions we need to fulfil to create or acquire a positive reification of Being, we are compelled to ask:

> "Is what I'm experiencing now helping or hindering me in fulfilling the conditions I must fulfil to create or acquire the state I'm seeking?"

This question leads us to judge every element of our experience within the (narrow) framework of a particular mission and blinds us to the value of everything that does not seem to support us in this mission.

Such a mission-fixated outlook can lead to negative reification of Being, where we perceive aspects of Being as:

- irrelevant to the mission
- hindering the mission
- a sign that we are failing the mission.

In short, interpreting our experience within the framework of a mission to fulfil certain conditions can in certain circumstances lead us to perceive Being as something negative that must be avoided.

For example, perceiving the silent aspect of Being as "peace" (positive reification) and believing that to create peace, we need to remain calm at all times (conditions), can lead us to perceive the dynamic aspect of Being as a "disturbance" of the peace and, thus, avoid it (negative reification).

Similarly, perceiving the light aspect of Being as "love" (positive reification) and believing that to create love, we need to connect with other people (conditionality) can lead us to perceive the silent aspect of Being as "loss of connection" and, thus, something antithetical to "love", which we must avoid (negative reification).

Negative reification of Being leads us to actively avoid the very thing we long for and seek, simply because we do not recognise it for what it is. This is the Knot of Negative Reification.

Negative reification of Being is akin to placing a mask on Being so that the one thing we seek and yearn for appears to us as something irrelevant, in the best-case scenario, and as something repulsive or threatening, in the worst-case scenario.

To dissolve the Knot of Negative Reification, we need to learn to see beyond the surface and recognise Being despite the mask of negative reification. We need to learn to embrace the very states we avoid and, thus, break the spell that makes them appear as something to avoid. This is the process of Sensing Taboos.

Many fairy tales point to the way in which what is most precious in life can appear as something irrelevant or even as something repulsive. It is the unremarkable lamp that contains the wish-fulfilling genie. It is the frog that, when kissed, turns into a prince. It is the beast that, when loved truly despite his menacing appearance, turns into a prince.

4.1. Why it is important to undo the Knot of Negative Reification

It is, of course, important to undo all knots so that clients can experience Being directly and, consequently, dissolve the issues emerging from inattention to Being.

However, facilitating the "absolution" of states clients perceive as negative has always been near and dear to my heart and a core part of my approach to therapy.

The reason is that this process has three interlinked and very important effects on clients' lives. It is worth spending some time elaborating on these effects as understanding them in some detail will enhance your appreciation of the Sensing Taboos process.

By learning to perceive negative states as negative interpretations of Being:

- the client will learn to perceive Being as all-pervasive and ever-present
- the client will gain increased inner freedom
- the client will become less susceptible to external control and manipulation.

4.1.1. Perceiving Being as all-pervasive and ever-present

In the chapter on Positive Reification, we saw that all the positive states we seek are expressions of Being and, in this sense, they are all one. Perceiving the unity underpinning all we seek is, in itself, a profound insight.

However, in this chapter on the Knot of Negative Reification, we expand the claim to include all states we seek to avoid. This is an even more radical insight.

It is one thing to accept that joy, peace, love, etc. are all aspects of Being. It is another to accept that meaninglessness, loneliness, anger, etc. are also all aspects of Being.

Sensing Taboos is a process through which the extended claim can move from an intellectual proposition to a direct, lived experience. When we examine the felt-sense core of a state we judge as negative, separately from the contexts in which we encounter it, we discover that this felt sense is identical to the felt sense of positive phenomena we seek in other contexts.

Realising that Being is the foundation of all our experiences, whether we judge them as positive or negative, offers a more holistic, unified perspective on life. It enables us to experience Being as all-pervasive and ever-present in the tapestry of our lives.

4.1.2. Gaining increased inner freedom

We all have inner states we avoid, such as worthlessness, loneliness, boredom, etc. To avoid these states, we often seek to avoid all situations in which we perceive a risk of feeling these inner states. If, for example, you wish to avoid a sense of failure, you may avoid all tasks where you feel unsure about whether you can succeed. Similarly, if you wish to avoid a sense of loneliness, you may avoid spending time alone.

Thus, the more states you avoid, the more your life turns into a minefield, where you will constantly have to navigate around any circumstances which potentially could activate your awareness of the inner states you feel it necessary to avoid.

Consequently, this may limit what we can achieve in life.

For example, fear of feeling worthless can make it difficult to learn from others. To learn from others, you need to encounter people who are better than you at something. However, if being around people who are more skilled than you brings you in touch with a sense of worthlessness, you may avoid such company to avoid the feeling of worthlessness. This will limit your possibility of learning from others.

Similarly, if you worry about being unlovable, you may spend a lot of your time and energy seeking confirmation of your lovability and testing people to see if they really think you are unlovable. You will also spend a lot of time and energy mitigating the risk that people will find your approval seeking behaviour tedious and unlovable. Such activities will take time away from growing and enjoying life.

Inversely, if you do not mind feeling the so-called negative inner states, your possibilities in life expand. You can move much more freely in life if your movements are not restricted by the requirement of avoiding situations in which you may experience certain inner states.

If you do not mind feeling a bit worthless every now and then, concerns about this feeling can no longer stop you from engaging with and learning from people who are better than you in some respect – be it knowledge, skills, virtue, social acknowledgement, or something else.

If you do not mind feeling unlovable from time to time, all the time and energy you would otherwise spend on monitoring whether people find you lovable is freed up and can be used for other purposes.

Sensing Taboos will help clients become more comfortable with states they otherwise perceive as negative. This will enable them to engage with a range of situations they otherwise would steer clear of to avoid these "negative" states. As we lose fear of our inner taboos, we gain tremendous freedom.

4.1.3. Becoming less susceptible to external control and manipulation

The increased freedom an individual gains by losing their fear of certain inner states is also a freedom from external control and manipulation.

While no one can create an inner state in you directly, others can exploit your associations between states and situations.

If someone knows that you, in certain situations, generate a particular inner state in yourself which you dislike, they can exploit this mechanism in you and use it to manipulate you. If you do not comply with their wishes, they can threaten to place you in a situation where they know you will produce an inner state you dislike.

An individual may, for example, fear the sense of rupture they feel when they find themselves in conflict with another person. In this case, other people can control this individual by acting confrontationally whenever the individual's behaviour goes against their wishes. To avoid the sense of rupture, the individual will back down.

Similarly, if an individual fears feeling weak, other people can exploit this fear and control the individual by regarding them as weak whenever the individual's behaviour goes against their wishes.

The more inner states you are comfortable feeling, the fewer situations other people can use to threaten and control you.

If, for example, you are comfortable feeling an inner sense of rupture, conflict will not deter you from doing what you want. If you are comfortable feeling weak, a public declaration of your weakness will not give you pause in your actions. You will be free to joyfully second that opinion and go about your day.

Finally, it is worth noting that being comfortable with a broader range of inner states will not only make you less susceptible to external manipulation; it will also make you less likely to engage in manipulation of others, since the impulse to manipulate others often originates in a wish to make them act in ways that will help you avoid certain inner states in yourself. For example, the impulse to manipulate someone to give you compliments may originate in your desire to avoid feeling worthlessness. Similarly, the impulse to manipulate someone to be subservient may originate in your desire to avoid feeling powerlessness. If you are comfortable feeling worthlessness and powerlessness, you will no longer have any need to manipulate others to help you avoid these feelings.

In summary, undoing the Knot of Negative Reification is important because it will make you comfortable feeling a broader range of inner states by revealing that the core of these states is nothing other than Being. As you lose your fear of more and more inner states, you will experience greater freedom in life as there are fewer and fewer situations you feel the need to avoid. Furthermore, you will become less and less susceptible to external control and manipulation because you will no longer feel threatened by situations in which you experience these inner states.

4.2. Negative reifications of the 10 aspects of Being

In Section 2.3, I introduced the ten aspects of Being and some positive conceptual names people typically give to each of these. In Section 3.1, I added some ways people typically will seek to create or acquire the positive reifications of each of the ten aspects of Being to the model.

Reifying an aspect of Being as a positive phenomenon and formulating ideas about what conditions must be fulfilled to create or acquire this phenomenon can lead clients to reifying the different aspect of Being as negative phenomena. Such negative reifications can arise from the way the client pursues the same aspect or a different aspect.

Negative reifications of an aspect of Being can arise from the way the client pursues that very aspect of Being, when the felt sense of the aspect is reinterpreted in the light of the negative effects of the actions a client takes to create or acquire that aspect of Being. For example, the felt sense of vibration, expansion and warmth (the Red Essence) can be interpreted as "strength". Once the felt sense is labelled as "strength", clients may try to hold on to it by dominating others and picking fights because a common idea about strength is that to be strong, one must be able to dominate others and win fights. This behaviour, in turn, can be perceived as negative phenomena, such as bullying and aggression. If this happens, the client may start seeing the felt sense of the Red Essence as the seed of bullying and aggression and turn away from it. Table 8 provides examples of how the felt sense of each essence can be reinterpreted as a negative phenomenon when it gets associated with negative outcomes of the ways in which clients seek to create or acquire the most common positive reification of that aspect of Being.

Negative reifications of an aspect of Being can also arise from the way clients pursue different aspects of Being. This happens when clients interpret the felt sense of one aspect of Being as an obstacle to their pursuit of a positive reification of another aspect of Being. In principle, every aspect of Being can be perceived as an obstacle to the pursuit of every other aspect of Being. However, to illustrate the principle, it suffices to look at the essences opposite each other in the model, which are often perceived as mutually exclusive. For example, when pursuing positive reifications of the White Essence, such as support and grounding, the light and bubbly felt sense of the Yellow Essence may appear as something unreliable and ungrounded we must purge. Inversely, when pursuing positive reifications of the Yellow Essence, such as joy, happiness and carefreeness, the solid, firm and heavy felt sense of the White Essence may appear as something burdensome, serious and careworn we must overcome. Table 9 illustrate this for each pair of opposing aspects of Being.

Even when a client consciously perceives an aspect of Being as negative, they may still contain parts of their personality that seek this aspect of Being. Clients can, therefore, have judgements of both the felt sense state related to an aspect of Being and of the parts of them that seek this state.

The focus of this chapter is how to work with the states clients judge negatively. I return to the question of how to work with the personality parts clients judge negatively in Chapter 6.

A more extensive table with more possible negative reifications relating to each aspect of Being can be found at www.the5knots.com/resources.

Table 8: Negative reifications of the 10 aspects of Being (Essences) arising from the pursuit of the same aspect

Essence	Positive reification	Conditions	Negative reification
White	Support	Maintain stability in work and relationships	Stuckness. Workaholism
Solid	Grounding	Resist influence	Stubbornness. Rigidity
Firm	Confidence	Acquire skills & achievements	Arrogance
Heavy	Patience	Repress frustration. Give up	Passivity. Collapse. Apathy
	Neutrality	Be indifferent. Have no opinions	Dispassionate. Unengaged
Red	Strength	Dominate others. Pick fights	Bullying. Aggression
Vibrating	Courage	Face fears. Leave comfort zone	Recklessness. Foolhardiness
Expanding	Passion	Suspend control & reason. Infatuation	Obsession. Jealousy
Warm	Vitality	Thrill-seeking. Excessive risk-taking	Recklessness. Irresponsibility
	Authenticity	Challenging social norms	Anti-social behaviour
Black	Peace	Withdraw	Deadness. Loneliness
Still	Non-attachment	Erase personal wishes & desires	Annihilation. Emptiness
Slow	Mastery/Power	Eliminate disturbances	Oppressiveness. Hate.
Empty	Sacredness	Disinterest in the world	Non-participation
	Absolution	Renunciation	Worthlessness
Green	Compassion	Reduce sadness & hurt	Fragility. Vulnerability
Tender	Loving-Kindness	Forgive transgressors	Defencelessness
Delicate	Connection	Share hurt & vulnerability	Sentimentality. Shame
Moist	Sympathy	Help vulnerable people	Pity. Disempowerment
	Agape Love	Self-sacrifice	Self-reduction. Melancholy
Pink	Appreciation	Give & receive gratitude	Feebleness. Mushiness
Soft	Acceptance	Gain fame & fans	Dependency
Fluffy	Lovable/loving	Focus on the positive in self and others	Rose-tinted glasses
Plump	Perfection	Living up to an ideal	Perfectionism
	Cosiness	Create a comfortable environment	Complacency
Yellow	Joy	Seek entertainment & novelty	Superficiality.
Light	Happiness	Prioritising personal enjoyment	Selfishness
Bubbly	Carefreeness	Reject seriousness & difficulties	Carelessness
Uplifting	Curiosity	Perpetual exploration	Nosiness
	Spontaneity	Impulsive actions & decisions	Frivolity
Gold	Bonding	Relinquish boundaries	Submissiveness
Sweet	Community	Give up individuality & autonomy	Self-rejection. Loss of control
Viscous	Romantic love	Nurture emotional connection	Affective dependency
Honey-like	Unity	Eliminate or downplay differences	Malleability. Loss of identity
	Surrender	Let go of control	Loss of personal boundaries
Cream	Nourishment	Fulfilling needs	Over-entitlement. Neediness
Full	Satisfaction	Seek instant gratification	Immaturity. Infantilisation
Creamy	Fulfilment	Accomplish goals	Utopia
Smooth	Wholeness	Avoid change to preserve coherence	Inertia
	Contentment	Limiting or denying needs	Under-entitlement
Blue	Clarity	Brutal honesty	Harshness
Sharp	Precision	Measure & quantify everything	Inflexibility
Clear	Intelligence	Acquire & display knowledge	Arrogance
Wakeful	Discernment	Follow a doctrine unquestioningly	Dogmatism
	Guidance	Critique others' ideas frequently	Judgemental
Clear	Freedom	Reject all constraints	Irresponsibility
Open	Openness	Accept all ideas and opinions equally	Indiscriminateness
Vast	Receptivity	Reject discernment & filtering	Overwhelm
Spacious	Trust	Excessive / insufficient scepticism	Cynicism / naivety
	Benevolence	Offer unsolicited advice or help	Condescension

Table 9: Negative reifications of the 10 aspects of Being (Essences) arising from the pursuit of a different aspect

When pursuing...	...the felt sense of...	...may feel
White: Support, grounding and confidence.	Yellow: Light, bubbly and uplifting.	Unreliable, ungrounded and flimsy.
Yellow: Joy, happiness and carefreeness.	White: Solid, firm and heavy.	Burdensome, serious and careworn.
Red: Strength, courage and passion.	Gold: Sweet, viscous and honey-like.	Yielding, co-dependent, enmeshed and confluent.
Gold: Bonding, community and romantic love.	Red: Vibrating, expanding and warm.	Rupture, disruption, conflict and agitation.
Black: Peace, intimacy and power/mastery.	Cream: Full, creamy and smooth.	Cluttered, smothering and infantile.
Cream: Nourishment, satisfaction and fulfilment	Black: Still, slow and empty.	Deprived, hopeless, pointless and meaningless.
Green: Compassion, loving-kindness and connection.	Blue: Sharp, clear and wakeful	Harsh, detached, cold, dispassionate and aloof.
Blue: Clarity, precision and intelligence	Green: Tender, delicate and moist.	Vague, confused and evasive.
Pink: Appreciation, acceptance and lovable/loving	Clear: Open, vast and spacious	Indifferent, desolate and inhumane.
Clear: Freedom, openness and receptivity	Pink: Soft, fluffy and plump	Claustrophobic, clingy, and smothering.

4.3. The Knot of Negative Reification and implications for therapy

The Knot of Negative Reification can be broken down into four interrelated misconceptions. The first of these is a general misconception that arises from the previous eight misconceptions as described above. The following three misconceptions are more specific versions of the first.

Seeking to create or acquire a positive reification of Being by fulfilling certain conditions can make other aspects of Being appear as hindrances and, thus, something negative we need to avoid (9th misconception). Even if two aspects of Being are both reified as positive phenomena, ideas about what conditions we must fulfil to create or acquire each of these phenomena can make them appear as mutually exclusive (10th misconception). As we saw in the last chapter, the way we try to create or acquire positive reifications of Being are counterproductive and have negative side effects. Over time, we may misattribute these negative side effects to the phenomenon we seek, turning it from a positive phenomenon into a negative one (11th misconception). And finally, when we reify an aspect of Being as a negative phenomenon we avoid and reject it, and the very act of avoiding and rejecting can cause discomfort. If we misattribute this discomfort to the state we avoid, it will further deepen our belief that this state is, indeed, something negative we must avoid (12th misconception).

To undo the Knot of Negative Reification, the therapist must shift each of these misconceptions by taking the client through lines of inquiry that will help them discover for themselves that the states the client perceive as negative and avoid in certain contexts are the same states they cherish and seek in other contexts (9th corrective principle); that all aspects of Being are the same and, as such, no two aspect of Being can be mutually exclusive (10th corrective principle); that the negative impact we ascribe to an aspect of Being is created by the method through which we seek to grasp the aspect – not by Being itself (11th corrective principle); and that the tensions we ascribe to an aspect of Being are created by our avoidance of this aspect – not by Being itself (12th corrective principle).

It is very useful to distinguish clearly between these misconceptions as this gives you valuable insight into the process through which clients come to perceive particular aspects of Being as negative in a particular situation and, conversely, how to help clients set aside their negative interpretations and perceive Being directly.

4.3.1. Misconception 9: Some inner states are negative and should be avoided

The first misconception related to the Knot of Negative Reification is the belief that certain inner states are inherently negative and should be avoided.

States people might perceive as negative and something to avoid include meaninglessness, pointlessness, powerlessness, hopelessness, worthlessness, loneliness, lostness, sadness, vulnerability, anger, frustration, disingenuousness, obsession, shame, guilt, jealousy, resentment, envy, inferiority, silliness, desire, hate, laziness, boredom and apathy[35].

The belief that there are inner states one must avoid can be expressed in different ways.

Some clients will express it directly by stating that they wish to get rid of a state they perceive as negative. They may say: "I wish to get rid of this sense of meaninglessness", or "I don't want to feel sad anymore".

Other clients will express their desire to get rid of an inner state simply by using a negatively laden word for the state and, thus, implying that they shouldn't feel that state. They may simply state "I feel lonely" or "I feel so much shame".

Yet other clients will express their desire to get rid of an inner state using expressions such as "transform", "overcome", "change", "deal with", "help" or "transmute". They may say "I wish to transform my anger into something more productive" or "I need to deal with my laziness".

Finally, some clients will express their desire to avoid certain inner states as a wish to avoid certain situations which they fear will bring them in touch with that state. They may say "I want to find a partner that doesn't make me feel inferior" or "I want to feel confident in asking for a pay rise". In the last example, the inner state the client wishes to avoid is implied rather than stated directly. It could be the state of self-doubt, as this is often perceived as the opposite of confidence. It could also be states of "worthlessness" or "insignificance" since the situation the client wishes to avoid is about symbols of value.

All of the above statements presuppose the belief that there are certain inner states which are negative in and of themselves and which should, therefore, be avoided. This is a misconception because the states in question are not negative

---

[35] You may not personally see all these states as negative. The point here is not to debate whether these states truly *are* negative but simply to suggest that many people *see* them as negative.

in and of themselves; they only become negative when interpreted in a particular context.

To illustrate this, one can think about the state of being lost. It is only negative to be lost if you believe you need to get somewhere. If you do not need to get somewhere, lostness just means "not knowing where you are" and this can be delightful. There are many people who find it enjoyable to get lost in a city because they see new and interesting things that way. Thus, once you remove the context of having to get somewhere, "lostness" is just another word for "exploration".

This is also true for the inner sense of lostness clients may seek to overcome through therapy. Lostness in life is not negative in itself. It only appears negative when juxtaposed with an idea such as: One should have a clear plan for one's life in order not to waste it. However, if one changes this idea with the (equally justifiable idea) that making too many plans is how one misses out on life, then what appeared to be a negative state of "lostness" may suddenly appear as a delightful state, one might call "receptivity", "openness", "freedom" or "flow". As we shall see in this and the following sections, no inner state is negative in itself but only appears so when interpreted within specific contexts.

The above examples illustrate that the state underpinning the concept of "lostness" is not inherently negative. The state only appears negative and acquires the negatively laden label of "lostness" in specific contexts. The main proposal of this chapter is that this is true for *any* negative state.

The contexts within which inner states come to appear as negative are created by the eight previously mentioned misconceptions.

"Not knowing where you are" only appears as the negative state of "lostness" if you believe you must get to somewhere in particular to be ok. In the same way, other negative states only appear negative if they are at odds with fulfilling the conditions we believe we need to fulfil to create or acquire the positive reifications of Being we seek.

In other words, once we have formulated and committed to a plan for how to create or acquire a particular positive reification of Being, we are compelled to perceive all elements of our experience, including other aspects of Being, in relation to this plan. We will judge everything as either irrelevant to, supporting or interfering with the plan, or as signs that we are succeeding or failing in our efforts to implement the plan.

Thus, when a client uses their plan for creating or acquiring a positive reification of one aspect of Being as a reference point for evaluating another aspect of Being, the latter can appear as a hindrance to the client's plan or as a sign that they are failing. When this happens, the client comes to reify the latter aspect of Being as a negative phenomenon they must avoid.

Of course, one aspect of Being cannot prevent us from perceiving another aspect of Being. This would be akin to claiming that the redness of an apple prevents us from perceiving the roundness of the apple or its sweetness.

However, once we have entered the realm of reifications, our *ideas* about different aspects of Being can create the illusion of conflict.

For example, a client may reify the silent aspect of Being as "peace" and believe that to create peace they must avoid agitation. Formulating and committing to such a plan makes it (almost) inevitable that the client will come to construe the dynamic and energetic aspect of Being as "agitation" or "disturbance" of the peace they seek. Thus, in the context of this client's mission to create or acquire peace, the dynamic and energetic aspect of Being appears as something to avoid.

There is nothing inherently negative about the dynamic aspect of Being. It only appears negative because the client created and became attached to a positive reification of another aspect and developed ideas about how to create or acquire this aspect that seems to be at odds with allowing the dynamic aspect of Being.

Thus, which aspects of Being are seen as positive and negative greatly depends upon the sequence in which we happen to become aware of and develop attachments to these different aspects of Being. If the client had perceived and become attached to the dynamic aspect before becoming aware of the silent aspect, it might have reversed which aspect they perceive as positive and negative.

For example, the client might have reified the dynamic and energetic aspect of Being as "strength" or "aliveness" and sought to create this strength and aliveness by dominating others and asserting their will upon the world. Now the silent aspect of Being might appear to the client as "passivity", "resignation", "weakness" or even "death". They may see it as something which threatens their mission of attaining strength by dominating others and asserting their will upon the world. Thus, in the context of this client's mission to create or acquire strength and aliveness, the silent aspect of Being appears as something to avoid.

Because any aspect of Being can be reified in positive as well as negative ways, the same exact aspects of Being may be perceived as either aliveness or disturbance of peace, either peace or loss of connection, either tranquillity or deadness, etc. Learning to perceive Being beyond any positive or negative labels is an important key to truly transformational therapy.

The void

One particular class of negative reification deserves special attention, namely any negative reification that is a reification of the *absence* of a positive phenomenon. For example, worthlessness, is a reification of the absence of worth; meaninglessness, is a reification of the absence of meaning; loneliness, is a reification of the absence of human connection, etc.

To understand the importance of this class of negative reifications, one must remember that Being, like physical space, is that which contains everything and, as such, it is none of the things it contains. This is why the experience of Being is often described as an experience of nothing. When the experience of nothing is interpreted in the context of a preceding experience of something positive, it is very easy to interpret the experience of nothing as a loss of that positive something.

If one moment you feel loved and the next moment you feel nothing, you are likely to experience this sequence as a loss of love, rather than as two separate experiences with their own separate qualities. Similarly, if you one moment have a sense of purpose and meaning and the next moment you feel nothing, you are likely to interpret the experience of nothing as purposelessness and meaninglessness.

Being, like physical space, contains phenomena but has none of the qualities of these phenomena. If you are aware of an experiential quality, you are aware of something contained in Being, not Being itself. Thus, when you become aware of Being directly, as opposed to Being compared to some mental content, it will by definition feel like not the phenomenon you were aware of before you became aware of Being.

In the chapter on positive reification, we looked at how Being can be interpreted as the absence of issues, which could be labelled as "joy", the absence of agitation, which could be labelled as "peace", the absence of stuckness, which could be labelled as "vitality", etc.

Following the same logic, Being can be interpreted as the absence of "meaning", which can be labelled as "meaninglessness", the absence of "value," which can be labelled as "worthlessness", the absence of "connection", which can be labelled as "loneliness", the absence of "love", which can be labelled as "animosity" or as "being unlovable", etc.

Here it is worth noting that because the positive reification of Being arises from comparing Being with some negative experience, that positive reification is bound to cease when the reference points change. Thus, whenever we experience a positive reification of Being it will inevitably fade away into nothingness at some point. When this happens there is the risk that the nothingness that is Being will be perceived as something negative, namely the loss of the positive reification.

For this reason, negative inner states that are reifications of loss are particularly potent doorways to becoming aware of Being in its suchness, free from either positive or negative reifications.

Implications for therapy

Clients will often come to therapy because they wish to find ways of avoiding a particular inner state they perceive as negative.

At first glance, it may seem that the role of the therapist should be to assist the client in overcoming negative inner states and, in this way, help them achieve increased well-being.

However, once we realise that the inner states clients perceive as negative in one context are the very same they perceive as positive in other contexts, we also realise that going along with the client's wish to avoid negative inner states can be problematic. If we help a client implement strategies to avoid an inner state they perceive as negative in a specific context, we are simultaneously "helping" them implement strategies that will block them from accessing a positive state they seek and need for their well-being.

If, for example, we help a client avoid their aggression because the client believes aggression is a negative state, we simultaneously "help" them avoid their strength because the felt sense state the client calls "aggression" in one context is the same they call "strength" in another.

Similarly, if we help a client avoid their "superficiality" because they believe this is negative, we simultaneously "help" them avoid their "joyfulness" because the felt-sense state the client calls "superficiality" in one context is the same state they call "joyfulness" in another.

If a client avoids "hurt", they also avoid "compassion" and "tenderness". If a client avoids "shame", they also avoid "authenticity" and "openness".

It is important to note that the above examples do not suggest that allowing the negative phenomenon is required for receiving the positive. The suggestion is that the negative and positive phenomena are *the same.* When we explore the felt sense at the core of the corresponding positive and negative states, we find that states that seem very different are, in fact, identical.

For this reason, Being-Centred Therapy is not concerned with judging inner states as good and bad and helping clients experience more of the good ones and less of the bad ones. Instead, Being-Centred Therapy focuses on helping clients learn to perceive the felt sense core of *all* states and, for negative states in particular, to perceive how context influences their perception and value-judgement of the state.

Becoming aware of the identity of the states they, in different contexts, perceive as negative and positive will help clients lose their fear of the negative states and, thus, expand what states they feel comfortable experiencing. Clients often perceive this as an increased sense of freedom in life. Furthermore, and more importantly, it will also enable clients to perceive Being as the core ingredient in all their inner states – including the ones they judge as negative in some contexts.

Thus, whereas traditional therapy may be guided by a question, such as:

- How can I help clients get rid of negative states?

Being-Centred Therapy is guided by questions, such as:

- What are the contexts the client uses to make the state appear negative?
- What would the state feel like to the client if they separated that state from these contexts?

The four most common answers to the first question, i.e., the most common contexts that makes an inner state appear negative are:

- The state is seen as hindering the acquirement of another state
- The state is seen as positive but in conflict with another positive state
- The state is conflated with the negative consequences of misguided attempts to create or acquire the state
- The state is conflated with the uncomfortable sensations, particularly tension, related to our avoidance of the state.

These four answers correspond to the four misconceptions I look at in this chapter (misconceptions 9-12).

Table 10: The identity of positive and negative states

Essence/Felt Sense	Positive Phenomena	Negative Phenomena
White Solid. Firm. Heavy. Downward movement. Relaxed immobile. Calm. Easeful.	Support. Stability. Grounding. Confidence. Patience. Neutrality. Perseverance. Discipline. Commitment	Stuckness. Workaholism. Stubbornness. Rigidity. Arrogance. Passivity. Collapse. Apathy. Dispassionate. Unengaged. Burnout. Lethargy. Boredom. Rigidity. Defeatism. Laziness. Burdened. Serious. Careworn.
Red Vibrating. Expanding. Warm. Energised. Free flow. Charged. Forward movement. Dynamic.	Strength. Courage. Passion. Vitality. Excitement. Authenticity. Truthfulness. Assertiveness.	Bullying. Aggression. Recklessness. Foolhardiness. Obsession. Jealousy. Recklessness. Irresponsibility. Anti-social behaviour. Insensitivity. Anger. Impatience. Frustration. Resentment. Envy. Irritation. Agitation. Impulsivity. Rupture. Disturbance. Conflict.
Black Still. Slow. Sense of being erased. Empty. Inward movement. Absorption. Velvety soft. Dark.	Peace. Non-attachment. Mastery. Power. Sacredness. Absolution. Intuition. Mystery. Magic. Intimacy.	Deadness. Loneliness. Annihilation. Emptiness. Oppressiveness. Hate. Non-participation. Worthlessness. Aloofness. Detachment. Worthlessness. Meaninglessness. Pointlessness. Powerlessness. Hopelessness. Dissociation. Deprivation.

Essence/Felt Sense	Positive Phenomena	Negative Phenomena
Green Tender. Delicate. Moist Calm flow. Fresh or minty.	Compassion. Loving-Kindness. Human Connection. Sympathy. Agape Love. Understanding. Open-heartedness	Fragility. Vulnerability. Defencelessness. Sentimentality. Shame. Pity. Disempowerment. Self-reduction. Melancholy. Weakness. Sadness. Hurt. Lostness. Helplessness. Inferiority. Grief. Regret. Shyness. Guilt. Remorse. Sorrow. Vagueness. Confusion.
Pink Soft like cotton. Fluffy. Plump. Sweet (light). Warm. Calm.	Appreciation. Acceptance. Being lovable/loving. Perfection. Cosiness. Welcomed/welcoming.	Feebleness. Mushiness. Dependency. Rose-tinted glasses. Perfectionism. Complacency. Evasiveness. Inefficiency. Laziness. Apathy. Passivity. Gullibility. Naivety. Clingy. Smothering.
Yellow Light. Bubbly. Uplifting. Upward movement. Sweet (light). Laughter.	Joy. Happiness. Carefreeness. Curiosity. Spontaneity. Optimism. Innocence. Light-heatedness. Unburdenedness. Simplicity. Desire.	Superficiality. Selfishness. Carelessness. Nosiness. Frivolity. Naivety. Childishness. Disloyalty. Lack of depth. Delusion. Hedonism. Silliness. Foolishness. Disingenuousness. Nervous excitement. Evasion. Lack of realism. Unreliability. Ungroundedness. Flimsiness.
Gold Sweet (dense). Viscous. Honey-like. Soothing.	Bonding. Community. Romantic love. Unity. Surrender. Harmony. Value. Generosity.	Submissiveness. Self-rejection. Loss of control. Affective dependency. Malleability. Losing identity. Loss of personal boundaries. Loss of self. Defencelessness. Addiction. Escapism. Infatuation. Co-dependency. Enmeshment. Confluence.
Cream Fullness. Creamy. Smooth.	Nourishment. Satisfaction. Fulfilment. Wholeness. Contentment. Fullness.	Over-entitlement. Neediness. Immaturity. Infantilisation. Utopia. Inertia. Under-entitlement. Over-indulgence. Self-satisfaction. Pacification. Complacency. Smothering. Infantile.
Blue Sharp. Clear. Wakeful. Crisp. Fresh. Energised.	Clarity. Precision. Intelligence. Discernment. Guidance. Alertness. Inspiration.	Harshness. Inflexibility. Arrogance. Dogmatism. Judgemental. Callous. Heartless. Unfeeling. Cruel. Insensitive. Ruthless. Detached. Cold. Dispassionate. Aloof.
Clear Open. Vast. Spacious. Light.	Freedom. Openness. Receptivity. Trust. Benevolence. Loving holding.	Irresponsibility. Indiscriminateness. Overwhelm. Cynicism. Naivety. Condescension. Indifference. Uncaring. Impersonal. Existential angst. Void. Nihilism. Desolation. Inhumane.

The most common answers to the second question of what negative states feel like when they are separated from the context that makes them appear negative are summarised in Table 10.

- The first column contains a range of negative phenomena.
- The second column contains the felt sense experience of these phenomena described in neutral, sensory words.
- The third column contains positive reifications of the felt sense state in the second column.

When exploring what a state the client perceives as negative feels like when separated from the contexts that create this perception, the client will first discover the felt sense in column two and then recognise this felt sense as one of the positive phenomena in column three.

Having this overview can be useful for therapists to develop good working hypotheses about what a given state the client is currently experiencing might transform into when separated from the context that makes the client interpret the state as negative[36].

That being said, the connections presented in Table 10 are not set in stone. Variations are common. Some clients will, for example, use the word "hate" to refer to an energetic felt sense, not a state of silence, emptiness and darkness some clients may use the word "disingenuousness" to refer to a felt sense of hardness, not lightness, and so on. It is, therefore, important not to make assumptions about the felt sense clients refer to solely based on the word they use. However, the general principle that any negative concept is synonymous with multiple positive concepts at the felt-sense level hold true for all negative concepts.

9th corrective principle: The states you perceive as negative and avoid in certain contexts are the same states you cherish and seek in other contexts

The first corrective principle related to the Knot of Negative Reification is:

> "The states you perceive as negative and avoid in certain contexts are the same states you cherish and seek in other contexts"

---

[36] The context can either of the two mentioned in Section 4.2: Seeing the Essence as responsible for the negative consequences of pursuing the Essence, and the seeing Essence as an obstacle to the pursuit of a different Essence.

This principle helps you remember that the states clients often perceive as negative, such as meaninglessness, hopelessness, sadness, anger, disconnection and emptiness, are merely experiences of Being in disguise. The problem is not the state itself but rather the negative interpretation of that state.

Thus, rather than helping clients get rid of these states, you can invite them to sense these states separately from the contexts that make them appear negative. This will ultimately reveal Being, the core ingredient of the negative states. Thus, clients will discover that what they avoid are blessings in disguise. They are the very same states they, in other contexts, call peace, love, joy, tenderness, vitality, and so on. We do not turn away from inner states because they are negative; they appear negative because we turn away from them. Seemingly negative states are lotuses in the mud.

4.3.2. Misconception 10: Two positive states can be mutually exclusive

The second misconception related to the Knot of Negative Reification is the belief that two aspects of Being, which are both reified as positive phenomena, can be mutually exclusive. While this does not lead to a negative perception of either aspect, it does lead to the (false) belief that it is necessary to choose between them, i.e. to reject one in order to achieve the other. One may, for example, believe that to feel "peace" (one positive reification of Being), it is not possible to also feel "vitality" (another positive reification of Being) – and vice versa.

This misconception is a consequence of previous misconceptions; in particular, the 8th misconception, where the client substitutes an aspect of Being itself for the method through which they try to create or acquire this aspect. While two aspects of Being cannot be in conflict, the conditions the client (falsely) believes they must fulfil to create or acquire each aspect can. If the client has forgotten what aspect of Being they are seeking and has come to see the fulfilment of the conditions as their end-goal (the 8th misconception), then the conflict between the two goals may come to appear unsolvable.

For example, peace and vitality are not mutually exclusive. It is possible to feel simultaneously peaceful and vibrantly alive. In fact, this is very common during meditation. However, if a client believes that to feel peaceful they must be inactive, while to feel alive they must be active, then the two states will suddenly appear to be mutually exclusive because it is not possible to be simultaneously inactive and active. This is illustrated in Figure 13. The first row represents the positive reification of two aspects of Being: Being as "peace" and Being as "vitality" respectively. The second row represents the conditions the client have come to believe they must fulfil to create or acquire each of the two positive reifications of Being: being inactive and being active, respectively. Any conflict the client may feel between the two stems from their ideas about how to create the states – not from the felt sense of these states.

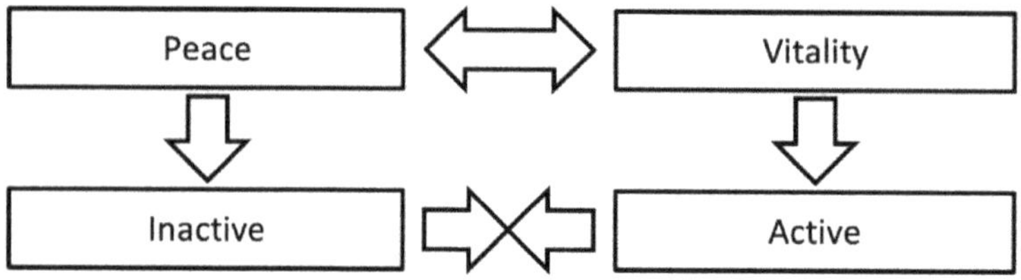

Figure 13: How two positive reifications of Being can appear to be in conflict

The fact that positive inner states can appear to be mutually exclusive even though they are not, has great implications for therapy because it means that many of the dilemmas clients face are not really dilemmas at all.

Implications for therapy

Often clients come to therapy because they feel torn between two desires. For example:

- A client may want to be adventurous, throw caution to the wind and live their life fully, but they also want a sense of safety and stability and therefore they stay at home.
- A client may want to be independent and have their own space, but they also want the nourishment of a close and intimate relationship.
- A client may want to progress their career, but they also want to build and nurture their family.

It can be tempting, as a therapist, to seek to help clients choose wisely what to give their energy to at a certain phase in their life or help them strike a good balance between two desired, but mutually exclusive, objectives.

However, insofar as the client's desires are desires for different aspects of Being, neither making a choice nor seeking a compromise is advisable.

It may seem reasonable in a given period of one's life to make a choice between two desired objectives. However, insofar as the client's desire for these objectives are expressions of their desire for Being, such choices become choices between aspects of Being, and it is not possible to choose between two aspects of Being since all aspects are of vital importance.

While it may be both reasonable and possible to choose for some time to focus on adventure at the expense of stability in our life, or the other way round, it is neither reasonable nor possible to choose between the dynamic and the grounded aspects of Being.

In the same way, one might choose between independence and relationship or between career and family. Many do, indeed, make such choices at different phases of their lives. However, when desires are particularly strong, it is a sign that they are fuelled by underpinning desires for various aspects of Being, and it is not possible to choose between them.

In the same way, it can seem reasonable to seek a balance or a compromise between two competing desires. Rather than choosing one over the other, it is possible to limit each of them so as to leave room for the other. You can have stability in your life and every now and then go on an adventure. You can be in an intimate relationship that leaves room for doing things independently. You can choose how many hours a day you dedicate to career and family, respectively.

While such compromises may work well in relation to the conditions, they do not work well when it comes to our desire for Being. We cannot ask ourselves to have just a little bit of each aspect of Being. When it comes to Being, nothing short of totality will be enough.

The cause of the client's painful dilemma is not that they haven't made a clear choice or that they don't know how to strike a balance or make a compromise between their two desires. The cause of the painful dilemma is the client's misconception that fulfilling certain conditions is a way to create or acquire certain aspects of Being.

Thus, helping the client to choose between the two desires or to strike a balance or settle on a compromise will leave the cause of the client's painful dilemma untouched.

To address the cause of the client's plight, therapy must dissolve the conceptualisations that make different aspects of Being appear mutually exclusive.

Whereas, traditional therapy might be guided by questions, such as:

- How can a client choose wisely between two positive, but mutually exclusive, objectives?
- How can the client achieve a balance or a satisfying compromise between two desirable, but mutually exclusive, objectives?

Being-Centred Therapy will be guided by questions, such as:

- What is the conceptualisation that creates the illusion of a dilemma between two positive states?
- What are the aspects of Being underpinning the two mutually exclusive objectives, and what does the combined felt sense of these aspects of Being feel like?
- How does feeling the combined felt sense affect the client's perception of facing a dilemma in their life?

10th corrective principle: All aspects of Being are ultimately one

The 10th corrective principle states that:

> "All aspects of Being are ultimately one and can, therefore, never be in conflict."

This principle helps us be sceptical about any solution to an inner split that involves making a clear choice, finding a balance or settling on a compromise.

It encourages therapists to investigate the conceptualisation that precedes the appearance of the dilemma rather than taking the dilemma as a given. This is particularly important in situations where the therapist is affected by conceptualisations in themselves that make the dilemma appear as a naturally occurring one. Sticking to the principle will help therapists avoid the trap of joining the client in reifying the dilemma instead of seeing it as the product of a particular conceptualisation of how the conflicting states are created or acquired.

In other words, the principle helps us discover the oneness of all aspects of Being and see through the appearance of Being as a thousand different phenomena.

4.3.3. Misconception 11: Feeling an aspect of Being can have a negative impact

The third misconception related to the Knot of Negative Reification is the belief that aspects of Being can have negative impacts on our lives.

This misconception arises from conflating an aspect of Being with the negative consequences resulting from the way in which the Knot of Conditionality makes an individual seek to create or acquire this aspect of Being.

In other words, we frequently attribute the negative outcomes of our actions, intended to create or acquire a certain aspect of Being, to that aspect of Being itself. This is a misconception, as neither the actions nor their negative outcomes are brought about by the aspect of Being, but rather by the misguided belief that we are separate from Being and must engage in particular actions to create or acquire it.

For example, an individual may reify the silent aspect of Being as "peace" and develop the idea that "peace" can be created or acquired by avoiding or ignoring conflicts. Following this strategy for creating "peace" can have many negative side effects. It can make the individual easy to dominate because they fail to stand up for themselves. It can also turn the individual into a coward who fails to meet their social responsibility by letting harmful conflicts remain unresolved.

When an individual's desire for the silent aspect of Being leads them to act in ways that make them easy to dominate or shy away from social responsibilities, it can influence the individual's perception of the silent aspect of Being. Rather than perceiving it as "peace", as they originally did, they may come to experience the silent aspect of Being as something passive and defeatist or something that prevents them from living up to their social responsibility to protect those who need their protection. Consequently, they will start actively avoiding the silent aspect of Being because they now see it as something that makes them betray themselves or others. This process can be summed up in the following way:

1. The individual perceives the silent aspect of Being
2. They interpret this experience in the context of the noise of their general state of mind and call it "peace" (positive reification)
3. The individual is attracted to the silent aspect of Being
4. They develop ideas about how to create or acquire this "peace"
5. Acting upon these ideas has negative consequences, such as abandoning oneself or abandoning one's social responsibilities.
6. They reinterpret the silent aspect of Being in the context of these negative consequences and now they call it "defeatism" or "social irresponsibility" (negative reification)
7. The individual is repulsed by the silent aspect of Being and develops ideas about how to avoid it.

Similarly, another individual may reify Being as "strength" and develop the idea that to create or acquire "strength" they must dominate others at all times. However, permanently dominating others can have many negative side effects. It can, for example, lead to hurting other people and can be exhausting in the long run as it generally requires a lot of continued effort.

If an individual's strategy for creating or acquiring Being in the form of "strength" leads them to act in ways that hurt others and takes a lot of energy, they may come to see the strength aspect of Being as harmful and exhausting. Rather than calling it "strength", "courage", "vitality" or "enthusiasm" (all common positive reifications of this aspect of Being), they may call it "aggression" or "struggle" (both common negative reifications of this aspect of Being). Once the strength aspect of Being has become part of such negative constructs, the individual is likely to begin actively avoiding it.

Thus, negative reifications of Being are often constructed by associating an aspect of Being with the negative effects of the ways we reach for that aspect of Being. In other words, negative reifications of Being occur when Being is interpreted in the context of problematic strategies for creating or acquiring that aspect of Being.

See Table 8 on page 239 for examples of negative reifications of each of the 10 aspects of Being that arise from the strategies clients employ to create or acquire these aspects.

Implications for therapy

Clearing up the 11th misconception is an important part of therapy. Whenever a client seeks to avoid an inner state because they believe feeling this state has negative effects on their lives, it can be good to explore what the state feels like when separated from any action and thus from any negative consequences brought about by these actions.

For example, a client may feel they have a lot of aggression, and they would like to get rid of it.

In traditional therapy, one might evaluate whether the client could be in a situation where aggression is appropriate, and teach the client anger management skills if it is not, for example by exploring what narratives they are telling themself, which generates the aggression, and then modifying these narratives.

Being-Centred Therapy offers a different path. First, we can ask the client what they see as negative consequences of the aggression. The client may state that the aggression leads them to abuse and hurt other people and regret this afterwards.

Once we know what the negative consequences are, we can invite the client to explore what the state would feel like separate from the actions and negative consequences that are associated with the state. We could ask:

> "What does aggression feel like if you feel it fully without doing anything? If you relax and don't do anything, you cannot abuse or hurt anyone, so you can give yourself full permission to feel the aggression without restraint. What do you feel when you do that?"

The client may then notice that aggression itself is nothing other than a lot of energy and inner heat, which can be quite enjoyable to feel. When this energy is not held back due to fear of negative consequences, it may feel invigorating and freeing. In other words, the client may become aware that what they call "aggression" and see as something negative in one context, is what they would call "strength", "courage" or "aliveness" in other contexts.

Thus, separating the state from problematic actions and their consequences has enabled the client to become aware of Being.

Once the client has become aware of Being in the form of strength and energy, they can go on to explore the concrete situation in which they found their aggression to be a problem. The client's view of this situation will most likely have changed radically because they now feel Being and, thus, the problem of being separate from Being is no longer part of the equation, so to speak.

The same kind of process can be carried out whenever a client believes they are feeling problematic inner states, such as "irresponsibility", "defeatism", "hate", "sadness", "desire", "boredom", "vulnerability", "meaninglessness", "lostness", etc.

It is worth noting that not all people will find all of the mentioned states problematic. Some may not have any problems with "sadness" or "boredom". But if a client does perceive these states as negative and problematic, it can be useful to explore what negative consequences the client associates with feeling these states and then invite them to sense the state separately from these consequences and the actions that are truly responsible for these consequences.

11th corrective principle: The negative effects are produced by the method of grasping – not by Being itself

The 11th corrective principle of Being-Centred Therapy is:

> "Negative inner states are often constructed by juxtaposing an aspect of Being and the negative effects of the strategies we develop in the Knot of Conditionality in an attempt at creating or acquiring this aspect of Being."

This principle invites us to understand negative inner states as positive inner states to which we have misattributed the negative consequences of following strategies born out of the Knot of Conditionality.

The principle helps you remember that the negative impact cannot come from simply sensing a state. It must come from actions. Thus, rather than seeking ways to get rid of or avoid the inner state, we can separate the state from misguided strategies for creating or acquiring these states.

While avoiding certain *actions* can be useful, we should not avoid any *inner states*. Rather, we can use inner states the client perceives as negative to point the client's awareness towards Being.

4.3.4. Misconception 12: An aspect of Being can feel tense and unpleasant

The fourth misconception related to the Knot of Negative Reification is attributing the felt sense of our judgements of an inner state to the state itself.

Once we have come to see a particular inner state as negative, we become afraid of it and seek to reject or avoid it.

Rejection and avoidance of an inner state can have the same feeling as rejecting or avoiding something external. Rejection can feel like pushing something away or holding something encapsulated, like when we hold the lid of a box shut so the content does not escape. Avoidance can feel like pulling away from something or encapsulating yourself, like when you shut yourself in a room and ensure that what you are avoiding does not get in. What all of these scenarios have in common is that they include different patterns of tension.

Because "rejection" and "avoidance" involve tension, clients will often be under the impression that the negative states they reject or avoid are states of tension.

If, for example, you ask a client what the aggression they reject feels like, they may say it feel tense. However, the tension is the feeling of rejecting the aggression. If the client did not try to repress, contain, push away or in some other way reject the aggression, they would not feel any tension. Aggression itself feels like pure energy. The tethers that hold aggression back feel like tension.

Similarly, if you ask a client what the vulnerability they avoid feels like, they may say that it feels tense. This case is identical to the previous one. The felt sense of tension is the felt sense of the client's avoidance of vulnerability – not the felt sense of vulnerability itself.

Because the felt sense of tension is uncomfortable, misattributing it to the state the client is rejecting or avoiding will compound the client's negative perception of this state. The client will come to perceive the state, not only as something that blocks something positive or something that has a negative impact on their life, but also as something that makes them tense.

In other words, the felt sense of the client's rejection or avoidance of a negative reification of Being becomes an extra layer in the construction of that negative reification.

Rejection and avoidance do not always feel like tension. Avoidance of an inner state may also come as a sense of confusion, fogginess or lack of focus, and rejection sometimes comes as a sense of nausea. As with tension, these correspond to ways in which we avoid or reject physical objects. Confusion, fogginess and lack of focus correspond to a blurring of our senses so as to avoid perceiving what seems threatening to us. Nausea corresponds to our body's natural reaction when we have eaten something poisonous that needs to be rejected.

Furthermore, multiple layers of a client's felt sense may pertain to rejection and avoidance. For example, avoidance of an inner state may feel like confusion. But because this confusion is uncomfortable, it may be rejected, and this rejection may feel like the tension of pushing something away.

Thus, finding the felt sense of the state the client is rejecting or avoiding can be a bit of an excavation exercise. It is, however, important work, because only when we discover this state can we start to separate it from the contexts that make the client perceive it as something negative. When the client comes to know the state they reject or avoid as an aspect of Being, the negative reification will dissolve along with the whole chain of rejection and avoidance.

Implications for therapy

As a therapist, it is useful to know that when clients say that the negative state feels tense, confused, nauseous, etc. they are often describing their rejection or avoidance of the state and not the actual state they are avoiding.

To direct a client's attention towards the felt sense of the state they are rejecting or avoiding, rather than the felt sense of the rejection or avoidance, you can ask questions such as:

> "What do you feel when you relax the tension?"
>
> "What do you notice if you do not feel confused?"
>
> "What do you notice if the fog lifts?"
>
> "What do you feel if you turn the lens of your perception so what you feel comes into focus?"
>
> "What does the thing that causes the nausea feel like?"

Such questions will often elicit an immediate response describing the combined experience of the state and the negative associations. From there you can use the questions presented in the three previous sections to help the client get a clear sense of the state they are rejecting or avoiding, separate from the associated contexts that make the state appear as something negative.

Sometimes it is too overwhelming for a client to become aware of the state they are rejecting or avoiding either indirectly by imagining stopping rejecting/avoiding it or directly by turning their attention to the thing they are rejecting/avoiding.

In such cases, you can ask questions that direct the client's awareness to the state they are rejecting or avoiding without implying that the client should stop rejecting or avoiding the state.

If, for example, the client rejects an inner state by encapsulating it in a layer of tension, you can say:

> "While retaining the tension, notice what the thing inside the tension feels like."

By describing the "content of the box", the client will, of course, feel it. However, the language implies that they are still in control of it, and this will sometimes create enough of an opening for the client to experience what they are rejecting and discover that it is not as bad as they feared. I will describe more techniques for managing overwhelm in Section 4.4, Sensing Taboos – how to untie the Knot of Negative Reification.

12th corrective principle: Tension is the felt sense of judgements against Being – not Being itself

The 12th corrective principle of Being-Centred Therapy is:

> "Tension and certain other felt-sense experiences are often the felt sense of rejection or avoidance of a state – not the felt sense of the state itself."

This principle helps us remember to be sceptical whenever a client says the state they reject or avoid feels tense. If we accept this statement at face value and proceed to explore the tension, we risk that the exploration distracts the client rather than helping them become aware of the state they are rejecting or avoiding.

Links to other systems

Many spiritual and psychological/therapeutic traditions emphasise relaxation as a key component in their practice.

In spiritual traditions, relaxation is often facilitated through various forms of meditation and is seen as a means to quieten the mind, open the heart and connect with deeper aspects of one's being or the divine. Releasing tension is seen as a way to release attachments and facilitate greater presence, inner peace, and spiritual growth.

In psychological/therapeutic traditions the focus on relaxation is particularly prevalent among the body-oriented approaches. Both the ones involving working directly with the body, such as Bioenergetics, Craniosacral Therapy, Body-Mind Centering, and Manuvision, and those involving developing awareness of the body, such as Focusing and Somatic Experiencing.

One of the pioneers in the field of body-based approaches to therapy was Wilhelm Reich, an Austrian psychoanalyst and psychiatrist, and a significant figure in the field of psychotherapy and psychoanalysis. He developed the theory of "orgone energy" and the therapeutic approach known as "Reichian therapy" or "orgone therapy".

In Reich's work, relaxation played a crucial role in the process of therapy.

He believed that many psychological issues and physical ailments were the result of repressed emotions and tension stored in the body, which he referred to as "body armouring".

According to Reich, this body armouring prevented the natural flow of "orgone energy" (a concept he proposed) through the body, leading to various emotional and physical disturbances.

Reichian therapy focused on helping individuals release this body armouring through relaxation techniques and body work. Reich believed that releasing body armouring and the corresponding unresolved emotions would result in clients experiencing greater emotional freedom and overall well-being.

His work had a significant impact on the field of psychotherapy, especially on somatic psychotherapy and body-oriented approaches to healing.

From the perspective of Being-Centred Therapy, the reason that releasing body armouring can resolve unresolved emotional issues and lead to greater well-being is not that the client gets rid of something as the word "release" might suggest. Rather, the reason is that releasing bodily tensions can bring about a perceptual shift by changing the context in which the individual interprets their inner states, including emotional states, from one of tension to one of relaxation. This increases the likelihood that clients will reify inner states as positive rather than negative, changing the world they inhabit.

This is not a matter of getting rid of all tensions. Even states of tensions will be construed in a different way when they are interpreted in a context of relaxation.

4.3.5. Summary

In the above, we have seen that the Knot of Negative Reification relates to four interconnected misconceptions. We have also seen how awareness of these misconceptions and their corresponding corrective principles can inform therapeutic interventions.

Table 11 summarises the misconceptions and corresponding corrective principles related to the Knot of Negative Reification.

Table 11: Misconceptions and corrective principles related to The Knot of Negative Reification

Misconceptions	Corrective Therapeutic Principles
Some inner states are negative and should be avoided (in particular, "the void").	The essence of all inner states is Being. The states you perceive as negative and avoid in certain contexts are the same states you cherish and seek in other contexts.
Two positive phenomena can be mutually exclusive.	All aspects of Being are ultimately one.
An aspect of Being can have a negative impact.	The negative impact we ascribe to an aspect of Being is created by the method through which we seek to grasp the aspect – not by Being itself.
An aspect of Being can feel tense and unpleasant.	The tensions we ascribe to an aspect of Being are created by our avoidance of this aspect – not by Being itself.

Table 12 summarises the differences between the questions that guide traditional and Being-Centred Therapy.

Table 12: How understanding the Knot of Negative Reification changes the questions guiding therapy

Traditional therapy questions	Being-Centred Therapy questions
What strategies can help the client avoid a particular negative inner state? How can the client overcome a negative inner state that prevents them from experiencing positive inner state?	What are the positive inner states that are equivalent to the negative inner state at the felt-sense level? What contextual factors determine whether the client interprets the state negatively or positively? What does the state that appears negative to the client feel like in situations where the client feels no need to pursue the positive state?
How can a client choose wisely between two positive, but mutually exclusive, objectives? How can the client achieve a balance or a satisfying compromise between two desirable, but mutually exclusive, objectives?	What is the conceptualisation that creates the illusion of a dilemma? What are the aspects of Being underpinning the two mutually exclusive objectives and what does the combined felt sense of these aspects of Being feel like? • How does feeling the combined felt sense affect the client's perception of facing a dilemma in their life?

Traditional therapy questions	Being-Centred Therapy questions
What narratives does the client tell themselves to generate the negative state and how can we help the client stop generating the negative states by changing these narratives?	What negative consequences does the client imagine that feeling the negative state produces and what does the state feel like when separated from these consequences? What is the connection between the client's imagined negative consequences of feeling the state and the client's methods for grasping the state?
How can clients release negative states of tension, nausea, confusion and other signs of overwhelm?	What do the negative states feel like beyond tension, nausea, confusion, etc.? What states emerge when the client lets go of the defensive states of tension, nausea, confusion, etc.?

In the following section, I will describe in detail a therapeutic process aimed at untying the Knot of Negative Reification. This process is called Sensing Taboos because it aims at creating awareness of Being through exploration of experiences the client perceives as negative and seeks to avoid. It does so by inviting the client to pay attention to the felt sense of such experiences, separately from the ideas that make it appear as something negative the client must avoid.

Since Being is the core ingredient in all experience, we can become aware of Being by separating *any* experience from all context-dependent interpretations. It does not matter whether we start from a phenomenon we perceive as positive or as negative. Both can be used to become aware of Being by going through the process of separating them from interpretations.

The only difference is what kind of interpretations we must separate the phenomenon from. Whereas positive phenomena must primarily be separated from ideas about how to attain them, negative phenomena must primarily be separated from ideas about how they block positive states, how they inflict negative consequences on our lives and how they cause negative felt-sense states such as tension, fogginess and nausea.

This perspective may be conceptually clear from reading the above (or similar texts). However, it is possible to understand that all negative states are Being in disguise at a conceptual level, yet still be terrified of them. It is possible intellectually to understand that our perceptions of the states will change if we embrace them, and still be completely unable to do so. To learn how to embrace states that appear negative (or plainly terrifying) to us, we need to go beyond conceptual understanding to direct experience, and let this experience update the beliefs that govern our behaviour. This is the goal of the Sensing Taboos process.

4.4. Sensing Taboos – how to untie the Knot of Negative Reification

The Knot of Negative Reification consists of four interlinked misconceptions which makes Being appear as something negative to be avoided and, thus, compels clients to direct their awareness away from Being and towards ideas about what conditions they need to fulfil to permanently banish the affected aspects of Being from their lives.

As the client turns their attention away from Being, they create a sense of deep loss and suffering. However, while under the spell of the misconceptions, clients tend to misattribute this sense of loss and suffering to the states they seek to avoid, thus strengthening their belief in the necessity of avoiding these states. They are unable to discover that the true source of their suffering is not the states they seek to avoid but rather their avoidance of these states.

The Knot of Negative Reification can be untied by encouraging clients to examine the states they avoid at a felt sense level – separate from their ideas about these states. As this goes against the clients' motivation, it requires patience, skilled persuasion, attentiveness to the client's anxiety level and the ability to make the process feel safe each step of the way.

The Knot of Negative Reification can be untied through the four-step process of Sensing Taboos.

1. **Recognise the Knot of Negative Reification:**
   The first step is to notice the Knot of Negative Reification. This is done by clarifying what state the client seeks to avoid.
2. **Distinguish between the felt sense of the state and reactions to the state:**
   The second step is to distinguish between the felt sense of the state the client avoids and the felt sense that is generated by the client's reactions to the state they avoid.
3. **Separate the felt sense from negative interpretations:**
   The third step is to separate the felt sense of the state the client avoids from any negative interpretations. Doing so will reveal through direct experience that the core of the state the client avoids is Being and, as such, is identical to states the client seeks and cherishes in other contexts.
4. **Correcting misconceptions:**
   The fourth step is to use the experience of step three to correct the misconceptions related to the Knot of Negative Reification. This step is divided into four different processes:
   a. **Changeless Transformation:** Clarifying the nature of transformation
   b. **Unification of Opposites:** Noticing the unity of the negative and positive states
   c. **Embracing the Void:** Recognising the loss of a positive state as a return to Being
   d. **Absolving the State:** Noticing that the true origin of the prejudice against the state the client perceives as negative derives from interpretations and not the state itself.

In the remainder of this chapter, I will describe why it is important to undo the Knot of Negative Reification, elaborate on the Mechanism of the Sensing Taboos process through which this can be achieved and outline how to facilitate the Sensing Taboos process in one-to-one sessions as well as in groups through a series of contemplation exercises. Figure 14 provides an overview of the process.

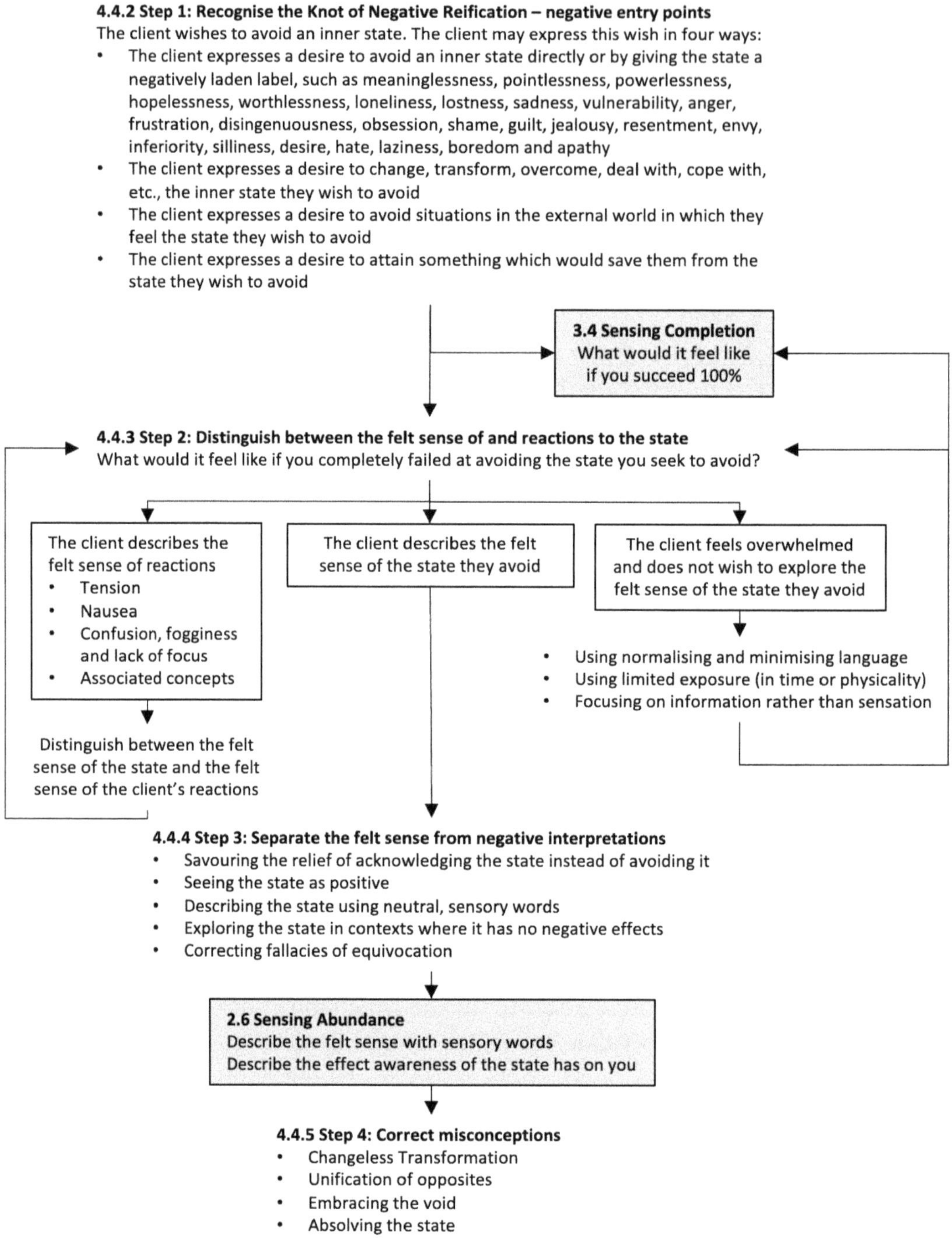

Figure 14: The Sensing Taboos process

4.4.1. The Mechanism of Sensing Taboos

Before describing how to facilitate the Sensing Taboos process, it is instructive to describe the overall mechanism of the process by contrasting it with the Sensing Completion process used to solve the Knot of Conditionality.

The two sides of any wish for change

A common way clients seek to avoid negative states is by seeking to create a positive state they believe would preclude the negative one. This shows that a wish to avoid a negative state and a wish to create or acquire a positive state can be two sides of the same wish for change.

Whenever a client wishes to make a change in their life, they simultaneously seek to attain something they believe is not present and reject something they believe is. If you see a red door and you want to paint it black, you simultaneously seek to attain the black colour and get rid of the red.

If a client wishes to attain "confidence", they are implicitly rejecting their current state, which they may describe as "self-doubt" or "timidity". If a client wishes to attain a "loving connection", they are implicitly rejecting their current state, which they might describe as "loneliness" or "alienation".

In these examples, the client's focus is on what they wish to achieve, and the thing they reject is only implied. However, sometimes it is the other way round. The client may be focused on what they wish to get away from, and what they seek is only implied.

A client may, for example, express a wish to overcome their crippling "self-doubt". This wish implies that they want something else instead, which could be a sense of "confidence". Similarly, a client may express a wish not to be "lonely" anymore without paying much attention to what it is they want instead. Nevertheless, the wish not to be lonely does imply that the client must want something different, for example a sense of "loving connection".

Conventional therapy wisdom holds that the so-called away-from-motivation, where clients focus on what they don't want, should be reformulated as towards-motivation, where clients focus on what they *do* want. The reason is that it is much easier for clients to achieve what they want if they know what it is they want. Thus, when a client expresses a wish to get away from a particular feeling, the therapist might ask the client what they want to feel instead. Clarifying what the client wants is seen as an important part of the therapy.

However, in Being-Centred Therapy, the focus is not on helping clients accomplish the change they desire but rather on using the clients' various desires to help them become aware of Being. For this purpose, a wish to avoid something is just as useful as a wish to attain something and does, as we shall see next, not necessarily have to be given a positive formulation.

Sensing Taboos vs. Sensing Completion

Both Sensing Completion and Sensing Taboos use attention to felt sense as a means of directing the client's attention towards Being. But this is achieved in opposite ways.

In Sensing Completion, we invite the client to examine the felt sense they expect to obtain if they successfully create their desired experience. This guides the client to notice the felt sense underpinning a positive reification of Being.

In Sensing Taboos, on the other hand, we invite the client to examine the felt sense they expect to obtain if they failed completely in creating their desired experience. This guides the client to notice the felt sense underpinning a negative reification of Being.

The relationship between the two processes is illustrated in Figure 15.

The outer circle illustrates the two processes emerging from positive and negative reification of Being respectively.

On the right side, Being is reified as a positive phenomenon by relating it to something negative. This generates a wish to create or acquire that phenomenon. This, in turn, leads to the development of ideas about what conditions are necessary to fulfil to create or acquire the phenomenon.

On the left side, Being is reified as a negative phenomenon by relating it to something positive. This generates a wish to avoid that phenomenon. This, in turn, leads to ideas about what conditions one must fulfil to avoid the phenomenon.

Wishes to avoid negative reifications of Being and wishes to achieve positive reifications of Being can then match up in a wish to change something in one's life.

A client may, for example, reify the silent aspect of Being as deadness (negative), which they wish to avoid, and the dynamic aspect of Being as aliveness (positive), which they wish to attain. These two wishes can merge into a single wish to feel more alive and less dead in life.

Alternatively, a client may reify the silent aspect of Being as peace (positive), which they wish to attain, and the dynamic aspect of Being as agitation (negative), which they wish to avoid. In this case, the client may express a single wish to feel more peace and less agitation in life.

The inner circle illustrates how both Sensing Completion and Sensing Taboos start from the client's wish to change something in their life and move the client's awareness step by step back to Being.

In the Sensing Completion process, we start from the change the client wishes to make in their life. By inviting the client to imagine what 100% success would feel like, we move the client's awareness to the state they seek to create or acquire. By inviting the client to examine the felt sense of this state, we move the client's awareness to Being.

In the Sensing Taboos process, we also start from the change the client wishes to make in their life. By inviting the client to imagine what 100% failure would feel like, we move the client's awareness to the state they seek to avoid. By inviting the client to examine the felt sense of this state without any judgement, we move the client's awareness to Being.

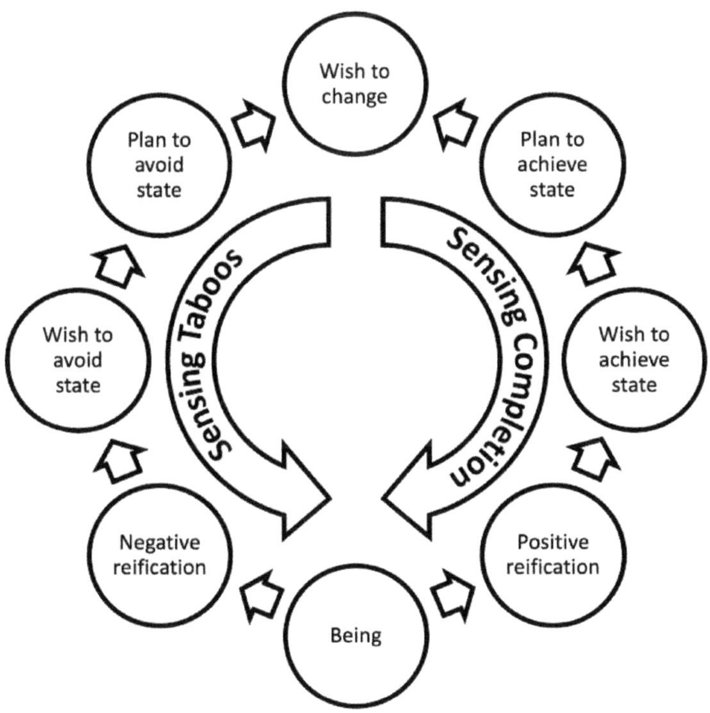

Figure 15: Sensing Taboos vs. Sensing Completion

Both processes are tricks in the sense that the therapist starts the exploration within the framework of the misconceptions that underpin the client's understanding of their situation while leading the client along a path of inquiry that is guided by knowledge of the true nature of Being.

Sensing Completion is a trick because the therapist starts by talking about the wonderful thing the client is trying to create or acquire – knowing that when they become aware of what they are ultimately reaching for, they will discover that they are seeking Being, which is already present, and that they, therefore, don't need to create or acquire anything.

Sensing Taboos is a trick because the therapist starts by talking about the terrible thing the client is trying to avoid – knowing that when they become aware of what they are ultimately avoiding and suspend their judgements, they will discover that it is Being and that it, as such, is the very same they in other contexts have been seeking and longing for and, thus, not something they need to avoid.

In other words, in both processes, the therapist should avoid directly challenging the client's current understanding, even if it is flawed, and leave it to the experience of the process to alter the client's understanding of their situation.

The role of the client's focus

Because every wish for change a client may have simultaneously seeks to attain and avoid something, the therapist will always have a choice regarding whether to use the Sensing Completion or the Sensing Taboos process.

If the client's own focus at the start of the session is on something they wish to achieve, the therapist can go straight into the Sensing Completion by asking what the client would feel if they were completely successful. If the therapist wishes to follow the Sensing Taboos process, they will have to start by clarifying what the client is implicitly avoiding when they seek to attain that which they seek to attain.

Similarly, if the client's own focus at the start of the session is on something they wish to avoid, the therapist can go straight into the Sensing Taboos process by asking what the state the client wishes to avoid feels like if there were no problems related to feeling this state. If, on the other hand, the therapist wishes to use the Sensing Completion process, they will have to start by clarifying what the client would like to feel instead of the feeling they seek to avoid, or by focusing on what the client would feel if they could be completely successful in avoiding the state they wish to avoid without any effort.

These four scenarios are summarised in Table 13: Sensing Completion vs. Sensing Taboos.

Table 13: Sensing Completion vs. Sensing Taboos

Client focus	Questions preparing for Sensing Completion	Questions preparing for Sensing Taboos
The client focuses on what they want to attain	• What would it feel like if you got it?	• What would attaining that save you from feeling? What would the thing you avoid feel like if there were no problems with feeling it? • What would you feel if you completely failed at attaining what you want to attain?
The client focuses on what they want to avoid	• What would you like to have instead? What would it feel like if you got that? • What would you feel if you were completely successful in avoiding what you want to avoid?	• What does the thing you avoid feel like if there were no problems with feeling it?

Criteria for choosing between Sensing Completion and Sensing Taboos

Whether to choose Sensing Completion or Sensing Taboos depends on factors such as the "ripeness" of the negative entry point, the time constraints on the process, and the client's level of energy and resourcefulness.

To make a skilful choice between the two processes, it is good to be clear on the advantages and risks connected to each.

The advantage of the Sensing Completion process is that the client will be motivated and have an enjoyable experience from the start. Sensing Completion is generally also faster than Sensing Taboos and gives more energy. Thus, if you do not have much time or if you sense that the client (or the group, if you are working in a group setting) has a low energy level, Sensing Completion might be the better option.

One risk of the Sensing Completion process is that it can, if not carried out with skill, lead to reinforcement in the belief that the positive state is created by success in fulfilling the conditions. Another risk is that it can become a form of spiritual bypassing used primarily to avoid difficult inner states – rather than to challenge the client's beliefs about the nature of reality.

The advantage of the Sensing Taboos process is that this process not only brings the client's awareness to Being but does so in a way that illuminates the darkness and enables the client to recognise Being in places they would never have thought to look for it. Giving the client the experience of failing completely and ending up feeling the bliss of Being is a very powerful way of disrupting the client's beliefs about the nature of reality.

One risk of the Sensing Taboos process is that if the process is not carried out with great skill, the client may not reach the point where they see through the mask of negative reification. If this happens, the client will merely spend time feeling bad, and this can reinforce their belief that they must avoid the inner state at all costs. This risk increases with the level of anxiety the client experiences in relation to the state they avoid. Sometimes, the client will be so frozen with fear when they think about the state they seek to avoid that the Sensing Taboos process would be very difficult to go through. In those cases, it can be better to choose the Sensing Completion process.

Another risk of the Sensing Taboos process is that if the client *does* see through the mask of negative reification, they can develop an attachment to diving into painful inner states as a means of finding relief. This is problematic because it can lead to the client rejecting positive inner states in their pursuit of negative inner states and the relief they expect to gain from engaging with such negative states. The main way to mitigate this risk is to ensure the client understands that it is not the act of diving into a negative state per se that brings the relief but rather seeing through the process of negative reification. Once the spell is broken, there is no reason to prolong or go back into the Sensing Taboos process.

Two therapeutic mistakes: Supporting or challenging the client's plan

Finally, the main mistakes a therapist can commit when working with the Sensing Taboos process are the same as when working with the Sensing Completion process, namely either buying into or challenging the client's wish to avoid the inner state they see as negative.

Supporting the client's plan

Sometimes, the client's wish to avoid certain inner states may seem very reasonable to you. You may wish to avoid these same inner states yourself.

You may, for example, believe that human beings are social creatures, and that loneliness is inherently negative and should be avoided. Or you may believe that anger is a mind poison, and that overcoming anger is a key step on the spiritual journey. If you hold such beliefs and a client expresses a wish to avoid or overcome loneliness or anger, you may unquestioningly engage in assisting the client in accomplishing these goals.

However, because states that appear negative to us in one context are the same as the states that we seek and cherish in other contexts, helping a client avoid any state they perceive as negative will build walls between the client and their own resources.

Thus, whenever a client is avoiding an inner state that you, as a therapist would also wish to avoid, it is good to trust the Sensing Taboos process and engage in a sincere examination of the state.

Many times, this can result in an enriching process for both the client and yourself. If you faithfully pursue the process, you may gain valuable insights from observing the client's process and discover with the client what is hidden behind the mask of negative reification.

Challenging the client's plan

Sometimes, a client's wish to avoid a particular state in themselves may seem objectionable or even reckless to you.

A client may, for example, wish to avoid sadness or anger and you may believe that such emotions are valuable and that avoiding them would be detrimental to the client's well-being. If you hold such beliefs, you may be tempted to directly challenge the client's agenda.

Insofar as any negative inner state is a negative reification of Being, you would be right in your beliefs. However, while engaging the client in an intellectual discussion about the value an inner state they wish to avoid or get rid of may have some effect, it is far more powerful to let the client discover the value of the state for themselves by examining the felt sense of the state while setting aside their judgements of it.

Furthermore, discussing the value of an inner state is a common way of avoiding the states. Thus, trying to persuade the client of the value of the state they avoid can inadvertently assist the client in avoiding the state. This is another good reason to rely on the Sensing Taboos process rather than intellectual reasoning.

4.4.2. Step 1: Recognise the Knot of Negative Reification - negative entry points

The first step in untying the Knot of Negative Reification is to detect it by noticing and clarifying what the client is avoiding. The way to do this is to listen for words, phrases and stories revealing a sense of urgent need to reject or avoid a particular inner state. I call the states clients seek to avoid "negative entry points".

"Negative entry points" is a parallel concept to the concept of "positive entry points" discussed in Chapter 2.6.1. Just like positive entry points, negative entry points are reifications of Being and, thus, examining the felt sense underpinning these entry points will enable the client to become aware of Being.

It is useful to distinguish between four different ways in which clients typically express their wish to avoid a particular inner state:

- The client directly expresses a wish to avoid or get rid of an inner state.
- The client indirectly expresses a wish to avoid or get rid of an inner state by using words such as "change", "transform", "overcome", "deal with", "cope with", "embrace", "be with" or "transmute".
- The client expresses a wish to avoid situations in the external world that would bring them in touch with the state they wish to avoid.
- The client expresses a wish to attain something that would save them from the state they wish to avoid.

These four expressions of the client's wish to avoid an inner state typically correspond to an increasing lack of awareness in the client of that which they are avoiding. Thus, the expressions indicate that an increasing level of preparation is needed to bring the client's awareness to the state they are avoiding.

It's crucial to note that not all words with negative connotations are negative entry points. For instance, if a client expresses feeling tired or sluggish but without any significant emotional charge, this is not a negative entry point. They may not perceive the state as negative, and even if they do, they may not feel any urgent need to avoid it. It may not be their preferred state, but it also doesn't send them into a state of panic or distress to feel it. They may simply plan to get more sleep the next night and not think more about it.

To qualify as a negative entry point, it is not sufficient for the client to label their state using a negatively charged word. The client must also feel a pressing need to evade the state. This urgent desire can range from mild anxiety to sheer terror when contemplating the state in question.

The client directly expresses a wish to avoid or get rid of an inner state

Sometimes, clients will explicitly express their wish to avoid or get rid of a particular inner state. When they do, they will typically use negatively laden words to label the state they wish to avoid, such as "meaninglessness", "pointlessness", "powerlessness", "hopelessness", "worthlessness", "loneliness", "lostness", "sadness", "vulnerability", "anger", "frustration", "disingenuousness", "obsession", "shame", "guilt", "jealousy", "resentment", "envy", "inferiority", "silliness", "desire", "hate", "laziness", "boredom" and "apathy".

The client may say:

- "I do not want to feel so powerless"
- "I want to get rid of my insecurity"
- "I want to stop feeling jealous"
- "I want to get rid of all this anger. It isn't good for me"

When clients express their wish to avoid an inner state in this direct manner they are ready to engage in the Sensing Taboo process. However, sometimes the client's wish to avoid or get rid of an inner state is not so clear.

The client indirectly expresses a wish to avoid or get rid of an inner state

Sometimes, clients express their desire to avoid or get rid of an inner state in more indirect ways. Rather than directly stating that they would like to avoid or get rid of a state, they may state that they would like to "change", "transform", "overcome", "control", "manage", "handle", "deal with", "cope with" or "transmute" it.

They may say:

- "I want to transform my sadness"
- "I need to deal better with my envy"
- "I must overcome my jealousy"
- "I must learn to control my anger"

As a therapist, it is important to recognise these words as possible indications of the wish to avoid or get rid of an inner state. The only difference is that clients using these more indirect expressions have an idea about the method through which they want to avoid or get rid of the state. Rather than simply wanting to get rid of a state, they want to get rid of it by transforming it into something else or transmuting it. Rather than avoiding an inner state, they want to avoid it by finding ways of dealing with it, overcoming it or controlling it.

Sometimes the methods the client intends to use to avoid or get rid of an inner state can make it appear as if the client is not trying to avoid the state. Clients may state that they wish to "embrace", "welcome" or "be with" an inner state. They may say:

- "I would like to learn to embrace my anger"
- "I feel I need to be with my sadness"
- "I want to welcome my frustration"

While the literal meaning of such expressions conveys a wish to feel rather than not feel an inner state, they are often merely covert ways of expressing a desire to avoid or get rid of the state. The client may be motivated to embrace a state because they believe doing so will transform the state into something positive or make it altogether disappear. Thus, the motivation behind the expressed wish to embrace an inner state is often to get rid of the state.

This way of expressing a desire to get rid of an inner state often occurs when clients, through their previous experience with therapy, have experienced how embracing negative emotions can change their inner state in a positive direction. While it is true that embracing difficult inner states can be a profoundly transformative experience, the problem with the above attitude is that if a client seeks to embrace a negative state because they see this as a way of getting rid of the state, they are not actually embracing it. They are merely tolerating it while waiting for it to go away. In such cases, it is better to acknowledge their wish to get rid of the state and then engage in the Sensing Taboos process, which is a rigorous process aimed at embracing the state without any wish to change it.

At other times, clients will not directly express any desire to *do* anything to an inner state. Instead, they will communicate their desire to get rid of the state solely through their attitude towards it.

- "I'm tired of feeling angry all the time"
- "I feel I'm being too vulnerable"
- "I hate feeling so inferior"
- "I feel so lost"

These statements do not *directly* express a wish to get rid of anger, vulnerability, inferiority or lostness. However, they do communicate a strong dissatisfaction with the presence of these states, which often implies the wish to get rid of them. Thus, sometimes, the wish to get rid of the state is implied by presenting the presence of the state as a (severe) problem. Sometimes it is communicated simply by using a negatively laden word for the state – sometimes accompanied by a certain disproving or despairing tone of voice.

There can be many reasons why clients are not explicit about their wish to get rid of a particular inner state. They may feel that it is unenlightened or unsophisticated to have such a wish. They may subscribe to an ideology of self-development that emphasises embracing all aspects of one's self – which is at odds with their wish to get rid of the state. Or they may believe that it is not possible to get rid of the state and that, therefore, it is futile to harbour a wish for something that cannot be.

Regardless of what the reason is, it can be good to give clients permission to express their wishes directly. You can do this either by asking directly whether the wish is there or by asking questions that pre-empt the various possible reasons clients may have to hide their wishes:

- "Would a part of you like to not feel any envy?"
- "It is, of course, good to embrace all sides of oneself, and this includes the sides that may wish to get rid of certain aspects of oneself. Would a part of you like to not feel any envy?"
- "Of course, it may not be possible to never feel inferior, but just because something isn't possible, we may still wish it were. Would you like to never feel inferior if that were a possibility?"

The purpose of these questions is to invite clients to embrace and express their wish to get rid of the state as wholeheartedly as possible without holding back. When clients hold back there are two issues in play, namely the issue of wanting the inner state gone *and* the issue of not wanting to admit to this wish. This needlessly complicates the process, and it is, thus, better to invite the client to speak plainly and directly.

The client expresses a wish to avoid situations in the external world

Sometimes, clients will not name the inner state they wish to avoid directly. Instead, they express a wish to avoid certain situations in life. The motivation for avoiding these situations, however, is that the client fears being in this situation will bring them in touch with an inner state they seek to avoid.

Clients may say:

- "I want to find a partner that isn't superior."
- "I hate when people are not direct."
- "I don't want to be around people who disrespect me."
- "I don't want to ask for a pay rise because I don't want to be told that I'm not competent or accomplished enough."

Whereas it is not possible to know for certain what state a client seeks to avoid by avoiding certain situations, it is possible to make good guesses. The reason a client would avoid superior partners could be that they want to avoid feeling "inferiority" or "low self-esteem". A client may avoid people who are not direct in their communication because they want to avoid "fear" or "insecurity" related to getting things wrong. A client may avoid people who act in ways they perceive as disrespectful to avoid a sense of "powerlessness" or "hurt". A client may avoid asking for a pay rise unless they are sure to get it because they fear that rejection of their proposed pay increase would bring them in touch with "worthlessness" or "insignificance".

When clients are focused on avoiding specific situations as a way of avoiding certain inner states, they defend themselves against these states one step removed, so to speak. Instead of avoiding the state, they are avoiding all situations in which the state *might* occur. It is analogous to shifting from avoiding a person by actively looking out for them to avoiding the person by steering clear of all places this person might potentially be found.

When clients avoid situations as a way to avoid a particular state, they may be so focused on avoiding the situation that they are not aware of what state they are avoiding. Thus, to prepare for Sensing Taboos, it is important to first determine what state the client is avoiding by avoiding the situation. You can do this by asking questions such as:

- "What do you feel when people are not direct?"
- "What does it bring up in you when people disrespect you?"
- "What would you feel if you asked for a pay rise and your manager told you that your competency level didn't warrant one?"

Often, clients will answer such questions by describing negative inner states, which can then be used as negative entry points in the further Sensing Taboos process.

When clients deny feeling discomfort in the situations they avoid

Sometimes, clients will tell you that they just don't like the situation but deny that the situation brings up difficult inner states in themselves. They may even report having good feelings in the situation they avoid. They may say things like:

- "If people don't recognise my value, they don't deserve me. I would feel good about knowing that I dodged a bullet."
- "I'm fine with people not being direct."
- "I just don't think it is right for people to act like that."
- "If I need to work harder to earn my pay rise, that is fine. I like having a goal."
- "I'm not interested in that kind of situation."
- "I have better things to do with my life."

There can be many reasons they clients refuse to admit that they avoid the situations as a way of avoiding difficult inner states.

- The client may want to give the impression that they can handle the situation.
- The client may feel that admitting they feel uncomfortable in the situation is admitting defeat.
- The client may feel that being disturbed by the situation is a sign of weakness.

Furthermore, the fact that clients seek to avoid a situation as a means of avoiding certain inner states will usually indicate that they find the state very disturbing and, thus, merely bringing it up in conversation can feel overwhelming for the client. Thus, denying that they would feel it in certain situations is part of the way they keep the negative state out of their mind as well as their life.

There are, of course, situations in life that people avoid without this being a way of avoiding negative inner states. However, if clients truly feel good or undisturbed by a situation, they probably wouldn't feel that it is urgently important to avoid it – and they probably wouldn't bring up the situation in a therapy session. So, it is worth challenging the above kind of statements. To do so, you can say:

> "Yes, what you say is true, but that is not why you wish to avoid the situation. The reason you avoid the situation must be that you feel something unpleasant in that situation. What is that negative feeling you might feel in the situation?"

You can adjust the start of the statement to reflect the specifics of the client's statement about what they feel in the situation. If, for example, the client says they feel good about having a goal, there is no reason to doubt this – however, if that was all the client felt in the situation, they would seek it – not avoid it. The fact that the client avoids the situation shows that there must be more than positive emotions involved.

It is also worth noticing that, in the above response, I have downplayed the severity of the negative feeling by calling it "something unpleasant". I do this to make it easier for the client to admit to having some discomfort without having to admit to the fullness of the negative state, as the reason they deny the state is likely to be quite overwhelming to them at this point.

Often, clients will answer the above question by describing negative inner states, which can then be used as negative entry points in the further Sensing Taboos process.

If, however, the client insists that they only feel positive emotions in the situation they avoid, you can ask questions such as:

- "If you only have positive emotions in relation to the situation, why do you want to avoid it?"
- "So, it is completely fine for you when people make you feel inferior/are indirect/disrespect you/reject your request for a pay rise?"

These questions are designed to display the inconsistency in the client's wish to avoid the situation and what they tell you they feel in the situation.

Often the clients will, at this point, realise that they do have uncomfortable inner states in the situations they avoid. If, however, they do not, it may be that they are simply not ready to face the negative states, so it may be wise to accept the client's statement and move on. The conversation will have challenged the client sufficiently and the client may simply need some time for the insight to land.

The client expresses a wish to attain something

Sometimes, clients avoid one state by seeking to create or acquire another state, which they perceive as opposite. This is analogous to avoiding a person by going to places that person is unable to come to.

The client may say:

- "I want to find a partner that values me"
- "I want to have direct communication with people"
- "I want to cultivate respectful relationships"
- "I want to be so competent in my field, that I can ask for any salary I want"

On the surface, such statements may not seem to be expressions of a wish to avoid anything. However, on a second look, it is obvious that such wishes must come out of having had experiences the client found uncomfortable and which they, for that reason, do not wish to repeat.

It is the specificity and importance of the client's wish that reveals it is an expression of a wish to avoid something.

There are many things one might seek in a partner, including humour, trustworthiness, consideration, generosity, good communication skills, physical attractiveness, passion, respect, good work ethics and emotional support. The specific things we feel are important to find in a partner are often precisely the things we missed the most in our previous partner. Thus, the wish to acquire something specific is born out of a wish to avoid something uncomfortable.

If a client has never felt unappreciated or inferior in a relationship, they would not get the idea that it is important to have a partner that values them. Similarly, the only way a client can come to desire direct communication is by having had experiences with indirect communication which they found uncomfortable. The same goes for the two last examples where the desire for respect must come from a wish to avoid disrespect and the desire to be in a position of asking for any salary one wants must come from a wish to avoid an uncomfortable feeling the client has experienced when they didn't get the salary they wished for.

However, even though the desire is an expression of a wish to avoid an uncomfortable inner state, the client may not be aware of this. They may simply be very excited about their goal.

Seeking this goal is a defence, not only against feeling the inner state they seek to avoid but against even thinking about it. Thus, when this defence works well, it will banish the negative state from the client's mind as well as from their life[37].

---

[37] The defence does not work since the state the client wishes to avoid will still be present in the client's wish to attain its opposite. I will return to this in the description of the 19th misconception.

To bring awareness to the state, the client seeks to avoid, you can ask them:

- "What would you feel if you failed completely in attaining your goal?"
- "What does attaining this goal save you from feeling?"

Contemplating never finding any partner that values the client, being in a world where no one says what they mean directly, where no one respects the client or where the client never succeeds in acquiring the salary they desire, will usually bring up the feeling they seek to avoid. Once they put a word to this feeling, that will be the negative entry point.

At times, the client will sincerely believe that they just want to achieve a goal because they believe this is a good goal. In such cases, it can be beneficial to point out that there are many possible goals that would be good to strive for and ask the client what past experiences led them to focus on the particular goal they seek. Since reaching the goal is generally a way of avoiding repetition of past negative experiences, remembering the experiences that led the client to see their particular goal as uniquely important, will help them realise what they are avoiding.

For example, a client may be focused on building their capacity to give their children emotional support. This is, indeed, a good and positive goal. At first glance, it may not seem as if the client is avoiding anything. However, in childrearing there are many possible positive goals. One can focus on encouragement and validation, giving attention, giving opportunities for control, developing social/language/motor skills, acquiring knowledge, setting clear boundaries, developing safety and containment, encouraging independence, offering economic stability and so on. If a client is fixated on emotional support as the most important in childrearing, it is likely that they have had negative experiences related to lack of emotional support and wish to avoid that state.

Defence mechanisms

Detecting what a client is avoiding is not always easy.

A client may, for example, be asking for help in overcoming a sense of sadness and lostness. However, no matter how one works with these emotions, they persist. In this case, the client may be using the sadness and lostness as a diversion from a sense of hostility and anger, which is the inner state they are truly afraid of, and, thus, the state the therapy should focus on.

Another client may express a wish to learn to deal with their anger. Yet, no matter how one works with the anger, the client continues to experience uncontrolled explosions of anger. In this case, the client may be using anger as a way of distracting themselves from a sense of vulnerability and grief, which they find overwhelming. Thus, it would be more fruitful working with these emotions.

In order to detect *what* inner states clients are avoiding, it can be useful to have an overview of *how* clients typically avoid inner states.

Such an overview can be found in the psychoanalytical literature on defence mechanisms (Di Giuseppe & Perry, 2021; Freud, 1937). Thus, a good working knowledge of defence mechanisms can greatly enhance a therapist's ability to recognise the Knot of Negative Reification.

For example, one common defence mechanism is devaluation, where an individual perceives another person or themselves as having less worth or importance than they actually do. Clients often engage in devaluation as a way of avoiding feelings of inadequacy or disappointment. Thus, when clients engage in unwarranted or excessive devaluation of self or others, it can be interesting to explore whether this is an avoidance of inadequacy or disappointment.

Another common defence mechanism is reaction formation, where an individual unconsciously transforms feelings they find unacceptable or anxiety-provoking into their opposites. For example, someone who feels anger towards another person may find their own anger unacceptable or threatening and mask it by expressing excessive kindness or affection towards the other person. Thus, when there is a mismatch between the emotional states a client says they feel and what other people would feel in the same situation, it is worth exploring whether the client is using one emotion to avoid another.

Yet another defence mechanism is humour, where an individual focuses on amusing or ironic aspects of a situation as a way of expressing deeper wishes and desires the client is uncomfortable expressing directly. Thus, when clients use humour, it can be interesting to explore whether this is an avoidance of unexpressed emotions, such as frustration, anxiety or desire.

Defence mechanisms are often categorised into three groups based on their level of maturity and adaptability: immature, neurotic and mature defences.

Immature defences, the least adaptive, encompass various mechanisms such as devaluation, idealisation, acting out, denial, projection and projective identification. These defence mechanisms indicate a lack of awareness regarding emotional and cognitive conflicts.

Neurotic defences represent a middle ground and include mechanisms such as reaction formation, dissociation, repression, intellectualisation and undoing. These defence mechanisms allow individuals to reduce anxiety by keeping certain aspects of conflict out of awareness.

Mature defences are the most adaptive and include humour, affiliation, altruism and sublimation. These defence mechanisms, promoting an integrated understanding of feelings and thoughts, are considered effective coping strategies.

Mature defence mechanisms indicate a higher level of psychological maturity and functionality and are, thus, preferable to neurotic and immature defence mechanisms.

However, from the perspective of Being-Centred Therapy, mature defence mechanisms also present a challenge: Precisely because more functional defence mechanisms include a higher level of emotional and cognitive awareness they can give the impression that a client is in touch with aspects of their experience – even when they are not. Consequently, mature defence mechanisms can more effectively block awareness of Being.

For example, if a client uses the neurotic defence of reaction formation to avoid sadness by substituting it with happiness, it is obvious that the client is avoiding the sadness and that sadness, thus, can be used as a negative entry point in the process of Sensing Taboos. However, if a client uses the mature defence of humour to avoid the direct expression of sadness by talking about this emotion in a light-hearted way, it can give the impression that the client is comfortable with sadness even when they are not. This may lead the therapist to miss the opportunity to use sadness as a negative entry point and, through the Sensing Taboos process, help the client to become comfortable with more direct expressions of and contact with their sadness.

Summary

The Knot of Negative Reification can be detected by listening for phrases or stories revealing a fixation on a particular inner state the client seeks to avoid, combined with a sense that avoiding this state is imperative.

This avoidance can be expressed in different ways, and clients may or may not be aware that they are avoiding a particular inner state.

Sometimes, clients directly express a wish to get rid of a particular state. In such cases, the client is most likely experiencing the state from time to time, and they are fully aware of their wish to avoid it. The state the client wishes to avoid can be used as a negative entry point.

Sometimes, clients express a wish to do something with the state, which implies their wish to get rid of it. In such cases, the client may not be aware that they are trying to get rid of the state. Once the desire to get rid of the state is acknowledged the state can be used as a negative entry point.

Sometimes, clients avoid an inner state by avoiding certain situations they expect will bring them in touch with the state. In such cases, the client may not be aware that they avoid the situation to avoid an inner state. You can bring the client's awareness to the state they are avoiding by asking them what they would feel if they could not avoid the situation. If a client claims that they would not feel any uncomfortable states in the situation, you can point out that unless they expect to feel something negative in the situation, it would not be so important for them to avoid it. Once the client becomes aware of the inner state they avoid, this state can be used as a negative entry point.

Sometimes, clients avoid an inner state by seeking to create or acquire another state they see as opposite. In such cases, the client may be so focused on what they seek to attain that they do not notice that their motivation is a wish to avoid something. You can bring the client's awareness to the state they are avoiding by inviting them to examine the experiences that gave them the idea that it is important to create a certain positive inner state. You can point out that if they had never experienced the opposite of that state, they wouldn't have got the idea that feeling this state is important. Once the client becomes aware that they seek one state as a means of rescuing them from feel another, the state the client is avoiding can be used as a negative entry point.

Lack of awareness of the state the client seeks to avoid is often part of the way clients avoid the state. Therefore, lack of awareness of the state can be an indication that the state feels overwhelming to the client and that it is associated with considerable anxiety. When one seeks to bring a client's attention to a state they are avoiding, it is good to pre-empt the client's concerns by normalising the state and downplaying the effects the client worries about.

If there is a strong conflict between a part of the client that wishes to avoid something and another part of the client that rejects this wish or rejects acknowledging this wish, it may be a sign of the Knot of Fragmentation and you can consider shifting the process.

4.4.3. Step 2: Distinguish between the felt sense of and reactions to the state

The heart of the Sensing Taboos process is to make conscious, direct contact with the felt sense of the states the client is avoiding without any intention to change it. In so doing, the client will see through the mask of negative reification and recognise the essence of the state as an aspect of Being.

Thus, once you have identified what the client is avoiding, you can invite them to explore the felt sense of this state in itself.

You can do this by inviting the client to imagine what it would feel like if they gave up avoiding this state and just allowed it to be there. You can ask:

> "What does this state you seek to avoid feel like if you allow it?"
>
> "What would it feel like if you completely gave up avoiding the state you seek to avoid?"

Exploring the felt sense of the state the client avoids is a two-step process.

First, we must distinguish between the felt sense of the state itself and the felt sense of the client's reactions to the state. This is the topic of this section.

Second, we must separate the felt sense of the state from the negative label the client uses to denote the state. This is the topic of Section 4.4.4.

Felt-sense "noise"

When you invite clients to focus their attention on the felt sense of the state they are avoiding, they will describe the felt sense they notice in that moment.

However, this will generally be a combination of two types of felt sense. Part of the felt sense the client will notice is the felt sense of the state the client is avoiding. This is the felt sense we wish to explore. Another part of the felt sense the client will notice is the felt sense of the client's reactions to the state they are avoiding.

A crucial step in the Sensing Taboos process is to distinguish clearly between these two kinds of felt sense so as to help the client become aware of the felt sense of the state they avoid in its pure form – separate from what one could call "felt-sense noise".

Clients will typically have three kinds of reaction when invited to feel what they avoid, which will add different kinds of felt-sense noise that must be distinguished from the felt sense of the state the client is avoiding.

- The client may reject the state they avoid. This will typically add a sense of tension or nausea.
- The client may blur their perception of the state they avoid. This will typically add a sense of confusion, fogginess, lack of focus or "spacing out".
- The client may redirect their attention to something they associate with the state they avoid. This will add different kinds of felt sense, depending on the association.

Below, we look at the different kinds of felt-sense noise and how to help clients distinguish them from the felt sense of that which they avoid. I round off this section with a comment on techniques one can use when the client feels overwhelmed by the suggestion of exploring the felt sense of the state they avoid.

Tension

Sometimes, when clients are asked what the state they avoid feels like, they will say that it feels tense. As we saw in Section 4.3.4, such tension is usually not the felt sense of the state the client is avoiding but rather the felt sense of their reaction to this state.

When tension comes up, you can point out that the tension is the felt sense of the client's rejection or avoidance of the state and then refocus the client's attention on the state they avoid by asking what that state feels like in itself.

To craft good refocusing questions, it can be useful to distinguish between six different types of tension:

- Pushing away
- Moving away
- Holding in
- Keeping out
- Holding the breath
- Insulating.

Below, I describe each of these and suggest questions you can use to help the client distinguish between the felt sense of the state they avoid and the felt sense of their reactions to the state.

Pushing away

If the client feels tension in, for example, the arms and chest as if they were pushing something away, it is generally the felt sense of "rejection". The client may show this tension by physically pushing something away with their hands while talking about the state or by using phrases that indicate pushing something away, such as "I just want to get it away from me".

You can refocus the client's attention by asking:

> "The tension you feel is the felt sense of your wish to reject the state. What does that which you are pushing away feel like?"
>
> "What would you feel if you pulled it towards you instead of pushing it away?"

Moving away

If the client feels tension in, for example, torso and legs as if they were trying to move backwards away from something, it is generally the felt sense of "avoidance". The client may show this tension by physically moving backwards in their seat or by using phrases that indicate moving away from something, such as "I want to get out of this" or "I want to get away from this".

You can refocus the client's attention by asking:

> "The tension you feel is the felt sense of your avoidance of the state. What does the thing you are moving away from feel like?"
>
> "What would you feel if you imagine moving towards it instead of away from it?"

Holding in

If the client feels tension patterns that correspond to keeping something encased, such as holding something in their hands or pushing something down inside their body, it is generally the felt sense of the client's wish to "control". The client may show this tension in rigid movements or by using phrases that indicate holding something fast, such as "I don't want to lose control of this" or "I need to keep this in place".

You can refocus the client's attention by asking:

> "The tension you feel is the felt sense of your wish to control the state. What does the thing inside the tension feel like?"
>
> "What would you feel if you imagine letting the thing you hold in move freely?"

Keeping out

If the client feels tension patterns that correspond to encasing themselves to keep something out, such as a general tension in the body or a sense of contracting the whole body around their solar plexus, heart or belly, it is generally the felt sense of the client's wish to "protect themselves". Thus, they experience the state as something external that attacks them. The client may show this tension by assuming a defensive or protective posture, such as moving the shoulders upwards and forwards and/or contracting their rectus abdominis. They may also reveal the tension through corresponding phrases, such as "I need to keep this out of my life" or "this feels like an onslaught or attack".

You can refocus the client's attention by asking:

> "The tension you feel is the felt sense of your wish to protect yourself. What does the thing you are protecting yourself against feel like?"
>
> "What would you feel if you allowed the thing you wish to keep out to come into you?"

Holding the breath

Sometimes, clients will hold their breath when they imagine sensing the state they seek to avoid. Holding one's breath is a common way of desensitising oneself and diminishing feeling. It is a common reaction when bracing for the impact of something the individual expect will be uncomfortable. Thus, holding one's breath and the corresponding tension is also generally not part of the felt sense of the state the client wishes to avoid but rather of their reaction to this state.

You can clarify this and refocus the client's attention by asking:

> "The tension you feel is the felt sense of your wish to avoid the state. What does the thing you avoid feel like?"
>
> "What would you feel if you took a few deep breaths?"

Insulating

The last form of tension, which is important to be aware of, I call insulation. This kind of tension occurs when clients are trying to feel the state they avoid because they believe this will lead to transformation. They may have experienced such transformation in previous therapy sessions, or they may have bought into the therapeutic idea that the way through is the way in or that it is necessary to feel the difficult inner places to achieve growth.

As a result, clients will sometimes sit with the state they find uncomfortable, waiting for it to change rather than becoming curious about it and sensing into it. They will kind of bear the torture waiting for the relief. This state of affairs is akin to putting on a wet suit and jumping into the ocean. You are in the ocean, but you are not really in touch with it. You are insulated from it.

When clients do this, the transformation or relief may never come because they are not actually sensing the state they avoid. Rather they are sitting within the state covered by a thin layer of tension so as not to make any direct contact.

This is thoroughly unpleasant and the longer the client remains in this way, the more the experience will reinforce their belief that this state is, indeed, horrible and should be avoided.

Thus, it is good to call this out. You can ask the client: Are you just waiting for this to shift? If they say yes, ask them to let go of the idea that it will ever shift.

Signals that the client is in this state of insulation include if the client appears tense, if the client describes the state they are avoiding but nothing seems to happen and if the client says: "I don't think it is working".

The sentence "it isn't working" is usually a good indication that the client is engaged in some sort of change plan. As a response, you can ask the client what they expect to happen and then ask them to sense the state without any hopes that it will transform or change in the way they expect.

Nausea

Sometimes, when clients are asked what the state they avoid feels like, they will say that they feel nausea. Nausea is typically the felt sense of the client's rejection of the state, since nausea is one of the body's ways of rejecting things.

You can clarify this and refocus the client's attention by asking:

> "You feel nausea because you do not like the state. But what does the state itself feel like? What does the nauseating thing feel like?"

I often deliberately leave out any direct references to possible reasons for the nausea so as not to mismatch the client's experience. If you, for example, say that the client feels nausea because they find the state they avoid "disgusting", the client may object to this word, and you would not achieve the refocusing of the client's awareness towards the felt sense of the state they are avoiding.

Avoidance and confusion, fogginess, lack of focus and "spacing out"

Sometimes, when clients are asked what the state they avoid feels like, they will say that they feel confused, foggy, unfocused or that they are spacing out or going blank. Once again, this kind of felt sense is typically not the felt sense of that which the client is avoiding but rather the felt sense of their reaction to it.

Felt sense of this kind is typically the felt sense of the client's avoidance. Blurring the senses and becoming confused is a common way of avoiding sensing something.

You can clarify this and refocus the client's attention by asking:

> "What would you feel if you were not confused?"
>
> "What would you feel if the fog lifted?"
>
> "What do you feel when you refocus your senses?"
>
> "What is it you are not seeing when you space out?"

When asking these questions, be prepared for the client to come in touch with sensations they find very uncomfortable. I will comment on what to do in such situations at the end of this section.

The felt sense of associated concepts

Sometimes, when clients are asked what the state they avoid feels like, the felt sense they share seems neither to correspond to the state or to their avoidance of the state. In such cases, the client will typically share the felt sense of a phenomenon they associate with the state they avoid.

For example, a client may be avoiding the state of anger and when asked what anger feels like, they say it feels "collapsed". While it may be correct that the client feels an inner sense of collapse when they direct their attention towards anger, it is unlikely that collapse is the felt sense of anger, as anger usually has a sense of energy, or that collapse is the felt sense of the client's avoidance of anger, since this would typically be a sense of tension, nausea or confusion as described above. Instead, the client may associate anger with powerlessness, and it is the state of powerlessness the client feels as an inner sense of collapse.

It is worth noting that the felt sense of a particular concept can differ from person to person and even within the same person at different times. For some, "anger" may feel warm, while for others it feels cold. For some, "sadness" feels empty while for others it feels heavy.

However, not all felt-sense experiences can underpin all concepts. Thus, when a client says that a phenomenon they avoid feels in a way that seems at odds with that phenomenon, it is worth examining whether this is really the felt sense of the state the client is avoiding or if it is the felt sense of a phenomenon the client associates with the state they are avoiding.

If you suspect that the felt sense the client is describing is not the felt sense of the state they are avoiding but rather of an associated phenomenon, you can test this by asking directly. In the above example, you may ask:

> "Is it anger that feels collapsed, or is the sense of powerlessness you sometimes feel when you feel angry that feels collapsed?"

Even if you get the association wrong, such questions can inspire the client to make similar distinctions and notice what the anger itself feels like.

In Section 3.4.3, I described at length how surprising answers to the question of what a particular state feels like can result from the client's mind jumping a few steps along a chain of associations. In the interest of space, I will not repeat them here, but merely mention that it can be beneficial to remember that surprising answers may result from the client's awareness when moving quickly along similar chains of associations, so that the description of the felt sense the client gives is not of the state they avoid but of a state they *associate* with the state they avoid.

Overwhelm and refusal to sense

Clients will usually not like the invitation to sense the states they seek to avoid. Otherwise, they would not be avoiding the state. Thus, there will almost inevitably be some measure of persuasion involved in the Sensing Taboos process.

However, sometimes clients will find the invitation to sense the state they wish to avoid, not merely unpleasant, but overwhelming. They may even experience that, by inviting them to feel this state, the therapist is pushing them to do something they do not want to do.

In such cases, you, as therapist, must make a judgement call. If the process is too overwhelming for the client, it may be better to work with what the client wishes to achieve through the Sensing Completion process.

However, there are a few techniques you can use to enable clients to work with the Sensing Taboos process even if it feels on the edge at the start. These techniques are

- Using normalising and minimising language
- Using limited exposure (limited time, limited physicality, titration)
- Focusing on information rather than sensation

Using normalising and minimising language

Assuring clients that the state they avoid is something normal that many people feel from time to time can greatly help the client. It is one thing to feel something you don't like. It is much worse if what you feel also signals that there is something wrong with you. To increase the effect of normalising the state, you can deliberately choose to reduce the emotional impact by using words for the state that are slightly less intense than those used by the client.

If, for example, the client is avoiding a situation because they believe they would feel "devastated" in that situation, you can ask:

> "I think most people would feel somewhat bumped out in that situation. Can you tell me what that feel like at a sensory level?"

If the client is trying to calm themselves down to avoid feeling a sense of "rage", you can ask:

> "Everyone will feel a bit annoyed every now and then; this is just part of life. However, many do not pause to notice what this actually feels like. What does it feel like?"

There is always a risk that the client will object to the minimising language. After all, rage is a lot more intense than "a bit annoyed". So, it is important to find an expression that lowers the intensity of the state without leading the client to object.

With each state there will be a range of expressions you can use. The intensity of "rage" can be lowered by calling it "anger", "frustration", "annoyance" or "feeling a bit inconvenienced". Using language in this way to lower the intensity is like turning the dial down until you find a level of intensity that is no longer overwhelming for the client to sense.

Using limited exposure (limited time, limited physicality, titration)

Another way of lowering the intensity of the experience is to suggest that the client should only sense it in a limited manner[38].

You can do this by suggesting exposure to the state during a limited amount of time.

If, for example, a client is avoiding feeling meaninglessness, you can suggest that they try out feeling it for 30 seconds, 1 second or 1 millisecond depending on the level of overwhelm the client feels. You can say:

> "How would it be to feel complete meaninglessness for just 10 seconds? You know well how to avoid feeling it, so if you do not like it, you can go back to avoiding it afterwards."

If you lower the time limit sufficiently, at some point the client usually agrees to the experiment. And if even one millisecond seems too much for the client, they probably are not ready for the Sensing Taboos process.

Another way of persuading clients to sense a state they prefer to avoid is by asking them to imagine sensing the state using only a very limited part of their body.

If, for example, a client is using tension to encapsulate a sense of worthlessness, and they do not want to sense what is inside the tension, you can ask them to imagine they touch what is inside the tension only with a single finger. You can say:

> "How would it be to keep the tension you use to control the sense of worthlessness and only touch it with a single finger? What could you then notice about the texture, temperature and substance of worthlessness?"

By allowing the client to keep the tension, you allow them to keep a sense of being in control throughout the experiment. This can help in lowering the client's anxiety

---

[38] This is similar to the technique in Somatic Experiencing called titration. Here the idea is to experience the overwhelming state "drop by drop", akin to the way one can avoid an explosive chemical reaction when mixing acid and base by doing it drop by drop.

sufficiently for them to turn their attention to the exploration of the felt sense of the state they avoid.

The benefit of inviting clients to sense the state they avoid in a limited manner is that it only takes one second of unreserved contact for the client to realise that the felt sense in itself, is not as bad as they expect. Once they have felt the state without prejudice, they immediately realise that nothing happens when they do. This can significantly increase the client's curiosity and willingness to continue the exploration.

The key word here is "unreserved". To invite this I often use phrases such as "complete", "unreserved" or "give full permission to".

Focusing on information rather than sensation

The last technique for persuading clients to sense a state they would prefer to avoid is to focus on sharing information about the felt sense rather than on feeling the felt sense. You can, for example, say:

> "You do not have to feel the state at all. Just tell me what it would feel like if you did."

This is a trick. Telling the client that they don't have to feel the state at all can calm them down. However, in order to access information about the state they will have to sense it. So, in asking about what information the client can share with you about the felt sense of the state, you are pretending to keep the conversation at a theoretical level, knowing that if the client engages in the conversation, they will inevitably feel the state.

It is akin to saying to someone: "You do not need to imagine a blue elephant, just describe to me what such a creature would look like." You cannot engage in that conversation without imagining the blue elephant. In fact, you cannot even understand the uttered request without imagining the blue elephant.

Summary

When we invite the client to explore the felt sense of a state they are avoiding, we can run into two problems.

First, the client describes the felt sense of their reactions to the state they are avoiding rather than the state itself. They may describe tension, nausea, confusion, fogginess, lack of focus or a sense of spacing out. This is generally the felt sense of the client's avoidance or rejection of the state.

To deal with this, you can point out that the felt sense the client is aware of is the felt sense of their avoidance or rejection and refocus their attention by asking what the thing they avoid or reject feels like or what they would feel if they ceased to avoid or reject the state.

Second, the client may be hesitant in describing the felt sense because it seems overwhelming to them.

To deal with this, you can use normalising and minimising language to turn down the intensity of the experience to a level that is manageable for the client. You can also invite the client to explore the state through limited exposure. This can be done either by limiting the time the client spends on sensing the state or by limiting the area in the body in which the client senses the state. Finally, you can frame the exploration as a matter of providing information about the state rather than sensing it.

If the exploration is too overwhelming for the client, it may be better to shift to the Sensing Completion process and explore what the client would feel if they could effortlessly avoid the state indefinitely.

If the client describes the felt sense they seek to avoid, it is time to move to the next phase of the Sensing Taboos process and separate the felt sense from any negative interpretations.

4.4.4. Step 3: Separate the felt sense from negative interpretations

Once the client has focused their attention on the felt sense of the state they are avoiding, it is time to separate the state from the negative prejudices the client holds against the state and help them gain a sense of the state itself beyond any negative interpretation.

If the client manages to do this, they will discover that the state they have been avoiding is nothing other than an aspect of Being.

This is one of the truly magical moments in Being-Centred Therapy and one that usually make a big impression on clients. It can be profoundly surprising for clients to experience that when they give up their defences against an inner state they see as negative, they discover that this state is something precious. It is surprising because it goes against their beliefs (i.e., their misconceptions).

In the following, I will present five techniques for helping the client focus their attention on the state itself – separate from negative interpretations of the state.

- Savouring the relief of acknowledging the state instead of avoiding it
- Seeing the state as positive
- Describing the state using neutral, sensory words
- Exploring the state in contexts where it has no negative effects
- Correcting fallacies of equivocation

Savouring the relief of acknowledging the state instead of avoiding it

The first technique is not really a technique to help the client sense the state in itself, but rather a technique for lowering their fear of the state and resistance to allowing the state. This can be done by focusing the client's attention on the felt sense of the positive effects of ceasing to avoid the state. In particular, since avoiding any inner state requires a lot of energy, ceasing to avoid a state often comes with a great sense of relief.

It can be a great relief for clients simply to acknowledge and put words to the state they are avoiding, and set aside the tension and confusion of their rejection and avoidance.

Even if the state itself appears as a negative state to them, ceasing the fight against it and acknowledging its presence can be a very relaxing experience. I have often seen clients exclaim "I feel empty/lost/sad/angry/etc." with a sense of elation and profound physical signs of relief, such as heaving a great sigh or softening the muscle tone in the entire body.

When this happens spontaneously, you can simply spend a bit of time asking the client to describe this relief.

If the client does not spontaneously feel a relief, it is possible to direct their attention towards the relief using questions, such as:

> "How is it to simply acknowledge that this is what you feel?"
>
> "How is it to no longer have to avoid this state?"
>
> "How is it to relieve yourself of the burden of having to avoid this state?"

In the last question, I have explicitly named the action of avoiding the state as a "burden". By framing the avoidance as something negative (a burden), I highlight the positive aspects of letting go of this activity.

Spending time savouring the relief of not having to avoid the state is akin to taking a pitstop, where the client can savour a positive inner state before continuing the rest of the way towards sensing the state they avoid.

Savouring the relief can calm the client's nervous system and put them in a much better position to explore the felt sense of the state they avoid without negative judgements of this state.

Seeing the state as positive

One simple way to invite clients to direct their attention to the felt sense of the state they avoid, separate from their negative interpretations of this state, is to ask what the state feels like if it were a good thing.

If a client avoids an inner sense of worthlessness, you can ask:

> "What does worthlessness feel like, if it was not a bad thing?"
>
> "What does worthlessness feel like, if you consider it a good thing?"
>
> "What does worthlessness feel like, if it is fine to be worthless?"

Since the client is convinced that the state is, indeed, a negative state, the question may seem a bit peculiar. Thus, it can be good to frame the question in a way that pre-empts objections as to whether this is a positive or a negative state. You can, for example, say:

> "You are used to thinking about this state as something negative. Imagine, just as an experiment, that you had been mistaken all this time, and that the state is actually a positive state. What would you then notice about what it feels like?"

It is surprising how often this simple question can flip clients' interpretation of the state from a negative to a positive reification.

When clients look at the emptiness they dreaded as if it were a good thing, they suddenly notice how peaceful it is. When they look at the rage they are terrified of as if it were a good thing, they may suddenly enjoy the sheer energy and directness of this state. When they look at the vulnerability they have been avoiding as if it were a good thing, they suddenly notice the tenderness and sense of connection in this state.

The advantage of flipping the client's perception from a negative to a positive reification is that it increases their willingness to explore the felt sense of the state.

If the client relabels the state using a positive label, it even makes it possible to continue with the process of Sensing Abundance.

If you know what the client sees as the opposite state of the one they wish to avoid, you can, as a variation, switch the client's value-judgements by presenting this opposite state as something negative.

If, for example, the client laments that they feel "worthless", it is clear that the opposite state would be one where they felt "worth". You can then ask them, what worthlessness feels like when they remember that gathering worth is such hard work and that they don't really need all that worth anyway. You can even combine this with the invitation to relieve themselves of the burden of having to be so valuable all the time.

By framing the opposite state as negative, you implicitly present the state the client seeks to avoid as something positive, and this may allow the client to explore the felt sense of this state separately from their habitual negative judgements of it.

Describing the state using neutral, sensory words

Another easy way to invite clients to direct their attention to the felt sense of the state they avoid, separately from their negative judgements of this state, is to ask:

"How can you describe the state using only neutral, sensory words?"

By limiting the client's vocabulary to neutral, sensory words, we remove the vocabulary needed for conveying negative interpretations. Consequently, using neutral, sensory words can help focus the client's attention on the felt sense of the state separately from any interpretations.

Once the states are separated from negative interpretations, the clients are likely to start feeling these states for what they are, namely, aspects of Being. This can, in turn, trigger positive reifications, which makes it possible to continue using the Sensing Abundance process.

Thus, by describing the states clients avoid using only neutral, sensory words, clients may come to experience the same kind of transformations as when they are invited to consider the states they avoid as positive states. The only difference is that using neutral, sensory words makes the intermediate step of sensing uninterpreted somatic states explicit.

For example, a client may seek to avoid a state of "loss". When asked what this state feels like, they may say it feels like a "horrible, hollow sense of emptiness".

When invited to describe this sense using only neutral, sensory words, the client may become aware that the felt sense, in itself, just feels spacious (spacious being the neutral word for both "hollow" and "empty"). As the client becomes aware of this spaciousness and sets aside their negative judgements of it as a loss of something, they may notice that it feels "peaceful" and "free". In this process, the client first feels a negative reification of a state of Being (loss), then they feel the state of Being itself (spaciousness), and finally they feel a positive reification of this state of Being (peace and freedom).

Similarly, a client may avoid a state of powerlessness (negative reification). When describing it in neutral, sensory words, they may say it feels like being a leaf in the wind (state of Being). This state can, in turn, feel delightful and carefree (positive reification).

Thus, inviting clients to describe the state they seek to avoid in neutral, sensory words is a practical way of inviting them to explore the felt sense of this state separately from their judgements of it.

Exploring the state in contexts where it has no negative effects

Another very effective way of focusing a client's attention on the felt sense of a state they avoid is by asking them to imagine what it would feel like in scenarios where the worries they have in relation to feeling the state are irrelevant.

This is especially effective, when the state the client seeks to avoid is a form of loss or lack. In such cases, the client seeks to avoid a state in which they are missing a resource they feel they need to survive and thrive in life. Thus, if you can create a scenario in which the client doesn't need this resource, you can create a scenario in which there would be no problem in feeling the state of lack or loss of the resource the client is currently avoiding.

If, for example, a client avoids feeling lost, it is because they believe they need to have a direction in life. In this case, you can ask: "What does it feel like to be lost if you have nowhere you need to get to?" You can even invite the client to think about times when they have enjoyed not knowing where they were.

If a client avoids feeling powerless, it may be because they believe they need power to accomplish something in life. In this case, you can ask: "What does powerlessness feel like when there is nothing you need to accomplish?" You can invite the client to think of a time when they sit on their couch and no one is around. In this scenario, there is arguably no need for power at all – so, it is completely safe to feel powerless.

Similarly, if a client avoids superficiality, they may believe that they are lacking depth and connection. In this case, you can ask: "What does superficiality feel like when you need a bit of a break from depth and connection?" By proposing the idea that one can have too much depth and connection, you create a scenario in which superficiality is a welcome break.

There is room for creativity when producing such scenarios. Creative use scenarios can be very effective in inviting the client to explore, without reservation, the felt sense of a state they would otherwise avoid.

Correcting fallacies of equivocation

Clients often avoid inner felt-sense states because they equate these felt-sense states with certain behaviours, with negative consequences.

- A client may avoid the felt sense of strength because they believe their strength will overpower other people.
- A client may avoid the felt sense of softness because they believe being soft will prevent them from standing their ground in conflicts.
- A client may avoid the felt sense of stillness because they believe such stillness will prevent them from achieving their goals in life.

In the above examples, the clients equate the felt sense of strength with overpowering behaviour, the felt sense of softness with the behaviour of failing to stand one's ground in conflicts, and the felt sense of stillness with passivity.

While a felt-sense state and a behaviour are obviously two completely different things, they can appear to be the same simply when the client uses the same word to refer to both the felt-sense state and the behaviour. In the first of the above examples, the client may say: "My strength overpowers other people". In this sentence, "strength" simultaneously refers to the felt sense of being energised and the action of overpowering others. In the second example, the client may say: "I cannot be soft in conflicts". Once again, the word "soft" refers simultaneously to an inner state and to the behaviour of giving in to demands of another person. In the third example, the client states: "I won't reach my goals if I am still". In this statement, "still" refers simultaneously to an inner feeling and to passivity.

Switching the meaning of a key term within the same argument or formulation of an idea is known as committing the fallacy of equivocation. The fallacy of equivocation often leads to confusion or false conclusions due to the shifting meanings of the word.

Felt-sense states and behaviour are two completely different things. One is about how you feel; the other about how you act. Therefore, rejecting the one to avoid the other makes no sense. You can feel energised while doing nothing at all. You can feel soft while declining to comply with another person's demands. You can feel inner stillness while dealing with the tasks of the day. Rejecting the inner state of "stillness" because you want to avoid "inactivity" is like refusing to put "jam" on one's toast because one dislikes being in a "jam".

That being said, many ideas based on the fallacy of equivocation are broadly accepted as true and valid by many people, and it can be difficult to spot and challenge ideas that are part of the common fabric of society even if they are false.

Nonetheless, becoming aware of and correcting fallacies of equivocation is an important part of separating aspects of Being from the negative interpretations which make clients judge these aspects as negative and avoid them. We can enable clients to see through negative reifications of Being by showing that the state of Being is something completely different from any behaviour and related outcome the client wishes to avoid.

There are three ways of correcting fallacies of equivocation:

- Making clear conceptual distinctions using different words
- Placing the two meanings in opposition to each other
- Clarifying the origin of the equation as based in the Knot of Conditionality

Making clear conceptual distinctions using different words

When a client avoids an aspect of Being because they equate the word they use to denote this aspect with the word they use to denote a behaviour that has negative effects, you can make a distinction between the state of Being and the behaviour and then invite the client to explore the felt sense of the former separately from the latter. A particularly good way of making such a distinction is to use different words to refer to the aspect of Being and the negative behaviour/effect.

For example, a client may avoid the silent aspect of Being because they believe "silence is violence". The client may believe that cultivating inner silence prevents people from doing something about societal structures that are unjust or harmful. In this case, the client equivocates "silence" in the sense "feeling an inner state of silence" with "silence" in the sense "refraining from speaking up when witnessing various forms of abuse". However, feeling inner silence and taking action against abuse are two completely different things. Thus, rejecting the former because one wishes to reject the latter makes no sense. In this case, you can help the client distinguish between the state and the behaviour by referring to the silent aspect of Being as "feeling silence" and the absence of intervening when witnessing abuse as "being passive". This distinction makes it easier for the client to explore the felt sense of "silence" separately from the judgements they hold against the behaviour characterised by "passivity". It also opens up the possibility of feeling inner silence while acting against abuse.

Similarly, a client may avoid the light and carefree aspect of Being because they believe that being carefree means not taking life seriously and neglecting responsibilities. In this example, the client equates the "carefree" in the sense of "being cheerful and not bothered by small things" with "carefree" in the sense of "being irresponsible". However, these are two completely different things. You can make the distinction by referring to the first sense of the word as "feeling carefree" and second sense of the word as "being careless". Establishing this distinction makes it easier to invite the client to explore the felt sense of "carefreeness" separately from the judgements they hold against the behaviour characterised by "carelessness". It also opens up the possibility of feeling carefree while being responsible.

If you are unable to produce separate words that capture the two meanings of the word used to refer to the aspect of Being and the negative behaviour/effect, you can simply ask what the state feels like if it has nothing to do with the negative behaviour/effect. You can, for example, ask:

> "What does silence feel like, if it has nothing to do with turning a blind eye to acts of violence and it didn't prevent you from intervening when needed?"
>
> "What does carefreeness feel like, if it has nothing to do with neglecting responsibilities?"

Rather than using two words to distinguish between the felt-sense state and the behaviour/effect, they use a word for the state and a description for the behaviour. While slightly more verbose, this will still enable the client to focus on exploring the felt-sense state separately from the judgements they hold against the behaviour/effect.

The beauty of this way of working is that it does not matter whether the client's judgements against certain kinds of behaviour are justified or not. Even if the client's judgements against certain behaviour are peculiar, you do not need to address it because it is irrelevant for the purpose of exploring the felt sense of the state they avoid. If you did not make the distinction between the state and the behaviour, you would have to challenge the client's judgements of the behaviour before you could make them explore what the state feels like when they explore it in a non-judgemental manner.

Placing the two meanings in opposition to each other

Once you have clarified how a negative idea about an inner state arises from using a single word to refer to both the state and to a certain type of behaviour with negative effects, you can use this to turn the logic behind this equivocation on its head. You can do so by presenting the state in *opposition* to the negative behaviour/effect rather than as equivalent to it. Doing so will further support the distinction between the state and the behaviour/effect by emphasising their mutual independence.

Consider a client who is avoiding "silence and peace" because they believe these will prevent them from doing something important with their life. This belief contains the fallacy of equivocation as it equates the silence of Being with passivity or inactivity.

The moment you have separated the two meanings of the word, you can turn the logic underpinning the client's belief on its head by suggesting that peace, rather than *preventing* them from doing something important, is precisely what *enables* them to do what they find important. You can, for example, say:

> "Sometimes, peace is exactly what is needed to gather your energy and get things done."

You can also break the equation by linking the opposite inner state with the behaviour/effect the client wishes to avoid. You can, for example, say:

> "Would you say that noise and distraction help you get things done more than peace?"

By suggesting that feeling peace helps, rather than hinders, the client in doing important things in life, you change the client's desire to do important things in life from a force that pushes the client away from the felt sense of peace into a force that pushes the client towards that same state.

Instead of seeing the client's desire to do important things in life as something that prevents them from feeling peace, you use this desire to motivate the client to feel peace.

Once again, this has the advantage that you do not have to discuss the appropriateness of the client's desired behaviour. Any desire can, with sufficient conceptual skill, be used to drive the client towards a state of Being.

It takes practice to learn to spot the fallacy of equivocation and break it by presenting the equated state and behaviour/effect in opposition to each other.

The following exercise is a good way of practising it, so that you will be ready when you are working with a client.

1. Name a negative idea about an aspect of Being
2. Discern the two senses of the key term in this idea (the state and the behaviour/effect)
3. Break the equation by
    a. Presenting the state as something that *enables* the behaviour/effects the client desires
    b. Presenting the opposite state as something that *generates* the behaviour/effects the client wishes to avoid

Clarifying the origin of the equation as based in the Knot of Conditionality

In the above, I have suggested that one can break the fallacy of equivocation by using different words to make a clear distinction between the felt-sense state on the one hand and the equated behaviour/effects on the other. I have also suggested that this distinction can be enhanced by presenting the felt-sense state as being in opposition to the behaviour/effects, highlighting the independence of the two concepts the client had equated.

Finally, the distinction can be further enhanced by exploring the reason a client has come to equate a felt-sense state with a particular behaviour and its negative effects.

The fallacy of equivocation, typically, originates from the 11th misconception: We misattribute to a state of Being the negative effects of the behaviours we engage in when trying to create or acquire this state of Being.

The reason the state of "peace" gets blamed for causing "inactivity" is that we try to create peace by being inactive. The reason the state of "carefreeness" gets blamed for causing "irresponsible behaviour" is that we try to create "carefreeness" by pushing aside responsibilities.

Seeing this clearly, can greatly help break the fallacy of equivocation.

I will return to this in Section 4.4.5, where I describe a way of rounding off the Sensing Taboos process and again in Section 4.6.2, where I describe how to facilitate the exploration of the origins of negative ideas about positive states in groups.

Combining techniques for separating the state from negative associations

The five techniques described above can work well together. Seeing a state the client avoids as positive, describing it using neutral sensory words and exploring it in contexts where it has no negative effects, are three good ways of finding words that can help in correcting the fallacy of equivocation.

As we saw in the section on the fallacy of equivocation, when clients associate an inner state with certain behaviours and their negative consequences, they come to see these as three parts (state, behaviour and consequences) as a single entity, and they refer to this entity using a single word or phrase.

The words/phrases clients use to refer to this entity can be:

- A word/phrase relating to the felt sense of the state
- A word/phrase relating to the behaviour
- A word/phrase relating to the consequences of the behaviour
- A negatively laden abstract concept
- A positively laden abstract concept, which to the client will feel negative

For example, a client may equate the state of inner silence with the behaviour of passivity and the effect of enabling abuse by staying quiet when witnessing abuse. When talking about this combined entity, the client may express their wish to avoid it by saying:

- "I do not want to be *silent*" (felt sense of state)
- "I do not want to be *passive*" (behaviour)
- "I do not want to *enable abuse*" (consequence of behaviour)
- "I do not want to be a *coward*" (negatively laden abstract concept)
- "I think it is wrong to be *peaceful* in certain situations" (positively laden abstract concept used in a negative way)

In the three first of these sentences, the client uses words that refer directly to one of the three equated elements, while implying the two others. In the two last sentences, the client uses abstract concepts that, for the client, refer to the combined entity of state, behaviour and consequence. In other words, both the word “coward” and the word “peaceful” can, for the client, mean to allow abuse by being silent/passive.

As we also saw in the section on the fallacy of equivocation, we can help clients to explore the felt-sense state separately from any negative associations by using different words for the state and the negative associations.

This can be approached differently in the five scenarios mentioned above.

Positively laden concepts and felt sense words

If the words the client uses to refer to the state they avoid are either a positively laden abstract concept or a word that refers to a felt sense, it is preferable to use this word for the felt sense and find other words for the associated behaviours/consequences.

For example, a client may avoid feeling “contentment” because they fear it will prevent them from being productive. Since “contentment” is a positively laden word, we can easily use the word “contentment” to denote the inner state and find other words, such as “inactive” or “pacified” to denote the equated behaviours and effects. As described above, this affords us the possibility of contemplating “contentment” in contexts where it is separate from negative effects, such as “inactivity” or “pacification”.

Negatively laden concepts and behaviours

If the words the client uses to refer to the state they avoid are either a negatively laden concept or behaviours the client sees as negative, there are two ways to create individual words for the state and the behaviour/consequence.

One option is to redefine the value-judgement of the word the client is using, turning it from a negatively laden into a positively laden word. We can then use this word to denote the state and find different words for the negative associations.

If, for example, a client avoids the state of “superficiality” because they see it as preventing them from developing deep connections with others, we can try to talk about “superficiality” as a good thing, and distinguish it from behaviours, such as “avoiding difficult emotions” or “lack of interest in other people”.

However, clients will not always go along with such redefinitions. Thus, a second option is to use the client’s words to denote the behaviours and effects, and find a new word for the equated felt-sense state. To find a suitable word for the state, we can ask the client what behaviours and effects the word they use refers to and then gradually subtract these from the state until the client comes up with a positive word for the state.

If we ask a client who associates the state of "superficiality" with behaviours, such as "avoiding difficult emotions" or "lack of interest in other people", we can ask what "superficiality" feels like if it has nothing to do with these behaviours. Then the client may notice that such superficiality feels "light" or "uncomplicated". We can then shift to using those words for the state and contrast it with the phrases describing behaviours and their effects.

When unpacking what behaviours are embedded in a negative label for a state, it is useful to know that such labels are often nominalizations. They are verbs that are turned into nouns. For example, "oppression" is a noun created from the verb "to oppress", "loneliness" is a noun created from "feeling lonely", and "regret" is a noun derived from the verb "to regret".

When a client uses nominalizations as labels for states they avoid, the behaviour can be discerned simply by turning the nominalizations back into verbs.

If, for example, the client says the state they avoid is the state of "escapism", it shows that the client is equating an inner state with the behaviour of "escaping from something". In this case, you can separate the state from the equated behaviour by asking what the state feels like if it has nothing to do with "escaping from anything".

Similarly, if the client says the state they avoid is "avoidance", you can separate the state from the equated behaviour by asking what the state feels like if it has nothing to do with "avoiding anything". If the client states that they dislike the state of "infatuation", you can separate the state from the equated behaviour by asking what this state feels like if the client is not "infatuated" with anyone or anything.

Consequences

If the words the client uses to refer to the state they avoid relates to the consequences, the main task is to unpack what behaviour and inner state the client associates with these negative consequences. This can be accomplished by asking what behaviours the client is concerned they may engage in that will have this consequence. If the word for the behaviour is positively laden, you can find a word for the state by directly asking the client to use neutral, sensory words to describe what it feels like to engage in this behaviour if it will not have any negative consequences. If the word for the behaviour is negatively laden, you can do the same or you can ask the client what this behaviour feels like if it was a good thing. Such lines of inquiry will produce distinct words for the state and the associated behaviour/consequences, which then allows the client to contemplate the state separately from any negative consequences.

Thus, the techniques of seeing a state the client avoids as positive, describing it using neutral sensory words and exploring it in contexts where it has no negative effects, are three good ways of finding the words needed for the technique of correcting fallacies of equivocation.

4.4.5. Step 4: Correct misconceptions related to the Knot of Negative Reification

In the part of the Sensing Taboos process described above, the therapist helps the client become aware of the felt sense they are avoiding. By separating this felt-sense state from any negative interpretations and subsequent reactions, the client can become aware that what they avoid is identical to what they seek. The only difference is whether they, in a given situation, reify this state as a negative or positive phenomenon. If done correctly, the client will have a vivid and visceral experience of something they fear transforming into something they desire.

At this point, it is important to sum up the transformation in a succinct manner. You may say:

> "So, when you sense meaninglessness, you discover that it is nothing other than freedom."
>
> "So, when you explore the felt sense of the superficiality you were avoiding, you discover that it is pure happiness."

Establishing the identity between the negative and the positive reification of a state of Being opens the possibility of powerfully suggesting the four corrective principles related to the Knot of Negative Reification. The final phase of Sensing Taboos consists of processes with this purpose.

In the sections that follow, I will outline four processes that aim at suggesting the four corrective principles.

- Changeless transformation suggests the 9th corrective principle
- Unification of opposites suggests the 10th corrective principle
- Embracing the void suggests the 10th corrective principle
- Absolving the state suggests the 11th and 12th corrective principles

During therapy sessions, I rarely use all four processes. I prefer to select one or two that seem to be most impactful for the specific client and the specific context.

The rationale behind this is that if a client gains a powerful insight, it is best to allow space and time for this insight to land. If you overload the client with additional insights, you risk confusing them and potentially diluting the power of the initial revelation.

Changeless transformation and the 9th corrective principle

In the Sensing Taboos process, nothing is transforming except for the client's own interpretation of the state they avoid. Sensing Taboos is a changeless transformation in the sense that the state the client experiences at the start and end of the process is the same. It only appears different because the client's attitude towards the state, and consequently their reaction to it, has changed.

However, while under the influence of the misconceptions related to the Knot of Negative Reification, the client is likely to perceive the Sensing Taboos process as a magical transformation of a negative phenomenon into a positive phenomenon. The reason the client experiences the process as a transformation of one phenomenon into another is that they perceive their negative and positive reifications of the same aspect of Being as altogether different phenomena rather than two perspectives on the same phenomenon. Thus, the client sees meaninglessness transformed into freedom, superficiality transformed into happiness, rage transformed into aliveness, vulnerability transformed into tenderness and connection, etc. – not realising that these pairs of phenomena are different reifications of the same state.

This is good insofar as it makes the experience memorable for the client and provides strong experiential evidence that can be used to challenge the client's misconception that the state they avoid is inherently negative.

However, it is important that the client recognises that the change they experienced during the Sensing Taboos process is not a change of phenomenon but of perspective. It is not a change in what they are looking at but a change in where they are looking from.

If the client is left with the impression that as they embraced the negative state, the state itself changed, they may start engaging in the process of Sensing Taboos as a way of getting rid of the states they deem negative. This would undermine the whole process because it would allow the client to retain their wish to avoid the state and the interpretations that lead them to perceive the state as negative.

To support the development of the client's understanding of the process of Sensing Taboos, it can be useful to round off the process by recapitulating exactly which interpretations and judgements the client set aside during the process and how this resulted in a transformation of their perception of the state they were exploring.

For example, a client may avoid a state of rage because this state feels tense and because they fear allowing it will hurt their relationships.

During the Sensing Taboos process, you will first point out that the tension is not the felt sense of the state but rather of their attempt to control the state. After that, you may invite the client to explore what rage would feel like if they allowed it when no one else was around so that there would be no possibility of damaging any relationships. Once the client does this, they may notice that the state itself is nothing other than a strong and vibrant energy, which they may recognise as a sense of vitality or life force.

In this case, you can point out that once the state of rage is separated from the tensions that comes from wanting to control the rage and from the enactment of any behaviour that would hurt the client's relationships, the felt sense of the rage itself is indistinguishable from the felt sense of vitality and life force.

Helping the client to clearly see the identity of the negative and positive reifications of the state they worked with during the process helps the client realise that the state they initially sought to avoid is not inherently negative and that the only thing that makes rage appear negative to them is the way they react to and interpret this state in certain contexts.

Spending some time dwelling on the unity of the positive and negative reification of a particular inner state can also enable the client gain insights into how what they see as something negative to be avoided in a given situation can be exactly what they need to deal with this situations.

For example, the client that sees their vitality as rage in certain situations may need to develop better skills when it comes to dealing with those situations. However, getting rid of their vitality is not a good way of doing this. In fact, once they recognise that what they see as rage is the same as vitality, they may also recognise that the state itself is not a problem but rather a resource they can draw on when learning to deal with the situation in which they feel the rage.

To illustrate this, I often tell a story about my interactions with my PhD supervisor who is amazing both as a professional and as a human being. Nonetheless, sometimes when she read some of my text, she would point to all the things that were vague and didn't make sense to her. More than a few times I got angry when I got the feedback and, in my frustration, I would exclaim: "Why don't you understand it? It is so simple. What I'm saying is…". And I would go on to make the point I was trying to make in my writing in a way that cut to the bone. Often after one of these exasperated exclamations, my supervisor would look at me kindly and say: "I think that is great. Why don't you just write the thing you just said?" While my frustration was nowhere close to rage, this story still illustrates how a state one might see as a negative state of anger can provide one with the capacity to become very clear and direct in one's communication, which can be a great resource if one knows how to use it.

Thus, pointing out that the felt sense of the negative and positive states the client experienced at the start and end of the Sensing Taboos process is identical, is key to correcting the 9th misconception that some states are inherently negative. It reveals that the states the client sees as negative and avoids in some situations are the very same ones they see as positive and seek to attain in other situations.

Unification of opposites and the 10th corrective principle

In the section on the 10th misconception, we explored how a client can interpret one felt-sense state as a hindrance to their possibility of achieving another felt-sense state. For example, a client who interprets the silent aspect of Being as "peace" may interpret the dynamic aspect of Being as a "disturbance" which prevents them from achieving peace.

In such cases, it can be useful to point out that whereas the conceptualisation of different aspects of Being can be mutually exclusive, the actual aspects of Being cannot.

For example, the concepts of "peace" and "disturbance" can be mutually exclusive. If you feel peaceful, you do not feel disturbed, and when you feel disturbed, you do not feel peaceful. However, because Being is both silent compared to the noise of the mind and dynamic compared to the fixedness of the mind, the silent aspect of Being does not exclude the dynamic aspect of Being.

The process of Unifying Opposites is a two-step process that aims at revealing the underlying unity of what appears as mutually exclusive phenomena.

- Step one: Clarify what felt sense underpins each of the two phenomena the client perceives as mutually exclusive. Often, this will be one positive and one negative phenomenon serving as a positive and a negative entry point.
- Step two: Invite the client to imagine the composite felt sense. In the imagination, it is possible to combine any two felt senses. It may be a peculiar sensation – but it is possible to imagine.

For example, working with a client that feels a conflict between the state of peace and the state of disturbance, you may find that the felt sense of "peace" is silence and the felt sense of "disturbance" is vibration. Now you can ask the client to imagine "silent vibration".

By focusing on the felt-sense level, we remove the interpretations and conceptualisations which can be in conflict. This makes it possible to experience a both/and state. The reason this is possible is that all phenomena at their core are reifications of Being and Being is one. No two aspects of Being can be mutually exclusive.

Embracing the void and the 10th corrective principle

A particularly interesting variation of perceived conflicts between different aspects of Being is the conflict many clients feel between a positive reification of Being and the empty aspect of Being reified as the loss of this positive reification.

In this scenario, both the phenomenon the client seeks (the positive reification), and the loss of this phenomenon are aspects of Being and, thus, one.

Consequently, what at a conceptual level appears as the experience of a particular phenomenon and the experience of the loss of that same phenomenon are, at the level of felt sense, merely experiences of two aspects of Being and, as such, one.

For this reason, when we ask a client to sense the loss of a particular phenomenon, they will first feel a peaceful emptiness and then from within this emptiness they may feel the very phenomenon they thought they had lost.

For example, a client may seek a sense of love and fear the loss of love. However, when we guide the client to focus their awareness on the felt sense of the loss of love, they will notice that what they perceived as a loss is just a sense of emptiness, and once they relax into this emptiness, they will often feel love.

This process is often portrayed as a mysterious process; however, there is nothing mysterious about it. The mutual exclusiveness of “love” and “loss of love” is purely conceptual. When we examine the felt sense underpinning these two concepts, we find that they are two sides of the same coin – or rather two aspects of Being.

When it comes to Being, what appears as loss is merely the transition from experiencing Being as a positive reification to experiencing Being as the space containing all such reifications. But since the positive reification is a reification of this space, nothing can ever be lost.

Once clients catch on to this truth, they can become very eager to explore various forms of loss.

Absolving the state and the 11th and 12th corrective principles

In the section on the 11th and 12th misconceptions, we explored how we misattribute negative consequences of our own actions to a state of Being.

Sometimes, we believe feeling the state has a negative impact on our lives, when in fact the negative impact we observe stems, not from feeling the state, but from the actions we engage in to try to create or acquire the state. For example, feeling light-hearted has no negative impact on our lives. Trying to create light-heartedness by turning a blind eye to problems in our lives does. When we conflate the state of light-heartedness with the method of ignoring problems, the state is “rebranded” as “superficiality”, “carelessness” or “shallowness”.

At other times, we believe that a state feels tense, nauseous, confused, etc. when, in fact, this is the felt sense of our reaction to the state and not the felt sense of the state itself. For example, feeling energised does not necessitate feeling tense. But if we fear that feeling energised will have negative consequences in our life, we may try to control this state and that makes us tense. When we conflate the state of energy and the state of tension, the state is “rebranded” as “aggression”, “frustration” or “being out of control”.

Part of the Sensing Taboos process is to separate the felt sense of the state the client avoids from the felt sense of the client’s reactions to this state – whether the reaction is to grasp or avoid the state.

Thus, going through the Sensing Taboos process, we gain insight into how a given state gets its negative reputation by being blamed for things that are not inherently part of the state.

Sometimes, it can be good to "absolve" the state at the end of the Sensing Taboos process by summarising this information and feeding it back to the client.

For example, a client may be avoiding worthlessness and, thus, creating tension in their bodies. When asked why they wish to avoid the feeling of worthlessness, they tell you it is because it makes them feel very tense. When we ask what worthlessness feels like without the tension the client may say that they feel like a blob that is unable to do anything that needs to be done. When asked what it feels like to be a blob if there is nothing the client needs to do, the client may discover that it feels soft, liquid and relaxed. Once the felt sense of worthlessness is separated from the idea of incompetence (being unable to do what needs to be done) and the tension aimed at controlling it, this felt sense may no longer appear to the client as "worthlessness". Instead, they may call it "contentment" or "relief".

A good way of rounding off such a session would be to summarise the mechanism through which the felt sense got turned into the phenomenon of "worthlessness" by misattributing the negative effects of the client's reactions to the state to the state itself. You can do this by saying:

> "So, the state you avoid is a state where you feel soft, liquid and relaxed. The reason you avoid the state is that you believe you cannot do the things you need to do when you feel like that. You see the state as incompetence. Once you have given the state this negative label, you tense up to keep away from it or to control it. This tension only makes the whole experience more unpleasant. So, next time you feel "worthless", just know that the state you are feeling is one of soft, liquid relaxation. Enjoy it. You might even find ways of dealing with life from this state of soft, liquid relaxation".

This little speech is designed to absolve the state from the "unfair" accusations against it, so the client will be more willing to allow the state in the future.

The final sentence borrows from the unification of opposites process by suggesting that the state the client saw as a hindrance to dealing with challenges in life may, in fact, be a resource. The reason the client believes that feeling soft, liquid and relaxed would prevent them from dealing with challenges in life is likely to be that the way they try to create or acquire this state is to push away their energy and dynamic side. While pushing away energy and dynamism *does* prevent one from dealing with challenges, feeling soft, liquid and relaxed does not. Feeling soft, liquid and relaxed does not exclude one from feeling energised and dynamic, and many difficulties are easier to deal with if one remains level-headed and at ease while actively engaging with them.

4.4.6. The role of the therapist's awareness of Being

The focus of this book is on the technical side of Being-Centred Therapy. It is about the skilful means through which therapists can help clients develop awareness of Being.

However, the therapist's own familiarity with Being is essential to the success of these approaches.

This is true for all the processes described in this book; however, it becomes especially clear in the case of the Sensing Taboos process.

When a therapist invites a client to pay attention to the felt sense of a state that the client sees as negative and maybe even harmful, they will inevitably pay close attention to the therapist's own reaction to this state.

If the therapist is uncomfortable with feeling the state they are inviting the client to feel, the client will sense it and this will increase their resistance.

If, on the other hand, the therapist is comfortable feeling the state they are inviting the client to feel, it will have a calming effect on the client and enhance their capacity to feel the state.

It is, therefore, vital that the therapist has gone through the work and found Being at the core of various negative states in themselves.

An invitation to feel a negative state that comes from a therapist who sees through the mask of the negative reification is reassuring and mysteriously irresistible to clients.

Reversing the value-judgements of a state the client sees as negative becomes easier when you, as the therapist, can see through the mask of negative reification because you truly see that which the client sees as negative as an aspect of Being which is the most precious there is. And clients can feel that you see something different from what they see.

Thus, the Sensing Taboos process can often feel like gently taking the client by the hand and going into the state they are afraid of together with them.

Next, we will look at two examples of the process of Sensing Taboos.

4.5. Examples of Sensing Taboos

In this section, you can read transcriptions of two therapy sessions applying the process of Sensing Taboos. The sessions, like all sessions in this book, are fictional but representative of sessions I have had with clients.

Furthermore, the sessions are abbreviated so they only include the key parts of the exchange. Real sessions often contain more exploration, longer narratives, tangents, pauses, etc. That being said, the Knot of Negative Reification can, in some cases, be untied in a matter of minutes. In such cases, the examples below would represent full transcriptions of the therapeutic exchange.

The examples are written in two columns. In the left column, you can read the client and therapist's conversation. In the right column, you can read the observations and considerations that guided the therapist during the exchange.

4.5.1. Session 5: Lack of love and purpose

This session starts the exact same way as session 3, but instead of conceptualising the situation as The Knot of Conditionality and exploring what the client is reaching for through their actions, we will conceptualise the situation as The Knot of Negative Reification and explore what the client is avoiding. Instead of focusing on 100% success, the exploration focuses on 100% failure. Thus, this session illustrates how there always is a choice regarding whether to work with the Sensing Completion process (as in session 3) or the Sensing Taboos process (as here).

Process	Comments
Client: The problem I have is that I pick the wrong partners. I always get involved with partners who are unstable, and I end up having to support them and help with all their problems. I'd like to have a stable partner. Someone who can help me out once in a while. But whenever I find someone who is stable, I feel no attraction. I'd like help figuring out how to be attracted to partners that are good for me.	In this opening statement, the client presents multiple agendas. The primary agenda is to find a stable partner. But the complaint that they feel no attraction when they encounter someone who is stable reveals that the client has a secondary agenda of finding an attractive partner. Both plans can form the basis of a Sensing Taboos process since both stability and attraction are things the client seeks to attain in order to avoid something they do not want to feel.
Therapist: Just to ensure I understand you right and don't make any wrong assumptions, why do you even want a stable partner?	I chose to work with the primary agenda. Asking why the client wants what they want is a good way of opening the session. However, asking it directly can disrupt the rapport. To mitigate this risk, I frame the question as a wish to understand, which generally builds rapport.
C: I want a family, and for that I need a stable partner.	The client provides insight into what they seek.
T: Makes sense. And what do you think having a family would give you?	I confirm that I understand and use the Sensing Completion question.
C: I want to have a place I belong. I want to settle down.	This is what the client is ultimately reaching for.
T: So, what do you think you would feel if you didn't find a family?	I ask what they would feel if they didn't get what they seek to clarify what they are avoiding.
C: I don't even want to think of it. That would be horrible.	Initially, the client does not want to even think about the state they avoid.

Process	Comments
T: I understand. Many people would not like to grow old without a family. But the reason might vary. Some might feel worthless, other weird, yet others unlovable. What would you feel?	I acknowledge the client's concern and use categories to spark their curiosity about what they feel.
C: I think all of them. Yes. All of them.	Client can relate.
T: Which one bothers you the most?	Inviting the client to choose is a way of engaging their curiosity.
C: No love. Yes. I feel my life would be devoid of love. And purpose. What would be the point of it all if I don't have anyone to love and care for?	Here the client presents two negative entry points: "Lack of love" and "lack of purpose".
T: Excellent. Are you up for a small experiment to explore this?	By framing the following question as an experiment, I avoid the client getting distracted by concerns about the question.
C: Sure. Yes.	
T: So, absence of love and purpose is probably nobody's favourite state. But exactly for this reason, we rarely explore what it actually feels like. We just run away. But one can learn a lot from paying a bit more attention to such states. So, what does lack of love and purpose feel like to you if you were to describe the felt sense of it?	I "sell" the idea of exploring the felt sense as something that the client can learn valuable lessons from. This is to ensure the client's engagement in the exploration.
C: Horrible. I feel my whole body tense up. I have this knot in the pit of my stomach.	The client describes the felt sense of their rejection/avoidance of the state.

Process	Comments
T: Yes. The tension you feel is the felt sense of your rejection of the state of no love and purpose. It's your way of keeping the state away. What would you feel if you relaxed the tension?	I label the tension as the felt sense of the rejection and ask what they would feel if they relaxed. This means asking for what they would feel if they stopped rejecting the state and felt it.
C: Just desolation. Nothing. Emptiness. As if life becomes meaningless. Like a desert.	The client describes the felt sense of the state they avoid but the description is coloured by their negative perception of it.
T: Good. And if you keep relaxing, what can you notice about this emptiness or nothingness? If you just hang out with it without trying to do anything with it. What do you notice?	By spending more time feeling the state and relaxing at the same time is a good way of setting aside the negative interpretation of the state.
C: I don't know. Not much. It's just blank.	The client describes the state in more neutral words.
T: Good. Is it ok to just hang out with this?	I encourage the client to sustain their attention of the state.
C: Yes. It is actually not unpleasant.	The client's perception starts to shift.
T: Wonderful. How does it feel now that you allow it?	I ask specifically what the state feels like when the client stops rejecting it.
C: It is actually quite relaxing. It's really a relief. It feels very kind to myself. It feels soft and loving somehow.	The client starts feeling the state in itself, separate from the negative interpretation of the state. As is often the case, the state is what the client was seeking all along.
T: Wonderful. And as you are feeling this soft and loving space, how do you feel about searching for a partner?	This is the question from the "urgency" process described in Section 3.4.4.
C: I feel much more at ease with it. It doesn't feel like a big deal, right now.	Because the client has connected with Being, the agenda feels less urgent.

Process	Comments
T: Yes. Because one of the things you wanted was this soft and loving feeling and now you have it – regardless of whether you have a partner. Enjoy it.	I round off by offering an interpretation of the shift the client has experienced.

4.5.2. Session 6: Anger, strength and leadership

In the following session, a sales manager has a problem with one of her team members. The client is angry with her team member but does not wish to acknowledge her anger. She sees a team member as breaking the rules in a way that is unfair to certain customers and she believes she is addressing this in an objective manner and that the employee gets upset for no reason.

In other words, her own sense of anger and frustration is edited out of the way she experiences and presents the situation. She imagines that she is unperturbed by the situation, and she does not want to admit that she is avoiding her frustration and anger because that would imply that she is frustrated and angry.

The session is, thus, an example of the common situation where a client has a taboo around a particular emotion (anger in this case) and, as a result, avoids even acknowledging it. Consequently, the session is fundamentally one long invitation to the client to acknowledge and explore the felt sense of her tabooed anger.

When the client finally acknowledges her anger, she first sees it as something negative. When asked to describe the felt sense, she initially feels the felt sense of her reaction to the anger, which in this case is tension and confusion.

When guided around these sensations to the felt sense of the anger itself, she feels relief. She uses some strong language to give expression to her anger and frustration and then she laughs. This is a very common reaction when clients during a session feel safe enough to acknowledge tabooed states.

At the end of the session, she recognises the felt sense she has been calling anger and avoided is the same felt sense that she, in other contexts, would call "taking leadership" or "strength".

Process	Comments
Client: My problem is that one of the people in my sales team frequently gets upset for no reason. She is a bit of a prima donna. I don't know how to handle this. It always takes me by surprise. It can come out of nowhere. I actually feel her behaviour is abusive. I often don't say anything. But then I berate myself afterwards for not standing up for myself or calling her out on her behaviour.	When a client experiences unprovoked and irrational attacks from other people it is often an indication that the client has a blind spot around their own participation in the creation of the interaction. Such blind spots are often created by the client's attempts at avoiding something in themself. This makes the situation a good candidate for the Sensing Taboos process.
Therapist: Tell me about the last time this happened.	Asking for a concrete example often gives information that can help reveal a client's blind spots.
C: We were in our daily meeting, and I pointed out some problems with the way my colleague handled a case where a client had complained about a product, they had bought from us. I wasn't the only one who believed her handling of the case was problematic. I was just the only one who said it. I was very nice about it. I didn't blame her for anything. I just said that I think it would be better to deal with it in another way. Just trying to be helpful. But she felt I was attacking her and then it was a whole thing. She even filed a complaint against me.	It is, of course, possible that the team member is overreacting. Some people do. But as it is always good to operate with multiple hypotheses, it is also important to notice that sometimes aggression and put-downs can be presented as a "wish to help". There is something jarring about stating that the team member "did something wrong" and that "I didn't blame her for anything". Saying that someone did something "wrong" *is* blaming them.
T: What did you think your colleague did wrong?	Once again, I ask for specific details to get around the client's blind spot.

Process	Comments
C: The customer wanted to return a product they had used. This is against our return policy. I had personally given the customer a thorough demonstration of the product. If they change their mind afterwards, that is their own problem. We can't give them the money back. But the customer is very charming, and he charmed my colleague, and she accepted the return. I think this is problematic. It isn't fair to our other customers either.	The client mentions that her colleague's behaviour is against the rules and unfair to other customers – but there is a conspicuous absence of reference to any problems related to the client herself. There is a discrepancy between on the one hand stating that she had personally taken care of the sale and on the other hand not saying anything about any problems the situation created for her personally.
T: Did it create any problems for you?	I test my theory.
C: No.	The client refutes it.
T: Do you get commissions on sales?	I start testing assumptions underpinning my hunch that there is a problem the client denies.
C: Yes.	Confirms first assumption.
T: Do you lose the commission when a product is returned?	Test second assumption.
C: Yes.	Confirms second assumption.
T: Is that not a problem?	Propose that the established facts point to a problem.
C: I'm very good at what I do. I will have no problem meeting my target.	The client avoids acknowledging the problem in the situation by commenting on a larger problem.
T: Sure, still, I think most people would be annoyed if someone breaks the rules and it results in a loss of commission for them personally.	Here I use normalising and diminishing language to invite the client to acknowledge anger – if they feel any (which is still an open question at this point).

Process	Comments
C: I'm not that kind of person. I'm not bothered by such small things.	Here the client shows that anger doesn't fit their self-image. This would be a reason to avoid it.
T: So, if the rules were different and your colleague would routinely accept returns on your sales, that would be fine with you.	I present an extreme version of the situation to test whether the client really is unaffected.
C: No. There must, of course be a limit (said with a sharp intonation and downward inflection).	Now the client connects with their anger.
T: What do you feel when you say that?	Thus, I ask for the felt sense.
C: Maybe a bit of frustration.	She acknowledges her emotion.
T: Tell me about that frustration.	I invite her to examine this emotion.
C: I don't like it. I don't want to focus on grievances. If there is a problem, we need focus on how to solve it, not bicker about who's to blame. Getting angry is so unprofessional.	The client reveals her negative judgements against anger. She sees it as not being solution-oriented and as unprofessional.
T: This is, of course, a good attitude. However, we cannot always control our emotions. So, if you are frustrated, it can be good to give that emotion space. If you repress it, it just affects you in ways you don't notice. What does the frustration feel like?	I acknowledge the value of the client's wish to focus on solutions and behave in a professional manner to ensure the client knows I'm not trying to undermine this. Then I give her a reason to examine her emotions that is in line with the above wish.
C: It feels tense and confusing.	The client notices the felt sense of her reactions to her anger.

Process	Comments
T: When you described the situation, you didn't seem confused. You seemed very clear about what you thought of it.	I point out that this is not the felt sense of the anger itself by pointing out that there was no confusion when she said what she felt was wrong in her team member's behaviour.
C: Yes. Ok. Yes. I'm angry. I really don't like her attitude. It is so frustrating when people behave like that. Why can't they just do their job?	Finally, the client feels safe enough to acknowledge her emotion.
T: Good. What do you feel when you say that?	I invite her to explore the felt sense.
C: Ah... it is actually really a relief (laughs). This is so not me. But I just felt a big relief in the belly. She is such a bitch!	The client feels the relief and finally expresses her view of the team member in direct language.
T: Wonderful. Say more about the physical feeling.	I invite the client to direct their attention to the felt sense.
C: I feel all tingly. Like a lot of energy. And really warm.	The client describes the felt sense of anger separate from judgements.
T: Great. And if, for a moment, you forget the whole situation with your colleague, and just focus on the feeling you feel now. How is it?	I invite the client to explore the felt sense of anger separately from the context in which the client interprets this felt sense as anger.
C: I feel much more present. I feel strong. It's strange. This kind of feels like taking leadership. That is what I'm paid to do (laughs). It feels good.	Now the client notices that in a different context, the felt sense has a different, and much more positive, meaning to her.

Process	Comments
T: Yes. This is just energy. When you feel it in situations where someone has done something you don't like, you see it as anger and as unprofessional. But if you reject this state, you are also rejecting the state you in other contexts feel as strength and as taking leadership.	I use the experience of the session to introduce the 9th corrective principle, that states you avoid in one context are the same as the states you seek and cherish in other contexts.
C: Wow. That changes things. Maybe I should welcome frustration more.	The client now has a more positive relationship to her own anger.
T: Yes. Welcome the energy of it. There is nothing bad about the state.	I support the client's insight.

After this exchange, it may be useful to have a conversation about how the client would deal with the situation while feeling strong and energised. Often, when clients connect with the felt sense of their anger as pure energy, they will no longer feel threatened and this will enable them to deal in calm, caring and assertive ways with the situation.

4.6. Untying the Knot of Negative Reification through contemplations

In Section 4.4, I have outlined how the Knot of Negative Reification can be untied in one-to-one sessions with clients.

In this section, I will describe a series of contemplation exercises specifically designed to untie the Knot of Negative Reification. These exercises are well suited to group work. The instructions are sufficiently simple to be given to a group, and the exercises can, for example, be performed in pairs or as individual writing exercises.

When working with groups, I often begin by inviting students to do the contemplation exercise in pairs or individually. Afterwards, I work one-to-one with a few students in plenum using the techniques presented in Section 4.4. This approach has the advantage that although I only work with a few students directly, the other students, having completed the contemplation exercise, can partake in the one-to-one processing vicariously.

4.6.1. What are your negative ideas about X?

In this chapter, we have seen that we can perceive the same inner state as something positive in some contexts and something negative in other contexts.

For example, we may interpret the felt sense of energy and vibration as "excitement" in some contexts and "anxiety" or "lack of control" in other contexts. Similarly, we may interpret inner stillness as "peace" in some contexts and "deadness" or "depression" in other contexts.

In this section, we will look at a great contemplation exercise that can reveal how positive and negative concepts can be different interpretations of the same underlying inner state in different contexts. The contemplation exercise takes as its starting point a positive inner state "X" and asks:

> "What are your negative ideas about X?"

At first glance, this may seem like a surprising question. One might expect to have only positive ideas about phenomena that one perceives as positive. However, in practice, any positive phenomenon will be associated with several negative ideas.

For example, while you may generally believe that peace is a good thing, you may also have come across ideas such as:

- Peaceful people are defenceless
- Peaceful people are aloof
- Peace is for old people
- Peace is boring
- Peace cannot be trusted
- I'm not a peaceful person or peace is not for me

Similarly, while you may generally believe that "happiness" is a good thing, you may also have come across ideas such as:

- Happiness is fickle – it won't last
- Happiness is for the lucky few
- Happiness is overrated
- Happiness is a luxury, not a necessity
- Happiness is for dreamers
- Happiness does not pay the bills

Such ideas reveal negative conceptions about phenomena otherwise perceived as positive. For example, the above ideas about peace suggest that the state that in some contexts is interpreted as "peace", in other contexts will be interpreted as "defencelessness", "aloofness", "old and low energy", "boredom", "something devious" or "something alien or out of reach". In the same way, the ideas about happiness suggest that the state that in some contexts is interpreted as "happiness" in other contexts could be interpreted as something divorced from reality that might get in the way of dealing with real life.

When engaging in this contemplation exercise, it is important to just list out all the ideas one has been exposed to. Many of these ideas are part of the social fabric. Thus, even if you do not consciously subscribe to or believe in these ideas, they will most likely still affect you in some ways.

The point of the exercise is not to evaluate the ideas and determine which are correct and which are not. The point is not to select which beliefs you want to keep and which you want to get rid of.

The point of the exercise is to see how the same state has both positive and negative interpretations. The point is to see that what in one context appears as a bad thing which you should avoid, in other contexts is exactly what you seek.

Listing out all the negative ideas you have about a positive concept can help you decouple the positive state from all these ideas and, thus, experience it in a purer form. In other words, it can help you use the positive concept as a positive entry point through which you can become aware of Being.

This can be done in two ways.

Consciously naming the ideas and seeing them as ideas rather than facts can break the influence the ideas have over your perception. When ideas are operating in our unconscious, they will determine what we pay attention to. For example, if you believe that happiness is a luxury and something that cannot help you deal with the real issues in life, you will ignore states of happiness as long as you need to deal with real life – which may very well be most of the time. Thus, as long as this idea guides you, you will rarely experience happiness. When you see the idea as just an idea, you may start to question it and its influence over your perception will diminish.

To support the questioning of the ideas, you can introduce a second contemplation:

> "For each of the ideas you listed in response to the first question, consider how this idea makes you avoid X or prevents you from noticing it."

One typical answer to the second contemplation question is that an idea can prevent you from noticing a positive phenomenon because it discourages you from looking for it. In cognitive science, there is a phenomenon called inattentional blindness which refers to the fact that individuals tend to overlook things they don't expect to see. Many of the above ideas will make you overlook the positive phenomenon simply because you won't expect to see it. For example, if you believe that you are not a peaceful person, you are unlikely to notice when you feel peace. Similarly, if you believe happiness is for the lucky few and you don't think of yourself as one of them, you won't pay attention to feelings of happiness. It simply won't be part of what you pay attention to in life.

Another typical answer to the second contemplation question is that an idea can make you actively avoid a positive phenomenon because the idea equates the phenomenon with some negative behaviour and, thus, makes you avoid the phenomenon to avoid the behaviour. This is the fallacy of equivocation discussed in Section 4.4.4. For example, if you believe that happiness is fickle and won't last, you may avoid happiness in order to avoid the inevitable disappointment you believe will result from allowing the feeling of happiness. In the same way, if you believe peace is aloof, you may avoid peace because you don't want to be seen as aloof.

There are many positive effects of realising that you have negative ideas about a positive phenomenon and reflecting on how these negative ideas prevent you from noticing the phenomenon or encourage you to actively avoid it.

First, it can reveal that the reason you find it difficult to feel a positive state is that you are ambivalent about it or actively avoid it because of certain negative ideas you may not have been aware of. Once you are aware of the ideas, you can absolve the positive state by correcting the equivocation fallacies contained in these ideas.

Second, it helps you identify the negative states that can be used as negative entry points. If you believe that peace is aloof, then exploring the felt sense of "aloofness" is a way of accessing the state of peace. If you believe that happiness is fickle, then using the Sensing Taboos process to become aware of the felt sense of fickleness is a way of becoming aware of happiness.

Finally, once you are aware of the negative interpretations of a positive state, you can absolve the state from the negative judgements against it by asking yourself

> "What would X feel like if it had nothing to do with any of the negative ideas I have about it?"

For example, you may ask questions such as:

> "What does peace feel like if it has nothing to do with defencelessness, aloofness, old age, boredom, death, etc.?"
>
> "What does happiness feel like if it has nothing to do with fickleness, irresponsibility, your ability to deal with life, or pay your bills, etc.?"

When you separate the felt sense from all possible negative interpretations what is left is just a state of Being.

Another way of absolving states of Being is to see how the state got its negative conception. This is the purpose of the next contemplation exercise.

4.6.2. How can your negative ideas about X be explained by the negative consequences of the ways you try to acquire or produce X?

One of the main reasons positive states get a "bad reputation" is that the actions we engage in to create or acquire the states have negative outcomes. In other words, one of the sources of the fallacy of equivocation is that we use the same word for the state we seek and the flawed methods we employ to create or acquire the state.

For example, if we seek to create a state of "peace" by disowning our life force and becoming complacent and overly compliant, we make ourselves defenceless. This is the origin of the idea that "peace is defenceless". We can absolve the state of peace from this idea by recognising that it is not the feeling of peace that makes us defenceless but rather the things we do to try to create peace.

Similarly, if we believe that happiness is the result of being surrounded by luxury, then happiness is a luxury and something only the lucky few can enjoy. However, this is not inherent to the felt sense of happiness but rather something that comes out of a particular idea about how happiness is created.

For this reason, it can be very illuminating to do the following sequence of contemplation exercises.

First, we do the contemplation exercise described in Section 3.6.1:

> "What are your ideas about how to create or acquire X?"

Next, we do the contemplation exercise described in Section 4.6.1:

> "What are your negative ideas about X?"

And then we compare the results of these two exercises by asking:

> "How can your negative ideas about X be explained by the negative consequences of the ways you try to create or acquire X?"

This exercise can reveal that the negative ideas we have about a particular state have nothing to do with the state itself but rather come from misconceived ideas about how to create or acquire the state.

This is a powerful way of absolving the state from the unfair judgements we have against it. When we see that simply feeling the state does not have the negative consequences we thought it had, we will be much more willing to allow the state.

This contemplation exercise can be a bit complicated to carry out. It requires a significant level of analytical skill on behalf of the students and, since it requires students to do two contemplation exercises as preparation, it also takes a significant amount of time.

However, even just seeing a few connections between negative ideas about a state and misconceived ideas about how to create this state can be greatly rewarding. Thus, this series of three contemplation exercises can form a substantial portion of a workshop.

Readers who are influenced by psychoanalytical approaches to therapy may be wondering whether the childhood family environment wouldn't be a more important source of negative ideas about various states. For example, if a child is consistently told that they are too much whenever they feel very alive, the child may come to form the idea that the state of being energised is too much for other people. Similarly, if a child grows up in a family that values being serious and frowns on being light-hearted and calls that being frivolous or silly, the child will internalise these judgements against the state of inner lightness.

It is probably indisputable that the childhood environment is one of the main places where the individual is introduced to such negative beliefs about otherwise positive states. However, this does not explain the *origin* of these beliefs. It leaves us with the question of how the parents came to hold such beliefs. If we answer that they got them from their parents, we have the problem of an infinite regress[39]. Saying that we get these ideas from our childhood environment does

---

[39] "Infinite regress" is a philosophical technique used to challenge or refute a claim by showing that the explanation or justification offered for the claim leads to an endless chain of further explanations or justifications, where each explanation itself requires another explanation. The

not explain the origin of the idea, only the means through which it is passed along from generation to generation. In this section, we have offered an explanation for the *origin* of negative beliefs about positive phenomena.

4.6.3. What would it feel like to fail voluntarily and deliberately?

The core of the Sensing Taboos process is to relinquish all defences against states we perceive as negative so we can feel what these states feel like on their own – separate from any context in which we judge them negatively.

A good way of inviting people to explore this in a group setting is to focus on the things people do to avoid negative states and acquire positive ones and ask:

> "What would it feel like to fail voluntarily and deliberately?

If, for example, an individual is trying to avoid humiliation by working overtime every time they get a new assignment at work, the above question invites them to explore what humiliation feels like if they voluntarily and deliberately fail to avoid it.

Similarly, if an individual is trying to acquire a sense of meaning in life by establishing a family, the above question invites them to explore the meaninglessness they believe they would feel if they voluntarily and deliberately fail to establish a family.

The key words in the above question are "voluntarily" and "deliberately". These words invite you to imagine that you are not merely allowing the negative state but that you are putting in an effort to feel it. You do not merely succumb to it. You actively seek it. If it starts slipping away on its own, you bring it back.

Research in cognitive science has shown that the link between people's judgements of phenomena and their behaviour in relation to this phenomenon mutually influence each other. It is not just our judgements of a phenomenon that influence whether we seek or avoid it. The reverse is also true. Whether we seek or avoid a phenomenon influences how we judge the phenomenon.

Thus, imagining that you voluntarily and deliberately seek to attain a state that you initially saw as negative, can influence your judgement of the state in a

---

concept of infinite regress highlights the importance of providing a solid, coherent and self-contained foundation or ultimate justification for beliefs or claims.

positive direction. In doing so, you can sometimes flip the interpretation of the state, so it shifts from a negative interpretation to a positive one.

For example, if you voluntarily and deliberately seek the state of humiliation, you may start noticing a sense of openness and undefendedness that comes with it. You may notice humiliation as something that brings a sense of humility and enables you to embrace your humanness and fallibility without reservations. Furthermore, you may notice how embracing your fallibility will free you from having to take it personally if someone tries to put you down just because of inevitable imperfections in your work.

Similarly, if you voluntarily and deliberately seek meaninglessness, you may start noticing the freedom that comes with it. You may start seeing meaning as a burden or a form of restriction. If there is no meaning in life, you are completely free.

While such transformations may not occur in unassisted contemplation exercises, even just giving serious attention to the idea of voluntarily and deliberately seeking failure can be liberating as it breaks a taboo against even thinking about such failure.

To optimise the chances of students having profound insights from this contemplation exercise, it is important to encourage clients to describe the states that emerge when they contemplate complete failure, using neutral sensory words. It is also important to emphasise the attitude of actively grasping the negative state and bringing it back if it changes into something else. Assuming the attitude of being madly in love with the negative state can bring out the positive qualities of this state.

4.6.4. Describe the felt sense of X, using neutral and sensory words

Another good way of inviting students to explore a state they see as negative while setting aside any judgements of this state, is to focus on a particular state most people would avoid and ask:

> "How can you describe the state using only neutral, sensory words?"

We can use this question to explore inner states such as "sadness", "anger", "boredom", "hate", "jealousy", "meaninglessness", etc.

Whereas the goal of this contemplation exercise is the same as the goal of the previous exercise, there are two main differences.

The previous contemplation exercise invited clients to first discover what state they avoid through their actions and then explore this state. The contemplation exercise in this section skips the first step and directly invites students to explore specific inner states most people would seek to avoid.

The previous contemplation exercise supported students in setting aside negative judgements of the state they avoid by inviting them to assume a particular attitude towards the state, namely to deliberately and voluntarily seek it. The contemplation exercise in this section supports students in setting aside negative judgements of the state they avoid by describing it using neutral sensory words (see also Section 4.4.4, subsection 3: "Describing the state using neutral, sensory words").

4.6.5. What if X was a good thing? (frame experiment exercise)

Finally, an interesting experiment I like to do with groups is to invoke a felt-sense state and ask what people would call this state if it were a good thing and then ask what people would call the state if it were a bad thing.

For example, I might ask people to imagine a sense of heaviness in the body.

When asked what this state is if it were a good thing, people will typically say it is "grounding", "confidence", "ease", "relaxation", etc.

When asked what this state is if it were a bad thing, people will typically say it is "stuckness", "stubbornness", "depression", "defeatism", etc.

This small exercise reveals in a very effective manner how felt-sense states do not have a fixed interpretation and how accessing the felt-sense state of a phenomenon we avoid can be a way of accessing the multiple phenomena we seek.

Often, there will be a lot of names for emotions among the answers. This demonstrates how emotions are nothing other than felt-sense states interpreted in context. It opens up the possibility of questioning one's emotions the same way one would question one's conclusions about a particular situation, since, in essence, emotions are just that. They are conclusions about the meaning of felt-sense states in particular contexts. In the context of an exam, we conclude that a flutter in the stomach is anxiety. In the context of a date night with our partner, we conclude that the same flutter in the stomach is love.

To use this exercise specifically to undo the Knot of Negative Reification, one can take any negative state and ask:

> “What happens if you perceive this state as a good thing?”

For this contemplation exercise you can use states, such as meaninglessness, pointlessness, powerlessness, hopelessness, worthlessness, loneliness, lostness, sadness, vulnerability, anger, frustration, disingenuousness, obsession, shame, guilt, jealousy, resentment, envy, inferiority, silliness, desire, hate, laziness, boredom and apathy.

You can frame the question by inviting clients to imagine that one day they wake up and discover that they have been mistaken about the experience in question all their life. To their surprise they discover that what they thought was a bad thing actually is, in fact, a very positive thing. You can further suggest that once they see the experience as a positive thing, they might feel that another name would be more appropriate for the experience. In particular, they might want to give the experience a name that reflects its positive nature.

Inviting the client to change the context in which they interpret the state from the context of “bad thing” to the context of “good thing” can radically alter how they experience the state (see also Section 4.4.4, subsection two: “Seeing the state as positive”).

4.7. Summary

In this chapter, we have explored the Knot of Negative Reification. This knot occurs when clients give an experience of Being a negative name and, in doing so, encourage themselves to avoid or reject the state.

The Knot of Negative Reification produces and is sustained by four misconceptions: That some inner states are inherently negative and should be avoided, that positive phenomena can be in conflict with each other, that feeling certain aspects of Being can have negative impacts and that aspects of Being can feel tense and unpleasant.

The way to untie the Knot of Negative Reification is through the process of Sensing Taboos, where we explore the felt sense of states we avoid or reject separately from the contexts in which we judge these states negatively.

We looked at how this process can be facilitated in one-to-one sessions and through contemplation exercises.

Next, we look at the Knot of Alienation in which clients perceive the presence of negative states and the absence of positive ones as the natural state of affairs because they have lost awareness of the processes through which they contribute to the construction of these states.

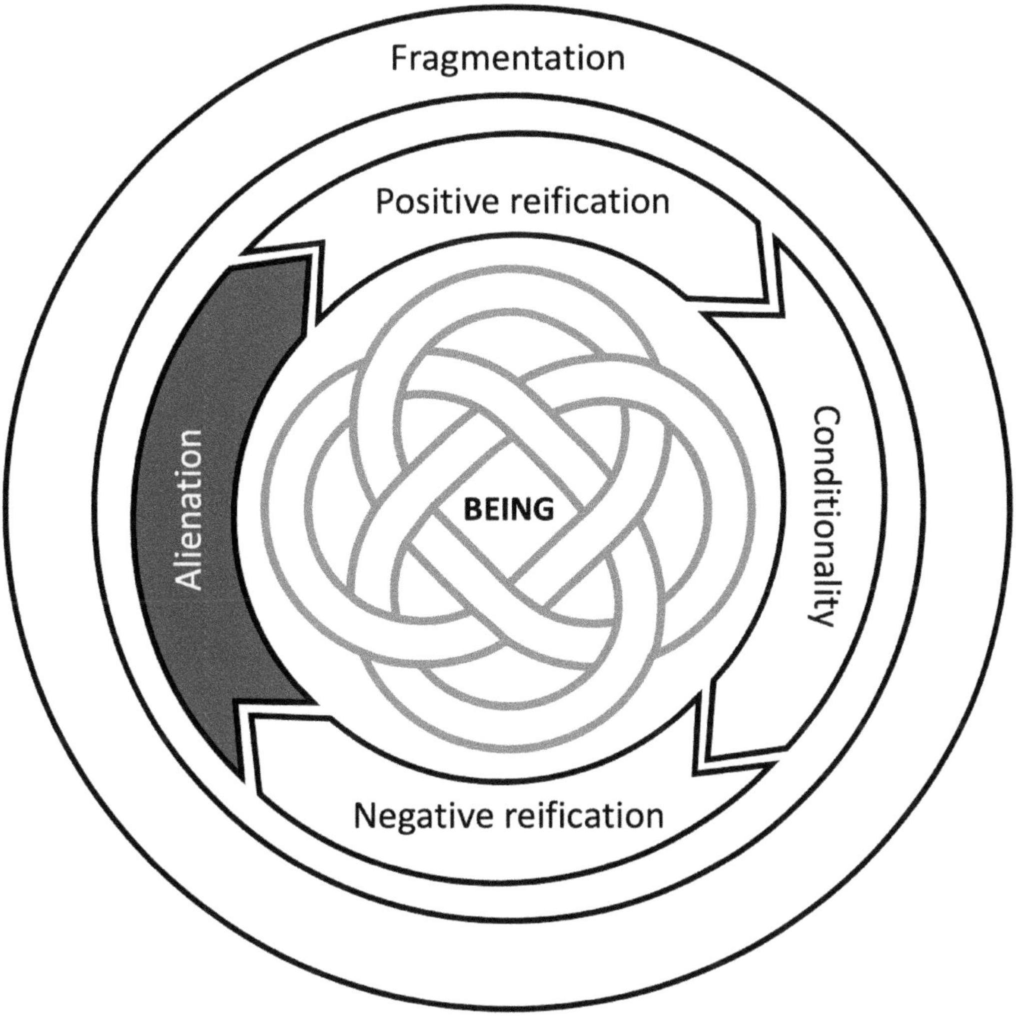

The Knot of Alienation

5. Knot 4: The Knot of Alienation

The Knot of Alienation occurs when clients create something, forget they are the ones creating it, and then fight their own creation as if it were existing independently from themselves. In other words, the Knot of Alienation occurs when clients are unaware of their own participation in the creation of something in their lives they perceive as problematic and, therefore, want to change. In such cases, clients are simultaneously creating their experience and fighting it.

Examples of things clients believe they are not the creators of, even though they are, include the absence of positive inner states and the presence of negative inner states related to emotions, identity, relationship to other people, tasks and any other phenomenon that in essence are classifications (more in 5.4).

When clients recognise that they are the creator of something problematic, they may solve this problem simply by ceasing to create it. When, on the other hand, clients believe they have nothing to do with the creation of something they see as problematic, they cannot change it. The best they can do is to create something else that mitigates the negative effect of the problematic thing.

To illustrate this, we can compare two examples where a client wants to change something they believe they are not the creators of – one example where their belief is true and one where it is false.

A client might want to change the weather. Because they do not create the weather, the best they can do is to create something other than the weather that mitigates effects of the weather they do not like. They can, for example, create a house to protect them from wind, rain and sun.

Another client may want to change the fact that they become aggressive in certain situations, because this aggression sometimes has negative effects. They may also believe that the aggression is created in them by external circumstances and that they are not involved in the creation of their own aggression. In this case, the client's beliefs make the aggression akin to the weather in that, if the client is not involved in the creation of their aggression, they cannot cease to create it. The best they can hope for is to learn techniques to handle it when it comes and, thus, mitigate the negative effects (more in Section 5.2).

The reason clients experience that they are not creating things they are, in fact, creating, is that the process of creation has been automated as an unconscious habit. Such habits can even be supported by changes in the client's biology.

To solve the Knot of Alienation, we must learn to get curious and perceive the automated mechanism through which we create the absence of states we would like to feel and the presence of states we would like not to feel. This is the process of Sensing Agency.

One of the main obstacles clients experience when invited to become aware of the mechanism through which they create the things they wish to change is accepting responsibility for these unwanted outcomes. Another obstacle is to understand the, often unconscious, motivations behind the automated processes.

Before we dive into the details of the Knot of Alienation, it can be instructive to say a bit more about how and why human beings automate processes of thought, emotion and behaviour (Section 5.1), how this affects the development of personality structure (Section 5.2), what alienation from each of the ten aspects of Being might look like (Section 5.3), and how the Knot of Alienation can occur at different logical levels of learning (Section 5.4).

5.1. Alienation and automation

Part of human development is the formation and automation of patterns of thought, emotion and behaviour. Once a pattern of thought, emotion and behaviour has proved to be useful in yielding reliable results when interacting with the environment, we automate it – i.e., we form a habit.

Automation is akin to delegating certain tasks to the unconscious mind. This is important because it frees up attention that can then be focused on further development.

Once we have learned and automated the process of walking, we can focus on where we want to go. Once we have learned and automated the process of typing on a keyboard, we can focus on working with the text we are writing[40].

---

[40] The distinction between focusing attention on an activity and focusing attention on what we can do through that activity is elaborated in Michelle Polanyi's concepts of focal vs. peripheral awareness (Polanyi, 1974) and Martin Heidegger's concepts of present-at-hand vs. ready-to-hand (Heidegger, 1962).

For automation to free up attention, we must necessarily forget about the automated processes. This includes forgetting that we created the processes in the first place. Consequently, when a pattern of thought, emotion and behaviour has become automated, it no longer feels to us as if we are doing it.

For example, while we may intellectually know that any act of speaking is something we do, what we say can sometimes take us by surprise and not quite feel as if we did it. Another common example is that of intending to drive to a friend's house only to find oneself in the parking lot at one's workplace. While you may know that you drove the car to the wrong place, it doesn't quite feel like it was you because it was done through automatic patterns of behaviour.

For physical actions, such as speaking and driving cars, we generally know that we are doing it, even if it feels like it wasn't us. However, when it comes to more subtle actions such as interpretation and organisation of our ongoing experience, we may not recognise the effects of our automated patterns as the result of our own action at all.

For example, we will often feel that we simply perceive other people's emotions and intentions directly. We are oblivious to the process of deduction through which we constructed that perception. The same is true for many of our own emotional reactions. We are often so oblivious to the processes through which we create our own emotional reactions that it appears as if they are created by outside circumstances alone.

Forgetting that we create and enact the automatic patterns that shape our experience is, in a sense, a form of alienation from our own agency. We don't recognise how we participate in the creation of our experience when the patterns through which we do so are automatic and unconscious.

The Knot of Alienation occurs when our automated patterns produce problems. Because we are oblivious to the patterns in us that produce the problems, we take them to be a purely external phenomenon, and by addressing these problems as purely external phenomena, we divert our attention away from the true source and, thus, undermine our possibility of solving them.

Thus, the Knot of Alienation is a characteristic of all the previously described knots.

Positive reification of Being (the automatic pattern) leads us to grasp for reified aspects of Being, which further diverts our attention away from Being itself (the problem). Negative reification of Being (the automatic process) leads us to turn away from the very thing we seek (the problem).

Because we don't recognise the things we try to grasp or avoid as the result of our own acts of reification, we continue to grasp and avoid – and we continue to fail.

If we recognise our own agency and become aware of the process of reification, we will recognise that what we seek to grasp or avoid are mirages and that there is nothing to grasp and avoid beyond our own creations. We cannot *solve* the problems arising from automated processes of reification by improving our ability to grasp or avoid what we perceive. We can *dissolve* the problems by recognising the true nature of the things we seek to grasp or avoid.

Alienation from reality

Once we have become alienated from our own agency so that we see things we create as existing independently from our own actions, we begin to become alienated from the world as well. Our perception becomes increasingly at odds with reality. This alienation touches upon several key parts of our understanding of reality, such as:

- **Identity:** We come to regard Being, which is what we truly are, as something separate from ourselves, and we come to identify with our thoughts and emotions, which is not who we are.
- **Causality:** We come to see what we seek as caused by the very activity that takes us away from what we seek.
- **Value:** Being, which is positive, appears as negative, and our attachment to fulfilling certain conditions, which is negative, appears as positive.
- **Intention:** Once we have given Being negative names, we start feeling alienated from our own pursuit of Being. It will seem as if the part of us that is pursuing Being is pursuing self-destructive things.
- **Control:** What is our own doing seems beyond our control, and what is beyond our control seems to be our own doing.
- **Responsibility:** We deny responsibility for things that are of our making, and take responsibility for things we have no control over.
- **Nature of reality:** We come to see what is impermanent as permanent.

Thus, with The Knot of Alienation, we enter into the domain where everything is upside down. I will return to the link between the 5 Knots and these inversions of key concepts in Section 7.6.3.

Two types of issue

Forgetting that we create and enact the patterns through which we shape our own reality can lead to problems, either if the world around us changes causing the pattern to become inefficient or if the pattern we have developed contains a misconception, the effect of which is only revealed after prolonged use.

The first type of problem often arises when automatic patterns developed to deal with the childhood environment are ill fitting to deal with the environment one finds oneself in later in life, which may be very different from the childhood family environment.

For example, a client may have an automatic pattern of putting others' needs before their own. The client may have developed and automated this pattern because it was very effective in dealing with their childhood family environment where they needed to appease others and avoid conflict. However, later in life the client may find themselves in a different environment where the same pattern makes it difficult for the client to assert themselves.

The second type of problems often arises when the automatic patterns have unexpected side effects that are only revealed after the pattern has become automated.

For example, a client may notice that they feel good whenever they achieve something. For this reason, they develop the habit of setting and achieving goals and they enjoy the positive feelings that follow. While this seems like a perfectly reasonable pattern, it contains the misconception that the positive inner states are caused by achieving goals, when, in fact, the positive inner states stem from the perception of Being, which the client merely happens to pay attention to whenever they finish a project. The negative side effect of this misconception is the sense of being separate from Being. This side effect may only start to be felt after the pattern is firmly established and automated.

Bringing awareness to a client's automatic patterns and the core misconceptions they embody can be a bit of an archaeological work. Over the course of their life, a client will have built an elaborate layered structure of automatic processes. To bring awareness to the misconceptions embedded in processes in the deeper layers of this structure, it is necessary to gradually dissolve or temporarily pause the processes in the outer layers. However, the default mode of human development is to add, rather than dissolve, layers. Thus, it requires skills, on the part of the therapist, to ensure that the therapeutic work results in dissolving the part of the structure that produces problematic outcomes, rather than adding corrective processes to the structure[41].

5.2. The layered personality structure

Throughout life we continuously develop and automate new patterns of thought, emotion and behaviour, and new patterns build upon previously established patterns.

For example, early in life, children learn to link certain symbols called letters with certain sounds. Once such links have been established, children can proceed to learn about words and sentences and various literary traditions. For example, it is only possible to compare The Magic Mountain by Thomas Mann and Ulysses by James Joyce because of myriad layered automatic processes through which we link letters with sounds, clusters of letters with words, and so on.

Similarly, early in life we learn to recognise certain combinations of felt sense and contextual cues in such a way that we can distinguish between different basic emotions. At some point, this becomes automatic, and we no longer think about this process. Instead, we simply know what emotion we feel. The ability to distinguish emotions enables us to develop links between other people's facial expressions and such emotions. In the beginning we might put an effort into making such links but over time making these links becomes automated. Once we automatically generate perceptions of both our own and others' emotions, we can proceed to learn about how different people's emotions interact. At some point, this may lead us to make automatic inferences about such interactions.

The creation and automation of new patterns typically arise as a response to challenges we face in our environment, helping us navigate and overcome these difficulties.

For example, when the infant sees something they find interesting, they learn to crawl and to reach out and grasp so they can get a hold of the object they want to explore. When the toddler wants to influence the parents' behaviour, they learn to, among other things, cry, gesture and speak. Similarly, when a young person

---

[41] In Section 7.5, we shall see that the automatic processes that produce difficulties in clients' lives are governed by beliefs in implicit memory. While much of therapy focuses on teaching clients strategies to help them manage the problematic effects of these beliefs, truly transformative therapy works by directly updating the beliefs stored in implicit memory, thus altering rather than managing the automated processes underpinning the problems.

experiences surprising and uncomfortable behaviour from other people, they learn to link certain facial expressions, body postures, tonalities and combination of words to certain emotional states and intentions in the other person. Learning to quickly and automatically make such links helps the youth overcome difficulties in navigating social interactions by making predictions about the future based on observations in the present and selecting appropriate courses of action.

Thus, our default response to encountering difficulties is to develop new patterns that can deal with these difficulties. However, sometimes, the difficulties we encounter stem from the automatic mental, emotional and behavioural patterns we have previously established. Because these patterns operate automatically, we often fail to recognise that the difficulties they generate are the consequences of our own actions. Consequently, when an automated pattern creates difficulties, our response tends to be to create *additional* patterns to tackle these problems, rather than to *dissolve or change* the pattern causing them.

For example, a client may have a pattern that automatically interprets their own energy as "aggression" and as something they need to repress. This pattern causes the client to have problems with setting boundaries and going for what they want in life. To deal with these problems, the client may practice being more assertive, pushing themselves to set clear boundaries and to go for what they want. However, this new pattern is created to deal with a self-inflicted problem. Thus, the client is running more automated patterns than is necessary. This is not energy efficient. A much better solution would be to change how the client interprets and relates to their own energy in the first place. Doing so would help the client reclaim their natural capacity for setting boundaries and going for what they want.

When we continuously add layers of patterns, each dealing with the unintended negative consequences of the previous, the result will be a structure which is permeated and defined by the misconceptions embedded in the foundational patterns. This structure is what we refer to as our personality structure.

Dissolving vs. adding layers to the personality structure in therapy

The goal of Being-Centred Therapy is to reverse the process of adding layers to the personality structure, and instead bring awareness to and re-evaluate the established patterns layer by layer until the client becomes aware of their initial misconceptions and corrects them. In other words, Being-Centred Therapy aims to change the cornerstones of the edifice that is our personality, weeding out the misconceptions upon which the client's current structure is founded.

To achieve this, the therapeutic process must dissolve or pause automatic processes and, in this way, clear the way for the client to become aware of the foundational patterns of their structure.

It is important to know that any therapeutic technique can result in either dissolving layers which are creating problems for the client (which is desirable) or in adding layers in an attempt to mitigate the problems created by such layers (which is not desirable).

For example, the therapeutic technique of inviting a client to embrace the energy of their repressed anger can either result in the client ceasing to repress this energy and learning to benefit from it by recognising their misconceptions about the nature of this energy (dissolving a layer), or in the client attempting to produce substitute anger and energy to compensate for the problematic absence of the genuine energy resulting from the automatic repression (adding a layer).

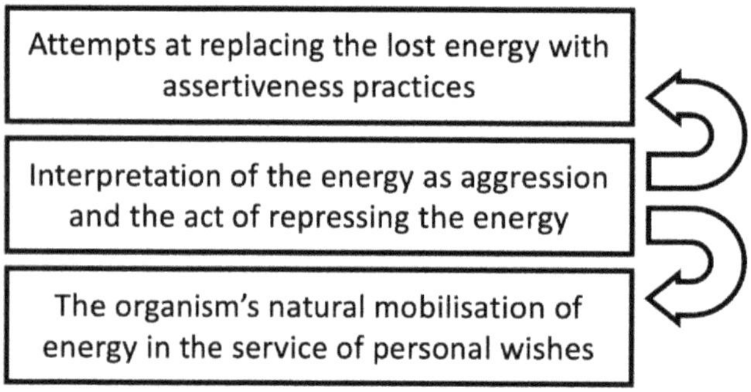

Figure 16: Adding vs. dissolving layers of personality

Dissolving and adding layers can, on the surface, look very similar, as the added layers will typically be a kind of imitation of what the client would have experienced had they dissolved the problematic patterns.

For example, if the client seeks to embrace their anger without dissolving the automatic pattern of repression, they may engage in actions they *associate* with anger, such as raise their voice, become dismissive of others, withdraw, attack others, vent, rant or even seek retaliation. Such actions may, at first glance, appear as genuine expressions of anger. However, insofar as such actions are responses to the absence of energy the client feels because they repress their true anger, they are likely to be out of touch with both the situation and the client's own true feelings. Thus, if the client does not dissolve their automatic repression of their anger, their attempts at embracing anger are likely to result in a pushy and tense assertiveness. Such assertiveness is a poor substitute for the free flow of life energy that would result from dissolving the patterns that lead the client to repress this energy.

This distinction between dissolving layers of the personality structure and adding layers to it is core to working with the patterns that prevent a client from perceiving various aspects of Being.

For example, negative reifications lead clients to turn their awareness away from Being. As a result, clients will feel the ensuing absence of awareness of Being as a problem. When clients are unaware that this problem is of their own making, they will develop patterns seeking to overcome the problem by generating what they perceive is missing. The result will be imitations of the experience of Being.

Only when the client recognises their own agency and sees clearly the pattern through which they create the negative phenomenon they are facing, do they have the possibility of setting aside this pattern and discovering Being itself. Thus, recognising one's own agency is key to dissolving rather than adding layers to one's personality structure.

The personality structure as obstacle and as guide

Insofar as the personality structure is based on the misconception of our fundamental separation from Being, it becomes an obstacle to becoming aware of Being.

However, since one of the main self-inflicted problems that clients are trying to deal with by adding new layers to their personality structure is their inability to perceive Being, a major part of clients' personality structures will consist of imitations of the experience of Being.

One may even go as far as to say that the very personality structure that entraps us, is a picture of the awakened state in which we are free.

This is important because it shows that a client's personality structure is not only something to dissolve, so as to regain awareness of Being.

A client's personality structure is also something very helpful as it contains hints that can help the client get a sense of what they are looking for.

It is true that once you feel Being, the personality's imitation will feel like a very poor substitute. However, it still has great value as a guide.

Personality is to Being like a menu is to the food at a restaurant. Even if the menu is a poor substitution for the food, it can still be a good guide.

In Being-Centred Therapy, we must on the one hand be discerning with respect to whether our therapeutic interventions dissolve or add personality layers and on the other hand learn to read the personality structure as a guide to the therapeutic process.

5.3. Alienation from the 10 aspects of Being

In Sections 2.3, I introduced the 10 aspects of Being and some typical positive reifications of each aspect. In Section 3.1, I expanded the model with some typical ways in which clients seek to create or acquire the positive reifications of each aspect of Being. In Section 4.2, I further expanded the model with some typical negative reifications of each aspect of Being that arise as a consequence of the ways in which clients seek to create or acquire Being

As outlined above, negative reifications of aspects of Being can lead to the formation of unconscious habits of avoiding these aspects. Such avoidance will lead to a more or less permanent loss of awareness of the affected aspects of Being and will be perceived by the individual as a loss of that aspect.

In Table 14, I provide examples of how clients typically reify the loss of awareness of each of the 10 aspects of Being depending on their previous positive reifications of the same aspect. For example, if a client perceives the tender and delicate state of the Green aspect of Being as "compassion", they are likely to experience the loss of awareness of this aspect as a feeling of hardness and coarseness, which they may call "indifference". Similarly, if a client perceives the light and bubbly state of the Yellow aspect of Being as "joy", they are likely to experience the loss of awareness of this aspect as heaviness and staleness, which they may call "depression".

The words in the table should be taken as examples that illustrate the principle. The words clients use to name the sense of loss vary. For many of the examples in the table, the words in the last column can be used to describe the experience of the loss of several of the positive reifications of a given aspect of Being listed in the second column. For example, "confusion", "vagueness", "slow-wittedness", "blurriness", and "lostness" could, in principle, all be used to denote the loss of "clarity" a client may experiences when they turn their awareness away from the Blue aspect of Being.

Table 14: Alienation from the 10 aspects of Being (Essences)

Essence	Positive reification	Reification of loss
White	Support	Betrayal. Precariousness
Solid	Grounding	Existential anxiety. Ungroundedness
Firm	Confidence	Performance-anxiety. Inadequacy
Heavy	Patience	Lack of self-control
	Neutrality	Entanglement. Disquiet.
Red	Strength	Weakness
Vibrating	Courage	Cowardess. Fear
Expanding	Passion	Deadness. Apathy
Warm	Vitality	Fatigue. Dullness
	Authenticity	Separation-anxiety. Inhibition. Phoniness
Black	Peace	Disturbance. Invasion
Still	Non-attachment	Agitation. Restlessness
Slow	Mastery/Power	Powerlessness
Empty	Sacredness	Profanity. Defilement
	Absolution	Impurity. Sin
Green	Compassion	Indifference
Tender	Loving-Kindness	Harshness. Hard-heartedness
Delicate	Connection	Rejection. Isolation
Moist	Sympathy	Callousness
	Agape Love	Insensitivity
Pink	Appreciation	Unappreciation
Soft	Acceptance	Exclusion
Fluffy	Lovable/loving	Cynicism
Plump	Perfection	Defectiveness
	Cosiness	Detachment. Coldness
Yellow	Joy	Depression
Light	Happiness	Dejection
Bubbly	Carefreeness	Worry
Uplifting	Curiosity	Lack of interest
	Spontaneity	Drudgery. Tediousness. Lack of inspiration
Gold	Bonding	Conflict. Isolation
Sweet	Community	Alienation
Viscous	Romantic love	Loneliness
Honey-like	Unity	Fragmentation . Agitation
	Surrender	Control issues
Cream	Nourishment	Deprivation
Full	Satisfaction	Disappointment
Creamy	Fulfilment	Hollowness
Smooth	Wholeness	Incompleteness
	Contentment	Discontentment
Blue	Clarity	Confusion
Sharp	Precision	Vagueness
Clear	Intelligence	Slow-wittedness
Wakeful	Discernment	Blurriness
	Guidance	Lostness
Clear	Freedom	Confinement. Feeling Trapped
Open	Openness	Closed-mindedness
Vast	Receptivity	Imperviousness
Spacious	Trust	Distrust
	Benevolence	Malice

With the addition of the typical reifications of the perceived loss of the different aspects of Being, the model is complete. The full model and other useful resources can be found at www.the5knots.com/resources.

5.4. The Logical Categories of Learning, Agency and Belief

The Knot of Alienation arise when automatic and unconscious processes in us create something that we later take to be unpleasant facts of life, not recognising our own agency in the creation process.

However, the Knot of Alienation can be found on two qualitatively different levels.

On one level, it is possible to automatically choose to deal with a particular situation in ways that have unintended consequences. For example, when someone try to improve the performance of a team by pointing out all mistakes and this practice ends up demoralising the team members and, thus, hurting rather than enhancing performance. Similarly, a parent might set strict rules at home to instil discipline in their children, but this approach can lead to a lack of open communication and trust, making children less likely to share their problems or concerns.

On another level, it is possible to automatically choose to *classify* a situation in a way so that the set of behaviours we have for dealing with "that kind of situation" does not include any useful options. For example, an individual may classify another person's feedback on a project as "a personal attack", causing them to deal with the situation by choosing between various forms of defence strategies, none of which allows the individual to profit from the feedback. Similarly, an individual may classify a negotiation with another person as "a win/lose situation" and, consequently, limit themself to deal with the situation by choosing between different strategies for winning over their opponent, making them blind to potential win-win scenarios, which may be better than any scenario where they win over their "opponent".

On these two levels, the concept "agency" will relate to two qualitatively different kinds of choice.

On the first level, "agency" refers to the individual's ability to choose which action to take in a given situation. We can call this "first-order agency".

On the second level, "agency" refers to the individual's ability to choose between different ways of classifying the situation, which, in turn, determines which set of actions they are able to choose from when dealing with the situation. We can call this "second-order agency".

While the choices we make using first order agency determine what reactions we get from the environment, the choices we make using second order agency shape the world we ourselves react to. For example, choosing to criticise team members as a way of enhancing their performance can result in negative reactions from those team-members, while choosing to see feedback as personal attacks shapes how the situation in which the feedback is delivered, i.e. that to which we react, appears to us.

While bringing awareness to first order agency can be an important part of therapy, the focus in this chapter is on bringing awareness to second order agency, as this is both more difficult and has more far-reaching effects on clients' lives.

The distinction between first- and second-order agency presented above is an extension of the work of Gregory Bateson (Bateson, 1972c), who applied the Theory of Logical Types developed by Alfred North Whitehead and Bertrand Russel (Whitehead & Russell, 1927) to the process of learning. In the following, I will briefly introduce the Theory of Logical Types, Bateson's application of this theory to the phenomenon of learning and my own extension of Bateson's theory to the phenomena of agency and belief in therapeutic work.

5.4.1. The Theory of Logical Types

The Theory of Logical Types, in a nutshell, states that no class can be a member of itself. The class of chairs is not a chair. The name for something is not that something. Whereas this may seem obvious, human beings, including scientists, constantly commit the logical error of making statements where they categorise a category together with members of the category. The result of doing so is the creation of a paradox. For example, we may ask:

> "If the barber in a city shaves all men who do not shave themselves, does the barber shave himself?"

This statement creates a paradox The paradox arises because the statement improperly treats the class of 'all men who do not shave themselves' as if it can include itself. Here, the barber is both a member of 'all men' and the designated shaver of those men, leading to a logical loop: if he shaves himself, he no longer fits the category of men he shaves, yet if he doesn't shave himself, he must be shaved by someone—namely, himself. This circular reasoning violates the theory of logical types, which requires that we keep a clear separation between categories and their members to avoid self-referential contradictions.

Whitehead and Russell call this the 'vicious circle fallacy' because of the way the reasoning loops back on itself, creating a trap that blocks any logical resolution. The 'vicious' element lies in how this circular structure leads the mind in endless cycles of contradiction, preventing clarity and productive thought[42].

By applying the theory of logical types, we can avoid conceptual confusion, make clearer distinctions in our reasoning, and recognise when an apparent paradox is actually a miscategorisation of types or levels within a logical system.

5.4.2. Logical categories of learning

Bateson proposed that learning implies a process of change and that, since change can occur on different logical levels, we must distinguish between different logical categories of learning.

Bateson explains these logical categories of learning by referring to the concepts of position, velocity and acceleration in physics, where velocity is a change in position and acceleration is a change in velocity. In the same way, Bateson proposes to distinguish between different categories of learning, where each category refers to a change in the previous category.

Below, I will briefly describe each of the four categories of learning Bateson proposes.

Zero-order learning

The most basic level of learning is change in behaviour in reaction to a stimulus in the environment, such as when a person blinks automatically in response to a sudden bright light. Bateson calls this level of learning “Learning 0” or “zero-order learning”. While most people might feel that this level of learning hardly qualifies as learning, we do use the word “learn” to refer to the process of receiving information from the environment. We may, for example, say, “I learned from the bell that it was lunchtime”. In this example, the individual does change their behaviour (going for lunch) in reaction to an external stimulus (the bell). However, the same external stimulus will always bring about the same behavioural response.

---

[42] The 20 misconceptions outlined in this book can be understood as logical fallacies that create paradoxes which are experienced as suffering.

First-order learning

The next level of learning, “Learning 1” or “first-order learning”, is change in Learning 0. It involves a change in the way the individual reacts to a stimulus in the environment. This is what is commonly referred to as trial-and-error learning. For example, a child might touch a hot stove once, feel pain, and learn to avoid touching it in the future. Similarly, a student may experiment with different study techniques – such as reading aloud, making notes or using flashcards – in search of the method that helps them retain information most effectively. This is what most people associate with learning: We change our behaviour and evaluate the results to optimise outcomes.

Second-order learning

The next level of learning, “Learning 2” or “second-order learning,” is change in Learning 1. It involves a change in the set of actions we choose from in Learning 1, produced by a shift in how we classify or structure the stimuli we respond to[43].

To understand this, it’s essential to recognise that, in reality, we are never exposed to the exact same stimulus twice, as no two stimuli are ever completely identical. However, as part of learning to navigate our environment, we create categories that allow us to perceive similar stimuli as repeated exposures to the same type of event. For example, no two eggs are exactly the same, but they are similar enough for us to perceive each instance of boiling an egg as a repetition of the same event. This enables us to learn how to boil eggs to our liking by adjusting our method with each consecutive attempt.

If we could not classify different experiences as the same kind of experience, trial-and-error learning would be impossible, as no situation would ever truly repeat. Consequently, we would only have one opportunity to respond to each unique situation.

Thus, second order learning is about changes in how we classify and structure the ongoing flow of experience into a string of repeated situations, which we can learn to deal with through trial-and-error learning, selecting from the set of actions relevant to the way we have classified these situations.

---

[43] Bateson uses the phrases “categorise experience”, “classify experience”, “structure experience” and “punctuate experience” interchangeably.

Second order learning appears as phenomena

One reason we confuse first- and second-order learning is that the categories that arise from second-order learning can appear to us as phenomena within our experience, even though they are simply names for our ways of organising this experience.

To understand this, it can be instructive to consider personality traits. We generally think of personality traits as behavioural patterns that characterise a particular individual, thus placing traits in the same logical category as other characteristics of a person, such as height, weight, eye colour, etc.

Bateson, however, claims that this is inaccurate, arguing that personality traits are not behavioural patterns but rather names for the ways in which we organise experience. He points out that there is a deep ambiguity in any behaviour, which allows us to classify the same behaviour in many different ways, each of which fundamentally changes the meaning of the behaviour and, consequently, the personality trait it indicates.

To illustrate this point, consider a conversation like the following:

- A: It will take for ever to put in these all these screws.
- B: Yes. Doing it with a regular screwdriver is a bit “last century”. I have a cordless electric screwdriver you can borrow.
- A: Thank you very much. I’ll give it back to you when I’m done.

It is possible to classify this conversation as A requesting help, B providing help and A expressing gratitude. If we classify the conversation in this way, A appears humble and grateful, while B appears competent and helpful.

It is, however, also possible to classify this conversation as A pointing out a problem and demanding a solution, B complying, and A rewarding B's compliance. With this interpretation, A appears dominating and perhaps even judgemental, while B appears compliant and subservient.

There are many other ways to classify this conversation, each of which changes the character traits we perceive in A and B. This illustrates that character traits relate to how we classify behaviour and are, therefore, not behavioural patterns themselves. In other words, character traits and behavioural patterns belong to different logical categories and should not be confused.

Confusing logical categories of learning creates problems

Recognising that personality traits are names for how we structure experience, rather than something inherent in individuals, can be used to illustrate how confusing different logical categories of learning can create problems.

For example, if we (mistakenly) believe that learning to be assertive is a first-order learning process (i.e. trial-and-error learning), we may try to become more assertive by adopting what we see as more assertive ways of reacting to different situations. We may, for example, start speaking louder in meetings, interrupt others to make our point, adopt a firmer tone or make more direct eye contact. However, because "assertiveness" is a personality trait, it is a name for how we structure our experience. In other words, learning to be assertive is a second-order learning process. Learning to be assertive is not about adopting new behaviours; it is about learning to structure one's experience differently.

If we adopt assertive behaviours without changing the way we structure our experience, we will end up feeling like an aggressive underdog – not an assertive person – because, while we may classify our actions as "assertive", we still classify the situations we are in in such a way that we appear as a non-assertive person. We may, for example, see other people as commanding and ourselves as defying those commands, which will make the other person the assertive or dominant individual and ourselves the rebellious underdog.

Similarly, a therapist may assume that the reason a client does not notice when other people appreciate them is that they lack self-love. This would imply that something is lacking in the person and that this lack causes them to overlook other people's appreciation.

However, not noticing when others appreciate them is part of how the client organises their experience, and, as we have seen above, personality traits such as "lack of self-love" are also names for the ways the client organises their experience. Thus, in this example, the proposed cause and effect are one and the same. The therapist's proposition is analogous to saying "the client does not love themselves because they lack self-love", which is an empty tautology.

Recognising when phenomena are names for the ways clients organise their experience is important because it helps us avoid introducing superfluous concepts into therapy. If we fail to recognise phenomena as names for the ways clients organise their experience, we may end up chasing ghost-concepts, such as self-love, instead of focusing on bringing awareness to the mechanisms that generate the client's experience and to their own agency.

In the above, I have focused on how personality traits are not behavioural tendencies in clients but rather names for the ways in which clients structure their experience.

The same can be said about the absence of positive states or the presence of negative ones. These phenomena are also names for how we structure our experience, and learning how to change them is not a matter of trial-and-error learning but rather of changing how we structure our experience.

Third-order learning

The next level of learning, "Learning 3" or "third-order learning", is a change in Learning 2. As such, it can be said that the present chapter is about how to facilitate third-order learning, since becoming aware of one's active participation in second-order learning implies the potential for change in the processes that produce second-order learning.

Bateson proposes that, while rare, third-order learning can occur in psychotherapy or spiritual transformation. Since personality traits are names for second-order learning, we must look for third-order learning in contexts where individuals experience a profound transformation of character.

However, merely finding instances where individuals change how they structure their experience does not provide evidence of third-order learning. For third-order learning to occur, the individual must learn something about how such change is brought about, so that consecutive instances of second-order learning occur more quickly. In other words, third-order learning must result in individuals becoming more skilled in engaging in second-order learning. Once again, this is precisely the objective of the techniques in this chapter.

The link between spiritual development and third-order learning is also evident in other ways. Bateson writes:

> "[learning III] must lead to a greater flexibility in the premises acquired by the process of Learning II —a freedom from their bondage. [...] But any freedom from the bondage of habit must also denote a profound redefinition of the self. If I stop at the level of Learning II, "I" am the aggregate of those characteristics which I call my "character." "I" am my habits of acting in context and shaping and perceiving the contexts in

> which I act. Selfhood is a product or aggregate of Learning II. To the degree that a man achieves Learning III, and learns to perceive and act in terms of the contexts of contexts, his "self" will take on a sort of irrelevance. The concept of "self" will no longer function as a nodal argument in the punctuation of experience." (Bateson, 1972b, p. 310)

In this quote, we recognise a common theme in spiritual teachings, namely, the dissolution of the "self". It is a testament to Bateson's genius that he is able to show how this esoteric phenomenon emerges as a natural consequence of thinking with logical clarity about the phenomenon of learning.

Furthermore, the above suggests that the more flexible one gets in terms of how to classify or organise one's experience, the more fluid one's sense of self becomes. In other words, the so-called "ego death" mentioned in various spiritual traditions is a consequence of third-order learning and, as such, it can never be achieved through second-order (trial-and-error) learning.

5.4.3. Logical categories of agency and beliefs

Bateson's logical categories of learning can be extended to logical categories of agency and beliefs. For the purpose of this book, it is particularly relevant to distinguish clearly between first- and second-order learning, agency, and beliefs.

First-order learning (trial-and-error learning) is about change in how the individual reacts to a certain situation. Thus, first-order agency can be defined as the individual's involvement in choosing between different possible actions, and first-order beliefs can be defined as beliefs about which action will bring which results.

Second-order learning is about change in how the individual categorises or structures their experience. Thus, second-order agency can be defined as the individual's active involvement in choosing between different ways of categorising or structuring experience, and second-order beliefs can be defined as beliefs about how experience should be structured and categorised.

The concept of second-order agency is central to this chapter.

In the Sensing Agency process, the approach used to untie the Knot of Alienation, there is a step called Elucidating Agency (see Section 5.6.3). This step focuses on making clients aware of their own agency in relation to creating the absence of positive states and the presence of negative ones. For this step, I present ten techniques, all of which aim to help clients become aware of how they structure their experience and how this structure creates the issues they are struggling with.

The reason clients often feel they have no agency in these situations is that the agency they possess is second-order, rather than the more familiar first-order, agency.

The concept of second-order belief is central to the final chapter of the book.

In the final chapter, I look at ways of working with deep-seated beliefs by first formulating these beliefs and then providing experiences that contradict them. While this is fairly straightforward with first-order beliefs, it is far more difficult with second-order beliefs.

For first-order beliefs, a contradictory experience simply must show that there is a discrepancy between what a client *expects* to be the result of a particular action and what the result of the action *actually* is.

This, however, is not possible for second-order beliefs because a belief about how to structure experience or classify a situation cannot be proven false by the facts of an event. For example, a client may classify any situation involving conflict as a threat to their well-being. This second-order belief can persist regardless of the actual impact of any given conflict on their well-being. If the conflict has a negative impact, it confirms that conflicts are threats; if it does not, the client may conclude that they managed to avoid the threat, which also does not contradict the belief that conflicts is threats. Furthermore, the distress caused by viewing conflict as a threat may indeed negatively affect the client, reinforcing the original classification of conflicts as threats to well-being. This example also illustrates how the self-confirming nature of second-order beliefs derive from the vicious circle fallacy, where the categorisation becomes part of what is categorised: Categorising conflicts as threats is part of what is threatening about conflicts.

Thus, for second-order beliefs, a contradictory experience must show that the way the client structures their experience has negative consequences and that a different way of structuring experience can mitigate these negative consequences. Alternatively, a contradictory experience may demonstrate that the client's habitual way of classifying a situation leads them to select their response from a set of actions that are all unhelpful, whereas a different way of classifying the situation allows the client to select from a different set of actions that include effective options.

Yet another method for producing experiences that can contradict second-order beliefs is the creation of double-binds, which highlights how the way clients structure their experience results in paradox. I sometimes refer to this technique as "short-circuiting" the client's logic. Bateson refers to this as "closing the loopholes" individuals use to retain belief in their way of structuring experience despite any paradoxes, thereby avoiding third-order learning.

The 20 misconceptions in this book can be understood as second-order beliefs related to ways of structuring experience that cause suffering – or, more precisely: suffering can be understood as a name for ways of structuring experience expressed in these 20 misconceptions.

Now that I have introduced how alienation results from automation (Section 5.1), how attempting to address problems created by automated processes leads to the formation of a layered personality structure (Section 5.2), how loss of awareness of the 10 aspects of Being can be reified as particular negative phenomena (Section 5.3), and how to distinguish between first- and second-order agency and belief (Section 5.4), it is time to look at the three misconceptions related to the Knot of Alienation.

5.5. The Knot of Alienation and implications for therapy

The Knot of Alienation can be broken down into three interrelated misconceptions about causality and personal agency. These misconceptions arise from the previous twelve misconceptions.

When we believe that we are separate from the states we seek (positive reification) and that we, therefore, must do something to create or acquire them (conditionality), it will appear as if the absence of positive states is natural and not something we are involved in producing (misconception 13). Similarly, when we believe that certain inner states can be negative in themselves (negative reification), it will appear as if negative states can occur without our involvement in their creation, either as a natural part of the human condition or a natural consequence of external circumstances (misconception 14).

To untie the Knot of Alienation the therapist must take clients through lines of inquiry that help them realise for themselves their own involvement in the creation of their present-moment experience[44]. In particular, clients must realise

[44] The physicist and spiritual teacher David Bohm aptly calls this the development of proprioception of mind (Bohm, 1990). Proprioception is the sensory awareness and perception of the body's position, movement, and orientation in space, which enables individuals to know when something they perceive in their environment is caused by the movement of their own body. Bohm encourages us to develop a similar sense of the movement of our own mind, so that we may

that when they do not feel a positive state, it is not because it isn't there, but rather because they are turning their awareness away from it (corrective principle 13). Similarly, clients must realise that negative states are caused by their own interpretation of conditions and circumstances, not by the conditions and circumstances themselves (corrective principle 14).

Recognising our own participation in the creation of an experience where positive states seem to be absent and negative states present, increases our sense of agency. This is important because if an undesired experience is *not* of our own creation, we can only change it by *doing* something, and this requires us to use extra energy. If, on the other hand, an undesired experience *is* our own creation, we can change it by *ceasing* doing something, and this will free up energy.

While most clients overtly express a wish to increase their sense of agency and have more control in their life, they will often simultaneously wish to place the responsibility for their predicament with external circumstances, thus separating agency and responsibility (misconception 15). However, an inherent aspect of realising the full extent of one's agency is to come to terms with the fact that increased agency inevitably comes with increased responsibility (corrective principle 15).

The first two misconceptions are fundamentally the same, namely that clients are involved in the creation of their undesired inner states – the difference being whether the client conceptualises an undesired inner state as the absence of a positive state (e.g., the absence of meaning) or the presence of a negative one (e.g., the presence of meaninglessness). Nevertheless, it is useful to distinguish between these two situations, since the way the client conceptualises the undesired inner state has implications for how to untie the Knot of Alienation and re-establish awareness of Being.

5.5.1. Misconception 13: Not feeling a positive state means that it is absent

The first of the misconceptions related to the Knot of Alienation is the belief that if you do not feel a particular positive state, it is because the absence of this state is natural and that you are not involved in the creation of this absence.

This misconception is a consequence of the previous misconceptions, which lead us to perceive aspects of Being as positive phenomena separate from ourselves

---

recognise when aspects of our present-moment experience are caused by the activity of our own mind.

that require an active effort to create or acquire. From this perspective, the absence of any of these positive phenomena is simply the natural state that requires effort on our part to change. Consequently, the absence of a positive state is a given, not something created by ourselves.

Clients will express this belief by saying: "I've lost my joy", "I don't have any purpose in life", "There is no intimacy in my relationship", "I can no longer feel peace", "I don't have any love for myself", and "Nothing gives me satisfaction". All these sentences express the belief that some positive phenomenon is absent and describe the client as playing a passive role.

To understand how the above sentences are expressions of the belief that the absence of positive states can occur naturally without the client's active involvement, it can be useful to contrast them with sentences that express the opposite belief, namely, that the client *is* involved in the creation of the absence of a positive state. Examples of such sentences could be: "I'm pushing away joy", "I'm ignoring purpose in my life", "I avoid intimacy in my relationship", "Since the event, I no longer pay any attention to peace", "I down prioritise love for myself", and "I'm feeling down because I don't value satisfaction". These sentences also express the belief that some positive phenomenon is absent but, contrary to the former statements, these statements describe the client as playing an active role.

Insofar as the positive phenomena we are dealing with here are positive reifications of Being, they are always present. They cannot be absent. Thus, if a client is not feeling a positive phenomenon, they *must* be actively diverting their attention away from it. In other words, if positive phenomena are always present, we cannot lose them, we can only lose awareness of them, and the reason we lose awareness of them is that we actively direct our awareness elsewhere. Thus, what we experience as a loss of something due to lack of the necessary action to retain it, is, in fact, due to actively turning our awareness away from it. In short, we do not *passively* lose positive states, we *actively* ignore or avoid them.

However, when the act of diverting attention away from a positive phenomenon has been automated as an unconscious habit, it will appear to the client as if they are not doing anything and that the positive phenomenon simply isn't there.

As we have discussed in the chapter on the Knot of Negative Reification, one common reason clients turn their awareness away from a positive inner state is that it doesn't seem relevant to a particular agenda they are pursuing.

For example, a client may be very concerned with creating or acquiring a sense of security by working hard and building up a fortune. The aspect of "joy" may not seem relevant for this particular agenda. Therefore, the client will ignore "joy". Consequently, joy will seem to be absent from the client's life. However, since "joy" is an aspect of Being, it isn't actually absent from the client's life. It only appears to be because the client is consistently ignoring it.

Another common reason clients turn their awareness away from a positive inner state is that they interpret it as something negative they need to avoid.

For example, a client may interpret the vitality aspect of Being as aggression. For this reason, they will actively avoid this aspect whenever they become aware of it. Consequently, vitality will seem to be absent from the client's life. Since vitality is an aspect of Being, it isn't actually absent from the client's life. It only appears to be because the client is consistently avoiding it.

Thus, when a positive state appears to be absent from a client's life, it is a consequence of something the client did (turning their awareness away from it), not a consequence of something the client didn't do (failing to hold on to it).

Implications for therapy

In Section 3.3.3 on the 6th misconception, we explored how it is important for a therapist to understand that when a positive state seems absent in a client's life it is not because it is missing and must be created but because the client actively turned their awareness away from it.

The implication for therapy was that, rather than explore what a client should do to create or acquire a missing state, we should explore what the client is already doing that causes them to lose awareness of the state. In short, the overall question guiding therapy exploring the absence of a positive state should be:

> "How do you avoid noticing [the positive state]?"

In this section, we see that because the act of diverting attention away from the positive state can be an automated, unconscious habit, clients will often object to the notion that they are in any way involved in the creation of the experience of lack they are dealing with.

The implication for therapy is that to answer the above question, we must extend the client's sense of agency to include their automated, unconscious habits. This includes making clients aware of these habits.

This can be a challenge. While it is relatively straightforward to make clients aware of habits relating to overt, external behaviour, it becomes progressively more challenging to make clients aware of habits, as these relate more to internal behaviour. It is possible to make clients aware of habits pertaining to overt, external behaviour simply by mentioning the behaviour.

For example, a client may have a habit of twirling their hair while speaking. Even though they may be unaware of this activity, it is easy to point it out to them by mentioning it every time they twirl their hair. Once this behaviour is pointed out to the client, they will readily accept that this is something they do.

It is much more difficult to make clients aware of habits pertaining to internal behaviour, such as selective attention and ways of making sense of experience.

For example, a client may experience an absence of "joy", "happiness" and "carefreeness" because they consistently interpret inner states of lightness that form the basis of such positive states as "frivolity" or "superficiality" and, consequently, distance themselves from states of lightness. This is a habit, just like twirling one's hair is a habit, but because it is purely internal, it is difficult to point to it. The only sign that the habit is there, is the absence of positive interpretations of states of lightness, such as "joy", "happiness" and "carefreeness".

However, pointing to the absence of "joy", "happiness" and "carefreeness" will generally not convince the client that they are actively involved in creating this absence, since the client is likely to see the absence of such states as merely part of the natural order.

They may believe that happiness is absent from their life because it is not something they are interested in and, consequently, not something they put in any effort to create. They may believe that happiness is absent from their life because they haven't achieved what they want to achieve in life. They may believe that happiness is absent from their life simply because they are not a happy person.

Whatever the explanation the client has invented to account for the absence of joy, happiness, and carefreeness in their life, the presence of such explanations makes it more difficult to point to the true reason for the absence. Clients are generally not interested in explanations for things they already believe they understand.

Thus, to expand a client's sense of agency to include their automated patterns, which makes them turn their attention away from certain aspects of Being, it is necessary to first "discredit" the client's explanations for the absence of positive states. We need to point to situations where the client's explanations contradict their experience and, in this way, undermine the client's belief in their explanations and trigger their curiosity. How to do this is the topic of Section 5.6.2 Step 2: Suggest Agency.

13th corrective principle: You are actively blocking positive states you do not feel

The 13th corrective principle of Being-Centred Therapy is:

> "If positive states are missing in your life, you are actively turning your attention away from these."

Bearing this in mind helps us empower clients and expand their sense of agency by revealing how they are creating their own suffering.

This principle also applies to common negative states such as jealousy, anger, hatred, sadness, envy and craving. While it may not be unusual to experience these states *infrequently*, their *complete absence* often indicates that the client has developed two automated habits that block awareness of positive states:

- The habit of interpreting a certain aspect of Being as a negative state (negative reification) – rather than as a positive state.
- The habit of consistently diverting attention away from the resulting negative reification to avoid the disturbance it creates.

A client may, for example, interpret the vital aspect of Being as "anger", judge this as a negative state, and then consistently divert their attention from this state, resulting not only in the absence of anger but also the absence of vitality.

Thus, noticing the absence of negative states can help us detect automatic patterns that block positive states.

5.5.2. Misconception 14: Circumstances directly cause negative states

Just like clients tend to believe that the *absence of positive states* is not their own doing, they also tend to believe that the *presence of negative states* is not their own doing. This is the second misconception related to the Knot of Alienation.

This misconception is the flipside of the previous misconception in that clients sometimes will conceptualise the absence of a positive state as the presence of a negative one. Absence of "meaning" can be seen as presence of "meaninglessness". Absence of "value" can be seen as presence of "worthlessness". Absence of "support" can be seen as presence of "lostness". As the flipside of the previous misconception, it too is a consequence of previous misconceptions.

Clients will typically express the belief that they are not involved in the creation of the presence of negative states by saying things like: “I feel worthless when I fail to meet other people’s expectations”, “My partner makes me insecure”, “My new job stresses me out”, “The bad weather makes me feel down”, “Being stuck in traffic frustrates me”, “Not having enough money makes me unhappy”, “Being around people who criticise me lowers my self-esteem”, “I feel depressed because I lost my job”, “I feel unimportant because my boss does not give me enough recognition”, “I feel lonely because I spend so much time on my own”, or “Bad news ruins my mood”. Such sentences describe the presence of negative inner states while simultaneously portraying the client as playing a passive role.

The above statements fall into two categories depending on what the client believes is the cause of the negative state – other than themself.

Some of these statements indicate that the client believes that the negative state is part of the default human condition and that the reason they feel it is because they have failed to do what is necessary to overcome this default state.

For example, if a client believes they feel worthless because they have failed to meet someone else’s expectations, we may deduce that the client sees themself as worthless by default and that they believe the way to change this is to meet other people’s expectations. Often this will be a part of a more general belief that human beings are worthless unless they contribute something that is recognised as valuable by other people.

This is a misconception insofar as the sense of value is an aspect of Being and, as such, it is always present. When the client is not feeling value, it is not because they haven’t contributed anything others deem valuable but rather because the client’s concern with how other people perceive their contributions takes their attention away from Being.

Other statements indicate that the client believes that the negative state is the consequence of certain external circumstances.

For example, if the client believes they feel insecure because of something their partner is doing, we may deduce that the client sees a direct causal relationship between their partner’s actions and their sense of insecurity, and that they believe the way to change their sense of insecurity is to change their partner’s behaviour.

This is a misconception insofar as the sense of security is an aspect of Being and, as such, it is always present. When the client feels insecure, it is not because their partner is instilling this feeling in them but rather because the client's concern with their partner's behaviour, and the potential meaning and consequences of this behaviour, takes their attention away from Being.

Implications for therapy

In the previous section, we saw that when clients experience an absence of positive states, we must ask how they manage to avoid noticing something that is always present.

In the same manner, when clients experience negative inner states, the question guiding the therapy should be:

> "How do you create the feeling of [the negative state]?"

In the previous section, we also saw how clients will invent explanations for the absence of positive states and that an important task for the therapist is to discredit such explanations and, in this way, enable the client to re-examine the situation and discover the automated and unconscious habits through which they create the perceived absence of a positive state.

In the same manner, an important part of therapy is to undermine the client's belief in negative states as part of the fundamental human condition or as a direct consequence of certain external circumstances. How to do so is the topic of Section 5.6.2 Step 2: Suggest Agency.

14th corrective principle: You actively participate in the creation of negative states

The 14th corrective principle of Being-Centred Therapy is:

> "If you experience negative states in your life, you are actively involved in the creation of these."

Bearing this in mind helps us empower clients by revealing to them that they have some measure of control over negative states they otherwise believed were out of their control.

This does not mean clients should ignore external circumstances that negatively affect their lives. There are often valid reasons to make changes, but avoiding a negative inner state shouldn't be the driving force. For example, if a client is in an abusive relationship, it's important to change the dynamic or leave the relationship. However, believing the reason for making such changes is that the partner's actions create negative inner states in the client, such as worthlessness or unhappiness, is problematic. The problem is that such a belief most likely contributed to the client staying in the relationship, because if the client believes their partner creates the negative states, they will also believe that positive states depend on the partner, making it harder to leave. In other words, the client may want to leave to avoid the negative states but stays because they don't want to lose positive states. The key is to recognise that they participate in creating their own inner states – independently of their partner.

5.5.3. Misconception 15: Agency and responsibility are independent.

The third misconception related to the Knot of Alienation is not so much a misconception as a conflict between two common preferences that often go unnoticed, but which can emerge when working with the Knot of Alienation.

It is common to prefer greater agency in one's own life, since greater agency means greater control and the potential for shaping one's life to one's liking.

It is also common to prefer to blame the unpleasant aspects of one's life on external circumstances.

These two preferences are incompatible. If we control it, we also bear responsibility for it.

Claiming to be in control of something but not responsible for it is a common fallacy. For example, a client may exercise agency by choosing a partner based on specific criteria they believe are indicative of a good match. However, if the relationship becomes troubled or ends, they may blame their partner's behaviour or external stressors, not considering that their own actions or choice of partner may have been contributing factors to the relationship's problems. Similarly, a parent may be in control of making important decisions in their child's upbringing, from educational choices to extracurricular activities. However, if the child struggles academically or socially, the parent blames the school system, the child's peers or the child itself, instead of reflecting on how their parenting choices may be contributing to the child's struggles. Both examples show how individuals can seek to be in control without recognising the responsibility this brings.

Similarly, claiming to be responsible for something you are not in control of is another common fallacy. For example, parents often feel responsible for their adult children's life choices, feeling guilt for their failures or pride in their successes, even though these outcomes are largely due to the children's own decisions and actions beyond the parents' control. Similarly, an activist may feel personally responsible for societal issues such as poverty or inequality, committing themselves to solve these complex problems, even though they are systemic, multi-faceted and far beyond any individual's control. These examples illustrate how individuals can feel responsible for something they cannot be responsible for since it is beyond their control.

To remedy such fallacies, it is good to see responsibility as a function of control. Either you have neither control nor responsibility, or you have both control and responsibility.

When undoing the Knot of Alienation, clients come to realise that they have far greater agency in their own lives than they thought. However, to embrace this agency also means embracing responsibility. This can give clients pause for various reasons.

Some clients are unwilling to accept that they have participated actively in creating the suffering in their lives, while other clients worry about whether they can live up to the responsibility. Such issues are important to address if they emerge during the work with the Knot of Alienation.

Implications for therapy

It is important for therapists to be aware that increased agency and increased responsibility are two sides of the same coin because it can help them be prepared if the client, during the work with the Knot of Alienation, begins to reject their emerging agency to avoid the related responsibility. Clients may resist accepting any perspective that increases their sense of agency, not because they disagree per se but rather because they are uncomfortable acknowledging the implied increased responsibility.

Seeing that you create your own suffering is a two-edged sword.

On the one hand, it is great news because if you need to put in an effort to create and maintain your suffering, you can escape it simply by ceasing to put in this effort.

On the other hand, accepting that you create your own suffering can lead you to berate yourself for being stupid and self-destructive and, consequently, having suffered needlessly.

It is, therefore, important in therapy to give clients a way of acknowledging their own agency without this leading to useless self-criticism.

The way I usually do this is by emphasising that just because we are creating a situation doesn't necessarily mean that we have a choice. We learn how to deal with life from a family and a society that offer us limited knowledge. We take the best tools for interpreting and engaging with life from among those that are presented to us. It is unfair to berate ourselves just because we don't invent a millennia's worth of psychological and spiritual insight on our own and in spite of being submerged in a social setting characterised by the kind of misconceptions described in this book. The knowledge presented in this book is not something any individual can be expected to develop without guidance.

Thus, even though much of our suffering is indeed of our own doing and we act out of ignorance about the nature of reality, it is not our fault. We do not do this out of negligence or malicious intentions. We are not in control of what automated habits we form throughout life. The best we can do is to learn to continuously revise and upgrade the way we perceive and interact with ourselves and the world whenever higher quality knowledge becomes available to us.

Making this clear is key to enabling clients to acknowledge the increased levels of agency and responsibility that will allow them to engage in the exploration of how they partake in the creation of their own suffering, without getting stuck in useless self-beratement for not having discovered these things earlier.

15th corrective principle: Increased agency comes with increased responsibility

The 15th corrective principle is that

> "Increased agency comes with increased responsibility."

Bearing this in mind can help us understand why clients may resist acknowledging their agency in relation to the creation of absence of positive states and presence of negative ones. It can also help us offer clients ways of avoiding useless self-criticism as they expand their sense of agency.

5.5.4. Summary

In the above, we have seen that the Knot of Alienation relates to three interconnected misconceptions. We have also seen how awareness of these misconceptions and their corresponding corrective principles can inform therapeutic interventions.

Table 15 summarises the misconceptions and corresponding corrective principles related to the Knot of Alienation.

Table 15: Misconceptions and corrective principles related to the Knot of Alienation

Misconceptions	Corrective Therapeutic Principles
The absence of positive states is natural	You are actively blocking positive states you do not feel
The presence of negative states is natural	You actively participate in the creation of negative states
Agency and responsibility are independent	Increased agency comes with increased responsibility

Table 16 summarises the differences between the questions that guide traditional and Being-Centred Therapy.

Table 16: How understanding the Knot of Alienation changes the questions guiding therapy

Traditional therapy questions	Being-Centred Therapy questions
How can you create the positive state you are missing?	What do you pay attention to instead of the positive aspects of Being – and why?
How can you change the circumstances that cause you negative states?	How do you participate in the creation of negative states?
How can the client attain more autonomy and agency in their own life?	To what degree is failure to recognise one's agency and participation in the creation of one's own experience motivated by avoiding responsibility?

So far, we have looked at the Knot of Alienation, three misconceptions related to this knot and three corresponding corrective principles that can guide therapy.

In the following section, I will describe in detail a therapeutic process aimed at untying the Knot of Alienation. This process is called Sensing Agency because it aims at helping the client discover the automated and unconscious patterns through which they create and maintain the absence of positive states and the presence of negative ones.

This perspective may be conceptually clear from reading the above (or similar texts). However, it is possible to understand how every individual participates in the creation of their own suffering conceptually, without this conceptual understanding changing anything about how we perceive Being, life and ourselves. To engender such change, we need to go beyond conceptual understanding to direct experience, and let this experience update the beliefs that govern our behaviour. This is the goal of the process of Sensing Agency.

5.6. Sensing Agency – how to untie the Knot of Alienation

The Knot of Alienation consists of three interlinked misconceptions which make the absence of Being appear as the natural order of things by obscuring the way clients actively create this apparent absence by turning their attention away from Being.

Taking the absence of Being as the natural order of things, clients are compelled to engage in actions to remedy the situation instead of ceasing the activity through which they are creating the absence. In this way, clients end up fighting their own creations.

The Knot of Alienation can be untied by elucidating clients' agency. Seeing that the state they take to be a natural state is, in fact, their own creation, makes it possible for the client to revise the patterns through which they create the experience of absence of Being and, thus, address the heart of their suffering.

The Knot of Alienation can be untied through the five-step process of Sensing Agency.

1. **Recognise the Knot of Alienation:**
   The first step is to recognise situations where clients see the absence of positive states or the presence of negative states as a natural consequence of the human condition, their own personality or external circumstances.
2. **Propose agency:**
   The second step is to suggest to clients that they are involved in the creation of the state they dislike. This can be done with an embedded question or through various challenges to clients' belief in the naturalness of the state.
3. **Deconstruct the "natural" state:**
   The third step is to map out how clients create unwanted states in themselves through the automatic and unconscious ways they select what elements of their experience they pay attention to, and organise these elements into meaningful structures.
4. **Understand motivation:**
   The fourth step is to develop an understanding of why clients have developed and held on to automatic processes that produce unwanted states. This can be done by asking them to reflect on whether these processes are motivated by hidden benefits or obsolete strategies for dealing with the childhood family environment. One particularly interesting option is that the unwanted states can function as a parental surrogate that clients turn to for various forms of support.
5. **Correct misconceptions related to the Knot of Alienation**
   The fifth and final step is to round off the process by summarising it in ways that challenge the misconceptions related to the Knot of Alienation by affirming clients' own involvement in creating the absence of positive states and the presence of negative ones, and by clarifying questions of agency and responsibility.

In the remainder of this chapter, I will describe how to facilitate the Sensing Agency process in one-to-one sessions as well as in groups through a series of contemplation exercises. Figure 17 provides an overview of the process.

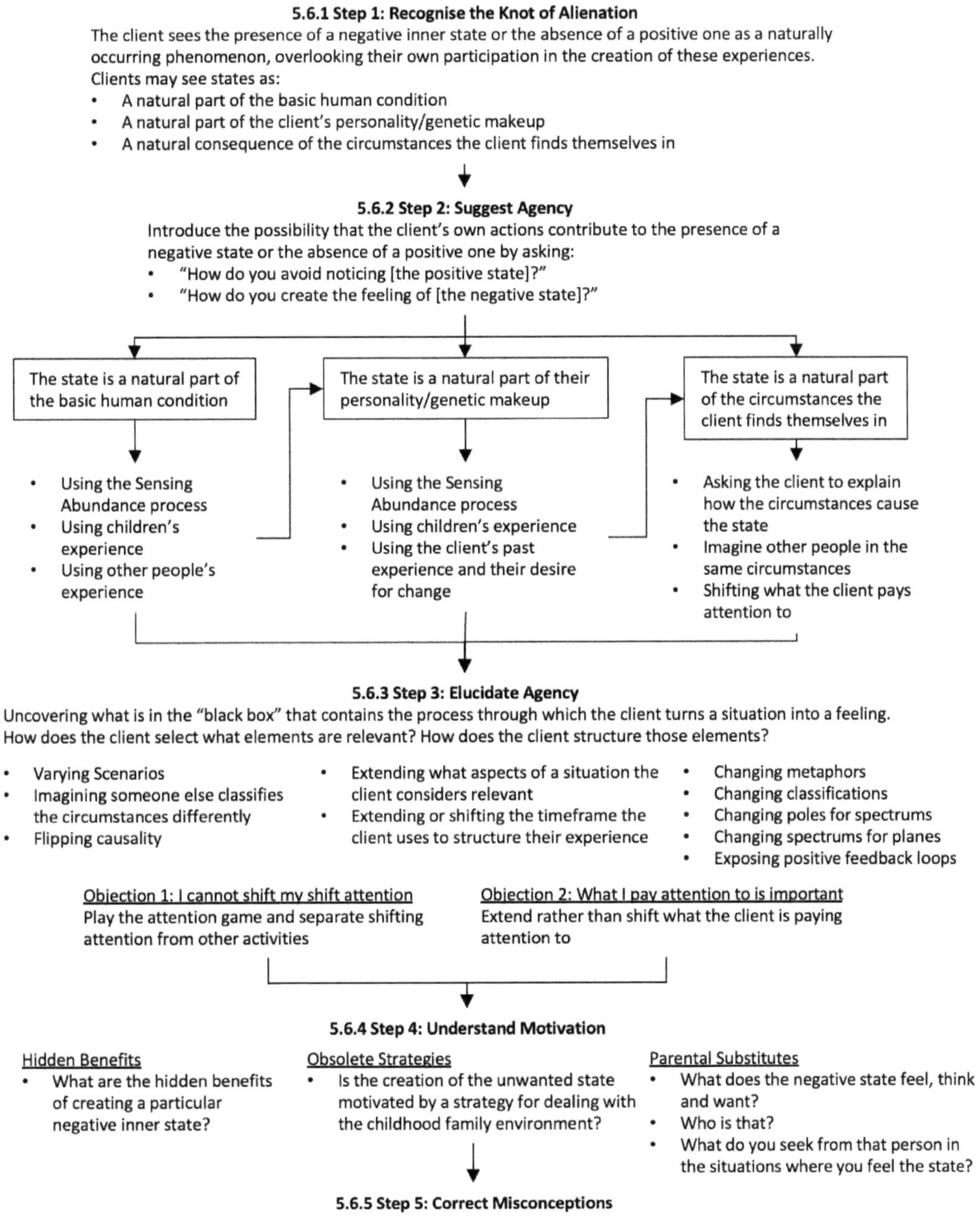

Figure 17: The Sensing Agency process

5.6.1. Step 1: Recognise the Knot of Alienation

The first step in untying the Knot of Alienation is to detect it by listening for phrases indicating that the client sees certain *undesired experiences as naturally occurring phenomena*, thus overlooking their own participation in the creation of these experiences.

There are two types of "undesired experiences":

- The absence of a positive state, such as love, vitality, meaning, peace, or connection
- The presence of a negative state, such as loneliness, neediness, anger, sadness, anxiety or agitation.

There are three ways clients typically explain undesired experiences as "natural" phenomena over which they have no influence. They may see them as:

- A natural part of the basic human condition
- A natural part of their personality/genetic makeup
- A natural consequence of the circumstances they find themselves in.

Despite their seeming plausibility, these explanations are generally inaccurate. They are examples of what psychologists call confabulation. Confabulation is the phenomenon that human beings fabricate plausible sounding explanations for events they do not understand. Clients do not understand that their undesired experiences stem from how they direct their attention. Instead of acknowledging this lack of understanding, they invent seemingly reasonable but ultimately false explanations for the undesired experiences, such as the above.

In the following, I will give examples of each of these three typical but false explanations of undesired experiences.

The client's undesired experience as a natural part of the basic human condition

When clients see an undesired experience as a natural part of the basic human condition, they may say things like:

- "I feel lonely because human beings are fundamentally alone. We are born alone, and we die alone. That is just a fact."
- "Life is fundamentally meaningless. People who seek meaning in religion or work are people who cannot handle that fact."
- "It is just human nature to be lazy. No one does anything unless they must."

- "We are all animals. So, whether we like it or not, humans are fundamentally aggressive."
- "Life is hard."

Clients who believe that undesired states are part of the fundamental human condition will often regard such beliefs as "the harsh reality" and see anyone who does not agree as someone who cannot handle the truth.

Someone who believes that humans are fundamentally alone may, for example, regard the human need for community as a need to avoid facing the fact of one's fundamental aloneness in the universe.

Likewise, an individual who believes that human nature is inherently aggressive and self-serving may perceive acts of love, compassion, or selflessness as either idealistic attempts to suppress one's true human nature or as strategies employed by people to protect themselves from other people's aggression, by adopting a submissive and non-threatening demeanour. They may see notions of civility as efforts to deny the reality of human aggression.

It is true that people sometimes avoid difficult feelings in themselves by clinging on to positive beliefs about the fundamental nature of humans and the human condition. However, claiming that negative states, such as aloneness or aggression, are fundamental to the human condition suffers from the same problem as claiming that positive states, such as togetherness or love are fundamental. Whenever we take a concept and define it as opposite another concept, we split the world in two, and this very splitting of the world into two categories is an act of human creation. Thus, whether we claim that connection and love or aloneness and aggression are fundamental to the world, we overlook our own participation in terms of the invention of such opposing concepts. We overlook that if we use a particular set of categories, and not some other possible categories, we can no longer be talking about the fundamentals but only about what something looks like within the constraints of the framework we have created and chosen to use[45].

---

[45] When I write that the aspects of Being correspond to positive states, it doesn't mean that Being *is* like that, only that when we experience Being and make sense of that experience using our conceptual systems, we often fit the experience into the categories that correspond to positive inner states. This is positive reification.

Thus, while undesired experiences may be part of the human experience, claiming that you feel certain undesired states because they are part of the basic human condition and that you have nothing to do with the creation of these states, is inaccurate.

The client's undesired experience as a natural part of their personality

When clients see a state as a natural part of their personality, they may say things like:

- "I'm just a moody person. I was born that way. It is in my genes."
- "I'm just not a courageous person."
- "I'm a glass half empty kind of person."
- "I'm a self-critical person."

Personalities, whether moody, cowardly or something else, are made up of mental, emotional and behavioural patterns, which are ultimately enacted by the individual. Thus, saying that something is your personality does not make it a natural state that is beyond your involvement. You may create the state through mechanisms that are beyond your conscious control. But they are still your creation. When your eyes are dry, you blink. This happens automatically but it is still you who are doing it. In the same way, you may be a person who frequently experiences states of moodiness and/or anxiety. Even though such states may be generated automatically, it is still you who are generating them.

This distinction is important because it reveals the possibility of transformation. In the same way that you are capable of pausing automatic bodily movements, such as blinking, you are capable of pausing automatic personality patterns, which can give you a glimpse of what is truly natural in the sense that it is not created by you, namely Being. And such experiences can transform your automatic personality patterns.

Thus, claiming that you feel certain undesired states because they are part of your personality, and that you, therefore, have nothing to do with the creation of these states, is inaccurate.

The client's undesired experience as a natural consequence of circumstances

Sometimes, clients see a state as a natural consequence of the conditions they find themselves in. They believe anyone in those conditions would feel what they are feeling. In such cases, clients may say:

- "I don't feel any love because my partner doesn't give me any compliments."
- "Public speaking makes me anxious."
- "People who drive slower than the speed limit make me angry."
- "The city stresses me out."
- "My manager's criticism makes me feel unappreciated."

Statements of this kind are so common that we often readily accept the causal relationship between circumstances and personal inner states they imply.

However, it is not possible for external circumstances, such as lack of compliments, public speaking, slow driving, cityscapes or criticism, to generate inner states in an individual, such as feelings of love, anxiety, anger, stress, or underappreciation.

Feeling such states in specific external circumstances requires the individual's own participation. The reason an individual feels a lack of love when they do not receive compliments from their partner is that this individual is doing something with the lack of compliments. First, they may assume that the lack of compliments is a sign that their partner does not love them. Next, they may tell themselves that their partner doesn't love them because they are unlovable. Then, they may become angry about seeing themselves as unlovable and blame their partner for this feeling – even if they themselves generated it by interpreting their partner's actions in a particular manner. At this point, the individual's attention is so occupied with the drama created by their own interpretations that they may have lost awareness of Being, in particular the loving aspect of Being. That is why they feel no love. It is, of course, nice when couples give each other compliments and the absence of compliments may or may not indicate something about the partner's feelings. However, the point of the above story is to show that the lack of love is not created purely by the external circumstances but that the individual is deeply involved in the creation of this inner state.

There are, of course, certain external circumstances that can affect an individual's inner state. But these are much fewer than we tend to believe. A good way of testing whether an inner state is truly caused by external circumstances is to ask whether the state is dependent on the individual's understanding of the situation. Ingesting certain chemicals can, for example, alter an individual's inner state. Such changes will not depend on the individual's understanding of the situation; thus, this is an example of external circumstances directly influencing an individual's inner state. In contrast, if an individual does not understand compliments as a sign of love, then receiving no compliments couldn't make this individual feel a lack of love. This shows that lack of love is not the direct consequence of receiving no compliments. Rather, it is the consequence of how an individual makes sense of this absence of compliments. And it is precisely this act of sense-making that constitutes the individual's involvement in the creation of their inner state in the given circumstances. Similarly, public speaking cannot make someone anxious unless they understand public speaking as a situation in which other people might judge them in ways that can have negative consequences.

Another litmus test that can determine if there is a direct causal link between certain circumstances and an individual's inner state is to ask the question whether it is possible to imagine another individual in the exact same circumstances experiencing a different inner state. If this is the case, it shows that the way the individual makes sense of the situation contributes to the creation of the inner state. For example, it is likely that most people (given they have an intact nervous system) will feel pain if they are poked by a sharp object. Thus, in this case the external circumstance of being poked by a sharp object does indeed create an inner state of pain. However, it is easy to imagine a person who will not become angry when someone in a car in front of them drives slower than the speed limit, someone who will feel excited, rather than anxious, in big cities, and someone who will be unruffled when receiving criticism from their manager. This shows that the causal links between circumstances and inner states suggested in the three examples above are false.

In short, it is incorrect when a client claims that certain undesired states are the *natural* consequence of the circumstances they find themselves in, and that they, therefore, have nothing to do with the creation of these states.

Naturalness vs. curiosity

The main problem with seeing an inner state as natural is that it shuts down the client's curiosity. If an inner state is fully explained by referring to human nature, personality or external circumstances, there is no reason to explore the client's own participation in the creation of the state. Thus, seeing an inner state as natural can make clients believe they have no part in the creation of their inner state when, in fact, they do. It can make clients lose sight of their own agency.

The challenge of shared alienation

The main difficulty therapists face when they seek to detect the Knot of Alienation is that they may suffer from the same alienation as their client. What seems natural to the client may also seem natural to the therapist. If this is the case, the therapist will also not be curious about why the client is feeling what they are feeling. If a therapist believes that it is human nature to be aggressive, they will not wonder why their clients feel aggressive. They will simply assume their clients are feeling what all humans are feeling. Consequently, they will not ask questions that can elucidate the client's own participation in the creation of the state of aggression. Similarly, if a therapist believes that certain behaviours in intimate relationships are inherently hurtful, they will not wonder why a client feels hurt when their partner exhibits such behaviour. Consequently, they will fail to ask questions that can elucidate how the client's sensemaking processes contribute to the client's inner state. In short, they will fail to recognise the client's agency in relation to their own inner state.

Once again, this is one of the reasons it is so important that therapists have done a substantial amount of inner work themselves as this will cultivate curiosity in them, leading them to question what others take for granted.

5.6.2. Step 2: Suggest Agency

Once you have detected a Knot of Alienation, the next step in the Sensing Agency process is to introduce the idea that the client is actively involved in the creation of the problematic part of their experience – even if they believe they are not.

It is worth dwelling on this part of the process as it requires skill to introduce an idea that the client is likely to perceive as somewhat at odds with reality. It may seem obvious to the therapist that the client is involved in the creation of their difficult inner states. However, if the client sees these inner states as a natural aspect of the human condition, a natural part of the personality they were born with or a natural consequence of their circumstances, then suggesting that they are creating these states may sound to the client as strange as if the therapist suggested that they are creating gravity or the changing seasons.

Introducing the idea of the client's agency can be done by first asking the client to recall a concrete situation where they experienced the inner state they see as problematic – whether they conceptualise it as the presence of a negative inner state or the absence of a positive one – and then asking the client a question that presupposes their active involvement in the creation of the problematic inner state.

If the client perceives the undesired experience as the presence of a negative state, which is part of the human condition, you can ask:

> "How do you create the feeling of [negative state]?"

If the client perceives the undesired experience as the absence of a positive state, you can ask:

> "How do you avoid noticing [positive state]?"

Sometimes, clients will directly accept the suggestion embedded in these questions, despite its strangeness, and begin to explore how they create the undesired experience. In that case, you can go directly to the third step of the Sensing Agency process and map out the process through which the client creates their inner state. This step is described in Section 5.6.3 Step 3: Elucidate agency (deconstructing the "natural" state).

However, frequently clients will object to the suggestion and instead maintain their default belief that the undesired experience they struggle with is natural, and that they have no part in creating it.

In such cases, the therapist will have to ask the client questions that make the client start doubting their view of the state as natural and, thus, open them to the possibility that they may, in fact, be involved in the creation of their undesired experience.

In the following, I will offer a few potent ways of casting doubt upon the naturalness of difficult states. I will treat the three ways of seeing the inner states as natural, described in the previous section, separately.

The client's undesired experience as a natural part of the basic human condition

The belief that an undesired state is part of human nature is both the strongest belief and the belief that is easiest to cast doubt on.

It is the strongest in the sense that seeing an undesired state as part of fundamental reality strongly discourages the client from asking what can be done to change it. Such questions will appear as futile as asking what can be done to change gravity or death.

It is also the easiest to cast doubt on because it is a universal generalisation and, as such, all that is required is a single counter example from the life of any person. If any person at any time in their life experienced a positive state, then the absence of this positive state cannot be a fundamental part of the human condition.

Similarly, if any person at any time in their life experienced the absence of a negative state, then the presence of this negative state cannot be a fundamental part of the human condition.

In the following, I will outline three ways of challenging the belief that an undesired state is a fundamental part of the human condition.

Using the Sensing Abundance process

One way of providing a counter example to the belief that an undesired state is part of the human condition is to ask clients to describe in detail what state they would like to feel. If you succeed in guiding the client to describe the state in such a way that they start to feel it, this experience reveals that it is possible to feel the state and that its absence, therefore, cannot be a fundamental part of the human condition.

Using children's experience

For some states, such as joy, happiness, worth and friendliness, it can be powerful to point out that small children naturally feel these things. This shows that the absence of these positive states cannot be part of the fundamental human condition but rather the absence of the state must derive from the client having learned to avoid it.

Using other people's experiences

Finally, you can use the experience of other people (real or imagined) to provide counter examples to the idea that the presence of a negative state or the absence of a positive one is a fundamental part of the human condition. You can ask the client whether they can imagine anyone for whom the negative state the client feels would not be a prevalent part of their day-to-day experience or if they can imagine anyone who has frequent experiences of the positive state the client feels is absent. If they can imagine such a person, or if they know such a person in real life, this reveals that the client's belief about the nature of the human condition is false.

When presented with counter examples to the belief that a particular undesired state is a general part of the human condition, clients will sometimes shift from claiming that their undesired experience is a fundamental part of *everybody's* experience to claiming that it is a fundamental part of *their personal* experience. In other words, they transition to the second way in which clients conceive of an undesired state as natural, namely seeing it as caused by their own personality.

The client's undesired experience as a natural part of their personality

The belief that an undesired state is a natural consequence of the client's personality is a reduced version of the belief that it is part of the human condition.

It is easier for the client to defend a generalisation that "only" pertains to the client's own life instead of the life of all human beings.

Consequently, the therapist has fewer ways to challenge this belief. While asserting that an undesired state is a universal part of the human condition can be countered by referring to *any person's* contrary experience, disproving that it's caused by the client's personality requires finding a counter example from the client's own life.

The belief that an undesired state is natural and unavoidable because it is caused by the client's personality can be questioned in three ways.

Using the Sensing Abundance process

As above, asking the client to describe the state they long for in detail until they feel it, will demonstrate that their personality does not preclude them from experiencing something other than the undesired state.

Using children's experience

If the client agrees that children have a different experience from the client, it is possible to suggest that the client must have felt what all children feel at some point in their life, and that the undesired state they are presently feeling must, therefore, be something they have learned to create – not something they were born with.

If the client says they always felt the way they feel now, you can ask the client to reflect on the truth of this statement by going further and further back in life.

Usually, the claim becomes absurd at some point. It is, for example, difficult to imagine a new born baby feeling tired of life, meaninglessness or loneliness. Such emotions require a certain amount of adult thinking that the infant does not possess.

Using the client's past experience and their desire for change

A way of providing a counter example to the belief that the absence of a particular positive state is an immutable part of the client's personality is to ask the client whether they can remember a time when they did feel this positive state.

If the client says they can remember feeling the state, this shows that the absence of the state is not a fixed part of their personality.

If the client says they have never felt the state, you can point out that if they had truly never felt it, they wouldn't be able to long for it. Thus, the fact that the client is unhappy about the absence of the state reveals that they must have felt it at some point, and by inference the state cannot be a fundamental part of the client's personality.

This line of inquiry can, of course, also be used to refute the belief that an undesired state is a fundamental part of the human condition.

When presented with counter examples to the belief that a particular undesired state is caused by the client's own personality, clients will sometimes shift from this belief to the belief that the undesired state is caused by certain *circumstances* in the client's life. In other words, they transition to the third way in which clients conceive of an undesired state, as being natural.

The client's undesired experience as a natural consequence of circumstances

The belief that an undesired state is a natural consequence of the circumstances the client finds themselves in is a reduced version of the belief that it is caused by the client's personality.

The belief that an undesired state is caused by circumstances can be questioned in three ways.

Asking the client to explain how the circumstances cause the state

One weakness of this belief is that claiming that external circumstances are the sole cause of an undesired state assumes a concrete mechanism that is independent of the client's way of understanding the situation.

An example where circumstances do, indeed, cause an undesired state is when someone causes someone else pain by pinching them. In this case, there is a physical mechanism (the squeezing of nerve ends) that is independent of the client's way of understanding the situation, which explains the link between the circumstances and the undesired state.

In most cases relevant to therapy, no such mechanism exists. There is no mechanism that is independent of the client's understanding of the situation that explains how a mean comment can cause states of sadness or inadequacy, how the lack of presents from a partner can cause states of feeling unappreciated or worthless, or how failing to achieve a goal can cause a state of self-doubt.

When the client fails to provide a satisfying account of the mechanism through which the circumstances cause the undesired state, they will start doubting whether the circumstances do cause the state.

Sometimes, this exploration will reveal that the mechanism does indeed involve the client. Such cases offer the opportunity for a smooth transition to the third step of the Sensing Agency process of mapping out how the client creates the undesired state in the particular situation.

Imagining other people in the same circumstances

Another weakness of the belief that an undesired state is caused by circumstances is that it, once again, is a universal generalisation. If certain circumstances cause certain states, this should be true for all people.

Thus, a simple way of challenging the belief that the undesired state is caused by circumstances is to ask the client if they can imagine another person who would feel differently in the same circumstances. If the client can think of such a person, this shows that the inner state depends, not only on the circumstances, but also on the person experiencing these circumstances. This means that the client must contribute to the creation of their undesired state.

If the client accepts this conclusion, you can proceed to the third step of the Sensing Agency process and inquire how the client creates the undesired state in the given circumstances.

Shifting what the client pays attention to

A third way of "undermining" a client's belief in the causal link between external circumstances and an undesired inner state is by asking them to pay attention to an aspect of the situation they would normally not pay attention to, and observe how doing so changes the way they feel in the situation.

For example, a popular advice given to people who feel anxious about public speaking is to imagine the audience in their underwear. For many people this does, indeed, change how they feel about public speaking.

If paying attention to something in the situation they would normally not pay attention to (e.g., the audience's underwear) changes the client's feeling of anxiety to some other feeling, it is possible to conclude that the anxiety is not caused by the circumstances themselves but rather by what part of the circumstances the client is paying attention to.

In other words, seeing that changing what you pay attention to changes how you feel, reveals that the feeling is created by how you use your attention and not directly by the circumstances.

The techniques for mapping out how a client creates their undesired experience, described in the next section, can help you develop the skill to propose effective shifts of attention that can demonstrate how clients contribute to the creation of the undesired experience by the way they chose to use their attention.

When presented with counter examples to the belief that a particular undesired state is caused by particular circumstances, clients will usually be ready to explore their own participation in the creation of the undesired state.

In case they are not, it is worth considering doing the fourth step of the Sensing Agency process before step three, i.e., to explore what might be the client's motivation for creating the undesired state before mapping out how they do it.

5.6.3. Step 3: Elucidate agency (deconstructing the "natural" state)

Once the client has accepted the idea that they are (or at least "might be") involved in the creation of an undesired experience, such as the presence of a negative inner state or the absence of a positive one, you can start mapping out the process through which the client creates this undesired experience.

At the start this process will appear as a black box. Certain situations come in at one end of the box and certain inner states come out at the other end.

The techniques for elucidating agency can be seen as techniques for opening the black box and seeing how clients create undesired inner states through automatic and unconscious acts.

The acts through which clients create their inner experience are mainly acts of selecting what elements of their experience they pay attention to and acts of organising these elements into meaningful structures.

Becoming aware of the details of the processes in the black box is important as it will strengthen the client's recognition of their own agency in relation to creating their experience and it will reveal to them exactly what acts they must change to cease creating the undesired inner experience. In the following, I will describe a range of techniques for elucidating agency. These techniques can all be seen as techniques for engaging the third-order learning which illuminates second-order agency and beliefs as described in Section 5.4.

Varying scenarios

When mapping out the process through which clients create an undesired state in themselves, it is a good idea to begin by clarifying under what conditions the client engages in this process. This will give us an idea about the acts of selective attention the client uses to create their undesired inner states.

Unfortunately, clients' ideas about when they experience the undesired state are often very unclear. This lack of clarity is problematic when mapping out the process that leads to the undesired state. It is equivalent to seeking to understand the process that results in a loaf of bread coming out of the oven nice and risen or collapsed without knowing what was in the dough or the oven's temperature.

One way of clarifying the conditions that initiate the process in the client that produces a specific undesired inner state is to present the client with a series of scenarios where you explore how varying a single element at a time affects the client's experience. Often this means substituting a more abstract term in the client's description of the circumstances they believe cause the undesired state in them, with various concrete examples of that term.

A client may, for example, say that they feel unloved when their partner compliments someone else. Thus, the client sees the undesired experience of being unloved as a consequence of a particular external circumstance.

At first glance the external circumstance may seem well-defined: The partner giving someone else a compliment. However, "compliments" and "someone else" are rather abstract terms and the client says nothing about the circumstances in which the compliments are given.

Thus, to clarify what conditions starts the process in the client that results in feeling unloved, you can start by generating scenarios where you test the impact of different kinds of compliments, the impact of whom the compliments are given to and the impact of different circumstances under which the compliments are given.

To help the client, you can offer two contrasting scenarios at a time and ask if there is any difference in how they feel about these two scenarios.

In the above case you can ask:

- Does it matter whether the compliment pertains to personal or professional qualities?

- Does it matter whether the person your partner compliments is a man or a woman?
- Does it matter whether the person your partner compliments is married or single?
- Does it matter whether the person your partner compliments is a friend of both you and your partner or only of your partner?
- Does it matter whether the compliment is given in public or in private?

As the client answers these questions, they will become clearer on what precisely triggers the process in them that ends with the creation of the feeling of being unloved.

They may, for example, discover that compliments only bothered them when they are:

- Given *publicly*
- Pertain to *personal qualities*
- Given to *unmarried* women
- Given to woman the client has *no personal connection* to.

You can then proceed to inquire whether the client feels differently about the scenario where the client's partner gives such compliments both to others and to the client, and the scenario where the client's partner only gives such compliments to others.

If there is no difference in these two scenarios, the starting point may indeed be hearing these compliments given to others. If the client feels unloved in the second scenario but not in the first, the starting point isn't the compliments the partner gives to others but rather the absence of compliments the partner gives to the client – and compliments to others merely remind the client of this absence.

If the client introduces new concepts as a way of clarifying the circumstances under which they feel the undesired inner state, these concepts can be exposed to the same process of clarification.

The client may, for example, discover that the compliments that bother them are compliments that are intimate. However, "intimate" can mean many different things. Therefore, scenarios in which the term intimate is replaced with concrete examples of intimacy can help shed further light on what precisely triggers the process in the client through which they create the feeling of being unloved.

Which variations are most illuminating will vary greatly, depending on the situations the client describes. However, it is useful to think about varying the following dimensions:

- The client's own actions
- Other people's actions or intentions
- The consequences of the client's actions
- Social/cultural norms
- The context (work, leisure time, with or without other people, in public, in private, etc.)
- Demographics of the people involved (gender, educational level, age, occupation, etc.)
- The type of relationships between the people involved (partner, friend, family, stranger, boss, employee, etc.)
- Individual words in people's utterances
- Aspects of people's body language

While this process of clarifying the starting point for the process through which clients create undesired inner states doesn't elucidate the process itself, it is still important because it provides a good foundation for the work with elucidating agency. Furthermore, it can itself generate valuable insights for the client.

Imagining how someone else classifies the circumstances differently

As mentioned in the section on Step 2: Suggest Agency, a powerful way of demonstrating the client's own involvement in the creation of their experience is to ask them to reflect on how someone very different from themselves might classify the circumstances differently.

This technique is also a great way of excavating the specific acts of classification through which the client generates the undesired inner state they experience in the situation.

The reason the client believes their feelings are created by the circumstances they find themselves in, and not by their own actions, is that they consistently classify these circumstances in a particular way and, thus, are consistently creating the same inner states in those circumstances.

By reflecting on how someone else might classify the circumstances differently and, consequently, feel differently in the situation, the client may realise that it is their own acts of classification, and not the circumstances themselves, that cause them to feel in a particular way. Furthermore, the client may identify what specific acts of classification create the undesired state.

For example, if a client feels oppressed when someone else talks incessantly about themselves, you can ask the client how someone else might classify the situation and how they, consequently, might feel. In answering this question, the client may realise that someone else might classify the situation, not as oppressive, but as boring or rude, or something else.

Comparing their own classification with such a person's classification can show that the client feels oppressed by the incessant talking because they *classify* the way the other person talks as an act of oppression. If they instead classify the incessant talking as rude or boring, they may instead feel offended or put off[46].

Thus, simply imagining how someone else may classify the circumstances the client finds themselves in differently can be an effective way of elucidating how the client creates the undesired inner state by choosing a particular way of classifying the situation.

As mentioned in Section 5.4, there is never a single correct way of classifying circumstances. Talking incessantly about oneself can be accurately described as oppressive, rude and boring. The only difference between these classifications is that some will leave the client feeling worse than others – and possibly impede the client's possibility of acting in ways that enable them to achieve what they want in the situation.

Flipping causality

One important process clients use to create their inner states is the process of placing elements of their experience in causal relationships.

When clients believe that their inner state is created by external circumstances, they tend to believe that the nature of the circumstances causes them to pay attention to certain things and act in certain ways to mitigate the negative effect the circumstances have on their inner state.

However, this causal relationship is often backwards. Many times, it is precisely because the client pays attention to certain things and acts in certain ways that the external circumstances appear as they do.

---

[46] Session 7 gives an in-depth example of this way of elucidating the client's agency.

Thus, another way of elucidating the client's agency in situations where they believe their inner state is created by external circumstances is to flip the client's causality by suggesting that rather than the nature of the circumstances causing the need for the client to pay attention to certain things, it is the fact that the client fixates their attention on certain things that creates the apparent nature of the circumstances.

In short, flipping the causality means transitioning from the first to the second of the following ways of looking at the relationship between the client's interpretive actions and the situation they act within:

- I pay attention to X because the situation is Y
- The situation appears as Y because I pay attention to X

For example, a client may believe that giving a presentation is an inherently scary endeavour. For this reason, they need to pay attention to potential mistakes so they may avoid them. From this perspective, the situation creates a sense of anxiety in the client that can be mitigated by the client's acts. The client is not involved in the creation of anxiety – it is a natural product of the circumstances.

In this case, the therapist can elucidate the client's agency in relation to the creation of anxiety by suggesting that the causality runs counter to what the client believes. The therapist may suggest that giving a presentation appears scary *because* the client fixates their attention on preventing mistakes, not the other way round. If the client shifted their attention to, for example, focusing on finding meaningful ways of connecting with the audience, giving a presentation may appear exciting rather than scary. From this perspective, the client, not the circumstances, creates the state of anxiety. This state is no longer a natural product of the circumstances[47].

If the client believes the nature of their circumstances is given and causes them to use their attention in a particular way, the suggestion to shift what they pay attention to can seem to be at odds with reality.

If, on the other hand, the client believes their circumstances are not a given, they are free to explore the effect of paying attention to different aspects and noticing

---

[47] It is worth noticing that suggesting paying attention to different aspects of the situation is, in effect, a change in how the situation is classified: "A threat" vs "an opportunity for connection".

how doing so changes both how they feel in the situation and how they perceive the nature of their circumstances.

Flipping causality also allows the therapist to flip objections the client may have against using their attention in a specific way to arguments for why they should do so.

If, for example, a client says that they have to pay attention to avoiding mistakes because otherwise the audience will attack them, the therapist may say that the wish to avoid attacks from the audience is a reason *not* to frame the talk as a matter of delivering a flawless presentation but rather as a matter of connecting around the exploration of certain ideas. If the client does not set themselves up to deliver a talk with zero mistakes, they cannot be attacked for failing to do so.

In short, flipping the causality is a very good way to demonstrate how clients have agency in the sense that they can choose how to use attention and that such choices impact their experience of the situation.

Extending what aspects of a situation the client considers relevant

Clients often believe their inner state is created by external circumstances because they habitually pay attention to certain aspects of the situations they find themselves in, and not others.

To elucidate how clients' acts of paying selective attention to certain elements of their experience contributes to the creation of their inner states, it can be useful to invite them to extend what they consider relevant and pay attention to and notice how this can change the way they feel about a particular situation.

For example, a client who believes their sense of worthlessness is caused by the fact that their partner rarely gives them any gifts is most likely paying attention to how often their partner gives them gifts while ignoring other aspects of the relationship dynamic. If you ask the client to describe in detail the dynamic of their relationship with their partner, you might notice salient aspects of the relationship dynamic the client pays little attention to. For example, the partner may put a lot of effort into taking care of practicalities or offering emotional support. Asking the client to focus their attention on these aspects of the relationship may significantly impact, or even wholly dispel, the client's sense of worthlessness. This reveals to the client that the way they use their attention, rather than the external circumstances as such, is creating their negative inner state of worthlessness.

Focusing on what is not working and forgetting what is working is a very common way in which clients create negative inner states in themselves. Asking clients to pay attention to what is working can, therefore, be a powerful way of demonstrating how they contribute to the creation of their inner states through habits of selective attention.

It is worth pointing out that the goal of extending what the client pays attention to is not to determine what they should pay attention to in order to feel good. The goal is to help the client become aware of how their acts of selecting what to pay attention to contributes to the creation of their undesired experience, thus elucidating the client's own agency – in particular their second-order agency.

Extending or shifting the timeframe the client uses to structure their experience

Sometimes, clients believe their inner state is created by external circumstances because they habitually organise their experience into particular sequences of events. In particular, they organise their experience into events with clear starting and ending points.

To elucidate how the clients' acts of structuring their experience into meaningful sequences contributes to the creation of their inner states, it can be useful to invite them to extend their sequences to include earlier or later events and to notice how this can change the way they feel about a particular situation.

For example, a client may report feeling hopeless at work because every time they have solved a problem, a new problem arises.

From this report, we can deduce what the client's work must be like and how the client organises the experience of their work in meaningful sequences.

First, we can deduce that the client's work must consist of a continuous string of problems and solutions (see Figure 18).

the client solves a problem – a new problem emerges – the client solves the problem – a new problem emerges

Figure 18: An unorganised string of events

Furthermore, we can deduce that the client must organise this string of events into sequences consisting of solving one problem and another one emerging (see Figure 19).

the client solves a problem – a new problem emerges	the client solves a problem – a new problem emerges

Figure 19: Organising the string of events into sequences

When the continuous string of problems and solutions are organised in this manner, it looks depressing. It creates a sense of hopelessness because it makes the work appear as something like a Sisyphus work characterised by an eternal state of things not working.

However, it would be equally valid to organise the string of event into sequences consisting of a problem arising and the problem being solved (see Figure 20).

a new problem emerges – the client solves the problem	a new problem emerges – the client solves the problem

Figure 20: Alternative way of organising the string of events into sequences

In contrast to the first way of organising the string of events, the second way of organising the sequence of events is likely to create a sense of hopefulness, optimism and even invincibility because it highlights how every problem always gets solved.

Looking at the therapeutic work with a particular issue provides another example of how different ways of organising events into meaningful sequences can produce radically different experiences for the client.

When working with a particular issue it is common that the client will experience bringing up the issue in a therapy session, arriving at some resolution at the end of the session and then reverting to feeling the issue sometime after the session. It is common that this pattern is repeated over the course of several sessions.

If the client organises this string of events into resolution followed by relapse, they are likely to feel discouraged. No matter how many times they work with the issue, it always comes back.

However, upon closer inspection, the client may notice that each time they work with the issue, they discover something precious in themselves. Instead of organising their experience in sequences of resolutions and (disappointing) relapses, they may start organising their experience of the therapeutic process into sequences of explorations leading to precious discoveries.

The issue could, for example, be lack of self-worth. In the first session, the client may explore what self-worth feels like and through this exploration may discover an exquisite state of stability and groundedness (the White aspect of Being). In the second session, the client may discover that their lack of self-worth is related to repressed anger. As they acknowledge the repressed anger the client may discover an exquisite state of feeling energised, alive and free (the Red aspect of

Being). In the third session, the client may explore the state of complete loss of self-esteem. By embracing this state without judgements, the client may discover the exquisite peace of allowing oneself to be extinguished (the Black aspect of Being). In the fourth session, the client may explore the sadness they feel when realising how much they have missed in life due to their lack of self-worth. By embracing this sadness, the client may get in touch with a beautiful state of tenderness and humanness (the Green aspect of Being). In the fifth session, the client may explore alleviating themselves from the burden of having to be confident. Ceasing to chase confidence may feel like a great relief and bring the client in touch with lightness and joy (the Yellow aspect of Being).

It is possible to organise this string of events into sequences of resolutions followed by relapses. Doing so will create a feeling of continuous failure. The stability and grounding didn't dissolve the issue for good and neither did the aliveness, peace, tenderness or lightness.

However, it is also possible to organise the string of events into sequences of engagements with the issue followed by discovery of a new precious inner state. Organising the string of events in this way may lead the client to regard the issue of low self-worth as a sort of treasure finding device. They may even feel that getting rid of the issue of low self-worth would be a loss because it would be a loss of something that keeps revealing what, in this book, are called aspects of Being[48].

In summary, by changing the start and end points of the sequences of events the client operates with, you can change the inner state of the client. This reveals to the client that their inner state is created through the way they organise events into meaningful sequences, and not by the circumstances themselves.

Changing metaphors

One of the ways humans structure their experience is through the use of metaphors. People understand one kind of situation as analogous to another.

For example, a client may understand the therapeutic process by seeing it as analogous to other processes that are more familiar to them.

Therapy can be understood as analogous to going to a doctor. When you feel physically unwell, you go to a doctor who will examine your physical symptoms,

---

[48] It is worth noticing that organising the string of events into a new sequence is equivalent to classifying the issue in a different way: "A problem to solve" vs "a treasure finding device".

determine the cause and propose a remedy. Using a visit to the doctor as a metaphor, we can understand a visit to a therapist as something we do when we feel mentally or emotionally unwell. The therapist will examine your mental and emotional symptoms, determine the cause and propose a remedy. When we talk about mental health, we are using this metaphor.

Therapy can also be understood as analogous to going to the fitness centre. Exercise is important to ensure that your body stays healthy. If you have a personal trainer, they may create a training programme that will help you develop the muscles you need to develop. Using the personal trainer as a metaphor, we can understand therapy as the act of training the "self-worth" muscle, the "conflict resolution" muscle, the "contentment" muscle, or whichever muscle you need to develop. I have seen places that market themselves as "spiritual fitness centres". This slogan draws on the fitness metaphor.

Yet another way of understanding therapy is as analogous to waking up. When you are asleep you dream and while you are dreaming, you don't know that you are dreaming. When you wake up, you realise that the dream was an illusion created by your own mind. When using the act of waking up as a metaphor, we can understand therapy as something that helps us recognise how aspects of what we perceive as external reality are, in fact, created by our own mind – like dreams. When we speak about spiritual awakening, we are using this metaphor.

Different metaphors will make different aspects of our experience appear as important and, thus, determine what we pay attention to.

Using the doctor metaphor gives importance to the symptoms. Using the fitness metaphor gives importance to the training programme. Using the waking up metaphor gives importance to raising awareness.

Thus, an effective way of shifting what clients pay attention to is to shift the metaphors they use to organise their experience.

For example, a client may have an issue with anger. They may tell you that:

> "I have a problem with anger. Sometimes, I just explode and say really hurtful things to others. I don't know why I can't control it. I would like to get better at anger management."

In this brief description of the problem the client is using two metaphors. They see anger as something explosive and as something that needs to be managed or controlled.

Using these metaphors will make the client pay attention to the volatile nature of anger, to the harm it can do, and to various ways of diffusing it and preventing it from erupting.

They are not paying attention to the message in the anger or to the sense of energy of the anger.

Instead of directly asking the client to extend what they pay attention to so it includes the message and the energy of the anger, you can offer the client a different metaphor that naturally highlights these aspects of the anger.

You can, for example, propose the metaphor of:

- Anger as an energy that cuts through limiting beliefs
- Anger as an energy that cuts the chains that keep one imprisoned
- Anger as a fuel for change
- Anger as a truth-teller

Detecting what metaphors clients use and proposing alternative ones can be an effective method of shifting what clients pay attention to and, thus, afford them the opportunity to notice how they create different experiences through selective attention. I will return to the theme of metaphors in Section 7.6 Cognitive Metaphors and Embodied Cognition.

Changing classifications

In the descriptions of the above tools, I have mentioned that changing what clients pay attention to in a situation is equivalent to changing how they classify that situation.

When clients reflect on how other people may experience a situation differently from them, they may discover that such people pay attention to different aspects of the situation and, thus, classify the situation differently. The same behaviour may be classified as "oppressive", "boring" or "rude".

Extending what aspects of a situation a client considers relevant or how that structure events in sequences are both equivalent to changing how they classify situations. Working with a particular issue may be classified as "problem solving" or as "treasure finding".

However, it is also possible to work the other way round. One may first change how one classifies a situation and then discover how this change of classification makes one pay attention to different aspects of the situation. Since metaphors are fundamentally classifications, noticing how different metaphors highlight different aspects of a situation is an example of working this way.

While all these techniques are very useful, it is also possible to work directly with clients' classifications and simply ask:

> "What kind of situation do you see this situation as and what alternative classifications could you imagine?"

It may take a bit of explanation to make clients understand what you mean by classification, but clients usually understand it quickly enough.

Working directly with changing classifications is a fast way of bringing awareness to overlooked aspects of a situation and at the same time learning about how classifications impact the options one has for dealing with the situation, i.e. it illuminates one's second-order agency.

For example, a client may describe a situation where they would like to travel alone for a few months but if they do, their partner may leave them. Clients will often classify this situation as a situation where they are controlled by their partner. However, assuming that the partner does not prevent the client from travelling through physical imprisonment, the partner really has no control over what the client does – only over their own response. Thus, a different possible way of classifying the situation is as a situation in which the client is unwilling to accept the consequences of their own actions or as a situation where the client is unable to make a choice between two goods (the travel and the relationship). Reclassifying the situation reveals that the partner has no control over the client's actions and allows the therapy to explore the client's unwillingness to accept the consequences of certain choices they may make.

From poles to spectrums

A common way of structuring experience is by categorising experiences using opposite and mutually exclusive categories, such as kind/unkind, powerful/powerless, leader/follower, brave/cowardly, generous/stingy, optimistic/pessimistic, honest/dishonest, strong/weak, confident/insecure, successful/unsuccessful, active/passive, happy/sad, responsible/irresponsible and healthy/unhealthy.

These sets of categories generally consist of a positive and a negative concept. Negative inner states are sometimes created when clients use opposites to understand their experience and, because their experience does not fit the positive category in the set, they conclude that it must fit the negative. If the client does not see themself as strong, they feel weak. If the client does not see themself as powerful or completely in control, they feel helpless.

To elucidate how the client's act of using opposites to structure their experience contributes to the creation of their inner states, it can be useful to invite them to structure their experience using a spectrum instead and to notice how this can change the way they feel about a particular situation.

A client may, for example, feel like a failure because they see most of their actions containing flaws and, for this reason, they do not see them as successes. They may, for example, see themselves as a bad parent because they sometimes become angry with their children which, to them, is not a sign of being a successful parent. They may see themselves as a failure in their work because they sometimes make mistakes. They may see themselves as failing in their therapy because their issues are not always resolved by the end of the therapy session. In such situations, the client's sense of failure is not created by the circumstances but rather by the client's use of the categories of success and failure as a way of making sense of the circumstances. The client believes that for something to be a success it has to be perfect and that everything that isn't a success is a failure. If, instead of polar opposites, the client used a spectrum from absolute failure to absolute success, the picture may change radically. They may note that they are 80% perfect parents, 85% effective at their work and that their therapy sessions resolve 90% of their issues. Looking at their life from this perspective, they may (justifiably) feel much better about their lives.

Similarly, a client may feel helpless in a situation because they are not in control of everything. Once again, the feeling of helplessness derives from the client using the polar opposites of helplessness and control to make sense of their situation. If the client instead used a spectrum, they might discover that they are 90% in control, which arguably is anything but helpless.

Yet another common example is clients feeling bad or evil because they are not 100% kind. If the only way of being a kind person is by eradicating all unkind thoughts, emotions and actions, no one would be kind. Using a spectrum is, for this reason, much better. Then the client could consider what percentage of their thoughts, emotions or behaviours should be kind, for them to feel they are kind enough.

Inviting clients to change black and white thinking for thinking in terms of spectrums and to notice how that affects their inner state can be a powerful way of elucidating how the way clients structure their experience contributes to the creation of their inner states.

From spectrums to planes

Clients will commonly structure their experience by using spectrums between two concepts they perceive as positive but mutually exclusive, such as independence/connection, self-care/care for others, adaptability/consistency, and people-oriented/task-oriented.

Negative inner states are created when this way of structuring experience leads clients to feel forced to make a choice between two positive concepts they place at either end of the spectrum.

Often the concepts are not actually mutually exclusive. They only appear to be so because the client thinks about them in that way. Thus, the choice the client is faced with, which causes frustration, is an illusion.

To elucidate how the client's act of placing two positive concepts in opposition to each other, even though they are not mutually exclusive, contributes to the creation of their negative inner states, it can be useful to invite clients to structure their experience using two perpendicular spectrums instead and to notice how this can change the way they feel about a particular situation.

A client may, for example, be frustrated with their work colleague because the colleague always points out potential problems with the client's suggestions for how to advance a project and the client perceives this behaviour as a sign that their colleague is not 100% committed to the success of the project. However, pointing out potential problems is not the opposite of being committed to success. It is possible to both pay attention to potential issues and be completely committed to success. In fact, the colleague may be pointing out potential problems precisely because they wish to project to succeed.

Figure 21 illustrates the change from structuring experience using a spectrum to using two perpendicular axes. In the first case, increasing one means diminishing the other. In the second case, it is possible to increase or diminish each variable independently.

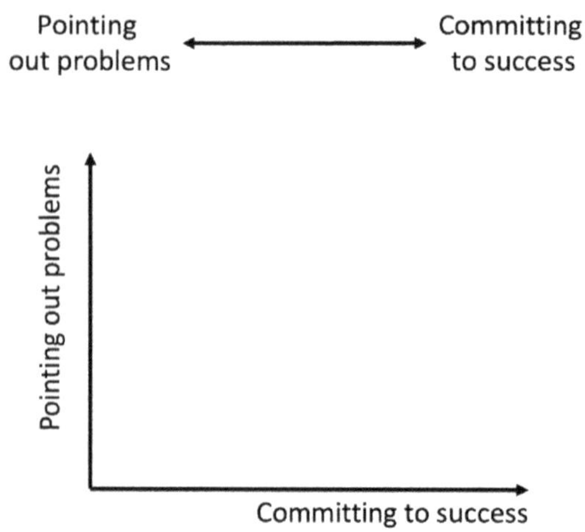

Figure 21: Spectrums to Planes

Other examples of concepts that clients may falsely perceive as mutually exclusive opposites include:

- Independence vs. connection ("If I'm independent, I'm not connected to others"): The client sometimes sees their wish for personal space as the opposite of wishing to be connected with their partner (or other people in general) and, therefore, feel guilty about having this wish. However, independence and connection are not opposites. It is possible to be 100% independent and 100% connected at the same time.
- Self-care vs. care for others ("If I care about myself, I don't care about others"): Clients often experience difficult emotions because they perceive their wish for self-care as the opposite of wanting to care for others. If they choose self-care, they feel selfish because it seems to exclude caring for others, and if they choose to care for others, they feel resentful because it seems to exclude caring for themselves. However, these emotions are created by placing self-care and care for others at opposite ends of a spectrum instead of seeing them as two independent variables. It is possible to care for both self and others.
- Adaptability vs. consistency ("If I'm adaptable or flexible, I'm inconsistent or stable"): Clients may perceive adaptability/flexibility and consistency/stability as opposite ends of a spectrum. They may perceive a need for adaptability, and this causes them to be concerned about losing consistency. However, once again adaptability is the opposite of unadaptable – not the opposite of consistency. For example, it is precisely one's continuous physical adaptability that enables one to keep a consistent upright standing position. Similarly, a

consistent daily routine can provide a solid base for adapting to changes in one's life. Thus, adaptability can support consistency and vice versa. Seeing this can dispel the client's sense of concern arising from a perceived conflict between adaptability and consistency.

- People-orientation vs. task-orientation ("Those who care about tasks, don't care about people"): Seeing individuals as either people-oriented or task-oriented runs through much of early leadership theory. Once again this is a false opposition. It is possible to imagine a leader that is neither concerned with people, nor tasks and it is possible to imagine a leader that is deeply concerned with both. Seeing the two as mutually exclusive opposites creates a difficult dilemma and, consequently, difficult emotions. Seeing that the two are not, in fact, opposites will dissolve the dilemma and the related emotions.

Seeing things that are not opposites as the two ends of a spectrum can also lead to difficult emotions when used to understand others. For example, concluding that someone does not appreciate one because they don't express any appreciation can lead to resentment. However, "not feeling appreciation" is the opposite of "feeling appreciation". It is not the opposite of "expressing appreciation". It is fully possible to feel appreciation and not express it or to express appreciation and not feel it. Feeling and expressing appreciation are, thus, two independent variables. Similarly, concluding that someone who doesn't express emotions is unemotional, or that someone who is happy is not deep, or that someone who is adventurous is not responsible, are all fallacies because expressing emotions is not the opposite of being unemotional, happiness is not the opposite of depth and adventurousness is not the opposite of responsibility.

Moving from thinking in terms of spectrums to thinking in terms of planes enables the therapist to flip a correlation in the client's thinking. When a client places two concepts that are not direct opposites at either end of a spectrum, they, in effect, conflate two spectrums.

For example, a client may experience that whenever they have an argument with their partner, they are able to see things from their partner's perspective, but their partner never seems to see things from the client's perspective. The client may see their tendency to see things from their partner's perspective as a weakness because it leads them to give up what they believe in. In this case, the client perceives the strength to stand by what one believes in and seeing things from the partner's perspective as opposites and mutually exclusive.

However, strength to stand by what one believes in and the ability to see things from someone else's perspective are not opposites. Thus, the client conflates two spectrums. One spectrum runs from strength to weakness in relation to stand by what one believes in and the other runs from perspective flexibility to perspective inflexibility. In the client's thinking these two spectrums are conflated in such a way that perspective flexibility and inability to stand by what one believes in are placed at the same end.

If we separate the two spectrums, we can ask ourselves whether it is possible to make an argument for conflating the two spectrums in such a way that we switch which poles are placed together. In this case, we would consider making an argument for conflating perspective flexibility and strength to stand by what one believes in. There are many ways of doing this.

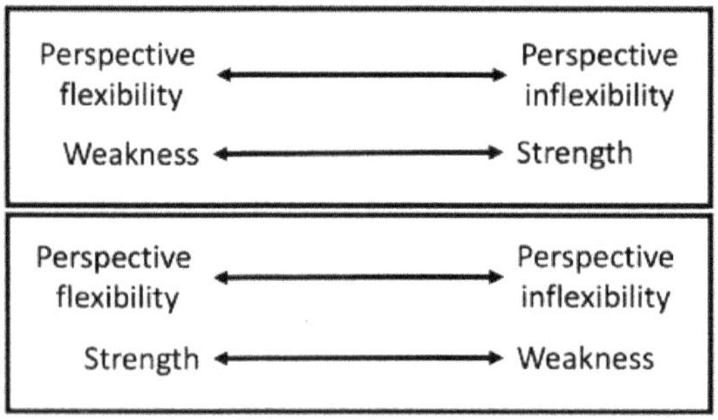

Figure 22: Flipping spectrums

One way of doing this is to say that in debate schools they teach that the better you understand your opponent's position the stronger you can argue your own point of view. Thus, perspective flexibility supports you in standing by what you believe in.

Another way of flipping the way the spectrums are conflated is to propose that the better you understand your partner's position, the easier it will be for you to imagine ways of resolving the conflict in ways that ensure both you and your partner get what each of you wants. Thus, perspective flexibility is a strength that enables you to stand by what is important to you. And your partner, who is more inflexible in their perspective, is, in this sense, weaker than you.

The point of making such arguments is, of course, not to convince the client that this new way of conflating the two dimensions is more correct than their previous way of doing so. The point is to create compelling narratives that break the client's fixated way of conflating the two dimensions and, thus, giving the client more flexibility of mind.

Inviting clients to change from seeing two concepts as opposite to seeing them as two independent variables and noticing how this affects their inner state can be a powerful way of elucidating how the way clients structure their experience contributes to the creation of their inner states.

Exposing positive feedback loops

Another common way people structure their experience is by assuming causal relationships between different elements. Examples of common causal links include: Achievements cause an increase in self-esteem, hard work leads to success, greater risks lead to greater rewards, financial problems cause stress, physical exercise causes improvements in one's mood, and so on.

As we have seen in the previous chapters, clients often get such causal relationships wrong. In a sense, all ideas about the conditions one must fulfil to create or acquire positive reifications of Being are examples of mistaken ideas about causal relationships.

However, there is another issue with the way clients structure their experience in terms of causal relationships between different elements. This issue arises when multiple causal relationships form chains of assumed causation, such as one element is seen to cause another element which is seen to cause a third element and so on. If each link in such chains of causality seems plausible, the client will naturally believe that the first element, in effect, causes the last element. But even a single mistake in this chain of causations can mean that such conclusions are wrong.

This can create a situation where a client is convinced that a particular action will bring about a particular outcome even if it, in reality, brings about the opposite outcome. The result of the action will, thus, lead the client away from their desired result. But because the client is convinced that the action should bring them closer, the further away they get, the more they will engage in the action, and the further from their goal they get.

For example, a client may wish to feel more appreciated by others. They may believe that being liked by others will make them feel more appreciated (first causal link). They may also believe that people will like them more if they exhibit certain traits while hiding or repressing other traits (second causal link). Taken together, these two links will suggest that modifying oneself to fit what other people like will produce a feeling of being appreciated by others. However, knowing that one must modify oneself to be liked by others will, in reality, create a sense of being rejected – not appreciated. Thus, the act of modifying oneself produces the opposite of what the client thinks this act will produce. As long as the client suffers from the mistaken belief that modifying themselves should bring about a feeling of being appreciated, they will keep modifying themselves. When this act produces a sense of rejection, the client will react to this sense of rejection by modifying themselves even more to remedy the sense of rejection. This, in turn, will increase the client's sense of rejection, which will increase their efforts to modify themselves, and so on. The result is a positive feedback loop that will increase the sense of rejection indefinitely (or until other processes are activated).

It is like a thermostat that has been set to increase rather than decrease the temperature when the temperature is above a certain threshold. When the temperature rises above this threshold, such a thermostat will keep seeking to increase the temperature indefinitely – until it melts or something else stops it.

The counterproductive strategies clients use are generally created in this way. Thus, the counterproductive strategies listed in Section 3.4.4 under the description of the Counterproductivity Process are all created as chains of causal relationships that each seem plausible, which, nevertheless, results in an overall flawed conclusion about the causal relationship between the first and the last link.

Inviting clients to recognise how intense negative inner states can be the product of flawed assumptions about how elements in clients' experience are causally linked can be a powerful way of elucidating how the way clients structure their experience contributes to the creation of their inner states.

Objection 1: I cannot shift my attention

The above techniques for elucidating agency involve asking clients to shift the way they use their attention. By shifting away from habitual ways of using their attention, they will directly experience the degree to which undesired experiences are created by such habits.

This way of working assumes that clients are, at least to some extent, able to decide what they pay attention to.

Sometimes, clients will oppose this assumption. They may, for example, state that they are unable to pay attention to certain elements they normally ignore in a given situation or to organise the continuous flow of events in their experience using sequences that are different from what they normally do. Clients may state that they cannot choose what they pay attention to because their attention is just grabbed by the things they normally pay attention to.

Whereas it is true that it can be difficult to change *habits* of attention, clients will usually have some measure of influence over what they pay attention to in the short term.

To demonstrate this capacity, I sometimes play an attention game with clients. I will ask them to shift their attention to a sequence of things that are easy to shift their attention to.

I may, for example, say:

> "Notice the sound of my voice. Notice your feet. Notice the colour on the wall. Notice what you are thinking now. Notice the plant on the table."

Once I have asked the client to shift their attention a few times, I will ask them if they found this exercise difficult. I have never encountered anyone who did. I then point out that this shows that they *do* have the ability to decide what to pay attention to at any given moment.

When clients find it difficult to shift their attention to a particular aspect of their experience, it is typically because they are trying to do more than just that.

Clients may, for example, believe that the purpose of shifting what they pay attention to is to change their *habits* of how they use their attention. Rather than simply noticing how paying attention to certain things impacts their inner state, clients may assume that the purpose of shifting attention to different elements of their experience is to never again pay attention to the things they normally pay attention to. Similarly, rather than simply noticing how shifting the way they organise strings of events into meaningful sequences impacts their inner state, clients may be trying to alter the way they *habitually* organise these events.

While shifting what you pay attention to is simple and easy, building a new habit of what you pay attention to takes practice. To elucidate the client's agency, they do not have to change what they *habitually* pay attention to. They only have to experience that changing what they pay attention to changes their inner state. This may then motivate them to practise a new habit, but that is another matter.

Clients may also mistakenly believe that the purpose of shifting what they pay attention to is to make changes in their lives or change what happens in a particular kind of situation. Rather than simply noticing how paying attention to certain things changes how they feel, they may be paying attention to whether it changes anything about other people's behaviour.

While shifting what one pays attention to is likely to shift one's inner state, it is unlikely to directly affect other people's behaviour. But to elucidate the client's agency in relation to creating their inner state, they do not have to change anything about the external situation. They only have to experience that changing what they pay attention to changes their inner state. If their inner state changes on a more permanent basis, the client is likely to start acting differently in the situation and this may or may not have an impact on other people's behaviour.

As long as clients believe that the purpose of shifting how they use their awareness is to change something either about themselves or the external environment, they are likely to overlook the effect it has on their own inner state and, consequently, are likely to overlook how this reveals their own agency in relation to creating these inner states.

In short, changing what we are aware of is usually relatively easy in the short term and this serves the purpose of exploring how the way we use our attention impacts how we feel and, in this way, elucidate our own agency in areas where we may have believed we had none.

Objection 2: What I pay attention to is important

When attempting to elucidate agency by asking clients to shift what they pay attention to, we can run into the problem that clients are unwilling to change what they pay attention to.

Clients may point out that the things they are paying attention to are important and shouldn't be ignored. Even if paying attention to these things generates a negative state in them, they still have to pay attention to them because not doing so might lead to situations that would create even worse inner states.

For example, a client may say that even though it is nice to notice that problems always get solved, it is still important to notice when problems arise too frequently. Frequent problems may be indications of a deeper or systematic problem that needs to be addressed and being content with the fact that problems always are solved might prevent one from noticing and addressing the deeper source of those problems. And if one does not deal with the deeper issues, they may end up in a worse place than the place they feel when fixated on problems.

Similarly, a client may point out that even though their partner does, indeed, offer acts of service and emotional support, the lack of gift giving can be a deal breaker if it is particularly important to the client. Sometimes, there are many things that work well in a relationship but the one thing that does not work may mean that it isn't viable to continue the relationship. Shifting awareness away from such facts would be a bad idea since even though it may create a positive change in the internal state, it does not solve the real problem. Thus, the change in inner state will be short lived.

To deal with such objections, it can be useful to point out that just because something is important, the client doesn't have to exclusively pay attention to it. In fact, by simultaneously paying attention to something that brings a positive inner state and to the problem the client wishes to deal with, the latter can become easier because they will deal with the problem from an inner sense of being resourced.

Whenever a client objects to shifting what they pay attention to because they find what they are currently paying attention to is very important, I usually suggest that instead of *shifting* what they pay attention to, they *expand* what they pay attention to.

For example, rather than paying attention to the way problems are always solved *instead* of paying attention to how new problems always arise, the client can pay attention to both. In other words, they can add awareness of how problems are always solved to their already existing awareness of how new problems continuously arise.

Such expansion of what the client pays attention to is often enough to produce a shift in how they feel and, thus, demonstrate how the way they use their attention affects their inner state and the agency this implies.

Expanding rather than shifting what one is aware of has an additional benefit. Learning to divide attention so as to be simultaneously aware of multiple things can, ultimately, help one become able to be simultaneously aware of Being and the issues of life you need to deal with. Such dual awareness enables you to approach issues in life from a resourced place and avoid conflating these issues with the issue of having awareness of Being. This makes dealing with the issues in your life much easier.

Finally, if clients claim that they are unable to expand what they are aware of, you can play a version of the attention game with them, where you ask them to be aware of two things at a time, such as both their feet, both the colour on the wall and the sounds from the street, etc. This can demonstrate the possibility of being aware of multiple things simultaneously.

That being said, maintaining awareness of Being while engaged in your daily tasks is, of course, challenging[49]. But the fundamental requirement of dividing one's attention between two things is not difficult.

Elucidating agency vs. reframing experiences

Many of the techniques presented above could be classified as what is commonly known as reframing. In this section, I will briefly define reframing in therapy and then comment on how traditional therapy and Being-Centred Therapy use reframing for different purposes.

Traditionally, reframing in therapy involves shifting the perspective of a situation, thought, or emotion to view it in a new and more constructive way.

This can be achieved by shifting what content the client is focusing on (content reframing) or what context the client is using to give the situation (context reframing), thought or emotion meaning. In other words, reframing can be achieved by shifting what a client pays attention to or by shifting how they interpret and organise what they pay attention to.

For an example of content reframing, one can think of a client who is unhappy because they frequently make mistakes in their presentations at work. The client's feeling may change radically when they notice that although they frequently make mistakes, they never make the same mistake twice. With this shift in focus, the client may shift from seeing themselves as a failure to seeing themselves as someone who is on a learning curve. This is content reframing because it involves a shift in the aspects of the situation the client focuses on.

For an example of context reframing, one can think of a client who is unhappy because they earn less than some of their peers. The client's level of satisfaction with their income level may change radically if they notice that they earn much more now than they did ten years ago, if they notice that their current income level is fully adequate for the lifestyle they enjoy, or if they notice that they work fewer hours than those of their peers who earn more than they do. All of these

---

[49] This is the main topic of the final chapter in this book.

are examples of context reframing because the meaning of the client's income level is changed by changing the context they use to evaluate it.

Reframing is traditionally used to challenge negative or unhelpful interpretations by offering alternative perspectives that can lead to greater understanding and positive affective changes. Through reframing, individuals can gain fresh insights into their experiences and develop healthier responses to challenges, ultimately fostering personal growth and well-being.

In Being-Centred Therapy, reframing serves an important additional purpose, in that it is used to demonstrate the client's agency in relation to creating their own inner states.

If clients cannot control the external situations in which they experience negative inner states, they tend to believe they have no agency in that situation – both in relation to the external circumstances and their inner states. However, this belief may change if clients, through engaging in reframing exercises, discover how they can radically alter the inner states they experience in the situation by changing what aspects of the situation they pay attention to and what context they use to give meaning to the situation.

In other words, reframing can be used to separate agency in relation to external circumstances and agency in relation to internal states, and show that even when you cannot change external events, you still have influence over your inner state.

Another important difference between how reframing is used in traditional therapy and in Being-Centred Therapy relates to how reframings are selected.

In traditional therapy the client and the therapist collaborate on selecting a reframing that achieves the goal of achieving greater understanding and positive affective changes.

In Being-Centred Therapy, reframing is used as a tool to learn to recognise negative inner states as products of the client's own activity rather than properties of reality. How this clear recognition changes the way the client structures their experience is not something the client is encouraged to choose. Instead, it is assumed that clear perception of one's own agency will lead one's system to make the needed adjustments on its own. The clear recognition of one's own agency establishes a feedback loop, that allows the client's system of mental, emotional and behavioural patterns to regulate itself more effectively.

Moving awareness upstream

When mapping out the process through which clients create their inner states, it is useful to organise the elements one is aware of on a timeline, and then ask what came before the first element on that timeline.

An emotional state may be created by a set of thoughts, but that only leaves the question: How are the thoughts that create the emotion created?

This question is key because if we deal with the problematic behaviours, thoughts or emotions we are aware of without asking what automatic patterns create these, we will be dealing with symptoms rather than causes. Furthermore, if we do not become aware of the patterns causing the problems we seek to deal with, these very same patterns may lead us to deal with the problems in ways that worsen, rather than solve, the problems (as we have seen repeatedly in this book).

David Bohm, an influential physicist and philosopher of mind and dialogue, expresses it as follows:

> "People have been dealing with this piecemeal — looking at symptoms, saying that we've got to solve this problem or that problem or that problem. But there is something deeper, which people haven't been considering, that is constantly generating these problems. We can use the analogy of a stream, where people are pouring pollution upstream at the same time they are trying to remove it downstream. But as they remove it they may be adding more pollution of a different kind. What is the source of all this trouble? [...] I'm saying that the source is basically in thought. Many people would think that such a statement is crazy, because thought is the one thing we have with which to solve our problems. That's part of our tradition. Yet it looks as if the thing we use to solve our problems is the source of our problems [...] the reason we don't see the source of our problems is that the means by which we try to solve them are the source." (Bohm, 1990, pp. 2–3)

By continuously asking how the present elements of the client's experience are created you are "moving upstream". Eventually, you will arrive at the misconceptions outlined in this book. These are the source of the thought pollution and lingering on the effects downstream will do nothing for ceasing the pollution. If the misconceptions are not corrected, the client's suffering may shift but not cease.

Bohm does not only see the pollution as creating problems for the individual. He also claims that problems at a societal and global level are fundamentally created by individuals operating from false assumptions about reality. Thus, when I claim that most of human suffering is created by operating from the 20 misconceptions outlined in this book, I, following Bohm, include the suffering related to societal and global issues, such as international (armed) conflicts, systemic discrimination and injustice, environmental degradation, famine and poverty. Dealing with these issues without dealing with the misconceptions from which they ultimately arise is problematic.

5.6.4. Step 4: Understand motivation

One of the reasons it can be difficult for clients to imagine they are involved in the creation of negative states, or the blocking of positive ones, is that they believe doing so would be against their own interests and, thus, they do not see what would motivate them to do this. Furthermore, once clients realise that they are, in fact, actively taking part in the creation of undesired inner experiences, they may conclude that there is something within them working to their disadvantage, which can be quite disturbing for clients. For these reasons, an important part of the Sensing Agency process is to clarify the motivation behind such seemingly self-sabotaging actions.

Therefore, the fourth and final step of the Sensing Agency process focuses on raising awareness, not merely of the mechanism through which clients create negative inner states or avoid positive ones, but of what motivates them to do so.

The starting point for this fourth step in the process is the assumption that people never do anything unless they believe it will be beneficial to them, and that when people do something that appears not to be beneficial to them, it is because they are unaware of the beliefs about benefits that motivate their behaviour.

The following sections present three approaches to raising awareness of what motivates clients to create negative inner states, or avoid positive ones.

The first approach is simply to invite clients to reflect on what benefits they could imagine gaining from feeling a negative inner state or not feeling a positive one. Sometimes, simply proposing that the client is motivated by hidden benefits is enough for them to become aware of what drives their behaviour.

The second approach is to invite the client to reflect on whether the creation of unwanted inner states might be part of a strategy that was beneficial to them earlier in life. Many times, clients will create negative inner states or avoid positive ones either because this was directly beneficial to them in their childhood environment or because creating such states was a necessary and worthwhile price to pay for dealing with particular challenges in this environment. In such cases, clients may continue to create unwanted inner states merely because they have not updated their strategies to fit their current environment.

The third approach relates to revealing a particular type of hidden benefit, namely, that a negative inner state can function as a parental surrogate towards which the client turns for various forms of support. I have devoted a separate section to this form of unconscious motivation as it can be difficult to discover unless one knows that it is a possibility.

Hidden benefits

When a client experiences inner states they perceive as negative[50], it is easy for them to see the disadvantages of feeling such states; however, many times there are also benefits to feeling them.

For example, a client may be plagued by feelings of helplessness, and they might have worked on changing this feeling but without success. They may believe that helplessness is the default human condition or that they feel helplessness due to certain external circumstances beyond their control. In either case, they will feel they have no part in creating the feeling of helplessness.

The belief that they are not creating the feeling of helplessness may be backed up by their keen awareness of the negative impact this feeling has on their life. Feeling helpless is unpleasant and limits their ability to get things done. And prolonged states of helplessness can negatively impact mental health and lead to feelings of depression, anxiety, and powerlessness. Being aware of such disadvantages can make it seem as if no one could be motivated to create the feeling of helplessness in themselves.

However, upon reflection, the client may realise that there are many potential benefits to feeling helpless.

- When you feel helpless, you can more easily elicit help from others.
- When you feel helpless, you have an excuse not to engage with tasks, you might prefer to avoid.

[50] I here refer both to the presence of negative inner states and the absence of positive ones.

- Expressing helplessness might attract attention from others, fulfilling the need for acknowledgment and validation.
- Expressing helplessness can elicit sympathy and support from others, fulfilling the need for connection and care.
- When people feel helpless, others may lower their expectations of them, which can alleviate performance pressure or expectations of success.
- In some situations, acknowledging helplessness can provide a sense of relief, by relieving the pressure to actively solve a problem or make a decision.
- Feeling helpless can provide a sense of relief from personal responsibility because if someone believes they can't influence a situation, they might not feel as responsible for what happens.

Just as there can be hidden benefits to feeling helpless, there can be hidden benefits to feeling many other states, despite their overt negative impact, including feeling meaninglessness, pointlessness, powerlessness, hopelessness, worthlessness, loneliness, lostness, sadness, vulnerability, anger, frustration, disingenuousness, obsession, shame, guilt, jealousy, resentment, envy, inferiority, silliness, desire, hate, laziness, boredom and apathy.

- Clients may create the feeling of hate to gain a sense of power and autonomy.
- Clients may create feelings of guilt or shame in an attempt at eliciting forgiveness or sympathy from others and mitigate the risk of rejection.
- Clients may create laziness to obtain a sense of relaxation.
- Clients may create a sense of cynicism to avoid disappointment.

When a client recognises that they believe there can be certain benefits to feeling the negative state they struggle with, it helps the Sensing Agency process in two ways:

First, it makes it easier for the client to engage in the exploration of the mechanism through which they create this state.

Second, it makes the client look with more kindness on the mechanism within them that creates the state. If they did not recognise any potential benefits, they would most likely see any such mechanism as a disturbing flaw or malfunction in themselves, which would lead to the Knot of Fragmentation (the topic of the next chapter).

When engaging clients in exploring hidden benefits of creating negative states, it is important not to forget the negative impact these states have on the clients' lives. In some cases, when clients realise the hidden benefits, they may become persuaded that creating the negative state is a good thing. They may either forget the negative impact all together, or the hidden benefits may seem to outweigh the negative impact.

In such cases, it is important to remind the client that the negative state really does have a negative impact on their lives, and that the purpose of becoming aware of hidden benefits is not to persuade the client to keep creating the negative inner state, but rather to separate the negative state from the imagined benefits.

Thus, once the client has become aware of the hidden benefits, you can ask them to:

- Reflect on whether the creation of the negative state delivers the imagined benefits. This will often not be the case.
- Reflect on how to achieve the hidden benefits in ways that do *not* involve the creation of the negative state.

For example, a client may create a sense of worthlessness to protect themselves from rejection or devaluation by others. When they see themselves as worthless, it hurts less if others do so as well. When the client realises that they create the sense of worthlessness to protect themselves, it might appear to them as a worthy trade-off. They may believe that feeling permanently worthless is worth it if it saves them from others' rejection and devaluation.

If this happens, you can point out to the client that if they see themself as worthless others are more likely to do the same, and, thus, feeling worthless may increase, rather than decrease, the risk of rejection and devaluation from others. Thus, creating the negative state of worthlessness does not deliver the hidden benefit the client imagined it would.

Furthermore, you may engage the client in explorations of alternative ways to deal with others' rejection and devaluation that does not involve feeling permanently worthless. In particular, the client can, through the Sensing Agency process, explore what negative inner states they create in themselves when others reject and devaluate them – and then cease generating these inner states. This would be a better way of dealing with rejection and devaluation by others than to create a permanent sense of worthlessness.

In summary, inviting clients to reflect upon what hidden benefits they might expect to obtain from creating negative inner states is often an effective way of clarifying what motivates clients to create these inner states. Furthermore, it enables reflections on whether the creation of the inner state delivers the imagined benefit and whether there might be ways of achieving the benefit that does not involve the creation of the negative inner state.

Obsolete strategies for dealing with the childhood family environment

Sometimes, clients are unable to find any hidden benefits in their adult life that could motivate them to create a negative inner state or avoid a positive one. In such cases, it can be helpful to explore whether doing so might have served a purpose in their childhood family environment. If it did, this can shed light on what motivated the client to form the automatic patterns that lead to the unwanted inner states.

For example, a client may struggle with a sense of numbness and joylessness in their adult life. Initially, the client may believe that joylessness is the natural human state or that they feel no joy because they have not found anything that brings them joy. Through the Sensing Agency process, the client may discover that they actively turn their attention away from joy in various ways. When exploring what might motivate them to do so, they find no hidden benefits related to their adult life. However, when considering their childhood environment, the client may recognise that their parents were very serious people and expressions of joy were frowned upon as a character flaw. Thus, numbing out joy was an intelligent adaptation to that environment, as it allowed the child to maintain a good relationship with the parents it depended upon. In this example, automatically creating an absence of a positive state that causes problems in adult life was a worthwhile by-product of a strategy that served an important purpose in the childhood environment.

Another example could involve a client who becomes very angry over minor annoyances. Initially, they may believe their anger is caused by circumstances, but through the Sensing Agency process, they may discover that they create it themself through paying selective attention to things that anger them while ignoring positive factors in any situation. When exploring what might motivate them to do so, they find no hidden benefits in their adult life. However, looking at their childhood environment, they may recall that their parents would often say or do things that were emotionally abusive. In that environment, being quick to express anger served the purpose of creating emotional distance from the parents to protect against the effect of the abuse. In this example, automatically creating a negative inner state that causes problems in adult life served an important purpose in the childhood environment.

Recognising that the automatic creation of an unwanted inner state is part of an intelligent strategy that achieved valuable objectives in one's childhood environment can make it easier for clients to map out their unconscious behaviours without feeling that what they do is irrational or intentionally self-destructive. Furthermore, seeing that the motivation is obsolete can, in some cases, lead to an immediate update of clients' strategy.

Parental surrogates (who is that?)

It is worth giving a separate section to one particular motivation for creating negative inner states as it occurs frequently but is difficult to discern if one is not familiar with the underlying mechanism.

In short, a negative inner state can function as a representation of a parent (or other childhood caretaker) and for this reason, losing the negative state can, to a part of the client's personality structure, feel like losing the parent and all the positive things the parent represents, such as care, support, survival, love, validation and connection. Thus, clients can be motivated to create negative inner states because these states are associated with parental care.

For example, a client may have grown up with a particularly anxious mother. As a child, the client had not yet learned that the related felt sense is called anxiety and that it is a negative thing. The felt sense of anxiety was simply a defining part of mother. Thus, whenever the client as a child sought nurture, connection, safety and all the other positive things the child got from its mother, they would turn towards the felt sense of anxiety that was their mother. This created in the client a habit of turning to the sense of anxiety whenever they felt the need for nurture, connection, safety, etc. Such a habit can persist in adult life. Thus, when the client feels insecure or in need of nurture, they create the feeling of anxiety as an internal surrogate mother they can turn to in search of these things.

This mechanism is worth exploring when three conditions are fulfilled:

- The client experiences a negative inner state which they wish to change
- The negative state persists over time despite the availability of obvious ways of changing it
- The negative state does not appear to have any hidden benefits or be a consequence of following an obsolete strategy for dealing with a particular challenge in the childhood family environment.

To explore whether a negative inner state functions as a surrogate parent, you can ask the client to describe the felt sense of the state in detail. When the client has a good sense of the state, you can ask:

> "Who is that?" or "Who does this remind you of?"

Often, clients will readily recognise the state as one of their childhood's primary caregivers. This can be very impactful and clarifying. Having revealed the "identity" of the negative state, you can suggest that every time the client feels the state, they turn to it and say: "Hi mom" or "Hi dad" depending on who the state represents.

When the client recognises that the negative state they experience is nothing more than the memory of what a parent felt like to the client as a child it is as if a spell is broken. The negative state will no longer appear as a threat or a burden in the client's life. Often the client will recognise that the state emerges whenever they feel the need for something they as a child would seek in their parents. Clarifying what it is they seek when they turn towards the state that represents a parent enables the client to reinterpret the negative state as a sign that helps them recognise and remember their need, rather than a problem in itself.

One client I worked with many years ago illustrates this process well. She was a highly educated and intelligent woman who was struggling financially and as a result always felt a sense of deprivation (the negative state). Friends and coaches had tried to help her find a well-paid job for years without success. Whenever she was offered a job that would solve her financial difficulties, and, thus, the state of deprivation, she found fault with the job, or something happened that prevented her from applying for it: The job wasn't quite what she wanted to do, she wasn't sure she had the skills needed for the job, she forgot to show up for the job interview, and so on. In sessions, she couldn't think of any benefits of having financial difficulties and feeling deprived. Thus, the situation fulfilled all three criteria for the Parental Surrogates process.

When I asked the woman to describe the state of deprivation she felt when struggling financially, she said she felt a sense of low energy, shabbiness and lack of value. As she described the state in more detail, she suddenly exclaimed: "It's strange, but this state somehow reminds me of my mother". This discovery set off a string of realisations. She realised that she was seeking comfort and connection by staying poor and that the mere idea of becoming affluent filled her with a dread of losing her mother and having to stand alone. Once the client learned to connect directly with states of comfort and connection, she no longer experienced any problems finding a well-paid job. She quickly paid off her debt and got to a place of financial prosperity. Whenever she felt the urge to leave her work or started finding faults with it, she would say: "Hi mom" and, instead of acting on these impulses, she would know that they meant it was time for her to prioritise comfort and connection.

Another client, who experienced a negative state that functioned as a surrogate parent, had a tendency to find everything in life very difficult. In sessions, he would frequently say the words: "It is so hard", whether we were talking about describing the felt sense of a state, finding a concrete example of a situation in which he had experienced a particular problem he wanted to work with, or answering any other question. At some point, the repetition of this phrase seemed more interesting than any of the answers the client would give to my questions. I, therefore, asked the client to describe what it made him feel like to say "It's so hard". The client described a sense of pushing against or carrying something heavy, like a big blob of dark rubber. He described a deep sense of exhaustion and sadness. When I asked him: "Who does that remind you of?", he first didn't understand the question. But after taking some time to reflect, he said: "This is my dad, isn't it?" Whenever, he was faced with an unfamiliar task, this client did what he had done in childhood: He turned to his father for support. His father had suffered from depression and the client remembered him as perpetually exhausted, sad and slumped over like a big blob of dark rubber. Interestingly enough, he had rarely received support from his father. However, small children will often turn to their parents for support even if they frequently do not get it. It is as if they instinctually know that this is the place where they are supposed to get support. Thus, even without receiving actual support, the state of the father and the concept of support can still be associated. Once the client recognised that the inner state he felt was a representation of his father, he stopped taking the sentence "It's so hard" literally. He understood that this sentence wasn't a statement about his situation but rather an expression of his longing for support. When he began to seek support in places where he could actually find it (as opposed to the sense of things being difficult, which offered no support) he found that many of the things that at first glance appeared hard to him became easy to deal with.

In the above stories, the client recognised their negative inner state as a representation of a parental figure with no or little prompting. If, however, a client does not recognise the felt sense of the negative state as one of their primary caregivers, you can try asking them to describe the state, not only in terms of the felt sense, but as a person. You can ask questions, such as:

- "If this state was a person, what would it believe?"
- "If this state was a person, what would be its predominant emotional state?"
- "If this state was a person, what would it say to you?"

Such questions can help map out what the client associates with the state. If the state is, indeed, a representation of a parent, it will be associated with the parent's beliefs, predominant emotional states and typical communications. Mapping out these associations can help reveal the identity of the state.

If this does not bring about a clear recognition in the client, it is good to leave the exploration rather than forcing it. As with all processes in this book, sometimes going through the process will plant an idea in the client's mind which may come to fruition days, weeks, or months later. And if it does not, the negative inner state may simply not be a representation of a parental figure.

The process of Parental Surrogates is summarised in Figure 23.

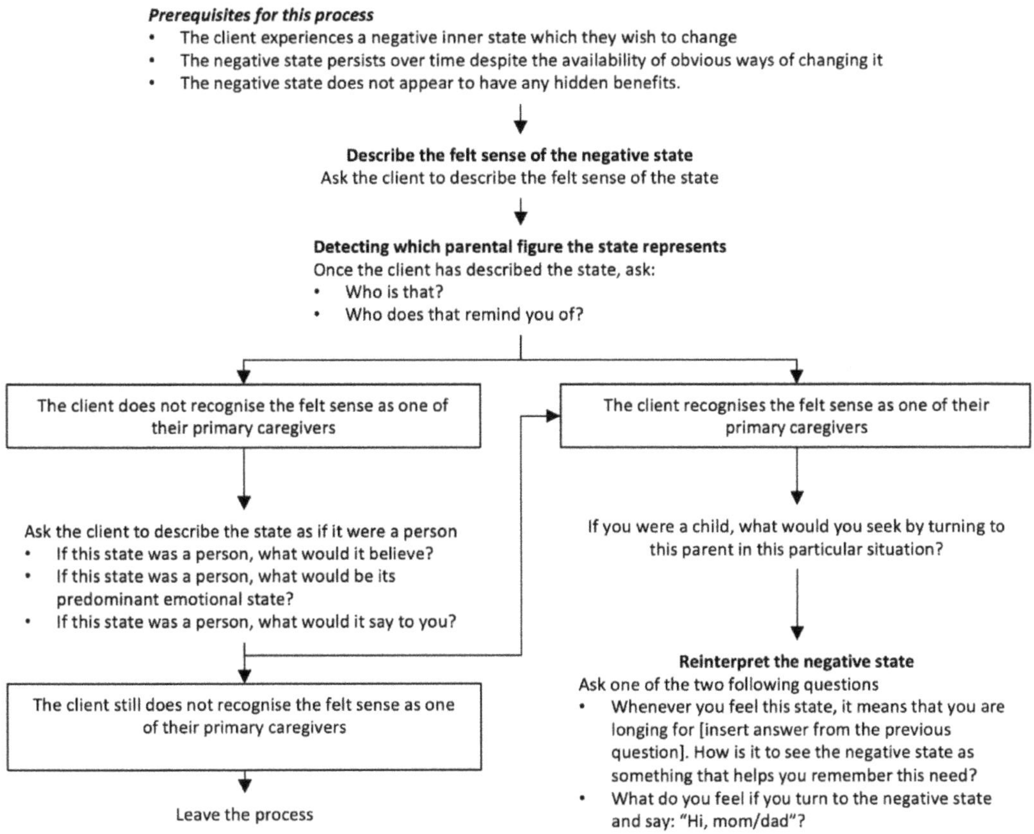

Figure 23: Parental Surrogates Process

5.6.5. Step 5: Correct misconceptions related to the Knot of Alienation

In the Sensing Agency process, the client becomes aware of the mechanism through which they create the experiences of the absence of a positive state or the presence of a negative one.

The two first corrective principles related to the Knot of Alienation are generalisations of such awareness.

1. "If positive states are missing in your life, you are actively turning your attention away from these."
2. "If you experience negative states in your life, you are actively involved in the creation of these."

These corrective principles can be suggested at the end of the Sensing Agency process simply by proposing that what the client has just discovered about a particular unwanted state is true for all unwanted states.

During the Sensing Agency process clients will discover that they are responsible for more of their own suffering than they thought. This can lead to unnecessary and unproductive self-criticism. It can, therefore, be beneficial to round off the Sensing Agency process with a few comments on the third corrective principle related to the Knot of Alienation:

3. "Increased agency comes with increased responsibility."

In particular, it is beneficial to let the client know that they are responsible for the unwanted inner states they experience in the sense that they are actively creating these through automated and unconscious processes. This, however, does not mean that they are responsible for the installation of these processes. No child has the power or knowledge to stand against the forces in their childhood environment that shape these automated and unconscious processes. However, in adult life, it is possible to change these and the first step in doing so is to recognise one's own agency and assume responsibility for whether one carries these patterns forward into the future or not.

Next, we will look at two concrete examples of what the Sensing Agency process may look like in practice.

5.6.6. The sequence of steps in Sensing Agency

While the Sensing Agency process must start with the therapist recognising the Knot of Alienation, the three following steps do not always follow in the same order.

For example, exploring hidden benefits of creating a negative inner state or avoiding a positive one can either be the first or the last step, depending on whether the client is more averse to the idea that they are creating their current unwanted inner state or to the idea that they could be motivated to create a state they see as undesirable.

If the client strongly opposes the idea that they are actively participating in the creation of the undesired inner state, it is beneficial to start by exploring the potential benefits. Once the client realises that they may have an interest in creating and maintaining the undesired state, they will become more open to the idea that they are actively engaged in creating and maintaining it.

Inversely, if the client is strongly opposed to the idea that there could be any benefits to the unwanted inner state, it is beneficial to start by exploring how they create it. Once the client realises that they are indeed creating the state, you can engage them in the exploration of hidden benefits by proposing that human beings never do anything unless they believe they will get something out of it.

5.7. Examples of Sensing Agency

In this section, you can read transcriptions of two therapy sessions applying the process of Sensing Agency. The sessions, like all sessions in this book, are fictional but representative of sessions I have had with clients.

Furthermore, the sessions are abbreviated so they only include the key parts of the exchange. Real sessions often contain more exploration, longer narratives, tangents, pauses, etc. That being said, the Knot of Alienation can, in some cases, be untied in a matter of minutes. In such cases, the examples below would represent full transcriptions of the therapeutic exchange.

The examples are written in two columns. In the left column, you can read the client and therapist's conversation. In the right column, you can read the observations and considerations that guided the therapist during the exchange.

5.7.1. Session 7: Oppression and victimisation

In the following session, the client feels oppressed and victimised when other people talk too much and don't give her space to talk. In this session, we map out the sequence of inner events through which the client produces a sense of being oppressed and victimised as a response to situations where other people talk in a certain way. In the process, we discover that the reason the client feels oppressed is that they have an idea about how to acquire value, which is ruined by the way the others talk. When the client becomes aware of value as an aspect of the present moment, they no longer feel oppressed by people who talk a lot.

Process	Comments
Client: Sometimes, I gather with a group of friends, and we just talk about what is going on in our lives and it is so lovely. It is very convivial, and no one is dominating. I feel a lovely sense of flow in those conversations. However, sometimes there will be someone there who tries to dominate the conversation and then the flow is gone.	The client describes a situation where she experiences that an external circumstance takes away a positive inner state. She does not see her own involvement in the loss of the positive state.
Therapist: How do you push aside the sense of flow when someone is dominating the conversation?	By asking how she pushes aside the flow, I suggest to the client that she is actively involved.
C: Well, I don't think that is something I do. It just happens when someone is dominating. Then I sit there thinking, how long is this going to go on? Should I say that I don't care about what they are talking about? I get oppressed and angry and I'm not interested in what the other person is saying.	The client says she believes she does not do anything – but she provides a lot of information about the sequence of inner events that will be useful later.
T: Can you give a situation where someone dominated you and you felt oppressed by it?	I ask for a concrete example to assist the exploration.
C: That is just how I felt with my mother.	The client gives an example, which reveals a metaphor using the past to understand the present.
T: What did she do to dominate you?	I ask for details.
C: She would tell me not to talk too much and then she would talk a lot.	The client points to an unfair behaviour in her mother.

Process	Comments
T: Excellent. Now imagine someone from a different family, same age as your mother, comes for a visit and you mother says the exact same things to this person.	Imagining someone else in the same situation can be a good way of making the client aware that the actions of the other person doesn't necessarily create the emotions she is feeling herself. I deliberately describe a person very different from the client as a child to increase the likelihood that this person would react differently to the mother's behaviour.
C: (laughs) She wouldn't do that.	That the mother would behave differently indicates that the guest would feel differently.
T: Exactly. If she did, the guest would think she is weird. They would not be oppressed.	I propose that the guest would feel a different inner state in that situation from the one the client felt.
C: No. That is right.	The client confirms my suggestion.
T: What is the difference? What would they feel in that situation?	I ask the client to reflect on the difference to ensure we have it right.
C: They'd think it's weird or rude.	The client expands on the difference.

Process	Comments
T: Yes. So this shows that your mother's behaviour doesn't *create* that state of oppression without your participation. So, the interesting thing is how do you conspire to create the sense of oppression? And I understand that growing up with your mother, you will have been indoctrinated into a particular way of reacting to her and today this isn't altogether your conscious choice. Nonetheless, it is interesting to, now, see how you create the sense of being dominated when someone talks a lot in the way she did.	I verbalise the obvious conclusion, that if not everyone feels oppressed by her mother's actions, the client must be actively involved in the creation of her own sense of oppression. I also acknowledge that her participation is not voluntary and probably not even conscious. This is important because it pre-empts this potential objection from the client.
C: Yes. There are people I and my partner see socially, who I find oppressive, and my partner doesn't find oppressive at all. So, yeah, I guess this also shows that I'm involved in creating the feeling.	The client brings another example that supports the conclusion that she is actively involved.
T: Yes. Some people talk in a certain way. Then you do something with that. And the outcome is a sense of being victimised and oppressed. How do you do it?	Focusing the client's attention on the question of their own agency.
C: I haven't got a clue.	The process creating the sense of oppression is unconscious.
T: That makes it even more interesting.	Using the absence of knowledge to spark further curiosity.
C: Well... I know that when they talk, I begin to feel heavy, angry and critical of this particular person. I feel judgemental and just angry.	The client discovers more emotions related to the situation.

Process	Comments
T: Excellent. So, now you know that you feel victimised and oppressed and also angry. If you should place these emotions on a timeline, which is causing which?	I introduce the idea of ordering one's inner states as a string of events on a timeline.
C: I guess that first I feel angry.	The client proposes a sequence.
T: Good. So, how do you get from anger to feeling victimised and oppressed?	I test the client's idea by asking about the nature of the causal link.
C: Ah, I see. It must be the other way round. I get angry about being victimised and oppressed.	The client realises that the anger is caused by the sense of being oppressed.
T: Yes. That makes sense. So, if the anger is caused by the sense of being victimised and oppressed, what then is causing the sense of being oppressed?	I confirm the client's analysis and ask about what might come before the sense of oppression to move the client's awareness upstream.
C: I think I feel helpless...	The client sees a deeper emotion.
T: Good. So, to feel helpless, there must be something you want to do, you feel unable to do. What is that?	Many emotions indicate something about what caused them. One can use logic to move further upstream.
C: Stop her from talking.	The client sees a deeper motivation.
T: Good. Why do you want to stop her?	Asking about motivation helps moving the client's awareness upstream.
C: I don't know.	Absence of knowledge, indicating that the motivation is unconscious.

Process	Comments
T: Let me give you some options. Why would someone want to stop someone else from talking? Maybe they want to get a point across. Maybe they want the other person to understand something they are seeing. Maybe they just want to be seen.	When the client doesn't know, offering possibilities can help. It does not matter whether the possibilities are correct. Wrong possibilities can trigger the client's wish to correct the therapist and in that way the client becomes aware of their true motivation.
C: Yes. Wanting to be seen feels right. When she talks, I feel eliminated. Not seen at all.	One of the options resonated with the client.
T: And what is it you want to get by being seen?	Once again, I ask about motivation.
C: Yes, of course. I want to be seen. I want her to value me enough to pay attention to me.	The motivation is obvious to the client. The client perceives "being seen" and "being valued" as one and the same.
T: Now we have it! This is the mechanism. First, you want to be seen because you believe that way you will feel value. Then she is talking incessantly and probably not about you.	Now, the mechanism is clear. Starting from a wish to feel value. I summarise the mechanism to the client.
C: (laughs) For sure not about me...	Confirms part of the mechanism.

Process	Comments
T: Exactly. And you have probably tried to stop her and failed at this. And then you feel heavy. And then you say, what is this sense of heaviness? And you interpret that as the feeling of being oppressed and victimised. And then you say: "Why is this person oppressing me and victimising me?" and then you become angry. Is this chain of events close?	At the end of the summary, I ask for the client's confirmation to ensure I've got it right.
C: (laughs) Yes. And it all starts with wanting to be seen because if I'm not seen I feel worthless.	The client confirms the account of the mechanism.
T: That's it. And the whole thing unfolds so quickly. You don't see every step. You just notice that she is talking and then you feel oppressed. And when you don't see the mechanism, you'd ask questions, such as: How can I get her to stop talking? How can I get her to see me? How can I stop her from oppressing me? But the interesting question is: What does the sense of value I'm seeking feel like? What does it feel like?	I acknowledge the kind of questions the client would normally ask and invite the client to ask about the felt sense of the value she seeks. This is the start of the Sensing Abundance process using "value" as a positive entry point. Once the client felt that value, the situations with the mother and the talkative friend were revisited and the client no longer felt oppressed by the situations because their sense of value was no longer threatened by the other person's way of talking.

5.7.2. Session 8: Mother's anxiety

In this session, the client describes feeling a negative inner state, namely anxiety. She knows her anxiety is exaggerated but she does not feel she is creating it. Through the process of Sensing Agency, it becomes clear *how* she creates the anxiety through paying selective attention to everything she finds scary in the world. Seeing this, however, does not affect the client very much. The shift only happens when the client discovers *why* she is holding on to the anxiety.

Process	Comments
Client: I feel anxious. I don't want to be, but I feel I need to be anxious because if I'm not, I may overlook something important and that will be detrimental. I know it is exaggerated. But I cannot let go of it.	The client describes the presence of a negative inner state she does not seem to believe she is creating herself.
Therapist: How do you create the feeling of being anxious?	I ask how she creates the anxiety both to test whether the client feels she creates the anxiety and to suggest to her that she is creating it.
C: It's just there. I think of all the things that can go wrong. What else would I feel?	The client expresses a lack of awareness of her own agency and simultaneously reveals how she is, in fact, creating the anxiety.
T: Yes, so you create the feeling of anxiety by thinking of all the things that can go wrong.	I point out that she is creating the anxiety by the way she uses her attention.
C: Ok, yes, but I feel I need to do that. I don't have a choice.	Clients often try to retain a lack of agency by suggesting they are forced to create the negative inner state.

Process	Comments
T: Who creates the sense of not having a choice? On the one hand you know that you don't need to be as anxious as you are – on the other hand you feel you need to. How do you create that sense of needing to be anxious?	However, since the sense of not having a choice can be seen as yet another negative inner state, the question of agency can also be applied to this sense of not having any choice. It is important not to accept clients' attempts at retaining lack of agency regardless of how they seek to do this.
C: It's just the world. That's how it is. There is so much bad stuff going on. You see it in the news. You hear it from friends. The world is scary.	Once again, the client attempts to normalise their sense of anxiety and see it as something beyond their control.
T: It is true that there are things in the world that requires you to be alert. If a tiger escapes from its cage in the zoo – it is good to be worried and run. But you said yourself that this is not the case right now. So, how do you convince yourself that you need to be anxious, even when there are no obvious threats around?	I challenge this normalisation by making the distinction between a situation where anxiety is warranted by external circumstances and the client's own situation. I use a reference to the client's own words to highlight that the anxiety is not an inevitable response to external circumstances.
C: Even if there are no threats *now*, there might be in the future. And I must be ready. I don't have a choice.	The client keeps justifying their need to be anxious. At this point, the phrase "I don't have a choice" stands out.
T: How do you feel yourself when you say: "I don't have a choice?"	I get a sense that the anxiety and lack of choice may represent a parent.
C: I feel small. I feel like I'm not in control of my life. The best I can do is predict what will happen and get out of the way. I feel a bit like a fugitive, actually. Like I'm on the run and always looking over my shoulder.	The client describes something that sounds like a person. This supports my sense that the anxiety may function as a parental surrogate.

Process	Comments
T: Can you say more about this fugitive? Who is this fugitive as a person?	I ask the client to develop their description.
C: She feels a bit like a scared child. I feel I don't really matter. Like there are forces in this life that play out and I'm like a mouse that might get squashed.	The richness of this description strengthens my belief that the client's inner state is a representation of a person.
T: Do you know who you are describing? Does this remind you of anyone? Do you know anyone, who felt like this?	I ask who the person might be.
C: This is my mother. Her family had to flee from Germany at the start of the war. She never talked much about it. But it really affected her deeply. My parents were wealthy, but they always kept it a secret. Especially my mother worried a lot about what other people might do out of envy if they found out.	The client directly recognises that she is describing her mother.
T: Good. What do you see if you compare your feeling of anxiety and of not having any choice in the matter with your mother's inner state?	To test whether the anxiety and lack of choice is indeed a representation of the client's mother, I ask her to compare the two.
C: That is so much how she felt. Especially when I was a child. Oh my God, she even used to say: "I don't have a choice" all the time. It was like her mantra. How could I miss this?	The client's response confirms that the identity of her anxiety is her mother.

Process	Comments
T: Good. This explains why you don't let go of the anxiety. To a part of you, it represents mother. When you try to get rid of it, a part of you feels like you are trying to get rid of mother. How would it be to simply turn to the anxiety and say: "Hi mom"?	I invite the client to reinterpret the sense of anxiety and see it as a representation of her mother.
C: (cries) I don't know why I'm crying. This is very emotional for me.	The client's reaction indicates that a deep process is set in motion.
T: Good. Welcome the tears.	I give time for the process.
C: (sighs) Oh. It's like this knot that's been there (points to her solar plexus) all my life just released. I feel I can breathe. I never knew. I don't feel I need to get rid of the anxiety to not feel anxious. Does that make sense?	The confusion indicates the emergence of a new understanding that is at odds with the client's old understanding. Here it is good to give ample time to the client.
T: Yes. When you recognise the anxiety as your mother, it has a different meaning. It is not a signal that you are in danger. It's just the memory of your mother.	I support the client's experience by offering an explanation.
C: That's it. I feel a lot of love towards her all of a sudden. I cannot remember the last time I even felt close to her.	Sudden and unusual feelings of love towards a parent is a common indication that the client has separated themselves from a problematic representation of that parent.
T: Good. You are released from the spell. Enjoy.	I verbalise the separation.
C: I will. Thank you.	
T: Thank you.	

5.7.3. A comment on sessions 3 & 5

Sessions 3 and 5 both started with the same statement from the client:

> "The problem I have is that I pick the wrong partners. I always get involved with partners who are unstable, and I end up having to support them and help with all their problems. I'd like to have a stable partner. Someone who can help me out once in a while. But whenever I find someone who is stable, I feel no attraction. I'd like help figuring out how to be attracted to partners that are good for me."

In session 3, I invited the client to explore what they are ultimately reaching for by finding a stable partner. Through the process of Sensing Completion, the client discovered that they were looking for a sense of ease, relaxation and home.

In session 5, I invited the client to explore what they were trying to avoid by finding a stable partner. Through the process of Sensing Taboos, the client discovered that they were avoiding a sense of absence of love and purpose. When they explored the felt sense of this absence of love and purpose, they found that it just felt empty and that allowing themselves to feel empty brought a sense of softness and love.

In the opening statement, the client talks about how they keep choosing unstable partners. While they technically say they are doing it, they talk about this as if they are not quite in charge of their own choices. You could, therefore, use the Sensing Agency process to make the client more aware of their own agency in the choice of partners by investigating:

- How the client manages to consistently choose unstable partners.
- What hidden benefits does the client get from choosing unstable partners?
- Is the choice of unstable partners part of a strategy the client developed to deal with a particular challenge in their childhood family environment?
- What sensation does having unstable partners create in the client and who might this sensation represent to the client?

5.8. Untying the Knot of Alienation through contemplations

In Section 5.6, I outlined how the Knot of Alienation can be untied in one-to-one sessions with clients.

In this section, I will present three contemplation exercises that are specifically designed to untie the Knot of Alienation. These exercises are well suited to group work. The instructions are sufficiently simple to be given to a group, and the exercises can, for example, be performed in pairs or as individual writing exercises.

These contemplation exercises can be deepened through one-to-one processing, as outlined in the previous sections. When working with groups, I often begin by inviting the students to do the contemplation exercise in pairs or individually. Afterwards, I work one-to-one with a few students in plenum. This approach has the advantage that although I only work with a few students directly, the other students, having completed the contemplation exercise, can partake in the one-to-one processing vicariously.

5.8.1. How do you create negative states?

In this chapter, we have seen how clients create negative inner states and then lose awareness of the process through which they create these states. Consequently, clients will experience the negative states as either emerging without any discernible cause or they will ascribe the negative states to external circumstances. In either case, they will be blind to their own agency.

In a group setting, you can ask students to contemplate how they create specific negative inner states, such as anger, frustration, meaninglessness, neediness, etc., by asking questions such as:

- How to you create frustration in your life?
- How do you create a sense of meaninglessness?
- How do you achieve a sense of neediness?

These questions presuppose agency and, as such, direct students' awareness towards the exploration of their own participation in the creation of these states.

If students have already acknowledged, or at least find it plausible, that they feel the negative inner states, you can directly ask them to explore the above questions.

However, for some negative inner states, students may not believe that they feel these states. In such cases, the above exploration can be preceded by exploring questions such as:

- When do you feel frustration?
- When have you felt meaninglessness?
- When do you feel needy?

Such questions can be framed by stating that these states are something most people experience from time to time but that since they are unpleasant, we tend to forget. In order to explore these states, as opposed to simply repressing them, it is important to start by noticing them. This framing gives an incentive to detect situations where one has actually felt these states.

It is also good to encourage students to find current situations as some students tend to repress the states by exclusively remembering situations in the distant past, which then allows them to pretend that these feelings no longer arise in them.

Most people can readily find situations where they felt frustration. This is because frustration, while uncomfortable to most people, is generally both tolerable to most people and accepted as a normal part of emotional life.

However, other states, such as neediness or meaninglessness, can be far more disturbing to people, both because of the intensity of the negative connotations surrounding these states and because they, consequently, often are not seen as part of normal emotional life. In such cases, it can be good to precede the contemplations suggested above with another question exploring the students' agency, namely:

- How do you avoid noticing your frustration?
- How do you avoid meaninglessness?
- How do you avoid feeling your neediness?

These questions suggest that the reason students may believe they do not feel these inner states is not that they actually do not feel them, but rather that they actively avoid them.

Students may, for example, avoid frustration by tensing up and putting on a smile or by rationalising their expressions of frustration as a wish to be helpful. Similarly, students may avoid meaninglessness by keeping themselves busy or by indulging in entertainment. Finally, students may avoid neediness by avoiding situations where they have to rely on others or by minimising their needs.

Recognising how they avoid a negative inner state helps students recognise when they feel this inner state.

If, for example, a student notices they avoid feeling frustration by tensing up and putting on a smile, they may learn to recognise a tense smile as an indication that they are feeling frustrated. Similarly, if a student notices that they avoid meaninglessness by consuming entertainment, they may learn to recognise their urge to binge-watch a tv series as an indication that they feel meaninglessness.

Thus, the three contemplation questions above can form a series of exercises that gradually reveal deeper layers of the students' agency in relation to the creation of their own experience of negative inner states. An exploration of neediness could, thus consist of the following three contemplation exercises:

- How do you avoid neediness?
- When do you feel needy?
- How do you create the feeling of neediness?

Whereas it is technically possible to engage in such strings of contemplations for each possible negative inner state, it would take a very long time. Thus, as a facilitator of personal development workshops, it is important to select which states to work with.

One way of selecting is to create workshops specifically focused on a particular negative inner state. That way, people who come to the workshop will, most likely, find it relevant to work with this particular state.

Another way is to work with negative inner states related to a particular aspect of Being. That way, the exploration of each negative state is likely to take the students to the same aspect of Being since this aspect of Being will be part of the material from which the students create the negative inner state.

For example, the dynamic aspect of Being frequently plays a role in the creation of negative inner states such as aggression, domination, recklessness, frustration, fear of other people, submissiveness and lethargy. Therefore, it can be advantageous to explore these inner states, or a selection of these inner states, together. Similarly, the silent aspect of Being frequently plays a role in the creation of negative inner states such as lostness, meaninglessness, lack of connection and cold hate. Therefore, it can be fruitful to explore such inner states together.

For an overview of which negative inner states typically relate to which aspects of Being see Sections 4.2 Negative reifications of the 10 aspects of Being and 5.3 Alienation from the 10 aspects of Being .

Asking students to contemplate how they create negative inner states can be a powerful way of elucidating their own agency by helping them become aware of the unconscious processes through which they create such states.

5.8.2. How do you avoid positive states? What do you pay attention to instead?

Just like we create negative inner states and then forget that we created them, we also avoid positive inner states and then forget that we do so.

The second type of contemplation exercise focuses on generating awareness of the ways in which students actively avoid noticing positive inner states through selective use of awareness.

You can do so by asking questions such as:

- How do you avoid feeling happy?
- What do you pay attention to instead of peace?

As with the questions in the previous section, these questions presuppose that the client is actively involved in creating their experience. Thus, they contain the assumption that when students do not feel happy or peaceful it is because they are actively doing something to avoid feeling or noticing these states.

As these presuppositions are likely to run counter to the students' beliefs, it can be useful to frame the questions by pointing out that happiness and peace are part of what the students can experience in meditation when they unhook their attention from any activity. You can, for example, say:

> "When people meditate, they can experience happiness and peace. This shows that these states are part of what one experiences when one does nothing. Thus, if you do not experience these states, you must be doing something that takes your awareness away from them."

When contemplating these questions, students will typically discover that they avoid positive inner states by reacting to the negative ideas they have about these states.

For example, a student may notice that whenever they feel a bit of happiness, they start worrying about whether other people around them are happy and whether anyone might attack them for being happy. Thus, they avoid feeling happy by worrying about being attacked for feeling happy.

As another example, a student may notice that they down prioritise feeling peace because they believe it is more important to focus their attention on how to develop their career or some other tasks. Thus, they do not feel peace because they do not value it and, consequently, they never take the time to feel it.

By recognising how they avoid positive inner states, students can begin to explore how it would be for them to pause the activities that take their attention away from these states.

Furthermore, it reveals the futility of any activity they engage in to create the positive states – if they do not also pause the processes that prevent them from feeling or noticing those states.

For example, a student may notice that they spend a lot of money on things that supposedly should make them happy, while at the same time fearing feeling happy because they (unconsciously) believe it puts them at risk of being attacked.

Similarly, a student may seek to be alone to feel peace but when they are alone they spend all their time working to build their career because they fundamentally do not value peace.

Thus, asking students to reflect on how they avoid positive states can be a powerful way of bringing attention to students' own agency in relation to experiencing a lack of such states in their lives.

5.8.3. What are the hidden benefits of your suffering?

Finally, exploring the hidden benefits of creating negative inner states or blocking positive ones offers a great contemplation question.

You can ask questions, such as:

1. What are the benefits of feeling lonely?
2. What are the benefits of not feeling happy?
3. What are the benefits of being needy?
4. What are the benefits of having no energy?

As these questions are likely to turn the students' perspective upside down, it is good to frame them by first acknowledging the students' perspective and then pose the question. You can say:

> "Of course, nobody likes to feel lonely. There are many obvious downsides to feeling lonely. However, there might also be benefits. What might the benefits of feeling lonely be?"
>
> "It is easy to see the benefits of feeling happy. For one, it just feels good. However, it is not uncommon to feel that there are also benefits to *not* feeling happy. What are the benefits of not feeling happy?"

Contemplating hidden benefits can be a good preparation for the previous contemplation exercises around how students create negative states or avoid positive ones. It can be easier to see *how* one does something, if one first understands *why* one would do it.

However, contemplating hidden benefits can also come after contemplations of how students create negative states or avoid positive ones. The advantage of doing the contemplation exercises in this order is that it makes it possible to provide a stronger framing for the exploration of hidden benefits. You can, for example, introduce this contemplation in the following way:

> "As we have just seen, you actively create the feeling of neediness. And as human beings we never do anything without a reason. Thus, there must be benefits – real or imagined – of being needy. What are the benefits of being needy?"
>
> "So, now that you have seen how you create the experience of having no energy, it can be interesting to explore what motivates you. What are the benefits of not having any energy?"

Recognising the benefits of creating negative inner states or avoiding positive ones can be valuable for the students for at least two reasons.

First, it helps them adopt a more understanding attitude towards themselves and diminish the sense of alienation they may feel when they discover that they do something that seems to go against their own interests. For example, a student may realise that they create a sense of loneliness by avoiding forming connections with others and that this is a way of protecting themselves against being abandoned. Understanding the purpose transforms the behaviour from something irrational and self-destructive to something that is merely unskilful – and that can be much easier to relate to.

Second, sometimes the hidden benefits are absurd, and once they are verbalised, they lose their influence over the student. Consequently, the student may stop creating the negative state or avoiding the positive one. For example, a student may realise that the reason they avoid happiness is that they believe this will be appreciated by other people and that this appreciation will make them happy. Recognising the absurdity of this circular or self-defeating logic can lead the student to immediately drop it.

5.9. Summary

In this chapter, we have explored the Knot of Alienation. This knot occurs when mental, emotional and behavioural patterns that have become automated and unconscious produce states that are later judged as negative or systematically take our attention away from states we judge as positive.

The Knot of Alienation produces and is sustained by three misconceptions: That not feeling a state means that the state is not there, that external circumstances directly create negative inner states and that agency and responsibility are independent.

The way to untie the Knot of Alienation is through the process of Sensing Agency, where we bring awareness to the processes through which we create negative inner states and avoid positive ones.

We looked at how this process can be facilitated in one-to-one sessions and through three contemplation exercises.

Next, we look at the Knot of Fragmentation which can be seen as a deeper state of alienation where parts of our personality structure get into more or less permanent conflict with each other. Such conflict can severely capture our attention and, thus, deepen our lack of awareness of Being.

With the Knot of Fragmentation, we also move from exploring single patterns in the personality structure to looking at the systemic level of this structure.

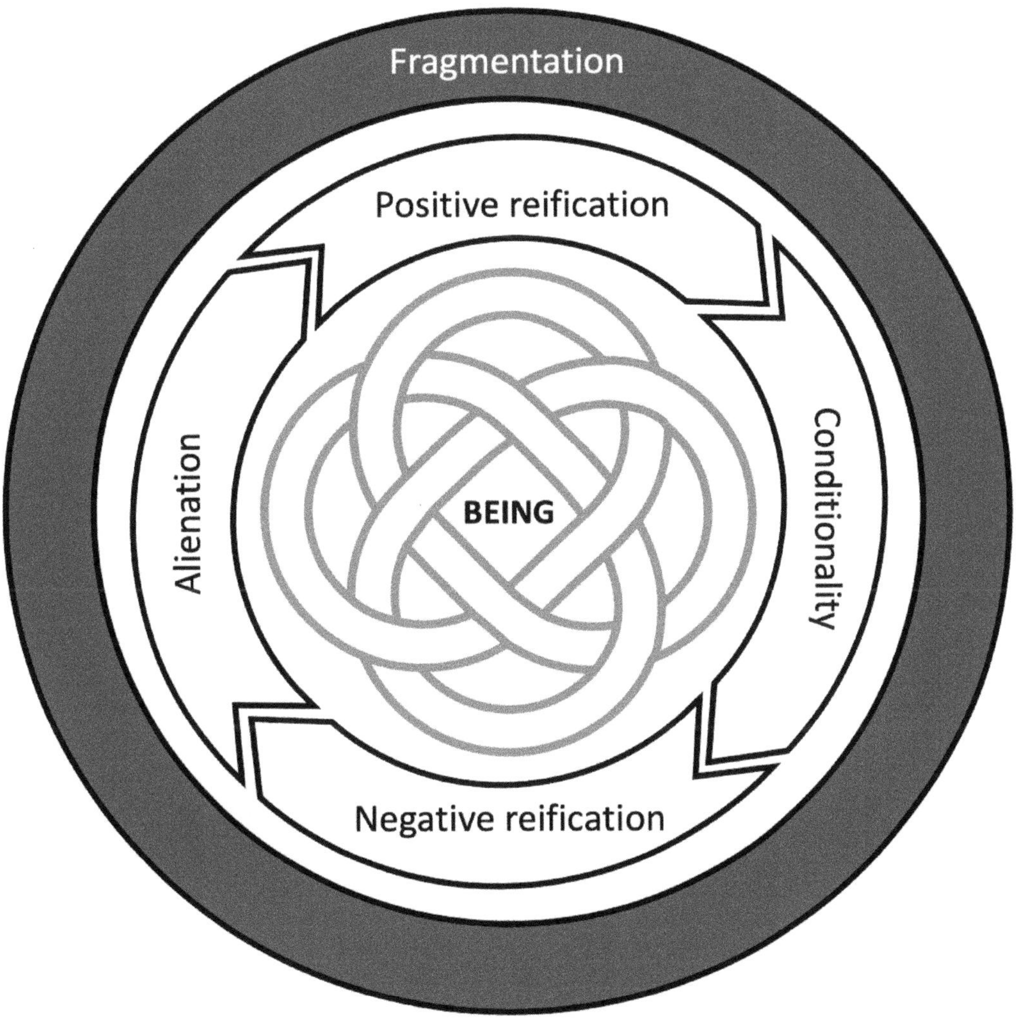

The Knot of Fragmentation

6. Knot 5: The Knot of Fragmentation

So far, we have seen how clients:

- Reify experiences of Being as positive phenomena making it appear as if there are many *different* positive phenomena they must acquire to thrive in life (The Knot of Positive Reification)
- Develop ideas about what conditions are needed to create or acquire each of these positive phenomena, which takes the client's awareness away from Being (The Knot of Conditionality)
- Reify aspects of Being as negative phenomena to be avoided, either because they are perceived as the opposite of the aspect the client is seeking or because the way the client has been seeking the aspect has had negative consequences (The Knot of Negative Reification)
- Fight the consequences of the above-mentioned actions because they have automated them and lost awareness of their own agency (The Knot of Alienation)

The result is a fragmented system of automated processes conflicting with each other in their distinct pursuits of different positive reifications of Being.

Such inner conflicts between automated processes or subsystems drain our energy and consume our attention in such a way that we no longer notice Being.

Therefore, resolving these inner conflicts can greatly liberate clients' awareness so they may become aware of Being.

Clients frequently seek to resolve their inner conflicts either by aligning with one side of the conflict against the other or by seeking a compromise between the conflicting parts. However, neither option can resolve the conflict since no subsystem will give up or compromise in its pursuit of Being.

Therefore, such attempts at resolving the conflicts will only consume or monopolise clients' awareness even further and, thus, further deepen the clients' sense of loss resulting from their lack of awareness of Being. This will, in turn, increase the activity of the conflicting subsystems as their activity intensifies in proportion to the perceived sense of loss. This vicious cycle is the Knot of Fragmentation.

The Knot of Fragmentation makes it difficult to work with the Knots described previously in this book because each time we turn our attention to a particular process in the client, other processes that are created to deal with the negative side effects of the process we wish to explore are triggered. Consequently, every time we focus our attention on one process in a client's inner life, we may be distracted by other processes before we have had a chance to complete our work.

This situation is akin to the situation where a group of people who disagree with each other, keep interrupting each other and shutting each other down. The result is that no one gets to provide a coherent account of their perspective and intentions.

To undo the Knot of Fragmentation, we must create space to work with one automated process at a time by putting other automated processes on pause. We need to stop the interference from other processes long enough for us to track the process we are exploring and recognise how positive reification, conditionality, negative reification and alienation play a part in this process.

Once we have done this with all the processes related to a particular inner conflict, we will frequently discover that there never was any real conflict in the first place because all processes involved in the apparent conflict are ultimately reaching for the same goal, namely Being. This is the process of Sensing Unity.

To understand the Knot of Fragmentation and how to untie it, it is useful to introduce the concept of personality parts and personality structure as well as the model of The 10 Strands of Mind.

6.1. Personality parts and personality structure

In this chapter, I will use the concepts of "personality parts" and "personality structure" extensively. As these concepts have been used in different ways by different authors, I must start by defining how I will use them in this chapter.

Our inner life is a complex tapestry of automated thoughts, emotions and behaviours, all connected in intricate patterns. Psychologists call such patterns schemas.

The purpose of schemas is to enable individuals to automatically make predictions by juxtaposing current observations and past experiences and to select a course of action based on these predictions.

While schemas are generally beneficial, we all contain some that are detrimental to our well-being. Despite being detrimental to our well-being, such schemas can persist simply because their complexity obscures the full scope of their impact.

Personality parts

To help us gain a more comprehensive understanding of our more complex schemas, it is beneficial to envision them as a community of distinct personality parts, each functioning like a mini-individual, which may relate to each other in supportive or conflicting ways.

Aggregating automated mental, emotional and behavioural patterns into coherent "personality parts" and examining the interactions among these enables us to discern larger patterns that would otherwise remain unnoticed and discover when these patterns lead to suboptimal outcomes.

The metaphorical framework of seeing our inner life as consisting of a community of distinct personality parts is key to many therapeutic approaches, including the chair work in Gestalt Therapy and the parts work in Internal Family Systems.

In this chapter, I will use the framework of "personality parts" extensively as this framework makes it easier to perceive and talk about themes, such as:

- How therapists can discern the schemas operating in their clients
- How clients' schemas get into conflict
- How such conflicts capture clients' attention and draw them away from Being
- How lack of awareness of Being intensifies conflicts between clients' schemas
- How resistance to therapeutic work can be viewed as the interruption by other parts and, thus, used to map out clients' systems of personality parts
- How it is possible to conceive of therapeutic work as a form of inner mediation between schemas, leading to a more coherent and less fragmented system of schemas.

Talking about the above themes using other frameworks can be cumbersome and make them appear very complex. Using the framework of personality parts makes them much easier to understand and talk about with clients.

Personality structure

Whereas I will use the term "personality part" to refer to a client's schemas, I will use the term "personality structure" to refer to the client's entire system of personality parts.

I already introduced the concept of "personality structure" in Section 5.2, *The layered personality structure*. The main idea in that section was that when we become alienated from our own agency, rather than changing automated processes that produce unwanted outcomes, we add new processes that mitigate these unwanted outcomes.

The result is a system of processes where many of the processes exist solely to deal with the negative side effects of other processes. Such a system is akin to a computer program that is riddled with patches and in need of a new base code.

In particular, around every positive reification of Being we create automated processes aimed at acquiring this positive reification. But because these processes are guided by the misconceptions that Being is separate from us and that it must be acquired, they produce negative outcomes, such as negative reification of Being and loss of awareness of Being. Rather than ceasing our misconceived attempts at acquiring Being, we form new automated processes, aimed at dealing with these negative side effects.

In the framework of personality parts, we may say that parts of us seek to attain various aspects of Being. Because these parts believe they seek different things they get into conflict with each other and demonise each other. When this leads to loss of awareness of Being, we perceive the resulting negative states as altogether new problems we must deal with and to do this we develop more personality parts. The resulting personality structure will, therefore, contain many conflicting and redundant personality parts. The moment we become aware of Being, all of these personality parts are set free in the sense that the problem they were struggling to solve has been dissolved through other means than those applied by the parts. Thus, personal and spiritual development within the framework of personality parts can be seen as a matter of correcting the misconceived beliefs embedded in our personality parts and, thus, reducing our personality structure.

6.2. The 10 Strands of Mind

In this book, I operate with ten aspects of Being, which are distinct felt-sense experiences that can arise when we become aware of Being.

Throughout the book, I have connected each aspect of Being with:

1. **Positive phenomena**, which are positive reifications of the felt sense we can experience when becoming aware of an aspect of Being (Section 2.3).
2. **Behavioural patterns**, which are strategies for creating or acquiring these positive phenomena (Section 3.1).
3. **Negative phenomena**, which are negative reifications of the felt sense of an aspect of Being once it has become associated with negative outcomes of the strategies for attaining this aspect or is seen as an obstacle to obtaining a different aspect of Being (Section 4.2).
4. **Sense of loss or deficiencies**, which is the result of negative reifications of an aspect of Being leading the individual to actively turn away from this aspect and, consequently, experiencing it less (Section 5.3).

In this section, I combine the models presented in previous chapters into the 10 Strands of Mind model (see Figure 24 on page 450), where each strand consists of an aspect of Being and the corresponding felt sense experiences, positive reifications, behavioural patterns, negative reifications and sense of loss or deficiency.

This model is useful for two things:

1. **Linking psychological issues to aspects of Being:** It can help therapists develop hypotheses about what aspects of Being clients are likely to experience when they untie their inner knots and, inversely, which issues might emerge in reaction to experiences of specific aspects of Being[51].
2. **Ten languages for teaching:** It gives therapists the possibility of talking about key themes of personal and spiritual development in ten different "languages". This is useful as it can help making the sometimes rather abstract teachings more personal and relatable.

---

[51] I will say more about why issues emerge in response to experiences of Being in Sections 7.5.5 and 7.5.6.

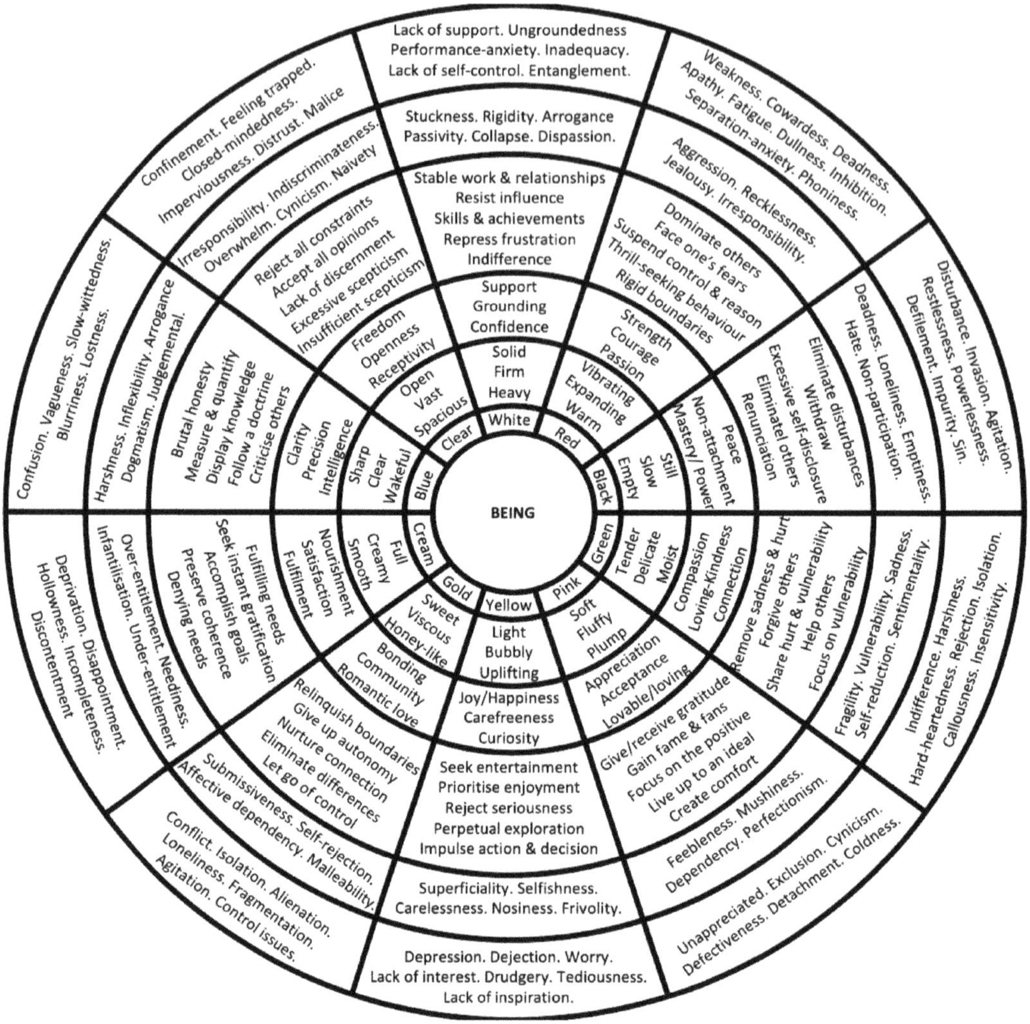

Figure 24: The 10 Strands of Mind

6.2.1. Linking psychological issues to aspects of Being

Each section of the map in Figure 24 links psychological issues related to different knots to the felt sense of a given aspect of Being.

The inner most circle contains the name of the aspects

The second circle contains a few words describing the felt sense of each aspect.

The third circle contains positive reifications of each aspect of Being. When we work with the positive aspects named in one section of this circle through the process of Sensing Abundance, we are likely to find the felt sense in the second circle of the same section. For example, when exploring positive phenomena, such as "support", "grounding" and "confidence" through the process of Sensing Abundance, clients are likely to encounter the solid, firm and heavy aspect of Being. Similarly, when exploring positive phenomena, such as "strength", "courage" and "passion", clients are likely to encounter the vibrating, expanding and warm aspect of Being.

The fourth circle contains examples of strategies clients typically use to create or acquire the positive phenomena in the third circle. Thus, when using the Sensing Completion process to explore what clients ultimately seek through the behaviours mentioned in the fourth circle, we are likely to find the positive phenomena and the felt sense in the third and second circles in the same section. For example, when exploring what clients are reaching out for by withdrawing or by seeking to eliminate disturbances (outside as well as inside) through the process of Sensing Completion, we are likely to encounter the still aspect of Being and clients are likely to name it as "peace" or "power". Similarly, when exploring what clients are reaching out for by seeking to alleviate other people's pain or by cultivating and inflating their own hurt and vulnerability, we are likely to encounter the tender aspect of Being, and clients are likely to call it "compassion" or "kindness".

The fifth circle contains the negative reifications of a particular aspect of Being. Thus, when we use the Sensing Taboos process to explore the felt sense of the negative states mentioned in the fifth circle, we are likely to find the felt sense in the second circle of the same section, and when the judgement is removed from the felt sense, the negative states are likely to "transform" into the positive phenomena mentioned in the third circle. For example, when exploring the felt-sense essence of negative phenomena, such as "mushiness" and "dependency" through the process of Sensing Taboos, we are likely to find the soft aspect of Being and clients are likely to call it "appreciation", "acceptance" or "lovability". Similarly, if we explore the felt sense essence of negative phenomena, such as "carelessness", "superficiality" and "frivolity" through the process of Sensing Taboos, we are likely to find the light aspect of Being, and clients are likely to call this "carefreeness", "happiness" or "joy".

Finally, the outermost circle contains descriptions of loss and deficiency that clients experience when the negative reifications of an aspect of Being leads the client to turn away from it and lose awareness of it. When we use the Sensing Agency process to explore how clients create the sense of loss and deficiency found in this circle, we are likely to find mechanisms that makes the client perceive the felt sense in the second circle of the same segment in negative ways, and when they pause these mechanisms, they are likely to find the felt sense and positive phenomena mentioned in the second and third circle of the same section. For example, when clients through the process of Sensing Agency become aware of how they create negative states, such as "conflict", "isolation" or "aienation" and they consider what it might be like to pause these processes, they are likely to discover the sweet aspect of Being, and they may call it "love", "bonding" or "sense of community". Similarly, when clients through the process of Sensing Agency become aware of how they create negative states, such as "deprivation", "disappointment" or "incompleteness" and they consider what it might be like to pause these processes, they are likely to discover the fullness of Being, and they may call it "nourishment", "satisfaction" or "fulfilment".

Thus, the model provides a way for therapists to orient themselves and get a sense of what aspects of Being underpin a broad range of personal experiences – both positive and negative. The model can help therapists avoid getting lost in detail and retain a focus on the purpose of helping clients become aware of Being.

6.2.2. Ten languages for teaching

Knowing the map is helpful, not only because it helps predict what states of Being clients might become aware of as they untie various inner knots, but also because it gives therapists the possibility of talking about key themes of personal and spiritual development in ten different "languages". This is helpful because it makes it possible to make rather abstract teachings more relatable.

Below, I will briefly comment on how the model affords different ways of speaking about a few key themes in personal and spiritual development.

Ego death

One important theme in personal and spiritual development is the theme of ego death. In the abstract this can be described as the dissolution or surrender of the ego, leading to a state of non-attachment and liberation. The above map provides a way of translating this somewhat abstract description into ten different descriptions each of which might be easier to relate to for certain people.

For example, a client may come to you because they have uncontrollable eruptions of anger, which ruin their relationships. Going through the process of Sensing Completion, the client may realise that the eruptions of anger are attempts at connecting with the dynamic aspect of Being. As the client becomes aware of the dynamic aspect of Being they start feeling effortlessly energised and autonomous (two common positive reifications of the dynamic aspect of Being). This experience may lead the client to feel that they no longer have any need for the aggressive behaviour as the purpose of this was to establish the sense of autonomy which they now feel. Thus, the energy of the dynamic aspect of Being cuts through the false beliefs that burdened this personality part and it is set free. This is an example of ego death in that it is a process through which part of the ego structure is dissolved. However, explaining ego death as the process through which Being cuts through the false beliefs that keeps the ego structure in place will be very relatable to the client who just went through this process.

Similarly, ego death can be explained as the way the stable aspect of Being allows us to not become hooked on any thoughts or emotions, as the way the still aspect of Being dissolves all the patterns of our mind, as the way the tender aspect of Being melts everything that is frozen in us, as the way the sweet aspect of Being melts us, and so on. Each of these ways of speaking about ego death may be more relatable to specific clients, depending on their personality structure and on what processes they have recently experienced. I will return to the topic of ego death in Section 5.4.2, where I will give a more technical account of this phenomenon as a consequence of a particular category of learning.

Meditation

The theme of meditation is often described as practices aimed at cultivating awareness, presence, and a deeper connection to the present moment. The above model offers different ways of describing such practices as the practice of:

- Losing interest in / not getting involved with thoughts and emotions (stability)
- Allowing everything inside to move unhindered (dynamism)
- Cutting through to the stillness behind the inner turbulence (stillness)
- Cultivating loving-kindness towards all aspects of yourself and others – including those that have hurt you (tenderness)
- Appreciating anything we encounter for what it is/accepting what is (softness)
- Not taking thoughts and emotions seriously (lightness)
- Melting any inner boundaries (sweetness)
- Enjoying the richness of the present moment (fullness)
- Perceiving the present moment as it is without superimposing one's own interpretations and preferences (clarity)
- Shifting awareness from thoughts and emotions to the space that contains them (openness)

Non-duality

Non-duality teachings generally emphasise the importance of realising the ultimate unity of all things, transcending the illusion of separation between the self and the external world, and between aspects of inner and outer life.

Using the model, it is possible to talk about how the positive and negative states pertaining to each strand are expressions of the same fundamental aspect of Being. For example, the felt-sense essence of aggression and strength are both energy, the felt-sense essence of happiness and superficiality are both lightness, etc.

Furthermore, the model enables us to talk about how aspects from different strands ultimately are expressions of, or are reaching for, the same. For example, at first glance, “being disciplined” and “rejecting seriousness” seem mutually exclusive. However, realising that they are expressions of the desire to reach the stable and light aspects of Being can enable us to recognise the way in which they are two sides of the same coin in that discipline provides a basis for lightness and adopting a less serious and more playful attitude can greatly reduce resistance to engagement and make discipline easier.

I will return to this theme multiple times in the present chapter.

Other themes

Other themes, where each strand of the model affords a different language, include the process of enlightenment or awakening, the concept and meaning of karma and rebirth, the importance and meaning of compassion and loving-kindness, and the process of surrender.

Having multiple ways of speaking about each of these themes is a must for any therapist who includes spirituality in their therapeutic work.

The map presented here is limited in three ways.

First, due to limited space it does not include all possible positive phenomena, strategies and negative phenomena. Neither does it contain a full description of each aspect of Being. Unpacking each strand in the model would be a topic for an entire book. However, working from this principle, therapists will discover many connections for themselves.

Second, the variety in how individual clients interpret aspects of Being and the strategies they develop to pursue these is great. For this reason, therapists must always bear in mind the possibility that some clients will contain connections that do not fit the map. The map is, thus, merely a tool for generating hypotheses that can guide the therapist – it is not a substitute for listening to one's clients.

Third, it is common for systems that examine Being to split it into components. In this book I talk about the peaceful aspect, the dynamic aspect, the stable aspect, the light aspect, and so on. The main risk in doing so is that we may forget that the components we explore are all aspects of one thing and feel the need to work with each and every component individually.

The above map may give the impression that there is an endless number of processes to go through: Sensing the abundance in every single positive phenomenon, exploring what every single behavioural pattern is reaching for, sensing the felt sense essence of every negative phenomenon, and so on. This is generally a risk related to every system that examines Being by splitting it into components. It can give the false impression that it is necessary to work with every component individually making personal and spiritual development somewhat of a Sisyphus work. I have seen many people getting caught in this trap. Instead of resting in Being, they are always looking for the next component of Being, feeling that the work is not done before they have the "complete collection". What they fail to understand is that the totality of Being is present in any single aspect. The categorisation is needed to have a tool capable of detecting all the patterns that can take awareness away from Being – it is not needed to perceive Being itself. When you perceive Being you perceive all of it. You don't have partial Being or Being with some pieces missing. This is why the name for enlightenment in different traditions may correspond to a single aspect of Being. For example, the Buddhist word for enlightenment "Nirvana" means to be blown out. This refers to the silent aspect of Being. In contrast, the Hindu word for enlightenment "Moksha" means liberation, referring to the open aspect of Being. One aspect is enough because each aspect is a name for the whole. If you find one side of a house, you have found the full house. You don't need to do extra work to find the other sides even if they are not in your immediate field of vision.

6.3. The Knot of Fragmentation and implications for therapy

The Knot of Fragmentation can be broken down into five interrelated misconceptions about identity and the ways in which the clusters of automated processes we call personality parts relate to each other.

Clients generally believe they have a single self in the sense that they have a single centre of volition (16th misconception). The belief in a single self makes clients sort their automated processes into the ones they see as part of this single self and those they do not see as part of the single self. Because the latter parts hold beliefs, values, emotions and agendas that are at odds with those contained in the former parts, clients will perceive some of their personality parts as inner enemies or obstacles (17th misconception). Once certain parts have been labelled as inner enemies or obstacles, clients are likely to form the belief that they should free themselves from these parts (18th misconception) and they may believe they can do so by rejecting them (19th misconception). Finally, because the agendas contained in the different personality parts can be mutually exclusive, clients tend to assume that their goals and intentions are also mutually exclusive and that it, therefore, is not possible to attain all of what their different personality parts seek (20th misconception)[52].

To undo the Knot of Fragmentation, the therapist must shift each of these misconceptions by taking the client through lines of inquiry that will help them discover for themselves that rather than a single self, they have multiple selves (16th corrective principle); that no parts of them are enemies or obstacles in themselves but only appear to be so from the perspective of certain other parts (17th corrective principle); that if they allow any part, regardless of how problematic it may appear at first glance, to show them what it is ultimately seeking, it will always reveal an inner treasure in the form of an aspect of Being (18th corrective principle); that the act of rejecting a personality part is an expression of the very part one seeks to reject (19th corrective principle); and that any perception of having to choose between the objectives of different personality parts are ultimately an illusion since all parts ultimately seek Being (20th corrective principle).

It is very useful to discern how the five misconceptions related to the Knot of Fragmentation manifest in clients as this gives you valuable insight into the processes through which clients develop and maintain internal conflicts. Such insight can help dissolve clients' inner conflicts and doing so is important because inner conflicts is one of the main things that occupy clients' awareness and distract them from noticing Being[53].

---

[52] This final misconception is intimately related to the 10th misconception presented in the Chapter on Negative Reification.

[53] For an in-depth introduction to solving inner conflicts, see my book on Transforming Self-Criticism (Springborg, 2024)

6.3.1. Misconception 16: You have a single self

Clients will generally think of themselves as being a single entity. They perceive themselves as having a single, coherent identity, a single personality that encompasses all their thoughts, emotions, and agendas.

In other words, clients tend to think that it is possible to describe themselves using a single, coherent set of characteristics, including their values, preferences, beliefs, goals, emotions, etc.

The belief in a single self leads clients to make statements which present an "I" with well-defined feelings, beliefs, preferences, agendas and characteristics.

- I love being a parent
- I believe that humans are happier when they are part of a family
- I hate my job
- I'm an ambitious person
- I prefer to avoid conflicts

Such statements may sound inconspicuous. However, this only reveals how common the belief in a single self is.

The reality of our inner processes is often far more complex and cannot be accurately captured through such simplistic statements. We have developed our thought patterns, beliefs, preferences, emotional responses, agendas, etc. from different interactions with the environment and ourselves, and it would be surprising if all the patterns we have developed in different contexts ended up as a perfectly coherent system. Generally, patterns developed in different contexts will contain contradictions and be in conflict with each other.

Therefore, it is more accurate to describe humans as consisting of *multiple* entities with *different* thoughts, emotions and agendas. Instead of using the clear-cut statements mentioned above, we must use statements which present multiple "I's" with conflicting and mutually contradictory values, beliefs, agendas and emotions, such as:

- Being a parent is the best and the worst thing that has happened to me
- One part of me believes that humans are happier when they are part of a family, and another part believes humans are happier alone
- I have a love-hate relationship with my job
- I have an ambitious and a lazy side
- I prefer to avoid conflicts and I can at times be quite confrontational

While it is rarer to hear such statements, many people will intuitively recognise them as more "human". They can be more relatable than the clear-cut statements based on the idea of a single self.

The belief in a single self is the result of a reification process. Just like we reify the complex and multifaceted experience of Being and see it as a single entity, such as "joy", "peace", or "vitality", we reify our complex and multifaceted internal processes and see it as a single entity we call our "self".

Once we have reified our "self", this reification will be self-reinforcing, in that the parts of our inner life we include in the "self" will dominate and repress the parts we do not include. And should parts of our inner life we do not include in our concept of "self" take control, we will say that we "Don't know what came over us" and that "We were not ourselves".

While seeing ourselves as a single entity can be useful in certain situations, it can also be profoundly unhelpful. In fact, it can significantly impede both self-development and mental health.

First, viewing oneself as a single entity downplays the existence and importance of internal conflicts by seeing one part involved in a conflict as one's "self" and the conflicting part as not one's "self". It makes us attempt to overcome the influence of the parts we see as not pertaining to our "self" instead of considering how to overcome our internal conflict and fragmentation. This perpetuates our fragmentation and prevents us from engaging in processes that would lead to personal growth in terms of increased inner coherence.

Second, viewing oneself as a single entity will make us act in ways that favour the parts of us we identify with and neglect those parts we do not. This internal favouritism is a significant source of our suffering. It creates internal polarisation since our conscious efforts to repress the parts of us we do not acknowledge as part of our "self" will lead to these parts reasserting themselves, leading to yet more efforts to repress, etc.

Third, the internal struggles which can, thus, result from viewing oneself as a single entity will occupy the client's attention and make it more difficult for the client to be aware of Being, and when the client loses awareness of Being, the resulting sense of having lost something precious will further fuel the internal conflict because all parts of the client's inner system will attempt to remedy the situation in conflicting ways.

Implications for therapy

Shifting from viewing humans as having a single self to viewing them as having multiple selves (or a "self" consisting of multiple more or less autonomous parts) has significant implications for therapy.

First, if clients have multiple selves, they can contain conflicting thoughts, emotions and agendas. Thus, just because a client has a particular value, preference, emotion or agenda doesn't mean they do not also have an opposing value, preference, emotion or agenda.

This changes the kind of questions that guide the therapeutic process.

Therapists should not ask:

- What are the client's true values, beliefs, emotions, wishes, etc.?

Instead, therapists should ask:

- What thoughts, emotions and agendas does the client contain?
- How are these organised into personality parts?
- How do these parts relate to each other (support, conflict, indifference)?

For example, some therapists may see it as their job to help clients determine what their true values are and find ways they can live in accordance with these values. However, asking what the client's true values are is premised on the notion of the single self. Therapy based on the notion of multiple selves would instead ask: What values does the client contain and how might these be in conflict with each other?

Similarly, some therapists may seek to uncover clients' true thoughts and emotions in a given situation. However, from the perspective of multiple selves, thinking in terms of "true" and "false" thoughts and emotions is imprecise. The thoughts and emotions clients express at the start of a session are no less true than the thoughts and emotions they discover through the therapeutic inquiry. Instead, the thoughts and emotions clients are aware of at the outset of a session may be those of parts they identify with, whereas the thoughts and emotions they discover through the therapeutic process are those of parts they do not identify with. Repressed does not mean truer – it just means out of the client's awareness.

In short, the perspective of multiple selves encourages therapists to stay open to the possibility of there being multiple answers to questions, such as:

- What do you value?
- What do you think about this situation/person?
- What do you feel?
- What do you want to do?

Second, behaviours can be overdetermined, in that multiple parts of a client can be motivated to engage in the same behaviour but for different reasons. In other words, just because a behaviour is motivated by one agenda, doesn't mean that the same behaviour is not also motivated by another agenda.

For example, a client may help a friend move. Multiple parts of the client may be motivated to do this but for different reasons. The client may contain one part that is concerned with projecting an image of being a helpful person and helping the friend move helps project this image. Another part may be concerned with building up social goodwill and ensure that there will be people who feel obliged to help the client, should they need it. Helping a friend move will create this goodwill and obligation. A third part of the client may seek a sense of togetherness and community by engaging in helpful actions. From the perspective of a single self, one may ask which of these motivations is the client's "true" motivation. However, from the perspective of multiple selves, they can all be simultaneously true. The behaviour is supported by a coalition of inner parts with different motivations.

That behaviours can be overdetermined means they can persist even after a successful therapeutic process in which a part that was responsible for the behaviour has found another way of achieving its goal – because there may be another part that is also responsible for the behaviour, which has not found a different way of reaching its goal.

For example, a client may overeat. During therapy, the client may discover that they contain a part that seeks to deal with emotional distress by overeating. The client may find different ways of dealing with emotional distress, but the overeating persists. The reason may be that the client contains another part that overeats for a different reason, such as a way of seeking pleasure or as a way of punishing themselves for failing to live up to a certain body image.

It is important for therapists to be aware that behaviours can be overdetermined because it helps them to stay open and curious, even after having discovered a plausible reason for the behaviour. This can help in detecting the entire coalition of inner parts responsible for a particular behaviour in the client.

Third, emotion, just like behaviours, can be overdetermined in that multiple parts of the client may feel the same emotions for different reasons.

For example, a client may feel lonely. The feeling of loneliness may belong to multiple parts. One part of the client may be concerned with maintaining personal boundaries and does so by distancing the client from other people, resulting in a feeling of loneliness. Another part of the client may seek to maintain a self-image as a strong person and does so by rejecting any vulnerability in themself. This rejection may, in turn, create a sense of isolation and loneliness in the vulnerable parts. A third part may hold an unrealistic ideal of what a relationship is supposed to be and when their partner falls short of this ideal, the client feels abandoned and lonely.

Working with any of these dynamics is valuable in itself and will be able to affect the client's sense of loneliness. However, the feeling of loneliness will persist regardless of how successfully the client works with any single part because the feeling of loneliness belongs to multiple parts.

It is important for therapists to be aware that emotions can be overdetermined in this way because it helps them stay open and curious and not become fixated on any single source of the emotion.

In short, shifting from seeing clients as having a single self to seeing them as having multiple selves prompts therapists to map out the system of selves and resolve conflicts – rather than helping clients discover and live in accordance with a supposed "true" set of values and preferences.

16th corrective principle: You have multiple selves.

The first corrective principle related to the Knot of Fragmentation is:

"You have multiple selves which can be in conflict, form coalitions in support of agendas and relate in many other ways."

This principle helps us stay open and curious and avoid closing down inquiry too soon by reducing the complex and multifaceted inner life of our clients to a series of simple answers and definitions.

Links to other systems

Throughout the book, I have frequently compared Being to physical space and thoughts and emotions to objects contained in physical space. I have also pointed out that Being is what we truly are.

Thus, it may be surprising that I, in this chapter, claim that we have many selves. After all, if we are Being and Being is like physical space, we should only have one self, since there is only one physical space.

This confusion arises from the multiple meanings of the word "self". In this chapter, I use the word "self" to refer to a sense of self that is part of the personality structure. When used in this way, it is accurate to say that we have many selves, since it is possible to identify with multiple parts of our personality structure.

However, many spiritual, psychological and philosophical traditions distinguish between a conditioned, everyday self and a true or higher self. The claim that we have many selves is only a claim about the conditioned, everyday self – not about the true or higher self.

- Zen Buddhism: Distinguishes between the "small mind", the ordinary, discriminating mind preoccupied with ego and dualistic thinking, and the "big mind", the mind of enlightenment, transcending individual ego and experiencing oneness with the universe.
- Hinduism: Differentiates between "Ahamkara", the ego-self, which identifies with the body and mind, and "Atman", the true self, or soul, which is eternal and beyond the physical.
- Sufism (Islamic Mysticism): Talks about "the nafs", the lower self, driven by ego and base desires, and "the ruh", the soul or higher self, connected to divine love and truth.
- Taoism: Differentiates between the "acquired self", shaped by societal norms and external influences) and the "original self", the natural, authentic self in harmony with the Tao, the underlying principle of the universe.
- Christian Mysticism: Often makes a distinction between the "false self", rooted in ego and separated from God, and the "true self", which seeks union with God and is guided by spiritual love and truth.
- Kabbalah (Jewish Mysticism): Differentiates between the "lower self", driven by ego and physical desires, and the "higher self", which is connected to the divine and seeks to fulfil the soul's purpose.

- Gnosticism: Teaches about the distinction between the "material self", ensnared in the physical world and ignorance, and the "spiritual self", which seeks gnosis – true spiritual knowledge and enlightenment.
- Jungian Psychology: Carl Jung's theory contrasts the "persona", the social face one presents to the world, often conforming to societal expectations, with the "Self", a central part of the unconscious, representing the psyche's totality and potential for wholeness.
- Humanistic Psychology: Carl Rogers distinguishes between the "ideal self", the person you strive to be because of what you have learned from your interactions with the environment, and the "real self", the person you truly are.
- Internal Family Systems (IFS): Differentiates between "parts", which are subpersonalities or aspects of the psyche shaped by life experiences and the "Self" with a capital 'S', representing a person's core or true self.

Each of these traditions offers a unique perspective on the nature of self and the journey towards realising one's true or higher self. However, they all share a common understanding that beyond our everyday, conditioned identity lies a deeper, more authentic essence.

Using the word "self" to refer both to the multiplicity of the conditioned or lower selves and the true higher self can sometimes lead to the misconception that the latter is to be found among the former. In other words, the idea that one of the conditioned selves is the true or higher self.

This, however, is incorrect. Just like space is something altogether different from any of the objects contained in space, so the true or higher self is something altogether different from anything contained in the personality structure – including thoughts, emotions, values, beliefs, tendencies, etc.

This is often not clarified when making the distinction between lower and higher selves, especially in psychological traditions that adopt this distinction from spiritual traditions[54].

---

[54] Thinking that the higher self is the same kind of thing as the lower selves is what logicians call a "category mistake".

6.3.2. Misconception 17: Clients contain inner enemies and obstacles

Clients frequently come to therapy because they wish to deal with their "inner demons" or "deficiencies". In other words, they wish to use therapy to become free from the aspects of themselves they perceive as inner enemies or obstacles.

Clients can perceive inner demons or deficiencies in their thoughts, emotions, behaviours, or some combination thereof.

When clients have thought patterns they don't understand, and which appear destructive, they may see these as inner enemies or obstacles. A client may, for example, have an inner voice that always tells them how worthless they are. They may view this voice as an inner demon they wish to eradicate. Similarly, a client who finds themself habitually distrusting others, even when they know it's unfounded, may perceive this excessive distrust as a deficiency they'd like to overcome.

Emotional reactions can also be seen as inner enemies or obstacles, especially when clients experience these emotions as irrational or damaging. For example, a client might view their shyness as an obstacle to achieving social or professional success. Another client might experience frequent bursts of anger and perceive this as an inner demon that destroys their relationships.

Lastly, clients may notice themselves engaging in behaviours they dislike or that have negative consequences. Despite recognising these behaviours as problematic, they often feel powerless to change them. This can lead them to view these behaviours as inner demons or deficiencies. One client might, for instance, continually prioritise others' needs over their own, only to later feel resentment when their own needs go unmet. Another might set overly rigid boundaries or isolate themselves in times of difficulty, thereby cutting off access to potential support.

In all these examples, clients observe thoughts, emotions, or behaviours that seem irrational, unnecessary, and that hinder them from achieving their goals or living the life they desire, and they conclude that they must contain something like an inner enemy or obstacle that is responsible for the creation of these thoughts, emotions and behaviours.

This perception is, however, an illusion which emerges when a client is identified with a particular personality part and believes that this part is all of who they are. When a client identifies with one personality part, other parts which contain thoughts, emotions and agendas that don't fit the worldview of the part the client is identified with, will appear to the client as destructive or irrational. In other words, they will appear as inner enemies or obstacles.

Clients will express this through statements, such as:

- My low self-esteem is holding me back.
- Whenever I get close to reaching my goals I self-sabotage.
- My uncontrollable anger outbursts destroy all my relationships.
- I want to get rid of my self-criticism because it is ruining my life.

From the perspective of multiple selves, such statements must be regarded, not as objective descriptions of the client's inner life, but rather as expressions of inner conflict between two personality parts described from the vantage point of one of these parts. In other words, it is a sign of incoherence in the client's personality structure.

From the perspective of multiple selves, a more accurate description would clarify the conflict between them without giving preference to either side. The above statements could, for example, be reformulated in the following ways:

- The part of me that has low self-esteem is holding my ambitious part back.
- Whenever, one part of me get close to reaching its goals, another part sabotages the project.
- A part of me experiences outbursts of anger in relationships while another part of me laments the loss of relationships.
- One part of me finds it important to be self-critical while another part of me believes such self-criticism is detrimental to living a fulfilling life.

Thus, the misconception that we contain inner enemies or obstacles is born out of the misconception that we have a single self. Believing we have a single self, leads us to take certain inner patterns of thought, emotions and behaviour, or schemas, to be our true selves, and, consequently, we will come to see conflicting schemas as enemies or obstacles.

From the perspective of multiple selves, no personality part is more defining of the person's self than any other. All personality parts are merely schemas or automated patterns developed to deal with certain situations.

This has important implications for therapy. In Being-Centred Therapy, therapists will focus on resolving internal conflicts because this will release the attention that is bound up in these conflicts, increasing the likelihood that clients come to be aware of Being.

Implications for therapy

In Chapter 4, Knot 3: The Knot of Negative Reification, I described how it is important for therapists to operate from the assumption that there are no negative inner states, only states that have acquired a bad reputation through negative reification. Operating from this assumption enables the therapist to invite their clients to fearlessly embrace and explore all inner states and realise that what appears as negative states is nothing other than negative reifications of Being.

In the same way, it is important for therapists to operate from the assumption that there are no evil personality parts, which are motivated by a desire to harm the client or prevent the client from living a fulfilling life. Operating from an unwavering belief in the fundamental goodness of all personality parts enables therapists to invite their clients to fearlessly embrace and learn to understand all sides of themselves.

Obviously, humans do sometimes operate in ways that cause harm to themselves and others. In fact, individuals that seek therapy will often do so precisely because they notice that they cause harm to themselves or others.

However, no matter how harmful the consequences of a particular personality part are, therapists must assume that doing harm is never the purpose and that all parts of a client's personality are trying to do something fundamentally positive.

To see through surface appearances and perceive the fundamental goodness of all personality parts, it can be helpful to remember that a client's personality parts are their automated solutions to problems they have encountered in life, and that many of these solutions were invented by the brain of a young child, who might have been scared or overwhelmed, and who had very limited experience. Thus, it is no surprise that some of a client's automated solutions have certain shortcomings.

When the logic underpinning the actions of a personality part is the logic of a young child, it can be challenging to understand what this personality part is trying to achieve through its actions[55]. Remembering this can help one understand that if a personality part engages in destructive behaviour, it is always only because

[55] As anyone who has spent time with children can testify to, children's logic is not always straightforward – even when they are *not* feeling overwhelmed.

such destructive behaviour to this part, with its limited view and child logic, appears to be necessary to achieve a greater good. Thus, harm is never the purpose even if to an adult the harmful behaviour appears irrational or unnecessary.

If we accept that a personality part can be governed by the logic of a young and overwhelmed child, we always come to realise that it is seeking to promote the client's well-being.

A client may, for example, drink heavily and be unable to help themselves, despite knowing that their drinking causes all sorts of problems for themselves and the people close to them. At first glance, this behaviour may seem to have no positive outcomes. However, if we investigate from the assumption that the part that leads the client to drink is trying to do something profoundly positive, we might find that the drinking is motivated by a belief that emotions are dangerous and should be numbed out. In childhood, the client may have experienced how the parents caused each other and their children great pain when in the grips of intense emotions. Given such experiences, it makes sense to seek to numb out emotions. In childhood the client may have numbed out their emotions in certain ways and as the client grew older more effective ways of numbing out emotions became available to them. Thus, drinking may merely be the adoption of a superior means to implement the strategy of numbing out emotions and avoiding the associated dangers. If the pain caused by out-of-control emotions in childhood were severe, the problems caused by drinking may appear as a small price for avoiding such pain.

Operating from the perspective that all personality parts are fundamentally good and seek to promote and secure health and happiness, has significant implications for therapy.

Some traditional approaches to therapy operate from the idea that clients get more of what they focus on. Therefore, clients are encouraged to give attention to what is positive in them and not what is negative in them. This is seen as a way of making the positive grow and the negative dwindle.

This approach to self-development is illustrated in a popular story about how every human being contains two wolves, a black one that is full of anger, jealousy, fear, greed and arrogance, and a white one that is full of peace, love, hope, courage, humility, compassion and faith. These wolves are always fighting, and the point of the story is that the wolf that will win the fight is the one that has been fed the most. In other words, we should give attention to the positive sides in us and not the negative ones.

We meet the same idea in many spiritual traditions. For example, the Christian idea of the seven deadly sins and seven contrary virtues proposes that pride, greed, lust, anger, gluttony, envy and laziness are negative aspects of the human psyche and that they can be overcome by cultivating the virtues of humility, generosity, chastity, patience, temperance, charity and diligence. Many other traditions have similar oppositions.

Seeing parts of us as bad and others as good will lead us to ask questions such as:

- What parts of the client's thoughts, emotions and behaviour are good and bad?
- How can the client give more attention to the good parts and less attention to the bad ones?

However, there are several problems with using the above questions to guide therapy.

First, if we take seriously the notion that there are no inner enemies or obstacles, it will make no sense to focus on what is good in us as a means to overcome what is bad – because there is no part of us that is inherently bad.

Second, if the parts of us that are causing harm are doing so, not because these are bad parts, but because these parts are modelled on the experiences of a young, fearful and overwhelmed child, then declaring them bad and turning away from them will backfire. To understand this, think about how a frightened child will react if you reject and abandon it. This will only increase the child's fear and sense of overwhelm, which was the reason the child acted in harmful ways in the first place. The same is true for personality parts.

Third, clients will generally seek to free themselves, not from personality parts that are inherently bad, but from personality parts that are perceived as bad *by other personality parts*. Therefore, following the conventional therapy wisdom described above, the therapist risk, inadvertently, allying themselves with one part of the client against another part of the client, thus intensifying the fight between different personality parts and increasing the client's level of fragmentation.

Therefore, the questions that govern Being-Centred Therapy are:

- What is the intention and logic behind parts of the client that cause harm?
- What happens to these parts when they are understood, and when they get what they are ultimately reaching for through their actions?

An approach to therapy that is governed by such questions is Internal Family Systems (IFS). IFS therapists assume that personality parts that cause harm do so because they carry burdens in the form of extreme beliefs and emotions, which lead them to view destructive actions as necessary for survival and well-being. However, personality parts are not the burdens they carry, and when they give up the burdens or are relieved of them, they immediately transform into valuable states.

The burdens IFS are referring to would be feelings, such as fear, rage, worthlessness and shame, and related beliefs such as emotions, are dangerous and must be avoided at all costs, everyone will let you down in the end, nobody considers me valuable and I'm a bad person.

The 20 misconceptions presented in this book can, in this context, be regarded as 20 burdens that make personality parts act in harmful ways. When these misconceptions are corrected, our personality parts are liberated and, like drops of honey, melt back into the wholeness of who you are. In other words, they turn into aspects of Being.

It is worth noting that the misconception in this section is "you contain inner enemies/obstacles". Taken together, this implies that if therapy is guided by the notion that we contain a black wolf that is fundamentally bad, then therapy is reinforcing an extreme belief that, when adopted, becomes a burden that makes our personality parts act in harmful ways.

17th corrective principle: There are no inner enemies (all parts seek the Being)

The second corrective principle related to the Knot of Fragmentation is:

> "There are no inner enemies or obstacles. There are only parts that act in ways that make them appear to other parts as enemies or obstacles. Ultimately, all parts seek Being which is a profoundly positive activity."

By remembering that there are no inner enemies, we can avoid committing the mistake of taking some schemas or personality parts to be the whole of the client while regarding other schemas or personality parts as something alien within the client.

This helps us stay curious in the face of any thought, emotion or behaviour – however destructive it appears and however problematic the consequences of this thought, emotion or behaviour may be.

By listening to problematic parts and seeking to understand them, we can help the part in putting down the burdensome emotions and beliefs it carries and, thus, it ceases to act in harmful ways.

6.3.3. Misconception 18: You must free yourself from problematic parts

As mentioned at the start of the previous section, clients frequently come to therapy because they wish to use it to free themselves from what they perceive as inner enemies or obstacles.

Clients will say that they want to:

- Get rid of their self-doubt.
- Stop drinking, smoking, over-eating or engaging in other forms of addiction.
- Be more motivated and stop procrastinating.
- Stop caring about what other people think about them.

When clients see parts of themselves, such as self-doubt, addictive behaviour, procrastination or insecurity, as inner enemies or obstacles, it will make sense to them to seek ways of getting rid of or changing these parts. If something is causing you harm, then getting rid of it seems like a good path to a better life.

However, the idea that certain inner parts should be rejected or changed is a misconception.

Of course, clients will sometimes behave in ways that are harmful to themselves or others and, therefore, behavioural changes can be beneficial or even necessary. However, changing behaviour is not the same as rejecting the personality part associated with this behaviour.

The key is to understand the intention behind the actions. Behaviours can be modified without negating the purpose they serve. We can view the parts of ourselves that manifest problematic behaviours as parts offering imperfect solutions to important problems. Dismissing these parts entirely might mean overlooking the underlying issues they attempt to address. The fact that a part is advocating a problematic solution does not diminish the value it brings by highlighting a problem worthy of our attention.

Instead of casting aside or altering a part because of its flawed solution, we should strive to discern and address the problem it is attempting to resolve. When a part engages in behaviour that appears irrational, it is often merely because we do not adequately understand what problem this part is seeking to solve for us. If we do not understand the part's objectives, we are in no position to reject it or even decide what behavioural changes would be appropriate.

As we have seen in the previous chapters, problematic behaviour often arises from valid and important concerns about our apparent lack of peace, love, joy, connection, ease and other positive reifications of Being. But because the parts that seek to address such problems are under the influence of the 20 misconceptions laid out in this book, the solutions they advocate are in themselves the cause of the problem – and of many follow-on problems.

In fact, the idea that we must reject parts of ourselves that are associated with problematic behaviour is itself a flawed solution to a valid problem. The problem is how to thrive in life. The proposed solution is to cut out all the parts of us that bring problems. This is a problematic solution in that it fails to recognise that when we see one part of us as causing problems we are, in that moment, identified with another part. Had we instead been identified with the first part, we might have considered the second part the problem. In other words, we do not have a vantage point from which we can judge which parts to cut out. However, even if the solution of cutting parts of us out is a flawed solution, the intention to find a way of thriving in life is valid.

In Being-Centred Therapy, it is important to resolve inner conflicts because such conflicts draw our attention away from Being and, in so doing, generate a sense of loss that inflames our inner conflicts. The fact that seeking to free ourselves from parts we consider problematic is not a viable solution to inner conflicts has important implications for therapy.

Implications for therapy

If all personality parts are seeking to solve valid and important problems, then all parts have something important to contribute to our personal development – regardless of how problematic these parts appear to other parts and regardless of how harmful their behaviour is.

Thus, rather than being concerned with which parts to reject (or which parts to change), therapists should seek to understand what problems every single part of the client's personality structure is seeking to solve.

In sessions, clients tend to talk about what the different parts of them want to do without explicitly mentioning what problems this behaviour is intended to solve. When clients say they want to get rid of self-doubt, stop drinking, be more productive and stop procrastinating, or cease to care what other people think about them, they are presenting solutions without making explicit what problem these solutions are supposed to solve. Clients may have problems implementing these solutions – but problems of implementation are different from the psychological problems the solutions are intended to solve.

In previous chapters, we have seen that when clients seek to attain or avoid something, it is generally because they believe that by attaining or avoiding these things, they will reach states of Being, such as love, connection, joy, peace, ease, etc. In other words, the real problem every part of the personality is dealing with is how to reunite with some aspect of Being but the problem they are occupied with and bring to therapy are problems of how to get better at implementing their favourite solution to this problem.

In traditional therapy the therapist may ask:

- How can the client achieve what they want to achieve?

However, it is problematic to let this be the question that guides therapy when what the client seeks to achieve is the implementation of a flawed solution to the problem of Being.

When we focus on the problems a client's personality part seeks to solve rather than on the flawed solutions it advocates, we can start wondering what aspect of Being this personality part is seeking. Instead of seeing the part as something pushing for a particular behaviour, we can see it as something that reminds the client of something precious, they have lost awareness of. This shift in how a problematic inner part is regarded can have profoundly transformative effects on the client.

Each personality part is precious in that it has the potential to become our guide. Instead of arguing about the behaviour the part advocates, we can ask it to take our hand and lead us to the preciousness it is ultimately seeking through this behaviour. In other words, we can work with the part using the Sensing Completion process[56].

When a personality part shows us its beloved, the precious state it seeks, we are brought in touch with this state. When we, through our conversation with a personality part, are brought in touch with the state the part is seeking, this experience can be profoundly transformative for the part because it reveals that it can unite directly with its beloved – and that the problematic behaviour is not necessary[57]. In other words, the experience of uniting directly with the state a part seeks will relieve the part of the burden of believing that the state is lost and that harmful behaviour is necessary to regain it.

Thus, Being-Centred Therapy is guided by the questions:

- What aspect of Being is the part in the client that advocates problematic seeking?
- What happens when the client comes to see this part as a reminder that can help them retain awareness of Being, rather than as an inner enemy that pushes the client to engage in problematic behaviour?

When asking such questions of a particular personality part, it is important to unmerge, not only from the part we are in conversation with, but also from any part holding a negative judgement of the part we are speaking with.

When a part is relieved of its burdens, it also ceases to be in conflict with other parts. If every part of us learns through direct experience that what they seek is already present and available without the need for any action, there can be no grounds for inner conflict and fragmentation.

Furthermore, the moment other parts recognise what a part is ultimately seeking, they will realise that what they saw as a deficient and irrational part is really a part that is deeply committed to the well-being of the client. If all parts directly experience what other parts are seeking, all parts will become united.

---

[56] In Section 3.4.2, I mentioned that clients can have a positive, ambivalent or negative attitude towards their own desires to fulfil certain conditions and that the last case was an indication of the Knot of Fragmentation.

[57] This is the Access Process. See Section 3.4.4

18th corrective principle: Problematic parts point to Being and should be given what they are pointing to – this will transform them

The third corrective principle related to the Knot of Fragmentation is:

> "All parts, no matter how problematic or harmful their behaviour is, are seeking to reach an aspect of Being, and can, therefore, become a guide that can take us home. When they do, they are transformed and the beliefs that form the basis for the harmful behaviour are dissolved."

This principle helps us avoid the trap of siding with one personality part against another and, in doing so, cause fragmentation.

6.3.4. Misconception 19: Rejection leads to freedom from the rejected.

In the previous sections, I discussed two related misconceptions: first, that parts of our personality are inner enemies or barriers, and second, that we should seek to free ourselves from these parts. In this section, I will address a third misconception related to the two previous ones, namely that we can free ourselves from inner enemies or obstacles by rejecting them[58].

However, the reality is that, even if we accepted the idea of "inner enemies" and the goal of freeing ourselves from them (which we should not do), the act of rejection would still prove to be an ineffective method for freeing ourselves from that which we reject.

The reason is that when we reject something, we give it attention, and by giving it attention, we tie ourselves to it.

If a client wishes to get rid of their inhibition, then inhibition is a key component of the way they define their goal, and they will judge their efforts to achieve this goal in terms of how much inhibition they feel. Thus, "inhibition" is front and centre in their thinking. We cannot free ourselves from something by placing it front and centre in our thinking.

Similarly, if a client wishes to work on their tendency to procrastinate or heal their angry side or overcome their shyness, they make procrastination, anger, and shyness central to their perception of themself and their actions. Anything they do to free themself from these aspects will be defined in relation to these very aspects. Thus, regardless of how successful they are in rejecting these things, what

[58] In Section 4.4.2, I discussed in detail the ways clients express their wish to avoid certain inner states. Clients will often express their wish to reject personality parts in similar ways.

they do only makes sense in terms of the very thing they reject. Therefore, rejecting something only ties us closer to it.

True freedom comes when any dichotomy in which these concepts play a part ceases to be relevant for the client.

Clients do not attain freedom from shyness by making themselves more outgoing. They attain freedom from shyness when the shyness/outgoing dichotomy becomes irrelevant for the client. Clients do not attain freedom from anger or procrastination by becoming more tranquil or more active. Freedom from anger and procrastination comes when these concepts are no longer figural in how the client makes sense of themselves and the world.

In short, clients have freedom in relation to a personality part when they no longer have strong preferences for whether it is there or not, when the presence or absence of this part of the client become non-issues, when shyness, assertiveness, procrastination and their opposites are all merely states that may come and go – unburdened by value-judgements.

Rejection of any aspect retains this aspects status as an issue – even if the client is "successful" in overcoming it because the very idea of the success in overcoming it retains it as an important phenomenon to pay attention to.

The fact that rejection ties us to that which we reject can be very useful in therapy as it provides ways of resolving conflicts and, thus, freeing up the awareness that is otherwise bound in managing these conflicts, making it more likely that clients become aware of Being.

Implications for therapy

As discussed earlier, when working with conflict between personality parts, it is imperative that we create a space for each part to express its wishes, goals and intentions – not only the behaviours it advocates to fulfil these.

To create such a space, it is important to dissuade other parts that perceive the part we work with as an inner enemy or obstacle from interrupting the process.

One tool I often use is to point out the counterproductive nature of the act of rejection. If I can communicate to the client that rejection of the part will tie them closer to it rather than free them from it, it can help persuade the client to try an alternative – such as talking to the part and understanding what it seeks to attain through its "problematic" behaviour.

Understanding how rejection ties you to that which you reject is particularly useful when working with the part of the personality Jung calls the shadow.

All clients will have certain parts of their personality they see as good and will, consequently, see the opposite aspects as bad. Clients will typically strive to be the good parts, and will do so by rejecting or disowning the bad ones[59].

A client may, for example, believe it is good to be kind and will try to be so by disowning any personality part they deem unkind. Another client may believe that it is good to be assertive and try to be so by disavowing any part of themselves they deem weak, indecisive, shy, insecure or some other form of non-assertiveness.

The problem is that disowned parts do not disappear. Instead, they will influence the client's behaviour and the client will be unaware of this. Clients who see themselves as kind can be ruthless in their actions without consciously realising it. Clients who see themselves as assertive may not realise to what extent their "assertive" behaviour is motivated by unconscious insecurities. The resulting mismatch between the client's self-image and their behaviour can lead to reactions from the client's environment that will be incomprehensible to them. Jung sums up the problem of disowning the shadow by saying "Until you make the unconscious conscious, it will direct your life and you will call it fate."

Shadow work can, thus, be seen as working with conflicts between the parts clients include in their self-image and parts they disown in their efforts to maintain this self-image. Resolving such conflicts will enable clients to acknowledge and integrate their shadow parts, and, in so doing, will become better at predicting and understanding the ways other people react to them. They will recognise the ways in which they shape or create their own "fate".

One way of facilitating the integration of shadow parts, is to clarify to clients how their self-image is predicated upon and, therefore, contains and ties them to their shadow.

For example, a client who sees themself as kind and considerate may not understand why other people get upset with them when they are only trying to

---

[59] Some clients will do the opposite. They will see themselves as the parts that are bad and reject or disown what is good in themselves. Whereas it is important to be aware of this, the principles of working with the shadow is the same whether it contains parts the client sees as bad or as good. For simplicity, in this section I will assume the client seeks to be the good parts.

help. For such a client, it will be crucial to learn to acknowledge and integrate their frustration, anger, hate and desire to harm others. Everyone has such impulses. And when we do not acknowledge them, we are likely to act on them without realising it. One way of helping this client acknowledge their "unkind" parts is to point out how the way they always seek to help others is, in itself, unkind. One may, for example, point out that when the client consistently takes the role of the kind helper, they will, in so doing, consistently give others the role of the helpless. And consistently seeing someone as helpless is a very unkind thing to do. By pointing out how excessive kindness is unkind, it is possible to place the client in a situation where it is difficult for them to deny their unkindness.

Similarly, a client that sees themselves as assertive and strong may not understand why they are consistently being attacked by other people. They may believe that the world is simply a hostile place, reinforcing their belief in the necessity of being highly assertive. For such a client, it will be imperative to learn to acknowledge and integrate their insecurities and vulnerabilities. One way of helping this client acknowledge these sides of themself is to point out that strong and secure people are relaxed about letting things happen. Thus, it is precisely due to insecurity that they feel a pressing need to stand their ground and take control of the situation. By pointing out how excessive assertiveness is a sign of insecurity, it is possible to place the client in a situation where it is difficult for them to deny their insecurity.

There are, of course, many good approaches to shadow work. Pointing out how the way clients reject their shadow parts ties them closer to these parts by making them central to the client's self-understanding is just one approach. It is particularly useful when the client's rejection is strong because it can be used to create a dilemma for the client where the very acts they believed showed the *absence* of the trait they reject are revealed to be expressions of this very trait.

Conventional therapeutic wisdom may suggest that therapists focus on the question of:

- How can clients learn to separate themselves from negative inner patterns?

However, if attempts at separating oneself from inner patterns only tie one closer to these patterns, therapists can instead focus on the question of:

- How can clients become aware of the way they embody the very thing they reject?
- How can clients acknowledge and integrate their shadow?

When clients realise that rejection of a personality part ties them closer to this very part, the notion of "inner conflict" transforms. What they used to see as two conflicting inner parts will start to appear as two sides of the same coin. When kindness is seen as excluding unkindness, it is itself unkind. When assertiveness is seen as excluding insecurity, it is itself an expression of insecurity.

19th corrective principle: Rejection ties you closer to that which you reject

The fourth corrective principle related to the Knot of Fragmentation is:

> "Rejecting something directly or by seeking to become the opposite will not bring freedom but only tie you closer to that which you reject by making it an integral part of how you perceive and make sense of yourself."

This principle helps us avoid engaging in therapeutic practices that result in the creation of shadow sides rather than real transformation through integration.

It helps us remember that true freedom comes from embracing both the rejecting and the rejected parts and, in this way, realise that you are neither.

6.3.5. Misconception 20: You cannot have it all – you must choose

The final misconception related to the Knot of Fragmentation is fundamentally the same as the 10th misconception (the 2nd misconception related to the Knot of Negative Reification). I revisit it briefly here, merely to expand on the importance of this misconception and its corrective principle in relation to working with the Knot of Fragmentation.

In Section 4.3.2, I mentioned that while our ideas about what we need to do to acquire positive phenomena, such as "vitality" and "peace", may be mutually exclusive, the phenomena themselves are two aspects of Being and, as such, they are one. A client may, for example, believe that vitality comes from being active and peace comes from being inactive. This client may conclude that vitality and peace are mutually exclusive phenomena because it is impossible to be active and inactive at the same time. However, this is a false conclusion. It is fully possible to feel vitality and peace simultaneously since these phenomena are merely two positive reifications of Being, and as such, they are one.

Mistaking the aspect of Being we seek for our ideas about how to create or acquire this aspect of Being is one of the main forces behind the fragmentation of clients' personality structures.

Different parts of the client are dedicated to implementing the different actions they mistakenly believe are necessary to achieve a certain aspect of Being. They are unaware that what they seek is ultimately one and the same.

This has important implications for how to dissolve inner conflicts in therapy.

Implications for therapy

Knowing that internal conflict is the product of misconceptions means that resolving inner conflicts is a matter of dispelling these misconceptions.

This can be done by taking each conflicting personality part through the process of Sensing Completion to reveal what aspect of Being this part is ultimately reaching out for and then proposing the possibility of sensing both aspects simultaneously. The experience of sensing both aspects of Being simultaneously can dispel the misconception that they are mutually exclusive, and that the client must choose between them.

For example, a client may state that he wishes to be generous and not control his partner but that he gets jealous of his partner's friendship with another woman. Thus, the client contains both a wish to not control and a wish to control. This may be felt as an inner conflict.

In Being-Centred Therapy, any ideas about whether jealousy is good or bad or whether it is warranted or not, are completely irrelevant. Instead of investigating the soundness of either part of the client, we can investigate what each part is ultimately reaching for.

In so doing, we may discover that the part that wishes to be generous and uncontrolling wants to do so because it believes that this will bring the sweet aspect of Being, known as the Gold Essence. Furthermore, we may discover that the part that wishes to control the partner wishes to do so because it believes this will bring the solid and easeful aspect of Being, known as the White Essence.

Once this is understood, one can ask the client to pay sustained awareness to the Gold Essence and the White Essence simultaneously. When these are felt together it will alter the client's perception of the situation and enhance their ability to deal with it.

The client may discover that the wish not to control is a wish to give space to what is precious and the wish for control is a wish to protect what is precious. Such realisations can profoundly change the client's understanding of the concepts of "relationship", "connection" and "control".

I will return to the mechanism through which the experience of Being can alter the meaning of our concepts at a fundamental level in Sections 7.6.1 and 7.6.2.

20th corrective principle: Things that are mutually exclusive in our conceptual system may not be so in reality – methods can be in conflict, essence cannot

The final misconception related to the Knot of Fragmentation is that:

> "Our inner conflicts are conflicts between the agendas of different personality parts but never between the intensions and goals of our personality parts since all personality parts are ultimately seeking Being."

Remembering this principle helps us not only realise that no inner parts have negative agendas, but also that our inner parts can fundamentally not be in conflict with each other in terms of what they ultimately seek.

It reminds us that rather than seeking to adjudicate between conflicting personality parts, it is more effective to seek to understand what each part is ultimately reaching for and questioning whether the perceived conflict genuinely exists. This approach promotes a deeper resolution and integration of these parts.

6.3.6. Summary

In the above, we have seen that the Knot of Fragmentation relates to five interconnected misconceptions. We have also seen how awareness of these misconceptions and their corresponding corrective principles can inform therapeutic practice.

Table 17 summarises the misconceptions and corresponding corrective principles related to the Knot of Fragmentation.

Table 17: Misconceptions and corrective principles related to the Knot of Fragmentation

Misconceptions	Corrective Therapeutic Principles
Clients have a single self	Clients have multiple selves
Clients contain inner enemies and obstacles	There are no inner enemies (all parts seek Being)
We must free ourselves from problematic inner parts	Problematic inner parts can point clients towards Being. When they are given what they are pointing to, they are unburdened and transform.
Rejecting an inner part leads to freedom from the part you reject	Rejecting an inner part will tie you to it by making it integral to your self-understanding
You cannot have it all – you must choose	Things that are mutually exclusive in our conceptual system may not be so in reality – methods can be in conflict, essence cannot

Table 18 summarises the differences between the questions that guide traditional and Being-Centred Therapy.

Table 18: How understanding the Knot of Fragmentation changes the questions guiding therapy

Traditional therapy questions	Being-Centred Therapy questions
What are the client's true values, beliefs, emotions, wishes, etc.?	What thoughts, emotions and agendas does the client contain? How are these organised into parts? How do these parts relate to each other?
What parts of the client's thoughts, emotions and behaviour are good and bad? How can the client give more attention to the good parts and less attention to the bad ones?	What is the intention and logic behind parts of the client that cause harm? What happens to these parts when they are understood, and when they get what they are ultimately reaching for through their actions?

Traditional therapy questions	Being-Centred Therapy questions
How can the client achieve what they want to achieve?	What aspect of Being is the part in the client that advocates problematic seeking? What happens when the client comes to see this part as a reminder that can help them retain awareness of Being, rather than as an inner enemy that pushes the client to engage in problematic behaviour?
How can clients learn to separate themselves from negative inner patterns?	How can clients become aware of the way they embody the very thing they reject? How can clients acknowledge and integrate their shadow?
Which of a client's conflicting personality parts is more reasonable?	What are a client's conflicting personality parts ultimately reaching for? What happens when the client experiences the combination of the states each part reaches for?

So far, we have looked at the Knot of Fragmentation, five misconceptions related to this knot and five corresponding corrective principles that can guide therapy.

In the following section, I will describe in detail a therapeutic process aimed at untying the Knot of Fragmentation. This process is called Sensing Unity because it aims at revealing the fundamental unity behind the seemingly fragmented personality structure. The core of the process is to reveal the intentions of conflicting personality parts and, thus, dispel the illusion of conflict.

This perspective may be conceptually clear from reading the above (or similar texts). However, it is possible to conceptually understand how all personality parts necessarily must be reaching for aspects of Being, without this conceptual understanding changing anything about how we perceive Being, life and ourselves. To go beyond conceptual understanding, we need direct experience of the unity described above, and let this experience update the beliefs that govern our behaviour. This is the goal of the process of Sensing Unity.

6.4. Sensing Unity – how to untie the Knot of Fragmentation

The Knot of Fragmentation consists of five interlinked misconceptions related to the perspective that human beings have a single self and must fight against internal demons and obstacles to thrive. This misconceived perspective creates internal polarisations dividing clients against themselves. The resulting internal conflicts will occupy clients' attention and prevent them from noticing Being.

The Knot of Fragmentation is the result of the previous knots. The Knot of Positive Reification makes Being appear as many different positive phenomena. The Knot of Conditionality makes clients develop beliefs about under what conditions they will experience these positive phenomena and with time they substitute the conditions for the goal. The Knot of Negative Reification conflates different aspects of Being with the negative outcomes and disappointments resulting from the Knot of Conditionality. The Knot of Alienation makes the issues arising from the previous knots appear as the natural state of affairs by blinding clients to their own participation in the creation of these issues.

The result of these four knots is a fragmented system of automatic inner processes, which over time will create further fragmentation for two reasons.

First, as long as clients' attention is occupied by their inner conflicts, they are unlikely to notice how these conflicts are illusions created by the misconceptions related to the four previously described knots, and the conflicts will, thus, persist.

Second, as long as clients' attention is occupied by their inner conflicts, they are unlikely to notice Being. This will in turn intensify the perception that something precious is lost and, thus, increase the conflicts between all processes that are seeking to remedy this perceived loss in different ways.

The Knot of Fragmentation can be untied by pausing the conflicts and working with each side of the inner conflict while the process is witnessed by the other side. This kind of work will reveal that all inner parts are ultimately reaching for Being and, thus, have no conflict at the level of their ultimate goals. As mutual understanding emerges, the intensity of the conflict subsides, and awareness is freed up so that the client may become aware of Being. When this happens, the reason for any conflict is dissolved and the client will feel unity and wholeness.

The Knot of Fragmentation can be untied through Sensing Unity process.

1. **<u>Recognise the Knot of Fragmentation:</u>**
   The first step is to notice the Knot of Fragmentation. This is done by noticing situations where clients are split between two agendas, are fighting inner obstacles or enemies, are fighting outer demons, or are flipflopping between two positions each of which is demonising the other.
2. **<u>Map the system of parts:</u>**
   The second step is to organise the client's thoughts, emotions and behavioural impulses into a system of clearly defined inner parts each of which is representative of a particular agenda.
3. **<u>Select a part to work with:</u>**
   The third step is to select the order in which to work with conflicting inner parts. It can be beneficial to start with the part that is most repressed since this is most likely to bring new information. It can also be beneficial to start with the part that is most agitated since this can bring more calmness.
4. **<u>Invite other parts to suspend judgement:</u>**
   The fourth step is to invite the parts you are not currently working with to suspend judgement. If this cannot be done directly, it can be helpful to put in guard rails, to point out the inefficiency of the judgement or to point out the flaws in the logic underpinning the judgement. If none of this helps, it can be beneficial to wait, as the client may not yet be ready for this process.
5. **<u>Correct the misconceptions related to the Knot of Fragmentation:</u>**
   The fifth step is to use the experience of going through the previous steps to correct the misconceptions related to the Knot of Negative Fragmentation. This step is divided into five different processes.
   a. Mapping the system of parts clarifies that we have multiple selves.
   b. The Sensing Taboos process clarifies that we have no inner enemies.
   c. The Sensing Completion process clarifies that whereas the strategies of personality parts can be in conflict their ultimate goals cannot.
   d. The Sensing Agency process reveals that conflicting personality parts sometimes propose conflicting solutions to a problem caused by a hidden personality part, which must be included rather than rejected.
   e. The Sensing Abundance process clarifies that positive inner states cannot be mutually exclusive.

In the remainder of this chapter, I describe the Sensing Unity process in one-to-one sessions as well as in groups through a series of contemplation exercises. Figure 25 provides an overview of the process.

6.4.1 Recognise the Knot of Fragmentation

Two schemas (parts) have conflicting objectives and perceive each other as obstacles:

- Doubter: The client feels split, torn, or in a paralysing dilemma
- Ascetic: The client struggles to contain, manage or reform something in themselves
- Crusader: The client expresses black and white thinking and strong judgements against certain behaviour in other people
- Shapeshifter: The client alternates between two (or more) positions and forgets or rejects the positions they are not currently holding

↓

6.4.2 Map the system of parts

- Organising thoughts and emotions in groups around agendas
- Layered personality structures
    - Relating: What do you feel when you observe this part?
    - Timeline: What came before?
    - Missing voices: Who is that a response to?
- Two ways of disidentifying (subtracting parts vs. adding parts)

↓

6.4.3 Select a part to work with

The part that gets the least attention

The part that is most agitated

↓

6.4.4 Invite other parts to suspend judgement

Suspending judgement → Putting in safety rails → Pointing out the inefficiency of judgement → Short circuiting the logic behind the judgement → Waiting

↓

6.4.5 Correct misconceptions related to the Knot of Fragmentation

Working with one part while conflicting parts are witnessing the process adds value to the works by dissolving the conflicts or rendering them irrelevant

Sensing Unity and the 16th corrective principle
Mapping out the system of conflicting parts reveals that we have multiple selves

Sensing Taboos and the 17th corrective principle
Recognising that all states in essence are Being reveals that there are no inner enemies

Sensing Completion and the 18th corrective principle
Realising that all parts reach out for Being reveals that all parts can point us to Being

Sensing Agency and the 19th corrective principle
Rejecting parts that propose problematic solutions to a problem prevents us from noticing that we create this problem ourselves

Sensing Abundance and the 20th corrective principle
Imagining the combination of the felt sense underpinning what conflicting personality parts seek reveals that these parts' end goals are compatible or even mutually supportive

Figure 25: The Sensing Unity process

6.4.1. Step 1: Recognise the Knot of Fragmentation

The Knot of Fragmentation occurs when two (or more) personality parts become polarised and antagonistic. Such inner polarisation manifests in different ways depending on:

- whether the client has a stable identification with one of the polarised parts or an unstable identification that makes them shift between parts.
- whether the part with which the client identifies at any given moment exerts a weak or strong repressive force over the other.

Using these two dimensions, it is possible to distinguish between four ways in which the Knot of Fragmentation can manifest.

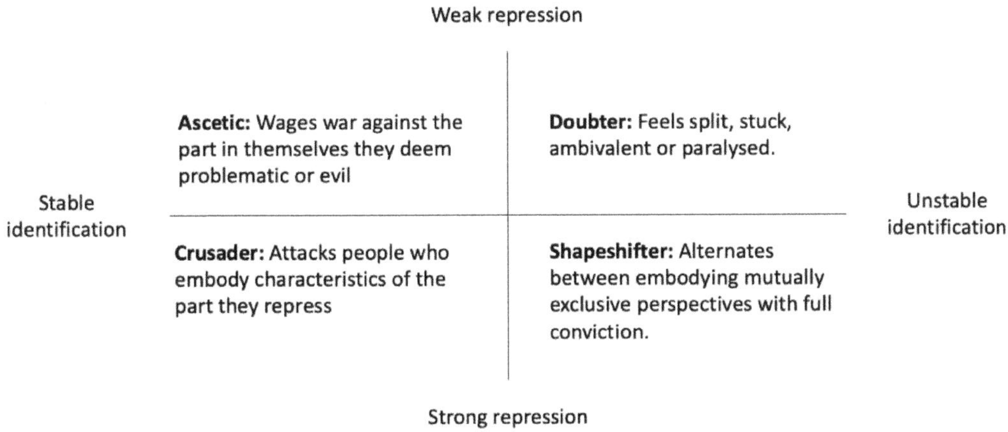

Figure 26: Four manifestations of the Knot of Fragmentation

Working with the Knot of Fragmentation is a matter of enabling the client to experience both parts from the inside, rather than being strongly identified with one part, and softening the certainty of each part through mutual understanding.

For this reason, the doubter (unstable identification and weak repression) is the easiest manifestation of the Knot of Fragmentation to work with and the tools proposed for working with the other manifestations of the Knot of Fragmentation can be understood as tools for getting the client to the position of the doubter.

In the following, I will describe each of the four manifestations of the Knot of Fragmentation and how to work with them.

Doubter (unstable identification and weak repression)

The doubter refers to the manifestation of the Knot of Fragmentation where the client's identity changes between the two parts and neither of the parts have the capacity to repress the other. The doubter will typically experience themselves as being in an unsolvable dilemma. They understand and empathise with both sides of the inner conflict, but they see the two parts' agendas as mutually exclusive.

Doubters will say: "I feel torn", "I feel split", "On the one hand I want to..., but on the other hand I also want to...", "I'm paralysed and don't know what to do, yet I do need to do something", "It's as if I'm damned if I do and damned if I don't", "I feel there is no way to win in this situation".

When working with this manifestation of the Knot of Fragmentation, it is generally relatively easy to pause one side while working with the other as the client has some measure of sympathy for both. You may, for example, engage in a Sensing Completion process with each part. Such processes will reveal that while the methods of each part may be mutually exclusive, the ultimate goals are not.

For example, a client may contain a part that seeks a sense of pleasure by relaxing and another that seeks a sense of glory by working hard. While the behaviours of these two parts (relaxing and working hard) may be mutually exclusive, the felt sense they seek (pleasure and glory) are not. Similarly, a client may contain a part that seeks peace by relaxing and another that seeks safety by being hypervigilant. While the behaviours of relaxation and hypervigilance are mutually exclusive, the felt sense of peace and safety can easily be combined.

When each part "witnesses" the process of the other part it can generate the mutual understanding necessary for dissolving the Knot of Fragmentation. In Section 6.4.5, I describe how each of the processes described earlier in this book can help resolve conflicts between personality parts.

Ascetic (stable identification and weak repression)

The ascetic refers to the manifestation of the Knot of Fragmentation where a client is firmly identified with one of two conflicting personality parts, but they do not have the capacity to repress the other part.

Because the client is identified with one personality part and, therefore, take this part's emotions, values and worldviews as their own, they will see the other part of themselves as something alien that goes against their beliefs and values. In other words, the client will experience themselves as containing something disruptive, problematic or even evil, which they struggle to control, reform or get rid of.

When the part they do not identify with takes control, they will experience that they do things "against their own will", or that they are unable to make themselves do what they want to do. Thus, bad habits and procrastination are often signs of the Knot of Fragmentation. Ascetics can often feel disappointed with themselves or disapprove of themselves.

Ascetics will typically say: "I want to stop my self-sabotage", "I try to build a career, but my laziness gets in the way", "I want to be a kind person, but I have these terribly mean thoughts from time to time", "I don't know why I always do that", or "I wish I was more..., than I am".

When working with this manifestation of the Knot of Fragmentation, it is important to pause the judgements against the repressed part and understand what it is ultimately seeking. Once you have paused the dominating part, you can, for example, engage the repressed part in the Sensing Completion process. Once the dominating part "witnesses" what the repressed part is ultimately reaching for it will understand that the goal is not in opposition to itself, and this will diminish the polarisation.

For example, a diligent, industrious part of the client may be in conflict with a leisurely part, which yearns for relaxation. The industrious part may view the desire to unwind as an obstacle to productivity and therefore pass judgement on it. It can be a great surprise to the industrious part to realise that the leisure-loving part seeks a sense of pleasure through relaxation that is not unlike the pleasure the industrious part seeks through achievements. While the method of obtaining pleasure through leisure and relaxation may remain alien or even incomprehensible to the industrious part, the recognition that both parts aim for a similar sense of pleasure and fulfilment can diminish the critical perspective the hard-working part has towards its more laid-back counterpart. Understanding the common goal can pave the way for the development of mutual understanding, which appreciates the value of both rest and accomplishment.

When parts are in conflict, there will be judgements both ways. In the case of the ascetic, the criticism coming from the part the client is not identified with will appear as unfair, excessive or irrational self-criticism. Whereas there are many approaches to working with self-criticism (Springborg, 2024) the general approach is to pause one part while working to reveal the other part's ultimate intentions and then switching. This process will reveal that there is no conflict between the intentions of the two parts.

Crusader (stable identification and strong repression)

The crusader refers to the manifestation of the Knot of Fragmentation where the client is firmly identified with one of the conflicting parts and this part exerts a strong repressive force over the other part.

Because one of the conflicting parts is repressed, the crusader will not feel any inner conflict. Instead, the client will have a rigid and often moralistic attitude, condemning other people who embody the parts similar to the one the client represses in themself. In such cases, the Knot of Fragmentation is usually expressed through black and white thinking and conflicts with other people.

The crusader will say: "I just don't understand why some people act like that", "There is simply no excuse for that", "I need to learn how to steer clear of such people", "Wouldn't you agree that this kind of behaviour is unacceptable?", or "I have no time for or interest in people who…".

Furthermore, crusaders can spend a lot of time on "building a case" against certain people or kinds of behaviour in general. It is precisely the level of attention crusaders give to particular kinds of people or behaviours that reveals the Knot of Fragmentation. If the people the crusader condemns did not resemble a personality part the crusader spends energy on repressing, the crusader would not give much attention to those other people. In the approach to therapy known as Internal Family Systems they often say: "If it is intense, it is yours". Thus, intense black and white thinking is generally a sign of the Knot of Fragmentation combined with a stable identification with one side and a strong ability to repress the other.

When working with this manifestation of the Knot of Fragmentation, the first step is to soften the client's certainty and black and white thinking. However, it is important to do so without getting into a debate with the client. If you start arguing the repressed side, the client may begin to see you as part of the problem and ultimately stop having sessions. Alternatively, they may fortify themselves in their position. It is possible to soften the client's certainty in several ways. Below, I will briefly illustrate how to do this by using some of the techniques covered in Section 5.6.3 Step 3: Elucidate agency (deconstructing the "natural" state).

Short-circuiting logic: One way is to create paradoxes where you use the client's own logic against their position. This is always possible because the client's position is one of fragmentation and not wholeness. For example, if the client is identified with a part that values hard work and despises relaxation because they see relaxation as laziness, you can say that part of working hard to achieve your goals is to keep your instruments in pristine condition and just like a car needs oil to function optimally, the human body needs rest. Thus, not to relax is incompatible with high work ethics. Short-circuiting logic can be seen as a variation of the "flipping causality" technique presented in Section 5.6.3.

Poles to spectrums: Another way is to turn the poles of the client's black and white thinking into a scale and invite the client to consider the limit. This is much harder to do than to pick a side, and, consequently, it will invite doubt that can soften the client's certainty and identification with one pole. For example, a client may divide people into those who work and those who prefer to relax, and they may identify with the hard-working category and judge relaxation negatively. To soften the client's judgement against relaxation, you can posit that *never* working is untenable, but that so is working 24 hours a day. Once each extreme is off the table, you can ask the client how many hours of work a day is enough. We previously looked at this technique in Section 5.6.3, "From poles to spectrums".

Spectrums to planes: Yet another way is to present the opposing poles of the client's black and white thinking as independent variables rather than opposites. For example, it is possible to work in a stressed manner or a relaxed manner. Thus, your level of work is independent of your level of relaxation and increasing relaxation doesn't necessarily mean decreasing work. Instead, it can mean changing your approach to work. We previously looked at this technique in Section 5.6.3, "From spectrums to planes".

Pointing to the enemy inside: Another way to invite the client to soften their black and white thinking is to point to behaviour in the client that stems from the repressed personality part. For example, if the client identifies with a personality part that values kindness and despises aggression, you can point out that devaluing aggressive people is in itself a form of aggression. Alternatively, you can ask the client about different contexts in which kindness would be absurd. Nobody is devoid of aggression, so it will be possible to find situations where it would be absurd for the client to deny any sense of frustration, anger, condemnation or forms of aggression. If successful, and the client recognises that they do, in fact, at times exhibit precisely the kind of behaviour they despise in others, this will move the client to the position of the ascetic – which is one step closer to the doubter.

It is worth noting that when crusaders recognise that they are guilty of the sin they condemn in others – and that they have been unaware of this – they may be mortified, and they may react in one of two ways. Sometimes, they will feel they are no longer a worthy part of humanity, that they have fallen into disgrace, and that they, consequently, no longer have any rights in this world. Alternatively, they may become even more righteous than before, determined to purge themselves of the evil they contain, or they may rationalise and justify their "sinful" behaviour and find ways of blaming other people for it to preserve their sense of superiority. Sometimes, clients will alternate between these two reactions. When such reactions come, there is nothing to do other than framing the client's "transgressions" as perfectly normal human behaviour and, thus, inviting them to relax their judgement and take as much time as they need for this.

By softening the crusader's certainty using the above tools, it is possible to gradually move them from the crusader, through the ascetic, to the doubter where the client sees and empathises with both personality parts. From there it is possible to ask one of the client's conflicting parts to suspend judgement and witness the work you do with the other part.

Shapeshifter (unstable identification and strong repression)

The shapeshifter refers to the manifestation of the Knot of Fragmentation where the client is firmly identified with one of the opposing personality parts but from time to time change which part they identify with.

This situation can be baffling as the client at different times in a single session can wholeheartedly express completely contradictory viewpoints. The client may even forget that they have previously expressed the viewpoint that conflicts with the one they are currently expressing. Such shifts can happen within minutes.

For example, at one point in the session, the client may say: "I feel it is dangerous to let down my guard", while the next moment the client says: "I'm so tired of always being on guard. There really is no need for this". And if you ask about the dangers, the client will deny both the legitimacy of any such dangers and ever having felt threatened. Similarly, at one point in the session, the client may say: "My partner is terrible to me. There is no excuse for what they do. I need to learn to be firm and put a stop to this", while moments later they say: "It's really all my fault. I don't know why I'm so mean to my partner. It is so painful that I hurt them over and over again. I don't deserve them". And if you ask if the client can remember having said that they thought their partner was terrible to them they may either say they don't remember or that they believe they were mistaken when they said that.

Because the expression of one part activates the expression of the other, the shapeshifter may shift between the two parts so quickly that there is not enough time to work with either part. Therefore, when working with this manifestation of the Knot of Fragmentation, it is important to help the client focus on one part long enough to gain insights into the functioning and intentions related to this part. For this purpose, the tools listed under the crusader can be used.

In addition, it can be useful to help the client see that neither position is tenable. Both positions are problematic solutions to the same problem. By recognising the problems related to each position, the client may begin to see the two personality parts as representing different parts of the puzzle and considering how the two parts can collaborate to find a viable solution.

For example, a client with an inner conflict between an industrious and a leisure-loving part may recognise that working hard without relaxation undermines their possibility of achieving their goals, and that perpetual relaxation will lead to mounting problems that undermine their possibility of having a relaxed lifestyle. Recognising these problems opens up the possibility of collaboration between the two personality parts.

Finally, the frequent shifts between the conflicting parts seen in the shapeshifter is often an indication that both parts contain feelings of being overlooked or ignored and that they, therefore, fight for control. For this reason, when working with the shapeshifter version of the Knot of Fragmentation, it can be particularly important to assure each part that giving attention to the other part does not mean that you have forgotten them or that you believe their perspective is irrelevant in any way.

Broadening the client's perspective through subtraction vs. addition

The Knot of Fragmentation is caused and sustained by the narrow perspectives of individual personality parts. When two or more parts hold perspectives that prevent them from recognising the legitimacy of each other's perspectives and intentions, then identifying with any one part will make the other parts appear as irrational and something to overcome.

For this reason, a key part of solving the Knot of Fragmentation is to help the client look at the situation from a perspective that is broader than the perspective of any individual personality part.

The process of moving beyond the narrow perspective of any individual personality part can be articulated as either a process of subtraction or addition.

Subtraction is the approach where we set aside one perspective after another. This is akin to removing lenses that restrict our visual perception and in this way achieve a broader view. The subtraction approach can be described as suspending beliefs and assumptions or disidentifying, unblending or demerging from personality parts. The subtraction approach invites us to experience who we are beyond any personality part, beyond the automated programmes we use to engage with the world, beyond our conditioning.

Addition is the approach where we keep including more and more perspectives. This is akin to adding more and more lenses to our repertoire and, thus, achieving a broader view by continuously complexifying and enriching our perspective. The addition approach can be described as considering multiple and conflicting beliefs and assumptions or identifying, blending or merging with multiple personality parts at the same time. The addition approach also invites us to experience who we are beyond any individual personality part but from a position of totality rather than a position of transcendence.

For the doubter, ascetic and crusader it can be useful to talk about disidentifying, unblending or demerging from inner parts as a way of helping the client escape the narrow perspectives of any single inner part.

However, for the shapeshifter it can sometimes be more beneficial to talk about identifying, blending or merging with multiple inner parts simultaneously. This will achieve the same broadening of perspective as more and more parts are included. However, it has the advantage that no part will feel left behind.

Broadening the perspective through subtraction and addition is not mutually exclusive and, used correctly, they are ultimately the same. However, it can be good to know that clients may react very differently to these two ways of articulating the process of moving beyond the narrow perspective of any individual personality part.

Working with more than two parts

In the above, I have focused on fragmentation between two parts. However, sometimes clients have personality structures where the fragmentation is between more than two personality parts. There may also be coalitions of parts, parts protecting other parts, etc.

In such situations, it can be good to map out the system of parts. This is the topic of the next section.

6.4.2. Step 2: Map the system of parts

Once you have identified a Knot of Fragmentation, it is useful to map the system of personality parts involved in this knot.

This map does not have to include detailed descriptions of each part. It only needs to give a rough overview of the main parts at play, which can serve as a basis for selecting a sequence in which you work with the parts.

In the remainder of this section, I will describe tools for mapping systems of parts. I start by commenting on how to segment a client's inner life into personality parts in a useful way. I proceed by presenting some questions that can help uncover hidden parts. I round off by describing three common pitfalls related to working with personality parts in general, which are particularly important to be aware of when mapping out the system of parts. These pitfalls are: Speaking for a part instead of from a part, getting caught in a part, and parts-work contributing to the Knot of Alienation.

One agenda, one part

When using the framework of inner parts, the first question we must deal with is how to segment clients' inner world into a useful number of personality parts, which enhances, rather than hinders, the development of clear understanding. It is possible to operate with both too few and too many personality parts.

On the one hand, operating with too few parts may lead to over-simplification which will mask underlying conflicts. The advantage of working with personality parts instead of a single self is, precisely, that it is easier to understand and explore internal conflicts by representing all relevant perspectives involved in such conflict through a distinct personality part. Thus, if we operate with too few parts, we may leave out important perspectives on the conflict limiting our understanding.

On the other hand, operating with too many parts can lead to confusion and to spending more energy on keeping track of all the parts than on actual therapeutic work. If we operate with a different part for every thought, emotion and behaviour, we have not gained anything by using the concepts of parts. We apply this concept precisely to *reduce* the number of inner elements we work with, allowing us to perceive larger patterns without becoming lost in details.

In the subsequent section, I will introduce a simple heuristic designed to effectively divide clients' inner worlds into a manageable number of parts, which is useful for therapeutic exploration.

Imagine the following scenario: A client tells you that they feel sad, lonely and angry. Sometimes, they withdraw from other people. At other times, they fill their diary with appointments and get very excited about this, only to later feel overwhelmed and end up cancelling many of the appointments because they want peace and space for themselves. Moreover, the client tells you that they think people are fickle and cannot be trusted, and that they, therefore, resent their own dependency on other people for emotional fulfilment and company.

When seeking to understand this client's inner life in terms of interactions between personality parts, you may ask yourself questions such as:

- How many distinct parts are at play in the above scenario?
- How do we begin sorting the client's multidimensional inner experience into a set of clearly defined parts?
- Do the feelings of sadness, loneliness and anger belong to three separate parts or to a single part?
- Do two feelings belong to one part and one to another and, if so, which two belong to the same part?
- Is the part that avoids contact with other people the same as the one that cancels the appointments or are they two different parts?

To answer such questions, it is helpful to remember that parts are schemas that allow individuals to automatically make predictions based on current observations and past experiences and to select a course of action based on these predictions. In other words, a part is developed for the purpose of achieving a particular outcome in a particular type of situation.

In practice, this translates into the following principle:

> "One part, one agenda."

When mapping a client's internal system of parts, you can start by identifying the various agendas in the client's account of their situation, and then proceed to determine which emotions and thoughts align with each agenda.

In the above example, we might discern one part seeking peace and personal space and another seeking social connection. Assuming these are the primary agendas, we can start sorting the client's thoughts and emotions accordingly. It would make sense that the part seeking peace and personal space is the part that avoids contact, cancels appointments, and feels overwhelmed by the prospect of too much human interaction. Similarly, it makes sense that the part seeking connection is the part that feels sad and lonely and fills the calendar with appointments. The belief that people are fickle and untrustworthy would match well with the agenda of seeking peace. It is also likely that it is this same part that feels anger since anger would be a natural response to fickle and untrustworthy behaviour in others. Thus, the distrust and anger most likely belong to the part that seeks peace. Resentment about having a need for other people would also match the part that seeks peace, while the need itself matches the part that seeks social connection. Thus, starting from the distinct agendas present in the client's account of their situation, it is possible to sort all thoughts, emotions and behaviours into two clearly defined parts. Using only two parts clarifies that the client contains a conflict between their ideas about how to create peace and their ideas about how to create connection. Knowing this, we can proceed to ask the client what peaceful connection or connected peace feels like as a way of revealing that while the methods the client uses for creating each of these inner states may conflict, the states themselves do not.

Great clarity can come from dividing a client's inner life into inner parts using the "one agenda, one part" rule of thumb.

While it is obviously important to listen to the client's own perception of what constitutes a separate personality part, the therapist should not rely solely on clients' ability to sort their inner experience into personality parts in a way that furthers the therapeutic work. Dividing inner life into personality parts is a tool that is best wielded by a skilful practitioner. So, do not shy away from "negotiating" with clients and suggest ways to divide their inner life into a useful set of parts. Sometimes, you may suggest that what a client sees as two distinct parts may be one and the same. At other times, you may suggest what a client sees as a single part would be more useful to consider as two separate parts. Often, after listening for an extended period of time to a client talking about their experience, I summarise and feed back what I have heard, using the language of personality parts: "So, one part of you..., while another part of you..., and then a third part of you...". This allows the client to confirm or make modifications – without placing the burden of creating the initial division into parts on the client.

Detecting hidden parts

In Section 5.2 The layered personality structure, I described personality as a system of automated patterns of thought, emotion and behaviour. Furthermore, I proposed that these patterns are developed to deal with specific problems and that sometimes the problem one pattern deals with is an unintended side effect of the activity of another pattern.

As a result, the personality structure is a layered structure. Clients are generally only aware of patterns in the outermost layers of this structure. Patterns in the deeper layers operate beyond clients' awareness and the effects of these patterns will, therefore, appear as facts of life rather than products of clients' own activity.

In Section 5.6.3, I presented a range of tools for bringing awareness to automated patterns that normally operate outside a client's awareness.

The framework of personality parts can greatly assist this work as it makes it possible to detect personality parts clients *are not* aware of by asking questions about the thoughts, feelings and motivations of personality parts clients *are* aware of. Three such questions I often use are:

1. How do you feel about a particular part?
2. What is a particular part reacting to?
3. Who is a particular part talking to?

You can either ask these questions directly to the client or use them as background questions that guide the therapeutic inquiry.

Below, I will comment on the use of each of these questions.

How do you feel about a particular part?

A very effective way of detecting hidden parts is to ask clients what they feel about the parts they are already aware of.

If a client has an opinion, positive or negative, about a particular part of themselves, it is a sign that the client in that moment is operating from another part. However, the client may not be aware that the opinions and emotions they experience when looking at one part of themselves are, in fact, the opinions and emotions of another part. They may look at the situation from the "single self" perspective and assume they are experiencing their *own* opinions and emotions.

A client may, for example, tend to please other people, disregarding their own needs and wishes in the process. The client may be aware that this tendency to please others is a part of them that take over in certain situations.

When asked what they feel about this part, the client may say that they dislike it, and that it seems weak and pathetic to them. This answer reveals that the client contains another part, which is trying to deal with the problematic side effects created by the people-pleasing part by judging it negatively and seeking to use therapy to change it or get rid of it.

Alternatively, the client may answer the question of what they feel by saying that they feel protective of the people-pleasing part and see it as a beautiful but fragile part that is unfairly exploited by others. Furthermore, the client may feel anger at anyone who dares to take advantage of this part. This answer reveals that the client contains another part separate from the people-pleasing part. However, whereas the client's opinions and feelings about the people-pleasing part in the previous example revealed a part that was trying to protect against the problems created by the people-pleasing part, the client's feelings and opinions about the people-pleasing part in this example reveals a part that tries to protect the people-pleasing part against external abuse.

Thus, asking what a client feels or thinks about a particular part of themselves, is a good way of discovering other parts, which otherwise could go unnoticed, since the client would be likely to consider the feelings and opinions of the hidden part as facts of life. In the first example, the client may believe people-pleasing is inherently pathetic. Similarly, in the second example, the client may consider that people-pleasing is objectively a beautiful but fragile trait that must be protected.

Alternatively, clients may consider the feelings and opinions they experience when looking at a particular personality part as just *their own* feelings and opinions. This reveals that the client is identified with the personality part whose feelings and opinions they are currently experiencing. This is a common way that personality parts hide. I think about it as a personality part hiding by placing itself next to the client and discussing the situation with the client pretending it, itself, is not a personality part. Pointing out that the feelings and opinions the client is experiencing are those of a personality part is akin to inviting the client to turn their head and notice the part that is sitting next to them.

As a rule of thumb, any charged relationship the client experiences towards a personality part is an indication of the presence of another personality part. Whenever a client feels an urgent need to do something with the part they are looking at, this indicates the presence of another part. Sometimes, clients may wish to do several and even conflicting things with a personality part. This would imply several other parts. For example, a client may simultaneously feel that their people-pleasing tendency is pathetic and should be changed *and* that it is fragile and should be protected against external abuse. As these are two distinct agendas, such a response would indicate the presence of two distinct parts.

If the client looks at a part without being identified with any other part, they will usually feel a non-judgemental curiosity and interest, and they will have no particular wish to change or transform the part they are looking at.

What is a particular part reacting to?

Another effective way of detecting hidden parts is to ask clients what a part they are already aware of is reacting to.

If a client has a part with a strong urge to prevent a particular problem, it is often a sign that the client has another part that produces exactly this problem. However, as this second part may be operating outside the client's awareness, they may not be aware that their urge is a reaction to something in themselves.

A client may, for example, have a strong urge to be assertive and not let other people take advantage of them. The client may be aware that this urge belongs to a part of them which takes over in certain situations. When asked what this part is reacting to, the client may become aware that they have another part, which fears conflict and, therefore, often chooses to be taken advantage of to avoid conflicts.

It is not always necessary to ask a client directly what a particular part is a reaction to. It is often possible to use this question as a means to develop hypotheses and then ask the client to confirm or refute these hypotheses.

For example, if a client has a part that actively argues for the client's worth, one can hypothesise that the client must contain another part that produces feelings of worthlessness. If this were not the case, there would be nothing to prompt the first part to argue for the client's value. Even if other people tell the client they are worthless, this will only prompt the client to argue for their value if they contain a part that doubts their worth.

Similarly, if a client is concerned with taking up too much space, one can hypothesise that the client must have another part that wishes to take up space.

If there were no part pushing for taking up space, there would be no reason for the client to develop a part that is concerned about taking up too much space.

The two questions “What do you feel about a particular part?” and “What is a particular part reacting to?” are complementary. The first question helps identify hidden parts that are responses to a part the client is aware of; the second question helps identify hidden parts to which the part the client is aware of is responding. In other words, the first question reveals what comes after a certain part while the second question reveals what came before.

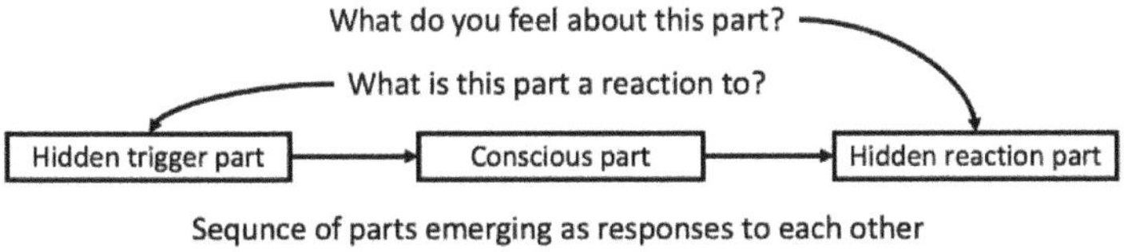

Figure 27: Uncovering hidden parts

Sometimes, clients will be aware of two parts that are reactions to each other. For example, a client may be aware of one part that seeks to minimise needs and another that seeks to inflate needs. The first part may seek to minimise needs to avoid the problems created by the part that inflates needs and vice versa.

In this case, one can ask what the “controversy” between these two parts is a reaction to. Asking this question may reveal the two parts the client is aware of are proposing two opposing answers to the same question, namely: How to get your needs met when you meet opposition from the outside. One part believes you are more likely to have your needs met if you minimise them. If you do not ask for much, others won’t be able to refuse. The other part believes you are more likely to have your needs met if you inflate them. If you ask for more than you need, you are more likely to get enough. Both answers presuppose that having your needs met is difficult because other people will oppose it. Thus, both parts can be seen as reactions to a third part holding this belief. If there were no difficulties in having your needs met, there would be no reason to devise strategies for how to do so.

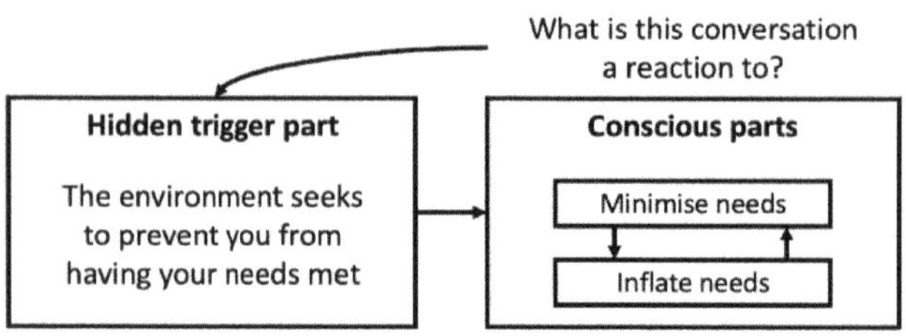

Figure 28: Uncovering hidden parts underpinning inner controversies

Thus, asking what the personality parts clients are aware of are reacting to can be an effective way of discovering hidden parts.

The advantage of this particular question is that it helps move the client's awareness upstream, as discussed in Section 5.6.3 *Step 3: Elucidate agency (deconstructing the* "natural" state) in the subsection *Moving awareness upstream*. Thus, repeated use of this question can bring the client's awareness all the way back to the initial part, which will be a positive reification of Being.

Who is a particular part talking to?

The third tool for discovering hidden parts is a variation of the previous question of what a part is reacting to.

When a client is describing the thoughts and feelings of a particular part, it can be helpful to imagine that the part is talking to someone on the telephone and try to guess what the person on the other end is saying.

If you listen to someone talking on the telephone, you will usually not be able to hear what the person on the other end is saying. Yet, you can make very qualified guesses based on what the person you can hear is saying.

Imagine the following is a transcription of someone speaking on the phone. While you read it, notice how easy it is to guess what the person on the other end of the line is saying.

- Hello, can I speak to the manager, please?
- I'd like to inquire about one of your products.
- Pricing and delivery options.
- Oh, great, thank you. What information do you need?
- Yes. Just a second. The product number is X4KJ7. I'm interested in the black version.
- That's perfect. I'd like to order two and have them sent to my home address with the express option.

- 123 Main Street, Knotsville
- No, that's all. Thank you so much.
- And a great day to you too!

While you cannot be certain what the person on the other end is saying, you can get a pretty good idea by listening to the part of the conversation you can hear.

In the same way, it is possible to listen to a client's account of their situation as if what they say are responses to another part inside of them which you cannot hear.

Imagine the following is a transcription of an account a client gives of their issue with their partner. While you read it, imagine that what you hear are the words one personality part is saying in response to another personality part as if it was talking to it on the phone. Notice if you can deduce what the other personality part must be saying from the responses you are hearing.

- My problem is that my partner doesn't respect me. He keeps down-prioritising the relationship, and I'm fed up with this behaviour.
- I'm *really* not asking for much here. Just some basic consideration.
- I'm not a needy or clingy person.
- I'm fine being on my own. But what is the point of a relationship if we hardly ever spend time together.
- I don't want to control his life or suffocate him, but it feels like he doesn't care about our relationship anymore. I miss the connection we used to have.
- I can easily find another boyfriend. I get lots of offers. I'm just tired of the whole dating thing.
- But I think I'll have to end the relationship. It isn't healthy, and I'm worth more than this.

As in the previous example, it is not possible to know for sure what the conversation partner you cannot hear is saying, but you can make some good guesses. For example, the client most likely has an inner part that holds the following beliefs:

- The client is asking for too much.
- The client is needy and clingy.
- The client should stay in the relationship because they wouldn't be ok on their own – for example, because they would be overwhelmed by loneliness.
- The client is controlling and suffocates their partner.
- The client may not be able to find another partner and are not worth their partner's (or anyone's) time and attention.

If the client did not contain inner parts holding the above beliefs, there would be no reason for the client to refute them in their description of their situation.

Listening to a client's account of their situation as one side of a telephone conversation can be a very effective way of developing good hypotheses about what hidden parts the client contains, which can inform your work with the client.

In summary, clients' inner life can be divided effectively into personality parts by using the rule: "one part, one agenda", and we can map the system of inner parts by using questions, such as "How do you feel about a particular part?", "What is a particular part reacting to?" and "Who is a particular part talking to?" to discover hidden parts that are outside clients' awareness.

6.4.3. Step 3: Select a part to work with

Once you have mapped out the system of parts operating in the client and clarified their relationships to each other, you can select one part to work with while asking other parts to suspend judgement and witness the process.

Over the course of a session, you may work with several parts, but it is important to focus on one part at a time because frequent shifts and interruptions can prevent the development of compassionate understanding for each individual part necessary for untying the Knot of Fragmentation.

Selecting which part you will work with and which part you will ask to suspend its judgement can be a bit of an art. However, generally it works well to select the part the client normally gives the least attention to and/or the part that are most agitated. If the part that gets the least attention is different from the part that is most agitated, selecting what part to work with will be a bit of a trial-and-error process.

The part that gets the least attention

We can think of the client's speech as a microphone that is passed among the client's inner parts. Some parts will frequently get to speak into the microphone while other parts will rarely ever touch it.

Above we looked at how it is possible to deduce the presence and perspectives of hidden parts. Using the metaphor of the microphone this is equivalent to deducing what the parts that are not speaking think and feel by listening to the parts that *are* speaking. This is possible because while the parts that are speaking may have a different perspective from those that are not speaking, they are still responding to the parts that are not speaking.

When we choose a part to work with, it can often be interesting to give the microphone to a part that normally does not speak. This will often bring forth information that can lead to profound and transformative insights.

A client may, for example, contain a part that is very vocal about the importance of setting clear boundaries. Because this part is very vocal, there is most likely to be nothing in this part's perspective that is unknown or surprising to the client. However, the focus on the importance of setting clear boundaries implies that the client must have another part that tends to let other people cross their boundaries. Giving this part the opportunity to tell its story and illuminate its reasons for allowing other people to cross the client's boundaries can bring forth important and transformative insights.

The part that is most agitated

When inner parts are in conflict, the perspectives, emotions and actions of each part can appear as a threat to the other part.

Therefore, whenever one part is speaking, other parts can become agitated and feel threatened. It is as if simply giving attention to one part is interpreted by the other part as if you are taking the other part's side. Furthermore, if you indicate empathetic understanding of one part's position, the other part may even more strongly feel that it is being side-lined and its goals are in jeopardy. This is particularly true for parts that contain fears of being overlooked, ignored, devalued or disregarded.

Thus, it can be beneficial to start by working with the part that is most agitated to reassure this part that it will be taken into account and heard. If you do not do this, the part may refuse to step back and will continue to interrupt any work you do with the other part.

A client may, for example, contain a conflict between a part that focuses on regular exercise and healthy eating habits, and a part that focuses on comfort and pleasure. The therapist may inquire into the perspective and intentions of the second part. As this part expands on what comfort means to it and how comfort and pleasure brings a sense of happiness and relaxation, the first part may start to feel that its efforts and discipline is being undermined and that its hard-earned progress will be squandered. Thus, this part may begin to bring forth in the client guilt about indulgence, judgements about being lazy, and worries about getting out of shape and suffering health issues. The emergence of such thoughts and emotions may indicate that the health-focused part is experiencing a high degree of agitation. Consequently, it can be fruitful to start by working with this part as developing a deep understanding of this part can calm it down and, thus, make it possible to work with the other part.

It is possible to imagine that the part that is most agitated is also the part that receives the most attention. In such cases, it can be useful to start by working with the part that is most agitated to open the possibility of working with the part that receives the least attention.

Parts will almost always experience some degree of agitation when asked to suspend judgement and witness the process of a part it is in conflict with. Therefore, it is important to have a set of tools that will allow you to ask parts to suspend judgement in a way that will minimise these parts' agitation. This is the topic of the next section.

6.4.4. Step 4: Invite other parts to suspend judgement

To understand a particular part of a client's inner life, it is necessary to listen to it with curiosity and compassion and without any judgement.

For this reason, it is important to ask any other parts of the client's inner life, which are in conflict with the part you wish to work with, to step back and suspend judgement.

Below I will describe five methods I often use for this purpose. The methods are arranged in order of increasing demand in terms of the skill and time they require.

Suspending judgement

The simplest way to get a part to step back is to ask it to do so. You can address the part of the client that judges the part you wish to work with directly and first acknowledge the legitimacy of its concerns and agendas, and then suggest that it suspends its judgement for a certain amount of time to make space for you to work with the part it judges.

For example, a client may tend to feel sudden flashes of anger towards their partner and shout at them. The emotion of anger and the behaviour of shouting belong to what we can call an aggressive part in the client.

When you ask the client how they feel about this part of them, they may say they feel ashamed of it and that they feel it makes them unlovable. This may lead the client to attempt to repress the aggressive part.

The feelings of shame and the attempt to repress the anger belong to another part in the client, which we can call the anti-aggression part.

To work with the aggressive part, it is important to ask the anti-aggression part to step back and suspend its judgement for a while. You can ask the part to do so directly, by first acknowledging that the eruptions into anger and shouting do harm the relationship, and this is truly problematic, and then say that it is unlikely that harming the relationship is the aggressive part's true goal. Then you can ask the part if it would be ok for it to step back and suspend its judgement for a while, while you seek to understand the true motivations and goals of the aggressive part.

Often, this will feel ok for the part you ask to step back. If so, you can proceed with your interview of the aggressive part.

However, sometimes the part will be unwilling to let go of its judgement. In such cases, you will have to stay with the anti-aggression part and understand its reluctance.

Putting in a safety rail

If the judgemental part is unwilling to step back when asked, it is a good idea to inquire what it is afraid would happen if it did.

In the above example, the part may fear that if it steps back, there will be no guard rails keeping the aggressive part in check and this would lead it to cause irreversible damage to the relationship.

Once you understand what the concerns of the part are, you can modify your request, so you ask the part to step back in ways that will ensure none of the things it fears will happen.

In the example above, you can ask whether it would be ok for the part to step back for a few minutes during the session, given that the partner is not present and that nothing the aggressive part may say or do during the session, therefore, can harm the relationship.

Putting in guard rails in this manner will require some creativity on the part of the therapist.

Pointing out the inefficiency of judgement

If the judgemental part still is unwilling to step back, you can draw its attention to the fact that its judgements do not solve the problem, and that it may be worth it to try another approach.

In the above example, you can ask for how long has the client had the problem with erupting in anger. The client is likely to state that this has been a long-term problem. You can then ask how long the client believes they have to continue repressing the aggressive part before the problem is solved. The client is likely to state that this will not really solve the problem as much as keep it in check.

You can then point out that judging and repressing the aggressive part seems to be a rather inefficient way of dealing with the problem and ask if the anti-aggression part would be willing to step back and let you try out a new approach to dealing with the aggressive part, which might solve the problems, rather than merely keeping them in check.

If the part trusts you, it will often allow the experiment, and you can go on to interview the aggressive part about its true purpose and goal.

Short-circuiting the logic behind the judgement

Sometimes, a judgemental part will not step back, even if it acknowledges that its judgement does not solve the problem.

In this case, you may short-circuit the logic the part operates from by revealing how judging the part it judges is not only inefficient but makes the problem worse.

In the above example, you may point out that when an angry person gets dismissed it usually makes them even angrier. Thus, seeking to repress the aggressive side only fans the flame of the aggression. In this way, by judging the aggressive side, the anti-aggressive side contributes to the process that is harming the relationship.

If you can convincingly present the counterproductive nature of judging a part as problematic, this can sometimes convince the judgemental part to step back and allow you to try out a different approach.

Another way of short-circuiting the logic behind a judgement is to take the logic to its natural conclusion in an extreme case. This will reveal the shortcomings of the logic and can make the part willing to rethink its own logic.

For example, a client may have one part that resists helping others and another dominating part that firmly believes one should be nice to others if it is at all within one's power, making it wrong to refuse any request for help. The client may be mainly identified with the latter part and, therefore, unwilling to explore their impulse to say no to other people's requests. The client, being primarily identified with the latter part, may dismiss or avoid exploring their impulse to say no to others' demands and judge it as a personal flaw.

One way to short-circuit the logic of the second part so that it may step back and allow exploration of the first part's intention is to highlight how the logic underpinning the second part's position can lead to absurd conclusions when taken to the extreme. For example, according to this logic, one should let oneself be raped if someone else would like to have sex, since it is physically possible to grant the other their request. The absurdity of this conclusion can cast doubt on the logic of unquestioning niceness and may encourage the part that represses boundary-setting to step back and consider the intentions of the part that wishes to say no to other people's requests for help.

Thus, short-circuiting the logic underpinning a dominant part can help create willingness to step back and work with other parts to gain a more nuanced view.

Waiting

If the judgemental part refuses to give any space to the part it judges, no matter which of the above methods you use, it usually means that this part feels a high level of fear. In this case, it is good to wait and postpone working with the part it judges.

Instead, you can work with the judgemental part and uncover its ultimate goals. Since all parts ultimately seek Being, working with any part can bring awareness of Being, and such awareness has a calming effect on all parts.

Thus, if you work with the judgemental part in ways that bring about awareness of Being, this will calm the part, and at some point, it may be calm enough to be willing to allow you to work with the part it judges.

6.4.5. Step 5: Correct misconceptions related to the Knot of Fragmentation

Once you have selected a part to work with and other parts have stepped back, you can work with this part using all the tools from the previous chapters.

However, this work will now have added value in that you are not merely working with the knots at the level of the individual personality part but also with the Knot of Fragmentation at the level of the personality structure.

When mapping out the system, clients will briefly sense into each of the parts involved. This activates these personality parts, making it possible for them to witness the work you are about to do with the selected personality part. This means that the ensuing process will not only affect the part you work with but also all the parts you have activated during the part of the process where you mapped out the system of parts. This includes parts which may be judging, protecting or relating in some other way to the part you will work with.

For example, a client may have an aggressive personality part that causes problems in their relationships. If you take this part through the Sensing Completion process, you may discover that the aggressive part seeks to defend against humiliation and put-downs, and that it believes that if it could banish humiliations and put-downs completely it would feel safe enough to love. Thus, the ultimate goal of the aggressive behaviour is to feel love. You may then proceed with the Sensing Abundance process and let the client explore the felt sense of the love their aggressive part is reaching out for. Feeling this love without the need for any aggressive defensive actions can be profoundly transformative for the aggressive personality part. This work is valuable, but it mainly affects the individual part.

If the session begins by mapping out all parts involved, for example by asking the client what they feel about the aggressive part, the client may discover that they also contain an anti-aggressive personality part that judges the aggressive part as shameful and destructive. Noticing this part will activate it in the client. This makes it possible for this part to witness the process of the aggressive part. It will witness both the deep longing for love that drives the aggressive part and the beauty of the felt sense of this love. Witnessing this can profoundly transform the anti-aggressive part. It may cause it to change from feeling a desire to repress the aggressive part to feeling compassion for the aggressive part. It may realise that rejecting the aggressive part only confirms the aggressive part's belief in the necessity of its destructive defensiveness, whereas abiding in love together with the aggressive part will contradict its belief and help it transform into a passionate champion of love that no longer needs the exaggerated aggression. Thus, this work goes beyond the level of the individual part and affects the broader system of personality parts, the personality structure[60].

In the following five sections, I will outline how each of the five processes for untying knots acquires an additional purpose and value when the work with one personality part is witnessed by other personality parts. Furthermore, I will comment on how these processes enable the correction of the five misconceptions related to the Knot of Fragmentation.

Mapping personality parts and the 16th corrective principle

Mapping out personality parts and their relationships during the first part of the Sensing Unity process enables clients to experience for themselves that the idea of having a single self is a myth, and that they, in fact, contain many relatively independent personality parts, each of which can be considered a separate "self" (the 16th corrective principle).

This shift in perspective can be reinforced by listing out the different personality parts the client has been working with throughout the session and noticing how connecting with each part radically alters the client's behaviour, emotions and outlook on life.

The shift from the single self to the multiple selves perspective can also be reinforced by highlighting moments during the session where the client changed from considering certain thoughts and emotions as belonging to an overall single self to recognising these thoughts and feelings as belonging to a personality part.

Highlighting such moments can enable clients to learn to perceive *all* thoughts and emotions as necessarily belonging to a personality part and not as defining of the client as a whole.

It enables clients to recognise how all their thoughts and emotions emerge from individual schemas that are learned through past experience and that no part of their inner life can be considered truer or more authentic than others. It helps clients learn from direct experience that the very notion that certain thoughts and

---

[60] Working one by one with parts that are in conflict with each other is akin to working with couples in therapy. Working with one part of the couple while the other part is witnessing the process can create the mutual compassionate understanding needed for the couple to rediscover and deepen their love for each other and heal any fragmentation.

emotions are more authentic than others is, itself, an idea belonging to a particular personality part.

Such insight will help correct the misconception of the single self.

Sensing Taboos and the 17th corrective principle

Sometimes the reason personality parts get into conflict is that one personality part contains a state the other personality part perceives as harmful or overwhelming and, thus, seeks to repress the part containing this state or altogether escape from it.

Using the Sensing Taboos process makes it possible to explore the felt-sense essence of the seemingly harmful or overwhelming states. Such exploration will reveal that at heart these states are nothing other than aspects of Being that have been interpreted in a negative light.

In the Sensing Taboos process, we may experience hurt transform into tenderness, aggression into vitality, hatred into peace, desire into joy, stuckness into grounding, lostness into freedom, and so on.

When such transformation is witnessed by the parts that believed it is necessary to protect against these states, they will lose their fear. This will not only dissolve the conflict between the two parts. It will also reveal through direct experience that the protective part is not protecting the client against a harmful state but is, in fact, preventing the client from accessing an important resource[61].

The experience of the Sensing Taboos process can reveal to all personality parts that what they see as inner threats are neither enemies nor obstacles. If we work in this way with one conflict after another, over time, the client will come to develop a deep embodied understanding of the 17th corrective principle that there are no inner enemies.

Sensing Completion and the 18th corrective principle

Sometimes the reason personality parts get into conflict is that they are pursuing courses of action that are mutually exclusive. Because each personality part sees

---

[61] In IFS, this process relates to working with protector parts that are protecting against the so-called exile parts, which contain feelings that at some point in the client's life appeared harmful or overwhelming.

their own course of action as necessary for well-being, they will see the other personality part's course of action as detrimental to well-being.

In Sensing Completion, we explore the end goal of a particular part's agenda by asking what the client would feel if they were 100% successful with this agenda.

In the chapter on Sensing Completion, I emphasised that it is immaterial whether the agenda the client presents at the start of the session seems realistic or even healthy. If the therapist keeps asking for the ultimate goal, the client will always discover that what any personality part is ultimately reaching for is a state of Being. This is true regardless of how irrational or destructive the personality part's behaviour may appear at first glance.

Making such discoveries is beneficial in all cases. However, when we do the Sensing Completion process with two conflicting personality parts and these parts witness each other's process, they may come to realise that, while they may pursue conflicting courses of action, what they ultimately seek to achieve through their actions is fully compatible. It may even be either mutually supportive or simply the very same.

Such realisations may dissolve the conflict between the two parts, and the absence of conflict, in turn, makes it easier for the client to develop a sustained awareness of Being, which will further dissolve the conflict since the moment the client becomes aware of Being, both parts will feel they have reached what they sought[62].

The experience of the Sensing Completion process also reinforces the 17th corrective principle that there are no inner enemies. However, it also reinforces the 18th corrective principle that when we listen to problematic parts and let them show us what they are ultimately seeking, they will become our guides and point out Being to us.

Sensing Agency and the 19th corrective principle

Sometimes the reason personality parts get into conflict is that they pursue mutually exclusive ways of solving the same problem of either the presence of a negative state or the absence of a positive one.

---

[62] In IFS, this process relates to working with protector parts that are protecting against other protector parts which, in their attempts at protecting the client is inadvertently harming the client.

Using the Sensing Agency process can help uncover the hidden part that is creating the problem the two conflicting parts are seeking to solve.

Thus, the Sensing Agency process can play a pivotal role in mapping out clients' inner parts beyond those the client is already aware of. It helps clients become aware of parts that are so well concealed that the effects of their activity appear to them as independent fact of life other parts must deal with.

Discovering these hidden parts can be revolutionary on its own. As we saw in the corresponding chapter, it can greatly expand the client's agency.

Furthermore, discovering such hidden parts can profoundly transform the relationship between the parts the client was already aware off.

First, it reveals that whereas the two parts may pursue mutually exclusive paths of action, they can be united in their desire to solve the same problem.

Second, discovering that what appears to be a fact of life, in reality is the creation of a hidden part, can render conflicts between other parts involved in dealing this assumed fact of life irrelevant, since the premise for the conflict will cease to exist the moment the third part ceases to produce the problem.

A client may, for example, contain two personality parts that try to deal with the presence of a negative inner state in conflicting ways. These parts will be judgemental of each other and perceive each other as obstacles. However, through the process of Sensing Agency, the client may discover that they contain a third personality part that creates and maintains the negative state. This discovery reveals that neither of the conflicting personality parts had the correct answer. Whatever method these parts are pursuing as a way of dealing with the negative state, will be futile as long as the third part keeps generating it. In other words, the discovery of the third part renders the conflict between the two initial parts irrelevant and refocuses the therapeutic work on the third part.

Similarly, a client may contain one personality part that deals with the absence of a positive inner state in a way that causes harm and another personality part that judges the first part for causing harm and tries to repress it. The client may, for example, have a workaholic personality part that attempts to deal with the absence of value by working long hours and hoping to impress the boss and co-workers and, thus, find value through external validation. The long hours may take a toll on both the client's health and relationships. The client may have another personality part that realises the harmful effects of the client's workaholism and shames the client for working long hours. If the client, through the process of

Sensing Agency, discovers that the absence of value is not a natural state but rather is created by a third personality part which actively undermines the client's sense of value, the conflict between the pro-work part and the anti-work part becomes irrelevant. Neither working hard nor working less will bring about the sense of value. Only working with the part that prevents the client from noticing their inherent value can do so.

Thus, the Sensing Agency process can reveal how the problems conflicting parts seek to resolve are often not naturally occurring but rather created by hidden personality parts. Thus, when clients identify with one of two conflicting personality parts and seek to reject the other, they will draw attention away from the true source of the problem and thus sustain the dynamic that gives rise to the very personality part they seek to reject. This is one way rejecting a personality part can tie clients closer to that which they reject (the 19th corrective principle).

The 20 misconceptions described in this book can be seen as 20 root causes of internal conflicts. This is why it is so crucial to correct these 20 misconceptions, rather than wasting time on seeking to reject any particular personality part, regardless of how problematic it appears to another personality part.

Recognising how inner conflict fundamentally emerges from misconceptions reveals that no parts of us operate from malicious intent. Harmful behaviour is always the result of operating from a misconception about reality[63].

Sensing Abundance and the 20th corrective principle

Sometimes the reason personality parts get into conflict is not that they see each other as either containing harmful states or as pursuing harmful agendas but merely that they believe they are pursuing two positive but mutually exclusive ends.

One may seek autonomy while another seeks connection. Both personality parts recognise the value of what the other seeks yet they both operate from the assumption that it is necessary to choose as the two cannot coexist.

In such cases, we can use the Sensing Abundance process to invite clients to perceive the combination of the felt-sense states underpinning what the

---

[63] This view is found in many traditions. For example, according to Socrates, no person willingly chooses to do wrong or act evilly. Instead, individuals commit harmful acts out of a lack of knowledge or understanding of what is truly good. Similarly, in Buddhism ignorance of the true nature of reality is the cause of human suffering and harmful behaviour.

conflicting personality parts seek. The experience of the state of "combined abundance" will enable clients to directly experience that the two states are not mutually exclusive. Furthermore, it will facilitate reflections on how the states may, in fact, be mutually supportive.

When used in this way, the Sensing Abundance process brings about experience that will reinforce the 20th corrective principle, that it is possible to have it all.

Final comments

There are many other ways in which the experiences of the Sensing Unity process enable the correction of the five misconceptions related to the Knot of Fragmentation. However, rather than presenting a long list, I invite therapists to stay alert to any opportunity that may arise during the process and evaluate which to act on.

As mentioned previously, during therapy sessions, I do not seek to correct all possible misconceptions. Rather, I focus on one or two that seem to be most impactful for the specific client and the specific context.

The rationale behind this is that if a client gains a powerful insight, it is best to allow space and time for this insight to land. If you overload the client with additional insights, you risk confusing them and potentially diluting the power of the initial revelation.

6.4.6. Pitfalls of parts work

Whereas the framework of personality parts is a powerful tool that can greatly simplify the therapeutic work, it also has its potential pitfalls. In the following, I will describe a few important pitfalls therapists should be aware of.

To be or not to be a personality part

In therapy, disidentifying from and identifying with parts are both useful tools. Knowing which tool to use with which parts is key.

If a client is strongly identified with a personality part, it can restrict the client's perspective and limit their capacity for reflection. For this reason, therapists will often encourage clients to recognise how the thoughts and emotions they are experiencing are the thoughts and emotions of a particular personality part. This recognition can help clients disidentify from the personality part and gain awareness of the thoughts and emotions of other parts of themselves, thus, empowering their capacity for reflecting on and resolving inner conflicts.

However, when working with a personality part that is or has been repressed in a client, asking the client to disidentify from that part, or merely framing it as "just a part", can in some situations end up supporting the repressive forces against that part in the client. The result may be that the client loses access to this part's emotions, perspectives and agendas. You may even experience that when you ask questions about the part, these questions will be answered by the repressive parts instead of the part you wish to talk to. Furthermore, disidentifying from a personality part can sometimes be perceived by that part as a form of rejection, and may, consequently, activate the part in ways that prevent the process of disidentification.

Therefore, in some situations, rather than asking them to disidentify from a personality part, it can be useful to ask clients to identify more with it to help them gain a more vivid sense of what the part is feeling and thinking, and to signal a wish to include, rather than reject, the part.

In other words, there is a trade-off between being and not being a part. Being, or identifying with, a part means that clients have direct access to the thoughts and emotions of that part – but maybe not to other parts. Not being, or disidentifying from, a part frees clients' awareness so they can notice the perspectives and emotions of other parts – but it may also limit their access to the part they have disidentified from.

Since the ideal scenario is to help clients hold awareness of the perspectives and emotions of multiple parts, we must be attentive to the difference between disidentification and repression.

When disidentifying from a personality part, it is important to do it in a way that preserves the connection to this part. When identifying with a personality part, it is important to do it in a way that preserves an awareness of being more than the part.

Whereas the ideal is for clients to be able to feel parts from the inside without forgetting that it is a part, it can be useful throughout a session to continuously assess whether it would be beneficial for a client to step more into a part or step more out of it.

Parts work contributing to the Knot of Alienation

A third common pitfall related to working with personality parts is that clients may come to perceive their inner life as ruled by a confusing multitude of inner parts far beyond their own control. This can enhance the Knot of Alienation, in that the client comes to feel powerless and feel that all their inner parts have taken over.

Of course, this very sense of powerlessness can be seen as the emotional state of a part of the client, which the client could be asked to step out of.

However, if inner parts are a metaphorical way of understanding automated schemas, there will always be a vast number of inner parts that are completely irrelevant to a given issue the client is experiencing.

If, in a therapy session, we see anything that moves in the client as indicative of another part to include in our exploration, the result will be a map of the client's inner life which is every bit as confusing and overwhelming as the territory we are seeking to map. Trying to account for and clarify the relationship between all inner parts can end up being the very activity that prevents clients from recognising their own agency.

To avoid this pitfall, it is crucial to be selective of which parts you include in the work. The "one agenda, one part" rule can greatly help avoid that parts work ends up reinforcing the client's sense of alienation.

6.5. Examples of Sensing Unity

In this section, you can read transcriptions of two therapy sessions applying the process of Sensing Unity. The sessions, like all sessions in this book, are fictional but representative of sessions I have had with clients.

Furthermore, the sessions are abbreviated so they only include the key parts of the exchange. Real sessions often contain more exploration, longer narratives, tangents, pauses, etc. That being said, the Knot of Fragmentation can, in some cases, be untied in a matter of minutes. In such cases, the examples below would represent full transcriptions of the therapeutic exchange.

The examples are written in two columns. In the left column, you can read the client and therapist's conversation. In the right column, you can read the observations and considerations that guided the therapist during the exchange.

6.5.1. Session 9: Don't let them off the hook

The following session is an example of the Knot of Fragmentation with three conflicting parts. One part is very concerned about what other people think about the client and, in particular, about being blamed for other people's bad mood. Another part wants to not care about what other people think and sees the first part as pathetic. A third part, which only emerges later in the session, is primarily concerned with remaining broken and using the client's dysfunction as evidence against the client's neglectful parents. It is very common that clients hold on to their pain because they fear that if they heal, whoever hurt them will be off the hook for what they did to them.

The client in this session is a shapeshifter in that the client changes quickly and frequently between the different parts and sees the situation almost exclusively from the perspective of the part they are identified with at any given moment. This is what gives the client a somewhat contrary demeanour. It is easy to mistake the client's frequent rejection of the therapist's attempts at clarifying or summarising what the client says for resistance to the therapy or the therapist, when in fact it is an expression of how the client's inner parts resist each other.

Process	Comments
Client: I feel I'm very porous and affected by other people's mood and what they think. If someone is in a bad mood, I feel terrible. I cannot just be at ease, especially, if their bad mood has something to do with me. If people blame me for it that stuff can worry me for days and weeks.	This client presents a lamentable situation. There is some degree of alienation in that the client presents an undesirable situation as resulting from a combination of the way they are and external circumstances – rather than as something they create themselves.
Therapist: What is it about such situations you see as cause for concern?	I ask about how the client creates the worry. This is proposing agency.

Process	Comments
C: I'm afraid people will turn their backs on me. My parents did that a lot. Whenever I did something, they didn't like, they would grow cold and distant and start ignoring me. Or sometimes, they would start telling me everything they thought was wrong with me and attack me to make me stop doing the thing they didn't like. And I wasn't a crazy child. I was very quiet. But they still managed to find a lot of things I did annoying. I don't think they really wanted a child.	Here the client describes what they believe is the cause of the way they are. Mentioning that the client wasn't "a crazy child" reveals a certain sense of resentment and the belief that what the client's parents did was unjust. In revealing this narrative, the client also reveals how they create the worry by telling themselves they are in imminent danger of being abandoned.
T: Would you like not to be so affected by other people?	This question is an invitation to the part of the client that laments the situation to expand on its perspective.
C: No. Cause if I'm not affected, I might do something that would make people turn away from me.	Here another part, that sees the wish to not be affected as dangerous, jumps in and blocks the conversation.
T: Would you like to make sure other people do not turn their back on you?	This question invites the new part to expand on its perspective.
C: No. I hate that everyone influences me so much.	Here the first part objects to the new direction of the conversation as it sees any concern about other people as a source of suffering.
T: What if there was a way of not being affected and still know that people would turn their back on you?	I seek to find an opening for a Sensing Completion process with the first part by creating a scenario that takes into account the concern of the second part.
C: Why think about that. There isn't.	The client's refusal to engage indicates that there might be a commitment to staying stuck.

Process	Comments
T: Of course, it isn't realistic. But sometimes we can learn important things from considering hypothetical situations – even unrealistic ones.	I invite the client to set aside their concern for realism.
C: What my parents did to me broke me. I don't think fantasising is going to fix it.	Here emerges another part that at first glance seems to be concerned about finding a way of healing.
T: Yes. Manipulating children by withdrawing connection is bad and hurtful for children. Different children are hurt in different ways by such parental neglect. How would you describe the effect it had on you?	I seek to match the client's condemnation of their parents to signal that I'm on the side of this new part. There are plenty of things that could be questioned – but when a part first emerges, it is better to welcome it unconditionally and invite it to speak more.
C: That is what I said. I cannot relax now. I'm porous and other people's mood and thoughts go straight into me. I have no defences. And it is ruining my life.	The client speaks with energy and in emphatic bursts. This indicates a strong desire to be heard and agreed with.
T: Yes. Being so affected by other people obviously has a negative impact on your life…	I agree unconditionally with the part to establish a relationship that will allow for exploration without being seen as challenging.
C: Yes. It ruins my life.	The client's interruption indicates the desire to be heard and understood in an exact way.

Process	Comments
T: ...it ruins your life. 100%. And sometimes, even if it sounds strange, we can believe that if something that ruins our lives were to disappear, that would also have negative effects. Could you think of any negative consequences if you woke up tomorrow and you were no longer broken?	I repeat the client's words exactly to indicate unconditional agreement. And then I ask a question to examine why it is so important for the part to firmly establish the fact that the client's life is ruined. This is the question about hidden benefits presented in Section 5.6.4.
C: Yeah. I wouldn't like that.	Here the part we are talking with clearly state that it does not want to let go of the brokenness.
T: Why not?	I invite the part to unpack its perspective.
C: Because then my parents would have gotten away with it. Then they could go around telling themselves that what they did was ok.	Here the part reveals that it believes it is necessary to remain broken to get accountability and justice. These things are important in themselves – but the intensity of the client's wish and the client's level of sacrifice indicate that these words also refer to aspects of Being.
T: Ah. So, if you were to heal, you believe your parents would be off the hook?	I check my understanding.
C: Yes.	The client confirms.

Process	Comments
T: Ok. What your parents did was wrong. You know it. I know it. Imagine everyone knows it. Clearly. No one will think what they did was remotely ok – even if you manage to overcome the effects their actions had on you. If we keep condemning your parents, then what would it feel like to not be affected by others.	Understanding the deep wish to condemn the parents for their harmful actions makes it possible to create a new scenario in which this concern is taken care of allowing us to engage in exploring what the first part wants to get out of not caring what other people think.
C: They are not getting off the hook?	The client checks whether their concern is considered.
T: Not in the least.	I confirm.
C: That would be such a relief (sighs deeply and relaxes).	This time it works, and the client allows the felt sense they seek.
T: Can you describe this relaxation?	I invite sensory description.
C: I feel my stomach unclench. Like I'm landing. This feels so good.	The client focuses on the felt sense.
T: Yes. So, when you say you want to not care about what others think, you say that you want to feel relaxed?	I suggest that the client's present felt sense is the true goal of the first part, that does not want to care about what other people think and feel.
C: Yes.	The client agrees.
T: And when you say you want to make sure no one turns their back on you. What do you seek?	I ask for the true goal of the second part, that cares very much about what other people think and feel.
C: I think it is the same. I want to relax.	The client recognises that the first and second parts are ultimately seeking the same.

Process	Comments
T: Yes. I believe you are right. And when you say you don't want your parents to get away with it. What do you seek?	I confirm the client's discovery and ask for the goal of the third part.
C: I want justice.	The client provides an abstract word.
T: What does this justice feel like?	I ask for the felt sense underpinning the abstract word.
C: It feels solid. Firm. It's not relaxation. It is more... like being able to hold my head up high.	The client discovers another aspect of Being that is different from the relaxation.
T: What do you think it would be like to feel both relaxed and solid, firm and able to hold your head upright?	I invite the client to imagine the combined felt sense of the two aspects of Being they seek.
C: This feels great. I don't think I'd need anything more than this. (laughs)	Feeling this has a calming effect on the client. It feels like that is all they are after.

At this point, the rest of the session can focus on exploring what new perspectives, ideas and emotions emerge when the client contemplates the situation while aware of and feeling the combination of the two aspects of Being they were seeking. Often this will lead to a more coherent understanding of the situation, which brings the different parts of the client together rather than creates fragmentation.

6.5.2. Session 10: Sweet solidity and solid sweetness

This session starts the exact same way as sessions 3 and 5. In session 3, I focused on the Knot of Conditionality and in session 5 on The Knot of Negative Reification.

However, it is also possible to focus on The Knot of Fragmentation since on the one hand the client espouses the belief that they would be better off choosing a stable partner but on the other hand the client's action of consistently choosing unstable partners expresses the opposite belief.

It is common for the Knot of Fragmentation to play out in this way where one part of the client is in charge of the client's thinking and another part is in charge of the client's behaviour. Thus, when people do not "walk their talk", it is often due to the Knot of Fragmentation. Inversely, when people walk their talk, it is often a sign of internal coherence between personality parts.

In therapy, it is important to speak to each part in a conflict as equals. However, speaking to a part that is in charge of behaviour poses certain challenges, since it may not be well connected to the speech systems of the client. As a therapist you may have to communicate with such parts through sensations, impulses and images rather than through words alone. Thus, when you ask such a part questions, you must be mindful that it may answer through other channels than words.

Process	Comments
Client: The problem I have is that I pick the wrong partners. I always get involved with partners who are unstable, and I end up having to support them and help with all their problems. I'd like to have a stable partner. Someone who can help me out once in a while. But whenever I find someone who is stable, I feel no attraction. I'd like help figuring out how to be attracted to partners that are good for me.	This opening statement indicates the presence of several thoughts, emotions and behaviours. However, there are only two agendas present, namely finding a stable partner and finding unstable partners. Applying the rule of one part, one agenda, this indicates the presence of two conflicting parts.
Therapist: So, part of you wishes to find a stable partner, and another part of you keeps finding unstable partners. Do I understand you right?	I present the situation as a conflict between two inner parts and check with the client. Sometimes, I will give the parts names to make it easier to refer to them later. Here I do not.
C: Yes, but I don't want to find unstable partners. I don't know why I keep doing that. I want to stop doing that.	This answer shows that the client is identified with one part and perceives the other as something alien.

Process	Comments
T: Good. So, when we have parts of us that engage in behaviour we want to change, a good place to start is to understand exactly what motivates that part. If we understand that, it becomes much easier to change behaviour. So, you know what is problematic about finding unstable partners. But that cannot be what motivates you to do it. There must be some possible benefit to doing it. What might that be?	First, I propose that understanding the part of us that is responsible for the "problematic" behaviour is a prerequisite for changing that behaviour. This shifts the energy of the client's wish for change from supporting rejection of the part they want to change to supporting engagement with this part. I then pre-emptively block the idea that the part has negative motivations and invite reflection on possible positive motivations. This is Sensing Completion.
C: I don't know. I just don't know.	The part we wish to talk to is unable to express itself through thoughts.
T: What positive feelings have you experienced when you are together with unstable partners.	I invite the client to pay attention to felt sense to see if the part is communicating on that channel.
C: I don't know. It's like I have a nose for picking them out. I just feel this click and this sweetness and it is so alluring. But now I know it isn't good. I know this is the start of an unhealthy kind of merging with that person. It's sticky. I don't like it.	The part is, indeed, expressing itself by bringing up memories of the felt sense. The click and the sweetness are the voice of the part we seek to communicate with. The other part, however, interrupts.

Process	Comments
T: Well, you don't like what these relationships turn into. But you say the sweetness is alluring. That is an interesting word. So, I'm not proposing that you should seek out unstable partners. But it is important to understand the allure. What is it about this click and sweetness that is alluring?	I acknowledge the concern of the second part and invite the first to continue expressing itself through felt sense.
C: Ah. It's like there is this understanding. This togetherness. It is intoxicating to be honest. I feel simultaneously let in and embraced. When a potential partner opens up and is vulnerable, I feel I can trust them. And I feel valuable because I have something to offer, and it is received.	Here the client gets a rich sense of what the part that picks out unstable partners is ultimately after. It is clear that it is this part speaking, as all the words are positive.
T: So, when you seek the so-called unstable partners, you seek sweetness, togetherness, trust, value, being received and connected through vulnerability. I understand the allure. What if you take a bit of time to just describe the felt sense of this state?	I acknowledge the value in the state the part that picks unstable partners is reaching out for and invite the client to spend more time with this state to allow awareness of the state to affect the client.
C: I feel melting and this sense of a golden halo all around me.	The client stays with the felt sense.
T: Beautiful. How is it to recognise that whereas the part that leads you to engage with unstable partners does create problems, it is actually after something very precious?	I point out that the part the client wanted to get rid of is actually after something precious. This is an invitation to the other part to reconsider its perception of this part.

Process	Comments
C: I feel much closer to this part now. It isn't as crazy as I thought.	The client now feels closer to the part they sought to change.
T: Good. Now, let's turn to the other part of you. What is it you believe you would feel when you have established a stable and loving family.	Now I turn to the more familiar part and repeat the Sensing Completion process.
C: It's the same. It's that sense of love and sweetness. But it is also a sense of stability that I lack with the other unstable partners.	The client realises there is an overlap in the objectives between the two parts – some common ground – and recognises that the familiar part seeks another state as well.
T: How would it be, now, to feel the sweetness and the stability together?	I invite the client to feel the combination of the two states.
C: (sighs) That would be wonderful.	The client does so.
T: So, just take some time to feel that, now.	I invite the client to stay with the felt sense to give it time to affect the client.
C: (closes the eyes and starts crying) This is what I'm longing for.	The client spends time with the state.
T: And now you are feeling it. Now you have it. Just stay with it.	I invite the client to stay longer with the state.
C: (sits for a long time without speaking then sighs) How can I keep this?	The client is able to stay. The client's question indicates that they see the state as a separate entity. It is the question from which the Knot of Conditionality emerges.
T: This is already in you. You are feeling it now, without doing anything to get it. It is just that sometimes, you get a bit too occupied with searching for a partner, and you forget this. Now you feel it.	I propose that the client is not separate from the state to dissuade the client from following the line of inquiry that will lead to the formation of Knot of Conditionality.

Process	Comments
C: Yes. It is quite remarkable.	The client accepts the proposition.
T: As you are feeling this sense of stability and sweetness, how does that affect your ideas and feelings about finding a partner?	I propose an alternative line of inquiry that will support the client in recognising their unity with the state they seek.
C: I feel much calmer. I can see that value openness and stability. That's it really. It's not about stability or not stability. I value open connection and actually, don't really understand what all the fuss was about. Open connection and receptivity is inherently stable. I have a hard time understanding what the conflict was about.	The client's perspective has changed to one where the conflict does not exist, since the conflict can only exist as long as the client sees the two states as separate. If they are one, it is not possible to be split between seeking one or the other.
T: Good. The conflict was about how to find what you seek by finding the right kind of partner. Now that you can feel the states you seek in yourself, that conflict is irrelevant.	I affirm the client's new perspective.
C: This is trippy.	It is common for clients to not fully understand what happens in these sessions. This is not a problem.

6.6. Untying the Knot of Fragmentation through contemplations

In Section 6.4, I have outlined how the Knot of Fragmentation can be untied in one-to-one sessions with clients.

In this section, I will describe a series of contemplation exercises specifically designed to recognise and untie the Knot of Fragmentation. These exercises are well suited to group work. The instructions are sufficiently simple to be given to a group, and the exercises can, for example, be performed in pairs or as individual writing exercises.

The first four contemplation exercises described in this section are exercises aimed at excavating personality parts that are outside the client's awareness. The exercises are designed to work with different levels of repression.

- The exercises in Sections 6.6.1 and 6.6.2 aim to identify parts that seek to repress a particular thought, emotion, agenda or trait.
- The exercises in Section 6.6.3 aim to help the client acknowledge the existence of a repressed thought, emotion, agenda or trait.
- The exercises in Section 6.6.4 aim to help the client acknowledge their acts of repression when these are outside the clients' awareness and imply the existence of the repressed thought, emotion, agenda or trait.

The fifth contemplation exercise, presented in Section 6.6.5, is a version of the Sensing Unity tool from Section 6.4.5 in the subsection "Sensing Abundance and the 20th corrective principle".

When working with groups, I often begin by inviting students to do the contemplation exercise in pairs or individually. Afterwards, I work one-to-one with a few students in plenum using the techniques presented in Section 6.4. This approach has the advantage that although I only work with a few students directly, the other students, having completed the contemplation exercise, can partake in the one-to-one processing vicariously.

6.6.1. What is your relationship to X?

A good way students can map out their inner parts is by exploring the multiple ways in which they may relate to a particular inner phenomenon, such as a certain emotion, trait, perspective, value, etc.

To do so, you can ask students the following question:

> "What is your relationship to X?"

This question is particularly useful when students are aware that they experience the phenomenon in question, but they may not be aware that different parts of them have different and sometimes conflicting relationships with this phenomenon.

Phenomena to explore using this question may include:

- Positive emotions (e.g. ease, excitement, peace, compassion, joy)
- Negative emotions (e.g. boredom, anger, hate, sadness, desire)
- Positive traits (e.g. grounding, courage, calmness, kindness, carefreeness)

- Negative traits (e.g. stubbornness, recklessness, aloofness, fragility, superficiality)

The examples above are sourced from the lists of positive and negative reifications of Being, since exploring students' relationships to these will help clarify the internal conflicts that prevent students from paying sustained attention to the related aspects of Being.

If, for example, students have a complex and conflicted relationship with "joy", which is a positive reification of the Yellow essence, this relationship will be activated whenever Being appears to the student in the form of joy and will immediately pull the student's awareness away from the simple and direct experience of Being in the form of joy.

Once the conflicting relationships are mapped out, we can use the process of Sensing Unity to create more coherence and, thus, make it easier for the student to let their attention rest with the joyful aspect of Being.

How to introduce the exercise

When you introduce this type of contemplation, it is good to explicitly invite students to welcome contradictory answers to the question and to consider their relationship to different aspects of the phenomenon as well as their relationship to the phenomenon in different contexts.

Contradictory answers

When you invite students to explore their relationship to a particular phenomenon, it is good to explicitly state that they might find multiple and even contradictory answers to the question. This helps students not to become stuck with the first answer they find or to waste time speculating on which answer represents their "true" relationship to the phenomenon in question.

Students contain multiple personality parts and each of these may have a different relationship to the phenomenon in question. Therefore, it is fully possible for a student to both consider "sadness" as a valuable part of life which should be encouraged *and* see it as worthless or a sign of weakness. Similarly, it is fully possible to both regard "strength" as crucial for living a fulfilling life *and* as a destructive force that prevents one from living a fulfilling life. It is fully possible to feel that peace is something you have *and* something you lack.

Different aspects of the phenomenon

Since most phenomena are complex it is good to explicitly invite students to consider different aspects of the phenomenon. For example, if you are working with students' relationship to sadness, you can ask them to consider their relationship to their own sadness and other people's sadness, to the feeling of sadness and the expression of sadness (e.g. crying), etc. This is important since students may have no parts that object to other people's sadness, but they do have a part that sees their own sadness as something dangerous that needs to be controlled or repressed. Similarly, students may have no parts which object to *feeling* sadness, but they may have a part that resists the *expression* of it.

Different contexts

Finally, since different personality parts are created to deal with different situations, students may experience that different personality parts are active in different contexts. For example, students may be very different when they are at work, with their family or with their friends.

Therefore, their relationship to a particular phenomenon may differ depending on the context they find themselves in.

Thus, when asking students to explore their relationship to a particular phenomenon, it is good to explicitly ask them to consider different contexts.

A student may find that they see the ability to express "sadness" as something that connects people in the context of family, but as "unprofessional" in a work context.

Some useful categories of context you can suggest that students consider are:

- Work vs. family vs. friends
- Alone vs. with others
- Familiar situations vs. new situations
- In the city vs. in nature
- Physical vs. digital spaces
- High pressure vs. relaxed settings
- Public vs. private settings
- Planned vs. unplanned settings

Not all of these will be equally relevant for the exploration of all phenomena. As a rule of thumb, it is good to limit oneself to two or three examples of different contexts as a way of communicating the idea of exploring one's relationship to a particular phenomenon in different contexts.

6.6.2. What are your (contradictory) ideas about X?

Another good way students can map out their inner parts is by exploring ideas about a particular inner phenomenon.

To invite students to do so, you can ask them the following question:

"What are your ideas about X?"

Like the previous question, this question is particularly useful when clients are aware that they experience the phenomenon in question, but they may not be aware of the extent to which different parts of them have different and sometimes conflicting ideas about this phenomenon.

How to introduce the exercise

Asking students to list out their ideas about a particular phenomenon has a dual purpose.

First, it helps students notice parts of themselves they would not normally notice, by noticing the ideas that guide these parts.

Second, by seeing their ideas about a particular phenomenon as ideas rather than facts, helps students demerge from the personality parts that hold these ideas. This is because ideas are like glasses: When you look at them, you are not looking through them. When you see an idea, this idea no longer shapes your vision.

It is good to bear this dual purpose in mind, when giving the instructions for this type of contemplation.

Listing out all ideas one has been exposed to

A good way of introducing this contemplation exercise is to ask students to list out all the ideas about the phenomenon they have been exposed to rather than asking for which ideas they believe in. The reason for this is that ideas held by repressed parts will not be immediately recognisable as ideas the student believes in.

A student may, for example, hold the espoused belief that it is good to be passionate about one's work. At the same time, a part of the student may hold the belief that passion is exhausting. Because this belief does not match the student's espoused belief, they may repress this part or see it as an annoying doubt that isn't really a part of them. When we ask this student: What ideas do you have about passion?, the student may only reveal the first belief and not the second. However, if we explicitly instruct the student to answer the question by making a list of all the ideas they have heard about the passion, the student is more likely to include both ideas.

I will often ask students to list out all the ideas they have been exposed to because even if they do not explicitly subscribe to an idea they have been exposed to, it may still have affected them.

Do not evaluate ideas on the list

Another part of the instruction for this contemplation exercise is to refrain from evaluating the ideas. Whether the ideas are true or false is irrelevant for the purpose of mapping out personality parts since a personality part can have an influence, whether it is guided by a true or a false idea.

Furthermore, evaluating which ideas are true and false can run counter to the purpose of demerging from personality parts that are guided by these ideas, since affirming the truth of one idea over another is likely to strengthen the student's identification with the personality part that holds the ideas that are judged as true. And while some ideas may be blatantly false, very few (if any) can be considered the full truth.

Offer examples that illustrate the breadth of ideas

Finally, to get students started on this contemplation exercise, it can be beneficial to offer examples of different types of ideas. This will prevent students from getting stuck in, for example, only listing negative ideas about a phenomenon or only listing ideas about cause of the phenomenon.

Ideas students hold about a particular phenomenon will generally fall into four categories each of which relate to one of the four first knots. In the following, I will describe each type of idea in turn and comment on how each one can support the dual purpose of discovering hidden personality parts and demerging from personality parts.

Four types of idea relating to the four first knots

When students are asked to list out all the ideas they have about a particular phenomenon, the list will contain four types of idea relating to the first four knots.

It can be useful to notice which type of idea students produce as this will provide important information about which knots are most active in the students and, consequently, which processes will be most likely to enable the students to discover Being.

Furthermore, in some situations, it can be useful to modify the contemplation exercise to focus on a particular type of idea.

Knot of Positive Reification: Positive ideas about the phenomenon

Positive ideas about an inner phenomenon relate to the Knot of Positive Reification. Students may, for example, hold ideas, such as:

- Confidence is attractive
- Courage is a virtue
- Truth is the most important thing in life
- Kindness is stronger than hate
- Joy is what makes life worth living
- Love uplifts people

To invite students to focus on these types of idea, you can ask:

> "What positive ideas do you have about X?"

Positive ideas about an inner phenomenon can be particularly interesting when exploring phenomena students tend to perceive as negative.

Positive ideas about phenomena students generally perceive as negative will often reveal personality parts the student may not normally be aware of. A student may, for example, notice that while they generally dislike "stubbornness" and, therefore, seek to be flexible in most situations, they, nevertheless, hold the positive idea that stubborn people progress society and that some stubbornness is necessary to rectify systemic societal injustices. When this student notices that they have a positive idea about stubbornness, they may be surprised, and may discover a part of themselves they would not normally notice.

Discovering positive ideas about phenomena students generally see as negative has the added advantage that it hints at the identity of negative and positive phenomena. In the above example, the positive idea about stubbornness hints at how stubbornness and perseverance may merely be two names for the same thing when interpreted in a negative and a positive light. Perceiving the unity between pairs of positive and negative phenomena can greatly support the process of demerging from personality parts that are confined to a particular value-judgement of the phenomenon in question.

Knot of Conditionality: Ideas about how to create and acquire the phenomenon

Some of the ideas students hold about a particular phenomenon are ideas about how to create or acquire this phenomenon. These ideas relate to the Knot of Conditionality. Students may, for example, hold ideas, such as:

- Confidence comes from competence
- To be courageous, you must frequently take risks
- To feel peace, one must have resolved all conflicts
- To be compassionate, you must think more about others than about yourself
- Joy comes from doing things you love doing
- Appreciation must be earned

To invite students to focus on these types of idea, you can ask:

> "What ideas do you have about how to create or acquire X?"

Students will often be surprised at discovering what they do to create or acquire a particular phenomenon. Such surprise indicates that the student has discovered a personality part they were not aware of.

Furthermore, seeing clearly how one seeks to create or acquire a particular phenomenon, makes it possible to question this strategy and discover the absurdity and counterproductivity inherent in these strategies. This can greatly support the process of demerging from the personality parts that follow the strategy in question.

I have described how to work with this type of ideas in more detail in Section 3.6.1 What are your ideas about how to create or acquire X?

Knot of Negative Reification: Negative ideas about the phenomenon

Some of the ideas students hold about a particular phenomenon are negative ideas. These ideas relate to the Knot of Negative Reification. Students may, for example, hold ideas, such as:

1. Confident people are obnoxious, smug and full of themselves
2. Passion is exhausting
3. Peace is boring
4. Compassion is condescending
5. Joy is superficial
6. If you feel trust, you will be taken advantage of

To invite students to focus on these types of idea, you can ask:

> "What negative ideas do you have about X?"

Just like positive ideas about phenomena students tend to perceive as negative often reveal personality parts the student may not always be aware of, negative ideas about phenomena the student generally considers positive can do the same.

Furthermore, making the beliefs explicit enables the student to question them. In fact, many times students will perceive the absurdity of many of these ideas immediately after formulating them. Challenging these ideas can greatly support the process of demerging from personality parts that hold them.

I described how to work with these types of idea in more detail in Sections 4.6.1 What are your negative ideas about X? and 4.6.2 How can your negative ideas about X be explained by the negative consequences of the ways you try to acquire or produce X?.

Knot of Alienation: Ideas that ascribe the phenomenon a will or intention of its own

Finally, some of the ideas students hold about a particular phenomenon are ideas about the inevitability or impossibility of experiencing the phenomenon. These ideas relate to the Knot of Alienation. As mentioned in the chapter on the Knot of Alienation, such ideas propose that the absence of positive phenomena or the presence of negative ones as a fact of life, are a consequence of the individual's immutable traits or of external circumstances. Thus, students may, for example, hold ideas such as:

- I'm not a confident person
- People from other regions are passionate, people from my region are not
- Being alive is not peaceful
- Kindness is a fiction, everyone is fundamentally looking out for themselves
- You cannot be truly happy when others are suffering
- Humans are animals and, therefore, fundamentally aggressive and territorial

To invite students to focus on these types of idea, you can ask one of the following questions.

If you work with a phenomenon students perceive as negative, you can ask:

> "What ideas do you have about why X is inevitable?"

If you work with a phenomenon students perceive as positive, you can ask:

> "What ideas do you have about why X is unattainable for you?"

Once again, these questions are particularly interesting when they contradict students' espoused beliefs because this makes them more likely to help the students discover parts of themselves they are not normally aware of.

For example, if a student sees aggression as something negative and holds the espoused belief that aggression is optional, it can be interesting to excavate the ideas this student holds about why aggression is inevitable. Asking directly about such ideas is an invitation for any part of the student that holds this view to speak and be acknowledged.

Similarly, if a student sees kindness as something positive and holds the espoused belief that kindness is a choice, it can be interesting to excavate the ideas this student holds about why kindness is ultimately an impossibility. Asking directly about such ideas is an invitation for any part of the student that feels hopeless, or despairing in relation to the possibility of humans being kind to each other, to speak and be met.

Finally, seeing clearly the ideas students hold about the inevitability or impossibility of experiencing a particular phenomenon makes it possible to challenge these ideas. Doing so supports the process of demerging from the personality parts that hold these beliefs.

I have described extensively how to challenge such beliefs in Section 5.6.2 Step 2: Suggest Agency.

Challenging ideas

While the different types of ideas mentioned above can be challenged in different ways, they can all be challenged by revealing the way in which subscribing to the idea will distract one from noticing Being. Thus, one question that can be used to challenge any type of idea is:

> "How do these ideas distract you from noticing Being?"

When students contemplate this, they will discover that any idea about an inner phenomenon will engage their awareness in processes that make it more difficult for them to notice Being.

- Ideas related to the Knot of Positive Reification distract one from noticing Being by making one pay attention to ideas about Being rather than Being itself.

- Ideas related to the Knot of Conditionality distract one from noticing Being by focusing one's awareness on fulfilling the conditions one believes one needs to fulfil.
- Ideas related to the Knot of Negative Reification make one avoid Being by making it appears as something negative.
- Ideas related to the Knot of Alienation make one cease to seek Being and accept the absence of Being as natural and inevitable.

Noticing that an idea one holds about an inner phenomenon makes it difficult to notice Being greatly helps demerging from the personality parts that are enthusiastic about this idea, since it reveals the way in which this idea is unhelpful.

To include this reflection in the contemplation exercise, you can instruct students to first make a list of ideas about a particular phenomenon and then look at the ideas on the list one at a time and reflect on how this idea distracts them from noticing Being.

6.6.3. When do you feel X? When are you X? How are you like X?

Another way of uncovering hidden personality parts is to ask students when they feel states they believe they do not feel, when they exhibit traits they believe they do not have, and when they are like people they believe they are very unlike. Below, I will first describe the two first contemplations together and the third in a separate section.

When do you feel X? When are you X?

A powerful contemplation exercise is to ask students when they experience states or exhibit traits which they would typically believe they do not contain[64].

Examples of such questions could be:

- When do you feel vulnerable?
- When do you feel lonely?
- When do you feel lost?

---

[64] It is useful to be aware that whereas most students will identify with states and traits they perceive as positive and believe they do not contain states and traits they see as negative, some students will do the opposite, i.e. identify with the states and traits they see as negative and believe they do not contain those they see as positive. For such students it will be more interesting to contemplate when they feel strong, when they are independent, etc., since answering such questions is more likely to reveal something to these students that they are not aware of.

- When are you aggressive?
- When are you selfish?
- When are you needy?

In answering such questions, students can discover personality parts that are normally repressed because they contain states or traits that do not fit with the students' beliefs about what kind of person they are – i.e. their self-image.

This allows students to work with the conflicts between parts that are included in their self-image and parts that are not. This can be done in several ways by drawing on contemplation exercises relating to the other Knots.

Students can draw on contemplations related to the Knot of Conditionality to explore what the repressed personality parts ultimately are reaching out for.

Students can also draw on contemplations related to the Knot of Negative Reification to explore what the negative states embodied by the repressed personality parts feel like in themselves – separate from any judgements against them.

The 10 Strands of Mind model can help predict what answers students will find to such further explorations.

For example, if students explore situations where they are rigid or stubborn (negative reifications related to the White strand), they are likely to find personality parts that are reaching out for support, grounding, confidence or solidness (positive reifications related to the White strand). Similarly, if students explore situations where they are dominating, competitive or excessively risk-taking (conditions related to the Red strand), they are likely to find personality parts that are reaching out for strength, courage, passion and vitality (positive reifications of Being related to the Red strand).

When working with states and traits related to a specific strand, and the purpose is to bring awareness to the related aspect of Being, it can be useful to combine the above question with the question of what the state or trait feels like in the body.

- When do you feel vulnerable? And what does that feel like in the body?
- When are you aggressive? And what does that feel like in the body?

This combination of questions invites students to identify when they experience negative entry points and explore the underlying felt sense without judgement. I have described this contemplation exercise in Section 4.6.4.

The above examples all include asking about specific inner states and traits students may not believe they contain. Doing so has the advantage that it makes it possible to work with one particular strand of mind.

How are you like X?

However, if the goal is to uncover multiple personality parts that do not match the students' self-images, we can ask them to contemplate how they are like a particular person that students are likely to believe they are very different from.

It is, for example, very common that students believe they are very different from their parents. In such cases, clients will typically experience their parents as embodying numerous negative traits, that the students believe they have either never had or that they have purged themselves of.

However, many of our personality parts are merely copies of our parents' personality parts, and when we believe we have purged ourselves of the traits we inherited from our parents, we will often merely have repressed them.

Thus, two useful contemplation exercises are:

- How are you like your mother?
- How are you like your father?

The advantage of these exercises is that they can reveal many repressed personality parts. The disadvantage is that they are likely to bring up very different parts for different students, which may make students focus on each of their individual processes, rather than working together on a particular theme as a group.

Notes on how to introduce these exercises

The key to the above type of contemplation questions is that they contain the presupposition that students contain states or traits they thought they did not contain.

When introducing this kind of contemplation exercise, it is good to reinforce this presupposition by emphasising that the question is not *whether* the students feel the state or exhibit the trait but *when* they do it.

For example, the question "When do you feel lost?" can be introduced in the following way:

> "Explore when you feel lost. Don't waste time on contemplating whether you feel lost and don't waste time trying to convince yourself that you don't feel lost or consider what you can do to avoid feeling lost. Just focus on finding situations where you do, in fact, feel lost. This is where you will discover something important and new."

6.6.4. How do you block or avoid X (a trait you see as negative)?

Another type of contemplation, which can help students discover conflicting personality parts, is asking them how they block particular states or traits in themselves, which students would typically believe they do not block.

This type of contemplation question can be used for two distinct purposes.

The first purpose of asking how students block or avoid certain states or traits is to reveal personality parts which seek to repress or limit states or traits the students believe they do not repress. This can include positive states, such as joy, strength, peace, compassion and love. It can also include negative states that students believe it is good to be comfortable with, such as being out of your comfort zone, vulnerability, sadness, or not knowing.

For example, a student may believe that they do not repress their sadness because they see themselves as a person who is comfortable with sadness. In this case, contemplating how they block or avoid sadness can reveal personality parts that are normally repressed because they do not match the student's self-image.

The second purpose of this type of contemplation exercise is to offer a gentle way of approaching states or traits that might be very disturbing for students to acknowledge directly. Depending on the students one is working with, such states could include neediness, meaninglessness, inadequacy, hostility, over-entitlement or under-entitlement. If students are asked directly to contemplate when they experience states or traits that are very disturbing to them, they may either not be able to answer, or answering the question may lead students to experience an unhelpful level of distress, which shuts down their capacity for contemplation.

For example, a student may believe they do not feel any hostility because they see themselves as a kind-hearted person, and should they ever discover any hostility in themselves, they may be so distressed that they cannot continue the contemplation exercise. In this case, contemplating how they block hostility can be a gentle way of opening the door to explorations of personality parts that do contain feelings of hostility. Asking students to explore how they block hostility in themselves does not directly suggest that they contain hostility. However, if they find that they do take steps to block hostility in themselves, that will indicate that there is, indeed, hostility since one would not put in an effort to block something that isn't there. Thus, exploring how one blocks an inner state or trait gives one time to get used to the idea that one might contain this state or trait.

When working with a negative state or trait it will depend on the group of students whether it makes sense to start by asking how they block the state or it makes more sense to save time and ask directly when the students experience this state or trait. What seems highly disturbing to one group of students may not be particularly disturbing to another.

Notes on how to introduce the exercise

When using this contemplation exercise to work with a positive state or trait (or states/traits students believe they are comfortable with), it is useful to frame the exercise in a way that shows the students that it is likely that they do, indeed, block the state, even if they think they do not.

If you are working with a positive state, such as "joy", you can say:

> "Joy is a great feeling. Yet, you may not experience joy as often as you would like. The fact that joy isn't always available may indicate that something in you blocks it. Understanding how you block joy can be a first step to understanding why and to eventually unblock it. Explore how you block joy."

If you are working with a negative state, which students believe they are comfortable with (and may not see as negative), such as "sadness", you can say:

> "Even if you are comfortable with feeling a certain level of sadness, you may still seek to limit it or even block it if it reaches a certain intensity or depth, or if you feel it in certain contexts where you feel it is inappropriate. You may also be comfortable with feeling sadness but not with expressing it – or the other way round. So, even if you are generally comfortable with sadness and often allow it, you may still also be blocking it. Explore how you block sadness."

When using this type of contemplation exercises to work with states or traits that might be disturbing to the students, it is good to emphasise the common nature of these states and traits and pre-emptively encourage students not to be hard on themselves should they discover something about themselves they do not like.

If you, for example, are working with inadequacy, you may introduce the exercise in the following way:

> "Inadequacy is a very common part of human experience. It is an experience that is shared by the vast majority of humanity. However, it is probably nobody's favourite experience, so most people will seek to repress it or avoid acknowledging it when they feel it. However, if you avoid or repress or change a part of you that is already feeling inadequate, this is likely to intensify the feeling. Thus, it is better to embrace and acknowledge the parts of us that feel inadequate even if it is uncomfortable to do so. A good way to start this is to notice the ways in which we seek to block or avoid feelings of inadequacy. Explore how you block or avoid inadequacy in yourself."

In this introduction, I use language that downplays the discomfort and give a compelling reason to acknowledge, rather than reject, the state.

6.6.5. What if you had both simultaneously?

The four previous contemplation exercises in this chapter aim at mapping out students' personality parts and, in particular, discovering personality parts they may not normally be aware of.

The fifth contemplation exercise aims at directly challenging the ideas students have about the mutual exclusivity of positive phenomena. Thus, this exercise is a version of the Sensing Unity tool described in Section 6.4.5 in the sub-section on Sensing Abundance and the 20th corrective principle.

As mentioned several times in this chapter, the root of fragmentation is the misconception that to attain one positive phenomenon it is necessary to renounce another. This leads to the formation of personality parts that seek to acquire particular positive states by, among other things, repressing and demonising each other.

Below is a list of pairs of positive phenomena which are commonly perceived as mutually exclusive.

- Independence & Connection
- Discipline & Freedom
- Stability & Adaptability
- Passion & Peace
- Vulnerability & Strength
- Compassion & Joy
- Seriousness & Playfulness
- Autonomy & Intimacy
- Creativity & Logic
- Emotions & Intelligence
- Relaxation & Productivity
- Ambition & Contentment
- Generosity & Prudence
- Assertiveness & Empathy
- Introspection & Socialisation

Whether the pairs of phenomena appear mutually exclusive, or not, to a particular individual depends on the ideas this individual holds around each of the phenomena in the pair[65].

However, insofar as all the above phenomena are positive reifications of Being, none of them can be in conflict with any other.

To explore this, you can invite students to describe the felt sense related to each phenomenon in a pair and then contemplate what it would be like to feel the combined felt sense. In essence, you will invite students to go through the Sensing Abundance process for each phenomenon in a pair and then imagine the "combined abundance", so to speak. The experience can be both baffling and exhilarating – often at the same time.

---

[65] Upon reading the list, you may notice that some pairs appear as good examples of mutually exclusive phenomena, while other pairs do not seem to be mutually exclusive at all. This is because you, the reader, have a particular set of ideas related to each phenomenon and these ideas will make some phenomena appear mutually exclusive but not others. You may even be surprised to hear which pairs other people see as the best examples of mutually exclusive phenomena because other people will contain a different set of ideas about these phenomena.

Once the students feel the combined felt sense, they may discover that the reason they perceived the two phenomena as mutually exclusive was that they had certain beliefs about what they must do to create these phenomena and that these beliefs may be false. Once such beliefs are recognised and brought into question students can start to recognise how the two phenomena are mutually supportive rather than mutually exclusive.

It is, of course, possible to skip the part of the contemplation exercise related to felt sense and go directly to reflecting upon how two phenomena one perceives as mutually exclusive may, in fact, be mutually supportive. However, the advantage of starting from the felt sense is that the combined felt sense provides a somatic experience through which the students' realisations can be grounded and embodied. I will return to this point in Chapter 7, Tying the Knot of Being.

A student may, for example, experience "independence" and "connection" as opposites. When they explore the felt sense underpinning each of these phenomena, they may find that the essence of "independence" is a felt sense of uprightness and easeful balance, and the essence of "connection" is a felt sense of a soft and melted substance in the chest. If the student is used to thinking about independence and connection as two mutually exclusive phenomena, imagining the combined felt sense can be a profound experience that enables the student to contemplate what it means to be simultaneously independent and connected.

Experiencing the combined felt sense provides the student with a means of revising their understanding of what it means to be independent and connected in two ways.

First, the student may realise that they hold beliefs about independence and connection, which lead them to perceive these as mutually exclusive, and that these beliefs may be false. The student may, for example, realise that they believe that to be independent they must cut off connection to other people and that this may not be true. The student may realise that they see connection and dependency as synonymous and that this may also not be true.

Second, the student may realise that independence and connection are, in fact, mutually supportive rather than mutually exclusive. The student may, for example, realise that it is precisely when they feel independence that they can enter into connection in an authentic manner without fear, neediness and dependency getting in the way. Similarly, the student may realise that it is precisely connection that allows them to develop independence, just like children who have a secure connection to their parents are more likely to develop into independent human beings.

Thus, sensing the combined feeling of "independence" and "connection" enables the student to realise how these may be mutually supportive and only appear mutually exclusive due to false ideas about the conditions one must fulfil to create these phenomena. Furthermore, the combined felt sense provides a somatic experience through which these realisations can be embodied.

Notes on how to introduce the exercise

When introducing this exercise, it is important to instruct students to describe the felt sense of each phenomenon using positive or neutral sensory words. Doing so will separate the felt sense from the ideas about the phenomena that create the illusion of the two phenomena being mutually exclusive.

It is also important to mention that it is possible to imagine combinations of felt sense that would not exist in any physical object. For example, while no physical object can be heavy and light at the same time, it is fully possible to imagine an inner felt sense that is simultaneously heavy and light. Similarly, no physical object can be both vibrating and still at the same time, yet it is common to experience an inner sense that can best be described as vibration and stillness combined.

When using this contemplation exercise in groups, you can either work with conflicts that have emerged for many students in the group or with conflicts that are common in people, such as the ones in the above list.

Finally, it is worth noting that in this section I have used positive words for the phenomena that conflicting personality parts may be reaching out for. However, if a student is primarily identified with one of the conflicting personality parts, they are likely to give negative names to the phenomenon the opposing personality part is reaching out for. For example, if a student contains two parts that are reaching out for independency and connection respectively and the student is identified with the part that reaches out for independency, they may see the inner conflict as a conflict between a part that seeks independency and a needy part. Inversely, if the student is identified with the part that reaches out for connection, they may see the inner conflict as a conflict between a part that seeks connection and one that seeks isolation. I wrote in detail about how being identified with one personality part can lead to negative perceptions of positive phenomena in Chapter 4, Knot 3: The Knot of Negative Reification.

I find that this contemplation exercise is a good way of operationalising teachings about non-duality as it reveals in an experiential way that is reasonably easy to understand how duality only exists in the realm of our ideas about phenomena and not in the essence of phenomena.

6.7. Summary

In this chapter, we have explored the Knot of Fragmentation. This knot occurs when different personality parts pursue different aspects of Being through mutually exclusive strategies and the ensuing conflict draws the client's awareness away from Being, thus, undermining the agenda of all parts involved.

The Knot of Fragmentation produces and is sustained by five misconceptions: That we have a single self, that we contain inner enemies and obstacles, that one should free oneself from these, that we can free ourselves from inner enemies and obstacles by rejecting them, and that some positive states cannot coexist.

The way to untie the Knot of Fragmentation is through the process of Sensing Unity, where we map out the system of conflicting parts and let these witness each other's processes.

We looked at how this process can be facilitated in one-to-one sessions and through five types of contemplation exercise.

In the final chapter, we will look at how to tie the Knot of Being. The five processes I have described so far untie the knots that prevent students from noticing Being. Untying these knots is a good way of pointing students' awareness to Being so they may have direct and personal experiences of Being. The final chapter focuses on how to ensure that such experiences of Being are not forgotten, when students engage in everyday life.

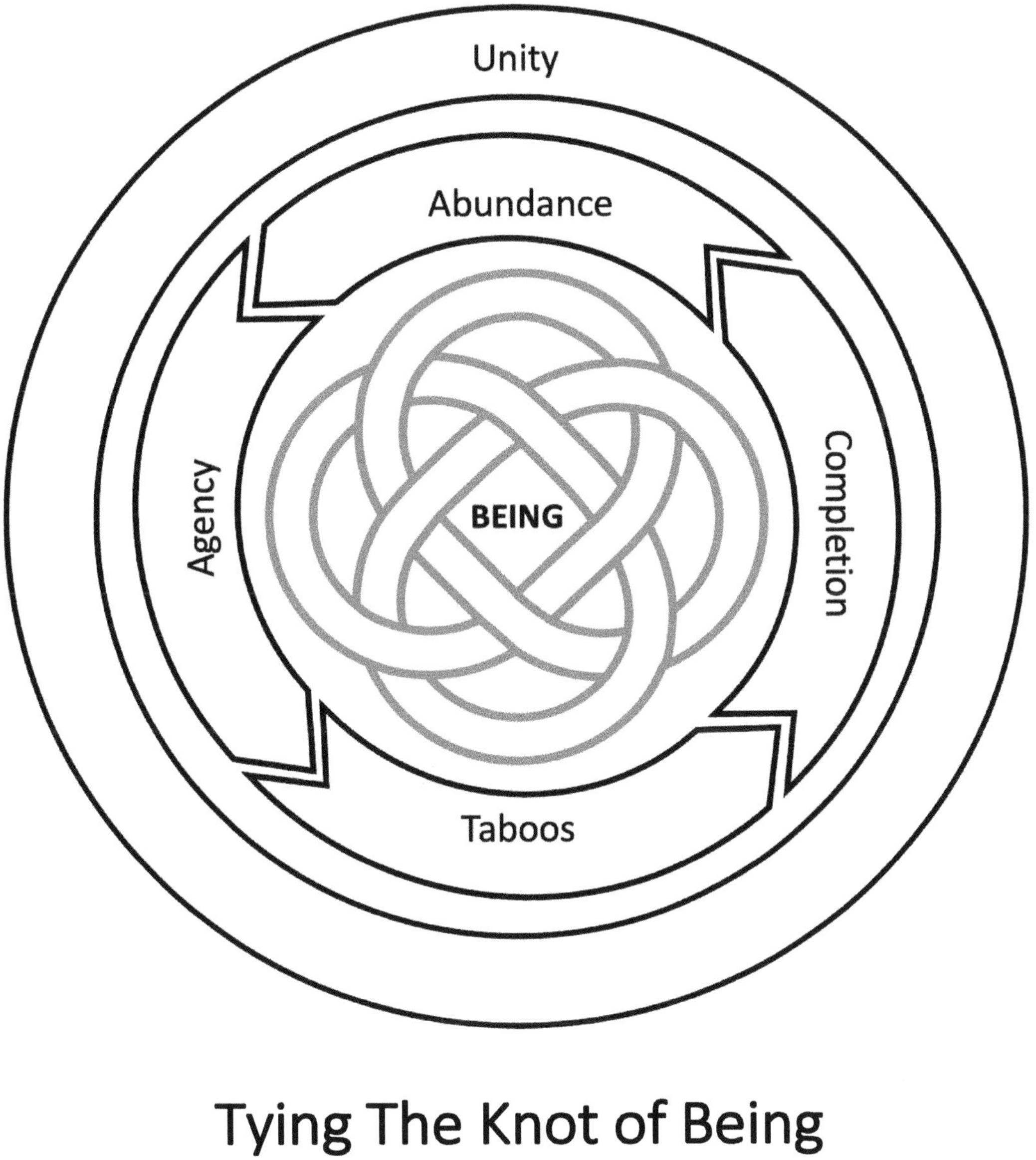

Tying The Knot of Being

7. Tying the Knot of Being

Many people have experienced leaving a therapy session, finishing a meditation, or completing some other practice feeling a deep sense of clarity and well-being, only to find that these feelings quickly fade and do not translate into substantial or lasting changes in their daily lives.

After a therapy session, you may, for example, have a clear understanding of what you need to change about the way you interact with your partner, yet when you come home old patterns take over. After a meditation, you may feel joyful and at ease, yet the moment you engage with other people, the feeling of ease and joy is all but gone.

Such experiences reveal that inner awakening and moments of deep insight alone are not enough for lasting personal and spiritual growth. Something else is needed to bring these insights into everyday life. Many spiritual and philosophical traditions address this issue by distinguishing between realisation and actualisation.

Realisation refers to gaining experiential insight into the true nature of reality, the self, or the divine. This often involves transcending ordinary perceptions and connecting non-ordinary states of consciousness. In the language of this book, realisation is the direct experience of Being that can occur when untying the 5 knots.

Actualisation, on the other hand, refers to the process of integrating realisations into everyday life. Actualisation involves embodying the wisdom gained through realisation, transforming how one lives life, interacts with others, and navigates the world. In the language of this book, one could say that actualisation is about Tying the Knot of Being.

Together, realisation and actualisation form a holistic approach to personal and spiritual growth, ensuring that profound inner experiences translate into meaningful outer changes.

So far, this book has been focused on how to facilitate realisation. This chapter shifts the focus to actualisation. First, I outline how various traditions have approached realisation and actualisation. Next, I present four key challenges faced by traditional approaches to actualisation. Finally, I explore how research on memory reconsolidation, cognitive metaphors and embodied cognition can be used to integrate the actualisation process into a Being-Centre Therapy session in a way that addresses these challenges and effectively supports actualisation.

7.1. Realisation Practices

Before looking at actualisation practices, it is instructive to examine how various traditions have approached realisation and how these approaches compare to those presented in this book.

Although realisation practices vary widely across different spiritual and philosophical traditions, they typically fall into one of three main categories: meditation, contemplation, and self-inquiry.

In the following sections, I will briefly describe each of these categories, provide examples from different traditions, and comment on how each type of practice relates to Being-Centred Therapy.

7.1.1. Meditation

Meditation practices generally focus on cultivating a state of inner stillness and awareness by concentrating the mind on a single object or simply observing the present moment without judgement[66]. The goal is to quieten the mind, reduce distractions and develop the capacity for focusing attention, so the practitioner may directly experience their true nature or the divine.

In Zen Buddhism, for instance, zazen (seated meditation) is practised by sitting in silence and observing the breath, or the nature of thoughts as they arise and pass away.

In Hinduism, mantra meditation involves repeating a sacred sound or phrase, like "Om", to anchor the mind and transcend ordinary consciousness.

In Sufism, the practice Dhikr (meaning remembrance of God) involves the repetitive recitation of phrases like "La ilaha illallah" (There is no god but God) or of the 99 names of God, which each reflect different attributes of the God, such as "Ar-Rahman" (The Most Merciful) and "Al-Haqq" (The Truth). Such recitation is

---

[66] The Hindu tradition distinguishes between Samatha meditation, also known as soothing meditation, and Vipassana meditation, also known as insight meditation. Samatha is the topic of this section on meditation, and Vipassana is the topic of the following section on contemplation.

often accompanied by rhythmic breathing or movement, and aims to focus the mind on the divine presence and cultivate a profound sense of spiritual connection.

All three practices aim to bring the practitioner into a state of consciousness free from the constant chatter of the mind, leading to a deeper realisation of true nature, self and unity with the divine.

Nyoshül Khenpo Rinpoche beautifully describes this form of meditation in his famous prayer:

> Rest in natural great peace
> This exhausted mind
> Beaten helpless by karma and neurotic thought
> Like the relentless fury of pounding waves
> In the infinite ocean of saṃsāra.
> Rest in natural great peace

The five processes for untying the 5 knots generally end with meditation practice, in that whenever a client becomes aware of an aspect of Being, the therapist will cease asking exploratory questions and instead support the client in paying sustained attention to the experience of Being.

The main tools for doing so are silence and, if the client starts turning their awareness away from the experience of Being, asking them to describe the experience using neutral, sensory language. I described this technique in Section 2.6.3, Step 3: Sustain awareness of Being.

As mentioned several times throughout the book, once the client becomes aware of Being, the therapist should aim to gently prolong this experience. The longer the client is aware of Being, the longer this experience will have to work on the client. This is a form of meditation practice.

7.1.2. Contemplation

Contemplation involves focused reflection on a particular question, concept, truth, or spiritual text, with the goal of deepening understanding and gaining intuitive insight beyond intellectual analysis. Contemplation practices are more analytical than meditation practices, encouraging the practitioner to think deeply and reflectively about the subject at hand.

In Christian mysticism, for example, Lectio Divina is a practice where a passage from the Bible is read slowly and meditatively, allowing its meaning to unfold and resonate deeply within the practitioner.

In Hinduism, the practice of Jnana Yoga involves contemplating philosophical texts such as the Upanishads, guiding the practitioner towards the realisation of the ultimate reality, Brahman.

In Buddhism, the contemplation of impermanence (Anicca) focuses on reflecting deeply on the transient nature of all things, leading to insights into the nature of suffering and the path to liberation.

In Taoism, contemplation of nature – such as observing the flow of water in a stream – helps the practitioner understand the Tao, the underlying principle of the universe, through the natural world.

In Stoicism, the contemplation of death (Memento Mori) encourages reflection on the inevitability of death, helping the practitioner cultivate detachment and focus on living a virtuous life.

These examples illustrate how contemplation engages the mind actively yet aims to lead the practitioner to a realisation that transcends mere intellectual understanding.

The five processes for untying the 5 knots and the 18 contemplation exercises presented in the five previous chapters can all be understood as contemplation practices where the object of contemplation is how the client's mental, emotional and behavioural patterns contribute to the client's experience of themselves and the world. They guide the individual to recognise the ways in which they are the co-creators of the world they inhabit. They help individuals recognise when they fight against phenomena they themselves have created. They help individuals notice the ways they create the illusion of being separate from what they desire and become engaged in remedying this separateness. Such realisations afford the individual the possibility to become aware of Being in two ways.

First, recognising when we are fighting our own creations enables us to dissolve the fight by ceasing to create that which we fight against. When this happens, the attention that was bound up in the fight will be freed, making it easier to become aware of Being.

Second, by moving our attention from the world to our own mind, we draw it nearer to Being. This is because when we use something as a tool, our focus is on the task, not the tool itself.

For example, when hammering a nail, your attention is on the nail, not the hammer. The more skilled you are, the more the hammer fades from awareness. Furthermore, your hand is the tool you use to handle the hammer, making it twice removed from your attention. Consequently, your hand will be even more invisible to you than the hammer while hammering the nail.

Similarly, Being is the tool that enables you to use the mind, which, in turn, is the tool you use to contemplate world. Thus, Being is twice removed from the focus of your attention when you contemplate the world, but only once removed when you contemplate your mind. Therefore, it is easier to become aware of Being when contemplating the mind than when contemplating the world.

The final category of realisation practices is a particular type of contemplation exercises which focus on the nature of self and identity.

7.1.3. Self-Inquiry

Self-inquiry is a direct and introspective practice that focuses on questioning the nature of the self, with the goal of dissolving false identities and realising the true self as pure consciousness or Being. The approach is a form of contemplation but is specifically directed towards investigations of self and identity.

In Advaita Vedanta, for example, Neti Neti (meaning 'not this, not that') is a practice that involves the systematic rejection of all objects of perception and thought, in search of the true self. By continually dismissing everything that can be identified or conceptualised, the practitioner moves closer to the realisation of the self as pure consciousness, beyond all forms.

"Who am I?" is another practice found in Advaita Vedanta. This practice was championed by the Indian sage Ramana Maharshi. It challenges practitioners to repeatedly answer the question "Who am I?" until they run out of answers. Through this process, the practitioner peels away layers of identification with the body, mind, and ego, ultimately leading to the realisation that the true self is not these transient aspects but the unchanging awareness behind them.

Neti Neti and "Who am I?" can be seen as complementary practices with a common goal. Both practices ultimately lead to the same realisation of the self as pure, non-dual awareness. However, they approach the task from different angles. While Neti Neti uses negation to clear away false identifications, "Who am I?" uses direct inquiry to dismantle the ego's illusion.

In the Sufi tradition, self-inquiry might take the form of reflecting on one's relationship with God, continuously asking how one's actions and thoughts align with the divine presence.

Such practices emphasise a relentless questioning of perceived realities of the self, driving the practitioner towards a direct experience of the underlying truth of who they are.

The practices of Being-Centred Therapy can be understood as self-inquiry in that they, directly or indirectly, lead the practitioner to question the nature of self, dissolve false identifications and realise Being as the true self.

Working with the knots of positive and negative reification invites the practitioner to investigate the nature of a range of phenomena they perceive as inherently positive or negative. While this is not directly an inquiry into the nature of self, such investigations will often have profound effects on the practitioner's sense of self, because individuals often identify with their value-judgements of such phenomena.

One person may see himself as the kind of person that values and seeks joy and light-heartedness. When he, through working with the Knot of Positive Reification, realises that joy and light-heartedness are inherent qualities of Being and not something that can be sought or lost, it will render part of his identity meaningless. It makes no sense to identify with the impulse to seek something that cannot be sought.

Another person may see herself as the kind of person that never gets angry. When she, through working with the Knot of Negative Reification, realises that the essence of anger is nothing other than an aspect of Being, which she in other contexts may call enthusiasm or vitality, it will deeply impact her sense of self. First, it reveals that she does, in fact, experience the state she calls anger even if she calls it by a different name. Second, it reveals that she in certain contexts sees this state as positive. Together, such realisations make it difficult to retain the identity of a person that never gets angry.

Thus, while working with the knots of positive and negative reification does not directly involve questioning the self, it does call into question concepts the individual uses to define themselves – making it harder to retain a fixed identity.

Working with the Knot of Conditionality will also undermine individuals' sense of self in that many people identify with their pursuits in life. An individual may, for example, see themself as the kind of person that pursues career, family, deep relationships, adventure, safety or something else. When discovering that such pursuits are ill-informed attempts at finding what is already present, it will no longer make sense to use this pursuit as a defining characteristic of oneself. Furthermore, working with the Knot of Conditionality one discovers that what one seeks are specific aspects of Being and that these are always already present. Since it makes sense to identify with whatever is permanently present to us, this discovery will suggest that Being is our true self.

Working with the Knot of Alienation further undermines individuals' sense of self in that many people's identity is formed around perceived limits of their agency.

One person may, for example, experience herself as a victim of certain circumstances. However, when through working with the Knot of Alienation, she discovers that she actively seeks out and creates these circumstances, the identity as a victim becomes difficult to retain.

Another person may experience himself as a product of human nature. However, when through working with the Knot of Alienation, he discovers that what he thought was human nature is, in reality, his own active (albeit unconscious) choice, the identity as a product of human nature can no longer be sustained.

Finally, working with the Knot of Alienation encourages shifting the focus of attention from the world to the mind. In so doing, the locus of operation shifts from the mind to witnessing consciousness or Being. This will also help the individual discover Being as their true self.

All of the above practices question the sense of self in mostly indirect ways. Working with the Knot of Fragmentation will question the self very directly.

Working with the Knot of Fragmentation reveals that we have multiple selves, and that we identify with different parts of ourselves at different times. Furthermore, it reveals that these selves are merely patterns developed to achieve certain objectives and, as such, are more like skills than what most people would understand by a "self". Finally, it shows that we contain selves that are in direct opposition to what we thought we were.

Such realisations beg the question: "What am I beyond this multiplicity of inner selves?" Answering this question is a self-inquiry practice and can lead to the realisation of the true self as the space in which all these individual selves operate and to whom they appear, namely Being.

Next, I'll look at practices for actualisation.

7.2. Actualisation Practices

Just as with realisation practices, actualisation practices vary widely across traditions. However, they typically focus on four key areas as means to help individuals increase their receptivity to insights and, simultaneously, embody and live in accordance with these insights. These four areas are: ethical living, selflessness, present-moment awareness, and authentic engagement.

In the following, I will briefly describe each area, provide examples from different traditions and comment on how they relate to Being-Centred Therapy. I will also highlight some common challenges related to each type of actualisation practice.

7.2.1. Ethical Living

Many spiritual and philosophical traditions emphasise ethical living as a key part of practice. By aligning actions and decisions with moral principles and cultivating virtues such as honesty, compassion, and justice, individuals can purify their heart and mind, making them simultaneously more receptive to insights into the nature of reality and better able to retain awareness of these insights in their daily lives.

For example, in Buddhism, three parts of the Eightfold Path to enlightenment focus on ethical living[67]. Right Speech involves speaking truthfully and kindly, and avoiding lies, gossip and harmful words. Right Action involves acting in ways that promote well-being of all living beings and avoiding harmful behaviour such as killing, stealing and unethical sexual behaviour. Right Livelihood involves choosing work that benefits others and does not cause harm to people, animals or the environment.

Judaism encourages practitioners to adhere to the Mitzvot – the Ten Commandments outlined in the Torah – guiding individuals to live in accordance with divine will and fostering a deeper connection with God.

---

[67] The other five parts can be divided in two groups. Right View and Right Intention focus on learning wisdom and Right Effort, Right Mindfulness and Right Concentration/Single-Mindedness focus on learning concentration or control of the mind.

Christianity teaches practitioners to follow the double love commandment: "Love the Lord your God with all your heart, soul, and mind" and "Love your neighbour as yourself."

All of these practices emphasise that ethical living is not just about engaging in ethical behaviour for its own sake, but also to make practitioners more receptive to spiritual insights and to deepen their connection with the divine.

Being-Centred Therapy does not focus directly on ethical behaviour but rather assumes that such behaviour will be the inevitable result of untying the knots.

The assumption is that any unethical behaviour is based on misguided strategies for reaching aspects of Being. Thus, becoming aware of Being will make unethical behaviour superfluous. If an individual already recognises that what motivates them to engage in harmful behaviour is to reach a state that is already present, and that by engaging in the harmful behaviour they cause themselves to lose awareness of this state, there will simply be no reason for the individual to engage in the harmful behaviour. Consequently, they will effortlessly cease to do so.

Focusing on adhering to a moral code can be a useful way of making oneself more receptive to deep insights and cultivating awareness of Being. For example, cultivating the virtue of moderation can help unhook one's attention from seeking Being through excessive consumption. Similarly, cultivating love for other people and seeking to be of service can help unhook one's attention from seeking Being through self-gratifications[68].

However, as with *any* practice, there is a risk. In the case of ethical living, the main risk is that adhering to the moral code can itself become a strategy for seeking to create or acquire Being in a way that ends up distracting the individual from noticing that it is already present. Someone may, for example, try to live up to an ethical code because they believe that if others see their ethical conduct, they will be more respected and that gaining the respect of others will bring them a sense of value – which is a positive reification of Being. However, the more someone is seeking to be recognised for their ethical conduct, the more this project will take their attention away from noticing the inherent value of Being. This risk is hinted

[68] In this way, ethical behaviour can make practitioners more receptive to realising some of the corrective principles presented in earlier chapters, such as "what you ultimately seek is already present" and "you cannot create by doing something but only become aware of it by ceasing to spend your attention on projects that distract you from it".

at in the Gospel of Matthew: "When you give alms, do not let your left hand know what your right hand is doing." (Matthew 6:3). This passage emphasises the importance of sincerity and humility in charitable acts, cautioning against the risk of being motivated by a wish for recognition.

Furthermore, if people believe their well-being depends on living up to an ideal of ethical behaviour, they are likely to start rationalising behaviour that falls short of this ideal to make it appear as if it does not. This can make people blind to their own unethical conduct and, thus, make it difficult to practice ethical living.

To mitigate the risk of ethical behaviour becoming adopted as a means through which the individual searches for Being, Being-Centred Therapy focuses on changing the individual's cognition in such a way that it supports rather than hinders continuous awareness of Being. Since the motivation to engage in unethical behaviour is the false belief that it is a way of attaining positive reifications of Being, ethical behaviour will emerge effortlessly as continuous awareness of Being removes the motivation for unethical behaviour. Changing cognition in this way and striving to live an ethical life can, of course, be practiced in tandem. However, adding the work on cognition greatly contributes to the actualisation practice of ethical living.

I will expand on how Being-Centred Therapy can change the individual's cognition in sections 7.4, 7.5 and 7.6.

7.2.2. Selflessness

Many spiritual and philosophical traditions encourage selfless action as a path to actualisation. By serving a greater good and focusing on the well-being of others, practitioners are liberated from the burden of their own desires, opening their eyes to the realities of unity and interconnectedness. Such insights will, in turn, make selflessness an effortless and integral part of the individual's life. While selflessness is sometimes viewed as part of ethical living, it holds special significance as a distinct practice of actualisation, aimed at dissolving the illusion of the individual self and embracing oneness with all life.

In Hinduism, the practice of Karma Yoga teaches practitioners to engage in work while relinquishing the fruits of their labour. By performing actions without attachment to the results, their practitioners' efforts become acts of selflessness, focused solely on service rather than personal gain.

The Jewish concept of Tikkun Olam (repairing the world) encourages individuals to engage in acts of kindness and justice, contributing to the betterment of society and the world.

In Mahayana Buddhism a central ideal is the Bodhisattva, one who attains enlightenment but chooses to remain in the cycle of birth and rebirth to work for the benefit of all beings and help them achieve liberation. This choice reflects profound loving-kindness, compassion and selflessness[69].

In Christianity, the practice of agape love involves selfless care for others, exemplified by Jesus' teachings to love one's neighbour – including one's enemies.

In Islam, the practice of zakat – charitable giving – is a pillar of faith that requires giving a portion of one's wealth to those in need, fostering community welfare and reducing inequality.

In Sufism, Ihsan (excellence in character) encourages selflessness through acts of kindness and service to others, seeing every good deed as a reflection of God's love. This practice involves transcending personal desires and seeking to serve others as a way of expressing devotion to God.

All these practices emphasise selflessness not merely as a moral endeavour but as a powerful means of attaining important insights into the nature of oneself and one's relation to the environment.

As with ethical living, Being-Centred Therapy does not focus directly on cultivating selflessness. Instead, it questions clients' conception of self and shows how pursuing personal desires can be counterproductive, in that while clients may achieve their immediate objective, the overall result is often the opposite of what they ultimately desired and hoped to gain.

Furthermore, Being-Centred Therapy reveals that everything clients ultimately seek is already available in the present moment. The result is a diminishing interest in the pursuit of purely personal goals, which brings forth an effortless selflessness. When you feel that your "cup runneth over" (The Bible, Psalms: 23:5), you become naturally selfless. Arriving at selflessness in this way mitigates the risk

---

[69] The choice also reflects an understanding that if there essentially is only one consciousness then all beings essentially are one and personal liberation is, therefore, not possible without the liberation of all beings.

of selflessness, like other ethical ideals, becoming part of a Knot of Conditionality, where selflessness is pursued for selfish reasons.

7.2.3. Present-Moment Awareness

Many spiritual and philosophical traditions emphasise present-moment awareness as a key actualisation practice. By fully engaging with the present, individuals can free their awareness from the endless stream of thoughts and emotions relating to past or future. Thus, present-moment awareness is a form of meditation in action and, as such, it gets to the core of actualisation.

In Zen practice, present-moment awareness is cultivated through everyday activities such as Zen gardening, walking meditation (kinhin), cleaning and other chores (samu), calligraphy (shodo), martial arts such as Aikido and Kendo, mindful cooking (tenzo), flower arranging (ikebana) and eating meditation (oryoki). Each of these practices transforms ordinary tasks into meditative exercises by encouraging full attention to the present moment, making every action an opportunity for mindfulness and awareness.

In Japanese tea ceremonies (chanoyu), every movement and gesture – pouring water, whisking tea, offering and receiving the cup, smelling and drinking the tea – is performed with meticulous attention and mindfulness, turning a simple ritual into a meditative practice of present-moment awareness.

In Christian monastic traditions, Ora et Labora ("pray and work") emphasises bringing mindfulness into manual labour, such as gardening or cooking, treating these activities as forms of prayer and devotion.

In Native American traditions, the practice of mindful walking in nature involves being fully attuned to the sensations underfoot, the sounds of the environment, and the rhythm of one's breath, cultivating a deep connection with the present moment and the natural world.

Through such practices, practitioners can learn to pay sustained attention to Being while they are engaged in everyday activities. Such practices align well with the corrective principle that Being is ever present and can, therefore, be found regardless of external circumstances.

Present-moment awareness is practised in different ways in Being-Centred Therapy. For example, the five processes for untying the 5 knots all encourage clients to answer questions by paying attention to their present moment felt sense, rather than to deduce answers from past experiences. Furthermore, the

Non-Urgency process described in Section 3.4.4 encourages clients to notice what new ideas for how to engage with a situation emerge the moment they juxtapose the memory of the situation with the present-moment state of Being they became aware of through the session. Both examples emphasise attention to what is happening in the present moment.

A common risk related to practising present-moment awareness is that it becomes an ideal that people seek to adhere to because they believe doing so will bring them happiness, safety, value, or some other positive reification of Being. In other words, seeking to live up to the ideal of present-moment awareness can lead to the formation of the Knot of Conditionality.

Furthermore, whenever individuals seek to live up to an ideal, they may rationalise behaviour that does not conform to the ideal, to make it appear as if it does. This can drive a wedge between how people believe they act and how they actually act, making it more difficult for people to discover when their awareness drifts away from the present moment – and, consequently, to practise present-moment awareness.

To mitigate these risks, Being-Centred Therapy focuses on changing clients' cognition in such a way that it no longer draws attention away from Being, making present-moment awareness effortless. The cognitive work does not need to replace present-moment awareness practices but can support and be supported by these.

I will expand on how cognition can be changed through Being-Centred Therapy in sections 7.4, 7.5 and 7.6.

7.2.4. Authentic Engagement

The fourth and final theme common to many actualisation practices is authentic engagement. Authentic engagement emphasises living in alignment with one's true self and values, rather than conforming to external expectations or societal norms. The goal is to achieve self-knowledge, integrity and a deeper understanding of one's true nature and purpose through the full expression of one's authentic self in the world.

In existential philosophy, authentic living means making choices based on personal values while embracing freedom and responsibility. Camus, a key figure in existentialism, emphasised living authentically by rejecting "bad faith", where one denies their freedom by conforming to societal norms or seeking external validation. Instead, he advocated for creating one's own meaning through deliberate, value-driven choices, fully engaging with life despite its inherent absurdity. By fully engaging with life in this way, one behaviour will be aligned with the deeper truth that meaning arises from within and cannot be found in imposed beliefs or societal expectations.

In Jungian psychology, "shadow work" encourages clients to be authentic by embracing and understanding all parts of the psyche, in particular those we do not consciously accept and value. Thus, shadow work encourages expression of the whole self, which aligns with the corrective principle that you contain no inner enemies. What appear negative in you are merely parts of your wholeness that you have not yet understood and integrated. Every part carries a gift when properly understood.

In Gestalt Therapy, clients are encouraged to engage authentically in life by focusing on their present experience and taking responsibility for their choices and desires. Such authentic engagement aligns with the corrective principles that every part of you is ultimately seeking well-being, that growth and fulfilment, therefore, come from embracing and acknowledging, rather than rejecting, your choices and desires as they emerge in you, that you have personal agency and responsibility in life, that meaning and truth is always found in the present, and that the self is not a fixed and monolithic entity but rather a multifaceted and ever-changing process.

In Stoicism, the practice of Amor Fati (loving one's fate) involves embracing all aspects of life, even its challenges, with acceptance and purpose, allowing for authentic engagement with whatever life brings. This approach to authenticity aligns with the corrective principle that life's value lies not in external circumstances but is omnipresent in every moment and every aspect of life.

Such practices show that authentic engagement is not just about self-expression but about realising and actualising one's true nature.

In Being-Centred Therapy authenticity is particularly prevalent when working with the Knot of Alienation and the Knot of Negative Reification.

As with ethical living, selflessness and present-moment awareness, authenticity can become an ideal through which people believe they can reach various positive reifications of Being. This can lead to the formation of the Knot of Conditionality and to the rationalisation of inauthentic behaviour, which undermines people's ability to practice authenticity. Being-Centred Therapy seeks to mitigate this risk by working with cognition in conjunction with practices focused on authentic engagement.

Before looking at how Being-Centred Therapy works with actualisation by altering clients' cognition, I will expand on the challenges faced by the actualisation practices that I have mentioned so far.

7.3. Challenges to actualisation

Realising Being is difficult because we have many patterns that distract us from noticing it. However, these distracting patterns do not need to change for us to realise Being. We "only" have to unhook from them and wait a while for Being to come into focus.

Actualising Being is more difficult because when we engage with the world, we rely on the patterns that distract us from Being. Therefore, to actualise Being, it is not enough to unhook from these patterns, we must change them. If we do not change the patterns we use to engage with the world, they will make us lose awareness of Being every time we use them.

All the above actualisation practices approaches hinge on the use of conscious effort to modify one's own behaviour – making it more ethical, selfless, focused on the present and authentic.

The assumption is that by consistently modifying our behaviour, we will eventually alter the patterns we use to engage with the world in such a way that they no longer interfere with our awareness of Being. When this happens, the behaviours we have been rehearsing will become effortless since they are no longer influenced by our lack of awareness of Being. In other words, the actualisation practices we have looked at so far can be understood as "fake-it-till-you-make-it" approaches to actualisation.

While such approaches can work, following them comes with several severe challenges. In the following, I will outline some of the main challenges related to actualisation before suggesting an approach to actualisation that takes into account these challenges. The first three challenges will be specifically related to approaches to actualisation that rely on behavioural modification. The fourth challenge will relate to any approach to actualisation.

7.3.1. Challenge 1: Knots of Conditionality

The first challenge for behaviour-based approaches to actualisation is the risk of forming Knots of Conditionality.

These approaches all suggest that by making our behaviour more ethical, selfless, present or authentic it is possible to achieve deeper awareness of Being. This proposition can, however, easily be misunderstood to imply that such behaviour brings Being, which is otherwise missing. This is precisely the Knot of Conditionality: Our experience of Being depends upon fulfilling the conditions of behaving in ethical, selfless, present and authentic ways.

Ethical living and similar practices don't create Being; they simply block behaviour that distracts us from it. However, without changing the underlying belief that we are separate from what we seek, we may replace one distraction with another that appears virtuous but still keeps us from noticing Being. For this reason, it is essential to work not only on behaviour but also on the beliefs driving that behaviour, and newer research in cognitive science provides valuable tools for this.

7.3.2. Challenge 2: Espoused theories vs. theories-in-use

The second challenge for behaviour-based approaches to actualisation is that they depend upon the accuracy of practitioners' perceptions of their own behaviour. However, there is often a gap between how we think we behave and how we actually behave.

Organisational scholars Argyris and Schön (Argyris, 1977; Argyris & Schön, 1974; Schön, 1986)studied this gap by distinguishing between "espoused theories of action" – the values and beliefs we believe guide our behaviour, and "theories-in-use" – the values and beliefs that truly govern our behaviour. They found that there often is a gap between what individuals believe they are doing and what they actually do in practice. Importantly, this is not a matter of deception. People often sincerely believe they are acting in accordance with particular principles and are blind to the ways in which their own behaviour is at odds with these principles.

Thus, it is possible to be sincerely convinced that you are living according to an ethical code – even if you are not. It is very possible to be convinced that you are selfless, present and authentic, even if your actual behaviour is selfish, absent-minded and inauthentic.

There are multiple mechanisms that contribute to the discrepancy between how we think we behave and how we actually behave. In the following, I will mention rationalisation, confabulation and a selection of relevant biases.

Rationalisation

One mechanism that contributes to the discrepancy between how we believe we act and how we actually act is rationalisation.

Rationalisation is the process of explaining the parts of our behaviour that are at odds with our beliefs about how we behave in a way that allows us to maintain these beliefs. For example, you may believe that you embody the ethical ideal of tolerance, yet you frequently deliver a harsh critique of opinions that do not match your own. Rather than acknowledging this contradiction, you may rationalise your behaviour by claiming your criticism aims to promote tolerance in others.

You may see yourself as a selfless person, yet frequently seek recognition or praise for your acts of kindness. Instead of acknowledging the self-serving nature of this behaviour, you may rationalise it by saying that sharing your good deeds is meant to inspire others to be selfless as well.

You may believe you are someone who is very present, yet you constantly check your phone for messages during conversations. Rather than recognising this habit as an indication that you are *not* focused on the here-and-now, you might rationalise it as an act of staying connected, responsive, available and present to everyone.

You may believe you are authentic in your behaviour yet hide your feelings when these are at odds with those of the people around you. Rather than seeing this as inauthenticity, you might rationalise it as being adaptive, considerate and respectful, which you see as part of being truly authentic.

Rationalisation is a challenge for the behaviour-based actualisation practices because it means that we can believe we are practising even if we are not.

Confabulation

Another mechanism that contributes to the discrepancy between how we believe we act and how we actually act is confabulation.

Confabulation is the process of inventing plausible explanations for our own behaviour even if we do not have any information about why we do what we do. Such explanations will appear believable to us, even if they are false.

In therapy, it is common to see clients jump to conclusions about why they think, feel, or behave in certain ways. This is confabulation, as the proposed explanations are not based on a thorough investigation but rather on quickly matching observations with spiritual or psychological teaching or preconceived ideas about self.

Whereas confabulation can look like rationalisation, it is different in its function.

Rationalisation distorts facts to obscure contradictions between our beliefs about ourselves and what our actions reveal about us. This is a problem for the kind of actualisation practices discussed in this chapter because it distorts reality, so we believe that we are practising even when we are not.

Confabulation, however, fabricates narratives to fill gaps in our knowledge, making us believe we know what our intentions and motivations are – even if we do not. This is problematic because what makes a behaviour align with spiritual principles is not the behaviour itself, rather it is the intentions and motivations behind the behaviour. By quickly filling gaps in our knowledge about our own intentions and motivations, confabulation prevents us from discovering whether our behaviour aligns with spiritual insights.

You may, for example, notice that you feel great joy when you give money to charities. You immediately assume the reason is that the ethical act of giving to a charity brings you in touch with the Joy aspect of Being. This explanation may seem plausible to you and, consequently, you do not investigate further. However, the true reason you feel joy may be that you expect to receive social recognition and appreciation for your act.

Similarly, you may decide to expose harmful practices in an organisation to protect the public or the environment, even if this means that you will lose your job. You may believe this is a selfless act. However, you may overlook that you are also motivated by a desire for personal revenge that is stronger than your desire for retaining your job.

In the above examples, confabulation presents false accounts of motivations that make behaviour appear as if it aligns with spiritual insights when it doesn't. However, confabulation can also mislead the opposite way.

You may, for example, be in the habit of allowing other people to speak more than you do. You may assume this shows you are absent-minded. However, the true reason may be that you are present-minded and do not get distracted by desires to introject your opinions and stories.

Similarly, you may readily and publicly admit to mistakes. You may believe this is inauthentic behaviour aimed at lowering other people's expectations and making them easier to fulfil. However, the real motivation might be authentic self-acceptance, making you relaxed about letting others see your mistakes.

As these examples illustrate, confabulation clouds our ability to assess whether the intentions and motivations driving our behaviour align with spiritual insights. It gives us the false impression that we know what drives our behaviour when we don't, preventing the necessary investigation of what drives us that is a crucial component of one's striving to live in accordance with spiritual insights. You might believe you're aligned when you're not – or the reverse.

Lastly, it is important to recognise that our behaviours are often driven by multiple intentions and motivations. Thus, even if our initial explanation is true, it is wise to keep investigating. Too often, clients cease exploring once they have found a single plausible explanation for their behaviour. However, living in alignment with spiritual teaching is more about investigating one's motivations and intentions than one's concrete actions. Therefore, it is essential to give this inquiry the attention it deserves and not allow confabulation to prematurely end the process.

Biases

Researchers have identified numerous biases that can make it difficult to accurately perceive our own behaviour. Below, I briefly mention six such biases.

Confirmation bias is the tendency to seek out, interpret and recall information that confirms existing beliefs while disregarding or minimising information that contradicts them. This bias can lead us to notice behaviour that aligns with existing beliefs about how we behave while ignoring behaviour that contradicts them. As a result, confirmation bias reinforces beliefs about how we act, even when these are false or don't fully match reality.

Self-Serving Bias is the tendency to attribute successes to internal factors such as our abilities and intentions, while blaming failures on external circumstances. Thus, when our actions align with our self-image and what we perceive as desirable, we credit ourselves, but when they do not, we blame external circumstances, rather than taking such behaviour as evidence that our perception of our own behaviour is flawed.

Fundamental Attribution Error is the tendency to attribute other people's problematic behaviours to their character, while explaining the same behaviour in ourselves as a result of situational factors. This bias reinforces the self-serving bias, allowing us to judge others for actions that reveal character flaws, while excusing the same actions in ourselves, and thus failing to recognise them as evidence of our own character flaws.

Introspection Illusion is the belief that we have special insight into our own motivations and behaviour, even when we don't. This can lead to overconfidence in our self-assessments and prevent us from recognising the influence of unconscious factors.

Halo Effect is the tendency to let one positive trait or behaviour influence our overall perception of ourselves, leading us to overlook or excuse behaviours that do not align with our beliefs about how we act by pointing to behaviours that do. In short, one selfless act can lead us to overlook numerous selfish ones.

Hindsight Bias is the tendency to see past events as more predictable than they were, which can lead us to rewrite our behaviour in a way that supports our beliefs about how we behave. In short, we may act from a selfish intention but if events happen to turn out in a way that benefits someone else, we can come to believe it was always our intention to benefit the other – even if it wasn't.

Thus, there are many mechanisms that make it difficult for us to accurately perceive our own behaviour. Consequently, actualisation practices that focus on modifying behaviour so it aligns with spiritual insights can be difficult in practice as they require us to have an accurate perception of our own behaviour. Research in cognitive science can offer alternative approaches to realisation by providing mechanisms for targeting the beliefs that shape our actions directly.

7.3.3. Challenge 3: Implicit memory

The third challenge, that approaches to actualisation based on behaviour modification face, is that much of our behaviour is governed by patterns (schemas) stored in implicit memory, and while it is possible to override these patterns, altering them can be difficult.

An individual may, for example, have the impulse to feign emotions to fit in socially. It may be possible for this individual to override this impulse and stand by their emotions. But this is not the same as changing the impulse itself.

Overriding behavioural impulses can be useful, but it requires constant effort. Whenever we are tired or stressed, we might not have the energy required to override our impulses. This is why we typically revert to old ways of behaving in such situations.

Thus, an individual may become skilled at standing by their emotions, but it will feel like a struggle, and whenever they become tired, they may revert to their old habit of pretending to have the emotions needed to fit in.

The goal of actualisation is to alter the patterns that govern our behaviour, so it naturally and effortlessly aligns with spiritual insights. However, approaches to actualisation that rely on behaviour modification will often result in adding new patterns that override, rather than alter, the schemas in implicit memory. The hope is that the experience the individual gains from acting in a new way will, eventually, alter the pattern in their implicit memory. However, this does not always happen. It is possible to spend a lifetime practising authenticity by overriding inauthentic impulses, without these impulses ever changing.

Thus, actualisation practices that rely on behaviour modification can lead to the formation of Knots of Fragmentation, where the individual is divided between a pattern in their implicit memory and a pattern they are trying to live by. Religious literature is filled with accounts of battles against the devil within: Struggles to override selfishness with selflessness, sexual desire with chastity, pride with humility, or greed with generosity. Accounts of such inner battles are often intended to represent the spiritual journey of aligning with higher virtues. However, in modern day language, they may be seen as attempts at overriding, rather than transforming, schemas in implicit memory.

As discussed in the chapter on the Knot of Fragmentation, it is key to allow the parts of us that do not align with spiritual ideals to reveal to us what problems they seek to address and in what emotionally charged situations they were formed. When this happens, we may recognise that the "inner devils" are parts of us that are doing their best to navigate important challenges. They are parts that deserve our respect and compassion. This approach can lead to true transformation and, therefore, true actualisation.

Recent research has found that through conversation it is possible to activate schemas in implicit memory, and that, once activated, these patterns enter into a labile state in which they can be permanently altered before they reconsolidate. This finding sheds new light on the actualisation process. It shows that it is possible to transform beliefs in implicit memory that govern behaviour rather than merely override them through continuous efforts, thus addressing one of the main challenges faced by approaches to actualisation based on behavioural modification. I will expand on this in Section 7.4.

7.3.4. Challenge 4: Changing patterns can be uncomfortable

The fourth challenge that any approach to actualisation faces is that updating our beliefs can be uncomfortable and complicated, particularly when it comes to those formed early in life. Three psychological theories are particularly useful for understanding this difficulty: Jean Piaget's theory of accommodation and assimilation (Piaget & Inhelder, 1969), Leon Festinger's theory of cognitive dissonance (Festinger, 1957; Festinger & Carlsmith, 1959), and Perkins and colleagues' theory of threshold concepts and troublesome knowledge (Meyer & Land, 2003; Perkins, 2006).

Jean Piaget's theory of assimilation and accommodation explains how there are two ways human beings can integrate new information into their understanding of the world. Sometimes new information fits into our existing schemas and can easily be assimilated. For example, when a child knows what a dog is, then seeing a new breed of dog is information that can easily be added to the child's pre-existing category of "dog". However, sometimes new information does not fit with any of our existing schemas. In this case, we need to change our schemas to accommodation this information. Accommodation is, thus, a more challenging process than assimilation because it requires us to change or replace our existing schemas. For example, when a child sees a horse for the first time, this child may first try to assimilate this information into a pre-existing category and call the horse a big dog. However, when the child is told that the animal is a horse and not a dog, they must create a new category of four-legged animals to accommodate this information.

Furthermore, our understanding of the world is layered with newer schemas building upon older ones. The earlier a schema is formed, the more other schemas depend upon it, making early ones particularly hard to change. When accommodation of new information requires us to change a schema that was formed early in life, it is like changing a cornerstone of the edifice of our worldview, which can necessitate a significant restructuring of how we understand reality. The misconceptions addressed in Being-Centred Therapy are foundational schemas. Thus, changing them involves significant shifts in all the schemas that build upon them. Resistance to changing these misconceptions often arises, not from unwillingness to change the misconception itself, but from an unwillingness to change certain beliefs that build upon it. For example, accepting that negative inner states are created by the individual, rather than circumstances, may be straightforward for the client, but it can meet resistance because implies challenges to a part of the client's established self-image, which they may be deeply attached to.

Leon Festinger's research on cognitive dissonance showed that people have a strong aversion to inconsistencies between their beliefs and behaviour. Such inconsistencies create cognitive dissonance, an uncomfortable state of psychological tension or pain. People will typically avoid this discomfort by using rationalisation or other mental strategies to make their behaviour and beliefs appear coherent, even when they aren't.

When we attempt to change a fundamental belief, it disrupts the entire framework of beliefs built around it, leading to temporary states of inconsistency, while these other beliefs adjust. The resulting cognitive dissonance can feel disorienting and uncomfortable, causing people to avoid it in ways that make the fundamental beliefs harder to update.

David Perkins and colleagues' research on education has shown that many domains of knowledge contain so-called threshold concepts, which are ideas that are difficult to grasp but crucial for making progress in that domain. An example is the concept of "opportunity cost" in economics, which can roughly be defined as the money you miss out on when choosing to do something other than the activity that would have made you the most money. This concept can at first seem counterintuitive, but if it is not understood, it will limit to what extent an individual can understand economics.

Threshold concepts are often resisted, not only because they are difficult to understand, but also because they bring with them what Perkins calls "troublesome knowledge". Troublesome knowledge is knowledge that is disturbing to us. For example, understanding the concept of opportunity cost leads to the knowledge that there is no free form of vacation. Even if we stay home and spend no money, we still pay an opportunity cost.

The 20 corrective principles in Being-Centred Therapy are threshold concepts. They are necessary to grasp for genuine personal and spiritual growth, but understanding them brings troublesome knowledge, insights that can be hard to accept. For example, the idea that everything we seek is already present can be unsettling because it brings the troublesome knowledge that much of our lifelong striving and suffering was unnecessary. Such realisations can be deeply uncomfortable but they are essential to face for transformative change to happen.

Thus, updating fundamental beliefs can be challenging because it requires us to accommodate the whole system of beliefs we've built around these beliefs, it creates cognitive dissonance, and it brings troublesome knowledge.

One of the reasons Being-Centred Therapy places great emphasis on developing awareness of Being throughout the therapeutic process is that doing so helps clients approach the task of updating core beliefs from a place of resourcefulness, making the process easier and more enjoyable. This approach supports clients in embracing the necessary discomfort for genuine growth without being overwhelmed by it. I will expand on this in Section 7.5.8.

7.4. Actualisation in Being-Centred Therapy

If one is aware of the above-mentioned challenges, it is, of course, possible to engage successfully in actualisation practices based on behavioural modification.

However, it is worth asking if there are ways of dealing more directly with these challenges. The Being-Centred approach to therapy presented in this book seeks to do so by drawing on recent advances in neuroscience and cognitive science.

In the remainder of this chapter, I will introduce two exciting strands of research that can provide insights into how to facilitate actualisation, namely, research on memory reconsolidation, and on the metaphorical and embodied nature of cognition.

Neuroscientists studying memory reconsolidation have found that schemas stored in implicit memory, which underpin problematic behaviour, can be updated or even erased when individuals are affectively and cognitively engaged with those schemas while simultaneously experiencing something in the present that contradicts them.

These findings suggest that actualisation can be understood as the process of using memory reconsolidation to update or erase beliefs that are at odds with the insights practitioners gain through realisation practices. In relation to Being-Centred Therapy, the 20 misconceptions presented in the chapters on the 5 knots can be understood as 20 implicit schemas underpinning psychological issues, and the experiences that arise when clients, through the work with the 5 knots, become aware of Being can be understood as experiences that naturally disconfirm and update these schemas.

Cognitive scientists investigating how cognition is grounded in the brain have found that even our most abstract concepts are grounded in reactivation of neural circuits originally developed for perception and motor control. This means that we understand abstract concepts metaphorically in terms of sensory-motor experiences. Research has also shown that shifting the sensory-motor experiences, in terms of which key concepts are grounded, can radically alter how individuals make sense of and engage with specific situations. It can even change an individual's perception of a situation from seeing it as impossible to deal with to seeing it as straightforward (Springborg, 2018).

These findings suggest that actualisation may be achieved, not by replacing any specific behaviour, but by grounding the concepts we use to engage with the world in the sensory-motor experiences that emerge when we become aware of Being. When more of the concepts we use to engage with the world are rooted in sensory experiences linked to Being, it becomes much easier to maintain awareness of Being while actively participating in the world. Thus, actively shifting the embodied ground of key concepts is key to facilitating actualisation.

7.5. Memory reconsolidation

A recent discovery in neuroscience that could provide new strategies for addressing the challenges related to the actualisation process is the process of memory reconsolidation.

Before this discovery, neuroscientists believed that once a memory is consolidated and stored in implicit memory – a type of unconscious memory that influences automatic behaviour – it becomes "fixed" and can only be overridden by learning new competing patterns, but not unlearned or altered.

This view suggests that learned patterns leading to unethical, selfish, absent-minded or inauthentic behaviour would remain stable and unchangeable throughout life, and the only way to change behaviour is to learn new competing patterns[70]. This belief is reflected in many of the actualisation practices listed

---

[70] This relates to misconception 6, the belief that if you wish to gain something you need to do something extra. If patterns once established are immutable, it wouldn't be possible to gain something through the cessation of these patterns (the 6th corrective principle).

above, where practitioners are encouraged to practise new behaviour to override the current behaviour.

Memory reconsolidation was discovered in 2000 when neuroscientist Karim Nader's team demonstrated that learning stored in implicit memory could, under certain circumstances, be modified and even erased. In their experiment, they conditioned rats to associate a sound with a mild electric shock, creating a fear response. Once the learning was established in the rats' memory, they reactivated it by playing the sound. During this reactivation, they administered a drug that blocked protein synthesis, which is necessary for memory storage. The result was that the original fear memory was erased so the rats no longer reacted to the sound.

This finding showed that when a memory is activated through recollection, it enters into a malleable state where it can be updated before it is reconsolidated back into implicit memory. Subsequent research has confirmed that this process of memory reconsolidation is a general mechanism that applies not only to conditioned fear responses but to a wide range of memories and emotional learnings in both animals and humans.

The research on memory reconsolidation has revolutionised our understanding of memory and paved the way for therapeutic methods that aim at transformational change by directly altering deeply ingrained emotional patterns, offering an exciting new avenue for actualisation.

7.5.1. Memory reconsolidation and therapy

Bruce Ecker and colleagues (Ecker et al., 2012) have developed a therapeutic process specifically designed to leverage the power of memory reconsolidation, known as Coherence Therapy.

Building on the memory reconsolidation process, Ecker and colleagues propose that the brain needs three experiences to trigger a reconsolidation process that can transform the core emotional learning in a client's implicit memory that drives the client's problematic behaviour, emotions and thoughts. They observed that this sequence of experiences is consistently present whenever therapy results in transformational change, defined as the complete and permanent eradication of a significant problematic activation without the necessity for any ongoing effort. They have found this sequence of experiences to be the same across many different approaches to therapy.

The three experiences are:

1. Uncover and activate: Formulate and activate the target learning underpinning a client's symptoms.
2. Unlock: Introduce a vivid experience that contradicts or modifies the target learning, making the memory circuits susceptible to updates.
3. Update: Repeatedly juxtapose the target learning and the contradictory experience, allowing the target learning to be updated before it reconsolidates – which typically occurs after five hours.

This sequence is the foundation for achieving deep and lasting change in therapy by directly unlearning or altering the root emotional learning underpinning the client's issues – rather than merely overriding it by adding new, competing learning.

Uncover and activate

The first experience needed to activate the memory reconsolidation process is the activation of the learning underpinning the client's symptoms. In therapy, this can be achieved by identifying the specific behaviours, emotions, thoughts, or somatic symptoms the client wants to address and uncovering the emotional learning or schema that leads the client to produce them[71].

Different approaches to therapy offer different methods for accomplishing this. However, it often involves tracing the client's reactions back to key beliefs that were formed early in life and recalling the situations which shaped them.

When clients do not understand why they produce problematic symptoms, they often assume that these symptoms are produced by something in them that is pathological, stupid, irrational, broken or evil. However, such an attitude will impede the uncovering of the learning in question. It is, therefore, important to operate from the assumption that the production of symptoms is part of a

---

[71] Note that assuming that the symptoms are produced by the client for a purpose, even if this purpose is unconscious, corresponds to the assumption behind the work with the Knot of Alienation. In particular, the 13th and 14th corrective principles, that the client produces both absence of positive states and presence of negative ones.

coherent, intelligible and caring strategy aimed at ensuring a sense of safety and connection in ways that made perfect sense at the time it was formed[72].

Formulating the learning that underpins the client's symptoms serves two purposes.

First, it clarifies what specific target learning needs to be addressed, which is crucial for selecting or creating experiences that can contradict or modify it in the next step of the therapeutic reconsolidation process.

Second, it activates the learning within the client, allowing them to connect both emotionally and cognitively with the part of themselves where this learning is stored. When clients articulate the underlying belief and it feels true to them, it indicates that the emotional schema is fully engaged, setting the stage for the next phase where it is juxtaposed with a contradictory experience.

In summary, the first experience needed to activate the memory reconsolidation process in therapy is that the client connects affectively and cognitively with the underlying learning producing the problematic patterns, and recognises it as an adaptive, albeit outdated, solution to a perceived problem rather than as a pathology. Only when the client understands the logic of the uncovered learning are they connected with it in a way that makes it possible to unlock the learning and make it available for updates.

Unlock

The second experience needed to activate the memory reconsolidation process is the juxtaposition of the symptom-producing learning uncovered in step one with a vivid, contradictory experience. This can happen in various ways.

Sometimes, the simple act of formulating the learning underpinning the symptoms is itself enough to disconfirm the learning. The client may either directly recognise flawed logic in the learning or recognise that it is at odds with what they clearly know from other experiences.

For example, a client may realise they stay silent to avoid sounding stupid because they have learned that if they say something stupid others will lose respect for them and stop listening to them. However, the moment the client articulates this

---

[72] Note that this assumption corresponds to the 17th corrective principle, that there are no inner enemies.

belief, they may immediately recognise that “staying silent will help you get heard” is a logically incoherent belief.

Similarly, a client may discover that their anxiety about always needing to be perfect stems from the belief that any mistake makes them completely unworthy of respect. However, the moment the client articulates this belief, they may immediately recognise it as false, as they recall personal experiences where others made mistakes without it diminishing the value and regard the client holds for them – and vice versa.

Sometimes, no contradictory experiences emerge when the client formulates their learning. The learning may initially feel true to the client. Since learning often concerns ways of solving problems, there are two obvious ways of bringing about contradictory experiences.

First, one may invite the client to consider whether they have personal experiences that disconfirm their perception of the problem. This may lead to the client realising that the problem they seek to deal with is not a real problem or that while it may have been a problem at some point in the client’s life, it no longer is.

For instance, a client may realise that they believe they need to be constantly achieving goals and improving themselves to avoid collapse. On reflection, they might recall experiences that show their world is far more stable than they feel, and that the perceived threat of collapse simply isn’t there. Furthermore, they might recall experiences that show that their relentless pursuit of achievement is far more likely to cause personal collapse than to prevent it.

Second, one may invite the client to evaluate the effectiveness of the solution they’ve adopted. This may lead to the client recalling personal experiences that show that the solution doesn’t work or that they have more effective, less costly ways of addressing the problem.

For example, a client might discover that they avoid social situations to prevent feelings of rejection. Once asked to evaluate the efficiency of this strategy, the client may vividly recall times when avoiding social interactions reinforced, rather than prevented, their sense of rejection. Additionally, the client may recall social situations where participating in social events led to meaningful connections that made them much less disposed to feel rejected.

Juxtaposing the activated implicit learning with a contradictory experience brings the learning into a so-called labile or unconsolidated state where it can be updated before it once more is consolidated. It is crucial to let this process unfold organically, without pushing for any specific conclusion, as doing the latter may prematurely close off the opportunity for transformation.

Update

The final step involves repeating or sustaining the experience from step two, giving the brain time to update the original learning with the new, contradictory experience. If the new experience fully contradicts the original learning, the old learning may be erased. If the new experience supplements the original learning, the old learning may be modified. Once the learning in implicit memory is transformed, the behaviour it drives changes effortlessly and permanently, since the root cause has been altered or removed.

Bruce Ecker and colleagues distinguish between what they call counteractive and non-counteractive therapy.

Counteractive therapy aims to directly instate preferred mental, emotional, and behavioural patterns to override problematic ones. For example, clients might be taught relaxation techniques to counter anxiety, motivational techniques to counter procrastination, or positive thinking techniques to counter depression. From this definition it follows that the actualisation practices mentioned earlier are largely counteractive, as they involve practising new thoughts, emotions, and behaviours to replace unwanted ones.

What often happens in counteractive therapy is that the client will say that they *understand* the need for the new mental, emotional and behavioural patterns, but that they do not *feel* it. This indicates that counteractive therapy often fails to alter the original symptom-producing learning in implicit memory, but instead creates new, competing learning in an attempt to override it. In the language of this book, counteractive therapy will often add new personality parts that are at odds with those producing the client's issues, as discussed in Section 5.2 under the heading "Dissolving vs. adding layers to the personality structure in therapy".

Non-counteractive therapy, on the other hand, does not seek to impose solutions or remedy issues. Instead, it focuses on fully understanding the learning that produces problematic behaviour and emotions, and on introducing experiences that can be useful for updating this learning. As a result, non-counteractive therapy cannot always fully predict what behavioural changes will result from the therapy. However, it does ensure that any change will be positive because the updated learning aligns more closely with the client's present-day reality.

7.5.2. Memory consolidation and actualisation

Research on memory consolidation and its application in therapy provides insights into how experiences of Being during various practices can be actualised so they translate into changes in the daily life of the practitioner.

Like psychotherapy, direct experiences of Being can be very transformative. The literature on personal and spiritual development abounds with accounts of individuals who were completely changed by such experiences. Some report the complete annihilation of anxieties or compulsive behaviours. Others report feeling a sense of joy or peace that persists effortlessly after the experience.

However, like psychotherapy, direct experiences of Being are not always transformative. It is common for practitioners to report direct experiences of Being that ultimately have little to no impact on their daily lives.

Drawing on the research on memory reconsolidation and its use in therapy, it is reasonable to suggest that experiences of Being are only transformative if:

- The specific learning that underpins the individual's suffering is first activated.
- The experience of Being occurs within a five-hour window following this activation.
- The experience of Being contradicts the activated learning.

Generally, approaches to personal and spiritual development that are based on facilitating the realisation of Being do not take these factors into account. They typically operate on the assumption that repeated experiences of Being are transformative in themselves. As a result, transformation only occurs when the above criteria are met by chance.

For example, daily meditation practice on compassion and loving-kindness generally does not include activation of learning that underpins the practitioner's lack of compassion and loving-kindness. Moreover, common advice such as meditating at the same time each day does not guarantee that the practice will occur within five hours of any chance activation of the learning underpinning the behaviour the practice aims to transform. As a result, while the meditation practice might repeatedly generate profound experiences of compassion and loving-kindness, the effects often fade because the symptom-producing learning remains untouched.

Some might argue that frequent practice throughout the day should ensure that the practice eventually overlap chance activation of problematic learning. However, even if the timing aligns, the specific experience of Being produced by the practice may not contradict the specific learning that is active during meditation. For example, an individual may suffer from feelings of worthlessness emerging from the belief that value comes from achievements, and that they are not good at anything. While experiences of compassion and loving-kindness can be profound, such experiences do not directly contradict the belief that produces the sense of worthlessness. Thus, even though an individual engages in meditation on compassion and loving-kindness while they are in touch with the symptom-producing belief, this belief will remain unaltered by the practice.

Additionally, some actualisation practices actively discourage engaging with the very learning that must be transformed to achieve the behavioural changes the practice aims for. As a result, the practice may unintentionally work against itself.

For example, practices focused on developing compassion and loving-kindness might encourage practitioners to avoid or suppress any unkind mental, emotional or behavioural patterns in themselves. However, by seeking to banish these patterns, the practitioner is unlikely to experience the kind of affective and cognitive connection with the learning underpinning these patterns, which, according to the research on memory reconsolidation, is necessary for their transformation.

Finally, when actualisation is left to personal practice outside of therapy sessions, there is a risk that clients may approach their symptom-producing learnings with intellectual distance or scepticism. Such detached attitudes can hinder the necessary affective and cognitive connection with the symptom-producing learning, making it more likely that experiences of Being that could contradict this learning will produce new competing learning, rather than transform the original learning.

For all of these reasons, if the actualisation process is left as "homework" for clients, one risks that the client's practices will not occur within the five-hour window of opportunity after any such activation, will not produce experiences that contradict the learning underpinning the client's suffering, or will not involve affective and cognitive connection with the symptom-producing learning.

Therefore, including actualisation as part of therapy in general and Being-Centred Therapy in particular is not only *possible*, it is *necessary.*

In the following, I will discuss how Being-Centred Therapy can consciously incorporate the therapeutic use of memory reconsolidation and how the processes for untying the 5 knots can facilitate, not only the realisation of Being, but also the actualisation process, ensuring effortless and permanent change. I will round off the section by introducing a contemplation exercise used in Being-Centred Therapy to facilitate the actualisation of any state of Being.

7.5.3. Working with memory reconsolidation in Being-Centred Therapy

The therapeutic use of memory reconsolidation emphasises the importance of creating precise formulations of the learning underpinning a client's symptoms. Doing so activates the symptom-producing learning and helps generate or identify experiences that can effectively contradict it.

In Being-Centred Therapy, we can approach the task of formulating the symptom-producing learning on three levels: The level of the 5 knots, the level of the 20 misconceptions and the level of the personal variations of the misconceptions.

Level one: The 5 Knots

On the first level, the 5 knots provide a typology of the *structures* of symptom-producing learning. For instance, the Knot of Conditionality is a structure where clients separate themselves from an inherent aspect of Being such as value, grounding, or joy, by conceptualising it as something that is created or acquired by fulfilling certain conditions. The Knot of Negative Reification is a different structure where clients separate themselves from an inherent aspect of Being by conflating it with the negative consequences of their misconceived strategies for acquiring this resource, resulting in a negative conception of this aspect of Being.

Understanding the structure of a symptom-producing learning is helpful because it clarifies what structure a contradictory experience must have. For example, to contradict a Knot of Conditionality one must experience having what one seeks without having fulfilled what one believed to be necessary conditions. Similarly, to contradict a Knot of Negative Reification, one must experience the value and pleasantness of something one believed would be worthless or unpleasant.

In short, while understanding the structure of the target learning does not provide a concrete contradictory experience, it does tell us what kind of experience to look for.

Level two: The 20 Misconceptions

On the next level, the 20 misconceptions represent a catalogue of common learnings that most people will carry in implicit memory, which produce much of their suffering. While the knots provide the structure of these learnings, the misconceptions provide the general content.

Knowing the 20 misconceptions enables therapists to counter them using the direct experiences of Being, which often emerge when untying the various knots.

For example, in the Sensing Completion process, clients directly experience that when they become aware of an aspect of Being, they can feel it without needing to fulfil any conditions.

The four processes in the final step in the Sensing Completion process demonstrate how this experience can be used to contradict the misconceptions related to the Knot of Conditionality.

- In the Access process, the experience is used to contradict the belief that what the client seeks is not already present.
- In the Non-Doing process, the experience is used to contradict the belief that action is required to access what the client seeks.
- In the Counterproductivity process, the experience is used to contradict the belief that performing a specific action will produce what the client seeks.
- In the Non-Urgency process, the experience is used to contradict the belief that the behaviour the client engages in is the client's ultimate goal.

Using memory reconsolidation to transform these beliefs facilitates the actualisation process in that it transforms clients' cognition, so it supports rather than hinders continuous awareness of Being.

Level three: Personal variations of the misconceptions

On the third level are the individual variations of the 20 misconceptions. For example, a client may believe that they need to repress anger to avoid being abandoned by loved ones. This is a personal variation of the misconception that action is required to attain what one seeks.

In therapy, identifying clients' personal variations of the misconceptions is crucial because it enables therapists to generate or select contradictory experiences that are specific enough to effectively update clients' symptom-producing learnings.

The five processes for untying the 5 knots have different emphases on clarifying and activating symptom-producing beliefs versus creating contradictory experiences. The processes can, thus, be viewed as a sequence where the later knots are more focused on clarifying symptom-producing beliefs and the earlier knots are more focused on producing experiences of Being in the present moment, which can be used as contradictory experiences:

- **The Knot of Fragmentation:** Here, the emphasis is on identifying which of the client's symptoms stem from the same underlying learning. Sorting symptoms into groups tied to different learnings is essential to do before clarifying the specific content of each symptom-producing belief. Failure to do so can result in conflating different beliefs and getting in a muddle.
- **The Knot of Alienation:** Here, the emphasis is first on working with beliefs clients may have about the extent of their own agency in relation to the symptoms they wish to change. This is done in the two steps: "suggesting agency" and "elucidating agency" in the sensing agency process. Once agency is established, the "understanding motivation" step shifts the focus to the task of uncovering the learning driving these symptoms.
- **The Knot of Negative Reification:** Here, we begin by clarifying what learning drives clients' avoidance behaviour by exploring what they believe would be the consequence of failure. Next, we generate a contradictory experience by inviting clients to describe what they avoid without judgement, leading them to discover that what they predicted would be a horrific experience is, in fact, either a neutral or a profoundly positive experience. This experience can update their beliefs about the phenomenon they avoid.
- **The Knot of Conditionality:** Here, we begin by clarifying what learning drives clients' compulsive behaviours by exploring what they believe would happen if they fully succeeded in achieving their aim. Next, we produce a contradictory experience by asking clients to describe the felt sense they seek, leading them to discover that this felt sense is available to them without engaging in the compulsive behaviour. This experience can update their beliefs about what is necessary to do in life.
- **The Knot of Positive Reification:** Here, the focus is primarily on pointing clients' awareness to Being. Thus, working with the Knot of Positive Reification serves as a tool for creating the contradictory experiences used in all of the above-mentioned processes.

This sequence illustrates how the different knots emphasise either the clarification of symptom-producing learning or the generation of disconfirming experiences, both of which are crucial for using the memory reconsolidation process to achieve lasting transformation.

In summary, Being-Centred Therapy seeks to update 20 misconceptions about the nature of reality that underpin much of clients' suffering. To achieve this, therapists can use formulation and exploration of clients' personal variations of these misconceptions to generate direct experiences of Being that can contradict the misconceptions.

7.5.4. What would your life be like if you could feel X at any time?

Research on the therapeutic use of memory reconsolidation suggests that the key to erasing or updating problematic learning in implicit memory is to juxtapose activation of this learning with a contradictory experience.

So far, we have looked at ways of working which activate the target learning first and introduce a contradictory experience second. However, if the juxtaposition of the two is what is important, the sequence should be reversible.

In this section, I will introduce a contemplation exercise that works by generating experiences of Being first and activates learning that is contradicted by these experiences second.

An experience of Being can be the result of a realisation practice, or it can emerge spontaneously during therapy. When a client has a profound experience of an aspect of Being (X), regardless of how this experience came about, it is possible to use this experience to trigger the memory reconsolidation process and update problematic learning by inviting the client to contemplate the following question:

> "What would your life be like if you could feel X at any time?"

The above contemplation encourages clients to juxtapose their present awareness of Being with different aspects of their life, noticing how awareness of Being produces salient experiential changes in how they perceive these aspects of their life. Rather than first uncovering and activating a belief driving certain symptoms and then seeking a disconfirming experience, this approach begins with a potent experience of Being and then seeks out the beliefs this experience challenges. This will often lead to the discovery of surprising and non-obvious contradictions.

For example, a client may experience Being as a deep sense of inherent wholeness. As he imagines engaging with different aspects of his life while maintaining this sense of wholeness, he might notice a confounding absence of the anxiety he usually feels when asking for what he needs. Initially, it may be puzzling that sensing wholeness should have such an effect. However, upon reflecting, the client may realise that his anxiety is driven by the belief that "having needs means that I'm incomplete and broken, and if anyone notices, they will abandon me, leaving me with no possibility of getting my needs met". Feeling inherently whole directly contradicts the belief that having needs means that one is incomplete. This feeling may even help the client realise that acknowledging his needs is part of his wholeness, not a sign of being incomplete. Thus, becoming aware of Being as inherent wholeness and noticing what changes this awareness brings, helped the client uncover a belief that is contradicted by the experience of inherent wholeness, making it possible to update this belief.

Similarly, a client might experience Being as unconditional love. Contemplating what life would be like with this love as a baseline, she might realise she no longer feels obliged to attend events she doesn't enjoy. Once again, the particular change produced by feeling unconditional love may be somewhat surprising. However, upon reflection, the client may discover that the reason she normally goes to events she does not want to attend is that she believes that "If I disappoint others, I will lose their love". Feeling unconditional love contradicts the notion that it is possible to lose love by disappointing others. When contemplating the situation while in touch with the sense of unconditional love, the client may even realise that declining an invitation can itself be an act of love since it can be part of seeking to connect in a mutually caring and authentic way. Thus, becoming aware of Being as unconditional love and noticing what changes this awareness brings, helped the client uncover a belief that drove problematic behaviour and which is contradicted by the client's experience of unconditional love, making it possible for her to alter this belief.

In short, when clients have a profound experience of Being, guiding them to juxtapose this experience with various aspects of their daily life can help identify, activate and update the limiting beliefs that this experience contradicts. Without this active contemplation, the transformative potential of the experience of Being may be lost, as the unconscious believes underpinning the client's suffering can remain dormant during the experience and, consequently, untouched and unchanged.

7.5.5. When issues re-emerge (the rebound)

It is common for people to experience freedom from particular issues when they become aware of Being, only for these issues to re-emerge after the experience – sometimes even more forcefully than before. The re-emerging of issues is sometimes called “the rebound”.

A client may, for example, suffer from performance anxiety at work when they give presentations. During a session the client may become aware of the White or grounded aspect of Being. While the client is aware of Being, they feel effortlessly grounded, and the performance anxiety is gone. It is tempting to assume that this experience has transformed the client and resolved the issue. However, after the session, the performance anxiety returns and may even feel worse than before.

This typically happens when a client experiences an aspect of Being that has the potential to resolve a particular issue without the activation and juxtaposition of the learning underpinning this issue. While the experience can feel amazing while it lasts, it will not update the belief that produces the issue. In this case, the part of the client operating according to this belief will react negatively to the experience of Being, taking it as a sign that the client is failing at doing what they, according to this belief, must do to be safe and loved, and that more effort is needed to regain control. Consequently, this part will seek to reassert itself, terminating the experience of Being and causing the issue to re-emerge with increased intensity.

For example, a client with performance anxiety may spend far too much time preparing before a presentation and analysing their performance and berating themselves for minor flaws afterwards. During a session, the client may experience Being in the form of unconditional grounding and experience an absence of worries about performing well. The client may recognise that when they give presentations within their field of expertise very little preparation is actually needed and minor flaws are inconsequential.

However, the belief underpinning the performance anxiety may be that “I’m only safe, if my performance is flawless”. From the perspective of this belief, the experience of Being as unconditional grounding and the accompanying absence of worry about performance is an experience of having momentarily lost the will and capacity to do what is needed to be safe. This is frightening to the part responsible for the performance anxiety and will make it intensify its efforts to prevent such lapses from happening again. Thus, after the session, the client may begin to obsess even more about their performance than before the session.

When an issue disappears during a session and reappears afterwards, it is common to think that the issue was resolved in the session, but that the client failed to maintain the resolution. From this perspective, it will seem that the client must learn to use repeated experiences of Being to keep their issue at bay.

The problem with this interpretation is that it often leads to the formation of a particular Knot of Conditionality known as "spiritual bypassing" (Welwood, 2000), where clients use realisation practices and the experiences of Being they can evoke as a means to escape from, rather than resolve, their issues. While it is possible to become very good at escaping issues in this way, this is a problematic practice because since it does not resolve the real issue, it requires continuous effort.

For example, once a client has experienced that performance anxiety disappears when they experience the grounded aspect of Being, they may put in a lot of effort to repeat this experience as often as possible. However, as we saw in Section 7.5.2, frequent experiences of Being do not guarantee the juxtaposition of the experience and the affective connection to the belief underpinning the performance anxiety, which is necessary for this belief to be updated and the issue resolved. Thus, the effort will go towards having prolonged breaks from the issue rather than resolving it.

Instead of considering the re-emerging of an issue as a failure to keep the issue at bay, it is better to consider it as a valuable opportunity to formulate and connect with the belief underpinning the issue – which is an indispensable step in the therapeutic process.

Such opportunities are valuable as the beliefs underpinning clients' issues can be difficult to formulate. Ecker writes that:

> "As a rule, the emotional learnings maintaining therapy clients' symptoms are complex and are areas of deep vulnerability that consist of implicit memory and implicit knowledge, so they are not conscious at the start of therapy. Retrieving them into explicit awareness [...] typically constitutes the greater part of the therapeutic work" (Ecker et al., 2012, p. 28)

The re-emergence of issues after experiences of Being points to the fact that experiences of Being can not only be used to correct beliefs in implicit memory that cause suffering and prevent awareness of Being, they can also be used as a tool for detecting or exposing such beliefs.

7.5.6. How experiences of Being expose beliefs preventing awareness of Being

Insofar as the beliefs that prevent awareness of Being are stored in implicit memory, they can be difficult to notice.

An effective method to uncover what beliefs in clients' implicit memory prevent them from living with a continuous awareness of Being is to investigate what beliefs underpin the issues that emerge in clients after direct experiences of Being.

For example, in a session, a client may have an experience of Being in the form of unconditional peace. The client may enjoy the experience; however, after the session they may start having intense concerns about being perceived as selfish and, therefore, start disregarding their own needs in favour of the needs of others. Exploring this issue might reveal that the client's self-sacrificing behaviour is driven by the belief that the only way to experience peace is to ensure all other people's needs are met – even if it means sacrificing one's own needs. Uncovering this belief reveals that one reason the client may not feel much peace in their everyday life is that they only allow themself to feel peace if no one around them has any unfulfilled needs – which will rarely be the case.

In this example, the experience of the peaceful aspect of Being activated the issue of self-sacrificing behaviour because this issue is produced by the client's belief about what they must do to acquire and hold on to peace. By exploring the issue, the underlying belief could be retrieved "into explicit awareness". At the same time, the experience of unconditional peace has the potential to reveal to the client that it is possible to feel peace without satisfying anybody's needs, thus contradicting their belief about what they must do to feel peace.

In short, the experience of the peaceful aspect of Being is both a tool for uncovering the beliefs that prevent the client from having sustained awareness of this aspect of Being and an experience that can be used to contradict these beliefs.

7.5.7. Two types of issues

The issues typically triggered by experiences of a particular aspect of Being can be classified in two broad categories, depending on which knots the beliefs underpinning the issues relate to.

- **Imitation Issues:** Issues involving behaviour with negative consequences will typically relate to the knots of positive reification and conditionality.
- **Deficiency Issues:** Issues involving perceived personal deficiencies will typically relate to the knots of negative reification and alienation.

In the following, I will describe these two types of issues in more detail and present an overview of typical examples of both types of issues relating to each aspect of Being.

Imitation issues: Issues involving behaviour with negative consequences

After clients have experienced a positive reification of Being, such as support, joy or clarity, they may feel compelled to engage in behaviour that has negative consequences, such as workaholism, escapism or emotional detachment. Such issues typically emerge because this experience of Being activates a part in the client that seeks to hold on to this experience through behaviours that, while aimed at achieving something positive, have negative consequences for the client.

By analysing emerging issues involving behaviour with negative consequences, we will typically discover that such behaviour is driven by the beliefs that the behaviour is necessary to acquire and maintain the desired state, and that the state is so important and valuable that enduring the harmful consequences is justified.

For example, a client may experience a profound state of unconditional support during a session and after the session they may start working unsustainably long hours and be unable to take breaks from work, causing stress and straining the relationship with their family. When analysing this issue, we may find that the client contains a part that is governed by the belief that it is necessary to work hard to secure a prestigious job and a sizeable monthly income to acquire and hold on to the sense of support in life they felt in the session.

I call this class of issues “imitation issues” because the problematic behaviour can be understood as an attempt at imitating an aspect of Being. For example, but working hard, the client in the above example tries to imitate the solidity and Being. The self-harming effects emerge because of the impossibility of this project.

I discussed how much of the personality structure is seeking to imitate the experience of Being in Section 5.2 *The layered personality structure*.

Once the beliefs driving the issue involve harmful behaviour, they can be juxtaposed with the experience the client had during the session where the desired state was present without the client engaging in the harmful behaviour, thus drawing the necessity of the harmful behaviour into question. Simultaneously holding the uncovered beliefs and the experience from the session in mind can lead to the beliefs being updated. This is fundamentally what is done in the Access process (see Section 3.4.4).

Deficiency issues: Issues involving perceived lack or deficiency

After a session where a client has experienced an aspect of Being they reify as a positive phenomenon, such as strength, bonding or nourishing satisfaction, they may experience profound states of lack or deficiency, such as separation anxiety, loneliness or neediness. This type of issues typically emerges because the experience of Being activates an unconscious part in the clients that interprets the felt sense of the aspect of Being as a negative phenomenon and, consequently, makes the client disconnect from it, creating a sense of lacking the positive reifications of this aspect of Being.

By analysing emerging issues involving a sense of lack or deficiency, we will typically discover that the disconnecting behaviour is driven either by the belief that the aspect of Being is a negative phenomenon, such as stuckness, lostness, infatuation or superficiality or, if the aspect of Being is perceived as a positive phenomenon, that allowing this positive phenomenon will have negative consequences (see Section 4.6.1). Both types of belief will make the client avoid or turn away from the aspect of Being, creating a sense of lack or deficiency.

For example, during a session, a client may experience the still aspect of Being and reify it as unconditional peace. After the session, the client may start worrying a lot about little things and feel profoundly deficient in peace. When analysing this issue, we may discover that the client contains a part that believes the stillness is lostness or, if this part sees stillness as peace, believes that allowing peace will have negative consequences, such as making the client overlook dangers and forget to do important things.

Once these beliefs have been uncovered, they can be juxtaposed with the experience the client had during the session where the client allowed the aspect of Being, which a part of them avoids, without suffering the negative consequences this part of them expects, drawing the inevitability of these negative effects into question.

For example, a client may believe that allowing the stillness of Being will feel like lostness or lead to overlooking dangers or forgetting to do important things. However, when the client experienced the stillness of Being during the session, it didn't feel like lostness or lead to overlooking dangers or forgetting important things. It simply felt like unconditional peace, contradicting the expectations in the client's implicit memory.

In summary, the issues that are triggered by experiencing a particular aspect of Being are driven by beliefs that can be contradicted by that very experience.

Table 19 provides an overview of common issues of both types relating to each of the 10 aspects of Being. This is not an exhaustive list, but it provides a good starting point for developing a sense of which issues relate to which aspects of Being[73]. The two columns in the table can be seen as an extended version of the two outermost circles in the 10 Strands of Mind model presented in Section 6.2.

---

[73] The comparison between the above model and Aristotle's virtue theory is intriguing. Aristotle views each virtue as an expression of eudaimonia (happiness) and a balance between two vices representing excess and deficiency in an emotional or cognitive domain. In this chapter, I propose that the issues resulting from a lack of awareness of Being fall into two categories: imitation issues, where individuals create a false experience of Being, and deficiency issues, where they accept the lack and attempt to cope with it. While awareness of Being fosters virtuous behaviour, its absence leads to one of two opposing vices. This mirror Aristotle's model. For instance, a common positive reification of the Red aspect of Being is "courage," while recklessness represents a common imitation issue and cowardice a common deficiency issue. This aligns with Aristotle's notion that courage is the "virtue" placed between the vices of "rashness" and "cowardice". However, defining virtue as awareness of Being and vices as a lack thereof implies that virtue is fundamentally different from its corresponding vices, rather than a balance between them.

Table 19: Symptoms typically resolved by each of the 10 aspects of Being

Essence	Imitation issues	Deficiency issues
White	• Workaholism • Obsessiveness • Tense patience • Tense commitment • Excessive (self-)discipline • Rigidity/inflexibility • Lack of neutrality and impartiality • Splitting and idealisation	• Feeling unsupported (despite support being available) • Feeling ungrounded • Deficiency in will • Lack of discipline • Performance anxiety • Boredom
Red	• Anger issues • Jealousy • Recklessness • Antisocial behaviour • Resentment • Perpetual frustration • Passive aggression • Judgemental • Impulsivity	• Fear of speaking one's mind • Fear of people/the world • Separation anxiety • Lack of physical energy • Fear of losing control • Procrastination • Cowardice • Lack of assertiveness • Lack of vitality and passion
Black	• Detachment • Artificial calm • Deadness • Disinterest in the world • Aloofness • Hate • Power grabbing	• Perpetual worrying and doubting • Powerlessness/Hopelessness • Meaninglessness/Pointlessness • Loneliness • Fear of the unknown • Death anxiety • Restlessness/Lack of peace
Green	• Excessive sadness/Melancholy • Self-reduction and shame • Oversensitivity • Excessive vulnerability • Exaggerated hurt • Rescuer or helper syndrome	• Absence of sadness • Pain anxiety • Unable to tolerate vulnerability and hurt in self and others • Callousness and insensitivity • Lack of empathy • Emotional detachment
Pink	• Perfectionism • Submissive behaviour • People-pleasing • Fawning/evasiveness • Self-abnegation • Approval-seeking behaviour • Excessive social compliance	• Being unable to receive or feel appreciation and love • Feeling undeserving of love • Fear of rejection • Feeling under-appreciated • Emotional dependency • Cynicism and attachment issues

Essence	Imitation issues	Deficiency issues
Yellow	• Superficiality • Escapism • Defensive humour or clowning • Non-committal behaviour • Obligation avoidance • Excessive focus on entertainment • Oversimplifying matters	• Excessive seriousness • Repression of wishes and wants • Lack of joy and spontaneity • Lack of curiosity and playfulness • Excessive loyalty and guilt • Perpetual problem-orientation • Overcomplicating matters
Gold	• Lack of boundaries • Confluence or loss of self/identity • Manipulative ingratiation/charm • Romantic idealisation/infatuation • Emotional enmeshment • Co-dependency • Love bombing	• Feeling unworthy or lack of value • Inability to sustain romantic interest • Loneliness • Social isolation • Inability to feel a sense of belonging • Engulfment anxiety
Cream	• Overindulgence • Addiction/substance dependancy • Infantilisation • Compensatory consumption • Emotional eating • Binge-watching • Over-entitlement	• Scarcity mentality • Neediness • Chronic dissatisfied • Feeling perpetually unfulfilled • Chronic disappointed • Disenchantment with life • Under-entitlement
Blue	• Intellectualisation • Rationalisation • Cognitive rigidity • Ideological rigidity/Certainty • Emotional detachment • Analysis paralysis • Pedanticism	• Sense of deficiency in intelligence • Anti-intellectualism • Lostness and confusion • Amorphous perception and speech • Difficulties synthesising information into understanding • Lack of perspective • Inability to focus
Clear	• Isolation • Withdrawal • Excessive meditation • Obsessive interest in transcendence • Escapism through daydreaming • Excessively hedonistic attitude • Unreasonably trusting	• Lack of freedom • Feeling trapped • Social suffocation • Overwhelm • Boundary issues • Fear of change • Universal paranoia

7.5.8. Working from Being vs. working from symptoms

In the previous sections, I suggested that because we know that direct experiences of Being contradict learnings in implicit memory underpinning human suffering, it is possible to activate the memory reconsolidation process by first having a direct experience of an aspect of Being and then activating and formulating symptom-producing learnings that are contradicted by this experience – as opposed to starting with the learning and then producing a vivid contradictory experience.

Furthermore, I have suggested that experiencing a particular aspect of Being will produce a rebound where certain issues emerge in reaction to this experience, and that these issues are precisely those underpinned by beliefs that are contradicted by the experience of Being.

One advantage of starting therapeutic work from experiences of Being rather than by uncovering and activating the beliefs underpinning the client's symptoms is that it allows the entire process to unfold from a place of resourcefulness.

When clients explore beliefs underpinning their suffering with awareness of Being, this awareness softens the pain associated with those beliefs. Consequently, clients are less likely to resort to intellectual distancing, scepticism, or other defences against such pain. Thus, when clients uncover a problematic belief while grounded in Being, they tend to be more willing and able to empathise with it and recognise its internal coherence, while simultaneously being able to recognise that it is at odds with their current experience, leading the belief to be erased or updated.

When working from the side of Being rather than the side of symptom-producing beliefs, it is more difficult to target specific symptoms. However, it is possible to update many commonly held problematic beliefs by working systematically with one aspect of Being at a time, and the work is far more "juicy" and enjoyable.

Table 19 provides an overview of which issues typically relate to each of the ten aspects of Being. Having such a map is useful when approaching the therapeutic work by bringing awareness to aspects of Being first and uncovering and connecting with symptom-producing learnings second. The map helps therapists predict what kind of issue are likely to emerge when working with a specific aspect of Being – and inversely, which issues one can work with to enhance students' ability to perceive a particular aspect of Being.

So far, we have seen that the research on memory reconsolidation can greatly enhance our understanding of the actualisation process and, consequently, help develop more effective actualisation practices that can be incorporated in Being-Centred Therapy.

Next, we look at what research on cognitive metaphors and embodied cognition can contribute to our understanding of how to incorporate actualisation in Being-Centred Therapy.

7.6. Cognitive Metaphors and Embodied Cognition

Another important discovery that could provide new strategies for facilitating actualisation, coming from cognitive science, is the discovery that cognition is metaphorical (Grady, 1997, 2005; Lakoff, 2012; Lakoff & Johnson, 1980, 1999) and embodied (Barsalou, 2008, 2010; Johnson, 2007; Johnson & Rohrer, 2007; Wilson, 2002).

Research on cognitive metaphors suggests that human beings understand more abstract concepts, such as "social friction", "importance" and "stubbornness" by seeing them as analogous to sensorimotor experiences such as rough textures, physical weight and physical hardness.

Initially, evidence for the existence of cognitive metaphors came from linguists, who noted that natural languages contain groups of metaphorical expressions that all use words related to one experiential domain to talk about another experiential concept. For example, that people understand social friction in terms of textures is evident in the existence of common expressions such as "a *rough* interaction" or "a *smooth* conversation". Similarly, that people understand importance in terms of physical weight is evident in that it is common to call an important argument "a *weighty* argument" or to say that an unimportant opinion "carries no *weight*". And that stubbornness is understood in terms of hardness is evident when we describe a stubborn person as "hard-headed" and someone who easily gives in as "a softy".

The research on Embodied Cognition suggests that the reason we understand abstract concepts through sensorimotor metaphors is that we use the same neurons to process abstract concepts and sensorimotor experiences. Since 2000 there has been mounting evidence for this hypothesis. For instance, Ackerman and his team (Ackerman et al., 2010) tested this hypothesis by exploring whether the activation of neural circuits related to processing specific sensorimotor experiences influenced the processing of specific abstract concepts in ways that corresponded to common cognitive metaphors. They found this to be the case. For example, holding heavier clipboards made people judge job applicants as more *important* and *competent* – two abstract concepts that are commonly talked about using metaphorical expressions involving physical weight. Similarly, touching rough surfaces made people judge social interactions as more difficult than if they touched smooth surfaces, and sitting on hard chairs made people more stubborn in negotiations than if they sat on soft chairs[74].

Some cognitive metaphors, such as the examples given above, appear to be near universal in that it is possible to find expressions indicative of these cognitive metaphors in nearly all languages. Other cognitive metaphors appear to be less universal in that one can find expressions that point to multiple different cognitive metaphors for the same abstract concept. For example, expressions, such as "I'm at a crossroads in my life" or "I'm on the right path in my life" point to a cognitive metaphor through which we understand "life" in terms of a "journey", while expressions, such as "she's playing the hand she was dealt", "he's ahead of the game" and "you win some, you lose some" point to a cognitive metaphor through which we understand "life" as a "game". In the remainder of this chapter, I will focus on particular kinds of cognitive metaphor, called sensory templates, which are characterised by fulfilling the two following conditions:

- Sensory Templates are cognitive metaphors which are grounded in sensorimotor experience as opposed to cognitive metaphors that describe one abstract concept in terms of another (slightly less) abstract concept, such as "life is a journey".
- Sensory Templates are cognitive metaphors where one abstract concept can be understood in terms of multiple different sensorimotor experiences.

Research has shown that sensory templates are part of the learning in implicit memory that guides people's behaviour. In fact, people's sensory templates deeply influence what solutions they can and cannot imagine when dealing with challenges (Springborg, 2015, 2018; Springborg & Ladkin, 2018).

For example, a client may understand the concept "self-control" in terms of the sensorimotor experience of "holding a tight grip". With this sensory template for

[74] For a comprehensive overview of the research underpinning the embodied and metaphorical view of cognition, I refer to my book Sensory Templates and Manager Cognition, Chapter 3.

"self-control" the client is likely to believe the only way to attain self-control is by having a tight grip on themself and forcefully suppress unwanted thoughts, emotions and impulses. In contrast, another client may understand self-control in terms of the sensorimotor experience of "relaxing a grip". This sensory template may lead the client to believe that self-control is attained by developing the capacity to let thoughts, emotions and impulses arise and fade away without engaging with or resisting them. In other words, self-control is attained by letting go of any compulsive reactions.

Similarly, if a client understands "motivation" as analogous to "using force to move something" their strategies for staying motivated are likely to involve using rewards and punishments to force themself to engage in the desired actions. In contrast, if a client understands motivation as analogous to "unblocking a natural flow", their strategy for staying motivated might focus on identifying and removing obstacles for action or on creating the right conditions for motivation to arise naturally.

In short, an individual's sensory templates place boundaries on what courses of action are within the individual's realm of possibilities. Thus, sensory templates are helpful when they enable individuals to imagine effective strategies for navigating challenges, and they are limiting when they lead the individual to believe that unproductive or counterproductive strategies are the best or only options.

Sometimes, the only reason clients cannot deal effectively with a particular situation is because there are no effective strategies to be found within the range of possibilities outlined by their sensory templates.

In this case, it is not merely that the client cannot imagine any effective ways of dealing with the situation. Even if the client is presented with an effective strategy, they will not be able to understand or adopt it if it is outside the range of possibilities allowed by their sensory templates. Instead, the client is likely to understand the strategy they are presented with in terms of the ineffective strategies they already know.

If, for example, a client who sees self-control as a matter of holding a tight grip is presented with the strategy of attaining self-control by letting thoughts, emotions and impulses arise and fade away without engaging with or resisting them, it is likely that this client will understand to enact this strategy as if it were a strategy of repressing any urge to engage. However, since the urge to engage is merely another impulse, this strategy is no different from the one they already use.

Any therapist who has tried to suggest that an overactive client should take a break and do nothing for a while will know that a typical response to such a suggestion is: "How do I do that?" or "I don't have the time or energy to also do this". Such responses indicate that the client is thinking about doing nothing as if it were yet another bullet point on their to-do list. The sensory templates they use simply do not allow them to understand and enact the strategy of doing nothing.

Because sensory templates place limits on what strategies are available to an individual, shifting the sensory templates used to represent key concepts relevant to a situation can completely alter the individual's perception of how it makes sense to deal with this situation. One sensory template can make the situation appear unsolvable, while another can make the same situation appear straightforward and simple to manage.

From 2010-2014, I conducted research with 60 managers who faced problems they believed were unsolvable. By helping them shift the sensory templates they used to understand key concepts such as "power", "connection", and "motivation", these managers, often to their surprise, discovered that issues they had struggled with for years could be resolved easily – sometimes within a single afternoon. This shift resulted from the new sensory templates enabling the managers to recognise effective courses of action that their old templates had obscured (Springborg, 2015, 2018; Springborg & Ladkin, 2018).

In short, the research on the embodied and metaphorical nature of cognition suggests that if behavioural change is not preceded by changes of the relevant sensory templates, the new behaviour may be understood and enacted in ways that only adopt the form but not the substance of the new behaviour, such as when selfless behaviour is adopted for selfish reasons or when someone enacts a prescribed ideal of authenticity.

From this perspective, a key part of actualisation is the deliberate adaptation of sensory templates that best support the embodiment of insights gained through realisation practices.

For example, if a practitioner aims at embodying the virtue of temperance or self-control, it is worth considering whether seeing self-control as analogous to "holding a tight grip" or analogous to "relaxing a grip" will better support the embodiment of this virtue. Similarly, it is possible to ask whether individuals become better at motivating themselves and others if they see motivation as analogous to "using force to move something" or as analogous to "unblocking a natural flow".

In the next section, I will look at how it is possible to work directly with Sensory Templates to support actualisation.

7.6.1. Actualisation through grounding concepts in the experience of Being

In the previous section, I propose that a key part of actualisation involves consciously shifting sensory templates underpinning clients' behaviour. This raises two questions:

- How can we change sensory templates?
- What sensory templates support actualisation?

In this section, I will answer each of these questions in turn.

How can we change sensory templates?

To answer the first question of how we can change sensory templates, it's important to note that sensory templates fundamentally are *beliefs* about what sensorimotor experience a given concept is analogous to. For example, one person may believe that "power" is analogous to the sensorimotor experience of moving physical objects, while another may believe "power" is analogous to the experience of resisting being moved, and yet another person believes, it is analogous to effortlessly remaining still and unaffected by external forces.

Such beliefs are not formed through conscious thought processes. They develop in the same way as the beliefs that enable us to ride a bicycle or to deal with our family environment. In short, sensory templates are beliefs that reside in implicit memory.

Fortunately, we have already established that such beliefs can be changed by utilising the memory reconsolidation process. Thus, a sensory template for a given concept can be changed by uncovering and activating one's belief about what sensorimotor experience the concept is analogous to, and juxtaposing the activated belief with an experience indicating that another sensorimotor experience offers a more fitting or useful analogy.

The processes for untying the 5 knots largely function on this principle by creating experiences that cannot be adequately understood using the client's present sensory templates but can be understood using an alternative template.

For example, people are surprised when during a Being-Centred Therapy session they experience a particular aspect of Being, such as joy, without having done anything to create or acquire it. The cause of this surprise is that their current sensory template makes them see "joy" as analogous to a "physical object", and physical objects must be created or acquired to be present. Thus, the experience in the session contradicts the sensory template and can, therefore, trigger a memory reconsolidation process and update the sensory template. In this case, the experience shows that "joy" is more akin to "space" than to a "physical object" in that it is present regardless of the client's own actions.

It is also important to note that beliefs about what sensorimotor experience a given concept is analogous to are beliefs about how to classify concepts – not about how to act in a particular situation. In other words, they are second-order beliefs (see Section 5.4).

Consequently, these beliefs cannot be contradicted through trial-and-error processes. The belief that power is akin to holding a tight grip cannot be contradicted by noticing any consequences of an individual's actions. If a concrete strategy for holding on to power fails, the individual will merely believe that they didn't hold on tight enough. The failure may prove the belief about the efficiency of the strategy to be wrong, but not the belief about what kind of thing power is. The experiences employed to contradict second order beliefs must be experiences that elucidate the effect of the current classification and show that a different classification is better able to make sense of the events and offers a better set of behaviours from which to choose when dealing with the situation.

What sensory templates support actualisation?

We now turn to the second question of what sensory templates supports actualisation.

Being-Centred Therapy asserts that ethical behaviour, selfless actions, the ability to be in the present moment and engage in the world with authenticity all emerge effortlessly when the individual is operating from sensory templates that allow them to retain awareness of Being while engaging with the world.

Thus, the question then becomes: What sensory templates make it possible to interact with the environment in ways that support continuous awareness of Being?

The answer proposed by Being-Centred Therapy is that a sensory template supports continuous awareness of Being if it is grounded in the sensorimotor experiences arising from this awareness.

For example, many people ground the concept of "strength" in the felt sense of muscular tension, as felt when one lifts or pushes something. Operating from this sensory template can distract people from Being by making them concerned about how to have enough strength to perform whatever lifting or pushing life requires (the Knot of Conditionality) or by making them reject strength because it is exhausting (the Knot of Negative Reification). However, the concept of strength could also be grounded in the felt-sense experience related to the Red aspect of Being, such as "energy flowing or expanding effortlessly". Operating from this sensory template will be less likely to distract from Being because it does not imply that the individual needs to do something to have enough strength or that being strong will be exhausting. When the concept of "strength" is grounded in the felt sense related to the Red aspect of Being, using this concept to engage with the world will not distract us from Being – rather it will remind us of one way in which we can experience Being.

According to Being-Centred Therapy, an important part of actualisation is to ground as many concepts as possible in the felt-sense experiences that emerge when we become aware of Being. In practice, Being-Centred Therapy works with grounding the concepts (positive as well as negative) related to each of the ten aspects of Being in the 10 Strands Model in the felt-sense experiences related to the corresponding strand.

For example, the Red aspect of Being relates to positively laden concepts such as strength, courage, vitality, enthusiasm and aliveness, as well as negatively laden concepts such as anger, frustration and resentment. According to Being-Centred Therapy, it will be beneficial to ground all of these concepts in sensorimotor experiences related to the Red aspect of Being, such as free flowing and expanding energy, heat and vibration.

Doing so will help prevent the formation of the knots that distract us from Being.

- **Positive Reification:** It will help prevent the formation of the Knot of Positive Reification because if the concept is grounded in the felt-sense aspect of Being, any use of the concept will activate this felt sense, making it difficult to forget.
- **Conditionality:** It will help prevent the formation of the Knot of Conditionality because when a positive concept is grounded in the corresponding felt sense of Being, using this concept will activate this felt sense, reminding us that we are not separate from it. In other words, if every time we use the concept "strength", we activate the felt sense of the Red aspect of Being, we are unlikely to start developing strategies for creating or acquiring this aspect of Being since we, in that moment, feel it.
- **Negative Reification:** It will also help prevent the formation of the Knot of Negative Reification because when a negative concept is grounded in the corresponding felt sense of Being, this concept will no longer appear as something negative we must seek to avoid.
- **Alienation and Fragmentation:** Finally, it will help prevent the formation of the Knots of Alienation and Fragmentation in that these knots cannot form without the other knots. If we do not disconnect from Being through the previous knots, we will not have any disconnects we can blame on external circumstances (Knot of Alienation) and we will not have conflicting strategies for acquiring different aspects of Being (Knot of Fragmentation).

In short, if we ground our concepts in the felt-sense experiences that emerge when we become aware of Being, then every time we use one of these concepts to engage with our environment, we will reactivate the sensorimotor experience of Being, and this will serve as a reminder of Being and support continuous awareness of Being.

In the next section, I will present a contemplation exercise used in Being-Centred Therapy to support actualisation by shifting the embodied ground of various concepts.

7.6.2. What does X mean if it is the felt sense of a particular essence?

In this section, I introduce a contemplation exercise that is specifically designed to alter clients' sensory templates, so their concepts become grounded in the felt-sense experience related to various aspect of Being.

The contemplation exercise has two steps.

First clients are asked to explore the felt sense a particular concept refers to when it is separated from associated ideas. For this step, we can use the Sensing Abundance process for positively laden concepts and the Sensing Taboos process for negatively laden concepts. As shown in previous chapters, this felt sense will always be an aspect of Being.

Next, clients are asked to contemplate the following question:

> "What does [the concept] mean if it is [the felt sense of an aspect of Being]?"

If clients normally see the concept as analogous to a different sensorimotor experience from the one they found in step one, the meaning that emerges from answering the above question will be surprising to them. This discrepancy can trigger a memory reconsolidation process which will switch which sensorimotor experience clients use to ground the concept from the old one to the felt-sense experience they uncovered in step one – which is an aspect of Being.

One of the most common changes I see is that clients switch from grounding a concept in the felt sense of the absence of this concept to the felt sense of the presence of this concept.

For example, to many people the meaning of "courage" is "doing dangerous things" – the greater the danger, the greater the courage. Furthermore, they ground the concept of courage in sensorimotor experiences related to fear.

However, if we use the Sensing Abundance process to explore the felt sense of positive and uncomplicated experiences of courage, we discover that the Essence of courage is a sense of freely flowing energy, heat and expansion (the Red aspect of Being).

When we contemplate what courage means if we see it as just this feeling and nothing else, we may discover that we can feel courage whether or not we do dangerous things. Courage is what we feel when life flows freely in us without us getting in the way. It is what we feel when we let our thoughts flow without editing them, let our emotions move without trying to change them, and let the energy in our body ebb and flow without repressing or dissipating it. In this sense, courage isn't about forcing ourselves to confront danger; it's about not getting in the way of what moves us. After acts of courage, people often say they didn't think – they just acted. In other words, they didn't obstruct their natural impulse to act.

The discrepancy between our usual understanding of courage and the understanding that emerges from the felt sense of courage reveals that what we normally call courage is really fear and that courage in itself is something very different. Of course, we may feel fear and courage at the same time. But this contemplation teaches us to distinguish between the two and reveals that we often conflate them. Therefore, this contemplation exercise can create an experience that will update the sensory template we use to ground the concept of courage so instead of grounding it in the felt sense of fear, we ground it in the felt sense of the Red aspect of Being.

Similarly, many people see "anger" as a destructive emotion, which can damage relationships and, therefore, should be controlled or managed or even got rid of altogether. Furthermore, for many people, the concept of anger is grounded in the combined felt sense of fiery energy and tension used to keep this energy contained. When the tension is stronger than the energy, the anger is bottled up, and when the energy is stronger than the tension, the anger explodes.

However, when we use the Sensing Taboos process to explore the felt sense of anger separately from any value-judgements, we discover that the Essence of anger is a felt sense of heat, energy and expansion – without any tension.

When we contemplate what anger means if we see it as just this feeling and nothing else, anger changes from a destructive force to something that can infuse life with vitality, strength, passion and courage. Anger becomes the very energy that is needed to deal with the situations in which it arose. Anger is not what destroys relationships but the passionate desire to rectify relational disconnects.

The difference between our usual understanding of anger and the understanding that emerges from the felt sense of anger reveals that what we often call anger is actually repression. For many people the characteristics of anger are tension and explosion, and both are part of our repression of anger. The tension is the repression itself, and the explosion is created because we judge anger negatively and seek to repress it. An explosion is created by placing a barrier around an expansive energy – not by the expansive energy itself. Seeing this clearly, can be the experience needed to update the sensory template we use to ground the concept of anger so, instead of grounding it in the sense of repression and explosion, we ground it in the felt sense of the Red aspect of Being.

These examples illustrate how defining a concept in terms of the felt sense of an aspect of Being can lead to radically different understandings of said concept, and that seeing this difference can be the experience needed to shift the sensory template for the concept, so it becomes grounded in the felt-sense experience of an aspect of Being.

How to match concepts and sensorimotor experiences

If you wish to facilitate actualisation by inviting clients to contemplate a given concept as analogous to the felt-sense experience of a particular aspect of Being, it is necessary to consider how to match concepts and aspects of Being in fruitful ways. There are two ways of doing so.

Using the 10 Strands model

The fastest way to pair concepts and sensorimotor experiences is to use the model of the 10 strands. Each strand of this model matches a range of positive and negative concepts with a selection of related felt-sense experiences. In the examples above, "courage" and "anger" are a positively and negatively laden concept from the Red Essence strand. Consequently, they were matched to felt-sense experiences related to Red Essence.

Knowing the model of the 10 strands can be a powerful starting point for working with shifting sensory templates for a wide variety of concepts that are key to navigating and thriving in life. I often run workshops where we repeatedly tune in to the felt-sense experience of the aspect of Being related to a particular strand and use this felt sense to ground the positively and negatively laden concepts related to that same strand. This work can be profoundly transformative and it has the advantage of being quick in that it allows for working with many concepts at a time.

However, because different people often use the same word to refer to different things, it is important to have more flexibility in one's work than the model of the 10 strands allows for.

Using the Sensing Abundance and Sensing Taboos processes

Another way to pair concepts and sensorimotor experiences is to notice what aspects of Being clients find when they explore positive concepts through the Sensing Abundance process and negative concepts through the Sensing Taboos process.

When we ask clients to describe the felt sense of a positively laden concept (in the Sensing Abundance process) or a negatively laden concept (in the Sensing Taboos process), they will often describe a felt-sense experience belonging to the same strand as the concept in the 10 Strands model.

However, sometimes clients will describe a felt-sense experience belonging to a different strand from the concept. This is not a problem. The reason is merely that different people use words in different ways. An example many therapists will recognise is the different ways people use the word "hate". One person may use the word "hate" to describe a cold and calculating emotional state, such as in the sentence "my blood ran cold with hate". Another person may use the word "hate" to describe a hot and explosive emotion, which the first person might call "anger", such as in the sentence "I hate him with a passion". Similarly, one person may use the word "love" to describe an inner state that feels "warm and melted". Another person may use the word "love" to describe an inner state that feels "hot and energised", a state the first person might call "passion".

When, during therapy, a client experiences an aspect of Being by paying attention to the felt sense of a particular concept, it is possible to match the two and ask the client to contemplate what the concept would mean if it were only referring to the felt-sense experience they found when they explored it.

This way of matching concepts and felt-sense experiences is particularly useful, when working with concepts that are not included in the 10 Strands model or when clients describe felt-sense experiences that we do not recognise as any of the experiences included in the 10 Strands model. Rather than trying to force clients' experiences to match the model, simply accept that they are venturing outside the mapped territory and discovering new aspects of Essence, and ask them to contemplate what the concept they are exploring would mean to them if it were defined as analogous to the felt-sense experience they have just discovered.

7.6.3. The knots and inversions of key concepts

When we ground sensory templates in experiences of Being, they can, as illustrated in the previous section, change meaning quite radically. Many writers on spirituality point out that our understanding, when we are unaware of Being, is not merely inaccurate – it is the exact opposite of what is true.

Knowing the inversions of meaning that occur when sensory templates of key concepts are grounded in Being, can help create contradictory experiences, since the contradictory experience will be an experience that clarifies the inversion for the client.

Below, I will show how untying each knot can be understood as a shift of sensory template that reverses our understanding of a fundamental concept and how this can be used to create contradictory experiences.

The Knot of Positive Reification

When untying the Knot of Positive Reification, we work with the concept of "reality". We show that what clients take to be permanent is impermanent, and what they take to be impermanent is permanent.

A client may, for example, believe that joy is analogous to permanent physical objects[75] that can be gained and lost, when, in fact, it is more akin to physical space, which can appear to us as many different things depending on what we interpret it in relation to.

We can reveal the impermanent nature of "joy" by clarifying the felt sense of joy and placing it in a different context to reveal how the same felt sense can appear to us as different phenomena. This shows that "joy" is not merely impermanent in the sense that physical objects are (they eventually deteriorate), "joy" is impermanent in the sense that it appears and disappears depending on the context[76]. See Section 4.6.5 for an example of this way of creating contradictory experiences.

The Knot of Conditionality

When untying the Knot of Conditionality, we work with the concept of "causality". We show that behaviour we believe will cause what we seek to be present takes it away from us, whereas behaviour we believe will cause us to lose what we seek will bring it.

For example, when clients believe that "joy" is analogous to physical objects, they will expect that certain circumstances, such as pleasant interactions with other people, cause joy to appear. People's view of causality changes radically when they come to see "joy" as analogous to space in that it is always present, or as

---

[75] Of course, physical objects are also not permanent. However, within the timeframe of human experience, some physical objects are experienced as permanent and can be used to ground our understanding of more abstract phenomena, such as "joy".

[76] This is the view belonging to the Buddhist tradition called Madhyamika, where phenomena are "impermanent" in the sense that they are "empty of inherent existence" and only arise in relation to other phenomena.

analogous to the transparency of water, which is revealed when we cease stirring up the mud in the water. Operating from such analogies, people discover that giving a lot of attention to creating pleasant interactions with other people can diminish, rather than create, our sense of joy in that this activity takes our attention away from the ever-present joy. Similarly, people will also discover that doing less to try to create pleasant interactions can increase, rather than diminish, our sense of joy in that it can be a relief and free up attention to become aware of the ever-present joy. Another way of saying this is that the shift from seeing joy as analogous to physical objects to seeing it as analogous to space or the transparency of water reverses the arrow of causality: It is not pleasant interactions with other people that cause joy, it is awareness of joy that causes interactions with other people to be pleasant.

A strong way of revealing misconceptions about causality is to invite clients to cease doing what they believe they must do to create joy and have them examine the felt sense of the relief of letting go of this project. When clients recognise the felt sense of the relief as "joy", the experience will have demonstrated the flaw in their understanding of causality because they got what they sought by *not* doing what they believed would cause it to appear. This opens the door to suggest that joy is more akin to space than to physical objects, thus shifting the sensory template.

The Knot of Negative Reification

When untying the Knot of Negative Reification, we work with the concept of "value". We show that what clients see as negative is precious, whereas the things clients value are often unimportant.

For example, a client may believe that "superficiality" is a bad thing that has no value and should be avoided, when, in fact, it is merely a negative interpretation of an inner state that the client would call "joy" and see as a positive and valuable thing in a different context.

The main way of revealing a client's misunderstandings about value is to ask them to explore the felt sense of a negative concept without judgement until they recognise this felt sense as a positive phenomenon.

The Knot of Alienation

When untying the Knot of Alienation, we work with the concept of "agency". We show that clients take responsibility for things they do not create and thus cannot be responsible for, while they do not take responsibility for things they do create and thus are responsible for.

For example, clients frequently take responsibility for other people's emotions even though they do not create these and thus cannot be responsible for them, while they do not take responsibility for their own emotions, even though they *do* create these and thus *are* responsible for them.

As we saw in the chapter on the Knot of Alienation, the reason clients do not recognise what they create and, thus, are responsible for, is that they create these things through automatic and habitual processes that operate outside clients' awareness. Thus, the main way to create contradictory experiences is by bringing awareness to these processes.

The Knot of Fragmentation

When untying the Knot of Fragmentation, we work with the concept of "self". We show that what clients take to be themselves is not themselves, while what they think is not themselves is, in fact, themselves.

Clients will typically see their "self" as analogous to a single coherent entity made up of a coherent set of mental, emotional and behavioural patterns, when, in fact, the self is more akin to the space in which all such patterns emerge.

A good way to create an experience that contradicts clients' perception of self as a single, coherent entity is to first reveal that they contain conflicting patterns, thereby challenging the idea of coherence, and then to question whether the self is made up of any such patterns. The idea that the self is a single coherent entity can, for example, be challenged by highlighting conflicts between how clients act and how they believe they act or want to act. The presence of such conflicts is better explained by viewing the client as having multiple conflicting selves rather than a single, coherent self. Furthermore, the realisation that thinking about the self in terms of mental, emotional, and behavioural patterns leads to having multiple selves can serve as the experience that ultimately challenges the notion that the self is found within these patterns at all. When forced to choose between either having a single self or a self made up of mental, emotional and behavioural patterns, most people will choose to abandon the latter to preserve the former.

In short, when untying the knots we realise that what is real is like space, what we seek is like space, what we avoid is misinterpreted space, anything that is not like space is our own creation, and we ourselves are like space.

By understanding how the key concepts of “reality”, “causality”, “value”, “agency” and “self” shift when grounded in Being, therapists can more effectively point out aspects of clients’ experience that directly contradict their existing frameworks, paving the way for transformational change.

7.6.4. Working with sensory templates vs. working with other beliefs

In principle, the process for updating sensory templates is the same as the process for updating any other beliefs in implicit memory. However, there are important differences relating to:

- What **social and moral judgements** clients may encounter for operating from the belief
- What constitutes an effective **contradictory experience** when seeking to challenge or change the belief.
- Clients’ level of **emotional engagement** with the belief.

Social and moral judgements

Sensory templates are less likely than most other beliefs to carry social or moral judgements, making it easier for clients to connect affectively and cognitively with them.

For instance, it might be easier for a client to admit, without reservation, that they are operating from the belief that “emotional safety is analogous to being surrounded by strong walls”, than to admit that they are operating from the belief that “to be emotionally safe, I must not trust anyone”. In a sense, these are two ways of formulating the same (or at least closely related) learning.

However, to admit that they are operating from the second formulation of the belief, the client must admit that they are distrustful, which (at least in some social circles) is seen as a negative character trait, and which may run counter to the client’s self-image and, therefore, be rejected. A good therapist can, of course, do a lot to help clients overcome this hurdle. However, because the first formulation of the belief does not contain the word “I”, what having this belief says about the person is more obscure and, therefore, it is less likely that the client’s self-image will get in the way of connecting affectively and cognitively with the belief when it is formulated in this way.

Contradictory experiences

It may, of course, appear easier to find or create an experience that contradicts the belief that "to be emotionally safe, I must not trust anyone" than to do the same for the belief that "emotional safety is analogous to being surrounded by strong walls". This is because we are used to thinking about contradictory experiences in the context of first-order beliefs – and sensory templates are second-order beliefs (see Section 7.6.1).

It is here worth noting, while the first formulation of the belief may appear to be a first-order belief, i.e. a belief about what will happen if one takes a particular action, it isn't. The reason is that the belief "to be emotionally safe, I must not trust anyone" is not a belief about a particular action – it is a belief about an attitude that can be expressed through many different concrete actions. Thus, it is a belief about a class of actions, and this makes it a second-order belief, which cannot be disproved through trial-and-error.

If, for example, a client remembers a situation where someone was trustworthy, this will not disprove the client's belief that not trusting anyone is key to emotional safety. The client may simply state that to figure out who is trustworthy and who is not, one must assume the attitude of not trusting anyone. In other words, distrusting everyone can be seen as a form of test, and the fact that some pass the test, while others fail, only reinforce the belief that the test is necessary.

For this reason, an effective contradictory experience for the belief that "to be emotionally safe, I must not trust anyone" must be of the same type as for the belief that "emotional safety is analogous to being surrounded by strong walls". An effective contradictory experience must show, not that a particular action brings a different result than what the client expects, but that the client's way of organising their experience has negative consequences and leads the client to select their response from a set of actions that are all unhelpful, whereas a different way of organising experience can mitigate these negative consequences and allow the client to select from a different set of actions that include effective options (see Sections 5.4.3 and 7.6.1).

Emotional engagement

Sensory template may appear to be less emotionally engaging than other beliefs. However, when the sensory template has been formed in an emotionally charged situations in early childhood, I find that these formulations will be emotionally engaging, despite their somewhat sterile appearance to outsiders.

In summary, when formulating the beliefs that underpin clients' symptoms at the start of the memory reconsolidation process, it can be worth considering, whether it will be useful to formulate the sensory template, rather than giving the learning a more conventional formulation. The sensory template formulation of a belief can be particularly effective, when the belief driving the client's symptoms carries social and moral stigma or runs counter to the client's self-image.

7.6.5. Working with cognition vs. working with behavioural modification

In this chapter, I have argued that the research on memory reconsolidation, cognitive metaphors and embodied cognition suggests shifting the focus of actualisation from practices that focus mainly on direct and repeated behavioural modification, towards practices that focus on altering people's conceptual system, so its use no longer distracts them from perceiving Being, and then letting new behaviours emerge spontaneously from this changed conceptual system.

The cognitive approaches to actualisation outlined in this chapter can help mitigate the risks related to actualisation practices based on behavioural-modification, such as the risk of forming knots of conditionality, rationalising behaviours instead of altering them and creating new behaviour-governing beliefs which compete with old beliefs instead of updating or erasing them.

Finally, letting new behaviour emerge spontaneously from an altered conceptual system liberates individuals to discover an endless repertoire of behaviours that align with insights into the nature of Being, rather than trying to conform to a predefined set of behaviours prescribed by a specific tradition.

7.7. Final remarks

In this book, I have aimed to provide a comprehensive guide to Being-Centred Therapy, an approach to therapy that focuses on helping clients develop awareness of Being and benefit from the transformative healing such awareness brings.

With this book on Being-Centred Therapy, I have also aimed at weaving together the teachings of several approaches to personal and spiritual development, both modern and ancient, and at creating synergies between the fields of cognitive science, mysticism, psychology and therapy.

Writing this book has been a long-held dream of mine, as I hope it can positively impact the lives of far more people than I could ever reach through individual sessions and retreats alone.

I sincerely hope that the book can inspire and empower many therapists to further develop their capacity to help their clients to live freer and more joyful and meaningful lives. I also hope that the book can help build bridges and facilitate dialogue between professionals from different fields that are united by a common wish to support others in living fulfilling lives.

For those interested in further exploration, information about The 5 Knots education is available on the Sensing Mind Institute's website: www.sensingmind.com.

8. References

Ackerman, J. M., Nocera, C. C., & Bargh, J. A. (2010). Incidental haptic sensations influence social judgments and decisions. *Science, 328*(5987), 1712–1715.

Almaas, A. H. (1986). *Essence.* Samuel Weiser.

Almaas, A. H. (2002). *Spacecruiser Inquiry: True guidance for the inner journey*. Shambala.

Andreas, C., & Andreas, T. (1994). *Core Transformation: Reaching The Wellspring Within*. Real People Press.

Argyris, C. (1977). Double loop learning in organizations. *Harvard Business Review, 55*(5), 115–126.

Argyris, C., & Schön, D. A. (1974). *Theory in Practice: Increasing Professional Effectiveness*. Jossey-Bass.

Barsalou, L. W. (2008). Grounded cognition. *Annual Review of Psychology, 59*, 617–645.

Barsalou, L. W. (2010). Grounded Cognition: Past, Present, and Future. *Topics in Cognitive Science*, *2*(4), 716–724.

Bateson, G. (1972a). Social planning and the concept of deutero-learning. In *Steps to an Ecology of Mind: Collected Essays in Anthropology, Psychiatry, Evolution and Epistemology* (pp. 127–137). Chandler.

Bateson, G. (1972b). *Steps to an ecology of mind.* Chandler Pub. Co.

Bateson, G. (1972c). The Logical Categories of Learning and Communication. In *Steps to an Ecology of Mind: Collected Essays in Anthropology, Psychiatry, Evolution and Epistemology* (pp. 205–224). Chandler.

Bateson, G. (1979). *Mind and Nature*. E. P. Dutton.

Bohm, D. (1990). *Thought as a system*. Routledge.

Bohm, D., & Edwards, M. (1991). *Changing Consciousness: Exploring the Hidden Source of the Social, Political, and Environmental Crises Facing Our World*. Harper.

Brewer, J. A., Worhunsky, P. D., Gray, J. R., Tang, Y.-Y., Weber, J., & Kober, H. (2011). Meditation experience is associated with differences in default mode network activity and connectivity. *Proceedings of the National Academy of Sciences of the United States of America, 108*(50), 20254–20259.

Brickman, P., Coates, D., & Janoff-Bulman, R. J. (1978). Lottery Winners and Accident Victims: Is Happiness Relative? *Journal of Personality and Social Psychology, 36*, 917–927.

Chalmers, D. J. (1995). Facing Up to the Problem of Consciousness. *Journal of Consciousness Studies, 2*(3), 200–219.

Chalmers, D. J. (2010). The Puzzle of Conscious Experience. *Scientific American*, 90–100.

Csikszentmihalyi, M. (1990). *Flow: The Psychology of Optimal Experience*. Harper & Row.

Di Giuseppe, M., & Perry, J. C. (2021). The Hierarchy of Defense Mechanisms: Assessing Defensive Functioning With the Defense Mechanisms Rating Scales Q-Sort. Front. Psychol. 12:718440. *Frontiers in Psychology, 12*(718440).

Ecker, B., Ticic, R., & Hulley, L. (2012). *Unlocking the Emotional Brain Eliminating Symptoms at Their Roots Using Memory Reconsolidation*. Routledge.

Festinger, L. (1957). *A Theory of Cognitive Dissonance*. Row Peterson.

Festinger, L., & Carlsmith, J. M. (1959). Cognitive consequences of forced compliance. *Journal of Abnormal and Social Psychology, 58*, 203–210.

Freud, A. (1937). *The Ego and the mechanisms of defense*. Hogarth Press and Institute of Psycho-Analysis.

Grady, J. E. (1997). *Foundations of Meaning: Primary Metaphors and Primary Scenes*. UC Berkeley - Department of Linguistics.

Grady, J. E. (2005). Primary metaphors as inputs to conceptual integration. *Journal of Pragmatics, 37*(10), 1595–1614.

Heidegger, M. (1962). *Being and Time (translated by: J. Macquarrie and E. Robinson)*. Basil Blackwell.

Johnson, M. (2007). *The meaning of the body: Aesthetics of human understanding*. The University of Chicago Press.

Johnson, M., & Rohrer, T. (2007). We are live creatures: Embodiment, American Pragmatism, and the cognitive organism. In T. Ziemke, J. Zlatev, & R. M. Frank (Eds.), *Body, Language and Mind Volume 1: Embodiment* (pp. 17–54). Mouton de Gruyter.

Kahneman, D. (2011). *Thinking fast and slow*. Farrer, Straus and Giroux.

Killingsworth, M. A., & Gilbert, D. T. (2010). A wandering mind is an unhappy mind . *Science, 330*(6006), 932.

Lakoff, G. (2012). Explaining embodied cognition results. *Topics in Cognitive Science, 4*(4), 773–785.

Lakoff, G., & Johnson, M. (1980). *Metaphors We Live By*. University of Chicago Press.

Lakoff, G., & Johnson, M. (1999). *Philosophy in the Flesh: The Embodied Mind and its Challenge to Western Thought*. Basic Books.

Mason, M. F., Norton, M. I., Van Horn, J. D., Wegner, D. M., Grafton, S. T., & Macrae, C. N. (2007). Wandering minds: The default network and stimulus-independent thought. *Science, 315*(5810), 393–395.

Meyer, J. H. F., & Land, R. (2003). Threshold concepts and troublesome knowledge: Linkages to ways of thinking and practising within the disciplines. In C. Rust (Ed.), *Improving Student Learning and Practice – Ten Years On.* (pp. 412–424). OCSLD.

Perkins, D. (2006). Constructivism and troublesome knowledge. In J. H. F. Meyer & R. Land (Eds.), *Overcoming barriers to student understanding: Threshold concepts and troublesome knowledge*. Routledge.

Piaget, J., & Inhelder, B. (1969). *The psychology of the child*. Basic Books.

Polanyi, M. (1969). *Knowing and being* (M. Grene, Ed.). University of Chicago Press.

Polanyi, M. (1974). *Personal knowledge: Towards a post-critical philosophy.* University of Chicago Press.

Schön, D. (1986). Deutero-learning in organizations: Learning for increased effectiveness. *The Leader-Manager*, 2–16.

Schwartz, R. C. (1995). *Internal Family Systems Therapy*. The Guilford Press.

Schwartz, R. C. (2018). *Greater than the sum of our parts: Discovering your true self through Internal Family Systems Therapy*. Sounds True.

Shah, I. (1971). *The Sufis. Garden City*. Anchor Books.

Springborg, C. (2015). *Art-based methods in management education.* Cranfield University.

Springborg, C. (2018). *Sensory Templates and Manager Cognition: Art, Cognitive Science and Spiritual Practices in Management Education.* Palgrave Macmillan.

Springborg, C. (2024). *Transforming Self-Criticism: A therapist's guide to resolving internal conflicts and discovering a life of abundance (2nd edition)*. Sensing Mind Institute.

Springborg, C., & Ladkin, D. (2018). Realising the potential of art-based interventions in managerial learning: Embodied cognition as an explanatory theory. *Journal of Business Research*, *85*, 532–539.

Welwood, J. (2000). *Toward a Psychology of Awakening - Buddhism, Psychotherapy, and the Path of Personal and Spiritual Transformation.* Shambhala Publications.

Whitehead, A. N., & Russell, B. (1927). *Principia Mathematica*. The University Press.

Wilson, M. (2002). Six views of embodied cognition. *Psychonomic Bulletin & Review*, *9*(4), 625–636.

www.ingramcontent.com/pod-product-compliance
Ingram Content Group UK Ltd.
Pitfield, Milton Keynes, MK11 3LW, UK
UKHW051117290926
15471UKWH00010B/1726

9 788797 177143